HISTORY
OF
BLACK AMERICANS

M
Bck STds.

HISTORY
OF
BLACK AMERICANS

From the Emergence
of the Cotton Kingdom
to the Eve of
the Compromise of 1850

Philip S. Foner

Contributions in American History, Number 102

Greenwood Press
Westport, Connecticut · London, England

Library of Congress Cataloging in Publication Data (Revised)

Foner, Philip Sheldon, 1910–
  History of Black Americans.

  (Contributions in American history; ISSN: 0084-9219
no. 40,)
  Includes bibliographies and indexes.
  CONTENTS: v. 1. From Africa to the
emergence of the cotton kingdom—v. 2. From the
emergence of the cotton kingdom to the eve
of the compromise of 1850.
    1. Afro-Americans—History. 2. United
States—Race relations. I. Title. II. Series.
E185.F5915   973'.0496073   74-5987
ISBN 0-8371-7529-1 (v. 1)   AACR1
      0-8371-7966-1 (v. 2)

Library of Congress Catalog Card Number: 74-5987
ISBN: 0-8371-7529-1 (v.1)
      0-8371-7966-1 (v. 2)
ISSN: 0084-9219

First published in 1983

Greenwood Press
A division of Congressional Information Service, Inc.
88 Post Road West
Westport, Connecticut 06881

Printed in the United States of America

10 9 8 7 6 5 4 3 2 1

Contents

Preface

In 1975 I published the first of what was to be a history of black Americans from Africa to the present in four volumes. But in projecting this ambitious study of this vastly challenging subject, I did not realize fully the dimensions to be covered just in the era of slavery. Consequently, I found it necessary to alter the number of volumes in this project and to devote three volumes to the more than two centuries of the black experience during slavery. The first volume began in Africa and ended with the emergence of the Cotton Kingdom around 1820. Volumes 2 and 3 will carry the history forward from the emergence of the Cotton Kingdom to the end of legal slavery in 1865. This volume deals with slaves and free blacks during the era of the Cotton Kingdom and traces the struggle against slavery from the emergence of Garrisonian abolitionism to the eve of the Compromise of 1850, analyzing in the process the nature of the antislavery movement and the role of black abolitionists. The third volume, shortly to be published, will continue the history of the antislavery movement from the Compromise of 1850 to the adoption of the Thirteenth Amendment following the Union victory in the Civil War. Here, too, special attention is paid to the contributions of black abolitionists and to black resistance to the Fugitive Slave Act of 1850. These three volumes will provide a truly comprehensive history of black Americans during the entire era of slavery.

As in volume 1, I have had the benefit in the present work of many people in its preparation. I wish especially to thank Jon Wakelyn of the Catholic University of America and Herbert Shapiro of the University of Cincinnati for reading the entire manuscript and making valuable suggestions. I also wish to thank Ronald Lewis of the University of Delaware and George Walker of George Mason University for the opportunity to read and discuss with them their unpublished studies in specific areas covered by this volume.

A large number of institutions gave me considerable assistance by enabling me to use their facilities. I wish to thank the library staff of Lincoln University,

Pennsylvania, for their kind cooperation in offering me the use of their fine collection of Afro-American materials and providing me with material through interlibrary loans. In addition the following institutions were helpful: University of Delaware, Washington State University, Georgetown University, University of California, Berkeley, University of California, Los Angeles, Louisiana State University, University of Chicago, University of North Carolina, University of Pittsburgh, Bowling Green State University, Columbia University, University of Illinois, Amherst College, University of Pennsylvania, Tulane University, Temple University, Lamar State College of Technology, University of Toledo, University of Santa Clara, Bowdoin College, University of Washington, University of Virginia, New York University, Brown University, City University of New York, Duke University, Fordham University, State University of New York at Buffalo, Pennsylvania State University, Washington University, University of Michigan, Florida State University, University of Buffalo, Harvard University, Howard University, Boston University, Boston Public Library, Library of Congress, Mississippi Department of Archives, Maryland Historical Society, Historical Society of Pennsylvania, Library Company of Philadelphia, Rhode Island Historical Society, New-York Historical Society, and the Delaware Historical Society.

PHILIP S. FONER

Professor Emeritus of History,
Lincoln University, Pennsylvania
February 1982

HISTORY
OF
BLACK AMERICANS

1

American Historians and Antebellum Slavery

In interpretations of the "peculiar institution" of the Old South offered by nearly all white historians of the nineteenth century, chattel slavery was condemned as a cruel system of forced labor. Unfortunately, however, this condemnation was accompanied by an acceptance of the racial inferiority of Negroes. The works of James Schouler, John Fiske, Herman Von Holst, John W. Burgess, John Bach McMaster, and James Ford Rhodes continued to present the stereotype of black Americans as docile, ignorant, and inherently inferior. To Fiske, the absence of any slave resistance was "one of the most remarkable facts of American history," and Schouler, in considering the same question, wrote that American Negroes were "a black servile race . . . brutish, obedient to the whip."

James Ford Rhodes, the dominant historian in the interpretation of slavery, was a prosperous Cleveland businessman who in middle age turned to the writing of history, with such success that his seven-volume history of the United States from 1850 to 1877, published between 1892 and 1906, strongly influenced the American generation prior to World War I in its opinions of the Negro. Even as Rhodes attacked the odious nature of slavery, he espoused with equal vigor the principles of white supremacy. He set down as "scientific truth" the fact that Negroes constituted "one of the most inferior races of mankind," and he described slaves as "indolent and filthy" on whose "brute-like countenances . . . were painted studipidity, indolence, duplicity and sensuality." He described Negroes as persons capable of only limited mental development, who turned early in life from intellectual to sensual pursuits, as incapable of love or affection, and as showing that a lack of chastity was "a natural inclination of the African race." Hence, according to Rhodes, slave women, except in isolated cases, yielded to the passions of their masters.

Rhodes did emphasize that slavery was an evil institution that subjected slaves to the harshest material conditions, but, for him, much of its horror was mitigated by the fact that the sorrows of the Negro were only transient. According to

Rhodes, the trouble with Southern apologists for slavery did not lie in their claim that "the negro race was inferior to the Caucasian," for that was "scientific truth," but rather in their use of this "fact" to justify slavery. This, he maintained, was "cruel as well as illogical."

This anti-Negro bias in the dominant historiography of these years was challenged by black historians—especially by George Washington Williams, W.E.B. Du Bois, and Carter G. Woodson. These scholars refused to accept the prevailing interpretation of the Negro's past; they sharply attacked the outright racism in the historical writings about slavery and brought to light a vast amount of material on black Americans that up to that point had been neglected by white investigators. This was particularly true of Carter G. Woodson, who in 1915 founded the Association for the Study of Negro Life and History and became, a year later, the editor of its publication, *Journal of Negro History*. With the material presented by Woodson and others, white historians were no longer able to claim ignorance as the reason for their distortions of the Negro's past. But Williams, Du Bois, Woodson, and other black scholars were ignored in white academic circles. After all, being black, how could they be objective?

And so the virulent display of racism in the writings about slavery continued. But now a new factor entered on the scene: the view that slavery had been beneficial rather than repressive.

ULRICH B. PHILLIPS AND THE PHILLIPS SCHOOL

The outstanding exponent of this viewpoint—that slavery was beneficial—was Ulrich Bonnell Phillips, whose studies of slavery made him the dominant scholar in the field from the eve of World War I until the late 1950s. A Southerner, the son of a Georgia merchant whose family was connected with the plantation gentry from the Old Dominion to the Gulf Coast, Phillips began publishing essays on slavery in 1903 at the age of twenty-six. By the time his principal work appeared fifteen years later, he had published twenty-eight articles and two books of documents. He made no pretense of objectivity. Indeed, he referred to himself as one who had "inherited southern traditions" and who gloried in the "innate kindness of the southern gentleman." Over the objections of his publisher, he insisted on dedicating his 1908 book, *A History of Transportation in the Eastern Cotton Belt,* "To the Dominant Class in the South who . . . wrought more sanely and more wisely than the world yet knows."

Phillips' intensive study of slavery culminated in the publication of his first major work, *American Negro Slavery,* in 1918, which was reinforced eleven years later by *Life and Labor in the Old South.* In all, his writings include six books, four volumes of edited source materials, approximately fifty-five articles, and fifty book reviews. Nearly all of them dealt with American Negro slavery and the plantation system.

The portrait of slavery and the slave that emerged from Phillips' *American*

Negro Slavery can be summarized as follows: Originally the Negro was brought to colonial America because of the shortage of white labor and because the Indian had failed miserably as a slave. Because of their barbarism, Negroes had to be held in check by slavery. When the invention of the cotton gin made the large-scale production of cotton profitable, the use of Negro slaves increased sharply. When the African slave trade was shut off, the domestic trade tried to fill the gap. The resulting scarcity of plantation hands increased their price and made the system a losing venture. But the primary role of the plantation system was not the organization of business but racial control. "Plantation life . . . was less a business than a life; it made fewer fortunes than it made men." Even though slavery was unprofitable, it had to be maintained because the slaveowners already had too much money invested in their human property, and they were afraid of the social consequences if the great mass of Negroes was suddenly freed. In fact, the slaveowners, by keeping the "barbarians" under control for so long, actually benefited the entire nation. Although antebellum slavery was a poor investment for masters, Phillips went on, it was the best available labor system and a boon to the black bondsmen. The institution of slavery was a civilizing factor; slaveholders were, in the main, kindly and sympathetic masters; slaves were almost all contented laborers. To be sure, there were "injustices, oppression, brutality and heartburning in the regime, but where in the struggling world are these absent?"

Phillips described slavery by giving specific illustrations dealing with the material conditions of slaves—housing and diet and hours of work, for example—drawn from planters' journals, account books, and letters. Although these illustrations provided some examples of ill treatment, his general picture was of slavery as a benign institution. This, he argued, was logical. First, the slave was a valuable piece of property: "The capital value of the slaves was increasingly powerful insurance of their lives and health," he wrote. Second, the day-to-day necessities of life on the plantation made adjustments necessary, which softened the harsher side of slavery. Although the planter could always resort to force, his relations with his slave, according to Phillips, were "largely shaped by a sense of propriety, proportion and cooperation." Paternalism—the adopting of a fatherly concern for one's slaves—was actually the only feasible method of labor control if the planter wished to preserve the morale of his work force. The "successful management" of slaves necessitated "a blending of foresight and firmness with kindliness and patience." Masters and slaves constantly made adjustment and readjustments, for the "slaves themselves were by no means devoid of influence." "The ideal in slave control," he wrote, "may perhaps be symbolized by an iron hand in a velvet glove."

Yet there were limits to what paternalism could achieve because the planters, after all, were dealing with Negroes who acted in "distinctly negro-like ways." Blacks, Phillips insisted, always were, and remained after slavery, lazy. The Negro was stupid, irresponsible, suffered from "inherited inaptitude," was incapable of taking care of himself, and therefore needed the white man's guidance and supervision. Phillips saw in the plantation system an educating and civilizing device. The plantations were "the best schools yet invented for the mass training of that sort of inert and backward people which the bulk of the American Negroes represented."

Another theme appearing in Phillips' works is that the Negro, because of his race, was naturally submissive and therefore suited for slavery. When Phillips compared Roman and American slavery, he placed great stress on race, observing that, unlike the Roman slaves, the American bondsmen were "Negroes, who for the most part were by racial qualities submissive rather than defiant, light-hearted instead of gloomy, amiable instead of sullen, and whose very defects invited paternalism rather than repression." Although he was ready to admit that occasionally there was a discontented slave, the vast majority were "more or less contentedly slaves, with grievances from time to time but not ambition." These traits were largely carried over into the twentieth century. After observing life at an army camp in 1918, Phillips wrote that the Negroes "show the same easygoing, amiable, serio-comic obedience and the same personal attachments to white men . . . which distinguished their forebears."

Thus, the severity of American slavery was minimized, its civilizing functions extolled, and the notion emphasized that the slave was submissive rather than defiant. This fundamental theme of black racial inferiority runs through Phillips' writings on slavery.

In reviewing Phillips' *American Negro Slavery,* W.E.B. Du Bois and Carter G. Woodson pointed to his blatant racial bias and emphasized a number of shortcomings that were only later to be fully recognized. In his review published in the *American Political Science Review* of November 1918, Du Bois noted that Phillips' use of sources, while impressive, was too one-sided; among other things, he used no Negro sources, which resulted in a "curiously incomplete and unfortunately biased work." Phillips had completely ignored the black as "a responsible human being," Du Bois wrote; "nowhere is there any adequate conception of 'darkies,' 'niggers' and 'negroes' (used liberally throughout the book) as making a living mass of humanity with the usual human reactions." Du Bois questioned the historical soundness of Phillips' characterization of slaves as "submissive," "lighthearted," and "ingratiating," as well as the view that the nature of blacks was "fixed and unchangeable," unaltered by a generation of freedom. Du Bois found Phillips' book, despite the labor and research that went into it, "deeply disappointing." "It is," he concluded, "a defense of American Slavery—a defense of an institution which was at best a mistake and at worst a crime—made in a day when we need sharp and implacable judgment against collective wrongdoing by cultured and courteous men. The case against American slavery is too strong to be moved by this kind of special pleading."

In his evaluation, published in the *Mississippi Valley Historical Review* of March 1919, Carter G. Woodson conceded the value of the book in furnishing information "about the management, labor, social aspects, and tendencies of the plantation." But he sharply attacked Phillips' "inability to fathom the negro mind," his failure to report the cycles in the history of slavery, and his willingness to develop conclusions totally unwarranted by the facts. Woodson also criticized Phillips for arranging the facts in such a way as to defend the institution of slavery and for asserting that the slaves were satisfied with their lot. "How can it be true," he wrote, "that blacks were contented when they from time to time resorted to servile insurrections until the institution became so well established that resistance was suicidal?" He criticized Phillips for failing to point to the evils of the domestic slave trade and the "cold-blooded fashion that . . . masters bartered them [slaves] away," separating families when it financially benefited them to do so.

Woodson also questioned the thoroughness of Phillips' research. "It seems," he wrote, "that Mr. Phillips has not exhausted the study of the plantation, for many of the records cited were those of the most enlightened and benevolent slaveholders of the Old South such as were never known to be the cruel and inhuman sort of masters who doomed negroes to torture in the lower south." In short, Phillips had either neglected or distorted the facts in order to defend an institution that was both immoral and inhuman. Woodson called upon other historians to search out new facts from the abundant material available so that a true history of the institution of slavery could be written.

Phillips, however, paid no attention to the reviews by Du Bois and Woodson, or to the facts published quarterly in the *Journal of Negro History*. His belief in the Negro's inferiority never changed. Even at the end, he saw the Negro as barely civilized, who could revert to a state of African savagery by any sudden relaxation of controls. As for Africa, he never paid attention to the abundant evidence increasingly being published that challenged his view of the "dark continent" as an abode of uncivilized barbarians.

Ulrich Bonnell Phillips set the tone for writing about slavery, and his scholarship lent credibility to the prevailing belief in the inferiority of the Negro. Phillips' influence was readily apparent in state studies of slavery and numerous other volumes dealing with the institution from 1918 to World War II. The volumes of the Phillips school were freighted with that historian's racial and methodological bias. The interpretation of slavery as a benign institution and of plantations as peopled largely by paternalistic masters and ignorant savages remained all-pervasive.

Several studies upheld and extended Phillips' economic conclusions. Of these, the most important was Charles W. Ramsdell's "The Natural Limits of Slavery Expansion," which appeared in the *Mississippi Valley Historical Review* in 1929. Ramsdell held that huge profits through the use of slave labor were possible whenever climate or soil conditions made cotton production possible. The incentive to capitalize on these profits was enough to stimulate the massive migration of planters with their slaves into new lands. However, there were certain natural factors that limited this migration. Among these were the "natural barriers" of climate, soil fertility, and land access. "By 1860 the institution of slavery had virtually reached its natural frontiers in the West," Ramsdell wrote.

"Beyond Texas and Missouri the way was closed. There was no ground for expectation that new lands could be acquired south of the United States into which slaves might be taken. There was, in brief, no . . . place for it to go." Ramsdell found slavery to be a "cumbersone and expensive system," which could show profits only if conditions were absolutely right. By the beginning of the Civil War, these conditions were no longer possible, and slavery was dying a natural death. Owners no longer found it profitable either to maintain large slave gangs or to continue to migrate with their slaves to new lands. Like Phillips, Ramsdell concluded that slavery had ceased to be profitable to the Southern planters.

CRITICISM OF PHILLIPS

The Phillips school of historiography did not go uncontested. At first, the dissenters came mainly from the ranks of black scholars. Since such people were considered obviously "prejudiced" and generally did not have full "standing" in the academic community, their findings, while not without influence, were unable, by themselves, to penetrate dominant intellectual circles. The first major white historian to criticize Phillips was Frederick Bancroft, who published his *Slave Trading in the Old South* in 1931. Rejecting Phillips' assumption that Southern planters were not involved to any great degree in slave breeding or slave trading, Bancroft maintained that "slave-rearing early became a source of the largest and often the only regular profit of nearly all slaveholding farmers and many planters in the Upper South." While Phillips had maintained that children were rarely sold, Bancroft cited evidence to show that "the selling singly of young children privately or publicly was frequent and notorious." In general, he maintained that Phillips knowingly perpetuated myths concerning not only the slave trade but also the relationship between master and slave, and he forcefully denied Phillips' contention that meekness and docility was characteristic of the slave. Bancroft, the first white historian to draw extensively upon slave sources, also criticized Phillips for spurning the use of slave narratives as reliable historical data.

Between 1938 and 1942 two works by white historians challenged Phillips' conclusions concerning slave contentment and presented a contrary picture of slave conduct. They were Joseph C. Carroll's *Slave Insurrections in the United States, 1800-1860,* published in 1938, and Raymond Bauer and Alice Bauer's 1942 article, "Day to Day Resistance to Slavery," published in the *Journal of Negro History*. Bauer and Bauer described basic forms of day-to-day resistance: work slowdown; destruction of property, including livestock; malingering; feigning illness and pregnancy; self-injury; suicide; and infanticide. The authors concluded that "the Negroes not only were very discontented, but . . . they developed effective protest techniques in the form of indirect retaliation for their enslavement."

In 1943, Herbert Aptheker published *American Negro Slave Revolts,* the most comprehensive work on the subject yet produced. Aptheker ridiculed Phillips' discussion of slave revolts under his treatment of "crimes." He argued that Phillips had presented limited data on slave revolts to maintain "racialistic notions that led him to describe Negroes as suffering from 'inherited inepitude,' and as being stupid, negligent, docile, inconstant, dilatory and 'by racial quality submissive.' " Aptheker insisted that "discontent and rebelliousness were not only extremely common, but, indeed, characteristic of American slaves."

But since Aptheker was a white Marxist historian, his influence on the dominant historiography was as slight as that of the black scholars. In 1944, Richard Hofstadter, another white historian, but hardly a radical, called Phillips' work "a latter-day phase of the pro-slavery argument," and revealed serious methodological flaws in Phillips' writings. His article, "U. B. Phillips and the Plantation Legend," published in the *Journal of Negro History,* noted that Phillips practically excluded nonslaveholding whites from his discussion of the Old South and devoted almost no attention to small slaveholders, concentrating instead on very large plantations, those with over two hundred slaves.

Despite all this, *American Negro Slavery* remained firmly lodged in the minds of the nation's teachers as the standard work on slavery. Nor did this change after the publication of a thorough refutation of Phillips by black historian John Hope Franklin in *From Slavery to Freedom: A History of Negro Americans,* published in 1947. Franklin rejected Phillips' thesis of the passive qualities of slaves and criticized the Phillips school for ignoring the extent to which slaveholders were dependent upon and involved in the domestic slave trade. Finally, he questioned the entire concept of paternalistic care for the slaves and their well-being under slavery.

Nevertheless, the fourth edition of the extremely popular college textbook in American history by Samuel Eliot Morison and Henry Steele Commager (*The Growth of the American Republic*), published in 1950, reflected Phillips' viewpoint. "As for Sambo," they wrote, "there is some reason to believe that he suffered less than any other class in the South from its 'peculiar institution.' "

Phillips' economic conclusions about the unprofitability of slavery also came under attack by several scholars during the 1930s and 1940s, especially by Lewis C. Gray. In his two-volume *History of Southern Agriculture in the United States to 1860* published in 1933, Gray maintained that slavery was a profitable system that displaced free labor systems throughout the South because it was cheaper and more efficient. In the long run, Gray argued, slavery's "ultimate influence upon the economic well-being of the South was pernicious," and it relegated the South as a whole to economic and technological backwardness. Nevertheless it had been a highly profitable form of business enterprise, which provided an economically superior means for the production of staples. Gray rejected the assumption of Phillips, and in particular of Ramsdell, that slavery had expanded to its limits by 1860 and was in the process of dying a natural death. "Far from being a decrepit institution," Gray wrote, "the economic motives for the continuance of slavery from the standpoint of the employer were never so strong as in the years just preceding the Civil War.''

In 1942, in his often-cited article, Thomas P. Govan answered the question, ''Was Plantation Slavery Profitable?'' in the affirmative. He argued that Gray was more nearly correct than Phillips. Using modern bookkeeping methods, Govan reached the conclusion that slavery yielded substantial profits for the masters. The group of historians led by Frank Owsley and Harriet Owsley also challenged Phillips' view of the unprofitability of slavery and his thesis that the institution was dying on the eve of the Civil War. On the contrary, they insisted, by the 1850s all economic levels of white southerners, and especially the lower ones, were experiencing a growing prosperity from the expanding slave economy and a substantial middle class existed in the antebellum South. Ownership of land and slaves was well distributed. Large numbers of farmers, especially nonslaveholders, were able to move into the owning class. Small landowners possessed soil as fertile as that of the large plantation owners. By the time of the Civil War, ''the white people of the South—the yeomanry—enjoyed with the planters a high degree of social and economic security.'' The plain folk of the antebellum South who were neither poor whites nor slaveholding planters actually constituted the largest group of whites in the region.

In the writings on slavery, Gray's thesis that slave labor was profitable was given either only token recognition or none at all. In the main, however, white historians accepted Gray's view (and that of the Owsley school) that slavery was the only institution that could have made effective use of savage Africans and their descendants.

The emergence of the civil rights movement, the growing sense of racial pride and identity among blacks, and the recognition by whites of the full implication of racism in America, all eventually had their influence on the studies of slavery. In the 1950s, young scholars began vigorously to assail Phillips' interpretation of slavery and launched a restudy of the minority anti-Phillips position in historiography heretofore largely neglected in academic circles. All this combined to set the stage for the anti-Phillips synthesis of slavery offered by Kenneth M. Stampp.

KENNETH M. STAMPP'S *THE PECULIAR INSTITUTION*

Stampp initiated his challenge to Phillips in 1952 in ''The Historian and Southern Negro Slavery,'' published in the prestigious *American Historical Review*. Calling for the rejection of Phillips, Stampp wrote: ''No historian of the institution [of slavery] can be taken seriously any longer, unless he begins with the knowledge that no valid evidence exists that the black race is innately inferior to the white.'' Stampp developed his anti-Phillips thesis fully in *The Peculiar Institution: Slavery in the Ante-Bellum South,* published in 1956, in which he rejected Phillips' generalizations concerning the nature of plantation life on the ground that they were based on limited evidence gained from the selective use of large plantation records, while neglecting other equally important sources, such as county and court records, census returns, and records of small farmers. The prime weakness of Phillips' work, Stampp contended, lay in his tendency to draw "loose and glib generalizations" about the plantation system from limited and questionably biased evidence. This was especially reflected in Phillips' discussions of slave treatment. "The evidence hardly warrants the sweeping picture of uniform physical comfort . . . that is sometimes drawn," Stampp wrote, "The only generalization that can be made with relative confidence is that some masters were harsh and frugal, others were mild and generous, and the rest ran the whole gamut in between."

Stampp also attacked Phillips' contention that blacks, in contrast to other races, were peculiarly suited for slavery and that the Negro's particular racial traits caused him to submit to the system with unusual ease. For one thing, Stampp insisted that it was impossible to generalize about an entire people and that "variations in the capacities and personalities of individuals within each race are as great as the variations in the physical traits." Then again, the Negro did not readily accept his lot; rather, there was a long history of slave discontent, which included everything from day-to-day resistance to open rebellion. Finally, the fact that the majority of the slaves appeared to accept slavery did not prove either a special fitness for the institution or contentment with it. "It merely proves that men can be enslaved when they are kept illiterate, when communication is restricted, and when the instruments of violence are monopolized by the state and the master class."Essentially antebellum bondage was a "system of labor extortion" that depended upon force, violence, and a measure of psychological terror.

Contrary to Phillips, Stampp maintained that slavery was not the great "school constantly training and controlling pupils who were in a backward state of civilization." He pointed out that the first generation of blacks born in the American colonies during the seventeenth century had learned the patterns of social behavior necessary for living in a free society. He insisted, too, that there was no truth in Phillips' assertions about paternalistic planters who lost money from a declining system but maintained slavery because of the hopeless future blacks would face once they were free. On the issue of profitability, Stampp developed and strengthened the anti-Phillips position already advanced by Lewis C. Gray. Although he criticized Gray for sharing Phillips' racial views of Negro inferiority, he gave high marks to Gray's analysis of plantation economics and lined up with him in the argument over the viability of plantation slavery in the late antebellum period. He did not accept the contention of the Owsley school that slavery benefited the majority of Southern whites; he insisted that the institution both oppressed blacks and worked against the interests of nonslaveholding whites. But he maintained that for the masters, it constituted an economically flourishing system with ample rewards in cash and power. Stampp blamed a combination of racism and inadequate research for having prevented Phillips from giving due credit to the successful employment of slaves in industry and to the numerous "experiments" demonstrating that bondsmen "could be used efficiently in a system of intensive, scientific and diversified agriculture."

Stampp conceded that the day-to-day resistance of slaves often resulted in breaking and misusing tools, abusing farm animals, and sabotaging efficient management. But he contended that Southern masters were able to overcome these obstacles and that a "reasonably efficient planter" could extract even more work from slaves than from free persons by a judicious blend of coercion and incentives, by demanding rigid discipline and longer working hours at critical times in the growing season, and by a much more systematic use of women, children, and older people.

Thus, Stampp rejected both the characterization of blacks as a biologically and culturally inferior, childlike people and the depiction of white planters as paternalistic employers wrestling with a vexing social problem that was not of their own making. The slaveholders, said Stampp, had built the system consciously. They had done so for profit, and they had been duly rewarded. Despite the brutal oppression to which the slaves had been subjected, black Americans had remained uncrushed in spirit and, in the end, unbroken in person. They had resisted not so much with mass rebellion but by day-to-day resistance. The meek, smiling slaves who were thought to be "contented though irresponsible" had protested their bondage "by shirking their duties, injuring the crops, feigning illness, and disrupting the routine." They were indeed "a troublesome property."

The Peculiar Institution drew fire from several historians associated with the Phillips school. Stampp was accused of hasty and inadequate research, even though he had patterned his organization after that in Phillips' *American Negro Slavery* and had used essentially the same sources. However, these critics charged, he had reached opposite conclusions from Phillips because of his latter-day abolitionist views on slavery. While conceding shortcomings in Phillips' major work, his followers still insisted that *American Negro Slavery* remained the best source of information on the institution of slavery and that Phillips "still overshadows . . . the subject of slavery in the Old South."

In Northern liberal circles, however, *The Peculiar Institution* was greeted as the definitive antidote to Phillips and as proof that slavery had been an oppressive institution. But it was not long before criticism emerged from a new source. In the mid-1960s black scholars noted that while rejecting the explicit doctrines of white racial superiority held by Phillips, Stampp nevertheless maintained that "innately Negroes are only white men with black skins, nothing more, nothing less." Although this reflected the view of many whites in the civil rights movement, who felt that what was needed was the integration of blacks into white society, blacks argued cogently that in making "whiteness" the desired goal, Stampp was accepting the basic doctrine of racism: the superiority of white society. Young white scholars joined in the criticism, and black and white historians alike criticized Stampp for presenting the story of slavery and of the slaves through white sources only, dismissing the validity of existing evidence from the slaves themselves. They pointed out that he had totally ignored a vast body of material in the form of slave narratives written in the nineteenth century by escaped or emancipated bondsmen and in the rich oral tradition of surviving former slaves as recorded by folklorists, particularly the Fisk University and WPA Federal Writers' Project Collections. Although these sources varied in quality and usefulness, it was clear that a large quantity of slave testimony had been neglected by Stampp (as it had been by Phillips) and still awaited systematic investigation.

Despite all this, *The Peculiar Institution* quickly established itself as the leading book to deflate *American Negro Slavery,* and its publication marked the end of Phillips' influence—at least for the time being.

The most controversial book on slavery appeared hard on the heels of Stampp's work. This was Stanley M. Elkins' *Slavery: A Problem in American Institutional and Intellectual Life.* Published in 1959, it immediately launched an extended and often stormy debate.

STANLEY M. ELKINS' *SLAVERY*

Elkins admired Phillips' scholarship, scope, depth of research, and use of original sources. But he went to great lengths to disagree with his contention that plantation slaves in the United States were inferior because the African cultures from which they came were barbaric and inferior. Elkins' premise was that North American slavery was altogether different from slavery anywhere else in the world; that it was, in fact, "peculiar." Building on the work of Frank Tannenbaum's *Slave and Citizen,* published in 1948, Elkins insisted that Latin American slavery was less harsh, exploitative, and closed than North American slavery. (So much did he lean on Tannenbaum that the thesis came to be known as the Tannenbaum-Elkins thesis.) It held that Roman law, imperial control from Madrid, Lisbon, and Paris, the influence of a powerful Catholic church, and the relative absence of racial prejudice in Spanish and Portuguese America mitigated most of the worst aspects of slavery. In North America, on the other hand, there was the virtual absence of "institutional arrangements." Neither government, the church, the law, nor any other institutional authority imposed any effective check on the uses the master made of the slave. The result was the general acceptance of the policy and practice of the master's absolute control and the acceptance, too, of the cruelty by means of which the control was exercised. The slave's need to adjust to this, then, accounts in large measure for the shape and content of the Negro personality.

Elkins' chapter, "Slavery and Personality," received the greatest amount of critical attention. In it, he contended that under North American slavery, the Negro, who in Africa had been a warrior or farmer, was reduced to a dependent, infantile child. This, Elkins argued, was in complete contrast to the slave in Latin

America, who, under a less restrictive system that "was not closed," had been able to retain an adult role and thereby remained both a man and a rebel. Not so, however, in the case of the slave in North America. The dominant slave type here was described in these words:

Sambo, the typical plantation slave, was docile but irresponsible, loyal but lazy, humble but chronically given to lying and stealing; his behavior was full of infantile silliness and by his talk inflated with childish exaggeration. His relationship with his master was one of utter dependence and childish attachment: It was indeed this childlike quality that was the very key to his being.

But what is the evidence for so stereotyping millions of black Americans? Elkins disposed of the problem of evidence by arguing that "the picture of Sambo has far too many circumstantial details, its hues have been stricken in by too many different brushes, for it to be denounced as counterfeit. Too much full knowledge, too much plantation literature, too much of the Negro's own lore, have gone into its making to entitle one in good conscience to condemn it as 'conspiracy.' " Instead of hard evidence, Elkins presented his hypothesis—and it is basically no more than a hypothesis—concerning the alleged mass infantilization of American slaves by the devastating brutality of antebellum American bondage. Using an amalgam of Freudian psychology—the concept of the father image, which in the case of the black slave was the master—together with the interpersonal theory of Harry Stack Sullivan and role psychology, Elkins argued that slavery "infantilized" the slave personality. For the slave, "docility" and "submissiveness" were virtues to be rewarded by white society, while "rebelliousness" and "discontent" were not acceptable and therefore dangerous and nonrewarding.

Elkins sought to buttress his hypothesis with the contention that the impact of enslavement on the personality and character of the Nazi concentration camp inmates was substantially identical with that which plantation slavery in North America had on the personality and character of enslaved blacks. The absolute power of a closed system produced an infantilization, a helpless dependency, and an identification with the oppressors, which prevented both the inmates of the Nazi death camps and slaves in America from offering resistance against their captors. The only way to survive was to play the role of the Sambo.

In part 4 of *Slavery*, Elkins dealt with abolitionism and the culture out of which the abolitionists emerged. He argued that unfortunately, the abolitionists were shaped by their culture to display a romantic, politically destructive antiinstitutionalism. Reflecting the Yankee culture around them, they found themselves hopelessly unequipped to view race oppression as a "problem of institutional arrangement." Instead they exhibited guilty self-righteousness and a romantic individualistic inability to subvert the Southern labor system without strangling all chances of a structured, permanent, and peaceful reform. By rejecting gradualism and a peaceful solution to the problems of slavery, by their intransigent, guilt-ridden stand, and by their inflamed rhetoric, the abolitionists had contributed to the outbreak of the bloody Civil War, which, though it did end slavery, ultimately denied equality to black Americans.

Elkins' *Slavery* was immediately hailed by most white historians as a master-piece, a seminal study of American bondage. Its appearance marked a meth-odological breakthrough and a turning point in American historiography, and, as a pioneering interdisciplinary study, it was to influence all subsequent works on the institution of slavery. Its impact was tremendous. Whereas Elkins simply stated that the widespread existence of Sambo "will be assumed" or will be "taken for granted," authors of monographs and textbooks asserted that he had proved the existence of "Sambo" as the "typical slave." Elkins, wrote many reviewers, had enabled Americans to disenthrall themselves from traditional ways of looking at slavery as benevolent or evil. He had explained better than anyone else the acquiescence of the slaves to bondage and the continuation of that acquiescence by the Negro for almost a century after emancipation.

But there were dissenting opinions, and they increased in volume as a furious debate developed among historians, sociologists, anthropologists, political sci-entists, psychologists, psychiatrists, and journalists. Some resented the author's magisterial tone and viewed *Slavery* as an annoyingly self-aggrandizing book, frequently underlining the significance of its discoveries and the scope of its revisionary enterprise. A number of critics observed that while Elkins disagreed with Phillips, he had reached the same conclusion about the lack of slave re-sistance as the Phillips school had. But where Phillips and his disciples attributed this to the innate racial traits of blacks and the benevolent nature of the system, Elkins attributed it to the extremely oppressive nature of the system and to certain sociological and psychological factors. In both accounts, the Negro emerged as a child. Like Phillips, too, Elkins paid no attention to accounts of slavery present-ed by the slaves themselves. To the extent that he used data and records, he relied mainly on those kept by men who had a vested interest in projecting the idea of the infantile character of black people.

A number of critics challenged the applicability of the Nazi concentration camp analogy. Others questioned the validity of the Tannenbaum-Elkins thesis and effectively refuted the view that Latin American slavery was less harsh and exploitative and that racial friction did not really exist in Latin America. The critics pointed to the essential similarities of all New World slave societies, noting the many common characteristics of slavery in the slave societies among the Anglo-Saxon, the French, Spanish, and Portuguese.

The literature on the Elkins thesis is immense. In 1971 *The Debate over Slavery: Stanley Elkins and His Critics* was published. Edited by Ann J. Lane, the volume includes primarily critical responses to Elkins' ideas in fourteen essays and Elkins' reply to his critics. Since the editor regarded Elkins' treatment of the abolitionists as the "least controversial aspect of his work," she included only one essay on this subject, by Aileen Kraditor.

Two contributors, Mary Lewis and Earl Thorpe, expressed the view that there never was a Sambo stereotype and that Elkins had failed to take into account the fact that slaves often acted like Sambo as a way of accommodating to slavery. They acted docile in order to protect themselves; they knew what they were doing, were capable of doing otherwise, and were simply "putting on" the slaveowners.

In his essay "Rebelliousness and Docility in the Negro Slave: A Critique of the Elkins Thesis," Eugene D. Genovese rejected Elkins' assertion that "Sambo" was a phenomenon unique to the United States. Instead he proposed that this was a situation that existed with all slavery. He further objected to Elkins' use of the concentration camp analogy, calling it confusing and misleading because Elkins had failed to recognize the crucial differences in the two experiences. Slaves were viewed as long-term investments, and therefore concern for their health was a major factor among slaveowners. Concentration camp prisoners, on the other hand, were of no monetary value, and hence their health and the necessity of keeping them alive were of no concern.

Genovese also criticized Elkins for assuming that the planter's power was absolute when, in reality, the slave system was based upon a series of compromises between blacks and whites. At the same time, Genovese defended Elkins. Noting that even though he "carelessly gives such an impression," he did not "equate childishness with docility"; rather he equated it with dependence. Genovese argued that the distinction was too subtle for Elkins' critics to discern, but it did not become any clearer as a result of Genovese's explanation. Indeed Genovese presented a refined version of the Elkins thesis, asserting that while "Sambo" could be seen in every slave, there was also within him an opposite tendency. However, the tendency toward infantilization generally proved stronger. Although Genovese did express reservations about Elkins' model of the slave personality, he concluded that his "generally remarkable book would long be remembered" for "the ingenious analysis" of social psychology. "Whatever the criticism of that analysis, it is a splendid beginning."

George M. Fredrickson and Christopher Lasch also questioned Elkins' conclusion concerning black resistance to slavery, but from a different standpoint. Elkins, they maintained, had failed to make clear what constituted resistance. He had assumed that noncooperation on the part of slaves and the few acts of open violence against whites represented resistance. But according to them, "resistance is a political concept . . . organized collective actions which aim at affecting the distribution of power in a community." While the few slave rebellions in the United States that can be documented tend to fall into this pattern, the two authors rejected the idea that resistance was widespread among blacks in the American slave system.

Fredrickson and Lasch also criticized the Nazi concentration camp analogy and suggested that a better one would be that of a penitentiary, where the relationship between guards and inmates is much closer to that of the plantation setting. Like the penitentiary inmate, the slave learned the need for adjustment and accommodation. The worst aspect of the slave system, they maintained, lay not in the brutality to which slaves were subjected "but in the degree to which slaves inevitably identified themselves with the system that bound and confined them." In essence, the slave did not revolt against the system because he identified with it. Adjustment and accommodation, not "Samboism," characterized the typical plantation slave.

In general, the critics in *The Debate over Slavery* rejected as false and inappropriate the analogy between the dehumanizing effects of American slavery and Nazi concentration camps, and, with the exception of one scholar—Herbert Klein—they rejected the analysis of comparative systems of slavery and the view that Latin American slavery was less harsh, exploitative, and closed than that in North America. They also argued that the day-to-day conditions of American slavery were not as severe as Elkins pictured, contending that although the slave's personality was scarred by slavery, he also learned under slavery the techniques of survival and so was not "Samboized." The system, they said, was more open than Elkins would have one believe, operating through a pattern of compromises.

In the concluding essay, "Slavery and Ideology," Elkins indicated that nothing the critics had written caused him to alter his views. He could only express regret that having written *Slavery* to "break out of a closed circle," he now found that the debate was again assuming the character of just such a closed circle.

While Elkins is certainly right in pointing to the need for an understanding of the effects of slavery on the personality of blacks, his assumptions do not meet the test of scholarship. He is attentive to only one model while inattentive to the rich sources that challenge his conclusion. No true scholar is so naive as to believe that all slaves were rebels, but to use such all-inclusive terms as the "typical plantation slave" is to fall into a fallacy. As Kenneth Stampp pointed out, "a historian utilizing the available evidence on slave behavior and master-slave relationship and taking account of all aspects of the personality theories used by Elkins will be forced to abandon his hypothesis that Sambo was the typical plantation slave."

EUGENE D. GENOVESE AND SLAVERY

While scholars were heatedly debating the portrayal of slavery and the slaves in Elkins' book, the influence of Ulrich Bonnell Phillips began to make its way back into the historical literature. To be sure, Wendell H. Stephenson, after studying Phillips' letters, papers, and notes, concluded that his errors were the result of a closed mind, that "his concepts were formulated" within a decade after he had obtained his doctorate, and that all of his basic views, especially his racism, "were the product of his early research and thought." But even while conceding all this, a number of white historians now insisted that Phillips' analysis reflected the realities of white racism in the Progressive era and that compared with some of his contemporary white scholars, Phillips "comes out looking much like a reformer."

Ironically, it was the man many scholars hailed as *the* American Marxist Eugene D. Genovese who contributed most to rescuing Phillips' work from oblivion. In an introduction to a 1967 reprint of *American Negro Slavery,* in an appraisal of Phillips that same year in *Agricultural History,* and in an edition of Phillips' essays on the slave economy of the Old South issued a year later, Genovese contended that Phillips' work, although dated in some aspects, contained valuable insights into antebellum society that Stampp and others had overlooked. He conceded that Phillips' discussion of Africa depended upon the work of discredited scholars and was "close to being worthless," and he acknowledged that Phillips was an "apologist for white supremacy." Nevertheless, Genovese insisted that Phillips' work was exceedingly scholarly and that the picture he drew of antebellum society was essentially correct in its most important aspects. Genovese went on to add: "I do . . . plead guilty to the charge that I believe his racism to have sharpened some of his genuine insights."

Several years later, Genovese adopted a similar approach to Phillips' racism when, in paying tribute to Phillips' "masterly essay" of 1907, "The Slave Problem in the Charleston District," he glowingly hailed the essay as providing "a model for similar studies"—this despite its comments about the "barbaric," "unambitious," "ever growing mass of half-savage Negroes" from the "African jungle" who exhibited "opressive sociability and friendliness" but "failed to acquire the English language in an intelligible form," despite efforts "in taming them to the ways of civilization."

Genovese's first major work on slavery was *The Political Economy of Slavery,* published in 1961. Having become convinced that slavery was far more than a "system of extra-economic compulsion designed to sweat a surplus out of black labor," Genovese attempted to depict the connections between slavery as an economic system and the political and social aspects of Southern civilization. In doing so, he linked Phillips' analysis of paternalism to the theoretical framework of the Italian Marxist Antonio Gramsci (1891–1937). Genovese used Gramsci's concept of hegemony to explain the complex and subtle ways in which a ruling class exercises domination over society. As defined by Gramsci, hegemony is "the predominance obtained by consent rather than by force, of one group or class over other classes." Genovese drew the conclusion that the antebellum planters were a "hegemonic" class in the South—shaping Southern society according to their own world view and legitimizing their authority by controlling the political, cultural, and religious superstructure.

Slavery, Genovese maintained, was far more than an alternative to free labor; it imparted to Southern society a complex of beliefs, attitudes, hopes, and faith— a unique world view. Southern plantation slavery was not a variant form of capitalism. The Southern slaveholders created a unique but anachronistic way of life—a "premodern" society in the preeminently "bourgeois" nineteenth century. The planters were a ruling class with an aristocratic, precapitalist spirit. They rejected the bourgeois values of thrift, hard work, rationalized production, and maximum profits. They emphasized instead family, status, and a strong code of honor, and they established an essentially paternalistic relationship with their slaves.

Whether it was neofeudal, as Genovese appeared to indicate, or prebourgeois, as he claimed in explaining his meaning, "Southern slavery was not mere slavery . . . but the foundation on which rose a powerful and remarkable social class." True, this class constituted "only a tiny portion of the white population," but it was able to impose its own "prebourgeois" quality upon the South. In order to ensure its hegemony, this class was either willing or compelled to wage war when the only alternative was to surrender its way of life. It was in defense of this aristocratic society, with its antibourgeois values, that the South took up arms in 1861.

In this special way of life, the plantation was a community, somewhat like an extended family with the master as the father and the slaves as children. The plantation was not a "total institution" but rather a place where the two classes, master and slave, significantly influenced each other, although the master class certainly had the upper hand.

Yet the economy upon which this civilization was built was both inefficient and defective. Alfred H. Conrad and John R. Meyer, in a much-discussed essay of 1958 (expanded into a book in 1964), had concluded that slavery was profitable for the typical slaveowner. Although this view (upholding Stampp's earlier conclusion about the profitability of slave ownership) began to be shared by virtually all other scholars, Genovese took issue with it. He reverted, instead, to Phillips' representation of slavery as an economically backward system of production, although he recast it in what he called "Marxian terms." He attributed the backwardness to the low productivity of slave labor, the low level of capital accumulation, the planters' high propensity for luxury consumption, the need to concentrate on a few staple crops, which led to soil exhaustion, the shortage of liquid capital, and the drain of much of the profits out of the region. Slavery prevented the significant technological advance that would have enabled the planters to increase the productivity of their plantations. The precapitalist ideology of the ruling planter class, the unsuitability of the mode of plantation organization for the conduct of diversified farming, combined with slavery's distorting effects upon the distribution of income and the structure of demand with the region—all served to obstruct the economic modernization of the South. Industrial growth was hindered by limited markets, a lack of capital and skills, and the subservience of commercial and industrial activity to the needs and prejudices of the planter class.

Agricultural reform could not aid the South. It would have required skilled labor and capital reserves, neither of which the South had in abundance. The Southern economy was faced with an economic impasse unless measures such as emancipation, urbanization, and industrialization could be adopted. These actions, however, would have totally undermined the economic, political, and social structure of the antebellum South. Slavery was the foundation of the planter's social position and political power. This, above all, had to be upheld.

In his second book, *The World the Slaveholders Made: Two Essays in Interpretation,* published in 1969, Genovese elaborated on his approach to slavery in the Old South. He portrayed the emergence of the Southern slavocracy as a reactionary, "seigneurial" challenge to nineteenth-century capitalism. He also advanced a comparative study of the slaveholding classes in the Western world. Basically he still saw paternalism as the particular form of slaveowner class rule, a paternalism that shaped the thought and action of the owners and that was also internalized by the slaves, resulting in what Genovese calls the "paternalistic compromise." In his view, this compromise led to the creation of the plantation community. But he paid little or no attention to either the slave community or the slaves themselves.

In the second essay, an analysis of the social thought of proslavery apologist George Fitzhugh, Genovese expanded his earlier argument that slavery was a precapitalist social formation and that the planter ideology, as expressed by Fitzhugh, posed a conservative alternative to the liberalism of nineteenth-century American capitalism. In his appreciative analysis of Fitzhugh, Genovese defended him against those critics who have argued that the Southern apologist for slavery was neither original nor very significant.

The reaction to Genovese's works varied from great praise to sharp criticism. Many agreed that at a time when Gramsci's writings were relatively unknown among American intellectuals, Genovese had made a contribution by focusing serious scholarly interest upon his Marxist thought. However, a number of radical critics accused Genovese of eliminating the part that the class struggle played in Gramsci's analysis when applying his concept to the antebellum South. Moreover, Genovese had concentrated all his attention on the ruling class and ignored the fact that the class struggle existed between masters and slaves and that any analysis of slavery must begin with the slaves themselves. Not only had he not focused upon class contradictions and struggle, as any Marxist should, but he had downgraded such slave protest as did exist, comparing it unfavorably with what happened in Brazil and the Caribbean and emphasizing throughout that the slave's response was to accommodate to the owner's paternalism. Genovese was also criticized for failing to recognize that the antebellum South was a capitalist, not a latter-day feudal, economy. His admiration for the planters' outspoken opposition to the bourgeois ethic also came under attack. "Genovese," wrote Arthur Zilversmit, in reviewing *The Political Economy of Slavery,* "seems to prefer the 'lords of the lash' to the 'lords of the loom.'"

In criticizing the same book, Thomas P. Govan argued that Genovese's work showed little hard research and that his conclusions were "products of deductive reasoning," not a factual description of the economy and society of the fifteen slave states. Similarly, in criticizing *The World the Slaveholders Made,* Kenneth Stampp noted that this was "Genovese's second undocumented volume," observing that "he supports his argument with virtually no evidence apart from the polemics of proslavery intellectuals." To black scholar and critic Ernest Kaiser, both books represented "made-up history."

Genovese's third, and most important, work was *Roll, Jordan, Roll: The World the Slaves Made,* published in 1974. As the subtitle indicates, Genovese turned his attention in this work to the slaves themselves. We will deal with this work in various later chapters, but here it is worth noting that Genovese altered a number of his basic concepts. This is especially true in the case of the role played by the slaves. Originally Genovese had viewed the slaves as a culturally dislocated people, who along with their white masters had helped to found a community on the plantation. He adopted Frank Tannenbaum's conclusion in this respect, writing in *The World the Slaveholders Made*: "The slave plantation, as Tannenbaum had eloquently and persistently argued, penetrated every aspect of slave life—economy and politics, religion, family, sexual mores and social relationships—and generated its own pervasive community ethos." In addition, Genovese expressed scorn for Herbert Aptheker's *American Negro Slave Revolts,* which he condemned as "mythology." Instead of the class struggle, which Aptheker had found to be endemic to the antebellum slave economy, Genovese argued that the slaves were relatively passive and unpolitical compared to slaves in other societies of the New World. He also expressed skepticism over the existence of an independent black political tradition and declared that slaves came to the Civil War with only a "dim awareness of oppression."

However, in *Roll, Jordan, Roll* Genovese asserts that "the slaves as an objective social class, laid the foundation for a separate black national culture while enormously enriching American culture as a whole." Previously arson committed by slaves was "nihilistic trashing about," but in *Roll, Jordan, Roll,* such acts by slaves are "brave deeds." He now found a many-sided struggle for survival and human dignity and declared that in *American Negro Slavery,* Aptheker had "demolished the legend of the contented slave." Whatever the limits of his work, he had "unearthed much evidence of insurrection, maroon activity, and other forms of physical resistance and compelled a new departure in the historiography of [slavery]."

Genovese still clung to the basic formulation, emphasized previously, that United States slavery was a precapitalist institution whose practices were guided by the nonpecuniary norms of an aristocratic upper class. While he also clung to the concept of paternalism and again characterized it as a system of "reciprocal obligations defined from above," he now paid more attention to how the slaves themselves modified paternalism, and he emphasized that slaves were often able to alter the terms of the relationship through their own initiatives. They persistently used their varied powers of resistance through subtle and manifold ways to frustrate their masters' or overseers' intentions; they malingered, broke tools, pretended to fail to understand orders, feigned childlike stupidity (which their masters took for real), and employed their wit and capacity for providing amusement—as well as working hard and at times joyfully—all in the cause of converting paternalism from mere obedience to the master's will into a complex relationship of reciprocal values.

Yet even this was basically a new twist to the old interpretation. The struggle for survival itself, Genovese argued, became a pillar of the system, for the slaves' "very strategy for survival enmeshed them in a web of paternalistic relationships which sustained the slaveholders' regime despite the deep antagonism it engendered."

Trapped in the system, slaves survived by retaining and rebuilding traditions of religion, music, song, and art and a relationship toward each other that was neither shared nor even much understood by their masters. Genovese believes that black religion "laid the foundation of protonational consciousness," and as such, it became "the slave's most formidable weapon for resisting slavery's moral and psychological aggression." But it did so at a price, because even as religion provided spiritual strength, it also, because it was developed in a paternalistic context, imparted political weakness. According to Genovese, black Christianity "enabled the slaves as a people to do battle against the slaveholders' ideology, but defensively with the system it opposed; offensively, it proved a poor instrument."

Nevertheless, Genovese asserts that while "Southern paternalism may have reinforced racism as well as class exploitation, . . . it also unwittingly invited its victims to fashion their own interpretation of the social order it was intended to justify. And the slaves, drawing on a religion that was supposed to assure their compliance and docility, rejected the essence of slavery by projecting their own rights and values as human beings." In the end, however, Genovese believes the slaves learned "to cohere as a people" in the space provided by paternalism, but that the process tended to deny the people the tools necessary for liberating themselves. This, as we shall see, was a one-dimensional, static interpretation of slavery.

Among the sharpest criticism of Genovese's concept of the quasi-feudal paternalism of the slaveowners, who supposedly rejected the ethos of unfettered capitalism that prevailed in the rest of the western world, are Paul D. Escott's *Slavery Remembered: A Record of Twentieth Century Slave Narratives*, published in 1979, and James Oakes' *The Ruling Race: A History of American Slaveholders*, published in 1982. In contrast to Genovese's analysis of a complex paternalistic relationship between master and slave, Escott argues that masters and slaves lived in separate worlds and "that blacks had a deeply ingrained awareness of themselves as an oppressed racial group and that this awareness reinforced their community while it guided them to their relationship with whites during slavery and reconstruction." He finds that not only did masters and slaves live in separate worlds, but that "physical proximity only heightened the sense of mental separation," and "that intimacy on the practical level did not lead to a common outlook." Escott concludes that "had the planters been able to see, they would have discovered anger and smoldering resentment."

In contrast to Genovese, James Oakes sees slaveholders as increasingly influenced by the nineteenth-century market economy. For most masters this meant that the paternalistic notion of master-slave relations yielded to the cruder needs for profits. On the ideal plantation of the agricultural journals, slaves were well cared for, but "in practice they were overworked, underfed, and dirty." The lash, in theory to be used sparingly, was altogether too convenient for disciplining bondsmen. While genuine paternalists did exist among the slaveholders, by 1860, they represented a relatively small group, mostly confined to the older Tidewater and Gulf areas. The minority of paternalistic masters were not at all representative of the mainstream of slaveowners. They were part "of a dying culture, not of an emerging one."

Sharply criticizing the fact that the "American historical profession . . . has accepted Genovese's scholarship as the legitimate Marxist interpretation of the slave South," Martin A. Kilian and E. Lynn Tatom demonstrate in depth "the inadequacies of Genovese's Marxian definitions and categories," and correctly conclude that "it is unfair to Marx for Genovese to label his approach Marxian." Genovese, they put it bluntly, "has romanticized the slave South." Genovese's latest work (in collaboration with Elizabeth Fox-Genovese), *Fruits of Merchant Capital: Slavery and Bourgeois Property in the Rise of Expansion of Capitalism* (New York, 1982)—with its insistence that the idea of a capitalist antebellum South must be abandoned—substantiates this opinion.

TIME ON THE CROSS

While historians and other social scientists were debating the various aspects of the slavery controversy, such as profitability, slave personality, resistance, and whether the slave system was capitalist or prebourgeois, reports began to appear that a study of slavery was underway that would bring the controversy to an end. This study was based on the techniques of econometric history (sometimes called "cliometrics"). This use of quantification for obtaining data relating to certain types of historical questions was by no means new, but the application of mathematical and statistical methods to history, as is done in cliometrics, was relatively new, because the economic, statistical, and mathematical methodology did not exist prior to the 1950s. These, plus the increasing sophistication of computers, made it possible for scholars to compare and analyze data that were too extensive for any individual to master.

The champions of cliometrics argued that, for the first time, historical conclusions could be reached objectively, since the computer, unlike the historian, had no prejudice or bias. Critics, however, while conceding the value of quantification, argued that the problem lay with the reliability of the data and their interpretation. The computer may have no bias, but the scholars who selected the data that went into the computer and interpreted the results could hardly be considered objective. A computer is a tool, and like any other tool, its value depends on the way in which it is used.

This dispute seemed largely academic until the long-awaited study of slavery based on computerized history made its appearance in 1974 with the publication of *Time on the Cross* (two volumes) by Robert William Fogel and Stanley L. Engerman, professors of economics at the University of Chicago and the University of Rochester, respectively. In preparation over eighteen years and relying on many thousands of hours of computer-aided research on what was described as "the most complete body of information ever assembled" on slavery, *Time on the Cross* promised to present for the first time a "scientific" picture of how the institution operated.

Fogel and Engerman's basic findings contrasted with what the authors called the "traditional" view of slavery. Far from being an unprofitable system, irrationally kept in existence by a precapitalist elite and "economically moribund" by the eve of the Civil War, slavery was a highly efficient and profitable capitalist enterprise. Southern agriculture was more efficient than that in the North, for slaves, far from being inept or inefficient workers, were more productive than free laborers. The material conditions of the slaves compared "favorably" with those of "free industrial workers." Unlike the popular view that "the destruction of slave marriages was at least a frequent, if not a universal consequence of the slave trade," the authors, citing invoices of slaves sold in New Orleans, concluded that "it is likely that [only] 13 percent, or less, of interregional sales [of slaves] resulted in the destruction of [slave] marriages." Unlike the popular view, derived from "antebellum critics of slavery," that slaveowners frequently exploited their black females sexually, the authors, citing the percentage of the population listed as mulatto in the 1860 census, concluded that the proportion of black "children fathered by whites on slave plantations probably averaged between 1 and 2 percent." The authors argued further that slaves were rarely punished, that the average pecuniary income actually received by a prime field hand was roughtly 15 percent greater than the income he would have received for his labor as a free agricultural worker, and that the diet of slaves "exceeded modern [1964] recommended daily levels of the chief nutrients." Thus, slavery had chalked up two great achievements: the economic success of the slave system and the "achievement" of black slaves as industrious, efficient workers.

"The principal cause of the myth of black incompetence in American historiography is racism." Thus begins the section headed "Toward an Explanation for the Persistence of the Myth of Black Incompetence." The authors bitterly attacked the abolitionists for promoting a racist image of the slaves. Abolitionists shared with proslavery advocates "the conviction that blacks were, for racial reasons, generally inferior to whites both as laborers and as human beings." The authors also attributed lingering racism to those neoabolitionist historians who perpetuated the denigration of blacks' performance as slaves even when they asserted it was due not to biological inferiority but either to mass infantilization or noncollaboration with the slaveowners.

Fogel and Engerman would have none of the argument that slaves were exploited, degraded, or brutalized in the antebellum South. If they were to concede this, then they would be viewing blacks as "the pitiful victims of a system of slavery so repressive that it undermined their sense of family, their desire for achievement, their propensity for industry, their independence of judgement, and their capacity for self-reliance." The authors reject such a "respectable and acceptable sociological justification" of black inferiority. Neither does evidence of resistance count as black achievement. To do so, according to the authors, would be to cast black achievement in an unfavorable light, for there is little evidence, the authors claimed, of "massive resistance" to slavery. Hence, if attention is focused on resistance, the slaves would be painted as "failures even at resistance—sympathetic failures but failures, nevertheless."

The initial reception of *Time on the Cross* was without precedent in the recent annals of historical scholarship. Heralded long before it was published, the work was the subject of television interviews, historical conferences, an unusually large number of lengthy published reviews in the United States and Europe, and numerous unpublished papers. Peter Russell, a Columbia University professor of economics, writing in the *New York Times Book Review*, was awestruck. "If a more important book about American history has been published in the last decade, I don't know about it," he observed. Yale historian C. Vann Woodward concluded a review with the observation that *Time on the Cross* was a book filled with "revolutionary findings" and likely to initiate "a new period of slavery scholarship." *Esquire* was so impressed with the "startling conclusions" that it predicted that *Time on the Cross* "may well abolish history altogether." *Time* was certain that the work "will relegate old-style historians to peripheral pursuits," while *Reviews in American History* raved: "It will be the *Das Kapital* of the literature on American slavery."

In the midst of these encomiums, Herbert Aptheker's two-part review entitled "Heavenly Days in Dixie: Or the Time of Their Lives" appeared. Aptheker minced no words in voicing his disagreement. He called *Time on the Cross* "the most ardent defense of slavery in the United States since George Fitzhugh's *Sociology for the South* was published in 1854, and the most brutal attack on the abolitionists since the Boston mob assaulted Garrison in 1835." He challenged the authors' use of antebellum census data "because of the racism that characterized the census work" and charged them with setting up "straw men" and presenting "caricatures of past literature in the field." Fogel and Engerman had produced a book that "Jefferson Davis could properly claim as his ideological offspring."

Although the first, Aptheker was not the only scholar to criticize *Time on the Cross,* even in these early days. But most of the criticism that did appear was mild. Within two years after publication, however, the situation had completely changed, and *Time on the Cross* was under sharp attack from all directions. Many historians bristled at the idea of a single "traditional interpretation" of slavery and insisted that there was no monolithic interpretation as *Time on the Cross* so vigorously asserted. Moreover, much of what Fogel and Engerman had said about antebellum Southern economic activity was already familiar to scholars. The econometricians had simply knocked down "easily destroyed straw men."

And what should be said of scholars who denounced all of their predecessors as "racists" yet rejected the record of slave resistance and pointed to "the record of black achievement" in submission, loyalty, and efficiency, and even criticized the abolitionists for continuing to view "slavery as oppressive and exploitative . . . even when slaves expressed a preference for bondage over freedom"? "The black achievement which Fogel and Engerman pride themselves in unveiling," wrote Eric Foner in *Labor History,* "seems to be little more than an internalization of the values of whites, and a successful adjustment to and willing participation in an institution based on their exploitation."

The attack also centered on the methodology used by the authors. The two volumes that comprise *Time on the Cross* are so arranged that the conclusions, findings, and interpretations are printed in volume 1, without footnote citations, while volume 2 contains the discussions of evidence and of methods. It soon became clear that many conclusions and findings rested on very slight evidence, and that many, too, were errors. Both *Reckoning with Slavery,* a collection of essays by well-known cliometricians, and *Slavery and the Numbers Game,* a critique by Herbert G. Gutman, went into great detail in establishing Fogel's and Engerman's errors. A partial list of such mistakes includes their estimate of the rewards and effects of whipping; the slave occupational structure; the rewards and incentive system under which slaves operated; the number of slave drivers; the number of black overseers; the frequency of slave sales; the effects of such sales on black families; the sexual behavior of slaves; the efficiency of the slaves; and the diets and medical treatment and long-term development prospects of the slave system.

Gutman charged, with evidence, that Fogel and Engerman were guilty of frequent and shocking errors, fabrication of facts, dubious quantitative data, exaggerated rhetoric, flawed assumptions, faulty inferences, inept research, incompetent reading, confused thinking, vague generalizations, and unfair treatment of abolitionists and historians. The authors, he added, had used their data to construct a model of slavery totally abstracted from actual history. In assuming that slave society was the same in 1720, 1800, and 1860, and making no allowance for change and development, the work was static. It was a collection of statistics from different times and places within the historical development of the South. Hence *Time on the Cross* ends up being "old fashioned."

Black critics like Julius Lester, Mildred C. Fierce, Kenneth Clark, and Ted Bassett called the work a new version of the proslavery argument. Black historian John W. Blassingame did not go so far, but he did highlight in detail the lack of adequate research and data for many conclusions and criticized the "assertions disingenuously presented as facts" in *Time on the Cross.*

In *Reckoning with Slavery,* the cliometricians concluded that "the number of factual props underpinning Fogel and Engerman's argument which have now collapsed is sufficiently large to warrant that the structure of the book be pronounced distinctly unsafe for continued occupancy." Indeed, by the time this judgment appeared, the general conclusion among a large number of scholars was that so much of the work had been proved worthless that "the intellectual edifice constructed by Fogel and Engerman lay in ruins." One critic even predicted that *Time on the Cross* would soon be forgotten and come to be regarded "as little more than an intellectual hoax." Unfortunately, as a number of black critics note, *Time on the Cross* had furnished "the theoretical basis for stepped-up aggression on the black population," and even the criticism of the work might not be able to overcome the influence of this "new slander on black people."

RECENT DEVELOPMENTS

By the mid-1970s, the slavery field had become one of the most active and exciting areas of American historical scholarship. Between 1970 and 1976 alone, there was an extraordinary outpouring of major works on slavery and closely related topics. Books, a great number of scholarly articles, and lengthy and stimulating conferences attested to the fact that slavery scholarship had become one of the richest and liveliest fields in American historiography. Interpretations and reinterpretations abounded of urban and industrial slavery, slave culture, the slave family, the environment of the slave quarters, and slave religion, and for the first time in American historiography, the most eminent scholars and researchers focused on the study of slavery.

Increasingly in the 1970s, slave research focused on the reconstruction of the slave culture. As far back as 1950, black historian J. Saunders Redding had evoked the culture of the slaves in *They Came in Chains: Americans from Africa.* But the extraordinarily complex nature and vitality of slave life only emerged with the 1970s. George P. Rawick's *From Sunup to Sundown,* published in 1971, and John Blassingame's *The Slave Community,* published in 1972, ushered in the new wave of scholarship on the slave's cultural history. Up to that time, most historians had stressed the influence of the slaveholders on shaping the slave's personality and culture. It had been a one-way flow of influence. But the new slavery historians, inspired by E. P. Thompson's assertions about the English workers in his classic *The Making of the English Working Class* (in which he attempted to discover "the degree to which they contributed by conscious efforts, to the making of history"), introduced the active black cultural involvement at all levels.

Blassingame rejected Elkins' argument that the testimony of slaves lacked objectivity. The slave, he argued, like the master, gave his view of the institution, and no one, not even the master, could provide a substitute for that perspective. Some years later, in 1978, Blassingame published *Slave Testimony: Two Centuries of Letters, Speeches, Interviews, and Autobiographies,* which revealed that slaves not only had a culture and a community but that they were sufficiently articulate to tell their own story in many different ways.

Rawick and Blassingame stressed the point that the psychology of Afro-America was reflected in the whole of a black culture. Eugene D. Genovese's *Roll, Jordan, Roll* (which could not have been written had it not been for this entirely new approach to the slave question) represented one side of the issue.

Genovese asserted that plantation slavery "brought white and black together and welded them into one people with genuine elements of affection and intimacy." In contrast to this view, which emphasizes a common master-slave culture, Herbert G. Gutman in *The Black Family in Slavery and Freedom, 1750–1925*, and Leslie Howard Owen in *This Species of Property* stressed the particular character of the Afro-American culture and focused on the extent to which it was autonomous from the slaveholder's mores. They recognized that in some way the slaves and masters had shaped each other's culture. Gutman informs us that many owners "encouraged the formation of completed slave families," and Owens documents the masters' influence in spreading Christianity among the slaves. Yet both are convinced that the slaves' beliefs were largely shaped by socializing experiences rooted within the developing Afro-American community. Gutman and Owens emphasize a common slave culture that was different from, and often opposed to, the slaveholder's culture.

Both Rawick and Blassingame have stressed that slaves maintained a viable family life in the face of great obstacles. But it was Herbert Gutman's *The Black Family in Slavery and Freedom, 1750–1925*, published in 1976, which firmly established the fact that slaves, in the quarters away from their owners, lived in stable families, lived as parents, and lived as persons who won respect and self-esteem in the society of their peers.

I have more to say about the slave family, black culture, and religion in chapter 6 dealing with the slave community. Here I but note that another important development of this period was the increasing use of the former slaves' testimony as a valuable research tool. This had long been urged but seldom heeded. Escaped slaves had written or dictated numerous narratives, but most of these had been dismissed as abolitionist propaganda. Voluminous interviews with ex-slaves had been neglected on the somewhat spurious ground that the survivors were too old to be reliable.

At the annual meeting of the Association for the Study of Negro Life and History in 1936, black historian Lawrence D. Reddick had criticized the narrow scope and "traditional" treatment of existing slave studies. He felt it to be a "waste of time" for historians to continue to base their research upon plantation records, planter journals, and the "usually superficial impressions of travelers," when there was "not yet a picture of the institution as seen through the eyes of the bondsman himself." In his 1944 critique of the "plantation legend," Richard Hofstadter recommended that future histories of slavery be "written in large part from the standpoint of the slave."

In 1945 Benjamin Botkin, the noted folklorist, published *Lay My Burden Down*, a collection of excerpts from the narratives. However, not until 1972 were historians able to use advantageously all of the testimony of ex-slaves in formulating their interpretations of the antebellum chattel system. In that year George R. Rawick published *The American Slave: A Composite Autobiography*, in eighteen volumes. The major source is the Slave Narrative Collection of the Federal Writers' Project of the Works Project Administration (WPA). This consists of two thousand interviews conducted in the 1930s. The other interviews were carried out in the late 1920s and had been collected by historians of Fisk University.

Although recognizing the limitations of the Federal Writers' Project material, most historians of slavery since 1972 have made significant and wide-ranging use of the interviews. However, while John Blassingame drew a good deal of evidence from slave narratives in *The Slave Community*, he excluded as sources the Fisk University and WPA interviews with slaves in the 1920s and 1930s. Blassingame defended his decision by noting that "uncritical use of the interviews will lead almost inevitably to a simplistic and distorted view of the plantation as a paternalistic institution where the chief feature of life was mutual love and respect between masters and slaves." Blassingame called for "a more sophisticated examination" of the interviews, which employed the skills of the linguist, statistician, folklorist, behavioral scientist, anthropologist, and African-ist. Only in this way would the investigator be able to "uncover the complexity of life on the plantation." By combining such systematic studies of oral interviews with critical examinations of the published narratives, scholars would be able "to write more revealing and accurate portrayals of slavery."

This is a tall order. Meanwhile, we shall have to be satisfied with the increasing number of studies of slavery that draw carefully and extensively, though not exclusively, on accounts left by the slaves themselves in writing the history of slavery from the viewpoint of the cabin rather than the big house.

The role of the slave driver has also come under recent study. Traditionally the slave driver, if studied at all, has been portrayed as a savage and cruel instrument of the slaveowners to maintain their domination. Even George Rawick concluded, after editing the slave narratives project, that the drivers were "the instruments of superbrutality."

The first major break with this version of the driver came with Eugene D. Genovese's *Roll, Jordan, Roll*. As interpreted by Genovese, the position of the driver was "fraught with ambiguity." On the one hand, the drivers had to carry out the bidding of the slaveowners and maintain discipline and production with all the power at their command, especially brutal whippings. Yet these men had to return at the end of the day and live among the people they controlled. Caught between two worlds, "the drivers' job ultimately became impossible," Genovese concludes.

Not so, says William L. Van Deburg in the 1979 study, *The Slave Drivers: Black Agricultural Labor Supervisors in the Antebellum South*. Far from being brutes as most historians have described them, an opinion found in many slave narratives, Van Deburg sees them as men who belonged to themselves and the larger slave community, men who represented the interest of their fellow slaves, acting as a buffer, and suffering along with the rest of the black population. In his picture many drivers foiled the system, gave fellow blacks extra rations, laid the whip on easily, and looked the other way when field hands eased up.

Van Deburg's defense of the drivers has called forth the criticism that he has closed his eyes to the reality of the way in which slavery operated. Melvin Drimmer, for example, charges that the author failed to "face up to the evidence that the drivers were part of the machinery of slavery, that this 'leadership elite' served as very effective collaborators, who, in fact, hindered black rebellion." He even questions the accuracy of the subtitle of Van Deburg's book, arguing that to call a driver a "labor supervisor" is to fail to understand "what the system is all about."

More research has yet to be done in this area before a definite conclusion as to the precise role of the slave driver can be reached. But the fact that this aspect of slavery is being finally studied is an important development in itself.

The result of the energetic research on slavery has been a series of studies that have provided a new view of a complex society. While some critics have charged that it also has produced "an essentially static version of slave culture" by ignoring its development in time and space, it is generally agreed that by illustrating the extraordinary vitality of slave life, these studies have destroyed whatever remained of the "Sambo" image drawn in 1959 by Stanley M. Elkins.

In his interesting study, *Slavery and Social Death: A Comparative Study,* published in 1982, Orlando Patterson concludes that the "Sambo" stereotype of the fawning, docile, childlike, and carefree bondsman has been "an ideological imperative of all systems of slavery, from the most primitive to the most advanced. It is simply an elaboration of the notion that the slave is quintessentially a person without honor."

I shall draw on this new research as well as other sources in the discussion of slavery that follows.

2

Rise of the Cotton Kingdom

THE INDUSTRIAL REVOLUTION

During the colonial period, cotton had been raised for home use, but because there was no real market for raw cotton, it had never become as significant a commercial crop as tobacco, rice, and indigo. Wool had long been the staple yarn in England and supplied a large part of the country's needs. It is significant that neither cotton spinners nor weavers were represented in the procession of trades during Manchester's celebration of the coronation of George III in 1763.

New techniques for spinning and weaving cotton goods resulted in their becoming a major fabric in Great Britain. In 1733, John Kay invented the flying shuttle, which greatly lightened the weaver's task and doubled his production. But not even cotton spinners working from morning until night on thousands of spinning wheels in thousands of cottages were able to supply the required yarn. James Hargreaves' spinning jenny (named for either his wife or his daughter), perfected in 1764, increased the production of yarn. Richard Arkwright's water frame (so-called because it operated by waterpower) produced a cotton yarn strong enough for warps. Arkwright, along with several partners, opened factories and equipped them with machinery for carrying out all phases of textile manufacturing from carding to spinning. He was the first to establish the factory system in the textile industry, and in 1773, he began to manufacture an all-cotton calico.

Related inventions followed. In 1779, Samuel Compton introduced the spinning mule (so nicknamed because it was a cross between the water frame and the jenny), which made possible the large-scale manufacturing of high-quality thread and yarn. Then Edmund Cartwright introduced machinery into the weaving process with the invention of a crude power loom, which he patented in 1785.

Machines, however, were so complex, so expensive, and so large that few spinners and weavers could buy and use them in their cottages, and so the factory system grew. When Arkwright introduced James Watts' rotary action steam engine in his cotton mill and demonstrated the feasibility of applying steam power to the new methods of producing textiles, the Industrial Revolution was fully underway.

John Kay's flying shuttle had increased the speed of the weaving operation, and its success created pressure for more rapid spinning of yarn to feed the faster looms. The mechanical spinners produced by Arkwright and Compton increased the output of cotton cloth. Then the replacement of waterpower by steam power increased the speed and output of power-driven machinery. But the supplies of raw cotton to fill the whirling spindles were inadequate.

Now that there was a market for raw cotton, Americans were desperate to supply it, but the cultivation of cotton was limited. The seeds of sea island, or long-staple, cotton suitable for the most delicate textiles, could be quickly removed by passing the bolls through two rollers, set closely enough together so that the seeds could not pass through. But sea island cotton could be grown only along the South Carolina and Georgia coasts; it could not be successfully cultivated inland. The short-staple, upland cotton could grow almost anywhere, but removing the seeds from the fiber was very difficult. Upland cotton had to be cleaned by hand, and it took a worker a whole day to produce one pound of the staple. Even with slave labor, the separation of the seed from the fiber was tedious and expensive.

Between 1783 and 1790, British imports of cotton had grown from 9 million to 28 million pounds. But the total cotton crop in the United States in 1791 amounted to less than 190,000 pounds, and the exports came only to a few hundred bags.

All this changed with the development of the cotton gin in 1793. After graduating from Yale College in the autumn of 1792, young Eli Whitney, a mechanic and inventor, went South to accept a position as a tutor in a gentleman's family. He ended up on the plantation of the widow of General Nathaniel Greene near Savannah. "During this time," he wrote to his father, "I heard much said of the extreme difficulty of ginning cotton—that is separating it from its seed. There were a number of very respectable gentlemen at Mrs. Greene's, who all agreed that if a machine could be invented which would clean the cotton with expedition, it would be a great thing both for the country and for the inventor."

According to some accounts, Mrs. Greene was the real inventor of the cotton gin and allowed Whitney, her boarder, to take out the patent on her invention, something the law prohibited women from doing. The usual story of the invention of the cotton gin, however, tells that within ten days after he had heard of the need for the gin, the newly arrived Yankee worked out a plan for such a machine. Ten days later, he made a successful model. By April 1793 he had built one. A simple apparatus, Whitney's device pulled cotton through a set of wire teeth mounted on a revolving cylinder, with the fiber passing through narrow slots in an iron breastwork too small to permit passage of the seed. The gin could be operated by manpower, horsepower, or waterpower. With the gin, a worker could produce ten pounds of cotton a day—fifty if he had a horse to turn the cylinder. It was now practical to clean the green seeds from the short-staple boll, which could be grown on almost any soil if the warm season were long enough.

Whitney patented his gin on March 14, 1794, and began with his partner, Phineas Miller, to attempt to exploit his discovery. He could not produce enough gins for the rapidly increasing crops to meet the hungry market in the British mills. Infringing machines were put into operation, and Whitney engaged in years of unsuccessful litigation in defense of his patents.

While Whitney himself reaped very little from his invention, the gin transformed cotton from a luxury item to the world's cheapest textile, stimulated the rise of the Cotton Kingdom, and fastened the plantation system and chattel slavery upon the South. In 1792, the United States exported 138,328 pounds of cotton; in 1794, the year Whitney patented the gin, 1,601,000 pounds were exported; the following year, 6,276,000 pounds, and by 1800, the production of cotton in the United States had risen to 35 million pounds of which 17.79 million were exported. In 1812, the year Whitney petitioned Congress (unsuccessfully) to extend his patent rights for the gin, of the 63 million pounds imported by England, close to half was grown and ginned in the United States.

While England was the primary market for the booming cotton crop, a secondary market emerged in New England. In 1790, Samuel Slater, an English mechanic, introduced the spinning machine into the production of cotton textiles in the United States. By 1812, there were 40 spinning mills in Rhode Island with thirty thousand spindles and 30 mills in Massachusetts with eighteen thousand spindles. (In England that year, there were at least 360 mills using 4.6 million mule spindles.) However, weaving was still being done in the homes on handlooms. Under such an arrangement, the development of the factory system was limited; in 1810, twenty times as much cloth was produced by household manufacture as by America's few cotton mills.

But a major transformation was about to take place. After returning to Boston from a trip through the British Isles where he investigated the textile industry, Francis Cabot Lowell engaged the services of a talented mechanic, and together they constructed a workable power loom. By 1815, the Boston Manufacturing Company was operating a factory in Waltham, Massachusetts, producing cotton textiles in a mill where spinning and weaving were done under one roof and all machinery was power driven, using waterpower.

But factory expansion at Waltham was limited by the waterpower capacity of the slow-flowing Charles River, and in 1820, a new site was selected some twenty-five miles from Boston. The community was renamed Lowell after Francis Cabot Lowell, who had died in 1817. The Merrimac factory was constructed in 1823, and by 1839, nine cotton textile mills were operating. The success of the Lowell mills (its dividends rarely fell below 10 percent) led to their expansion throughout New England.

WESTWARD EXPANSION

Cotton cultivation meant expansion. Soil exhaustion, brought about by repeated cotton plantings, caused planters to pack up and move to new land. In 1816, 60 percent of the nation's cotton crop was produced in South Carolina and Georgia, most of it in the Piedmont region. But the land was being used up, and the phenomenal gross returns from the cotton crop of 1815 (with cotton bringing thirty cents a pound) was $18,526,589—sufficient to buy more land to bring into cultivation.

Settlers flocked to the dark, rich soil of the cotton lands in Alabama and Mississippi. Both of these Southern territories had been opened up to settlement after Andrew Jackson's defeat of the Creek Indians in 1814 and soon after by the Creeks' cessions of lands. By 1820, these two territories had become states: Mississippi in 1817 and Alabama in 1819.

The panic of 1819, the first modern American depression, ended a period of rapid expansion and growth in the South. The average price of cotton, 29.8 cents a pound in 1817, dropped to 14.3 cents in 1819. Tracts of land that had been valued as high as $69 an acre were now sold for $2. The depression lasted about six years. By 1825, the economy recovered, and the Southwest entered a new period of economic development as the westward march of the Cotton Kingdom accelerated. Between 1820 and 1830, the cotton area of Georgia was greatly expanded as the Creek Indians were once again forced to cede their territories.

Spanish control of East Florida before 1821 and the presence of the Seminole Indians had confined white settlers from the United States to the towns of St. Augustine and Pensacola, even after the purchase of Florida from Spain in 1819. But as reports reached Georgia, the Carolinas, and Virgina that the combination of soil and climate of Florida "possesses superior advantages and is well adapted to the cultivation both of the short and long staple cotton," planters flocked into the new state with their families and slaves. Others pushed into Alabama, Mississippi, Louisiana, and Arkansas, cutting through the wilderness to clear land for the cultivation of staple crops, among which cotton took first place.

The demand for cotton, accompanied by spiraling land and cotton prices, stimulated further expansion into Indian lands. Before he became president in 1829, Andrew Jackson had already opened large portions of Indian land to cotton cultivation. "He had supplied the expanding Cotton Kingdom with a vast and valuable acreage," notes Michael Paul Rogin. As president, Jackson pursued a policy of Indian removal to areas west of the Mississippi, and in the process, a 25 million acre domain was opened to the expansion of cotton production. As Jackson asked in his message to Congress in December 1830:

What good American would prefer a country covered with forests and ranged by a few thousand savages to our extensive Republic, studded with cities, towns, and prosperous farms, embellished with all the improvements which art can devise or industry execute, occupied by more than 12,000,000 happy people, and filled with all the blessings of civilization and religion?

Martin Van Buren, Jackson's hand-picked successor to the presidency, continued the process of Indian removal for the benefit of cotton producers. He assigned to General Winfield Scott the task of forcing the removal of the Cherokee Indians from western Georgia. The Indians were forced to abandon their homes and leave their property, crops, and livestock behind. During the Cherokee exodus to the site of present-day Oklahoma—along what has been called the "Trail of Tears"—several thousand men, women, and children died as a result of malnutrition, exposure, cholera, and the physical hardships of the journey.

In 1842, the War Department informed President John Tyler that although there were still some Indians residing east of the Mississippi River, "*there is no more land east of the Mississippi, remaining unceded, to be desired by us.*" The land had been delivered over to white planters to cultivate cotton with slave labor.

In 1820, the Alabama-Mississippi area had 200,000 people; ten years later, the population had grown to 445,000. From 1822 to 1824 the area produced 46,000 bales of cotton, and between 1827 and 1829, 80,000 bales. For the decade of the 1830s, Alabama's population increased 76 percent and Mississippi's population a fantastic 154 percent. The slave population of Alabama increased 114 percent and that of Mississippi, 197 percent. In 1834, the coastal states of the Southeast produced 160 million pounds of cotton; Alabama, Mississippi, Arkansas, Louisiana, and other newly settled areas supplied 297.5 million pounds.

The panic of 1837 and low cotton prices only temporarily slowed the growth of the Cotton Kingdom. In 1824, the first planters had come to Texas, then part of Mexico, to obtain cheap and fertile soil for growing cotton. But the revolution of Texas against Mexico caused temporary chaos in the Texan economy, and while the annexation of Texas to the United States in 1845 opened millions of acres upon which cotton could be produced, the Mexican War the following year curtailed emigration. After the war, however, the "Gone-to-Texas" fever swept the South. Even planters in Mississippi and Alabama moved with their families and slaves to the rich, fertile lands of Texas to begin cotton cultivation. From 1850 to 1860, thousands of planters, caught up in the "Texas fever," sold their plantations and moved to Texas. During the same decade, the total population of Texas increased from 212,593 to 604,215, its slave population from 58,161 to 102,566, and cotton production from 58,072 to 431,463 bales.

By the 1850s, cotton had become the major cash crop in central Georgia, in the rich black belt of central Alabama, and in the alluvial Mississippi River delta from Memphis southward almost to Baton Rouge, Louisiana. By 1860, Mississippi had become the nation's leading cotton state with a production of 1,202,207 bales, followed by Alabama, Louisiana, and Georgia. Texas was also rapidly becoming a major cotton producer. In 1861, the Southwest accounted for over three-fourths of the 4 million bales of cotton exported from the United States.

The following table shows the relative importance of the principal Southern ports during the year ending August 31, 1860. The table shows the number of cotton bales handled, minus transshipments.

Number of Bales Handled by Principal Southern Ports

Ports	Number of Bales
New Orleans	2,139,425
Mobile	843,012
Galveston	252,424
Apalachicola, St. Marks, and other Florida ports	192,794
Savannah	531,219
Charleston	509,308

To sum up, at first, cotton cultivation clung to the South Carolina and Georgia coasts. It gradually crept inland, covering these two states; by 1820, their production constituted more than half the total crop. The 1830s saw cotton engulf Alabama, Mississippi, and part of Louisiana, and by 1840, the outline of the Cotton Kingdom had been drawn. Eager cotton growers continued to pour in, fleshing it out, as victims of the "Texas fever" poured into Texas. By 1860, the Cotton Belt covered almost 300 million acres in a huge arc running 1,600 miles in width from eastern North Carolina to western Texas.

The Industrial Revolution, the invention of the cotton gin, and the availability of fertile lands all combined to stimulate the emergence of the Cotton Kingdom. But this still would not have happened without slavery. Without the use of abundant, cheap, forced labor, the rapid expansion and increase of cotton culture could never have been achieved. The settlement of the Gulf Coast was inseparable from slavery. The more labor a planter could get, the more acres he could work and the more cotton he could sell. But whites were not willing to migrate into the wilderness and work for wages. For decades, indentured servants had been an alternative, but by the nineteenth century, this solution was no longer available. The solution was black slavery.

THE ILLEGAL AFRICAN SLAVE TRADE

A number of these slaves still came from Africa, despite the act of 1807 abolishing the African slave trade. The absence of specific enforcement machinery led to multiple violations of the act. The enormous profits were irresistible as the demand and the price for slaves rose, especially after the War of 1812. So notorious was American participation in the slave trade after 1808 that President James Madison informed Congress in 1810 of the necessity of devising further legislation for its suppression. This was attempted with the passage of two acts: one, enacted in 1818, promised that one-half of the fines and forfeitures secured from slaving penalties would go to informers; the other, passed in 1820, labeled direct participation in the slave trade as piracy, with those convicted liable to punishment by death. By the time the act of 1820 was passed, estimates of importations in the preceding decade were as high as 60,000. A ready market for contraband slaves flourished in the Southern states and the West Indies, and the precautions forced upon the slavers to evade the law only increased their profits.

In his 1896 study, W.E.B. Du Bois condemned government "apathy" toward stamping out the illicit trade, noting that the act of 1807, supplemented by those in 1818 and 1820, came very near to being a dead letter. In his 1963 work, *American Slavers and the Federal Law, 1837–1862*, Warren S. Howard found it ironic that despite the many prohibitory laws, the trade continued to flourish. The government's efforts to halt the traffic were indeed feeble. The sum designated by Congress for suppression of the slave trade in 1819 was $100,000, but thereafter it decreased annually as Southern influence increased. With inadequate funds and an officer class inclined, because of its Southern connections, to look the other way, the U.S. Navy was in no position to prevent illicit importations.

On May 24, 1824, Richard Rush, an American minister to the Court of Saint James, negotiated a convention with the British to give the naval forces of both nations the right to search and seize ships of either nation suspected of engaging in the trade. The document, elaborately bound and with the seal of the United States attached, was signed by President Monroe and Secretary of State Adams. When it was presented to the Senate for approval, amendments by the Southern senators so emasculated the agreement that Great Britain subsequently rejected it.

By 1840, Great Britain had signed up all the major maritime powers except one to a treaty of "reciprocal search and seizure" to help enforce the antislave trade declarations. The lone exception was the United States. Under these treaties, the British Navy acquired the right to board the signatory nations' ships at sea and, if evidence of slaving were found, to seize them and send them into port for legal penalties. But the United States refused, insisting that only U.S. Navy vessels could examine ships flying the American flag. Apart from the fact that the federal government lacked the zeal to do anything on its own, the U.S. Navy did not have the resources to cope with the crafty slave traders. Hence the U.S. flag became a refuge of slave traders of all countries and "the protector of every slaver bold enough to fly it." The zest with which England put down the slave trade after it had served its purpose inevitably brought the charge of "holy hypocrisy." But the zeal with which the United States sabotaged the British efforts gained it the reputation of being the "champion of the unholy traffic."

After years of prodding, Congress in 1842 joined Britain in suppressing the slave trade and granted the British Navy the right to search. In 1843, the United

States established its own African Squadron to suppress the slave trade, but Southern influence resulted in a lack of adequate equipment, money, and personnel, all of which hamstrung the squadron. It simply had too few ships to patrol a coastline almost three thousand miles long, and, as Robert Wetherall points out in his study, "The African Squadron, 1843–1861": "For its first sixteen years, the African Squadron was never provided with enough ships to make even a dent in the 'Guinea Trade.' " Cuba and Brazil were the most important slave economies that continued the slave trade far into the nineteenth century. But until after the Civil War, the United States was the third, and until then American planters and slave traders managed to foil all attempts to end the trade.

THE DOMESTIC SLAVE TRADE

There is a considerable debate over the magnitude of the illegal foreign slave trade, with W.E.B. Du Bois, Daniel P. Mannix, Malcolm Cowley, Peter Duigan, Clarence Clendenon, Warren S. Howard, and Kenneth M. Stampp maintaining that it was an extensive trade, while Ulrich B. Phillips, W. H. Collins, and Eugene D. Genovese argue that it did not amount to more than a drop in the bucket. But whatever the extent of the illegal African trade to the United States, it was replaced in large part by the growth of the domestic or internal slave trade. The expansion of cotton production to the Southwest brought about an increased demand for slaves, which the planters of the upper South, in the main, were willing to supply and slave traders willing to transport. For while the lower South was booming, the upper South remained in a period of steady economic decline. Virginia was especially affected by declining agricultural production, a decrease in population, and generally a depressed, outmoded economy. Virginia's rate of population growth from 1820 to 1830 was 13.5 percent, a large decrease from 37 percent in the previous decade.

The emerging Cotton Kingdom was hungry for blacks, and the upper South had surplus slaves in large quantities to sell. Tobacco, the staple of the slave-manned plantations of the upper South, had become an increasingly unprofitable crop. Edward S. Abdy, an English visitor, described the scene between Alexandria and Warrenton, Virginia, as one of "exhausted soil, miserable hovels, thinly peopled villages, half-ploughed fields, and spontaneous vegetations in rank fertility, usurping the place of healthy and profitable crops."

Declining tobacco production created a large slave surplus in both Virginia and Maryland. In 1820, Virginia's slave population numbered 425,148, and Maryland's was 107,397. Both of these Southern states (and Kentucky, North Carolina, and Missouri, which also grew little or no cotton), found a ready market for their excess slaves in the rapidly expanding cotton states to the south. The closing of the African trade drove slave prices upward, with attendant monetary gains for the planters of the slave-selling states.

Outside of Fredericksburg, Virginia, James Silk Buckingham, an Englishman touring the Southern United States, observed a sight that was increasingly to be seen in the South. Buckingham noticed a coffle of slaves marching to a slave market in the Deep South:

The men chained together in pairs, and the women carry the children and bundles, on their march to the South, the gang was under several white drivers, who rode near them on horseback, with large whips, while the slaves marched on foot beside them; and there was one driver behind, to bring up the rear.

This was just one of thousands of coffles that traveled from Virginia, Maryland, Kentucky, and Tennessee to the lower South in the domestic or internal slave trade during the era of the Cotton Kingdom. How extensive was this trade? The first serious attempt to estimate mathematically the extent of the internal slave trade was made in 1904 by W. H. Collins in his book, *The Domestic Slave Trade of the Southern States*. He divided the South into two categories: the states that were net sellers and those that were net buyers. In the former category were Virginia, Maryland, and Kentucky, and later South Carolina and Missouri. Starting in 1820, these states began shipping southward five thousand slaves per year. In the 1830s, a peak of over eleven thousand slaves per year were sent to the buying states. For the next twenty years, selling leveled off first to six thousand and then to eight thousand annually.

In 1931, Frederick Bancroft's *Slave Trading in the Old South* was published. By combining the results of earlier research with new research and findings of his own, Bancroft came to the conclusion that a vast exodus of slaves had been flowing from the border slave states to the areas of the Southwest. He estimated that between 1830 and 1840, 113,681 slaves should have been added to the Virginia slave population as a result of natural increase. After computing the effects of emancipations and runaways, Bancroft concluded that 117,938 slaves were exported from Virginia for the decade, or about 11,800 slaves a year. Not all were sold and exported by traders; many migrated south with their masters. Bancroft demonstrated the way in which the increase of Negro slaves allowed many Virginia planters to remain solvent. Impoverished planters did not usually wish it known that they sold slaves, for this would have publicized their economic plight. Nevertheless, they sold them.

Virginia was only one of the states exporting slaves to the Southwest. In discussing the slave trade in Kentucky, Bancroft refuted the view that it was of minor importance because the papers of the period and the Louisville commercial directories contained little or no mention of slave traders. Bancroft demonstrated that the traders were called by other names—agents, general agents, general commission merchants, or auctioneers—and concluded that the slave trade flourished in Kentucky until the Civil War.

In South Carolina, as in Virginia, Bancroft showed, many of the most prominent citizens were dependent on the sale of their slaves; such transactions were far more profitable than the use of slave labor in agriculture.

On the question of emigration, Bancroft declared that of all the slaves who finally reached the South, one-third at best did so by moving with their owners. In this respect, he differed sharply from Collins, who believed that in areas like Virginia, from 50 to 60 percent of the slaves who went south were chattels who had emigrated with their masters.

In 1956, Kenneth Stampp published *The Peculiar Institution* in which he listed Virginia as providing the heaviest traders, with Maryland and Kentucky sharing the second place. Over a thirty-year period prior to the Civil War, 150,000 Virginia slaves ended up in the Deep South. For Maryland, the figure was 75,000. These included both those traded and those who emigrated, since Stampp made no effort to make a distinction between the two.

A number of scholars have argued recently that the notion that the domestic slave trade was extensive is without foundation in fact. In 1972, William Calderhead insisted that Maryland did not participate extensively in the interstate slave trade, and he pointed to a number of factors that, he claimed, limited the trade. While slavery as a system of labor in Maryland was no longer profitable, the practice of renting out slaves was, and there was some economic incentive to rent rather than sell one's chattel to customers to the South. Again, many slaves in the upper South were promised freedom, but the liberation was delayed for years. In such a situation and usually by law, a slave could not be sold beyond the state.

In their book, *Time on the Cross*, published in 1974, cliometricians Robert Fogel and Stanley Engerman estimated that between 1810 and 1860, slave traders in Virginia, Maryland, and the Carolinas exported only an average of twenty-five hundred slaves a year. They claimed, moreover, that slave trading played a minor role in the transportation of slaves to the south and West. Slave traders, they maintained, transported only 16 percent of the total number of slaves who migrated to the new cotton lands, while the remaining 84 percent of all slaves traveling from the Old South to the New South went with their masters.

But when one realizes that Alexandria alone often exported twenty-five hundred slaves annually, the same amount Fogel and Engerman cite for the entire four-state average, the figure they reach is certainly very small. Indeed the Chesapeake Bay area slave-trading cities of Washington, D.C., Richmond, Baltimore, and Alexandria easily equaled the two thousand five hundred yearly average, and this leaves out such important slave-trading cities as Annapolis (Maryland), Norfolk and Petersburg (Virginia), Lexington (Kentucky), and Columbia (South Carolina). In all of these cities, moreover, slave trading was a fully operating business and played an important role in the transportation of slaves. The view that most slaves accompanied migrating planters and were not bought and sold by slave traders is hardly tenable. "The evidence is ample enough to conclude that a substantial interstate trade in human beings took place," writes Richard Sutch. He estimates that over one-quarter of a million slaves were exported from the selling states to the buying states during the last decade of slavery, nearly one slave out of every fifteen. A conservative estimate values these slaves at $200 million, or approximately $20 million per year.

As early as 1800, Alexandria and Washington, D.C., had become depots for the collection of slaves, but the continuing illegal African slave trade hindered their full development as slave markets. By 1825, professional slave traders began to appear in these cities. On February 15, 1825, the *Alexandria Gazette* carried the following advertisement:

SLAVES WANTED

The subscriber will at all times, pay the highest price in cash for slaves, either single or in families. Letters addressed to me in Alexandria, will be promptly attended to. Sixty or seventy slaves at this time, expressly to go to Tennessee.

E. P. LEGG

Similar notices began to appear in newspapers in the large cities and small county seats of the upper South. The number of slaves demanded in each advertisement ranged from a low of twenty to twenty-five to a high of one thousand. Young slaves were stressed, the terms were cash, and the seller was promised the highest prices.

At first, most of these advertisements were placed by a single trader who moved through the exporting states until he collected the group of slaves. He then escorted them to the importing states, selling where he could or at times selling them in a block to a local trader. There were even a few amateur slave traders who sought a quick fortune in a few ventures. They were usually planters who contacted other planters, either relatives or friends, about the possibility of selling slaves for profit in the Deep South. "My object," wrote one of these amateur slave traders in 1834, "is to make a fortune here as soon as possible by industry and economy, and then return to enjoy myself."

While the largest class of traders in terms of numbers consisted of single traders, the business of slave trading soon resulted in the emergence of larger organizations. On May 17, 1828, the *Alexandria Gazette* carried the following advertisement inserted by Franklin, Armfield & Co.:

CASH IN MARKET

The subscribers having leased for a term of years the large three story brick house on Duke street, in the town of Alexandria, D.C. formerly occupied by Gen. Young we wish to purchase one hundred and fifty likely young negroes of both sexes between the ages of 8 and 25 years. Persons who wish to sell will do well to give us a call, as we are determined to give more than any other purchasers that are in market, or that may hereafter come into market.

Franklin Armfield & Co., a partnership established by Isaac Franklin and John Armfield on February 28, 1828, consisted of a slave-trading agency in Alexandria and distributing agencies in New Orleans and Natchez. The establishment in the East was for buying and shipping slaves, while the ones in New Orleans and Natchez were for receiving and selling them. At the time they established their partnership, there was no precedent for such a setup. It was a complete slave-trading organization, eliminating all middlemen. They established a system of collecting agents, a stockade in Alexandria, a large and dependable slave transporting fleet, and outlets for their slave merchandise. Through this organizational structure, Franklin, Armfield dominated the Virginia slave market in the 1830s.

Large slave-trading firms like Franklin, Armfield had "houses" in their buying and selling areas where a member of the firm resided. In the exporting area (states of the upper South), slaves were brought by their owners to the house and sold to the traders. Agents in outlying areas sent the slaves they purchased to the house—a combination hotel and jail—where the chattels were kept. In some cases small traders would sell some slaves to the larger traders instead of taking them into the lower South. The purchased slaves were collected at the house until a number sufficient to warrant shipment to the importing states had been obtained. From these houses, or pens, the slaves left for the lower South by ship or land.

In Alexandria, the city's minor traders used Franklin, Armfield's holding and transportation facilities, since they were able to accommodate large groups of slaves. Franklin, Armfield so dominated the Alexandria slave market that others participating in the city's slave trade became official agents of the company. The firm's successful activities helped make Alexandria the most important slave exporting city in the upper South, at least until the 1850s. Even Austin Woolfolk of Baltimore, one of the leading traders on the Atlantic Coast, advertised in the *Alexandria Gazette*.

George Kephart, a small Maryland trader, became Franklin, Armfield's principal Maryland agent. He had impressed the firm with his manner of collecting slaves. Instead of waiting for planters to bring in their slaves, he would visit plantations, taverns, and hotels seeking slaves for sale. In 1837 Kephart purchased Franklin, Armfield's slave pen and the *Isaac Franklin,* its best ship. His first advertisement on March 14, 1837, read:

NEGROES WANTED

I will give the highest cash prices for Likely Negroes, from 10 to 25 years of age, Myself or Agent can at all times be found at the establishment formerly owned by Armfield, Franklin & Co., at the west end of Duke Street.

Geo. Kephart.

When federal troops entered Alexandria in 1861, they seized Kephart's business correspondence, and selections from it were published by British abolitionist Moncure D. Conway. Introducing the letters, which covered the period from 1837 to 1857, Conway remarked that "the firm of Kephart and Co., Alexandria, Virginia, was, ever since I can remember, the chief slave-dealing firm in that state, and perhaps anywhere along the border between the Free and Slave States." The letters give insight into the activities of a leading slave trader. The first eight are concerned with the correspondence between Kephart and other traders in Richmond and New Orleans. Bacon Tait, a successful Richmond trader, wrote to Kephart warning him against selling "inferior negroes" in the

Louisiana market, noting that while "trash and defective" were "very frequently sold at a profit for the time being; yet the sales often recoil upon the vendor with detriment more than counterbalancing such profit." The second letter was from Thomas Bondar, a New Orleans trader, replying to an inquiry from Kephart on the sale of children. Bondar replied: "You ask about little boys and girls. . . . All I can say is that they are always ready sale; but they must be purchased right, or they do not pay much profit." Most of the other letters dealt with the sale of individual slaves. A letter from an agent of Bacon Tait of Richmond concerns the sale of a sickly female servant. "Today Rachel Lockhert is sold for $587.00. This is the best offer we have had since she was sick affecting her eyes so that she had to be blistered on the back of the neck." The agent urged Kephart to send him "some young Negroes" since there was "some activity in the market."

The last letter, from George Carter of Louden County, Virginia, went: "I have a mulatto female servant, twenty years old, a first-rate seamstress, capable of cutting out both men's and womens apparel, hearty, robust. She is for sale and if you wish to buy her, and will stipulate to send her to New Orleans or to the South, you shall have a bargain in her."

There were three methods by which slaves in the upper South were usually sold to the lower South. The most common was by a standard bill of sale. In this legal instrument, a contract was made between buyer and seller naming the slave purchased, his or her price, and the place of residence of the seller and slave, as well as the slave's name. The next important means was through the settlement of the personal estate of someone deceased. Since there were thousands of slaveholders in the upper South, all of them inevitably destined to leave their chattels behind, a large base of sales existed from this source. Traders liked the opportunities that sales of estates offered.

The third source of sales for the domestic slave trade was through the state's legal authorities. Although it varied from state to state, it was usually as a form of punishment, except for serious crimes for which hanging was to be the penalty, that slaves could be sold out of state. Then too, slaves who had been guilty of several escape attempts, slaves guilty of helping others escape, and all slaves completing a penitentiary sentence had to be sold out of state. In practically every case, slave traders got nearly all of these "cast-offs."

There were two additional ways in which slaves were sold. One was by kidnapping free blacks or even slaves and then selling them South. The other was through the legal instrument of the land deed. Usually land and slaves were sold separately, but a small percentage of the upper South's land sales also involved the slaves who worked the land. But usually traders had little interest in such a sale.

Kenneth Stampp points out that there were two different types of slave sales: "involuntary" and "speculative." An auction sale or administrative sale, to ease the financial troubles of an estate, was considered involuntary, but to sell a slave for profit was speculative and, according to Stampp, frowned upon by many planters. An advertisement in the *Alexandria Gazette* of June 13, 1835, read: "The undersigned, a planter in Mississippi and a native of Virginia, wishes to purchase for his own use and not for speculation, thirty or forty negroes of good character." General sales of surplus slaves, made in the belief that this would decrease the threat of slave uprisings, were widely approved.

The majority of the upper South's white population accepted the domestic slave trade as a natural part of the Southern way of life, but a few protested. In 1827, a small group of citizens organized the Benevolent Society of Alexandria for Ameliorating and Improving the Condition of the People of Color. The group resented the presence of slave traders in their city. They spoke of the harshness and misery that was visible when traders drove slaves through the city streets and then confined them in "loathesome prisons." They especially stressed their concern that such scenes tended to corrupt the entire population:

These enormous cruelties cannot be practiced among us, without producing a sensible effect upon the morale of the community; for the temptation to participate in so lucrative a traffic, though stained with human blood, is too great to be withstood by all, and even many of those who do not directly participate in it, become so accustomed to its repulsive features that they cease to discourage it in others.

But few other white southerners shared these fears, and no real movement emerged to check or reverse the growing domestic slave trade.

"Preeminent in villainy . . . stands the hard-hearted negro trader," a contemporary work, *Social Relations in Our Southern States*, argued. A widely held view of the interstate slave trade is that those who engaged in it were looked down upon and even despised by their contemporaries. Yet one of the largest and most successful traders, Isaac Franklin, married the daughter of a Presbyterian minister, and other prominent southerners have been identified with various aspects of the trade.

ORGANIZATION OF THE DOMESTIC SLAVE TRADE

While some trading did take place throughout the year, it appears that the majority of the slaves were sent South after the harvest. The mode of transportation could be by foot, with some of the women and children being allowed to ride in wagons, while others were sent by ship, especially for the long trip from Maryland and upper Virginia to Louisiana. In later years some slaves were shipped by rail.

An 1834 description of the slave ship *Tribune,* owned by Franklin, Armfield, read: "The hold is appropriated to the slaves, and is divided into two apartments. The after hold will carry about eighty women, and the other about one hundred men. On either side were two platforms running the whole length; one raised a few inches, and the other half way up the deck. They were about five or six feet deep. On these the slaves lie, as close as they can stow away."

The transportation of slave cargoes from port to port was regulated in a manner similar to transported cargo of merchandise in general. The African Slave Trade Act of 1807 established the framework for domestic slave trading. Any ship over forty tons could transport slaves between American ports but only after duplicate manifests were made out for each transported slave and presented to the port collector before sailing. Vessels weighing less than forty tons were prohibited from transporting slaves, and those violating this provision were subject to a fine of $800 for each slave on board. There were, however, no provisions to deal with the seaworthiness, safety, or health conditions of those vessels of over forty tons, nor was there any restriction on the number of slaves carried on them. The captain and shippers each had to sign a statement declaring that the slaves on board "had not been imported into the United States, since the first day of January one thousand eight hundred and eight."

The manifests that accompanied the slave cargo included the names of the slaves, their ages, height, color, the name and residence of the shipper and consignee, the name of the ship's captain and that of the vessel, its tonnage, and the ship's destination. One manifest remained at the port of departure, and the other accompanied the ship to its destination. After the manifest was checked at the arriving port by the port official and the cargo checked for contagious disease by the port collector, the slaves entered the port city and waited for their eventual sale. Any ship violating these statutes would be forfeited to the United States, and the ship's master would be fined $1,000. Any captain who failed to present a manifest to the collector was subject to a $10,000 fine.

Generally the domestic slave trade was regulated by federal law, but there were a few laws regulating the trade peculiar to the District of Columbia. To engage legally in the slave trade there, for example, the slave trader paid a fee of $400 to the district government for a slave-trading license.

Many traders preferred the water route to overland transportation because more slaves could be transported in a shorter period of time. However, during January and February, the Potomac River often froze or filled up with ice, closing the ports to shipping. Shipwrecks and mutinies were the major dangers of the sea routes. It was possible for traders to insure a slave cargo against the risks of the sea. A typical policy, issued by the Louisiana Insurance Company, insured the slaves of William Kemmer & Company of Alexandria

on the sea against men of war, fire, enemies, pirates, rovers, thieves, jettison, letters of mart and counter mart, surprisals, taking at sea, arrests, restraints and detainments of all kinds, prices or people of what nation, condition or quality soever, barrating of the master and mariners, and all other perils, losses and misfortunes that have or shall come to the hurt, detriment or damage of the said goods or merchandise, or any part thereof.

The policy stated that the company was not responsible for "insurrection, elopment, suicide, and natural death." The premium for the one hundred slaves, valued at $40,000, was 1.25 percent.

The alternative to shipping was transporting slaves by the overland route to the Ohio River, where they were placed on boats and sent to New Orleans or Natchez. Many descriptions of these slave gangs were given by visitors to this country. One Englishman, on passing through the trans-Allegheny in 1834–1835, wrote:

Just as we reached New River, in the early grey of the morning, we came up with a singular spectacle, the most striking one of the kind I have ever witnessed. It was a camp of Negro slave drivers, just packing up to start, they had about three hundred slaves with them . . . who had bivouacked the preceding night in chains in the woods; these, they were conducting to Natchez on the Mississippi River, to work up on the sugar plantations of Louisiana.

They had a caravan of nine wagons and carriages in which the whites and any slave who had become lame could ride. The females were sitting on logs, and children were warming themselve by the fire. Two hundred men stood in a double file, chained together. The observer continued:

I had never seen so revolting a sight before. Black men in fetters, torn from the lands where they were born, from the ties they had formed . . . and driven by white men, with liberty and equality in their mouths, to a distant and unhealthy country to perish in the sugar mills of Louisiana where the duration of life for a sugar mill slave does not exceed seven years.

The white slave drivers, "tolerably well dressed," were "standing . . . laughing and smoking cigars."

In July 1835, Ethan Allen Andrews visited the Alexandria stockade of Franklin, Armfield and witnessed the preparations for an overland trip. The tailor shop provided each slave with two suits of clothes before departing. They were not to be worn until they reached market. A Franklin, Armfield agent told Andrews that "as it is an object of the first importance that the slave should arrive at their place of destination 'in good order and well conditioned,' every indulgence is shown to them, which is consistent with their security, and their good appearance in the market."

The narratives of slaves who experienced the slave coffle are hardly in keeping with the idea that "every indulgence" was shown to the slaves. Charles Ball described how he was placed with a group of thirty-two other slaves, men and women. The women were tied together with a rope, "about the size of a bed cord, which was tied like a holster round the neck of each," while a strong iron collar was fitted closely by means of a padlock around each man. The men were chained together, and the slave to whom Ball was chained "wept like an infant when the blacksmith fastened the ends of the bolts that kept the staples from slipping from their arms." After the day's march, the master ordered a pot of mush for their supper.

Reverend W. B. Allen, born a slave in Alabama, recalled the cruel and callous treatment at the hands of the slave traders:

The slaves were driven by men on horses who, at times, drove them on the run until they fell from exhaustion. The drivers always carried whips, 12 to 15 feet long, which were made from 8 strands of plaited rawhide. These whips were fastened to short, heavy hickory stocks; and a driver, seated on a horse, could split a Negro's hide with one of them from a distance of 15 or 20 feet. With such a ''persuader'' to hurry them along, the slaves would often travel at a fast gait for hours—until they dropped in the road. All that lagged behind or failed to keep the pace set by the horsemen were literally slashed to ribbons. The drivers were often hard drinkers, and while under the influence of liquor they bloodied their slaves fearfully.

William Wells Brown described the plight of women and children in his reminiscences of the slave coffle. Often, he wrote, young children, many too young or unsophisticated to understand the gravity of the situation, grew very noisy. The ''driver'' would complain of a child's crying and warn the mother to stop the noise. If the crying persisted, ''drivers'' would take the child away from its mother and give it away to the first home the ''gang'' came across. The mother would run up to the ''drivers'' and fall on her knees, begging for him to return the child to her. Clinging around his legs, she might cry, ''Oh, my child! my child! master, do let me have my child! Oh, do, do. I will stop its crying, if you will only let me have it again.'' After one such occurrence, a feeling of horror would shoot through every mother on the coffle, as all would imagine this happening to them.

Contemporary observers noted the increase in slave cargoes on the railroads in Virginia during the 1850s. In 1854, Frederick Law Olmsted reported seeing two freight cars of about forty slaves; ''such kind . . . of activity . . . is to be seen every day.'' Lyman Abbott observed that ''every train going south has just such a crowd of slaves on board, twenty or more and a 'nigger car' which is very generally also the smoking car, and sometimes the baggage car.'' During a trip between Fredericksburg and Richmond, Charles Dickens wrote that ''in a negro car belonging to the train in which we made this journey were a mother and her children who had just been purchased.'' Fares for transporting slaves by rail generally were half that of the price of a full fare for a passenger. Some railroads allowed Negro children in the slave trade to travel free.

On the road, a slave coffle might average about twenty to twenty-five miles on a good day. On the major railroad lines leading to the cotton plantations of the lower South, slaves were transported much more swiftly.

After seven or eight weeks of traveling through the wilderness, the coffles reached the Mississippi, and on its banks, the slaves were sold to the planters of the Southwest. Natchez, Mississippi, was the western terminus for slaves sent overland, and one mile outside the city there was a settlement called ''Forks of the Road,'' devoted exclusively to the display and sale of slaves.

Slaves sent by sea to the Southwest were usually sold in New Orleans, the greatest slave-trading center in the South—"The Mistress of the Trade," according to Frederick Bancroft—and a larger market than Richmond and Charleston combined. The slaves were taken to one of the many trade yards or pens that dotted the city. The housing quarters for the slaves usually consisted of three floors of room in each building. There were two entrances to the pen, one for the slaves, the other for visitors and buyers. The windows in front, which overlooked the street, were heavily barred, as were those overlooking the yard.

Men and women were separated, and both were segregated from the children. Conditions for the slaves in the pen were much improved over those they had had to face in the coffle. They were fed regularly, washed, shaved, combed, and "plucked" (an activity performed upon the old slaves, which included the pulling out of gray hairs). Those who were too grey to be plucked without making them bald had their hair dyed.

But there was also the flogging room. Screwed into the floor of this room were several rows of wooden cleats, through which was passed a long cord. There were floggings every day, but it was a rule not to flog with any instrument that would cut the skin in order not to depreciate the value of the "property." Punishment was inflicted with a flogging paddle, which contained the flogs of leather, about a foot-and-a-half long. Flogging was inflicted for various reasons but especially for "not speaking up and looking bright and smart" in the presence of a potential buyer.

The final step in the trading process was the sale, generally conducted in a large hall or at an open-air auction block. Interested planters or traders sat around the block upon which the slave was placed, with the auctioneer standing beside the chattel to be sold.

To ensure the highest possible price, slaves were attired in their "Sunday best." Men wore good-quality blue cotton suits, with vests, ties, white shirts, well-shined shoes, and hats. Women were adorned in multicolored calico dresses with bright silk bandannas. The idea was to create a pleasing appearance of cleanliness and well-being. The men, to show they were spirited, were often given a drink of gin or whiskey. Sometimes each slave would be given a silver coin to put them in a happy mood or to make them seem cheerful.

Prospective purchasers usually examined Negroes carefully to make sure there were no physical defects or scars from whippings. Scars found on a slave's back were considered evidence of a Negro's rebellious or unruly spirit and could hurt the sale. The age of the Negro also helped to determine value. Planters were hesitant to purchase blacks whose advancing years would prevent a profitable output of work. There were some exceptions, such as house servants and skilled blacks, who might be used as cooks, nurses, carpenters, bricklayers, or blacksmiths. The average purchaser, however, preferred to buy young Negroes.

The customer would dwell upon the good or bad qualities of each slave, and many would make the "merchandise" hold his head up and walk briskly back and forth. They might feel his hands, arms, and body, or order the slave to open his mouth and show his teeth, "precisely as a jockey examines a horse which he is about to barter for or purchase." Sometimes a man or woman was taken to a private room in the yard, where they were stripped and inspected more minutely.

Slaves who were to be sold were instructed to look "spry and smart," to hold themselves up well, and to smile cheerfully. Despite the emotional impact of the proceedings, the slave was forced to look bright and lively, for the slave's general appearance influenced the price.

When the customers finished examining the "merchandise," the traffic in human flesh began. The auctioneer, according to numerous accounts, would usually begin:

Gentlemen, here is a likely boy; how much? He is sold for no fault; the owner wants money. His age is forty. Three hundred dollars is all that I am offered for him. Please to examine him; he is warranted sound. Boy, pull off your shirt—roll up your pants—for we want to see if you have been whipped. I have just been informed by his master that he is an honest boy and belongs to the same church as he does.

Although the purchaser inspected the slave, it was entirely possible that a defect might be overlooked or deliberately concealed—hence the importance of the announcement that the slave was "warranted sound." In a number of cases, the court ruled that although the purchaser had had an opportunity to examine the slave, under the warranty of soundness, "the vendor is answerable for any defect which is not obvious to the senses." In one case a Negro girl was sold with a warranty of soundness but died within eight months after performing ordinary domestic duties for several months. The court ruled that the purchaser was entitled to "the difference between the value of the slave, if sound, and her value with the disease or unsoundness."

In many areas of the South, the price of cotton directly determined the price of slaves. However, during times of speculation, slave prices were not related to cotton prices. Rather, slaves became an independent speculative commodity. A Georgia editor wrote in the 1850s:

A fever is raging in Georgia for buying slaves. . . . men are borrowing money at exorbitant rates of interest to buy negroes at exorbitant prices. . . . The old rule of pricing negroes by the price of cotton by the pound—that is, if cotton is worth 12 cents, a negro man is worth $1,200—does not seem to be regarded. Negroes are 25 percent higher now with cotton at 10-½ cents.

By 1860, while the price of cotton remained constant, the price of prime field hands doubled or sometimes tripled. (Prime field hands were generally thought to be healthy males aged between eighteen and thirty.) Some specific factors, however, continued to determine the price of slaves. When Negroes were sold in groups, their average price was less than when sold separately. A light skin brought a lower price because it facilitated escape. Generally craftsmen—good carpenters and cabinetmakers—brought two to three times as much as prime field hands. Generally, too, according to Ulrich B. Phillips, the average price of slaves was about one-half that of prime field hands. Slave traders also helped to regulate the price of slaves to some extent just by contracting the number of slaves available for the market. A small number of slaves in the market would certainly raise a slave's selling price.

Here are some specific examples. A bill of sale for the purchase of two Negroes by John Finlayson of Florida in 1838 at Annapolis, Maryland, shows that he paid $600 for a Negro woman, Dinah, and her child with a guarantee that "both were sound in body and mind and a slave for life." (Bills of sale guaranteed that the slave was sound in body and mind, an assurance for the buyer that the chattel had no mental or physical defects.) In May 1838, Mrs. Charlotte Thornton of Virginia sold a large number of slaves to Mr. A. Glassell of Alabama. One woman of thirty-three years brought $500, and a woman Venus, with four children, went for $1,200. A girl, age seven, was sold for $400, and one infant for $150. In 1840, Jeremiah Morton of Virginia bought six male slaves for $4,000, an average of $666 apiece.

In the District of Columbia in 1835, an eighteen-year-old male was sold for $750, an eighteen-year-old female for $650, a first-rate male field hand for $900, and a mechanic for $1,200. In Alabama in 1835, males were selling for $1,000 and females for $750. Prices in the Virginia area for prime field hands in 1836 and 1837 ran from $830 to $930, and some sold for about $1,200 to $1,300. In 1838, a year after the panic, the price of slaves dropped to about $800 or $900, a price decline that continued until 1846. But by 1853 a slave broker in Richmond listed the following prices:

Best men (18–25) $1,200 to $1,300
Fair men (18–25) 959 to 1,050
Boys, five feet in height 850 to 950
Boys, four feet 375 to 400
Young women 800 to 1,000
Girls, five feet 750 to 850
Girls, four feet 350 to 430

In Texas, the prevailing selling price for slaves in 1853 was as high as $1,500 for a man and $1,250 for a woman. Although the depression of 1857–1858 drove some planters into bankruptcy, it does not seem to have altered the price being paid for slaves. When the crisis forced Pierce Butler to sell his share of the slaves on the family plantation in Georgia in order to pay his debts, the appraised price for a forty-year-old plantation blacksmith was $1,350 and for a much younger carpenter, $1,300. A total of 429 blacks realized $303,850.

On the basis of prices compiled by U. B. Phillips and others, the prices for slaves in the lower South and New Orleans for the period 1849–1860 break down as follows:

Lower South			New Orleans	
	Prime Hands	*All Slaves*	*Prime Hands*	*All Slaves*
1849–1850	$1,109.00	$509.50	$1,062.50	$531.25
1851–1855	1,215.00	607.50	1,250.00	625.00
1856–1860	1,585.00	792.50	1,605.00	802.50

One scholar sees the high prices as a "blessing to the slave class" because it raised the standard of care bestowed upon them in return for their labor: "A fifteen-hundred-dollar slave deserved better care, since he was a valuable piece of property." Actually, the high price of slaves during the 1850s caused an increase in the number of free Negroes kidnapped, and it also caused an increase in another means of acquiring Negroes: the device of stealing a slave from his owner and carrying the stolen property to another part of the state or another state.

SLAVE BREEDING

Did slave traders relieve planters in the upper South of unwanted slaves, or did many upper South planters develop an extensive system of slave breeding, deliberately producing slaves for sale to the lower South? The evidence of slave breeding is contained in the testimony of leading figures of the period. In 1818, Thomas Jefferson, concerned about the heavy mortality among infants on his plantation, admonished his overseer to provide adequate leisure for pregnant slaves and nursing mothers. "I consider," he wrote, "the labor of a breeding woman as no object, and that a child raised every 2 years is of more profit than the crop of the best laboring woman. In this, as in all other cases, providence has made our interest and our duties coincide perfectly."

In 1832, Thomas R. Drew of Virginia asserted that western migration "induced the master to attend to the negroes to encourage breeding, and to cause the greatest number possible to be raised. Virginia is, in fact, a *negro* raising state." That same year, Thomas Jefferson Randolph, a Virginia state legislator, declared that "Virginia had been converted into one grand menagerie, where men are reared for market, like oxen for the shambles." And Edmund Ruffin, Virginia's fire-eating agricultural reformer, insisted that "the cultivations of eastern Virginia derive a portion of their income from a source quite distinct from their tillage. . . . This source of income is, the breeding and selling of slaves."

Visitors to the South also reported evidence of slave breeding. Edward S. Abdy, an Englishman, stated in 1833 that the planters of Virginia "bred slaves as graziers bred cattle for the market." In his account of his visit to the seaboard slave states in the 1850s, Frederick Law Olmsted reported that many planters prided themselves on their stock of "breeding women" and encouraged them to produce children. One planter boasted that his women were "uncommonly good breeders and he did not suppose that there was a lot of women anywhere that bred better than his." The planters provided the slave women with favorable conditions and rewards if they produced. Olmsted concluded:

In the states of Maryland, Virginia, North Carolina, Kentucky, Tennessee, and Missouri, as much attention is paid to the breeding and growth of negroes as to that of horses and mules. . . . Planters command their girls and women (married or unmarried) to have children; and I have known a great many negro girls to be sold off because they did not have children. A breeding woman is worth from one-sixth to one-fourth more than one that does not breed.

Others corroborated Olmsted's points about rewards and punishment. Fanny Kemble noted that slave women were induced to breed by the "consideration of less work and more food." When two girls of a South Carolina slaveowner ate dirt, thereby, in his opinion, rendering them "unprofitable as breeding women," he sold them. On the other hand, a Virginia planter regularly gave a small pig to the slave mother of a newborn child.

The autobiographies of ex-slaves furnish ample evidence of slave breeding. The Fisk University autobiographical records of ex-slaves report that some masters would buy one female and one male and put them together as though they were cattle. Some masters had breeding farms and raised slaves to sell on a regular basis. Frederick Douglass told the story of a slave woman who was bought as a "breeder" and kept in the finest of material comfort in the hope she would provide a fortune for her master. James Roberts reported that on his plantation, fifty to sixty females were kept solely for breeding. From twenty to seventy-five children a year were bred on this plantation, and as soon as they were ready for market, they were taken away and sold. A Georgia ex-slave recalled that "a few 'stud bucks' were granted unusual privileges." He himself had eight brothers who belonged to this special class, and he estimated that before the war, these brothers "musta been de daddies o' at least a hunnert head o' chillin scattered all over Harris county." Often it was "a race between these large, powerful black men to see which one could beget the largest number of children in a year."

In 1862, British economist John Elliott Cairnes published *The Slave Power: Its Character, Career and Probable Designs*. Cairnes argued that the domestic slave trade led inevitably to slave breeding and converted Virginia and Maryland into breeding grounds to fill slave ranks thinned by hardships suffered in the Deep South. Furthermore, had slave breeding not been profitable, slavery would have disappeared from both Virginia and Maryland. Devastation of the land would have progressed to a point where "instead of the slave running away from his master, the master would have run away from his slave."

Several twentieth-century historians agreed with Cairnes. Frederick Bancroft asserted that "slave rearing early became the source of the largest and often the only regular profit of nearly all slaveholding farmers and of many planters in the upper South.'' Rewards to stimulate fecundity, he noted, often served as ''virtual premiums.'' Kenneth Stampp does not go as far as Bancroft, noting that while ''slaves were reared with an eye to their marketability, the evidence of systematic slave breeding is scarce indeed.'' But this was due in large part to the fact that written records of such activities were seldom kept, and Stampp does point out that planters ''overtly interfered with their [the slave women's] sexual activity'' to encourage slave fecundity. Commonly a slave woman who did not bear any children was sold off to the traders.

Alfred H. Conrad and John R. Meyer have demonstrated with care that the economics of slavery was geared to slave breeding. Thus, they concluded in their 1964 study that ''breeding returns were necessary to make the plantation operations in the poorer lands as profitable as alternative contemporary activities in the United States.'' Recently Richard C. Sutch has demonstrated the validity of this conclusion in his quantitative study, pointing out that among exports of slaves from the upper to lower South, males outnumbered females from 14.3 to 29.8 percent. He concludes that slave breeders were more often kept at home.

A number of scholars have demonstrated that evidence of slave breeding appears in the higher price that younger women with children drew in the slave-trading market. The value of a ''prime field wench'' (one who produced from five to ten marketable children in her lifetime) was from one-sixth to one-fourth more than that of a woman who was not fertile. Moreover, the fact that the price of a fertile woman was higher in Virginia than in the lower South is evidence that Virginia planters realized the importance of the child-producing slave woman.

It would have been an ''act of economic insanity'' if they had not realized this, as Herbert Gutman points out: ''Enslavement, after all, meant much more than the use of human chattel as labor. It also required—after a time and especially after the abolition of the overseas slave trade—that the slave labor force reproduce itself. Few realized this requirement better than the slaveowners themselves.'' The steady increase in the price of slaves, furthermore, intensified the significance of slave rearing.

Nonetheless, a number of historians have insisted that there was little, if any, deliberate breeding and selling of slaves from the upper to the lower South. Lewis Cecil Gray defended this viewpoint from a simple racist stance, writing: ''Given the irresponsible Negro character and the fact that the parent suffered no deprivation for the rapid increase of his progeny, a premium on breeding was unnecessary.'' Others maintain that a distinction must be made between the process of transferring surplus populations and a system of deliberate breeding. The former existed; the latter was largely a myth. ''The legend of 'slave breeding' must be dismissed,'' conclude J. G. Randall and David Donald. Robert William Fogel and Stanley L. Engerman include a section in their work, *Time on the Cross,* entitled, ''The Myth of Slave-Breeding,'' in which they say: ''The evidence put forward to support the contention of breeding for the market is meager indeed.''

But while there may be an absence of plantation records or diaries that conclusively prove the practice of widespread slave breeding by planters, there is
plenty of evidence to sustain Frederick Bancroft's conclusion that "slave-rearing
was the surest, most remunerative, and most approved means of increasing
agricultural capital." Most planters were enthusiastic about "good breeders"
among their slave women and encouraged unions among slaves, even setting
intended couples to housekeeping in the same cabin.

SEPARATION OF FAMILIES

"Nothing demonstrates his powerlessness as much as the slave's inability to
prevent the forcible sale of his wife and children," concludes John W.
Blassingame in his study, *The Slave Community*. Although the threat of the
disruption of a slave family varied from owner to owner, the evidence indicates
that when economics dictated the profitability of such action, husband and wife
were separated, and children were sold separately from their mothers. It is true
that owners occasionally directed in their wills that their slave families be kept
together when property distributions were made to beneficiaries and that some
planters saw it in their own interests to keep families together to ensure peaceful
operation of the plantation. Again, it would seem that house servants had a much
better chance of being sold as a family.

But the great majority of slaveholders chose business over sentiment. After
studying the wills of a large number of slaveowners, Kenneth Stampp concluded
that the financial returns constituted the overriding consideration in determining
whether families were to be kept together or broken up. In the case of the slave
trader, the evidence is overwhelming that if a trader found it more profitable to
sell a slave as an individual and break up a family, the decision was usually made
to separate the family. Some traders did advertise that they did not separate
families, but their claim is hard to substantiate. In New Orleans, it was illegal to
sell a child under eleven separate from his or her mother, but despite this law,
almost 10 percent of the sales in that city were children younger than eleven, sold
separately. And there was no law in any of the other Southern states that restricted the separation of a slave mother and her children or a husband and wife.
One Washington trader, Joseph W. Neal, was asked if he ever bought a wife
without her husband. Neal replied: "Yes, very often; and frequently, too, they
sell me the mother while they keep her children."

How many of the thousands of slaves who were sold in the domestic slave
trade represented the separation of man and wife and children is still an unsettled
subject. Blassingame believes that the slave trade was so extensive and masters
so indifferent to marriage bonds that roughly one-third "of the unions were
dissolved by masters," and he considers this estimate, which he derived from the
records of the Freedmen's Bureau, to be understated. Herbert Gutman points out
that "families were frequently broken just by the movement of an owner with his

resident slaves to the lower South.'' Eugene D. Genovese, on the other hand, argues that the extent to which marriages were destroyed by the slave trade is less than has been supposed. He emphasizes instead the ''painful uncertainty'' created by ''the potential for separation—whatever the ultimate measure of its resolution.''

Fogel and Engerman admit that the interregional slave trade resulted in the destruction of some slave families but insist that no evidence supports the accepted view that this trade resulted in widespread division of slave families and destruction of slave marriages. New Orleans sales records over a sixty-year period, they argue, ''indicate that 84 percent of all sales over the age of 14 involved unmarried individuals. Of those who were or had been married, 6 percent were sold with their mates; and probably at least a quarter of them were widowed or voluntarily separated.'' But critics have noted that the conclusion of the authors of *Time on the Cross* is based more on suppositions and assumptions than real evidence. Not only did Fogel and Engerman make no effort to establish the accuracy of the records or how representative they were—the five thousand sales they cite comprise, by their own figures, less than one-quarter of 1 percent of the over 2 million slaves during these years (1804-1862)—but the sales invoices themselves contain no information about the marital or familial status of the slaves sold.

Because the marriage contract of slaves was not legally binding, masters had the right to separate couples. One slave preacher who married couples always noted that they were joined ''until death or *distance* do you part.'' Some slaves were clever enough to persuade planters and traders to keep their families intact. But even the sensitivity of kind slaveholders could not keep families together when the law forced slave sales to pay the debts of deceased planters. Slave families were parted for many other causes, including the spite of a jealous wife or the misbehavior of a stubborn slave. But in most instances, the cause was profit. Basically slaveowners and slave traders were in the business to make money. Slave couples who had lived together for decades were separated in the drive for profit. Although Donald M. Sweg refers only to one leading slave trader (John Armfield), he sums up the prevailing practice: '' . . . John Armfield was neither iniquitous barbarian nor enlightened humanitarian, but a good businessman. When it was good business to divide families and sell young children, he did so. When it was better business to maintain the slaves in family units he did that.''

Slaveowners often dismissed the charge that separation of families was a brutal practice by claiming that slaves had no deep feeling for wives, husbands, children, brothers, or sisters. One owner who sold his slaves and separated the families wrote: ''The negroes . . . are quite disconsolate—but this will soon blow over. They may see their children again in time.'' All the slave narratives, however, not only call attention to the separation of families occasioned by the slave trade but describe the bitter and sorrowful reaction to the sale. John Thompson described his feeling on seeing a coffle pass with his wife in it:

For God's sake, have you bought my wife? He [the trader] said he had; when I asked him what she had done, he said she had done nothing, but her master wanted money. He drew a pistol and said that if I went near the wagon on which she was, he would shoot me. I asked for leave to shake hands with her, which he refused, but said I might stand at a distance and talk with her. My heart was so full that I could say very little. . . . I have never seen or heard from her from that day to this. I loved her as I loved my life.

"What should I now see in the very foremost wagon," recalled Henry "Box" Brown as he described a slave coffle, "but a little child looking towards me and pitifully calling, 'father,' 'father!' " Josiah Henson's account of the agonies of family separation is especially poignant:

My brothers and sisters were bid off first, and one by one, while my mother, paralysed by grief, held me by the hand. Her turn came and she was bought by Isaac Riley, of Montgomery county. Then I was offered to the assembled purchasers. My mother, half-distracted with the thought of parting for ever from all her children, pushed through the crowd, while the bidding for me was going on, to the spot where Riley was standing. She fell at his feet, and clung to his knees, entreating him in tones that a mother only could command, to buy her *baby* as well as herself, and spare her one, at least, of her little ones. Will it, can it be believed that this man, thus appealed to, was capable not merely of turning a deaf ear to her supplication, but of disengaging himself from her with such violent blows and kicks, as to reduce her to the necessity of creeping out his reach, and mingling the groan of bodily suffering with the sob of a breaking heart? As she crawled away from the brutal man, I heard her sob out, "Oh, Lord Jesus, how long, how long shall I suffer this way?" I must have been then between five and six years old.

Lydia Maria Child, a white abolitionist who collected and recorded narratives dictated to her by fugitive slaves, reported the bitter and violent reaction of slave mothers when their children were sold. In one instance in Marion County, Missouri, in 1834, a slave trader bought three small children from the slave mother. The mother became so violent that she was lashed and tied with ropes. During the night she managed to escape, went to where the boys were sleeping, took an axe, chopped off their hands, and ended her own life with the same instrument. The sole concern of the trader whose "unrighteous bargain drove the frantic mother to this act of desperation," according to Child, was his financial loss.

William Still, the black compiler of the records of fugitive slaves, tells of another slave mother who became so distraught upon being informed of the imminent sale of her children that she threw three children into a well and jumped in with them. Such slaves, said William Wells Brown, experienced conflicting emotions at the death of their children. The first was that of joy, for their children were beyond the reach of the slaveowner. The second was grief over the loss of a loved one. Brown reported, too, that some slave women openly expressed the wish that their children be stillborn. Solomon Northup occasionally heard slave women who had been separated from their children talking to them in the cotton fields as if they were present.

Perhaps the most ironical aspect of this brutal part of slavery involved a case concerning a slave husband in Missouri who had given a watch as a gift to his wife prior to his having been sold apart from her. The new owner went to the wife for the slave's clothing and the watch. After he had received them, the wife's owner sued for damages. The court of Missouri ruled that while the principle was clear that "the property of the slave belongs to his master," it was "not for strangers to interfere and deny the validity of any transfer of his property which a slave may make."

The watch being the property of the negro man, he gave it to his wife. What is more natural than that a man about to be separated from his wife, should be willing to give her a portion of the property he may have? What possible inference can be drawn from the refusal of the man to receive the watch, but that it was his wish that the wife should have it? The master of a slave not objecting to the disposition of the of the property, who else shall gainsay its validity?

What inference can be drawn from the fact that under the law it was perfectly proper for a slave wife to keep a gift from her husband after he was separated from her in the slave trade—so long as her master did not object—and that this was all that was permitted to remain of the marriage?

"The law of God acknowledges infidelity to the marriage convenant as the only justifiable cause of the dissolution of the contract," declared the Charleston Presbytery in 1854. "But slaves are sometimes separated by other causes which lie beyond their control." The question that concerned the presbytery was not the practice of separating husband and wife but what to say about "a new marriage . . . contracted after such compulsory separation." The answer the clergymen gave was to treat involuntary separation as equivalent to death and to allow remarriage.

3

Urban and Industrial Slavery

URBAN SLAVERY

In the United States rural slaves almost always accounted for more than 90 percent of the total slave population. It is not surprising, therefore, that in dealing with American Negro slavery, historians traditionally have emphasized the rural patterns of the institution and neglected the contingents of slaves dwelling in Southern towns and cities. In 1964, Richard C. Wade wrote his groundbreaking *Slavery in the Cities: The South, 1820–1860*, in which he demonstrated that slaves constituted an important group in Southern cities and that urban bondage differed substantially from its rural counterpart. Since then, other studies have supplemented the picture Wade presented, and some have altered it. For example, Wade confined his study of urban slavery to ten of the largest cities in the antebellum South on the assumption that in "small as well as large towns," slavery "was fundamentally the same wherever it existed, and that similarities of urban life were more important to the institution than differences in settlement, region or age." But studies of slavery in smaller Southern cities point out that small-town slavery deviated significantly from both the rural and more highly urban patterns of the institution.

By the 1830s, slaves comprised at least 20 percent of the population in most Southern cities. Frequently, as in Charleston, South Carolina, where blacks outnumbered whites, the proportion was much higher. However, no accurate record was kept of the slave population in any Southern city. One reason was that census takers depended on masters to enumerate their Negroes, and since most towns had a tax on slaves, owners tended to minimize their holdings. Also runaway slaves who crowded into the cities zealously avoided being counted. Consequently, the number of slaves in Southern urban centers was always underestimated in official figures.

According to census figures, the slave population of Baltimore in 1850 was 2,946; Charleston, 19,532; Louisville, 5,432; Mobile, 6,803; New Orleans, 17,011; Norfolk, 4,295; Richmond, 9,927; St. Louis, 2,656; Savannah, 6,231; and Washington, D.C., 2,113. Thus, in 1850, nearly 77,000 slaves were being kept in the ten largest Southern cities.

In all of these cities, except Richmond, female slaves outnumbered men— 10,901 to 8,631 in Charleston and 10,193 to 6,818 in New Orleans. This imbalance between male and female slaves reflected the practice on the part of owners to sell their younger males to planters in the cotton and cane country.

Probably the major jobs of slaves in cities were house servants, cooks, washerwomen, maids, valets, butlers, carriage drivers, hair dressers, gardeners, and general handymen. Many worked as carpenters, longshoremen, draymen, bakers, butchers, plasterers, coopers, wagonmakers, and shoemakers, and a few even became typesetters. Almost all cities used slaves on public works projects. Slaves built and cleaned the streets, put out fires, and performed the countless other tasks associated with life and labor in the cities.

In 1848, slaves constituted 45 percent of the work force in Charleston, About 43 percent of Charleston's carpenters, 73 percent of its coopers, 87 percent of the blacksmiths, 32 percent of the painters, and 49 percent of the ship carpenters were slaves. Slaves also worked in other trades: 43 percent of Charleston's butchers and 45 percent of its blacksmiths were slaves. And they were used in Charleston's stores and shops as salesmen and clerks.

Businessmen connected with the railroads, the ports, the shipping trade, and other commercial enterprises owned and hired large numbers of slaves. Although most Southern cities did not have large-scale manufacturing, smaller industries such as those connected with the building trades used slaves to meet the needs of the area. Commerce, and particularly the cotton trade, gave rise to a service sector composed of hoteliers, grocers, lawyers, clerks, and doctors, many of whom owned and hired slaves.

Some cities had a large number of slaves working in industrial pursuits. Richmond had the largest industrial slave labor force; its tobacco factories were manned almost exclusively by slaves, and by the 1850s its iron foundries had switched to slave labor. New Orleans used slaves in its sugar refineries, and the city's gasworks had a Negro compound with all facilities for the slaves' room and board. Even the overseer was a slave. The Savannah & Georgia Railroad and the Central Railroad Banking Company each had more than fifty slaves. Other large users of slaves in the city were painters, saddlers, merchants, and physicians. About one-quarter of Savannah's slave users listed ten or more slaves, with some businesses employing large numbers. On the other hand, in Baltimore, Louisville, St. Louis, and Washington, D.C., relatively few slaves were owned or hired by individual users. In fact, over one-half of the total slaves in Baltimore and Washington, D.C., were employed by persons who had only one slave. The majority of these slaves were probably used in domestic activities.

SLAVE HIRING

Although the institution of hiring out slaves developed in rural areas in the eighteenth century, the cities soon became the major slave-hiring centers. The owner might be a farmer or planter from the surrounding area who did not need his entire work force at all times of the year; he would come to the city and hire out his slaves at a set price. Or he might own no plantation or farm, keeping slaves for the sole purpose of hiring them out. In four to five years, even the most expensive Negro would, through the annual hiring-out fee, pay for his original purchase price, for the cost of the upkeep of a hired-out slave was transferred to the person employing him.

Slaves were hired out in three ways: by personal contact between the owner and the lessee, by personal contact between an agent in a major city to whom the owner had assigned his slaves and the lessee, and by public auction. Newspaper advertisements by agents suggest that they were widely used. Richmond alone had eighteen hiring agents. Auctions were usually held on the courthouse steps around the first of January, and newspaper accounts of this practice indicate that this may have been the most popular method of hiring slaves. Slaves who were to be hired out by their owners congregated at the courthouses, sometimes in the master's company and sometimes in that of his agent.

Slaves were hired out by the day, week, month, and year. Sometimes, as the following advertisement indicates, the period was longer:

WANTED TO HIRE

Wanted to hire, twelve or fifteen Negro Girls from ten to fourteen years of age. They are wanted for the term of two or three years. E. H. and J. Fisher.

The usual period of hire was fifty weeks, beginning in early January and ending shortly before Christmas. The hirer paid a cash rent and assumed the costs of feeding, clothing, and housing the slave, as well as the payment of medical expenses and slave taxes. By the beginning of the nineteenth century, the courts had defined the responsibilities of lessor and lessee in instances of the death, injury, or escape of a hired slave. An important 1806 decision in Virginia declared, "Where one hires a slave for a year, that if the slave be sick or run away, the tenant must pay the hire; but if the slave dies without any fault in the tenant, the owner and not the tenant, should lose the hire," because such death was an act of God.

The average rate of hire in the Southern states prior to 1850 was less than a hundred dollars for the year. During the 1850s, the average rate increased, and yearly hire ranged from $100 to $400.

Many urban slaves, especially those who were skilled, hired out their own time. Hired out slaves frequently "found" themselves, which means that they engaged their own lodgings and meals and paid for their own clothing. Some were able to earn and keep money over and above that demanded by their owners, but this was an exceptional and generally frowned-upon arrangement. Some enterprising slaves even hired out other slaves, but this, too, was discouraged. Indeed most Southern cities legislated against the practice of self-hire. Mobile, in addition, specifically legislated in 1858 against slaves' hiring the time of other slaves. Charleston provided that slaves who worked for other slaves must wear badges. But all such legislation was difficult to enforce.

Usually the slaves who hired themselves out saw little of their masters except periodically to turn over a stipulated portion of their earnings. Many of them lived virtually free of whites, and some were employed long distances from their owners, who often instructed friends or relatives to check on them. The *New Orleans Daily Picayune* complained on January 27, 1853, of the slaves' liberty "to engage in business on their own account, to live according to the suggestions of their own fancy, to be idle or industrious . . . provided only the monthly wages are regularly gained."

A slave who lost time through sickness within the year was obliged to make it up. Whatever the weather or the availability of work, the master had to receive his fixed amount at the end of every month. Of those who did not, many withdrew the hiring-out privilege, and the quasi-freedom the slave enjoyed would be lost.

If the hiring-out system was profitable for owners, it was because it made blacks work harder. It led to a more systematic exploitation of slaves, including slave children, and also to the separation of these children from their families. Few material goods were furnished to slaves in return for their labor. An employer who engaged a worker for a brief period of time did not have a vested interest in the slave's future well-being. His prime concern was in obtaining suitable labor at the lowest possible cost and exacting the greatest amount of work in the shortest period of time. The only deterrent to maltreatment was the realization that a hirer of labor could be held legally responsible for injury to a worker in his employ. In 1853, a South Carolina judge stated as an accepted fact that "hired slaves are commonly treated more harshly, or with less care and attention, than those in possession of the owner."

For the slaveowners, the practice also brought with it a number of disadvantages. Hiring out meant that physical control of the slave was removed from the owner. Tight control was even more difficult to maintain when the slaves were allowed to hire themselves out. Such slaves would have to support themselves and to compensate their masters, but this in effect reinforced their sense of independence. It also intensified the slave's desire for freedom as he came to question the sharing of his earnings with his master. The fact that the slave was sometimes permitted to retain a percentage of his earnings was proof that he was entitled to all of them. Discontent among this class of slaves grew, and many began looking for means of escape.

NATURE OF URBAN SLAVERY

The bulk of the urban slaves lived, dressed, and ate much better than those in the countryside. If their masters or employers did not furnish a sufficient supply of food, the town slaves could turn to grocery stores, bake shops, the markets, and hucksters. Shops catering to slaves also sprang up. Legally, merchants could not sell to slaves who did not have a written order from their owners, but this was seldom enforced. The urban setting, moreover, furnished opportunities for slaves to acquire the basics of learning. Although the law prohibited teaching slaves to read and write, there were many places in a city where the slave could pick up the rudiments of reading and writing, opportunities rarely presented to plantation slaves. In general, both contemporary observers and historians pointed out that slavery in cities produced a more independent and self-reliant individual than that of the country plantation. "A city slave is almost a free citizen," declared Frederick Douglass, who had experienced life both in Baltimore and on the plantations of the Maryland Eastern Shore. "He enjoys privileges altogether unknown to the whip-driven slave on the plantation." Urban slaves were, as Richard C. Wade has written, "more advanced, engaged in higher tasks, more literate, more independent, and less servile than those on plantations."

Although slaves in Southern urban centers had considerably more freedom than plantation laborers, they were bound by the same laws that affected slaves in the rural areas and were also subject to a set of restrictions governing activity specific to the city. Urban leaders imposed restrictions on the mobility of blacks by requiring them to register with the mayor's office and to wear metal identification badges, carry identification passes, observe curfews, and submit to a variety of other controls. In New Orleans, loitering by slaves in front of a tavern or a warehouse was deemed a crime. Slaves were also prevented from riding in public vehicles without their masters' approval or from purchasing any article over $5.00 without written permission from their masters. The New Orleans city fathers proclaimed: "All slaves are forbidden to quarrel, yell, curse or sing obscene songs, or in anyway disturb the public peace, or to gamble on the streets, roads or other public places, or on the levee."

Everywhere in Southern cities, ordinances stressed the need for stringent control of slaves during the nighttime. Throughout the antebellum period, even after the streets were lit and regularly patrolled, laws continued to reflect a fear of a slave conspiracy planned in the night. Everywhere, too, urban slaves were subject to severe punishment if they were found guilty of violating any one of a whole catalog of restraints designed to control the black bondsmen. "The whip was always there," notes Wade, "and that none was immune threw a pall over nearly every aspect of his existence." The reality of urban slavery is indicated by the fact that many slaves ran away from their masters, some hiding in the city and others seeking freedom in the North.

DECLINE OF URBAN SLAVERY

Reporting of his travels in the South in 1859–1860, John S. C. Abbott re-produced the following conversation. " 'The cities,' said a gentleman to me, 'is no place for niggers. They get strange notions into their heads, and grow discon-tented. They ought, every one of them, to be sent back to the plantations.' " While not every one was so sent back, the proportion of the urbanized Southern slave population declined during the 1850s. The absolute number of slaves in the two American cities with the largest slave population—Charleston and New Orleans—declined by 29 and 21 percent, respectively, and the aggregate slave population residing in the South's twenty-two largest cities declined by 4 per-cent. Historians have generally held that the declining fortunes of urban slavery were manifestations of an inherent incompatibility of slavery and urban life. According to Wade, who has developed this thesis in great detail, urban slav-ery's decline "did not stem from any economic reason" but rather from so-ciological incompatibility. Basically the city environment weakened the structure of slavery and threatened to dissolve the web of restraints on which the institution rested. The urban milieu provided a freer life for its slave inhabitants. But these very freedoms granted to city slaves were responsible for the decline in the urban slave population that occurred between 1850 and 1860. The complex institution of slavery was subject to an irreconcilable internal conflict. On the one hand, the granting of certain freedoms to slave labor was necessary for the efficient provi-sion of urban goods and services. But these freedoms created fears of slave rebellion in the minds of the urban citizenry and threatened the important social and economic distinctions between freemen and slaves. Many slaves lived apart from their masters, hired out their own time, married other slaves or free blacks, and raised families of their own. They were, in Wade's words, "beyond the master's eye."

It was not just a lack of control, according to Wade, that destroyed slavery in the cities. The institution of slavery underwent a fundamental change, being transformed from a chattel-master to a worker-employer relationship. The roots of this deeply entrenched institution were eroded in cities because urban life demanded certain freedoms for slaves, and these freedoms, in turn, made slaves almost independent. Urban slavery collapsed from within; slavery was incom-patible with the cities.

In his study of slave hiring, Clement Eaton reached the same conclusion. "In the towns and cities," he wrote, "the growing practice of obtaining the service of slave labor by hire instead of purchase was inevitably loosening the bonds of an archaic system. . . . Plantation Negroes who were sent to the cities and towns to be hired lost much of their submissiveness and became more sophisticated in the milieu of city ways." Many masters feared that slaves who were hired out in the city would become "uppity" and hard to handle. One South Carolinian spoke of the "baneful effects of hiring out slaves because it produced in them an unwillingness" to return to the regular life and domestic control of the master.

The easier acquisition of knowledge, the greater possibility of association, and the greater confidence and assurance that city life developed, as compared with country life and agrarian activities, were widely recognized as dangers associated with the growth of a large urban slave population. The cities also contained large numbers of free blacks whose existence made it easy for slaves to escape. As escapees became more numerous, the expected value of an urban slave decreased, and the demand for the services of such laborers diminished. Urban slaves could be sold to rural areas, where control was less of an issue. In addition, the threat of mass rebellions or insurrections was real enough to convince potential urban owners of slaves not to purchase and to persuade those who already owned to sell. Over time, the cost of keeping slaves in the cities compared to that for the rural areas rose. And policing, jailing, and adjudicating costs were shifted from the community at large to the owners of slaves through the imposition of specific taxes and license fees on slaves. Urban slavery, according to many scholars, placed great strain on the bonds of the institution; sheer numbers increased the fear of rebellion, and costs made the use of the slaves less attractive.

In 1976 Claudia Dale Goldin published *Urban Slavery in the American South 1820–1860: A Quantitative History*. Taking issue with Wade and other scholars, she concluded that cities and slavery were not incompatible. The cities were just subject to more dramatic shifts in slave populations due to the availability of substitute labor and to other factors, which made the urban demand for slaves more elastic than that for rural areas. Although some forces unique to urban areas created an inhospitable environment for slavery, they were relatively weak. The additional costs that were imposed on urban owners and hirers amounted to a very small percentage of total costs and do not appear to have increased to any great extent over the years.

Goldin's own explanation for the numerical decline of urban slavery is, unlike Wade's, entirely economic, the result of an economically rational shift of labor in response to differences in urban and rural supply and demand. Rather than urban slavery declining because of its social and economic incongruity, slaves shifted from urban to rural areas because the demand for slaves was increasing faster than their supply. While free labor, particularly immigrant labor, provided a substitute for urban slaves, there was no substitute close at hand for slave labor in rural areas. However, Goldin concedes that it is "not yet entirely clear" why immigrants could not be substituted for slaves in the cotton fields.

Jane Riblett Wilkie advances another reason for the decline of urban slavery in the 1850s, using Edna Bonacich's split-labor-market theory as an explanation. The central tenet of the split-labor-market theory is that when the price of labor for the same work differs by ethnic (racial) groups, a three-way conflict develops among business, higher-priced labor, and cheaper labor, which may result in extreme ethnic antagonism. The price of both slave and free black labor, Wilkie points out, was cheaper than that of white labor. Capitalists, benefiting from cheaper labor, would support the urban employment of blacks, while higher-priced white workers, fearful of displacement, would attack it. Racial antagonism on the part of white workers threatened by the labor displacement of blacks in urban areas would have induced slaveowners, who were becoming increasingly dependent on the proslavery support of white laborers, to shift black workers from urban to rural areas.

As we shall see, however, slaveowners in the cities either ignored the protests of white workers against the use of slave labor or defeated their efforts to halt the practice. But what the slaveowners could not defeat was the influence of city life on the slave. As John S. C. Abbott put it in 1859:

The city with its intelligence and enterprise is a dangerous place for the slave. He acquires knowledge of human rights, by working with others who receive wages when he receives none; who can come and go at their pleasure, when he from the cradle to the grave must obey a master's imperious will. . . . It is found expedient, almost necessary, to remove the slave from these influences, and send him back to the intellectual stagnation and gloom of the plantation.

INDUSTRIAL SLAVERY

Some scholars have contended that rather than the urban environment being hostile to slavery, slaves were more suited for agriculture than for industry; hence, slaves were more highly desired in the country than in the cities. According to this view, slaves were "incapable of all but the rudest form of labor." Slaves, wrote Ulrich B. Phillips, could be profitable only "if the work required was simple," for then the "shortcomings of Negro slave labor were partially offset by the ease with which it could be organized." Lewis Cecil Gray believed that the Negro was "primitive" and difficult to control. Thus the plantation system was adopted because it "afforded more powerful stimuli than the rewards of industry."

With few exceptions, studies dealing with the economic aspects of the slave system have followed this avenue and have concentrated upon the relative efficiency and profitability of the institution in an exclusively agricultural context. Until recent years, little attention was concentrated upon the industrial use of slaves in an agricultural society. Although it was well known that the slave was a skilled craftsman on plantations, where he made furniture, nails, and a wide range of other articles, many historians expressed the view that the bondsmen "were not suited to the handling of machinery."

Recent studies, especially those by the late Robert S. Starobin, have demonstrated that while the economy of the antebellum South was basically agricultural, by 1861, industrialization had forged ahead to such an extent that the slave states accounted for more than 15 percent of the capital invested in the nation's industry. While some establishments employed both whites and slaves at the same factory, mine, or transportation project, most of the industrial enterprises in the South employed slave labor almost exclusively. In the 1850s, about 200,000 slaves—nearly 5 percent of the total slave population—worked in industry.

The development of industry in the slave society of the antebellum South created problems for the slaveowners, who found themselves caught on the horns of a dilemma: what was the better form of labor, black slave or free white? More than simply a question of who would perform what type of work, the issue reflected a concern about that kind of society the South would constitute. The plantation slaveowners, Eugene D. Genovese has indicated, "had to view industrialization with either slave labor or free with misgivings," for while planters favored increased Southern manufactures in order to reduce dependency upon outside suppliers, too much industry threatened their way of life. Because of a relative loss of control over blacks in such a fluid setting, planters "looked askance at the social consequences of industrial urban slavery." On the other hand, planters had even less control over a free white industrial proletariat. Sporadic labor militancy and working-class animosity over competition with slaves made planters fear the creation of such a class. Since they dominated southern society, either alternative presented a threat to the status quo.

James H. Hammond, a leading South Carolina planter and future governor of the state, expressed the major concerns of many slaveowners. Hammond feared that "whenever a slave is made a mechanic he is more than half freed," and usually he became "the most corrupt and turbulent of his class." He reminded the slaveowners that "wherever slavery has decayed, the first step in the progress of emancipation, has been the elevation of slaves to the ranks of artisans and soldiers. We have no doubt that the same causes will produce the same effects here." For Hammond, poor, white labor provided the most logical solution to the South's industrial labor problem. Through steady employment in the growing number of factories, Hammond hoped to uplift poor white workers from economic destitution and squalor. Then, rather than constituting an alienated and latently antislavery group of malcontents, the "unruly" white workers would become a pillar of support for the planter-dominated aristocracy.

Actually the labor shortage so characteristic of the early American economy forced many southern manufacturers to employ any kind of labor available. Frequently this meant a labor force of free whites and blacks, both free and slave. Starobin argues that while the debate over industry in the South assumed an inherent black-white conflict and although racial hostilities did occur, "they were much less significant than the striking extent of interracial harmony among workers at almost all integrated industries." Indeed what was surprising was not racial antagonisms at integrated work places but "the depth of racial tolerance, considering the racist foundations upon which slavery rested." In the final analysis, since slaveowners so dominated the political economy of most Southern regions, they had the power "to integrate work forces if they chose." Those opposing integration were powerless to halt the process. Regardless of the wishes of white workers or of the ideologists warning against it, "slave-employing industrialists and planters had sufficient economic and political power to use slave labor however they wished."

Part of the mythology of the antebellum South was that blacks could not learn mechanical skills and that the use of slave labor in the region's industries was "visionary" and "impractical." But many operators of cotton mills simply disregarded such opinions and employed thousands of blacks. In South Carolina, cotton mill operators founded the textile industry in the region by the sweat of black slave labor. Between 1816 and 1838, every textile mill constructed in South Carolina, except possibly one, used slaves as factory hands. In the 1830s, the use of slave labor was expanded to encompass the Southern textile industry as a whole. Cotton mills employing slave labor were found in Virginia, Tennessee, North Carolina, South Carolina, Alabama, and Mississippi. In a number of them, white and black operators worked side by side. A visitor to Georgia in 1839 reported "white girls working in the same room, and at the same loom with black girls; and boys of each colour, as well as men and women, working together without apparent repugnance or objection":

In one of them, the blacks are the property of the mill owner, but in the other two they are the slaves of planters, hired out at monthly wages to work in the factory. . . . The negroes here are found to be quite as easily taught to perform all the required duties of spinners and weavers as the whites, and are just as tractable when taught.

Although several textile mills in the antebellum South never abandoned their use of slave operators, after the 1830s, there was a shift away from slave labor. One reason given for the limited use of slave labor is that prejudice and the proslavery argument made white workers unwilling to labor in the same mills with black bondsmen. But since slaveowners were usually able to prevent racial hostility from halting the use of slave labor, this was not a decisive factor. Mainly it was the result of the rise in cotton prices in the 1850s and the fact that the boom in agriculture made the cost of buying or renting slaves much greater. With many planters wanting all of their slaves for the raising of cotton, factory owners found themselves unable to hire any bondsmen. By 1860, only a few cotton mills in the South still operated with slave labor.

Slave labor played a large role in all phases of production at iron furnaces in the Old South. An average charcoal blast furnace required some sixty or seventy slave workers in addition to a white manager and a handful of skilled laborers. Slaves were used to chop wood, man charcoal pits, and haul the charcoal to the furnace site. At the ore banks, slave miners dug iron ore, while other miners extracted limestone to use as flux in the manufacturing process. Other slaves fed measured amounts of iron ore, charcoal, and limestone into the blast furnace, day and night, until the blast was completed.

As founders, colliers, miners, teamsters, wood choppers, and general furance hands, slaves constituted the bulk of the laboring force. Black youths, working under the guidance of black craftsmen, acquired the skills of blacksmiths, colliers, founders, and forgemen. Not infrequently, black women worked in the mine banks, and some labored in the furnace and forge.

In the 1850s, 160,000 to 200,000 slaves worked in industry. About four-fifths of these industrial slaves were directly owned by industrial entrepreneurs; the rest were rented by employers from their masters by the month or year. Most were men, but many were women and children. They lived in rural, small-town, or plantation settings, where most Southern industry was located, rather than in large cities, where only about 20 percent of the urban slaves were industrially employed.

Industrial and urban slavery in the South were thus not synonymous. Much industry was an integral part of the agricultural part of the agricultural economy and was rural in location, and much urban slave labor had no connection with manufacturing. In the case of iron production, however, industry was both rural and urban. Farming operations were also conducted at most Southern iron works, and a constant interchange of slave labor between industrial and agricultural tasks took place at furnaces and forges, allowing ironmasters to employ their extensive labor force all year.

Richmond's most important iron establishment, the Tredegar Iron Works, differed in organization from the rural charcoal iron plantation model. Founded in 1836 in an urban commercial and transportation center by several Richmond businessmen and industrialists, it "represented both physically and symbolically, the emergence of the modern corporate organization in the upper South." In 1848 it was bought by Joseph R. Anderson, manager of the operation, who made Tredegar the most important ironworks in the South.

When Anderson started with Tredegar in 1841, he introduced black slave labor into the mill, at first in subordinate capacities and later in highly skilled positions. But when he tried to install black slaves to be trained for the most skilled and high-paying positions at the works, the skilled white workers, fearing they would be discharged once the blacks had been trained, refused to accept them. On May 23, 1847, skilled whites decided to strike to prohibit the employment of black slaves in skilled positions. Anderson informed the white strikers that they had *"discharged themselves."* In a letter to the *Richmond Enquirer,* he wrote that

those who enter into his employment must not expect to prescribe to him who he shall be at liberty to employ; and that he would not consent to employ men who would unite and combine themselves into an association to exclude slaves from our factories. It was because the late workmen asserted such a pretension that he determined that their employment should cease. . . . In that aspect, he regarded it as a matter in which the whole community was concerned; it must be evident that such combinations are a direct attack on slave property; and if they do not originate in abolition, they are pregnant with evils.

The city's newspapers applauded Anderson for his stand. The *Times and Compiler* noted:

The principle is advocated, for the first time we believe in a slave-holding state, that the employer may be prevented from making use of slave labor . . . this principle struck at the root of all the rights and privileges of the master, and if acknowledged, or permitted to gain foothold, will soon destroy the value of slave property.

The white strikers failed to influence either Anderson or the city officials to whom they appealed, and large numbers of blacks went into the Tredegar rolling mills. In 1848 Anderson reported: "I am employing in this establishment [the Tredegar works] as well as at the Armory works adjoining, of which I am President, almost exclusively slave labor except as to Boss men. This enables me, of course, to compete with other manufacturers."

The experience of the white workers at the Tredegar Iron Mill illustrates the fact that while slavery technically constituted a status reserved for blacks, a variety of legal and economic forms of compulsion, in the words of Richard B. Morris, "measurably reduced the freedom of white workers in the slave states." Slavery provided a form of control over white workers, as well as slaves. The personal freedom and security of all labor, black or white, was severely weakened in the slave states.

Small wonder, then, that labor organization in the South lagged behind that in the North. In the South, Richard B. Morris has written, "the courts were openly antagonistic to striking workers" because many Southern officials believed that "strike action, like anti-slavery agitation, was an attack on their 'peculiar' institution." The fact that slaves could not strike and form trade unions was an important reason for the increasing use of slave labor in the 1850s.

Slaves provided the backbone of the labor force at most Southern mining establishments. Whether in coal, lead, iron, or gold mining, slaves played a crucial role in the development of the mining industry. In the summer of 1843, Henry Howe, a Virginian, visited the Midlothian mines and recorded the impressions of that descent into what constituted America's deepest coal pit. Howe observed that "the Midlothian mines employ in all their operations some 150 negroes," a sizable establishment even by present standards.

While some black coal miners were free, most Southern mines utilized slave labor. One Alabama mine owner observed in 1859:

Every day's experience confirms my opinion that it is next to impossible to prosecute my mining interest successfully with free labor. . . . No reliance whatever can be placed upon it. . . . I have now not a white man in my work . . . with a force of 20 hands, 16 could be kept inside and 4 do all the outside work. . . . I must have a negro force or give up my business.

Because of the dangerous working conditions in antebellum coal pits, mine operators often found slaveowners reluctant to hire their bondsmen for mine labor. One way owners and employers alike tried to minimize the loss of their human property was through insurance. Midlothian advertisements noted that "the lives of slaves hired to the Midlothian Company can be insured at a reasonable premium, if desired by the owners." By the late 1850s, however, insurance companies had become wary of underwriting the lives of slaves who worked in coal pits with a known history for accidents.

Further complicating the recruitment of an adequate labor force was the fact that some slaves themselves refused to work in the coal mines, fearing loss of life, and had to be forced to do so. Many of those who were forced to work in the mines made it clear by running away that they did not intend to risk their lives willingly.

Before the invention of refrigeration, salt was a vital food preservative. From its inception along the Great Kanawha River in 1808, the western Virginia salt industry "rapidly became the largest area for the basic necessity in the antebellum United States." Faced with the labor scarcity characteristically felt by manufactures, salt producers turned to the employment of slaves, especially from eastern Virginia, which had a surplus slave population. In 1850, thousands of Kanahwa County slaves were employed in all phases of the manufacturing process.

Frequently salt makers owned their skilled hands, but normally they hired skilled and unskilled laborers. To obtain maximum production, they ran their furnaces twenty-four hours a day and often seven days a week, paying both hired and owned slaves an extra amount for Sabbath labor.

Starobin has concluded that four-fifths of the industrial bondsmen in the Old South were company owned. But the proportion of owned slaves in the salt industry was much lower. Often 30 to 45 percent of a salt company's slave labor was leased, and in some cases, the percentage was as high as 90 percent. In most phases of the salt industry, the occupations were dangerous, especially in coal mining, where slaves labored to supply the fuel to salt furnaces. Hired slaves usually occupied the most dangerous positions. While some slave hirers stipulated that the lessee would not work the slaves in unsafe pursuits, this did not restrain either salt makers or managers. Slaveholders were continually suing salt makers for the injuries and deaths that resulted in the loss of their valuable assets.

The location of the Kanawha salt industry so close to the Ohio River offered both advantages and disadvantages to the manufacturers. While it facilitated the transportation of products, it proved a hazard to owners anxious to guard their human property. To the slave the Ohio River, as a pathway to Cincinnati, presented the hope of freedom.

During the colonial era, hemp was used for the manufacture of linen, lace, and "coarse" cloth for clothing. Normally the fiber and products derived from it were manufactured privately in the home. During and after the American Revolution, the manufacturing process was removed from the home and into centralized public and private factories. But by the antebellum era, cotton textiles had largely replaced those made of hemp, and the major producing center had shifted westward to Kentucky. There, bagging and twine were manufactured for baling Southern cotton. One of the most striking features of the Kentucky hemp industry was its almost total reliance upon slave labor. From planting to finished product, black bondsmen performed nearly every task. "Without hemp, slavery might not have flourished in Kentucky," observes James F. Hopkins. "On the hemp farm and in the hemp factories the need for laborers was filled to a large extent by the use of Negro slaves, and it is a significant fact that the heaviest concentration of slavery was in the hemp producing area." In the factories, the slaves were owned by the operator of the enterprise or hired for a period of time.

The numerous commercial fisheries in the South constituted, as Frederick Law Olmsted pointed out, "an important branch of industry and a source of considerable wealth." Many Southern fisheries were significant enterprises, with "the largest sweep seines in the world," usually manned by slaves and free blacks.

Most of the estimated 182,000 slaves in Texas at the time of secession worked on plantations. However, thousands of bondsmen learned the cowboy's skills from *vaqueros* from Mexico or Indians. All-Negro crews were common in eastern Texas.

Describing lumbering in the Great Dismal Swamp of the lower South, Frederick Law Olmsted observed that "labor in the swamps is almost entirely done by slaves," most of them hired hands. Numerous slaves also labored in the cyprus lumber industry of the lower Mississippi valley. They toiled at all occupations from logging, to sawmill work, and as crewmen on log rafts and lumber flatboats. Moreover, many of them spent much of their time out from under the eyes of their employers.

John Hebron Moore examined the experience of Simon Gray, a hired slave who worked as chief boatman for a Natchez lumber company between the 1830s and the Civil War. According to Moore, "almost every aspect of Simon Gray's career violates our modern conception of the slave in the lower South." "Contrary to law and custom," Gray was relatively well educated, traveled freely, earned a regular wage, and lived with his family. He also acted as an agent for his employer, exercised authority over workmen, black and white, and carried a weapon with the permission of his employer. Moreover, according to Moore, Gray's status differed only in degree from that of other slaves who worked for the same employer. Although Gray enjoyed an exceptional degree of freedom, he points out, many slave lumbermen led semifree lives, with little direct supervision. Moore concludes that the available research does not make clear whether the treatment accorded slaves working for that particular lumber company was typical of lumber companies specifically or nonagricultural enterprises in general. However, the evidence implied that the "privileges these industrial workers enjoyed were not unusual."

During the two decades before the Civil War, the number of Southern tobacco factories expanded. Concentrated primarily in the upper South, the tobacco industry of Kentucky and Virginia-North Carolina employed thousands of slaves. In *The Tobacco Kingdom*, Joseph Clarke Robert points out that when adapted to the manufacture of tobacco products, the "peculiar institution" underwent "conspicuous modifications." He found that tobacco factory slaves gained a significant measure of social freedom, which inevitably created fear among the already jittery Southern city whites. As in most other industries, tobacco manufacturers relied upon cash incentives to motivate slave workers and provided their hired hands, usually half of the employer's force, with a small amount of money to find room and meals for themselves. Moreover, by the 1850s, hired tobacco slaves commonly chose their own employers. These practices continued unabated until the end of slavery, despite complaints from many sources that such indulgences "ruined" bondsmen. Robert even implied that hired tobacco hands held a certain amount of power to affect the nature of their bondage, since they had the option of hiring themselves to employers who provided the best working conditions.

Most of the labor in the tobacco factories was performed solely by blacks, principally hired slaves. Males predominated, although with the expansion of the industry in the 1850s, more women were employed, usually as stemmers or cooks. By 1860, women made up over 33 percent of the hands in Petersburg, Virginia. As a rule, the slaves were managed by white overseers. However, in describing the tobacco town of Lynchburg, Virginia, J. Alexander Patten wrote in 1859 that the superintendent of a number of tobacco factories was

an intelligent slave. He was a man some forty years of age, large-framed, and seemingly of an amiable disposition. He could read and write; and, we were informed, wrote letters of business for his master. He was not only perfectly familiar with the qualities of tobacco, and all the details regarding its manufacture, but he gave a clear and interesting account of the whole operation.

Perhaps no other Southern industry relied upon slave labor so thoroughly as the construction of roads, railroads, canals, and other internal improvement enterprises. Except for a few border-state lines, all Southern railroads were built by slaves owned by contractors or by hired bondsmen. Most Southern canals and navigation improvements were excavated by slave labor, and most other Southern transportation facilities were dependent upon slave work forces. Slave labor also played a pivotal role in the construction of American ships in the Southern port towns of Baltimore, Norfolk, Charleston, and New Orleans.

Slave women made up one-half of the work force at South Carolina's Santee Canal. They built Louisiana levees, and the Gulf Coast lumber industry employed thousands of female slaves. Southern entrepreneurs concluded that "in ditching, particularly in canals . . . a woman can do nearly as much work as a man."

CONTROL AND TREATMENT OF INDUSTRIAL SLAVES

The complex problem of the control of industrial slaves was a factor that caused many Southerners to oppose the use of slave labor in the region's industries. Along with James H. Hammond, they doubted "whether their [the slaves'] extensive employment in manufacturers and mechanic arts is consistent with safe and sound policy." According to Starobin, the most intelligent masters of industrial slaves found effective ways of controlling and increasing the productivity of their workers. Although "all discipline rested upon violent coercion," he points out that brutality was not characteristic of industrial slavery. Industrial masters utilized practical day-by-day techniques, such as cash incentives, to increase the productivity of their slave force rather than relying on "the indiscriminate application of terror."

This improvement indicated, however, only that the institution was changing its face to make the system more efficient. In fact, an examination of "the manner, timing, history, and effects of cash incentives suggests that they were not a step toward emancipation" but a technique that had buttressed the institution since colonial times. Industrial slavery required a mixture of force and subtle rewards, and to emphasize one over the other was to overlook the complexity of the unique variety of human bondage.

The treatment of those slaves who were hired out to industry is a subject of controversy among historians. In the view of a number of scholars, slave hiring and industrial work were among the most brutal and exploitative aspects of the American slave system. With only a temporary interest in their welfare, these historians argue, employers totally ignored anything but the profits to be obtained by overworking the hired slaves. "Slaves hired to mine owners or railroad contractors," Kenneth Stampp concludes, "were fortunate if they were not driven to the point where their health was impaired."

Other students of slavery have presented a somewhat different picture. Clement Eaton and Richard B. Morris see slave hiring and industrial work as contributing to the development of improved living conditions for slave laborers. Morris, moreover, argues that these improvements represented a "trend toward upgrading slaves into a shadowland of quasi-freedom" in the late antebellum era. Eaton concludes that the hired slave "possessed strong weapons, if he chose to use them, for obtaining good treatment from the employer," and, "despite abuses, hiring was often a form of upgrading of slave labor and loosening the bonds of servitude." Indeed, according to Eaton, hiring frequently constituted "an intermediate state between bondage and freedom."

"The goals of production had priority over the interests of the slave," concludes John Edmund Staley in his study of slave labor in the manufacture of salt. By leasing rather than purchasing slaves, losses in case of accident could be minimized, "because it was not one's own property being killed or maimed. The only threat was a lawsuit, but an adverse result could be defeated on appeal, delayed, or avoided with the plaintiff residing in a distant locality." In short, as far as the salt industry was concerned, hiring simply intensified the exploitative nature of slavery.

On the other hand, Ronald L. Lewis, in assessing the role of slave labor in the Chesapeake iron industry, argues that for reasons of practicality and profitability, ironmasters found it necessary to rely upon more sophisticated techniques than "brute force." Because many ironmasters hired their slave laborers, Lewis found that black ironworkers often skillfully utilized the conflicting economic interests of owners and employers, which were inherent in the hiring system, in order to improve the conditions of their daily life. This measure of power exerted in practice by slave ironworkers, according to Lewis, helped deflect the psychologically debilitating effects of the "total" power exercised by the masters in theory.

In an article, "Disciplining Slave Ironworkers in the Antebellum South," Charles B. Dew came to the same conclusions as those advanced by Lewis. Dew analyzed the variety of nonviolent techniques used to control and discipline slave workers. These methods, he found, had the effect of providing slaves with psychological space, which enabled them to "carve out" some semblance of a private life and limited direct control over their daily existence. While Dew does not contend that industrial slavery was a light burden, the "central tendency" was to operate by "mutual accommodation" rather than by "outright repression."

But in a study of the Negro ironworker in antebellum Virginia, Samuel Sydney Bradford presents a different view of the nature of bondage at the ironworks. Characterizing the ironworks regimen as repressive, Bradford emphasizes the severe discipline and harsh daily existence for slave ironworkers and argues that such severity resulted from the "peculiar conditions in the use of hired slave labor." Since the hired bondsman was separated from his master, he became vulnerable to the employer, whose only interest in the slave was to get as much labor from him as possible, no matter what the human cost in life or the health of the hired bondsman.

The observations concerning industrial slavery derived from both contemporary spectators and modern historians frequently differed from those of the bondsman himself. Not all boatmen in the lumber industry, for example, were quite as fortunate as Simon Gray. Moses Grandy, a slave, hired his own time barging lumber from the backwaters of the upper Chesapeake to port towns in the bay. While Grandy also lived a quasi-free existence, that status did not rest lightly on his shoulders. The anxiety and frustration arising out of being permitted to arrange one's daily affairs, while realizing full well that as a slave he could never control his ultimate destiny, almost crushed his spirits. No amount of either "quasi-freedom" or wages earned could replace the right to dream about one's future. Forced to purchase himself three times before it became a reality, he concluded that "slavery will teach any man to be glad when he gets his freedom."

William Wells Brown's perspective on the nature of "quasi-free" slavery also differed substantially from that held by many contemporary masters and modern historians. While a slave, Brown labored as a field hand, but he also worked as a hotel servant, steamboat porter, assistant to a newspaper editor, house servant, and as a "soul driver" or slave trader. Working in several cities along the Mississippi River, Brown did not find the institution easy-going anywhere, but he observed that "no part of our slaveholding country is more noted for the barbarity of its inhabitants than St. Louis." Brown also reflected the ambivalence frequently experienced by industrial slaves who, while escaping the regimentation and fixed relationships that bound master and field hands, nevertheless suffered more anxiety than their plantation brethren from the more constant exposure to the uncertain whims of whites.

Even though industrial slaves might enjoy certain advantages and liberties unavailable to their brothers and sisters on plantations, emotionally they often experienced high levels of anxiety and sometimes great physical violence from having their lives so intimately bound with their white oppressors. Skilled white artisans traditionally opposed the use of slave labor, and many of the slave narratives note the hostility they encountered, including brutal physical abuse, when they attempted to practice their skills.

Although he lived better at a fishery maintained by a Carolina planter, Charles Ball was "compelled to work all the time, by night and day, including Sunday." He gladly returned to plantation work where a few hours a week were his own.

Because of the hazards in hiring out slaves who performed dangerous work in the Southern industrial system, owners took steps to protect their large investments, even to the extent of carrying slave life insurance. But no such concern was expressed for the slaves themselves, working in industries with crude technology and often under inexperienced management. Hazards of work were ever present, and thousands of slaves lost their lives or suffered serious injuries. Slaves working on ships were killed by cotton bales that crushed them or knocked them overboard to a watery grave. Black miners were in constant danger of losing their lives or suffering severe injury in pits that flooded.

The average industrial slave worked twelve hours a day, but such occupations as fishing and steamboating required much longer working days. Some owners worked their slaves seven days a week for months at a time. Steamboat slaves were often forced to work at the beck and call of the captain. Many slave steamboat crews worked like beasts "for thirty or forty hour stretches." Black firemen who stoked steamer furnaces stood watches, working all day and part of each night for seven or more days in succession.

While free workers could and did quit under intolerable working conditions, slave workers were helpless before the employers' compelling urge for profits.

They could and did run away, but if they were recaptured, they could be severely punished. The slaveowner who hired out his slaves soon learned that if he was too particular about his slaves' welfare and set limits that would impair the employers' ability to exploit them for profit, the contract would be voided and the slaves returned to the owner, who was then denied his income. The increase in the hiring of slaves provided increased profits to owners who rented the bondsmen. But it also meant that owners with slaves to hire were less inclined to concern themselves about how their slaves were treated by industrial employers.

Rather than slavery being unsuited for industry and slave labor lacking the skills to be used in industrial pursuits, recent studies have demonstrated a greater potential for industrial growth and expansion in the antebellum South than historians generally acknowledge. But even if slave labor in Southern industries was profitable, efficient, and economically viable, as Robert Starobin, the leading scholar on this subject, insists it was, the fact is that the antebellum South did not rank as an industrial power. The limited size of the Southern market for manufactured goods, with slaves kept at subsistence levels and poor whites lacking purchasing power, the limited urban market, with many of the city inhabitants being slaves or free blacks, and therefore possessing minimal purchasing power, the absence of technological development compared to the North, and the fact that agriculture outbid industry in the competition for capital, are among the deterrents to industrialization in the antebellum South.

4

Plantation Slavery

In the literature on slavery, a large slaveholder has usually been defined as one who had a minimum of fifty slaves. In 1860, less than one-fourth of all slaves lived on plantations in the large-size class. Most lived either on medium-sized units, with fifteen to fifty slaves, or on small, family-operated farms with fewer than fifteen slaves.

THE PYRAMID OF AUTHORITY

The organization and management of a plantation depended on whether it was a large, medium-sized, or small unit. Nevertheless, certain features were fairly uniform.

At the top of the whites' pyramid of authority was either the resident owner or the steward of an absentee planter's several estates. Directly below the planter or steward was the overseer of an individual plantation who might occasionally have an assistant or an apprentice overseer. In the working of the slave force, the overseer could make use of one or more black drivers. If there were several of these black supervisors, one would likely be designated "head driver" or "over-driver" and the others "under-drivers." Beneath, or at the same level of authority as the black field leaders, were slave foremen responsible for certain industrial or craft operators. Then there were slaves assigned specific duties, such as caring for the stock, ministering to young or sick slaves, or keeping the farm implements in good working order.

Black slave drivers were bondsmen who managed slave laborers. Their responsibilities included directing labor in the fields, maintaining discipline, time and account keeping, guarding the crops, distributing weekly rations, and other similar duties. The driver, a slave himself, combined the tasks of foreman, manager, superintendent, gang boss, and more. He was chosen by the planter to work either under his direction or that of an overseer. Occasionally the driver functioned alone, taking care of the plantation without an overseer and in the absence of the owner.

A number of planters found the use of slave drivers in place of overseers to be economically profitable. The fee of an overseer, which ranged from $100 to $2,000 per year, was eliminated, as was the cost of furnishing overseers with lodging, provisions, a servant, and often other fringe benefits. Drivers often knew more about plantation management of crops and the work force than did the whites, and upon occasion, planters accepted drivers' advice on plantation operations. Some planters who employed overseers required them to consult and respect the advice of the drivers on important points. One planter urged his colleagues to follow this pattern, assuring them that "a great deal of useful experience may be gained by conference with them." Frederick Law Olmsted visited a Georgia rice plantation and found that the planter used an overseer because the law required it. In practice, even his most trusted overseers had to consult the black drivers. The drivers were directly in charge of the field people. They made the major decisions about the timing and amount of the water flow into the fields. Their advice was generally taken on all matters pertaining to the administration of the plantation.

In assigning the various plantation duties, slaveholders created an occupational structure that was very similar to that existing in white Southern society. Men were virtually never spinners, weavers, seamstresses, or nurses, and female slaves rarely rose to the rank of drivers. When a woman did appear as a supervisor of field labor, it was usually as the leader of the "trash gang," a laboring unit of "irregulars" formed from the ranks of children, the elderly, and female slaves in advanced stages of pregnancy.

THE WORK SYSTEMS

Two work systems were used on plantations: gang and task. Large slave gangs predominated in the production of rice and sugar, which employed approximately one-fourth of all Southern slaves. Cotton was particularly suited to the task system, but all planters used a combination of both to a greater or lesser degree.

Under the gang system, the more commonly used, slaves were worked in groups under a black driver who supervised and set the work pace of the slave gang. The driver's duties were not only supervisory; he worked alongside the blacks in the fields and often produced more than any of them. Under the gang system, the slave was compelled to work the entire day with the exception of periods allowed for meals and rest. To make each gang as uniform in efficiency as possible, the hands were divided into several gangs according to strength.

Under the task system, a slave's daily routine was sharply defined. Hands were assigned a certain amount of work for each day: so many rows to be sowed, so much cotton to be picked, so much grain to be threshed. Upon completion of the task, the slave could use the rest of the day as he wished. After meeting the master's minimum work requirements, the slaves generally left the field in the early afternoon in time to tend their own gardens.

It was thought that the idea of free time for the slave would increase the hand's incentive to finish the task and not loiter. Planters and supervisors hoped this method would also create a competitive spirit and greater efficiency. Another advantage was noted by a Georgia planter who wrote: "As . . . the task of each [slave] is separate, imperfect work can be readily traced to the neglectful worker."

On all plantations, operations of one growing season overlapped into the next. During the winter months, the men and women, in addition to working the fields, spent time clearing new lands, stripping and burning bushes, and digging ditches. The hours of work and number of days worked varied from crop to crop. On the tobacco plantations, the work was continuous from morning until dusk and on some days through part of the night. The hands labored by moonlight or candlelight during the winter. There were no idle seasons on sugar plantations. The work lasted the entire year, and planters kept their hands employed at all times. The autumn cutting and grinding season was especially taxing, since at that time work intensity reached its peak, and periods of rest and sleep were severely contracted. Slaves were not allowed to sit down long enough to eat their dinner. Due to the demands of the sugar crop, Sundays and holidays—even Christmas, if necessary—had to be sacrificed.

Some sugar planters employed Irish workers to dig ditches because they were afraid the work was too strenuous for their slaves who, after all, represented a considerable investment. An English traveler in the Louisiana sugar region in 1861 observed: "The labor of ditching, trenching, clearing the waste lands, and hewing down the forests, is generally done by Irish laborers who travel about the country under contractors, or are engaged by resident gangsmen for the task." But not all planters could afford the high prices asked by the contractors for Irish workers, and some had to use their slaves for the heavy and dangerous work.

The task system was the mode of work organization in the low country along the coastal regions of South Carolina and Georgia, not only for rice and sea island cotton but for lumbering and such secondary plantation activities as cultivation of corn, fencing, barrelmaking, and carpentry. Under the task system and with the cooperation of the black drivers, slaves were often able to set aside a portion of the day for their own use.

Three-quarters of the slaves were employed in cotton fields, and the variety of duties involved in cotton production and the degree of regimentation during the yearly round of labor tells us much about the life and labor of the majority of American slaves. The routine of work of cotton growers was generally the same everywhere, although there were some variations from planter to planter and some differences in the time of planting. The planting season ran from late March to late April, a period of heavy labor demands. "Drills," or light furrows, were opened in the corn, and cotton seeds were sown in these drills. The seed was covered by hand or with a harrow. Some replanting was necessary. Vegetable gardens were cultivated, and corn fields were plowed and hoed.

From May to August, the cotton was "barred," a process that consisted of running a bull-tongue plow around the cotton row. The object was to provide a small ditch on each side of the row for drainage and to furnish greater warmth to the roots. Planting cotton in drills made it necessary to thin it, and this was accomplished by chopping the cotton with hoes. Weeds and grass were also killed in this manner. Cotton and corn were cultivated until the middle or latter part of July. After the crops were "laid by," there was an interval of rest until the crops ripened enough to be picked. In August, new ground was cleared, fodder was pulled, the blades were stripped from the corn stalks, and the gin house was cleaned.

From September to December, cotton was picked, ginned, pressed, and shipped. The field was picked three times. Each slave carried a sack suspended about the waist into which the cotton was deposited as it was gathered. The gathered cotton was placed temporarily on scaffolds to dry. The seed cotton was taken from the scaffolds to the gin house and left to "sweat" for several days before ginning. During these same months, peas were gathered, corn and fodder were hauled, potatoes were dug, corn was shucked, ditches were cleaned and repaired, fences were mended, wood was hauled and cut, and new ground was cleared.

During January and February, the hands completed picking, ginning, and pressing cotton and hauling it in wagons to the point of shipment. In the period before the Civil War, the picking of 150 to 200 pounds a day was required of field hands, although more was reported on occasion. After the harvest, the slaves were kept busy by other plantation work. Hogs were killed and cut and their meat salted. Wood was cut and hauled, as were fence rails. Buildings and tools were repaired; manure was spread; new ground was cleared; cotton fields were ploughed; and vegetables were planted.

On a typical day on many plantations, the driver awakened the sleeping field hands while it was still dark by blowing a horn or ringing a bell. After the slaves had prepared a hasty breakfast for themselves and the working stock, a second signal was given for the field hands to assemble at some central point. Following a quick check of the cabins in the slave quarters by the driver or overseer to determine if all hands were present, the driver led the workers to the field.

Upon arriving at the site of the day's labor, the driver assigned the tasks or began to lead or supervise his gang. When he determined that the hour of the midday meal had arrived, he called a halt to the work and directed the feeding of the field hands and their draft animals. The slaves ate the provisions that they had carried from home or that were brought to them from a common plantation kitchen. Work was then resumed until the driver decided that the day's agricultural activities were completed.

Throughout the day, the driver administered punishment to any hand who was deemed to be falling behind in his work. Sometimes such punishment was administered or supervised by the overseer, but usually it was the driver who did the whipping. The drivers also had the responsiblity of policing the slave quarters after the day's activities. When the hands had eaten their evening meal, the driver would once again blow a horn, ring a bell, or simply yell, "Oh, yes! Oh, yes! Ev'body in an' do's locked"—thus signaling the end of both the slaves' physical labors and the brief time available for family and social life.

If a slave was found to be missing during the subsequent evening check, it was the responsibility of the driver to report the absentee to the master or overseer. Even if all appeared to be well on the estate, he was often required to turn in a nightly verbal report of the preceding day's activities and accomplishments.

WOMEN AND CHILDREN

While both black men and women suffered under slavery, Eugene Genovese has pointed out that "the women field hands generally had a longer day than their men. . . . In addition to the usual work load, the women had to cook for their families, put the children to bed, and often spin, weave, and sew well into the night." Genovese quotes an ex-slave who recalled his mother's returning exhausted from the field and having to cook for her husband and children. The son wrote, "Lots of times she's so tired she go to bed without eatin' nothin' herself." Fannie Moore, an ex-slave from South Carolina, told an interviewer: "My mammy she work in de field all day, and piece and quilt all night. . . . I never see how my mammy stand such hard work." Children had to help their mothers. The same Fannie Moore recalled helping her mother spin enough thread every night to make the four cuts required by the white folks:

Why sometimes I never go to bed. Have to hold de light for her to see by. She have to piece quilts for de white folks too. Why, dey is a scar on my arm yet where my brother let de pine drop on me. Rich pine was all de light we ever had. My brother was a-holdin' de pine so's I can help mammy tack the quilt and he got to sleep and let it drop.

In her very perceptive article on black women under slavery, Jacqueline Jones sums it all up when she concludes: "The drive for cotton profits induced slaveowners to squeeze every bit of strength from black women as a group."

To add to the slave women's woes, the owners established for themselves the right not only to their labor but to their sexual services as well. Planters assumed that sexual access to slave women was simply another of their prerogatives. Eugene Genovese argues that many slave women escaped "white lust" because the whites knew they had "black men who would rather die than stand idly by." There were also black women who resisted, but at a terrible cost. Lewis Hayden's slave mother was approached by a white man who "made proposals of a base nature to her. When she would have nothing to say to him, he told her that she need not be so independent, for if money could buy her he would have her. My mother told old mistress, and begged that master might not sell her. But he did sell her.'' But "she would not consent to live with this man, as he wished; and he sent her to prison, and had her flogged, and punished in various ways, so that at last she began to have crazy turns. . . . She tried to kill herself several times, once with a knife and once by hanging. She had long, straight black hair, but after this it all turned white, like an old person's.''

Many Southern white women, who saw their husbands' features stamped on the mulatto children around them, could testify to the widely practiced sexual exploitation of slave women by white men. Complaints about the notoriously free sexual access of white men to black women filled the diaries and reminiscences of Southern women. Nor were they impressed by the argument that the availability of slave women minimized the need for prostitutes, or that under slavery, white men "could satisfy their sexual needs while increasing their slave property." "I saw slavery in its bearing on my sex," wrote one Southern woman. "I saw that it teemed with injustice and shame to all womankind and I hated it." In her famous *Diary from Dixie,* Mary Chesnut wrote on the eve of the Civil War:

Our men live like patriarchs of old, surrounded by their wife, family, and concubines.

The young woman who waits on me at morning is my niece. The young man who drives my coach is my children's half brother.

You can go to any plantation and the mistress of that plantation can name the father of every child on every plantation but her own.

Ours is a monstrous system.

Some white men had liaisons with black women in their wives' beds, boasted about their black lovers, insisted on keeping their black mistresses in their homes, and publicly denounced their wives when they objected.

On many large plantations, slave children destined to become field hands were not put to work until they were between the ages of ten and fourteen. Those trained to be house servants began much earlier. But most children between the ages of six and ten were given miscellaneous chores around the plantation. They tended sheep, milked cows, gathered firewood, carried water, helped with the cooking, assisted at the nursery, swept the yard, ran errands, and did other odd jobs. Between the ages of ten and fourteen, young blacks began actual fieldwork. At first they were assigned special tasks. On cotton plantations, they were given the job of gathering the first bales from the lower part of the stalk, where it opened months before the rest was ready for picking. On tobacco plantations, one of the principal jobs of the younger children was to pick worms off the tobacco leaves.

On many plantations an older field hand was assigned to teach the children how to do fieldwork. As they grew older and stronger, the children were given regular tasks. Olmsted noted that all field hands "are divided into four classes, according to their physical capacities. The children begin as 'quarter-hands,' advancing to 'half-hands,' and then to 'three-quarter hands'; and finally, when mature, and able-bodied, healthy and strong, to 'full-hands.' ''

By the time they had become full-fledged field hands, the young slaves knew that the whites not only held them as slaves but intended to use their power to make them behave like slaves. Many did not have to wait that long; even as children, they had learned what slavery really meant. Describing the attitude of overseers on the Maryland plantation where he lived as a slave child, James Pennington recalled: "These men seem to look with an evil eye upon children. . . . They seem to take pleasure in torturing the children of slaves, long before they are old enough to be put at the hoe, and consequently under the whip.'' Josiah Henson saw his father appear one day with a bloody head and lacerated back: "His right ear had been cut off close to his head, and he had received a hundred lashes on his back. He had beaten the overseer for a brutal assault on my mother, and this was his punishment.'' William Wells Brown remembers watching his mother being whipped for tardiness in going to the fields and how "the cold chills ran over me, and I wept aloud.'' "Other children,'' Thomas L. Webber reports, "saw their friends divested of a finger for attempting to learn to read, escapees tortured, and grandparents put off the plantation and told by the white authorities to fend for themselves.''

SLAVE PRODUCTIVITY

Estimates of the productivity and work patterns of plantation slaves vary widely. Some historians argue that the slaves were efficient and contented laborers who identified with their masters' interests. Others contend that slaves performed well below their capacity because of the preindustrial attitudes toward time, work, and leisure, which discouraged steady, routinized labor. Since the plantation economy required extraordinary exertion at critical points of the year, notably during the harvest, planters settled for measures that would capitalize on the slaves' willingness to work in spurts rather than steadily. Hence, according to Genovese, the slaveowners only got enough work out of their slaves to make the system pay at a level necessary for their survival as a slaveholding class in a capitalist world market. During the longer working days in the summer, "masters generally compensated their slaves with a midday break of two hours or more'' and even gave them "breaks to rest or go swimming.'' When the work got hard during the harvest season, everybody pitched in: "masters, overseers, hired whites and blacks, house slaves, mechanics and craftsmen all worked together under conditions made as festive as possible.''

Yet it is difficult to see how masters grew so rich if they tolerated such a low level of work performance by the slaves. The narratives of ex-slaves and the testimony of former slaves emphasize the herculean pace they were required to maintain and make no mention of slaves' receiving breaks to rest or go swimming. In fact, Christmas appears to have been the one extended period during the year when slaves were free from labor.

All of the slave narratives call attention to the long hours of labor, of a working day from sunup to sundown, or from "dark to dark," six days a week, with minor variations depending upon the season, crop, and location. And, of course, there was also the slaves' labor for their own needs—cooking, tailoring, shoe mending, furniture repairing, and the tending of personal gardens, permitted by some masters as a supplementary source of nourishment. Henry Bibb, an escaped slave, recalled:

I have known the slaves to be so much fatigued from labor that they could scarcely get to their lodging places from the field at night. And then they would have to prepare something to eat before they could lie down to rest. Their corn they had to grind on a hand mill for bread stuff, or pound it in a mortar; and by the time they would get their slippers it would be midnight; then they would herd down all together and take but two or three hours rest, before the . . . horn called them up again to prepare for the field.

In evaluating slave work patterns, one must not overlook the fact that on most large plantations, the overseer, not the master, determined the amount of work— and overseers were under considerable pressure to produce a large crop. The overseer of a cotton plantation in the lower South was given one year—if he were lucky—in order to prove his ability. If he did not harvest a bountiful crop during his initial year of service, he was likely to find himself looking for a new position the following year. The amount of cotton bales produced was the sole criterion. An English traveler, writing to the *London Daily News* from Mississippi in 1857, declared that "*the future of the overseer depends altogether on the quantity of cotton he is able to make up for the market.*" An Arkansas planter, observing that "a very decided and commanding man must be had to make anything on a plantation without the presence of the owner," dismissed his overseer because he had not pushed the slaves sufficiently hard.

When negotiating salary terms with their overseers, planters made it clear the figure would have to depend on the amount of staple produced under their direction. "One unfortunate result of such pressure upon the overseer," writes William Kaufman Scarborough, "was to increase the latter's tendency to disregard the welfare of the Negroes in his determination to make a good crop."

Plantation owners drew up detailed regulations for their overseers to follow in the management of slaves, and they often warned against overworking the labor force. But since the overseer was rewarded generously for producing a large crop, the warning was not very effective, especially if the owner was absent from his plantation for long periods. In any case, the low pay the overseers usually received, the demand from the planters for a large crop, and the frequent turnover made overseers indifferent to the care of the slaves under their charge. Possessing no property or investment in the slaves, they did not even have the influence of self-interest to check their abuses.

While there is no doubt that the number of black overseers who managed plantations is much larger than generally was believed, the view of Fogel and Engerman that 72 percent of the overseers on plantations of more than fifty-one slaves were black and that "on a majority of the large plantations, the top nonownership management was black" has come under sharp criticism. (Scarborough has argued that over 90 percent of plantations with more than a hundred slaves had white overseers.) In any event, while slaves and black overseers might conspire to cut down the work requirements, overseers, whether black or white, were under intense pressure to produce a large crop. In the main, the black overseers helped to make the plantation a functioning operation and acted as agents for the planters in the control of the field workers.

An old slave who rowed Fredrika Bremer, a visitor from Sweden, across a South Carolina river pointed to plantations along the banks and said, "Good master" or "Bad master." "Slavery was owing who you were with," another bondsman told her. A former North Carolina slave explained that "slavery wus good an' bad according to de kind of master you had."

FOOD AND CLOTHING

Although the conditions of slavery varied from plantation to plantation, certain features were common to most. Diet in general consisted of pork and corn, with various additions. For most slaves, the principal, and indeed frequently the only, cereal was corn. Slaves customarily were issued an average of one peck or more of cornmeal weekly. Pork was the other major source of protein for slaves, and they received it in quantities ranging from some two and one-half to four pounds weekly. However, the pork was normally "fat pork," mainly because it was inexpensive. The cornmeal was made into bread loaves, johnnycake, or mush. During the harvest season, there was some fresh meat, rice, sugar, coffee, and an allowance of whiskey. Coffee usually was ersatz, the result of roasting corn, okra, or other grains.

Ex-slaves recalled that sometimes the slaves got enough to eat, and sometimes they did not. One woman recalled that "we didn't have nothing to eat but sour milk," and another remembered:

At some places where I have worked, I have known that the slaves had not a bite of meat given them. They had a pint of corn meal unsifted, for a meal,—three pints a day. I have seen the white men measure it, and the cook bake it, and seen them eat it: that was all they had but water—they might have as much of that as they wanted. This is no hearsay—I've seen it through the spring, and until the crop time, three pints a day and the bran and nothing else.

In contrast, Fogel and Engerman in *Time on the Cross* present a mouth-watering description of the slave diet: a "careful reading of plantation documents shows that the slave diet included . . . beef, mutton, chickens, milk, turnips, peas, squashes, sweet potatoes, apples, plums, oranges, pumpkins, and peaches.'' They concluded, the ''slave diet was not only adequate, it actually exceeded modern [1964] recommended daily levels of the chief nutrients.''

This evaluation of the nutritional value of the slaves' basic diet is not accepted by most other scholars. On the contrary, many of them have concluded that the slaves' caloric intake was totally inadequate and that their diet was not sufficient to ensure either sound bodies or the stamina necessary for sustained labor. An analysis of the narratives of ex-slaves reveals that those who relied solely on the rations provided by masters were famished most of the time. Often, however, slaves supplemented the diet furnished by their masters by fishing, hunting, raising fowl, keeping gardens—and stealing from the masters. During the op- posum season when the animals were plentiful and fat, slaves would often be permitted to go hunting. Upon returning from the hunt, they would steal and kill two or three fat pigs, skin them, and bury the skins and entrails. Then they would skin the opposums, bury the bodies, and put the pigs, dressed in the skin of the opposum, into kettles to boil. When the master came upon the party of slaves and inquired what was in the kettle, ''a fat opposum'' was the reply, accompanied by the presentation of appropriate proof.

Raids on the master's house were quite common, and even though this was considered stealing by both the master and overseer, to the slaves it was merely taking that for which they worked, and they ''could see no reason why, since we were compelled to work without wages, we should not eat the fruits thereof.'' It has been determined from an analysis of ex-slaves' testimony that stealing was more than six times as frequent on the plantations of masters who provided meager rations as on those of masters who provided more ample provisions.

Slave children were breast-fed by their mothers, and as they were weaned, the mother's milk was supplemented with cow's or goat's milk and ''the liquid from boiled cabbage, and bread and milk together.'' The older children who were still too young to work ate lunch and sometimes breakfast at the nursery, or the ''cook's house.'' The fare was usually bread and milk for breakfast and corn- meal dumplings and greens for lunch. Upon the return of the older slaves from the fields, the children went to their own cabins for their evening meal.

Frederick Douglass recalled that as a slave child, he was ''so pinched with hunger that I have fought with the dog . . . for the smallest crumbs that fell from the kitchen table.'' Those slave children whose fathers supplemented their diets by fishing, trapping, and gardening were more fortunate. Louisa Adams of North Carolina remembered: ''My old Daddy partly raised his chilluns on game. He caught rabbits, coons, and 'possum. He would work all day and hunt all night.'' But Lizzie Williams of Mississippi recalled:

Dey didn't give us nothin much to eat. Dey was a trough in de yard what dey poured de mush an milk in an us chillun and de dogs would all crowd 'round it an eat together. Us chillun had homemade wooden paddles to eat with and we sho' had to be in a hurry 'bout it cause de dogs would get it all if we didn't.

By way of contrast is the recollection of Isaiah Turner, a former Virginia slave:

Great times in the Big House. Folks had plenty of money, and what they didn't buy, we raised for them. I remember the big parlor. Company all the time, and the folks had big dinners. Fine ladies! Beautiful and they dressed like princesses.

As a general rule, slaves' clothing for all but privileged house servants was barely adequate. The usual clothing distributed to male slaves consisted of a coat and trousers of "osnaburgs" (a coarse linen of flax and tow) for winter, and cotton trousers, sometimes with a jacket, for summer. To these were added two pairs of shoes, three shirts, one blanket, and a felt hat. Women were given two dresses—one for summer and one for winter—and one or two pairs of shoes.

Children wore a single garment made of varying types of cloth, which fitted like a long shirt reaching to the ankles. "Boys until they got up large enough to work wore little slips," an ex-slave relates. "We called them shirts; they'd sew it up like a sack and cut a hole in the neck for your head to go through, and you wore that till you were ten or twelve years old. There was not much difference in the dress of girls and boys." "We never wore underclothes, not even in the winter," recalled Robert Anderson, a slave who spent his childhood in Maryland, "and a boy was ten or twelve years old before he was given a pair of pants and a shirt to replace the sack garment. We never had more than one at a time, and when they had to be washed we went naked until they had dried. . . . When one child outgrew a gown, it was handed down to someone smaller. The fit was immaterial, because there was no shape to these one-piece garments, other than that of a sack." Many slave children complained that the coarseness of the shirts scratched and irritated their skin.

Slave children rarely received shoes. "On frosty mornin's when I went to de spring to fetch a bucket of water," Will Sheets recalled, "you could see my feet tracks in de frost all de way dar and back." Children often wrapped their feet in bagging sacks to help keep warm. Hats for children were also rare. In general, plantation owners let the parents clothe those children who were too young to work. "Little children," a former slave recalled, "wore what their parents put on them."

HOUSING AND HEALTH

Most slaves were housed in what was called "the quarters." On plantations of moderate size, there was usually only one quarters, consisting of cabins several hundred yards away from the owner's family's "great house," near a spring and a supply of fuel from the nearby woods. On large plantations with more than seventy or eighty slaves, there were often two quarters: an "upper quarter," consisting of a set of cabins near the more distant fields, and a "lower quarter," which was a set of cabins closer to the great house.

In addition to household cabins, the quarters of the large plantations often contained a number of work houses, a "children's house" or nursery, a "sick house," and a bachelor quarters where unmarried males lived together. On some plantations, the cabins in the quarters were arranged in a circle; on others, they were put up haphazardly, whenever the need arose.

Slaves usually preferred to have their cabins some distance from the great house, and this desire often met with the owners' approval; they did not want to have the sight and sounds of the quarters disturb the peace and beauty of the great house. The cabins of the house servants were usually whitewashed and closer to the great house so that the Negroes could be easily summoned.

The typical slave cabin consisted of one large room, about sixteen by eighteen feet. They were usually constructed of wood logs daubed with mud and sticks and with holes in the walls with wooden shutters for windows. Slaves frequently and bitterly complained about what their masters considered "adequate" housing. Margaret Nillin of Texas pointed out that the so-called windows let "flies in durin' de summer an' col' in durin' de winter. But if you shuts dat window dat shut out de light." John Brown complained that "the wind and rain will come in and the smoke will not go out." Another ex-slave recalled that when the dirt fell off from between the logs in the cabin he lived in as a slave, "You could look out and see the snow falling. Sometimes you would get up out of your warm bed and the side towards the wall would be full of snow." And Austin Parnell, recalling his Mississippi slave cabin, declared:

I laid in bed many a night and looked up through the cracks in the roof. Snow would come through there when it snowed and cover the bed covers. . . . Before you would make a fire in them days, you had to sweep out the snow so that it wouldn't melt up in the house and make a mess.

The mud-and-sticks-chimneys often caught fire. "Many of the time we would have to get up at midnight and push the chimney away from the house to keep the house from burnin' up," recalled Richard Carruthers, who had lived as a slave in Texas.

Most slave cabins housed at least two families. The 260 slaves on the plantation where Charles Ball was enslaved shared 38 cabins. The average was 6.8 slaves per cabin. Lewis Hughes lived on a plantation with 160 slaves, and there were 18 cabins, with an average of 8.8 slaves per cabin. Josiah Henson commented that 10 to 12 people shared each cabin on his plantation. The great majority of the slave cabins in the 1850s appeared to have housed five to six slaves.

The furnishings of the cabins were simple, consisting of homemade chairs, tables, and beds. Boxes were often used for everything from bureaus and chairs to storing food. Gourds of varied sizes, which slaves grew, served many purposes. Robert Shepherd, who lived as a slave in Georgia, recalled: "Us loved to drink out of gourds. Dere was lots of gourds raised every year. Some of 'em was so big dey was used to keep eggs in and for lots of things us used baskets for now. Dem little gourds made fine dippers'' Most slaves also possessed at least one big wooden water bucket and perhaps an even larger wash barrel. Many slaves did much of their cooking at the fireplace in a large three-legged black pot nicknamed "the spider."

Generally the slaves worked hard to make their cabins as comfortable as possible for themselves and their children. Many worked late into the night in order to build some simple furniture; some spent long hours cementing the chinks between the logs of their cabins or inserting mud in them so that they and their children might gain some protection from storms and the cold.

Although slave cabins were severely crowded, there was usually a separation of sexes. The kitchen area might be segregated for males, while the young women would huddle together in the area set aside for the parents. "Gals slept on one side of de room and boys on de other," noted Georgia Baker, who grew up on a Georgia plantation.

William H. Russell, correspondent for the London *Times,* visited the slave cabins on a Louisiana plantation and noted that "not a sign of ornament or decoration was visible." While most cabins were foul and wretched, some masters required that the overseers see that "the houses and quarters are cleaned up once a week."

The health of a slave was presumably a matter of grave concern to a master. At the very least, illness meant a loss of time from work; since an unhealthy slave depreciated in value, it meant the loss of a valuable capital investment. Theoretically, therefore, this should have resulted in the slaves' being protected medically against illness. But Charles Ball, an ex-slave, wrote: "I have seen many of our poor people compelled to pick cotton when their frames were shakin' so violently by the ague that they were unable to get hold of the cotton butts without difficulty."

Foul drinking water, spoiled or badly prepared food, and generally unsanitary conditions caused a high degree of dysentery and other ailments among slaves. While many planters maintained extensive health rules on their plantations and insisted that all reasonable complaints receive prompt attention, Henry Bibb wrote of the overseer of the plantation where he labored:

He always pronounced a slave who said he was sick a liar and hypocrite; said there was nothing the matter, and he only wanted to keep from work. His remedy was most generally strong pepper tea boiled till it was red. This would operate on the system like salts, or castor oil. But if the slave should not be very ill, he would rather work as long as he could stand up, than to take this dreadful medicine.

Many planters spent money on medical attendance for their slaves, but most refused to call a doctor for any complaint. Consequently they either tried their own hands at medicine or had other slaves take care of sick bondsmen. In discussing slave health conditions, Leslie Howard Owens writes: "During all their sufferings, physical and mental, slaves largely treated slaves." In general, when the master failed to supply medical care, slave doctors took over and cared for and cured fellow slaves.

In an age of high infant mortality, the death rate of slave children within the first year of life was much higher than that of white children. During her pregnancy, a slave woman usually continued her backbreaking labor until a few weeks before her child was born. The slaveowner, solicitous for the health of the new child out of a common business sense, would release the mother from labor after the birth for a lying-in time, which might last for a few days, a week or two, or a month, during which she nursed the infant. After the mother returned to full-time work in the fields, the new child was usually cared for during the day at the plantation nursery, in the case of a large plantation. Here the children were tended by one or two women who were too old to work in the fields and who were assisted by the older brothers and sisters and even cousins of the infants. The child's mother would be released from work to nurse the infant two or three times during each workday.

On smaller plantations, the mother either carried the infant to the field with her or returned to her own or the grandparents' cabins at intervals during the day to nurse the child. Whether he was being cared for at the nursery, at his grandparents' cabin, or in his own home by one of his older sisters or brothers, many slave children were fed irregularly or improperly. Suffering from a variety of ills and treated poorly, black children died in droves.

While a number of scholars have recently stressed the care lavished on the slave's health, Southern agricultural journals before the Civil War often complained about the lack of such care. The editor of the *Carolina Planter* warned that overseers were killing their employer's investment by their refusal to allow proper care and rest for slave women before and after childbirth. Small wonder, it noted, that the slave states, with 38 percent of the population, had 45 percent of the stillborn and infantile deaths in the year ending June 1, 1860.

An important criterion for arriving at some conception of the general standard of living of slave field hands is the amount a master spent for a slave's upkeep. Frederick Law Olmsted quoted a South Carolina planter as asserting in 1846 that food and clothing for a "full tasked hand" cost fifteen dollars annually, and his own observation, made ten years later, led him to declare: "In fact, under formidable circumstances, on the large plantations the slave's allowance does not equal in quantity or quality that which we furnish rogues in our penitentiaries."

In 1852, a Louisiana court accepted a $15 estimate as the amount required yearly to sustain a slave, but that figure was just that—an estimate. A more reliable figure is provided by the 1856 case of *Sheriff* v. *Boyle*, in which a Louisiana judge awarded $420 as recompense for board, clothing, and medical attention for eleven slaves detained one year under a writ of sequestration. This amounted to an average of $38.18 and is close to Kenneth Stampp's estimate of an annual expenditure of $35 for each slave. Of that sum, probably $26 was spent for food. In many instances the food might have been produced by the slave on the plantation after his normal workday. In any case, the total annual maintenance cost of the slave was between $35 and $36, this for a fully adult field hand.

It is now becoming clear that the debilitating effects of long hours in the fields, under a dehydrating sun, coupled with the nutritional deficiencies of slave diets, resulted in a lack of the necessary nutrition and energy for bondsmen. Both stamina and the capacity to labor were thereby reduced, and productivity was diminished. Yet many historians have assumed that planters made sure to provide their slaves with adequate food, clothing, housing, and medical care in order to keep their investments productive. Still, the slave was dependent on the master's arbitrary power. Since the master alone was responsible for food, clothing, shelter, and medical care, it was his interests, not those of the slaves, that dictated the quantity and quality of the provisions. Self-interest would not necessarily make the master treat the slaves well. Solomon Northup, an ex-slave, put it succinctly in 1853: "In the estimation of the owner, a slave is most serviceable when in rather lean and lank condition."

THE LASH

By the nineteenth century, the practice of whipping had fallen out of favor as an acceptable form of punishment in the free states, but it continued in the South because it was an integral part of the system of discipline and motivation in slavery. Some plantations had jails to confine slaves, and in Southern cities, owners often sent slaves to prison to be lashed or otherwise punished. Imprisonment, however, was never the standard means of punishment for slaves because the resulting loss of time was the master's loss and not that of the slaves. Thus whipping was more logical. "De white folks was hard on us. Dey would whup us 'bout de leas' li'l thang," Mingo White, an ex-slave from Alabama, recalled. Indeed punishment was often inflicted when no offense had been committed, and on many estates, the whip was regularly in evidence. "Never do to be too slack with niggers," was a common remark. The diary of Bennett H. Barrow, a Louisiana slaveowner, shows that slaves were whipped regularly. At times, the whole crew of cotton pickers would be whipped for not picking as much as their master thought they should. Barrow records whippings administered for being up too late and out of the cabins, inattention to work, talking to white workmen, careless planting, slowness about work, and being late for work. He also chained two slaves "for general bad conduct for a year and better."

Public opinion and "gentlemanly honor" were supposed to protect the bondsmen, but they proved to be uncertain guarantors. A number of Southern states passed laws making it a crime for any person "cruelly or inhumanely to torture, beat, wound, or abuse any slave in his employment, or under his charge, power, or control." But the laws themselves revealed how fragile was the slave's claim to protection, since they allowed punishment by sticks or whips. It was only *unusual* punishment that was prohibited. Moreover, it was extremely difficult to obtain a conviction unless white witnesses could and would testify against the defendant. As a rule, however, outsiders almost always hesitated to interfere.

Consequently mistreated slaves had nowhere to turn. Many were unaware of the laws giving them protection, and all were powerless in the courts. "Warn't no law sayin' dey got to treat slaves decent," an ex-slave avowed. The slave was totally vulnerable, with only the master's sense of humanity for a shield. Mary Boykin Chesnut, the wife of a slaveowner, declared that she hated slavery for many reasons, but that a major one was its cruelty. Under slavery, she said, men and women were punished "when their masters and mistresses are brutes, not when they do wrong." While there were many masters who were not brutes or psychopaths, there is plenty of evidence to establish that a large number not only used whippings regularly to keep their slaves in line but often used cruel and barbarous methods of punishment. Interviews with ex-slaves are a source of countless stories of horror.

Anne Clark's tale was typical:

They'd whup us with a bullwhip. We got up to 3 o'clock, at 4:00 we done et and hitched up the mules and went to the fields. We worked all day pullin' fodder and choppin' cotton. Master'd say, I wan' you to lead dat field today, and if you don't do it I'll put you in de stocks. . . . When women was with child they'd dig a hole in the groun' and put their stomach in the hole, and then beat 'em. They'd allus whup us.

Frances Foster, a woman of eighty-six, told an interviewer for the Federal Writers' Project how she was beaten by her mistress. Indicating her jaw and her speech impediment, she said, "That's what slavery did."

Mary Chesnut described the torture a neighbor inflicted on slaves. He had a penchant for putting "negroes in hogsheads with nails driven in all around" and then rolling" the poor thing downhill." Olmsted tells of a slaveowner who "had tied up a slave in a fit of anger, and had drawn a live cat down his back, so she would strike her claws into his skin and tear it. The slave was seriously injured."

The Coroner's Book of Inquisitions, 1851–1859, for Edgefield District, South Carolina, contains reports of the deaths of a number of slaves. One, "Randal the negro," received about "five hundred lashes," after which he had saltwater thrown on him. The "negro woman Aggy" received 150 licks with a leather strap fastened to a handle. A short while later she died.

On December 15, 1811, in Livingston County, Kentucky, a slave named George broke a pitcher. His master, Lilburne Lewis, with the help of his younger brother, Isham, both nephews of Thomas Jefferson, committed a grisly murder when they decided to teach all their slaves a lesson in obedience. They herded the slaves into the kitchen cabin, which stood apart from the main plantation house, and bolted the door so that none could escape. Lilburne Lewis then seized an axe and sank it deep into George's neck, after which the brothers compelled one of the other slaves to complete the dismemberment of George's body. As the pieces were cut off, they tossed them onto the roaring fire in order to destroy all evidence of the crime. During the several hours required to behead and dismember the slave's body and burn his remains in the kitchen fire, Lilburne lectured the horror-stricken slaves on their duties to their master and warned them that if any one of them so much as whispered anything about George's murder, he would receive the same punishment.

The crime might have gone undiscovered were it not for a severe tremor that rocked the Mississippi Valley and toppled the Lewises' kitchen chimney, leading to the discovery of the slave's skull. The brothers eventually were indicted for their crime but they never stood trial. Lilburne died in the family graveyard, in a botched suicide pact, but Isham, the younger brother, survived and later broke out of prison and disappeared.

Perhaps nothing illustrates the methods of punishment inflicted on slaves better than the many advertisements in newspapers for runaway slaves. They reveal how commonplace was the mutilation, burning, and torturing of slaves. "Lately branded on the left cheek"; "very much scarred about the neck and ears, occasioned by whipping"; "I burnt her with a hot iron the left side of her face"; "much scarred with the whip"; "has a burn on his buttock from a piece of hot iron, in the shape of a T"; "has an iron bar on her right leg"; "has a small scar over her eye, a good many teeth missing"—these extracts from advertisements are testimony to the brutality of the slave system. So, too, was the description of the sight that greeted an onlooker when black recruits for the Union Army during the Civil War were stripped for physical examination in Louisiana:

Some of them were scarred from head to foot where they had been whipped. One man's back was nearly all one scar, as if the skin had been chopped up and left to heal in ridges. Another had scars on the back of his neck, and from that all the way to his heels every little ways; but that was not such a sight as the one with the great solid mass of ridges from his shoulders to his hips.

When men are given such despotic power over others who have no recourse to law, it is not surprising to find such serious abuses, especially when those who exercised this absolute power viewed the blacks as subhuman. The British consul in Charleston wrote in 1854: "My next-door neighbor, a lawyer of the first distinction and a member of the *Southern Aristocracy*, told me himself that he flogged all his own negroes, men and women, when they'd misbehaved. . . . It is literally no more to kill a slave than to shoot a dog." These were almost the precise words of an overseer in Alabama, who told Olmsted he felt not the slightest qualm about beating a slave—in fact, "Why, sir, I wouldn't mind killing a nigger more than I would a dog."

Advertisements in Southern papers publicized "Fancy Whips to be used on black backs," and "For Sale. Ivory Handled Planters' Whips." The 1857 publication, "Maxims for Young Farmers and Overseers," carried the following assurance: "Africans are nothing but brutes, and they will love you the better for whipping, whether they deserve it or not. Besides, by this manly course you will show your spunk.''

Even if many planters were restrained in their treatment of their slaves, what shall we say about those who blatantly brutalized the bondsmen? And what about the psychological damage done to all slaves by the atrocities inflicted on some? Enough vulnerable blacks experienced inadequate care, physical and sexual abuses, and other forms of mistreatment to make all of them aware of the terrible possibilities, the uncertainties, and the insecurity they faced.

"After twenty years of rich historiographical debate," David Brion Davis concludes, "it is now clear that slavery in the United States was characterized by comparatively positive scores on every quantifiable index: nutrition, health, clothing, housing, family stability, life expectancy, and so forth." The slaves had a different view. After submitting a significant portion of the Federal Writers' Project material of slave narratives to an exhaustive statistical survey, along with two volumes produced at Fisk University, Paul D. Escott concludes that an overwhelming majority of former slaves saw their masters as "pursuing a selfish advantage"; a great majority reported personal experience with whippings or beatings; hard work was almost a universal source of complaint; food, clothing, and shelter were simple but barely adequate in quantity; terrible physical abuse often did occur; and roughly one-fifth reported at least a partial breakup of their families under slavery as a result of slave sales. In essence, slavery was a harsh and heavily exploitative social system.

5

The Techniques of Control

"The techniques of control," Kenneth Stampp noted in *The Peculiar Institution*, "were many and varied, some ingenious, some brutal. Slaveholders generally relied upon more than one." The first step in controlling the slave was to define blacks as a naturally inferior people cursed by God to be slaves to white people. The story of the "curse of Ham" was drummed into the minds of slaves, and they were told that all humanity was descended from the household of Noah, the single family that survived the Flood, and that one branch of the family of man—Africans descended from Ham, son of Noah, whose children were cursed—was doomed to perpetual slavery. They were also made to believe that their immediate ancestors were "African savages who were innately barbaric, . . . immoral and stupid."

RESPECT FOR WHITES

The slave was trained to show total respect for his master. He was also to do the same for every other white man and woman in order that he might be constantly reminded of his station in life. He was required to remove his hat in the presence of a white man and to keep his eyes downcast when conversing with him—in short, to avoid any indication of insubordination. John Brown wrote in his slave narrative that he had been "forced to watch the changes of my master's physiognomy, as well as those of the parties he associated with so as to frame my conduct in accordance with what I had reason to believe was their prevailing mood at any time." Frederick Douglass explained in his narrative:

Does a slave look dissatisfied? It is said he has the devil in him. . . . Does he speak loudly when spoken to by the master? Then he is getting highminded, and should be taken down a buttonhole lower. Does he forget to pull off his hat at the approach of a white person?

Then he is wanting in reverence. . . . Does he venture to vindicate his conduct when censured for it? Then he is guilty of impudence, one of the greatest crimes a slave can commit.

One plantation owner Olmsted interviewed said that he disliked any poor whites living near him because "it is best that they [the slaves] do not see white men who did not command their respect, and whom they did not always feel to be superior to themselves and able to command them." Although the slave might look down on "poor white trash," nevertheless he was to show respect to them, if only because they were white.

ROLE OF RELIGION

Although the institution of slavery was justified in the South as an instrument in a crusade to convert pagan barbarians to Christianty and thus give a large number of blacks the gift of "eternal salvation," the religion of the master class was imposed upon the slave community primarily, in the words of a Southern minister, to "prove to be a stronger fortress against insubordination and rebellion than weapons of brass and iron." Some owners even believed that the only way to compel their work force to accept bondage was through the indoctrination of conservative religious ideas among the field hands.

The concept that religion could be used as an element of behavioral control for the slave community had long existed within the South, but it did not win widespread endorsement until 1822, with the discovery of the planned Denmark Vesey rebellion in Charleston. When the rebellion was exposed, the churches of the South were quick to point out that none of their slave members had taken part in it. "The reason for this," declared the Protestant Episcopal church in Charleston, in a typical statement, "is because in the sober, rational, sublime, and evangelical worship of the Protestant-Episcopal Church there is nothing to influence the passions of the ignorant enthusiast; nothing left to the crude, undigested ideas of illiterate black class leaders." The implication was clear: the church had been an ally of the slaveowners.

The concept conveyed to the slave was that God's chosen people were the members of the master class of the South. As one of the prayer books for slaves in use during this period pointed out: "Masters and Mistresses are God's overseers . . . do service for them as if you did it for God himself."

Since every Southern legislature banned any measure to educate slaves—a ban sometimes explained to slaves as necessary "to keep them ignorant of anti-Scriptural doctrine"—it was decided to rely on oral instruction to them during their religious training period—hence the slave catechism, in which the questions and answers would be repeated numerous times until all had committed the content to memory. The white instructor would then turn to all of his charges, pose the questions, and receive the correct answers from them.

A favorite subject of these questions and answers was the God-given right of their masters and mistresses to own them and their duty to obey them:

Q. Who gave you a master and a mistress?
A. God gave them to me.
Q. Who says that you must obey them?
A. God says that I must.
Q. If a master be unreasonable, may the slave disobey?
A. NO—the Bible says, "Servants be subject to your masters with all fear, not only to the good and gentle, but also to the forward."
Q. If servants suffer unjustly, what are they to do?
A. They must bear it patiently.
Q. Is it right for the servant to run away, or is it right to harbor a runaway?
A. NO!

The edict of God that a slave must submit was considered to be one of the most important lessons that could be imparted through religious instruction. Reverend William Meade's *Sermons Addressed to Masters and Slaves* was widely circulated among clergymen of the Protestant Episcopal church in Maryland and Viginia during the eighteenth and nineteenth centuries. Ordained a priest of the Protestant Episcopal church in Virginia and a bishop of the Virginia diocese from 1841 to his death in 1862, Meade was famous for the slave sermons that he edited and published. A believer that slavery was divinely sanctioned, his short sermons and catechisms for slaves stressed this theme, using such phrases as "your masters and mistresses are God's overseers." Here is a typical section:

There is only one circumstance which may appear grievous that I shall now take notice of; and this is CORRECTION. Now, when *correction* is given you, you either deserve it, or you do not deserve it. But whether you deserve it or not, it is your duty, and Almighty God requires that you bear it patiently . . . and leave your cause in the hands of God. He will reward you for it in heaven, and the punishment you suffer unjustly here shall turn to your exceedingly great glory hereafter.

West Turner, an ex-slave of Virginia, recalled: "This the way it go: 'Be nice to Massa and Missus, be obedient, an' work hard.' Dat was all de Sunday school lesson dey teach us." Frank Roberson, another ex-slave, described the sermon preached to a group of slaves by a white preacher:

You slaves will go to heaven it you are good; but don't ever think that you will be close to your mistress and master. No! No! There will be a wall between you, but there will be holes in it that will permit you to look out and see your mistress when she passes by. If you want to sit behind this wall, you must do the language of the text, "Obey your master."

A South Carolina slaveowner testified to the value of the slave catechism, writing in 1845:

A near neighbor of mine, a prominent member of the Church in which he belonged, had contented himself with giving his people the usual religious privileges. They gave him a good deal of trouble, especially in their family relations. About six months ago he commenced giving them special religious instructions. He used Jones' Catechism, principally. His people soon became interested; the children were pleased with the Catechism; and at this time, there is apparently an entire change in the views, feelings, principles and tempers of all without a single exception. He states that he has now comparatively no trouble in their management.

There is no doubt that some slaves were convinced by such sermons. One bondswoman wrote to her mistress:

I try . . . to be contented at all times and am determined not to let anything make me unhappy; we are taught to resemble our Maker and He is always happy, therefore it is our duty to be happy, too, knowing that his divine Providence is over all our changes. . . . My mind is continually aspiring to that heavenly place where all our sorrow will terminate.

And a house servant on a South Carolina plantation declared: "I hope and prays to git to hebben. . . . I wants to be in hebben wid all my white folks, just to wait on 'em."

It is with such slaves in mind that the Alabama Baptist Association adopted a resolution in 1850 declaring that "intelligent masters with the light of experience before them will regard the communication of sound religious instruction to their slaves as the truest economy and the most efficient policy and as tending to the greatest utility, with regard to every interest involved."

Some plantations had black preachers, both bond and free, who held mid-weekly meetings in the quarters and preached to the slaves every Sunday in the master's church. According to fugitive slave Henry "Box" Brown, at each of such meetings and sermons, there were always some white men present to take note of what was preached. If the topic, or even the words used, were deemed insubordinate or antislavery, the meeting was quickly stopped, and the preacher was lectured about his mistake and in some cases even barred from preaching there again.

Some owners tried to manipulate the slave's superstitions as a means of control. This was used, for example, to keep slaves from roaming about at night. When the fear of the whip was not enough to keep slaves at home, masters attempted to accomplish this by spreading ghost stories. "Superstition and fear of ghosts were promoted among slaves," notes Gladys-Marie Fry, "so that they would be more fearful in their movements, especially at night." Numerous stories of ghosts chasing slaves home at night helped the owners convince the Negroes to stay home rather than face the unknown.

The slaves also had their own religion in the quarters, and keen observers on plantations sometimes realized that although the masters believed that religion was an effective means of control, it might become a two-edged sword of truth, which would free the slave.

Keeping slaves in ignorance was also a major technique of control. Although the education of slaves had been frowned upon since colonial times, it was during the 1830s, when there was a widespread fear of slave uprisings, that statutory prohibitions to teach slaves to read and write were enacted in Mississippi, Delaware, Florida, Alabama, and the Carolinas. (Georgia already had such laws.) Missouri did not legislate against schools for blacks until 1847, and Tennessee, Kentucky, and Maryland never actually forbade them. Virginia, on the other hand, made the teaching of free blacks, as well as slaves, to read and write a crime punishable by imprisonment. North Carolina's law of 1838 forbade not only the teaching of slaves but even giving or selling them books or pamphlets. The statute held:

Whereas the teaching of slaves to read and write, has a tendency to excite dissatisfaction in their minds, and to produce insurrection and rebellion, to the manifest injury of the citizens of this State: Therefore,

Be it enacted by the General Assembly of the State of North Carolina, and it is hereby enacted by the authority of the same, that any free person, who shall hereafter teach, or attempt to teach, any slave within the State to read or write, the use of figures excepted, or shall give or sell to such slave, or slaves any books or pamphlets, shall be liable to indictment in any court of record in this State having jurisdiction thereof, and upon conviction, shall, at the discretion of the court, if a white man or woman, be fined not less than one hundred dollars, nor more than two hundred dollars, or imprisoned; and if a free person of color, shall be fined, imprisoned, or whipped, at the discretion of the court, not exceeding thirty nine lashes, nor less than twenty lashes.

Of the three states that did not forbid the education of slaves—Tennessee, Kentucky, and Maryland—not one made public provision for their education. In parts of Maryland, there was such opposition to Negro education that even free blacks had little opportunity to learn to read and write. Levi J. Coffin wrote that although both of his parents were free, his mother had to teach him secretly to read.

REWARDS AND INCENTIVES

Although the whip was the most enduring symbol of the "peculiar institution," some owners argued that if the slaves could be won over to their side through a system of rewards and incentives, this would solve many of the problems of control. "Now I contend that the surest and best method of managing negroes is to love them," wrote a Georgia slaveowner. "We know . . . that if we love our horse, we will treat him well, and if we treat him well, he will be obedient, . . . and if this treatment has this effect upon all the animal creation . . . why will it not have the same effect upon slaves?"

One of Solomon Northup's masters believed in managing his slaves by kindness. Although he "lost nothing by his kindness," Northup observed, he was regarded by the majority of the surrounding slaveowners as "not fit to own a nigger.'' The general feeling was that to treat blacks with kindness would only ruin them. Nevertheless, most masters realized that an occasional act of kindness could be helpful in exercising control because of its very contrast to the general hardships of slavery. True, those masters who held Saturday night parties for their slaves did so partly to cut down on the number of their bondsmen's illicit gatherings. It was to the owner's advantage to be able to control such gatherings rather than to have his slaves hold them free of his control. If the master did not provide the food for the party, the slaves could help themselves. Mrs. M. E. Abrams, an ex-slave of South Carolina, recalled: ''We'in used to steal our hog ev'er Sa'day night and take off to de gully whar us'd get him dressed and barbecued.'' Finally, the master decided ''dat de best plan wuz to do away wid de barbecues in de holler'' by holding a party for the slaves.

Some owners sanctioned the growing of gardens as a means of control; they had the effect of keeping the slave attached to his home and made him ''feel that he has more than a passing interest in the things about him.'' Others, however, felt that it undermined the feeling of dependency on the master or that the slaves needed their nighttime and Sundays for rest in order to prepare for the next day's work. Some feared that the slaves would conserve their energy while working for their masters so that they could tend to their own gardens. ''They labor at night when they should be at rest,'' complained the *Southern Cultivator*. ''Like all other animals, the negro is capable of doing only a certain amount of work without injury.''

Although many masters contented themselves with merely giving their slaves the negative incentive of avoiding physical punishment as a means of maintaining control, others utilized the more positive means of offering rewards. These might include a pass to visit a nearby town or neighboring plantation. Even masters who were quite liberal with their whippings gave their slaves monetary rewards and gratuities at harvest or Christmas time. Money could be given directly, but more often the owner would make purchases for the slaves at their direction. A Louisiana planter gave three of his slaves suits bought in New Orleans ''for their fine conduct picking cotton, etc.'' At one Christmas celebration, he gave all his male slaves pants as presents. Some slaves on Louisiana sugar plantations were even permitted to accumulate and dispose of capital and property, despite the lack of legal protection for such activities.

DIVIDE AND RULE: PRIVILEGED BONDSMEN

For all the techniques they developed for control, including punishment, rewards, and incentives, if the slaveowning class had not applied the rule of ''divide and conquer,'' it could not have lasted a year. Hence the creation by masters of a divisive hierarchy within the slave community—a group of slaves who have been called ''privileged bondsmen''—the drivers and house servants. They comprised an elite group of about 5 or 10 percent of the total slave population. These slaves usually lived under conditions that were unrepresentative of those of the field hands, and through rewards, authority, pride, and other features of paternalism, they were induced, in many cases, to identify with the master's interests. In any event, masters expected total allegiance from the "privileged bondsmen" to the exclusion of any concern for their fellow slaves.

"The head driver is the most important negro on the plantation," wrote James H. Hammond, the South Carolina planter and agricultural reformer, in his *Plantation Manual*. "He is required to maintain proper discipline at all times. To see that no negro idles or does bad work in the field, and to punish it with discretion on the spot." Planters gave drivers most of the symbols of authority: whips, high boots, and great coats. They let them do all the whippings. One advantage was that the driver and not the master would be blamed.

On most plantations, whether with or without an overseer, the driver's responsibility was to maintain discipline and order. The driver was responsible for awaking the slaves for work in the morning and ensuring their retirement at night. He was responsible for the proper performance of tasks. He set the pace for the slaves in the field and kept them moving. He had permission to use the whip on slack hands and to flog slaves for breaking plantation rules. He had to report everything he saw "going wrong, or that he believes to be wrong, whether the person guilty of the crime is under his particular orders at the time or not." He had to make sure that the slaves did not leave the quarters without his permission and to make certain that the slaves did not keep or drink "spirituous liquors of any kind."

His tenure depended on how well he maintained discipline and order on the plantation and on whether he secured the proper amount of production in the field. Slaveowners believed that since the driver was chosen from among the slaves and lived in their quarters, he would be more effective than a white overseer in controlling the slaves. The slaves, in other words, would have less difficulty in relating to a black driver than to a white overseer because of the bond of kinship. In this connection, it was felt that the best combination for control of the slaves was to have a driver who was also a preacher. Olmsted met one such driver, whose master told Olmsted he felt himself fortunate: "He [the driver] drives the negroes at cotton all week and on Sunday he drives them at the Gospel."

On the other hand, masters were concerned lest their drivers get too close to their fellow bondsmen or treat them with respect. A very capable driver was severely reprimanded because he addressed the slaves as "brothers and sisters." Drivers were forced, on pain of punishment to themselves, to keep the hands at work and to maintain discipline. Solomon Northup was chosen to be a driver on a Louisiana sugar plantation. He was given the whip with instructions to use it upon any slaves caught idle. If he failed to obey, he was warned, there was another whip for him.

Drivers punished slaves for slackness in work, feigning illness, fighting, stealing, or running away. Sometimes they were able to convince the master and overseer that the slave was being severely punished even though the whip hardly touched the field hand's back. But too often drivers were brutal in punishing the slaves, and one ex-slave spoke for many when he said, "We might a done very well if the ole driver hadn' been so mean, but de least little thing we did he beat us for it."

In return for their services, and especially if they worked well, the black overseers received privileges and rewards. Masters gave drivers better clothes, more food, and special favors as long as they remained faithful. A few drivers were given larger meat allowances. If prime hands received two-and-a-half pounds, a driver received three pounds. Occasionally gifts of from one to ten dollars were given at the end of the year. They were also provided with better quarters and more frequent and extended passes. Some drivers were allowed to leave the plantation at their own discretion to purchase supplies.

The position of driver was passed down within slave family groups, and usually the son of a black foreman inherited the job when his father died. In this way, many, but by no means all, drivers became devoted to their masters and thoroughly alienated from their fellow slaves. "They are the same as white men," a former slave said in disgust. "Some of them will betray another to curry favor with the master." Although the driver was able to protect the slaves from unlimited abuse by masters and overseers, the system of promoting trusted slaves to slave foremen and the rewards given them for faithful service constituted a major technique of control. Apart from all other considerations, slaves chosen to be drivers were the most intelligent, motivated, and perceptive slaves. Paradoxically, they were also the type of slave most likely to become involved in revolts. Some were frequent runaways who had been converted by bribes of special treatment. Thus, the encouragement of privileges and rewards provided a means of reducing slave resistance.

Another privileged group were the house servants, who often lived in the "big house," in close contact with the white family and the cultural influences of the planter class. The feeling that they were a "slave aristocracy," superior to field hands, was encouraged by white owners, who sought to get them to identify their own interests with those of the owners. Owners often chose mulattoes as house servants and made them feel they were a superior group in the slave hierarchy. Henry Bibb, who spent years as a slave, revealed that "the distinction among slaves is as marked as the classes of society are in any aristocratic community." He went on to assert from experience that "the domestic slaves are often found to be traitors to their own people, for the purpose of gaining favor with their masters." Austin Steward, another ex-slave, similarly declared that a domestic slave would, "for the sake of his master and mistress, frequently betray his fellow-slave. . . . He is often rewarded by his master who knows it is for his interest to keep such ones about him." Although this was not universally true, the fact is that many former slaves emphasized that the existence of what Frederick Douglass called "a sort of black aristocracy" of house slaves was an important instrument of control. Labor in the "big house" often protected domestic servants from many of the injustices that the field hands suffered, and, as a result, Douglass noted, "the distance between these favored few, and the sorrow and hunger smitten multitudes of the quarter and field was immense."

SLAVE PATROLS

Behind the owner and his personal agents stood an elaborate and complex system of military control. In the cities, there were guards and police, and in the countryside there were patrols, an important part of the system of social control over the slaves. The patrols were designed to maintain order among the bondsmen and particularly to ensure that slaves neither went abroad at night without written passes from their masters nor congregated for unauthorized meetings. Composed of white males, the patrols were supposed to visit each plantation in the area at least once every week or two. Any slave found outside his owner's property was questioned, and the patrol could search slave cabins for firearms and disperse any gathering of seven or more bondsmen.

All white males were subject to patrol duty, and theoretically no adult male, regardless of status, was exempt from such public duty. But in reality, slaveowners were often able to evade patrol duty, a situation that frequently aroused resentment among the poorer whites who had to serve. They, in turn, often took out their resentment on the slaves, and with the slightest provocation, they would enter the slave quarters at night and whip men and women alike. Ida Henry, an ex-slave from Oklahoma City, recalled how patrollers tormented the slaves:

De patrollers wouldn't allow de slaves to hold night services, and one night dey caught me mother out praying. Dey stripped her naked and tied her hands together and wid a rope tied to de handcuffs and threw one end of de rope over a limb and tied de other end to de pummel of a saddle on a horse. As me mother weighed 'bout 200, dey pulled her up so dat her toes could barely touch de ground and whipped her. Dat same night she ran away and stayed over a day and returned.

A song all the slaves knew went:

> Run, nigger, run,
> De Pateroll git you!
> Run, nigger, run,
> De Pateroll come.
>
> Watch, nigger, watch,
> De Pateroll trick you!
> Watch, nigger, watch,
> He got a big gun.

The patrols were authorized by statute, but Solomon Northup reported that any white man could seize a Negro without a pass and whip him. Poor whites would often stop and examine a slave, since catching a runaway was a way of earning money. If, after advertising, no owner appeared, the black was sold to the highest bidder, and fees were given to the finder for his services.

Behind the patrols were the state militias, numerous and well-trained voluntary fighting organizations, and, as a last resort, the federal government. In 1860, Olmsted wrote of the South: "There is . . . nearly everywhere, always prepared to act, if not always in service, an armed force, with a military organization, which is invested with more arbitrary and cruel power than any police in Europe." But then, as Governor Robert Y. Hayne of South Carolina reminded the squeamish: "A state of military preparation must always be with us a state of perfect security. A period of profound peace and consequent apathy may expose us to the danger of domestic insurrection."

To slaveowners, the presence of the free black posed one of the major obstacles to control, and free Negroes were condemned as "the most dangerous incendiary element to our existing institution of society." Many efforts were made to curtail their freedom, but the law also prescribed severe penalties for any white southerners whose actions posed a threat to the slave system. All Southern states declared it a felony to write or say anything that directly might lead to discontent among the slaves. At the same time, realizing that nonslaveholders were important to the maintenance of slave control, the slaveowners made an intense effort to win the support of the almost 75 percent of Southern whites who owned no slaves. They never fully achieved their goal, but they did win the allegiance of many nonslaveowning yeoman farmers, poor whites, and the commercial bourgeoisie. This they did partly by instilling in them a desire to become slaveholders themselves but mainly by convincing them that slavery and its accompanying restrictions upon blacks not only preserved the dominant status of all whites but also provided less tangible benefits by controlling the social and economic competition of Negroes. J.D.B. DeBow, editor of the most influential pre-Civil War periodical in the South (*DeBow's Review*), was the author of *The Interest in Slavery of the Southern Non-Slaveholder*. One of these "interests" was in preserving an institution in which blacks were at the bottom of the ladder:

The poor white laborer at the North is at the bottom of the social ladder, whilst his brother here has ascended several steps and can look down upon those who are beneath him at an infinite remove. . . . No white man at the South serves another as a body servant, to clean his boots, wait upon his table, and perform the menial services of the household.

Frederick Douglass explained this propagandistic appeal by noting that even though both the poor, laboring white men and blacks were "plundered under slavery"—the white being robbed by the slave system "of just results of his labor, because he is flung into competition with a class of laborers who work without wages''—the poor whites were blinded to this competition ''by keeping alive their prejudices against the slaves as *men*—not against them as *slaves.*'' The slaveowners appealed to their pride, warning them that if slavery was abolished, the tendency would be ''to place the white working man, on an equality with negroes.'' By this means, slaveowners succeeded not only in diverting the minds of the poor whites from the real fact that by the rich slave master they were regarded as ''but a single remove from equality with the slaves,'' but also in converting them into part of the apparatus of slave control.

SLAVE CODES

Frederick Douglass once defined slavery in these terms: ''Slavery in the United States is the granting of that power by which one man exercises and enforces a right of property in the body and soul of another. The will and the wishes of the master are the law of the slave.'' They were also the law of the slave states and a fundamental means of slave control.

Each slave state regulated the condition of slavery through codes of laws. Although the slave codes of each state had unique provisions, all shared a common feature: they placed the slave completely under his master's control. The slave could not own personal property, rent real estate, make any civil contract, or lawfully be taught to read and write. His position before the courts was seriously limited in every respect. Thus he could not bear witness against his master, nor could he institute a suit in his own behalf. The law assumed that the master's interests were synonymous with the physical well-being of the slave. Slaves could lawfully be sold away from their families, and their marriages lacked legal sanction.

Relations between slaves and free blacks were outlined precisely in the codes, the duties of white patrols spelled out carefully, and penalties set for failure to perform duties when called. The patrol was authorized to inflict up to a specified number of lashes on a slave found at an unlawful assembly or off the plantation without a pass. Any slave off the plantation who refused to submit to investigation could be killed summarily by any white.

Slaves could be punished for gathering in unlawful assemblies, commiting trespass, or making seditious speeches. A prison sentence could be imposed on anyone helping a slave to escape, forging a pass for a slave, harboring a runaway, or inciting a black to defy a white. The death penalty was prescribed for blacks convicted of such varied offenses as assaulting or molesting a white woman, maliciously setting fire to a barn, preparing any poison, or conspiring to revolt. ''A ring leader or chief instigator of any plot to rebel or murder any white,'' a Tennessee law stated, ''may be lawfully killed on sight.''

The codes contained elaborate provisions for the apprehension, detention, and return of runaway slaves. Procedural rights of slaves accused of crimes were spelled out, and the punishment, after conviction, was specified. In criminal cases against slaves, either slaves or free blacks could be competent witnesses for or against the accused. In civil actions where all parties were Negroes, both slaves and free blacks could testify. But in criminal cases against white persons or in civil actions in which one or all parties were white persons, blacks, whether free or slave, could not testify.

Every Negro, no matter how much white or how little black blood he had, was presumed to be a slave; slavery was considered the general condition of Negroes and mulattoes in Southern states. Thus, with one exception, the burden of proof was upon the Negro or mulatto to prove that he was a free person. The exception was Louisiana, which had inherited from the period of French and Spanish colonial rule a different approach to social and racial patterns. The supreme court of Louisiana declared in 1845: "It has been the settled doctrine that persons of color are presumed to be free . . . and the burden of proof is on him who claims the colored person as a slave." By contrast, in 1827, the circuit court for the District of Columbia held that "every negro is, by rule of evidence well established in this part of the country, *prima facie* to be considered a slave, and the property of somebody, and he, who acts in regard to him as if here were a free man, acts at his peril." This was the pattern in the antebellum South.

Ulrich Bonnell Phillips minimized the impact of the admittedly harsh slave codes and insisted that "most provisions of the repressive legislation were dead letters at all times." It is true that laws restricting the slaveowners were rarely enforced. Thus, owners were seldom prosecuted for permitting their slaves to hire out their services, even though this was forbidden in codes at different periods, and, as a result, the custom continued unabated. However, after 1830, with the rise of abolitionist agitation in the North, augmented by the fear of another Nat Turner rebellion, Southern whites became more determined than ever to guarantee their own safety while continuing their domination over their slaves. The laws regulating slaves became more restrictive, and they were enforced. Actually, new and more elaborate slave codes were always being adopted in the slave states. As the preamble to one of South Carolina's revised slave codes stated, "The laws heretofore enacted for the government of slaves, free negroes, mulattoes and mestizos have been found insufficient for keeping them in due subordination."

THE COURTS

Restrictions imposed on slaves did not end with codes and other laws. The blacks were also subject to unwritten law or common custom. In 1847, for example, a South Carolina appeals court ruled that slaves could be punished for insolence to whites, even though such behavior was never prescribed in statute law. It was understood, ruled Judge D. L. Wardlaw, that all slave statutes in South Carolina "contemplate throughout the subordination of the servile class to every free white person." In June 1852, Judge Nash of the North Carolina Supreme Court declared in a decision:

What acts in a slave towards a white person will amount to insolence it is manifestly impossible to define—it may consist in a look, the pointing of a finger, a refusal or neglect to step out of the way when a white person is seen to approach. But each of such acts violates the rules of propriety, and if tolerated, would destroy that subordination, upon which our social system rests.

After agitation from grand juries in Southern states complaining of the wanton killing of blacks, laws were enacted making murder of a slave a capital offense. Usually such laws provided that if the killing occurred ''in heat and passion,'' the penalty would be a $500 fine and six months in jail. But because of the laws barring the testimony of Negroes against any white person, these measures, in most instances, remained dead letters. Similarly, when after years of struggle in the courts, slaves won the right to defend themselves against clear attempts to take their lives, it was almost impossible for them to present their case in such an event, since they could not testify in court against whites. As critics of slavery correctly pointed out, this rule compelled Negroes to suffer illegal treatment in silence. Even when laws were enacted restraining masters in their behavior toward and treatment of their slaves, the restrictions on slave testimony made enforcement difficult. It was white men who executed and interpreted laws protecting the slave, and the Negro was left with no protection.

Because of this legal restriction on blacks, even white men suffered unredressed injuries. When Professor George Whyte of William and Mary College was poisoned by his nephews, the culprit could not be convicted because the principal witness against him was a Negro, legally incapable of testifying against a white man. A tobacco planter had part of his crop stolen by white boatmen to whom it had been entrusted for transportation from Lynchburg to Richmond, and the boatman's Negro assistants could have described what had happened. Yet the planter knew that it would be useless to enter suit because the blacks could not testify in court against the white thief.

In *A Sketch of the Laws Relating to Slavery,* published in 1856, George M. Stroud summed up the entire situation:

The evil is not that laws are wanting, but that they cannot be enforced; not that they sanction crime, but that they do not punish. And this rises chiefly, if not *solely,* from the cause which has been more than once mentioned,—the exclusion of the testimony, in the trial of a *white* person, of all those who are *not white.*

In most slave states statutes were enacted extending to slave offenders on trial most of the procedural rights of white men. These included trial by jury, challenge of jurors, counsel, and appeal to the supreme court of the state. But the right to a trial by one's peers is necessary to give meaning to the right of trial by jury, and the acts providing trial by jury for slaves stipulated a jury of twelve slaveowners to hear the cases. Usually these cases involved a crime the punishment for which extended to life or limb. Jury trial was rarely extended to slaves charged with minor offenses; they were tried before a single justice of the peace.

But as Kenneth Stampp has noted, regardless of the manner of trial, it was "difficult [for a slave] to get a fair trial."

With few exceptions, slaves were prosecuted only for acts of violence committed against whites. If a slave stabbed a Negro belonging to another master, it was usual for the two planters to settle the difficulty without going to court. Actually the state willingly granted the slaveowner the power to act as the law, or above the law, in many matters relating to his slaves.

In the 1829 decision of Judge Thomas Ruffin in *State* v. *Mann,* the absolute power of the master over a slave and the lack of any rights on the part of the slave were clearly set forth. Before the court was the question of whether it was a criminal offense to subject a slave woman to "a cruel and unreasonable battery"—shooting her. The defendant, who had committed the act, had hired the slave woman. In dismissing the case, the judge ruled that the hirer of a slave could exercise the full legal authority of a master for a time and that the punishment in question did not go beyond the legal authority of the master. But the attorney general, who represented the state of North Carolina, argued that a master's authority over the slave was analogous "to those existing between parents and children, masters and apprentices, and tutors and scholars," and was limited to the same extent. Judge Ruffin, however, rejected the analogies:

There is no likeness between the cases. They are in opposition to each other, and there is an impassable gulf between them. The difference is that which exists between freedom and slavery—and a greater cannot *be imagined.* . . . With slavery . . . the end is the profit of the master, his security and the public safety; the subject, one doomed in his own person and his posterity to live without knowledge and without the capacity to make anything his own, and to toil that another may reap the fruits.

The court went on to emphasize that a slave was to "labor upon a principle of natural duty," to disregard "his own personal happiness"; a slave "had no will of his own" but had surrendered his will "in implicit obedience to that of another." There was no alternative. "The power of the master must be absolute, to render the submission of the slave perfect." It had to be so:

There is no remedy. This discipline belongs to the state of slavery. They cannot be disunited, without abrogating at once the rights of the master, and absolving the slave from his subjection. . . . It is inherent in the relation of master and slave. . . .

That there may be particular instances of cruelty and deliberate barbarity where in conscience the law might properly interfere is most probable. . . . [But] we cannot allow the right of the master to be brought into discussion in the courts of justice. The slave, to remain a slave, must be made sensible that there is no appeal from his master; that his power is in no instance usurped; but is conferred by the laws of man at least, if not by the laws of God.

Then, finally and ironically, Ruffin concluded that the decision of the court not to interfere with the absolute power of the master was not only to protect the value of slaves and to uphold the principle that the security of the master and public tranquility depended upon the slaves' subordination, but also because it was designed for "most effectually securing the general protection and comfort of the slaves themselves."

Judge Ruffin's statement was reaffirmed in the declaration of Judge Field in *Souther* v. *Commonwealth of Virginia* (1851). The case was almost as brutal as the one involving Jefferson's nephews. The master, Souther, had tied his slave to a tree and beat him with switches until he himself became tired. He then ordered another slave to take up the beating, this time with a shingle, and "applied fire to the body of the slave, about his back, belly, and private parts." He proceeded to wash the slave with hot water filled with red pepper, kicked and stamped upon him, and finally choked the slave with a rope, continuing this process of "correction" until it resulted in death. Arrested, Souther maintained he did not intend to kill the slave—proof of intent was necessary for conviction—and thought his slave "was feigning and pretending to be suffering or injured, when he was not." The decision of the court read:

> It is the policy of the law, in respect to the relation of master and slave, and for the sake of securing proper subordination and obedience on the part of the slave, to protect the master from prosecution in all such cases, even if the whipping and punishment be malicious, cruel and excessive.

But a white man had witnessed the brutal deeds and testified against Souther, so the court felt compelled to sentence him to five years' imprisonment.

The decision of the Virginia court in the 1848 case *Peter* v. *Hargrave* is revealing. After winning their freedom suit, Peter and other manumitted slaves sued for the profits of their labor that had accrued since their illegal detention in slavery by their emancipators' administrator and children. They alleged the willful disregard of their right in freedom, which began at the emancipator's death, by the administrator and children. But the trial court ruled against their claim to profits on "authority too clear to be doubted."

On appeal, the court unanimously denied the manumitted slaves the profits they sought. Despite the manumittees' illegal detention in slavery from the time their title to freedom accrued, the court did not regard them as free from that time. On the contrary, it regarded them as slaves because "persons in the status of slavery are, in the contemplation of the law, slaves, whatever may be their right to freedom." Moreover, the "mere acquistion" of title to freedom did not remove the manumittees from the status of slavery because only "legal adjudication" could remove that status. In short, the court's opinion denied the manumittees the right to sue for profits on the broad principle that "persons in the status of slavery have no civil rights, save that of suing for freedom when entitled to it."

In *Time on the Cross*, Fogel and Engerman contend that slaves convicted of capital crimes were more likely to be banished than executed, since banishment represented no loss of capital. However, in a study of executions following death sentences in antebellum South Carolina, Maurice S. Hindus establishes that blacks were executed "at a high rate." Moreover, since owners of executed slaves received reimbursement from the state, the argument of loss of capital did not apply. In short, the economics of slavery did not save slaves from the gallows.

It certainly proved of little value to Celia, a slave whose master repeatedly forced her to have sexual intercourse with him, although she had been pregnant for some months and was ill. On the night of June 23, 1855, Celia warned her master that she was very ill and threatened to hurt him if he did not cease forcing her to sex relations. When he ignored the warning and attacked her, Celia killed him.

During August 1855, Celia was formally indicted for murder by a Calloway County (Missouri) grand jury. Her court-appointed attorneys cited a Missouri statute of 1845 that states that "any attempt to compel any woman to be defiled by using force, menace or duress is a felony," and implied that any woman who defended herself in such a case, even to the extent of committing murder, would be judged innocent. The attorneys insisted that the words "any women" embraced slaves as well as free white women and asked the jury to find Celia not guilty on this ground. The court, however, rejected the interpretation of the statute and instructed the jury to disregard the section cited because it did not cover slave women. Celia was found guilty of murder in the first degree.

When two days later the attorneys for the defendant filed a motion asking the court to set aside the verdict and grant the defendant a new trial, the motion was immediately overruled, sentence was pronounced, and Celia was ordered to be executed by hanging on November 16. The supreme court of Missouri denied Celia's subsequent appeal, but the execution was delayed until after the birth of her child. On December 13, 1855, the day after the child was born, Celia was hanged.

Examining appellate cases involving slaves convicted of crimes and whites convicted of abusing slaves, some scholars have recently argued that Southern judges imposed some limitation on the extent to which blacks could be beaten and killed and found technicalities to spare black lives. A. E. Keir Nash, in particular, has published a series of articles stressing the liberality of Southern judges and extolling the treatment of blacks by "State Supreme Courts of the Old South." But Judge A. Leon Higginbotham, Jr., is not impressed:

The denial of marriage, the denial of the right to own property, the debasement of a man and his children living as slaves in perpetuity reduce Professor Nash's findings to miniscule significance in evaluating the justice in slavery. With millions enslaved and denied the above rights, there is only slight solace in Professor Nash's findings that a few Southern appellate courts were concerned about procedural fairness to the relatively few cases where whites—usually strangers—were prosecuted for brutalizing slaves.

Despite the liberality of courts of appeals, the slave, in the end, was legally powerless. Although he believed slavery to be a good institution, Thomas Reade Roots Cobb conceded the slave's legal impotence in his 1858 *An Inquiry into the Law of Negro Slavery in the United States of America. . .*

On account of the perfectly unprotected and helpless position of the slave, when his master is placed in opposition to him: not being allowed to accumulate property, with which to provide means for the protection of his rights; his mouth being closed as a witness in a court of justice; his hands being tied, even for his own defense . . . ; his time not being at his service, even for the purpose of procuring testimony; and his person and conduct being entirely under the control of him against whom he stands arrayed.

Perhaps the following typical definition found in many slave codes sums it up best:

A slave is one who is in the power of a master to whom he belongs. The master may sell him, dispose of his person, his industry and his labor. He can do nothing, nor acquire anything but what must belong to the master. The power of the master must be absolute, the submission of the slave perfect.

6

The Slave Community

THE QUARTERS

Most of the slaves lived in quarters away from the master's house and removed from his constant scrutiny. The slave quarters became the center of their lives. There they were able to enjoy some social life that was not controlled by their masters. There they found ways to alleviate the worst features of the system. There, too, they devised means for hunting, fishing, gathering wild crops, and other ways to supplement their meager rations. It was in the slave quarters that there evolved the stories, folk sayings, and beliefs; the songs, dances, and entertainment; the recipes, clothing, and house utensil styles; and the medicines and other forms of healing. In the hours between sundown and sunup; men would travel to other slave quarters, where they passed the night talking, singing, smoking, and drinking, often with the driver turning his eyes the other way.

It is true that in many ways the slave community was often insecure. Slaves were sold or forced to accompany their masters to other areas, far away from family and friends. Slaves who were hired out might live on a different plantation every year, suffering separation from their spouses, children, and friends. Nevertheless, there developed among the slaves a sense of community, not only with those on their own plantations and in their immediate neighborhoods, but also with those in far-off places. Even when they were sold, slaves were usually able to adapt themselves to their new community, for they would find people who shared a common destiny with them and who would help them adjust to their new life. While the slave narratives and interviews reveal regional differences among slaves, they also point up the similarities of their experiences.

Harriet M. Farlin, a former slave of Colonel Jesse Chaney in both Texas and Arkansas, vividly recalled the slave quarters:

Colonel Chaney had lots and lots of slaves, and all their houses were in a row, all one-room cabins. Everything happened in that one room—birth, death, and everything. . . . I loved to walk down by that row of houses. It looked like a town, and late of an evening as you'd go by the doors you could smell meat a-frying, coffee making and good things cooking.

Many of the quarters, to be sure, did not give evidence of "good things cooking," but everywhere the quarters were the centers of slave life. There, on pleasant evenings, after the daily work and chores had been completed, the entire slave community brought benches and chairs outside the cabins and sat around telling stories and singing. In cold weather, the fireplaces of the slave cabins became the centers of gatherings. Parents and children, grandparents, aunts, uncles, cousins, and adopted children whose parents had died or been sold, or who had themselves been sold, were all part of the household circle that gathered around the fireplace.

Holidays, especially Christmas, crop-laying-by time, the Fourth of July, and Easter, were special times for community and family gatherings in the quarters. But throughout the entire year, the slave community met to make common decisions, plan events in secret, provide for common physical and recreational needs, "and generally organized itself to be as independent as possible from the whims of the white personalities and the strictures of plantation rules and regulation."

In the quarters, parents taught their children how to survive and escape the rigors of slavery. They were taught to conceal their true feelings and hide their personalities in order to escape punishment. Most children grew up understanding that their parents' submission was really a role played in order to avoid suffering.

In spite of the most rigorous efforts of the masters to keep the blacks in ignorance and make them content to spend their lives working to enrich others, most slave parents instilled in their young a sense of skepticism about what the white master and mistress told them. This even extended to what they were told by the minister when he read to them from the Bible—the "master's Bible," they called it. They told their children that the black slaves were superior to white people; that they were more efficient, stronger, and able to work longer and more effectively than their white masters and overseers, whom they considered lazy and dissolute and incapable of running profitable plantations.

The economy of the quarters was partially controlled by the slaves, since distance from the masters allowed them a certain autonomy in small matters. Slaves occasionally slaughtered stock, without permission, ate some of the meat, and traded the surplus chickens, sheep, and swine to fellow slaves and even to white peddlers and merchants. The excitement and dangers of stealing the master's livestock were shared by the entire community. Emphasis was placed not on the commandment, "Thou shalt not steal," but rather on the section of the gospel that went, "Where ye labor there shall ye reap." Thus in Henry Bibb's view, it was not simply need that justified a slave's taking his master's goods—it was a matter of the worker's right to the fruits of his labor. "I did not regard it as stealing then, I do not regard it as such now. I hold that a slave has a moral right to eat and drink and wear all that he needs, and that it would be a sin on his part to suffer and starve in a country where there is plenty to eat and wear within his reach. I consider that I had a just right to what I took because it was the labor of my hands." Some slaves even rationalized their deeds by asking, If the slave was property, how could he steal from his master? How could a piece of property steal another piece of property? But most of them felt that, living as they did under a system that was built on cheating, lying, and deceit, there was nothing wrong in stealing from the master. Charles Ball recalled:

I was never acquainted with any slave who believed that he violated any rule of morality by appropriating to himself anything that belonged to his master, if it was necessary to his comfort.

The master might call it theft, and brand it with the name of crime; but the slave reasoned differently, when he took a portion of his master's goods, to satisfy his hunger, keep himself warm, or to gratify his passion for luxurious enjoyment.

The slave sees his master residing in a spacious mansion, riding in a fine carriage, and dressed in costly clothes, and attributes the possession of all these enjoyments to his own labor; whilst he who is the cause of so much gratification and pleasure to another, is himself deprived even of the necessary accommodations of life.

On the other hand, to steal from a fellow slave was considered a serious offense. As a rule, said ex-slave John Brown, most slaves thought nothing of stealing from the master but "would have allowed themselves to be cut to pieces rather than betray the confidence of their fellow slaves." The slave's own moral code made a careful distinction between "taking" from the master and "stealing" from another slave, which was regarded as a serious wrong.

Most of the slaves received no education at all, and in all of the slave states, the great masses of the blacks were kept illiterate. There were plantations with hundreds of slaves, not one of whom had the merest rudiments of education. Yet slaves did manage to learn to read and write. In the slave community, they taught one another. Slave parents who had enough knowledge to do so sometimes secretly taught their children to read. Some planters, ignoring the law or customs prohibiting slave literacy, did nothing to hinder their slaves' efforts to learn. An occasional master even deliberately educated his slaves so that they could be more useful. (A brother of Jefferson Davis educated a slave to be a plantation accountant.) Slaves sometimes educated themselves while assisting printers or clerks. A few slaves—Frederick Douglass among them—were helped to learn by friendly whites, especially children.

After he had learned to read, Douglass tried to start a school to teach other slaves. This was broken up, but he then started another, which met secretly. In Savannah, Georgia, a black woman secretly taught a black school for over thirty years in defiance of law. In South Carolina, the young white, Sarah Grimké, the future abolitionist and women's rights advocate, disobeyed the law by secretly teaching her maid to read, keeping the door of her room closed, and even the keyhold plugged. Robert Edmond, a Scot who came to South Carolina in order to teach planters' children, was so shocked by the degradation of the slaves that he tried to teach some of them to read. His actions became known, however, and a band of disguised white men came to his schoolroom, dragged him away, and covered him with a coat of tar and feathers. Edmond fled to the North. In North Carolina, the young Quaker and future Underground Railroader, Levi Coffin, taught neightborhood slaves until their masters threatened him.

Despite stultifying restrictions, small numbers of slave children managed, covertly, to learn to read and write.

DRIVERS AND FIELD HANDS

The narratives of fugitive slaves and ex-slaves abound with testimony about the drivers who ruled their field hands with brute force, and in much historical literature, black slave drivers are viewed as barbarous half-savages, so debased by slavery that they found sadistic pleasure in inflicting pain on their hapless brothers in bondage. Yet there is also considerable evidence revealing that while some drivers flogged slaves without mercy, others assisted bondsmen by faking whippings, secretly distributing extra rations, fighting with violent overseers, and behaving in other ways that were decidedly not in the master's interest.

Solomon Northup, who was a driver for eight years on a Louisiana plantation, learned, out of consideration for his fellow bondsmen, to handle the whip with marvelous dexterity and precision "throwing the lash within a hair's breadth of the back, the ear, the nose, without, however, reaching either of them." When the overseer appeared, he would lash vigorously, and by prearrangement, the slaves would "squirm and screech as if in agony." Other drivers' dexterity with the whip rivaled Northup's. They, too, "didn't like dat whippin' bus'ness," and carried through the form, but not the intent, of the master's orders.

Some drivers refused to beat slaves when ordered to do so by the overseer. After inflicting forty-five blows upon the back of a slave woman, one driver refused to lash her any more though threatened with a lashing himself. An Alabama driver pleaded with the overseer to stop beating a severely hurt woman slave. On another occasion, this driver defied the overseer and refused to whip a sick slave woman. When ordered to whip two other women for not performing their tasks, the same driver had to whip one of them because the overseer watched until the full 150 lashes had been applied. However, as soon as the overseer left, the driver refused to whip the second woman and instead hit the tree to which she was tied. He did the same when compelled to lash one of the male slaves.

Drivers also often reduced the work norms. They measured a task according to the particular slave's ability and assigned him to the proper gang according to his ability to do the work. Or else they would make certain that the different groups on the plantation were not given more work than they could complete in a day. They might also arrange for the slaves to work in family groups, so that the younger and stronger members of the family could assist their older and slower relatives.

Some drivers provided slaves with additional food. On one plantation, whenever the slaves felt their rations to be inadequate, they would tell the driver, and "he seed to it that us got plenty." Drivers frequently connived with their fellow slaves to plunder the master's food supply. Although many drivers were illiterate, a few who could read provided the slaves with some educational benefits. And some drivers not only escaped from slavery but also worked to free bondsmen who remained enslaved. Driver Josiah Henson escaped to Canada but returned to the South to lead slaves to freedom.

The drivers' position between owners and slaves was a difficult one. The key to understanding their actions lies in the realization that they had their roots in the slave quarters. They had stronger emotional bonds with their fellow slaves than with their masters, and, as members of the slave community, they were part of its family, religious, and social life. The core of their identity lay in the quarters, which provided them with the psychological protection they needed to withstand the forces of dehumanization that might have made them brutes. Fellow slaves were especially appreciative of the favors the drivers bestowed. In responding to the charge that the drivers were more brutal to the slaves than masters and overseers, a former slave wrote:

This is the way the slaveholders take to hide their own wickedness. They say the colored driver is more cruel than the white overseer, and use this as an argument against the poor colored man, to show how cruelly they would treat each other if they had the power. Pardon me, readers, if I say this is an insult to God; since my own experience teaches me better. Reader, when they say that colored drivers is this, Is it the fault of the colored people, or is it the fault of the white man? Good sense answers to every thinking mind, and says that the poor negro is not the greatest transgressor here, but the white men are the tyrannical instigators of this wrong.

HOUSE SERVANTS AND FIELD HANDS

Although the house servants were better off than most of the field hands, they also carried an unbearable load. Their life consisted of unending toil under the close supervision of the owner or his wife, who demanded service from the time the slave was awakened early in the morning until the household was ready for retirement. Young girl slaves were pressed into service waiting on the women and children of the home and learning laundering, cooking, and cleaning. They were exposed to the whims and passions of every member of the family and were often forced into intimacies by the master or the master's sons.

Some cooks and house servants were even deprived of the food they themselves had prepared. Lunsford Lane, a slave who had bought his freedom, speaking of his wife's experience as a cook, related: "her master was so particular in giving it out to be cooked, or so watched it, that she always knew whether it was all returned; . . . the stern old lady would sit by and see that every dish was put away and then she would turn the key upon it."

House slaves sometimes considered themselves less free than field hands. A former slave in Tennessee "liked the field work better than . . . the house work. We could talk and do anything we wanted." The slave quarters, after all, was the only place where black men and women were relatively free from supervision, where they could "lower the mask" that a good house servant always had to wear before master and mistress. They were required, according to numerous exslaves, "to leave dry tongues in de quarters." If the field slaves envied the more adequate material provisions of the domestic slaves, they did not envy the demands upon their leisure time and their lack of contact with their families and other slaves, even on weekends. Martha Shownley of Roanoke commented on her career as a chamber maid:

We had to be doin' somethin' all day. Whenever we was in de presence of any of de white folks, we had to be standin' Never was 'lowed to set down in de Big House whilst de sun was showin'. In de afternoon whilst old Missus was takin' her nap, I would set on de back stairs and res' awhile. Didn's dare to sleep myself, 'cause she might wake up any minute an come lookin' for me.

The opening lines of an old poem of black people throws light on the real life of many house slaves:

> That old kitchen done killed my mamma
> That old kitchen done killed my mamma
> That old kitchen done killed by mamma
> Lord help that kitchen from killing me.

Indeed former domestic slaves rejected the widespread notion that their material needs had been adequately met. On the contrary, they emphasized that were it not for the fact that they were in a position to steal food, they would have suffered privation. Mary Raines, a former slave, commented:

If you didn't get better rations and things to eat in de house, it was your own fault, I tells you! You just have to help de chillun' to take things and while you doin' dat for them, you take things for yourself. I never call it stealin'. I just call it takin' de jams, de jellies, de biscuits, de butter and de 'lasses dat I have to reach up and steal for chillun to hid 'way in der little stomachs and me, in my big belly.

Peter Randolph, who led a field hand's existence, wrote of the house slaves that though "dressed and fed better than others," they had "to suffer alike with those whose outward condition is worse. . . . You may examine their persons and find many a lash upon their flesh. They are sure of their whippings and are sold the same as others." As Randolph noted, the lash was used as a means of punishment for the domestic servant as well as for the field hand. And if the lash was used more frequently on the field hand, the domestic servant could have her ears boxed for trifling mistakes or simply for being within reach of the master or mistress at an inappropriate moment.

When the intensity of the crop increased during harvesting, house servants were often drafted to do field work. This gave them greater contact with field hands and made many understand their grievances better. They learned that they shared a common oppression with the field hands. Some even acted to help their fellow slaves by giving them food stolen from the master. While many served as informers for the slaveowners, there were those who functioned in this capacity for the field hands. Byrd Walton of Danville recalled the following incident:

Mother was a housemaid fo' Missus Walton, an she never could leave de house to go to de quarters till dinner was done. One time de slaves was plannin' a big dance over to de folkses' place, an mother was aimin' to go. But dat evenin' Jerry de footman come in from court wid' Marsa, an' he say to mother right in front of Missus, "Howdy, Mary, did you know dey was bugs in de wheat?" "What you talkin' 'bout, Jerry?" Missus ast. "Nothin." But Mother know what he meant. De bugs was de ole patterollers, and dey was comin' round to de Quarters dat night.

Most house slaves yearned for the companionship of the slave quarters, and on arriving there, the house servant "would regale other members . . . some of whom had never set foot in the Big House, with tales of 'master' and 'missus,' would take them off in speech and gesture so faithfully that the less privileged would shake with laughter."

Even the supposedly ever-faithful "Mammy," whose duties were mainly connected with the care of the children of the slaveowner, was drawn into close relationship to the field slaves, although rarely to the same extent as others in the big house. Actually it was only on the very large plantations that a specialized role existed for the Mammy. On the majority of the plantations, the Mammy did much of the housework "and even occasionally helped with special field chores." The Mammy had very little time for her own family, and her children were usually cared for by others, such as the plantation nurse or slaves too old for field work. In other cases, they were brought to the big house to serve as playmates for the white children. But the view that the Mammy loved the white children better than her own is highly questionable.

Thus while many house slaves identified with the master's interest, there is a difference between this and complete submission. A sense of solidarity developed between many house slaves and the field hands. Family ties, cultural identification, and common oppression reinforced a sense of unity and common purpose among all slaves, the "privileged bondsmen" as well as the field hands. Indeed the dependency of the masters on their servants and drivers and the fact that these slaves also had connections with the quarters led to problems of control and complicated its entire character.

RELIGION IN THE QUARTERS

The religion of the slaves was a particularly significant area for the development of the black community. Historians disagree, however, as to the nature of the religion that emerged in the slave community. According to some, slave religion was largely borrowed from white Protestantism and served as a balm by holding out the promise of relief in heaven. They argue that all African mores and beliefs were completely eradicated during the "Middle Passage" and subsequent enslavement in the New World. Other historians argue that the slaves' religion kept alive their African past, that it was the product of the accumulated historical experience of the slaves, and that the beliefs brought from Africa were part of that tradition. Even though they were transformed in the American South, the key ingredients of the African religion remained and shaped Afro-American Christianity, turning it into an African and Protestant amalgam. When mixed with the evangelical preaching of the Southern Protestant ministers, it provided an adhesive mix, which bound together the Afro-American community.

Still another difference among scholars concerns the extent to which slave religion was aligned with the religion of the planters. Genovese argues that while Afro-Christian cults of the Caribbean and Latin America played a vital role in the slaves' resistance and in the development of a tradition of revolutionary leadership, the Afro-American Christian religion in the antebellum South could supply the slaves only with the tools for survival but not for revolutionary action to overthrow slavery. The slave preachers preached and practiced a religion of compromise, accommodation, and resignation, and even the conjurors and medicine men were integrated into the system of white domination.

Other historians contend that slave religion became a weapon of open resistance, which, through messianic preachers like Denmark Vesey and Nat Turner, envisioned an immediate, revolutionary release from servitude. (A number of scholars have stressed the response to Vesey's and Turner's religious appeals as the principal motivating factor behind the planters' interest in converting slaves.) Herbert Aptheker has noted that "many of the leaders of slave rebellions were deeply religious men, often leaders of the worshipping activities of their comrades." Of course, to the extent that black preachers emphasized the Christian virtue of submission, they were tolerated and encouraged by the white masters. But when their sermons contained allusions to events in the Bible that tended to create restlessness among the enslaved, they were feared by the whites and sometimes suppressed. Genovese argues that the message of the black preachers lacked "a politically militant millennial and prophetic tradition" that might have stirred a revolutionary ardor in the slaves. But the *Tuskegee* (Alabama) *Republican* of January 1, 1857, complained: "Preaching by negroes ought to be utterly abolished. Negro preachers are almost invariably the corrupters of the slaves, and they are the head of all this mischief that is brewed among them."

Most slaves refused to identify with the religion of their masters, which sanctioned their enslavement. They also rejected the slaveholders' gospel of obedience to master and mistress. Lunsford Lane recalled that a "kindhearted clergyman . . . who was very popular with the colored people" made the mistake of preaching "a sermon to us in which he argued from the Bible that we should be slaves, and our masters be our owners." Immediately, Lane reported, "many of us left him." Charles Colcock Jones, a slaveholder who was a preacher to the slaves, recalled the same reaction to a sermon he delivered before a slave congregation in 1833:

I was preaching to a large congregation on the *Epistle of Philemon:* and when I insisted upon fidelity and obedience as Christian virtues in servants and upon the authority of Paul, condemned the practice of *running away*, one half of my audience deliberately rose up and walked off with themselves, and those that remained looked anything but satisfied, either with the preacher or his doctrine. After dismissal, there was no small stir among them; some solemnly declared "that there was no such as Epistle in the Bible"; others, "that they did not care if they ever heard me preach again!" . . . There were some too, who had strong objections against me as a Preacher, because I was a *master*, and said, "his people have to work as well as we."

By the eve of the Civil War there were actually two intertwined religions in the slave community. Although not all slaves were Christians and some who accepted Christianity were not members of a church, the doctrines, symbols, and vision of life preached by Christianity constituted the established religion in the community. But the slaves did not absorb the religion of the masters, which they did not consider the "true Christianity." Rather, they took Christianity, infused it with Africanisms of all kinds—from spirit possession, baptism, and the call and response form of gospel singing—and adapted it to their own needs. This fusion of the black religion of Africa with Christianity became a distinctive form of Christianity, an "invisible institution." As Albert J. Raboteau points out, the religion of the slaves was "both institutional and noninstitutional, visible and invisible," formally organized and spontaneously adapted:

Regular Sunday worship in the local churches was paralleled by illicit, or at least informal, prayer meetings on weeknights in the slave cabins. Preachers licensed by the church and hired by the master were supplemented by slave preachers licensed only by the spirit. Texts from the Bible which most slaves could not read were explicated by verses from the spirituals. Slaves forbidden by masters to attend church, or, in some cases, even to pray, risked floggings to attend secret gatherings to worship God.

The slaves went to great lengths to direct their religious affairs independently of the master. They held religious gatherings in the quarters, often without the knowledge of the planters. Elizabeth Ross Hite, a former slave of a Catholic master in Louisiana, recalled that all slaves on the plantation were "supposed to be Catholics," but "lots didn't like that religion." Consequently the slaves would "hide behind some bricks and hold church" themselves beyond the master's scrutiny. Almost every slave narrative mentions the secret prayer meetings where the intense relationships between preacher and congregation reflected African religious practices. The slaves called these "hush-harbor meetings," and at them, the slaves listened to one of their own choosing, while drivers frequently looked the other way. More importantly, they shared in this emotional release of frustrations against the master and the system. Drivers, in fact, often preached at and presided over these unauthorized prayer meetings. Josiah Henson reported that a common theme at these meetings was that not only did Heaven harbor no overseers and whips but that God wanted them "to clear the earth itself of both of these instruments of the Devil." Henson reported, too, that many slaves believed that somewhere, there was a real bible that came from God but that the bible being used by the master was the "master's bible."

While many masters merited Henry Bibb's indictment for callousness regarding the slave dead and his complaint that "less care was taken care of their [the slaves'] bodies than if they were dumb beasts," and Frederick Douglass was only slightly exaggerating when he said that it was "worth but half-a-cent to kill a nigger and half-a-cent to bury him," slave communities went to great trouble to make certain that dead slaves received proper burials. James Weldon Johnson has written that the slave burial sermon delivered by the slave preacher on behalf of the grieving slave community was a part of the process by which slaves "of diverse languages and customs who were brought here from diverse parts of Africa and thrown into slavery were given . . . unity and solidarity."

At the "hush-harbor meetings," black preachers emphasized passages from the Old Testament history of the early Hebrews. The stories of oppression and slavery in Egypt were full of meaning to the men and women in Southern bondage, and they responded enthusiastically to sermons that issued calls for a "Moses" who would lead the black people out of bondage and into the promised land—sermons that, if delivered within earshot of the whites, were bound to get the preacher into trouble.

Identification with the children of Israel was important for white America too, and the slaves often described the settlement of the New World as similar to the exodus of the Israelites from the bondage of Egypt. But this theme clashed with the experience of the slaves for whom, as Vincent Harding has observed, the Middle Passage had brought a new Egypt under new pharaohs. For the slaves, the characters, scenes, and events from the Old Testament became alive and present, and identification with the children of Israel became a key aspect of the slaves' religious experience.

THE SPIRITUALS

The richness of protest symbolism in Negro spirituals has often been noted. There is, of course, the interpretation that the black spirituals represented the slave's eager expectation that in the hereafter, he would experience those joys denied him in life on earth, and his faith in a heavenly future in which justice would prevail would be confirmed. In this sense, it is argued, the spirituals, by serving as a sustaining element for the oppressed, were basically a support for the system itself. But other scholars have insisted that the spirituals represented a hidden spirit of revolt against the slave's circumstances in this life and that they often relayed messages on how to resist the system itself. Lawrence W. Levine has recently pointed out that it would be a mistake to read in the spirituals an urge that was "exclusively outworldly." They reflected the common view that the slaves were God's "chosen people," that God himself was the enemy of slavery, and that he would deliver his "chosen people," even as he delivered the Israelites from the oppressions of the Egyptians:

> No slav'ry chains to tie me down,
> And no mo' drivers ho'n to blow for me,
> No mo' stocks to fasten me down,
> Jesus break slav'ry chain, Lord
> Break slav'ry chain, Lord
> Break slav'ry chain, Lord,
> De Heben gwinter be my home.

The spiritual about the blind Samson who brought down the mansion of his conquerors probably contained more for slaves than mere biblical implications. Many writers have insisted that slaves who sang the line, "And I'll tear this building down," were referring to tearing down the structure of slavery itself.

The spirituals reflect a whole sacred world raised in contradistinction to the actuality of slavery, a world pervaded not only by the black version of the Christian God but by the spirit of things. The slave, Levine insists, did not patiently bear the painful present in the hope of heavenly reward, although that is an element in the religion, but instead constructed a world view that provides for the transcendence of the present. Their sacred world encompassed the seen and the unseen, the earthly and the heavenly, the past, the present, and the future. Their spirituals emphasized their worth rather than their degradation. It is difficult to believe that when the slaves sang of how the Lord delivered Daniel, the spiritual had no wordly concern for the black man in bondage:

> He delivered Daniel from de lion's den,
>   Jonah from de belly of de whale,
> And de Hebrew children, from de fiery furnace,
>   And why not every man?

Frederick Douglass pointed out that for him and many of his fellow slaves, the song, "O Canaan, sweet Canaan, I am bound for the land of Canaan," symbolized "something more than a hope of reaching heaven. We meant to reach the *North*, and the North was our Canaan." Douglass also wrote that the lines of another spiritual, "Run to Jesus, shun the danger, I don't expect to stay much longer here," had a double meaning, which first suggested to him the thought of escaping slavery.

Although it would be a mistake to view the spirituals as serving only a secular function, it is possible to see in them symbols of the slaves' desire for freedom and the deceptions used to prevent the masters from learning of their plans to upset the system. Masters were deceived into thinking that their slaves were happy and were absorbed only in terms of the rewards in the next world. But spirituals abound with hidden meanings, and many writers have maintained that such spirituals as "Steal away, steal away, steal away to Jesus" were used as explicit calls to secret meetings. Similarly, they point out that the word *chariot* in the spiritual, "Swing Low Sweet Chariot," means any way of escape the slaves could utilize to get to their goal in the North and freedom. The "River Jordan" referred to the Mason-Dixon line, "home" was the North in the free states or Canada, and Harriet Tubman, the Moses of her people, was the "band of angels":

> Swing low sweet chariot, coming forth to carry me home.
> Swing low sweet chariot, coming forth to carry me home.
> I looked over Jordan and what did I see, coming forth
> to carry me home!
> A band of angels coming after me, coming forth to carry
> me home
> Swing low sweet chariot, coming forth to carry me home.

This use of the spirituals as a means of secret communication was pointed to by an ex-slave who recalled that when he and his fellow slaves believed one of them was acting as an informer, they would sing while working in the field

> O Judas he wuz a 'ceitful man
> He went an' betray a mos' innocent man.
> Fo' thirty pieces of silver dat was done.
> He went in de woods an 'e 'self he hung.

Recent scholarship has cautioned against viewing the spirituals as "coded protest songs," but it does not fail to note that while for some slaves a particular verse might have only a spiritual meaning, for others it carried a protest significance because of their particular experience. Moreover, since the composing and singing of spirituals was a group activity, they became a vehicle through which a slave's specific experience became part of the group's consciousness. Thus, when asked about the origin of a song, a former slave declared:

I'll tell you; it's dis way. My master call me up and order me a short peck of corn and a hundred lash. My friends see it and is sorry for me. When dey come to de praise meetin' dat night dey sing about it. Some's very good singers and know how; and dey work it in you know; till dey git it right; and dat's de way.

More than five thousand spirituals were composed by slaves as they rewrote the Scriptures. While many had different meaning for different slaves and at different times, they made religion a practical vehicle, both for enduring their suffering under slavery and for helping them escape from bondage.

There were, of course, other songs of the slaves in addition to the religious songs of work and play. These offered opportunities for a wide variety of expression. However, as Frederick Douglass noted: "Once in a while among a mass of nonsense and wild frolic, a sharp hit was given to the meanness of slaveholders." Bitter derision was clear enough in the song:

> We raise de wheat,
> Dey gib us de corn;
> We bake de bread,
> Dey gib us de crust;
> We sif de meal,
> Dey gib us de huss;
> We peal de meat,
> Dey gib us de skin,
> And dat's de way,
> Dey take us in;
> We skim de pot,
> Dey gib us de liquor,
> And say dat's good enough for nigger.

Slaveowners often claimed that the fact that the slaves so frequently sang was a sign of their contentment. Frederick Douglass felt otherwise; he said that it proved only that the slave possessed a strong spirit and that even slavery was not entirely able to kill off that spirit. The songs that slaves sang, Douglass wrote, told of woes and bitter anguish. Every song was a diatribe against slavery and a prayer for liberty. To the person who equated song and contentment, Douglass responded:

The singing of a man cast upon a desolate island might be as appropriately concluded as evidence of contentment and happiness, as the singing of a slave; the songs of the one and of the other prompted by the same emotion.

And John Little, a former slave, wrote:

They say slaves are happy, because they laugh, and are merry. I myself and three or four others, have received two hundred lashes in the day, and had our feet in fetters; yet, at night, we would sing and dance, and make others laugh at the rattling of our chains. Happy men we must have been! We did it to keep down trouble, and to keep our hearts from being completely broken: that is as true as the gospel! Just look at it, must not we have been very happy? Yet I have done it myself—I have cut capers in chains.

Whatever they may have symbolized, the songs certainly did not give any evidence that the slaves identified with their masters. Despite constant interaction between slaves and masters for more than two centuries, they remained fundamentally apart. In most instances, they did not inhabit the same world. Slaves came to view themselves as a captive people in need of a leader like Moses to lead them out of bondage—a people destined for martyrdom but, as descendants from Africans, a people whose religious tradition taught them that there was little distinction between the physical and spiritual world. The blacks thus were sustained by a belief that in the real world, a real Moses would end their bondage.

In many instances Afro-American beliefs were simple and direct. But often what appeared on the surface as merely a religious utterance was in fact a political expression couched in biblical symbols. Similarly, slave folk tales, such as those of Brer Rabbit, while dealing with the victory of the weak over the strong in the animal world, referred in reality to that of the slave over the master. Through the humor slaves wove into their songs and folk tales and through their sardonic remonstrances of the master, they made clear their hatred of the system under which they were forced to live.

THE SLAVE FAMILY

The independent community formed by black people in North America under slavery found one of its most significant expressions in family life. For a long time, historians held firmly to the view that the black family under slavery was totally destroyed. Even those scholars who believed that it was not altogether shattered conceded that the slave family was, of necessity, weak. Thus, even the black historian, E. Franklin Frazier, in his famous 1932 study, *The Negro Family in the United States,* after contending that there were factors that tended to promote family consciousness among slaves, nevertheless concluded that the institution of slavery did not permit the black family to exist, that it deprived black males of authority and responsibility, and that it encouraged sexual looseness. Other scholars who followed were even more convinced that the black family suffered a historical pathology traceable to slavery. "In the life of the slave," Kenneth M. Stampp wrote in *The Peculiar Institution,* "the family had nothing like the social significance that it held in the life of the white man. . . . Parents frequently had little to do with the raising of their children. . . . The husband . . . was not the head of the family, the holder of property, the provider of protection. . . . The male slave's only function within the family was that of siring offspring.'' The ''typical slave family'' as reconstructed by Stampp was ''matriarchal in form, for the mother's role was far more important than the father's.'' The husband was at most ''his wife's assistant, her companion and sex partner.''

In *Slavery: A Problem in American Intellectual and Institutional Life*, Stanley M. Elkins listed four reasons for the destruction of the black family: sexual exploitation, separation, miscegenation, and restrictive legal codes. The law could permit ''no aspect of the slave's conjugal state to have an independent legal existence.'' In his examination of the urban South, Richard C. Wade reached the same conclusion: ''For the slave, no matter where he resided, a house was never a home. Families could scarcely exist in bondage. The law recognized no marriage.''

The conclusion that the black family was matrifocal (mother centered) and disorganized received its most publicized exposition in the 1965 study by Daniel Patrick Moynihan, *The Negro Family: The Case for National Action*. Moynihan, then adviser to President Lyndon B. Johnson, asserted that ''slavery vitiated family life. . . . Since many slaveholders neither fostered Christian marriage among their slave couples nor hesitated to separate them on the auction block, the slave household often developed a fatherless matrifocal family.''

Like many other aspects of slave life, however, the view that slaves had no real family underwent vigorous revision by scholars in the 1970s. In 1970, Eugene D. Genovese observed that the ''typical plantation unit in the South was organized by family unit'' and that the slaves, ''from their own experience, had come to value a two-parent-male-centered household, no matter how much difficulty they had in realizing the ideal.'' John W. Blassingame reached a similar conclusion. ''Although it was weak, had no legal existence and was frequently broken,'' he noted in his 1972 study *The Slave Community*, ''the family was in actuality one of the most important survival mechanisms for the slave.'' It provided companionship, love, sexual gratification, and opportunities for the development of self-esteem and cooperation among its members. The family furnished ''an important buffer, a refuge from the rigors of slavery.''

George P. Rawick, editor of the slave narratives recorded by the Federal Writers' Project and Fisk University in the 1920s and 1930s, reached substantially the same conclusions about the slave family. The law notwithstanding, under slavery there existed ''socially recognized marriages in which father and mother lived together under the same roof with their children. The entire living unit functioned socially and economically as a single family unit, not dissimilar to the European-American kinship pattern, although sometimes broken by the sale of members of the family to different masters.''

The works of Genovese, Blassingame, and Rawick pointed up the fact that the black family played a positive and meaningful role of socialization within the slave community, which enabled it to withstand the vicissitudes of slave life without succumbing to disorganized or pathological behavior. In spite of the high rate of forced separations, a significant number of slave marriages endured, with the nuclear-headed household being the most prevalent form for all slaves and the single-family household predominating. Finally, the slave family was not matriarchal, and slave fathers played strong, positive roles within their families.

The major revisionist challenge to the traditional view of the slave family as being disorganized, unstable, and matriarchal was posed by Herbert G. Gutman, first in a series of papers written between 1968 and 1972 (most of which are still unpublished) and then, in 1976, in *The Black Family in Slavery and Freedom, 1750–1925*. On the basis of his survey of a vast number and variety of sources— records of probate courts, plantation and Freedmen's Bureau manuscripts, and censuses, as well as oral accounts of whites and blacks—Gutman concluded that the black familial ties developed and survived under slavery; that slaveowners' behavior had only a negligible impact on black families; that blacks, by active choice, have always depended on their own peer group culture and kinship system to develop familial roles; and that the result, until recently, was an average black family as patriarchal as its white counterpart.

Gutman's study shows that the majority of slaves lived in two-parent house-holds and that many slave marriages tended to be remarkably enduring, except when they were prematurely broken by sale. Children were raised as nearly as possible by both parents, and when marriages were dissolved, usually as a result of the strains placed on them by slavery, they were done so with formality and not carelessly tossed aside in favor of less binding liaisons. There are numerous accounts of the importance that black families placed on staying together, whether through buying members out of bondage or running away. Moreover, we know from advertisements for runaway slaves that the number of fugitives in quest of their "spouses" was legion. Slaveowners advertised the fact that they knew that their escaped field hands would remain within the state and attempt to reunite themselves with their wife and children. Then, too, much of the mobility of blacks after the Civil War was a result of efforts of individual blacks to find wives, husbands, and children separated from them in the antebellum period.

Thus for both slaves and masters, the two-parent household was the norm. Once a couple had come together—each from another family within the planta-tion or, often, from outside it—it was a permanent marriage, with the children living with both parents and with the father very much present. But beyond the nuclear household structure, the slaves' family structure was more or less unique in kinship patterns, marital rules, and sexual norms. Bereft of legal resource to defend marriage bonds, blacks learned in self-protection to define kinship broad-ly even to the inclusion of "fictive kin" to whom they were not related by blood. The blacks transformed kin obligations into communal care for orphans. They had great respect for elders, and they used kin titles ("uncle," "aunt") as terms of respect for nonrelatives.

The great bulk of slave marriages had a de facto standing a number of years before the Civil War. But after the war, Gutman reveals, blacks showed a strong desire to legalize marriage. Thousands went to U.S. Army and Freedman's Bureau posts and to county clerks to register marriages that had begun in slavery. This indicated that

the slaves had created and sustained very important familial and kin sensibilities and ties. The choices so many made immediately upon their emancipation and before they had substantive rights in the law did not result from new ideas learned in freedom and were not reflections of beliefs learned from owners. Such behavior had its origins in the ways in which Africans and their Afro-American descendants had adapted to enslavement.

Gutman challenges the view that plantation owners were interested in preserving the slave family. So long as offspring resulted, most of them professed indifference to the specific kinds of sexual arrangements existing in the quarters. It was the slaves, not the masters, who placed a high value on the family. Despite the master's control of the plantation, much of the slave's family life remained their own affair and was guided by their own values. In his study of surnames, for example, Gutman shows that masters were not able to dictate child-naming practices. Children were named after blood kin. The slaves took last names according to a varied set of rules, which violated those of the masters and of which the masters were unaware. Naming patterns, in other words, were indicative of a strong consciousness of kinship ties rather than a master's influence.

From his study of the slave family, Gutman concludes that slaves named their children most frequently after the father, dead siblings, grandparents, aunts and uncles, and sometimes great-aunts and great-uncles, in that order. Whereas sons, especially first or second born, frequently had their father's name, daughters almost never had the name of the mother. Gutman also suggests (although here the data are admittedly inclusive) that grandparents may have played a prominent role in the naming process.

Gutman emphasizes the function of the kinship network among slaves as a major force in developing an Afro-American culture that enabled blacks to survive under difficult circumstances. He challenges the view of most other scholars that the slave family deepened dependency ties between slaves and their masters. He argues that the content of slave kinship ties was not usually dictated by the masters and that, in significant ways, these ties developed without the masters' even understanding what was happening. These kinship ties helped reinforce behavior that lessened dependency upon the master and provided the basis for some autonomous activity.

The slave family was not a pathetic reflection of the master's views. Rather, slave behavior reflected a belief system particular to the slaves themselves. Gutman's study of birth registers reveals that cousins almost never married. This practice of exogamy contrasted sharply with the master's practice of endogamy. According to one contemporary observer, "the marriage of cousins" among slaveowners was "almost the rule rather than the exception." Its frequency is undeniable. At the upper level, 38 percent of slaveholding couples in a rich district of Alabama were first cousins in the two decades beginning in 1861. It is quite probable that slaves derived from African kinship practices the view that marrying blood relations was wrong. Similarly, slave sexual patterns depended on their own codes of behavior. In contrast to the slaveowners' Victorian sexual codes, slaves did not view prenuptial intercourse as "licentious" or subversive of marriage but rather as "a prelude to settled marriage."

In essence, the slave community functioned like a large family, or what anthropologists called a "generalized extended kinship system" in which all adults looked after all children, in which there was always some older person to take care of children, and in which everyone helped maintain their family ties under great pressure. In the slave community and within the family, slaves found ways of alleviating the worst impact of the cruel system.

The texts of two advertisements for fugitive slaves in the *Lynchburg Virginian* are revealing: "He has a wife at Major Smith's plantation on Flat Creek, where I have but little doubt he is lurking." "He has a wife at the Forge, near Rocky Mount, and he is no doubt lurking in that neighborhood." Of course, the use of the word *wife* by slaveowners was ironical. There was no law regarding the marriage of slaves. The general custom of slave marriage in the South involved, literally, jumping over a broom. But undefended by the law, the slave family endured. It was not a legal institution, for slaves were prohibited from making a marriage contract. The family structure was constantly threatened with disruption, for families were broken up and sold and their members scattered. The masters and other white men sexually exploited the women of the slave family. Yet plagued in every way, the slaves succeeded in maintaining a strong and flexible family structure. That the Afro-American family now appears to have both survived and adapted to enslavement is no proof of the mildness of American slavery. Rather, it is a tribute to the resilience and viability of the slave community.

Although he is critical of Gutman's tendency to minimize the tragic and negative effects of slavery on the black family, Dan T. Carter concludes that *The Black Family in Slavery and Freedom* is "a sustained and at times genuinely moving tribute to the resourcefulness of millions of nameless black Americans who managed to forge strong family ties and personal relationships in the midst of slavery and a debilitating caste system."

Clearly, the slaves fashioned their own independent community on the basis of a creative reworking of older elements of West African culture and life, combined with the influences of European-American society. The slaves created a subtle and extensively organized cultural system, which was fundamentally different from and even opposed to that of those who ruled over them and whose social structure and status were largely determined by values and traditions within the slave culture rather than reflecting the values held by the master class. Furthermore, it does not appear that much of life in the slave community derived from "paternalistic compromise" or that the slaves significantly internalized paternalistic values as the price of survival. On the contrary, more and more evidence is accumulating which demonstrates that, far from being the passive, deculturized beings who accepted the values of the master class and offered little resistance, as they are depicted by many historians, the slaves emerge as members of a vital community of their own, with roots in both Africa and America, with values quite different from those of the master class, and with their own models rather than those promoted by the slaveowners.

All this does not mean that slavery was not a horrible institution, but as John W. Blassingame has pointed out, because the slave quarters allowed frequent interactions among slaves, in a setting where they were "not solely dependent on the white man's cultural frames of references for their ideals and values," the rigors of bondage "did not crush the slaves' creative energies." As Lawrence W. Levine has written, slavery "never pervaded all the interstices of their [the slaves'] minds and their culture," and in the gaps they were able to create "a distinctive voice" through which they expressed their dammed-up feelings—a voice of disguised imagery and indirect statement and one also of resistance to enslavement. That many slaves maintained their identity as persons, despite a system bent on reducing them to a subhuman level, was certainly due in part to the strength of the slave community.

7

Slave Resistance in the Antebellum South

Shortly after the bloody Nat Turner slave rebellion in 1831, a Virginia legislator reassured himself and his colleagues by announcing: "Our slave population is not only a happy one, but it is a contented, peaceful and harmless one." The myth of slave docility thus expressed flourished for over a hundred years, dominating both popular and scholarly white views of blacks in bondage. Beginning in about 1940, the myth came under severe attack by scholars. Since then, many historians have clearly demonstrated that slaves were not contented, that they gave the appearance of docility only in order to protect themselves, and that they knew what they were doing, were capable of doing otherwise, and were simply "putting on" the slaveowners. The slave narratives also indicate that, in order to survive, slaves spent a good portion of their lives within a framework of deception, wearing a mask, as the black poet Paul Laurence Dunbar put it:

> We smile, but O great Christ, our cries
> To thee from tortured soul arise.
> We sing, but O the clay is vile
> Beneath our feet, and long the mile;
> But let the world dream otherwise,
>   We wear the mask!

The truth is that from the very beginning of slavery in this country, slaves proved that it was only a mask. I noted in volume 1 that blacks started to fight physically for their freedom as soon as they landed in America and continued this struggle throughout the subsequent history of slavery. In every part of the antebellum South—both urban and rural—slave resistance remained one of the most difficult problems facing both slaveowners and slave hirers.

DAY-TO-DAY RESISTANCE.

While slaves did not usually engage in sizable revolts, they did conduct a conscious struggle against their continued bondage. They did this through individual acts of witholding or sabotaging production and by other acts of violence, as well as by stealing from their masters. Slaves managed to avoid work by pretending to be sick or by inventing other plausible excuses. Sometimes their work was so inefficient that it gave rise to the suspicion that they were deliberately sabotaging the crop. A term commonly applied to slave labor was *eye service,* which meant that a slave performed well only as long as he or she was closely watched. When confronted with a cruel overseer, the slaves would sometimes work badly and cause him to lose the crop, thus discrediting him and bringing about his replacement by an overseer more to their liking.

Slaves willfully destroyed the master's property by breaking tools, mistreating animals, and setting fire to storehouses, dwellings, and other plantation buildings. So many fires were set by slaves in protest of their oppression and as a means of avenging their exploiters that a number of insurance companies put an end to the practice of insuring property in slave areas. There were also slave strikes that were often either partially or totally successful. After some particular incident of brutality on the part of the master or overseer, a slave or a group of slaves would take off for the swamps or woods where they would hide out. Annie Coley, an ex-slave from Mississippi, recalled one such incident:

But ole Boss Jones had a mean overseer who tuk 'vantage of the women in the fiel's. One time he slammed a niggah woman down that was heavy, an cause her to hev her baby— dead. The niggah womens in the Quarters jumped on 'im and say they gwine take him to a brushpile and burn him up. But their mens hollored for 'em to turn him loose. Then big Boss Jones cam en made the womens go back to the Quarters. He said, "I ain' whipped these wretches for a long time, en I low to whip 'em dis evenin'." But all de womens hid in the woods dat evenin', en Boss never say no more about it. He sent the overseer away en never did hev no more overseers.

Not all strikes were settled so quickly, and after some time, the slaves who were hiding out would send in a representative to arrange for a conference. Often they lost, and that meant being whipped or, at times, subjected to even more severe punishment. Nevertheless, the strikes continued.

The ultimate protest a slave could make against his bondage was to commit suicide, although this was less common among slaves in the United States than it was in Brazil and the Caribbean sugar islands. The fact that masters and overseers found it necessary to refuse to give the slave's body a decent burial—in the hope that this would serve as a deterrent—indicates that this type of protest was not too uncommon.

"The slaves armed themselves with sticks, racks, hatchets, etc. to resist the overseer." So read the charge in the case of *Emmanuel and Giles (slaves)* v. *State of Mississippi,* April 1859. Most slaves were unwilling to resist a white man, but when driven to desperation they did. Such was the reaction of a slave driver, Summer, whose overseer, William Jacobs, punished the driver's wife. Jacobs related the incident in a letter to his employer's wife in 1837:

I received your few lines . . . as to the difficulty with Summer, it arose from my having hit his wife a few light liks. . . , after which I proceeded to the field where Summer left his work to the distance of 20 or 30 yards with his cane knife in his hand and very much inraged, and Said that I had abused his wife and that he was not going to put up with it and that I was an unjust man, and that I might go get my gun, kill him and bury him but that he was not going to put up with any other punishment of himself or family.

Similarly revealing is the following incident from the early life of Frederick Douglass. Determined to crush young Douglass' spirit, his master hired him out to Edward Covey, a professional slave breaker. From January to August 1834, the young slave was overworked, flogged daily, and almost starved to death. After six months of such treatment, he was indeed "broken in body, soul and spirit." There seemed nothing left to do but either to kill Covey and then commit suicide or to fight back. Steeled by a combination of desperation, hope, and fear, the youth found the courage one day to turn on and soundly thrash his tormentor. The result was that Covey abandoned the whip and ignored Douglass for the four remaining months of his hire. The slave never forgot the episode:

This battle with Mr. Covey was the turning-point in my career. I was a changed being after that fight. I was nothing before. I was a man now . . . with a renewed determination to be a free man. . . . The satisfaction afforded by the triumph was a full compensation for whatever else might follow, even death itself. . . . I now resolved that, however long I might remain a slave in form, the day had passed forever when I could be a slave in fact.

Solomon Northup recalls a somewhat similar experience in his narrative. On one occasion, when his master ordered him to strip to receive a lashing, Northup refused. His master then seized him by the throat and raised the whip with the other hand to strike him; the slave seized the owner and pushed him to the ground:

Putting one arm around his leg, and holding it to my breast, so that his head and shoulders only touched the ground, I placed my feet up on his neck. He was completely in my power. My blood was up. . . . In my frenzy of my madness I snatched the whip from his hand. He struggled with all his power; swore that I should not live to see another day; and that he would tear out my heart. But his struggles and his threats were alike in vain. I cannot tell how many times I struck him.

Douglass and Northup were fortunate in that they suffered no reprisals. But other slaves learned that resisting punishment could lead to death. A Louisiana slave lost his life when he defied both his driver and overseer. The overseer, Albert Forester, later testified at the coroner's inquest on July 5, 1857:

I asked Samuel if he had refused to get down for punishment when the driver ordered him, he answered at once, yes, by God, I did and I am not going to be whipped by anybody, either black or white. I told him to stop, as I allowed no negro to talk in that way, and that he knew that. I then ordered him to throw down his hoe, and to get down, he swore God damn him if he would I repeated the order, and he again swore he would not. I ordered my horse nearest to him when he turned and ran off. I kept my horse standing and called to the rest of the hands to catch that boy, not one of them paid the least attention to me but kept on at their work. I then started after Samuel, myself, and overtook him and turned him. I ordered him to throw down the hoe and stand he swore, God damn him if he would, and again ran off. I ran at him again and again and turned him and repeated my order and got the same answer he started again and I after him got again 4 or 5 yards when he wheeled round, with his hoe raised in both hands and struck me with his full force my horse swerved aside and passed him his hoe descending I think within one or two feet of my head, pulled my horse up, and drew my pistol. Samuel was then standing with his hoe raised. I fired across my Bridle arm when he fell.

The overseer was not charged and went free, despite the fact that the post mortem examination revealed that Samuel had been shot in the back, with the bullet lodging near his spine.

How many "proud . . . vengeful and . . . daring" slaves like Samuel were, in the words of W.E.B. Du Bois "sent to heaven" for resisting slaveowners and overseers, we do not know. But there were many, and as Albert Forester's testimony indicates, they had the respect of the slave community, which refused to aid in their persecution.

Despite the tendency of Southern newspapers to play down these stories, there were numerous accounts of white masters and overseers being beaten, or even murdered, by their slaves. Northern newspapers frequently reprinted such accounts. The following appeared in the *Boston Courier* of July 20, 1827:

BURNING ALIVE

The slave had killed his overseer. It was decided that the negro should be immediately burned to death. The wretched black was tied to a tree, a large quantity of pine knots collected and thrown around him, and notwithstanding the remonstrance of several gentlemen, was, in a short time, burnt to death.

Murders by slaves were most often performed by axes, razors, knives, and occasionally, guns. But another slave weapon was illustrated by the poisoning of three of her master's children by a woman slave in Prince George County, Virginia in 1834. The poison most often employed was arsenic, but corrosive sublimate, strychnine, and laudanum were also used.

Thus, despite the rigors and severity of slavery and despite the well-developed system of control, slaves were never completely subdued. In one form or another, they expressed resentment over their lot, sometimes in individual acts of resistance and sometimes collectively, sometimes through passive and sometimes through violent resistance. In his study of the plantation and household slaves of Mississippi's John Anthony Quitman (the Southern fire-eater Congressman who described his slaves as "faithful, obedient, and affectionate"), Robert E. May points out numerous examples of resistance by Quitman's slaves, including running away, suicides, work slowdowns and other forms of sabotage, and adds: " 'Pampered' house servants also manifested displeasure with their condition despite the privileges accorded them. Such resistance usually took the form of sullenness, sloppy work, and infringement of household regulations. . . . Household servants also ran away."

FUGITIVE SLAVES

"The problem of slavery as a rule," Daniel Goddard, a South Carolina ex-slave, told an interviewer, "was a question of wits, the slave to escape and the master to keep him from escaping." Slaves began to "vote with their feet" against slavery very early in American history and continued to do so until the abolition of slavery. Escape has been called "the most common overt form of resistance to slavery."

Many of the slaves who ran away did so temporarily and escaped to nearby regions of the South rather than to the North. This was particularly widespread when slaves lived in the proximity of swamps. The Dismal, Pasquotunk, and Great Okefenokee swamps and the bayous of Louisiana were favorite refuges for runaways. But slaves were often reported "lurking" near plantations all over the South and either stealing food from their former owners or receiving food supplies from slaves who were not "lying out." Describing "a nest of runaway negroes" situated in the fork of the Alabama and Tornbeckbee rivers, a Charleston paper reported in 1827: "Some of them had been running away for years, and had committed many depredations on the neighboring plantations." The "nest" was "broken up" by the militia, and three of the slaves were killed. But other groups of runaway slaves built regular encampments, or "maroon" colonies, where they lived an independent existence for years. These relatively permanent settlements of runaways were found in the swamps and backwoods in many parts of the South. Maroons built homes, raised cattle, cultivated the land periodically, raided plantations for supplies, and even carried on trade with people neighboring their communities.

It has been estimated that during the era of the Cotton Kingdom, an average of perhaps one thousand slaves per year escaped to the North and freedom, while many times that number tried and failed. Trying to establish an exact total of runaway slaves is a very difficult, if not impossible, task. Only with the 1850 census did the federal government start to collect material on escaped slaves. Moreover, the records gathered for both 1850 and 1860 are incomplete, since the tabulations noted only the slaves who escaped in the year preceding each survey. These census statistics represent only two years in the mid-nineteenth century.

The 1850 census showed that 279 fugitives escaped from Maryland in 1849. Kentucky was second with 96, and Lousiana, with 90 runaways, was third. In 1860, Kentucky lost 119 slaves, Virginia 117, and Maryland 115. Delaware reported 12 fugitives. These statistics did not include the number of slaves who escaped from their owners and were apprehended before they could cross the Mason-Dixon line. In any case, according to the inadequate statistics of the federal census, several hundred slaves did escape during these two years.

Most fugitives who escaped to the North ended up, if successful, in Northern free states. Many, however felt safe only in Canada:

> I'm on my way to Canada,
>   That cold and dreary land;
> The sad effects of slavery,
>   I can no longer stand.

> I've served my master all my days,
>   Without a dime's reward;
> And now I'm forced to run away,
>   To flee the lash abroad.

> Farewell, old master, don't think hard of me,
> I'm on my way to Canada, where all the slaves are free.

In 1793, the same year the Fugitive Slave Act was passed by Congress, Upper Canada began to provide for the gradual abolition of slavery, and in 1833, by act of British Parliament, slavery was abolished in all British dominions. This meant, of course, that any British territory within reach of escaping United States slaves became a refuge for the fugitives. Some escaped to the Bahamas, Bermuda, or Nassau. But because of the long border between Canada and the United States, it was natural that many of the fugitives would go to Canada. Windsor, Ontario, just across the river from Detroit, was the point of entry for many. By 1860, there were 60,000 blacks in Upper Canada alone, three-fourths of them fugitive slaves.

Mexico offered a sanctuary for some fugitive slaves. A Texan described to Frederick Law Olmsted the escape of one of his slaves: "He got into them bayous, and kept swimming from one side to another. If he's got across the river . . . the Mexicans'd take care of him." A "Free Colored Floridan" urged slaves to turn toward Mexico because of its convenient location, its mild climate, its generous land policy, and its lack of color prejudice.

Recent scholarship has questioned the importance of the Underground Railroad in helping slaves escape to the North. Larry Gara, for example, minimizes the significance of a highly organized abolitionist escape system and suggests that more attention should be focused on the individual bondsman, who found his way, often unaided, to the North, than on the abolitionists who helped them once they arrived. Gara sought especially to dispel what he called the myth that the white conductor of the Underground Railroad was "the leading figure in the drama." While striking a balance is desirable, in the process Gara practically eliminated consideration of the Underground Railroad altogether. Nevertheless, there was an Underground Railroad and especially a Black Underground, in which Negro men and women risked their lives by organizing escape routes and aiding slaves to flee to safety in the North and to Canada.

Free blacks in the South often assisted fugitives with free papers, a hasty meal, temporary lodging, or the drawing of a crude map or providing other travel instructions. A few former slaves even returned to the South to guide slaves to freedom, as did some whites. But most slaves who risked their lives to escape from their bonds usually depended upon their own self-reliance and their knowledge of the north star to guide them to freedom.

Careful planning was important for the ultimate success of every escape plot. Harriet Tubman, the most famous of the former slaves who returned South to help her people escape, actually mentally planned the first day of her escape trip long before she actually left the Maryland Eastern Shore for freedom.

Timing was an essential element of every planned escape. Many successful escapes occurred on weekends when slaveowners traditionally extended travel privileges to slaves. This gave an escaping slave, equipped with a pass, one or two days' travel in relative safety. Moreover, slaveholders were often absent from their plantations on weekends, visiting friends and relatives or staying at recreational facilities, and they would not be able to take any action to recover the fugitive until they had returned to the plantation. The holiday atmospheres that prevailed during the Christmas and Easter seasons and the Fourth of July also presented bondsmen with the opportunity to escape. While the Christmas holidays were poor for the fugitive's purposes because of the cold weather and the scarcity of fruit trees, the unusual festivities made it easier for the slave to slip away.

Stages, railroads, and ships engaged in coastwise or ocean traffic were all employed by fugitives. A number of fugitives escaped by waterway. William Grimes stowed away on a steamer going from Savannah to New York, living on bread and other food hidden with him until he landed safely at a Northern port. Henry Watson, a Mississippi slave, escaped from his master after making preparatory arrangements with a ship captain sailing for Boston. Slave women also stowed away on ships. They usually boarded the vessels by carrying what appeared to be freshly laundered clothes for some of the passengers. Black crewmen helped to stow away fugitive slaves on ships leaving Southern ports for the North. Seamen Edward Smith and Isaac Gansey were wanted in Virginia for "having abducted slave Isaac," and $3,000 was offered for their delivery to the jailer at Norfolk.

The majority of the fugitives fled on foot. Some took a horse from the master's stables to speed their arrival in the North, but most realized that any mounted black was quite conspicuous and susceptible to challenge by patrols. To travel alone on foot as a fugitive from any part of the South, but especially the lower

South, to the North and even to Canada, was no mean accomplishment. One fugitive traveled 1,200 miles from Alabama to New York without any help. He journeyed at night, subsisting on roots and berries. Another fugitive took an entire year to reach Cincinnati from Alabama. He, too, traveled after sundown and spent his days hiding in the woods or thickets.

The fear of detection caused escaping slaves to consider practically everyone as a potential slave catcher. And there were indeed individuals who supplemented their incomes by capturing and returning fugitives, motivated by the rewards offered for the successful return of an escaped bondsman. Such offers usually appeared in newspapers with the amount of the reward and an accurate description of the male or female fugitive. The female fugitive "Esther" who escaped from a plantation near Reisterstown, Maryland, was described as "rather between a mulatto and black, short chunky, with thick lips and somewhat freckled in her face; she is about 22 years of age; she had on a light calico frock when she went away, and a cloth overcoat, olive colour." The reward for return of "Esther," who escaped in 1825, was $50. Over the years the amount increased, and by the mid-1850s, it was not unusual for advertisements and handbills to offer $500. Slaves who remained behind on the farms and plantations often aided the runaways by destroying descriptive handbills.

Who were the fugitive slaves who sought to escape their servitude and start a new life in the North? Information based on three hundred Maryland fugitives, drawn from Pennsylvania and Maryland newspapers and from the records of the Philadelphia Vigilance Committee, suggests that the majority were young adults. The average age for male fugitives was 25.5 years and for females 26.5. The male slaves outnumbered the females by five to one.

Not surprisingly, the same average seemed to operate in the other slave states as well. The physical hardships associated with an attempted escape must have disheartened many elderly bondsmen. They probably concluded that their chances for surviving a period of prolonged hunger and exposure were slight. Even escape from Maryland to Pennsylvania required a seven- to ten-day journey, mostly at night, and only young adults could survive it without adequate nourishment. Abraham Harris escaped from his owner in Charles County, Maryland, and lived for nine days without eating. After reaching Philadelphia, he collapsed and died from malnutrition.

Exposure to harsh climatic conditions was another obstacle. It was not unusual for fugitive slaves to arrive in the North with swollen feet, broken bones, and frostbitten limbs. Elizabeth Williams, escaping from Baltimore County in 1857, found it necessary to have her frostbitten toes removed by a Pennsylvania surgeon.

The young adults who set out for freedom used a variety of methods. One was to borrow free papers from a black who resembled the person contemplating escape. To effect his escape, Frederick Douglass sought the help of free Negro sailors whom he had come to know in the Baltimore shipyards and who showed that they were sympathetic to the plight of the slaves. From a seafaring friend named Stanley, who was his height, he borrowed a sailor's suit and a sailor's "protection," a paper listing the physical features of its owner who, as a free American sailor, could move about the country. (The suit was later returned to its owner by mail.) Douglass hopped the last car while a friend, Isaac Rhodes, threw his bundle into the moving train as he left the Baltimore station for Philadelphia. In this way he avoided buying a ticket, which would have subjected him to close scrutiny by the ticket agent who was required to check the description on the "protection."

Fortunately, the conductor on the train was satisfied with the "protection." Nor did he pursue the matter further when Douglass replied, on being asked for the "free papers" that all free blacks were required by Maryland law to produce on demand, that his "only pass was an American Eagle." Having passed the conductor's inspection, he arrived in Philadelphia in the late afternoon of September 3, 1838.

Henry Bibb had no trouble escaping, for, as the *New Haven Palladium* noted, "his color was almost clear white." Fugitives who were light skinned usually escaped by posing as white travelers. This was the method used by Ellen Craft, who, with her husband, William, devised a bold plot to achieve freedom. Ellen was fair enough to pass as white, and they decided to escape by having her act the part of the master, while William posed as her servant. Ellen cut her hair short, wore clothing stolen from her master, and, to disguise her beardless face, muffled it in a shawl, pretending she was suffering from severe toothache. They knew that they would have to register at hotels in the course of their travels, but neither could write so they placed Ellen's hand in a sling. Anticipating queries, they concocted the story that William's young master was very ill and traveling to Philadelphia in search of medical care. To make the story even more plausible, Ellen wore dark glasses, limped slightly, walked slowly with a cane, and was said to be almost totally deaf. In this way, hotel clerks and strangers would be discouraged from prolonged conversation. At Baltimore, they were held up while transportation authorities requested a bond for the "servant." However, by impressing the need for quick medical attention, the two were able to proceed without giving bond. They started out from Macon, Georgia, on December 21, 1848, and arrived safely in Philadelphia on Christmas morning.

Henry "Box" Brown's escape from Richmond, Virginia, was among the most dramatic of the fugitive slave experiences. While praying, Brown claimed he heard a voice saying, "Go and get a box and put yourself in it." He obediently went to the railroad depot and measured the largest box that could be freighted and asked a carpenter to make one that size. Despite the carpenter's warning that no one could live in a container three feet, one inch long, two feet, six inches wide, and four and a half feet high, Brown got into it and asked a friend to nail it shut and ship him north. Because the railroad workers ignored the "this side up" label on Brown's temporary home, he had a difficult journey. However, he arrived safely in Philadelphia, where he was met by members of the Vigilance Committee, an organization formed to aid fugitives in a variety of ways. William Still, the committee's black secretary and one of the four receiving agents, pried off the lid, whereupon, Still recalled, "the marvelous resurrection of Brown ensued. Rising up in his box, he reached out his hand, saying, 'How do you do, gentlemen?'"

The sensational escape produced a song entitled "Escape from Slavery of Henry Box Brown," the opening stanza and chorus of which went:

> Have you seen a man by the name of Henry Brown,
> Ran away from the South to the North;
> Which he would not have done but they stole all
>   his rights,
> But they'll never do the like again.
>
> (Refrain)
> Brown laid down the shovel, and the hoe,
> Down in the box he did go;
> No more Slave work for Henry Box Brown,
> In the box by express he did go.

A similarly dramatic escape was that of a young slave woman who had herself boxed up in Baltimore in the winter of 1857 and conveyed as freight to the depot, to be shipped to Philadelphia. William Still described what happened next: "Nearly all one night the box remained in the depot with the living agony in it, and after being turned upside down more than once, the next day about ten o'clock it reached Philadelphia." When the lid was pried off, the slave woman was discovered in the straw. After three days in bed, she told how she had survived the ordeal. "She had a pair of scissors with her, and in order to procure fresh air she had made a hole in the box, but it was very slight. How she ever managed to breathe and maintain her existence, being in the condition of becoming a mother, it was hard to comprehend." After she recovered, the Vigilance Committee helped her settle in Canada.

Slaves sometimes escaped in groups. Seventeen fugitives once arrived at the home of Levi Coffin, the Cincinnati Quaker who was the reputed "president" of the Underground Railroad. They had planned well, escaping from Kentucky where they paid a skiff owner to transport them across the river near their plantation. Other arrangements were necessary for their escape, and after crossing the river they made their way to Cincinnati. On another occasion, thirteen slaves escaped from a Virginia plantation after several weeks of planning and arrived in Pennsylvania three weeks after leaving their starting point. The leader of the band told a Pennsylvania abolitionist: "We traveled only at night, and in day time we lay in swamps where the thickets were almost as dark as night itself. There were plenty of fruits in Virginia, but we didn't find any in Maryland. Sometimes we were two or three days without anything to eat."

In June 1844, five slaves—John W. Jones and two brothers from the Elzy plantation in Loudon County, Virginia, and two men from a neighboring plantation—met at a secret designated place on the Elzy plantation. They took a change of clothing and food, which they hoped would last them for four days. To protect themselves from capture on the way to the North, each man carried a pistol and a sharp knife. They traveled at night, hiding during the day, until they reached Maryland, when they began to grow a little bolder and more daring by traveling during daytime.

One day at cross-roads in Maryland, three well-armed slave catchers appeared and attempted to capture the runaway slaves. But when the fugitives drew their pistols, the slave catchers withdrew, fearing the determined slaves. Before they set out again on their northward journey, all members of the party took an oath to fight to the death in case they were pursued "and never to be taken back into slavery again." By the end of the month, the five fugitives were in Pennsylvania. They passed into upstate New York, and near the city of Elmira, more dead than alive, they came to the farm of Nathaniel Smith, and crawled into the haymow of the barn. Here they remained nearly a week, aided by the physician and his wife who were both active in the antislavery movement. On July 5, 1844, the five escaped slaves arrived in Elmira, New York, where they decided to settle instead of going on to Canada.

Some fugitives, especially female slaves, singlehandedly brought their entire families across the Mason-Dixon line. A mother and from three to seven children would often escape together. Frequently they stole carriage wagons in order to accommodate infants and children. Such escapes were usually from Maryland because of the short distance to be traveled. In 1845, some one hundred slaves made a mass escape from southern Maryland. Most of the runaways were captured, but some made it to freedom in Canada. In 1857, three brothers escaped from Maryland, and, in addition, carried their mentally retarded brother to Pennsylvania with them so that all four might enjoy freedom.

Families who escaped usually armed themselves to resist capture. In Frederick County, Maryland, one family of eight bondsmen were overtaken "but stabbed three of the whites and made their escape." In 1856, a Maryland paper reported that "a man slave . . . and two women and two children ran away Sunday night [from Hagerstown] and were overtaken before they reached the Pennsylvania line, but made a stout resistance and succeeded in getting away." The typical runaway was a young man who fled alone. "Slaves often gave runaways moral and material support," Michael P. Johnson points out, "but most slave women and older men were restrained from running away alone by their familial obligations and community bonds." But he also notes that "the same community ties that had to be severed to run away alone could and did strengthen slaves of both sexes and a wide range of ages to run away together, in groups." After a careful analysis of advertisements for groups of runaway slaves that appeared in the Charleston, South Carolina, newspapers from 1799 to 1830, Johnson concludes that almost a thousand slaves ran away in the company of one or more of their co-workers or family members, and that life in the slave community strengthened the determination and the ability of slaves to run away in groups.

Although attempts were numerous, slave escapes were not often successful. Most runaways returned voluntarily from their brief escape in the woods, usually driven by hunger, or else they were hunted down and returned to their masters. The lack of sheltered places of refuge, the vast distances to be covered, and the slave's high visibility combined to make successful escape difficult. Yet despite these obstacles, slaves did succeed. They did so by dint of tremendous courage and endurance, traveling at night over hundreds of miles of hostile territory, guided by the north star, hiding in swamps and forests, as they made their way slowly to freedom. A jubilant Harriet Tubman remembered that after crossing the Mason-Dixon line, "I looked at my hands to see it I was the same person. There was such glory over everything . . . and I felt I was in heaven."

SLAVE CONSPIRACIES AND REVOLTS

Theft, arson, murder, suicide, and escape were the most common forms of resistance to the institution. But the danger of slave insurrection led a Tennessee court to rule in 1844 that slaves should not practice medicine for fear that "such doctors might fomment [*sic*] insurrection":

A slave under pretense of practicing medicine, might convey intelligence from one plantation to another, of a contemplated insurrectionary movement, and thus enable the slaves to act in concert to a considerable extent, and perpetuate the most shocking massacres. . . . It was thought most safe to prohibit slaves from practicing medicine altogether.

Black scholars, such as Carter G. Woodson, W.E.B. Du Bois, and Benjamin Brawley, always stressed the importance of rebellions in the history of slave resistance, but most historians did not take this seriously until 1937, when two white historians, Herbert Aptheker and Harvey Wish, presented the first detailed work on the history of slave rebellions in the United States in a pair of scholarly articles. A year later, Joseph C. Carroll's full-length study, *Slave Insurrections in the United States, 1800–1865*, was published. It was superseded in 1943 by Aptheker's *American Negro Slave Revolts*, still the definitive work on the subject.

Aptheker defined a slave rebellion as one in which "a minimum of ten slaves were involved; freedom was the apparent aim of the disaffected slaves; [and there were] contemporary references labelling the event as an uprising, plot, insurrection, or the equivalent of these terms." Using this as his gauge, Aptheker claimed that there were at least "two hundred and fifty revolts and conspiracies in the history of American Negro Slavery." Aptheker not only tabulated and described the slave revolts and conspiracies that occurred, but he showed how pervasive the fear of the slave was in determining the policy of the Southern masters. He also demonstrated that the tactics for the prevention or suppression of mass rebelliousness among slaves constituted one of the major considerations in the formulation of the legal, social, and theological aspects of pre-Civil War Southern life.

It is indicative of the state of American historiography concerning the black experience at the time that Aptheker's book was published that nearly all other white historians flatly rejected his conclusion, calling his evidence suspect and based on "inference and rumor." Since the publication of *American Negro Slave Revolts*, the prevailing view among white historians has been that while the book provides a useful corrective to the view that the slaves "were almost uniformly contented," it is deficient in failing to distinguish between slave revolts and conspiracies, and rumors of conspiracies. However, a number of historians, black and white, have not only substantiated many of Aptheker's conclusions but have revealed even more instances of resistance, which found both individual and group expression among the bondsmen.

As a result of Aptheker's study and subsequent works by other historians, it has been established that between 1520 and 1860 there were more than two hundred slave revolts for which there are definite records. In all probability, there were also numerous minor uprisings, which were quickly suppressed before they reached public notice. Some half-dozen uprisings can be considered large scale, and three of these were notable: Gabriel Prosser's insurrection in Virginia in 1800, Denmark Vesey's insurrection in Charleston in 1822, and the Nat Turner insurrection of 1831 in Virginia.

I have dealt with Gabriel's insurrection in volume 1. As I noted, the plan never came to fruition. A heavy storm occurred the day of the scheduled uprising, bringing with it a flood, which prevented the majority of the insurrectionists (most of them slave artisans) from assembling at the appointed place outside Richmond. Two slaves told their master of the conspiracy; the Virginia state militia was called out and the entire white community alerted. The leaders of the planned insurrection were apprehended, along with a number of their followers. On October 7, 1800, Gabriel Prosser and fifteen other rebels were hanged. In all, thirty-five slaves were executed for their role in the aborted uprising. The laws governing the conduct of slaves and free blacks were applied more severely.

Historians argue about the scope of Gabriel's insurrection and as to whether its constituents numbered thousands, hundreds, or even under a hundred men, but no one disputes the existence of the conspiracy. However, the existence of the slave revolt led by Denmark Vesey has not been accorded such universal acceptance.

DENMARK VESEY'S CONSPIRACY

Denmark Vesey, the slave of a sea captain, had traveled abroad with his master and had learned to read and write. He purchased his freedom after winning a lottery in 1800, and as a master carpenter, he became a leading member of

Charleston's free black community. For several years, thoughts of conspiracy dominated his mind. He had read widely and knew a great deal about the Old and New Testaments, the Missouri debates in Congress, and the Saint Domingue revolution in the 1790s, the only successful slave rebellion in history, which led to the formation of the black republic of Haiti. He had, according to a contemporary report, "rendered himself perfectly familiar with all those parts of the scriptures which he thought he could pervert to his purpose and would readily quote them to prove that slavery was contrary to the laws of God." Even while walking down the street, he was not idle; if his companion bowed to a white person, he would rebuke him, observing that all men were born equal and none ought to degrade themselves in front of others. Vesey also occasionally debated with whites on the subject of slavery in a bold manner and was overheard doing so by groups of slaves and free blacks. Small wonder that he became both widely known and respected among the city's black population.

Vesey began actively recruiting conspirators in the winter of 1821–1822, and he soon had "five principal officers": Rolla and Ned, the two slaves of Governor Thomas Bennett of South Carolina; Jack, slave of Mrs. Purcell; Peter, slave of Mr. Poyas; Gulla Jack, who belonged to Mr. Pritchard; and Monday, slave of Mr. Gell. Vesey employed these five slaves and "some others . . . to travel about the country adjacent to Charleston [to gain support among the slaves in the rural areas]. . . . He engaged great numbers to join in the intended insurrection."

The leaders exercised great caution in enlisting conspirators. Few domestic servants were asked to join, since they were generally distrusted. As Peter told the others: "But take care and don't mention it to those waiting men who receive presents of old coats from their masters or they'll betray us." Special enlistment efforts were made to recruit blacks, both hired and working out.

A Negro blacksmith who had been accustomed to making edged tools was employed to make pike heads and bayonets with sockets, to be fixed at the end of long poles. By June 16, 1822, one hundred of these pikes were said to have been made, in addition to from two hundred to four hundred daggers. Other rebels obtained daggers, swords, fuses, powder, and a few firearms. The plantation slaves, hundreds of whom came to Charleston in canoes on weekends, were supposed to bring additional weapons. The city's draymen, carters, butchers, and liverymen, many of them free blacks, were in charge of providing the horses for the rebel cavalry.

Vesey and almost all of his lieutenants were leaders and deacons in the African Church of Charleston, and several plotters testified to the intensity of Vesey's religious convictions. "His general conversation was about religion which he would apply to slavery," said one. Another added, "He studies the Bible a great deal and tried to prove from it that slavery and bondage is against the Bible." In the Vesey plot, African religion was also represented, in the person of Gullah Jack, an Angolese witch doctor who, it was said, had the power to make the rebels invulnerable.

Vesey wrote two letters to Haiti asking for assistance, which were carried to a vessel departing for the black republic. In May 1822, Vesey set July 14, the anniversary of the French Revolution and the darkest night of the month, for the beginning of the revolt. July 14 was also a Sunday, a day when many whites left Charleston and, conversely, when blacks came in from the countryside.

The plan was to attack arsenals, guardhouses, and armories where arms and ammunition were stored. The rebels, wearing wigs and false whiskers made of white men's hairs, planned to capture the arms and supplies and then seize Charleston by a seven-pronged assault. Peter was to lead one group to seize an arsenal and guardhouse; Ned was to lead another from the countryhouse; Rolla to lead another; and a fourth party from the country and partly from Charleston was to meet at Gadsen's Wharf and attack the upper guardhouse. A fifth, consisting of country blacks, was to assemble at a farm two-and-a-half miles from the city, seize the powder magazine there, and then march into the city. A sixth, under Vesey's command, was to march to the guardhouse. Simultaneously a number of rebels were to ride on horseback through the streets and prevent any whites from assembling or sounding an alarm. The rebels would kill most of the whites and some of the blacks who had refused to join the conspiracy, and, if necessary, escape to Haiti or Africa.

In late May, William Paul, one of Vesey's lieutenants, attempted to recruit the domestic slave of an important Charlestonian, who promptly informed his master. As a result, Paul was arrested, and the authorities slowly amassed the evidence that enabled them to crush the conspiracy. Vesey advanced the time for the rebellion to midnight June 16, and the leaders destroyed all records. But further disclosures followed, and on June 15 and 16, military forces were deployed at strategic points in the city, while Vesey and his lieutenants tried unsuccessfully to communicate with their supporters on the plantations before going into hiding.

The uprising never materalized, but between June 17 and 27, about two dozen more slaves were arrested, tried before a special court of magistrates and freeholders, and sentenced to death. On June 22, Vesey was captured at his wife's house, tried and convicted the next day, and executed. The trials continued until July 26, when twenty-four more slaves were hanged, bringing the total number of executions up to this point to thirty-four. Altogether, seventy-one men, sixty-seven of them Negroes, were convicted for their part in the plot; twenty-five of the Negroes were hanged, and forty-two condemned to banishment. Four white men were convicted of the misdemeanor of "inciting slaves to insurrection" and were sentenced to prison terms and stiff fines.

The relatives of the blacks who were hanged were not allowed to bury their dead, since the authorities regarded the bodies of slaves, even in death, as property. The bodies were turned over to surgeons for purposes of dissection.

Because of the great secrecy maintained by the leaders, it is impossible to determine the exact number of participants, but Denmark Vesey's conspiracy has long been viewed as the most extensive slave insurrection in the antebellum

South. "In boldness of conception and thoroughness of organization there has been nothing to compare with it," wrote Thomas Wentworth Higginson in 1861. Herbert Aptheker described it as "one of the most serious, widespread, and carefully planned conspiracies."

In 1964 Richard C. Wade, writing in the *Journal of Southern History,* contended that "there is persuasive evidence that no conspiracy in fact existed or at most that it was a vague and unformulated plan in the minds or in the tongues of a few colored townsmen." On the basis of an appraisal of the trial record, Wade argued that there were serious inconsistencies and "deliberate" discrepancies in the rebel testimony so that "little confidence can be placed in the authenticity of the official account." Wade concluded that all that existed was "loose" talk among a number of slaves and hysterical fears among the whites and that these fears alone resulted in the execution of thirty-five blacks.

While conceding that in all slave conspiracies there is an inevitable uncertainty about what really happened and that we must reconstruct the story of the Vesey plot from admittedly fragmentary sources, most students of the insurrection in South Carolina, such as Herbert Aptheker, John Lofton, and, more recently, William W. Freehling, Robert Starobin, and Max L. Kleinman, have clearly demonstrated that a plot did in fact exist. Lofton points out that the severe repressive action that followed the uncovering of the conspiracy led to a debate in South Carolina between those of the slaveholding class who sought ruthlessness and those who sought more "mildness." These differences, in turn, induced tampering with the records of the trial, which led Wade to cast doubt upon the existence of an actual slave conspiracy. Starobin argues that the testimony of the important witnesses is consistent in all major points and that the three weeks between the arrest of William Paul and the other arrests gave Vesey plenty of time to destroy evidence. Aptheker notes that following the arrests of the conspirators, a plan was formulated for the rescue of the prisoners. Indeed on the day of Vesey's execution, there was another attempted insurrection, but the state troops held the slaves in check. Finally federal troops were sent in because the slave opposition was so "determined." Clearly, then, the conspiracy had the support of many blacks who were prepared to suffer terrible consequences in order to save their would-be liberators.

The evidence of the existence of the Vesey conspiracy and its reality, as set forth in the writings of a number of scholars, is overwhelming and makes it clear that its scope was such as to present a great danger to the white inhabitants of Charleston.

Despite its failure, Vesey's conspiracy contributed substantially to the fear among whites of a general slave war. The *Charleston Times* branded blacks "the Jacobins of the country . . . the anarchists and the domestic enemy; the common enemy of civilized society, and the barbarians who would, if they could, become the destroyers of our race." The determination to forestall further insurrections sparked both the enactment of a more rigorous slave code and the first in a series of Negro seamen acts designed to isolate Charleston's large black population from dangerous contact with free black sailors by providing for their detention while in South Carolina ports. In addition, the legislature forbade blacks leaving the state ever to return, placed a tax on free blacks, required them to have guardians, and prohibited self-hiring by slaves.

INTERLUDE

The inhabitants of Edgecomb County, North Carolina, were much distraught in December 1825 "by the partial discovery of an insurrectionary plot among the blacks," and in December 1830 the citizens of Sampson, Bladen, New Hanover, Jones, Onslow, and Duplin counties in the same state petitioned the general assembly for military assistance in searching for runaways and for authority to shoot them on sight. The petitioners complained that the slaves were "becoming almost uncontrollable. They go and come when and where they please, and if an attempt is made to correct them they immediately fly to the woods and there continue for months and years committing grievous depredations on our Cattle, hogs, and Sheep." The petitioners also stated that patrols hesitated to act for fear of having their houses burned. A few days later the residents of New Bern, Tarboro, and Hillsboro were terrified by slave unrest. The inhabitants of New Bern, "being advised of the assemblage of sixty armed slaves in a swamp in their vicinity," called out the militia, surrounded the swamp, and killed the entire group of insurgents. In January 1831 a resident of Wilmington reported that there had recently been "much shooting of negroes" in that neighborhood, "in consequence of symptoms of liberty having been discovered among them."

But it was an event in neighboring Virginia that same year of 1831 that threw the entire South into a state of greater hysteria than ever before in the history of slavery.

NAT TURNER'S REBELLION

In 1800, the year of Gabriel Prosser's slave uprising, Governor James Monroe of Virginia gloomily observed that "unhappily while this class of people exists among us we can never count with certainty on its tranquil submission." That same year, a man was born in Virginia who was to substantiate fully the truth of Monroe's prediction. He was Nat Turner, leader of the third great slave revolt of the nineteenth century. This insurrection, generally referred to as the Southampton Insurrection or the Servile Insurrection of 1831, has been characterized by one historian as "the largest and most celebrated slave insurrection in the United States," by another as the "single instance of sustained revolt of slaves against their masters in American history," and by still another as "the bloodiest slave insurrection in Southern history, one that was to have profound and irrevocable impact on the destinies of Southern whites and blacks alike."

The question posed by a Richmond newspaper in 1831—"Who is this Nat Turner?"—is difficult to answer. In what is probably the most comprehensive single source book on the Turner rebellion (*The Southampton Slave Revolt of 1831: A Compilation of Source Material*), Henry Irving Tragle concludes that "we know almost nothing of the historical Nat Turner in any context other than as the leader of a band of rebels." Much of what we do know about his life prior to 1831 comes from *The Confessions of Nat Turner*, which Turner dictated to the white lawyer, Thomas Gray, while awaiting trial, and which goes into vivid detail about Turner's visions and religious ideas. Although some scholars have argued that it is difficult to tell how much of it is Turner and how much is Gray, Herbert Aptheker considers the *Confessions* genuine. Recently Stephen B. Oates has thrown new light on Nat Turner's life through research in the census records and local archives. While taking into account the lack of much hard historical evidence, we can offer a reasonable view of Nat Turner's life.

Nat Turner was born on October 2, 1800, on the farm of Benjamin Turner in Southampton County, Virginia, located about fifteen miles southwest of Jerusalem, the county seat. It was mostly a small farming area, with cotton fields and apple orchards, the latter supplying a potent apple brandy. Most of Southampton's white citizens farmed small holdings, and only a handful of its most prosperous ones owned more than twenty-five slaves. The average in 1830 was around three or four slaves per family. Southampton was one of the counties in Virginia that had suffered economic decline after the War for Independence, and a number of the whites, finding the soil too poor for extensive tobacco or cotton cultivation, had moved on to new cotton lands in Georgia and Alabama. The result was that Southampton's population in 1830 (16,074) was 60 percent black. Of the 9,500 blacks, moreover, 1,700 were "free persons of color," an unusually high proportion in a rural area.

Nat Turner was the son of two strong-minded parents, an African-born mother who, tradition had it, had to be restrained from killing her infant son rather than see him grow up in bondage, and a father who escaped to the North while Nat was a boy. Nat early learned to read and write, and from an early age, his parents imbued in him the idea that he was "intended for some great purpose." He intentionally held himself aloof from the rest of the slaves. "Having discovered [myself] to be great," he told Gray, "I must appear so, and therefore studiously avoided mixing in society, and wrapped myself in mystery, devoting my time to fasting and praying."

Nat was also influenced by his grandmother, who taught him to pray and to take pride in his superior intelligence. His ability to read and write prompted those who knew him to remark that he had too much sense to be raised in bondage—he "would never be of any service to anyone as a slave," one of them said.

In 1810, Benjamin Turner died, and Nat became the property of Turner's oldest son, Samuel. He used every opportunity to improve his knowledge. He studied the white children's school books and experimented in making paper and gun-powder. But religion was increasingly becoming the dominant influence in Turner's life. He spent many hours reading and memorizing the Bible. Soon he started preaching at black religious gatherings and rose to prominence as a leading exhorter in the slave church. Although not ordained and never a member of any church, he was accepted as a Baptist preacher by the slaves, and he even baptized a local white man. Turner's status as a slave preacher gave him considerable freedom of movement, and he came to know most of Southampton County intimately.

Sometime around 1821, Nat Turner disappeared. His master had put him under an overseer, and he was evidently whipped. Thirty days later, he voluntarily returned. His fellow-slaves "murmured" against him, Turner told Gray later, "saying that if they had any sense they would not serve any master in the world." But he explained that "the Spirit appeared to me and said I had my wishes directed to the things of this world, and not to the Kingdom of Heaven, and that I should return to the service of my earthly master."

When Turner first experienced his miraculous religious visions is not known. But the story is that one day while he was praying, a Spirit approached him, saying "Seek ye the kingdom of Heaven and all things shall be added unto you." Through the Spirit he was able to see a whole series of miracles. While working in the field, he said, he discovered drops of blood on the corn. In the woods, he found leaves with hieroglyphic characters and numbers on them. Other leaves contained forms of men—some drawn in blood—like the figures in the sky. Once, against a darkened sun and thunderous sky, he witnessed a battle between black and white spirits in which streams of blood flowed in the air; another time, the Spirit revealed to him "the knowledge of the elements, the revolution of the planets, the operation of the tides, and changes of the seasons." Finally, on May 12, 1828, Turner said he had a vision in which he "heard a loud noise in the heavens, and the Spirit instantly appeared to me and said . . . the time was fast approaching when the first should be last and the last should be first." In the same vision, he was told that "until the first sign appeared, I should conceal it from the knowledge of men."

Nevertheless, he told Thomas Moore, his third owner, that slaves ought to be free and would be "one day or other." For this dangerous talk from a slave, Turner received a whipping. This was not the only taste he had of the brutality of slavery. Turner had married a young slave named Cherry, who lived on Samuel Turner's place with her husband. But in 1822 Samuel Turner died, and they were sold to different masters—Cherry to Giles Reese and Nat to Thomas Moore.

Moore died in 1828 and Turner's nominal ownership passed to Moore's nine-year-old son, Putnam. Within two years the widow Moore married a local wheelwright, Joseph Travis, who moved into her house and set up business in the place.

On February 12, 1831, there occurred an eclipse of the sun, and this appeared to Nat Turner to be the sign he had been awaiting. In his words, "The seal was removed from my lips, and I communicated the great work laid out for me to do, to four in whom I had the greatest confidence, (Henry, Hark, Nelson and Sam)."

The first date chosen for the beginning of the uprising was July 4, 1831, but Turner tells us that this date had to be abandoned because "I fell sick." Then on August 13, there occurred a day-long atmospheric phenomenon, during which the sun was seen only faintly and appeared to be of a greenish hue. This occurrence, which caused widespread consternation in many places in the eastern United States, was accepted by Nat Turner as a direct communication from God. He told his followers that "as the black spot passed over the sun, so shall the blacks pass over the earth."

After alerting those whom he had originally chosen as his primary lieutenants and recruiting two more, Turner arranged a meeting on Sunday, August 21, deep in the woods near the Travis homestead at a place called Cabin Pond. Hark Travis (called "General Moore" by his fellow slaves) brought a pig, and Henry Edwards some brandy. The slaves roasted the pig and drank the brandy. Later in the day, Nat Turner appeared and noticed a newcomer in the group: "I saluted him in coming up, and asked Will how came he there, he answered, his life was worth no more than others, and his liberty as dear to him. I asked him if he meant to obtain it? He said he would, or loose [sic] his life. This was enough to put him in full confidence." Turner then explained the nature of his mission. When one of the men expressed apprehension because of the small size of the group, Turner said he had intentionally avoided involving too many slaves in his planning. Other plots, he said, had "always leaked out," and he intended "that their march of destruction and murder should be the first news of the insurrection." After dining and drinking into the night, these seven slaves, under the leadership of Turner, set out on their mission.

In contrast to the traditional view, Nat Turner's revolt was not a spontaneous uprising, and the slave rebel leader, aware of the danger of betrayal, appears to have been a careful strategist. But there seems to have been no preparation of arms and ammunition or any prior secreting of these weapons and supplies. Evidently Turner was confident that slaves and free blacks alike would rise up and join him. He also appears to have seen himself as an instrument acting for a higher power, which would provide all that was necessary when the time came.

We know little about Turner's ultimate objective. It may have been that he wanted to fight his way into the Great Dismal Swamp some twenty miles to the east, a region that had long been a haven for fugitives. Or, as was reported at the time, perhaps the rebels intended to march to Norfolk, seize ships, and sail to Africa. But probably the objective was nothing less than the destruction of every white person within reach. In the words of the *Confessions* "we should commence at home (Mr. J. Travis') on that night, and until we had armed and equipped ourselves, and gathered sufficient force, neither age nor sex was to be spared."

We will probably never know with certainty the precise motives that led

Turner to lead his rebellion. When Thomas Wentworth Higginson wrote "Nat Turner's Insurrection" in 1861, he attributed the revolt to Turner's having suffered the indignities and injustices of slavery. He had a wife whom he could not protect from sexual "outrage," scars on his body that may have come from white hands, and his followers were men who "had been systematically brutalized from childhood" and who "had seen their wives and sisters habitually polluted" by white ravishers.

Over a century later, Stephen B. Oates explained Turner's mandate for rebellion as social frustration—the rage born in a proud and godly man "blocked from his potential." Having experienced a spiritual call to greatness and having gained eminence in the black religious community as a powerful exhorter, "he felt betrayed by false hopes," Oates concludes, and "felt humiliated that he remained a lowly field hand . . . while less intelligent Negroes became privileged domestics."

The most cursory glance at the famous *Confessions* reveals a man for whom religion was the center of life and one who developed a deep religious commitment. As a self-appointed Baptist preacher, Turner had an immense influence among Southampton's slaves and, after experiencing a series of religious visions, he became convinced of his divine mission to lead the "fight against the Serpent." We can probably accept as genuine his statement to Gray: "It was plain to me that the Savior was to lay down the yoke he had borne for the sins of men, and the great day of judgment was at hand." In short, Turner's vision was that of redemption and the establishment of earthly justice, a view that he found in the Gospels.

Beginning at about two o'clock in the morning of Monday, August 22, the rebels, led by Turner, made their silent way through the woods to the Travis farm. Turner ascended a second-story window by means of a ladder, opened the doors for others, and Travis and his family were murdered. Salanthiel Francis, the owner of the rebels Sam and Will, was the next victim; he was killed in his farmhouse six hundred yards away. As the rebels moved from farm to farm, they gathered axes and hatchets, muskets, swords, and other weapons, and acquired horses. Their numbers slowly increased—from seven to fifteen, to forty, to sixty. By dawn they had visited half a dozen houses and had killed more than twenty men, women, and children. No white along the route was spared, with the exception of one family so poor that, Turner observed, they "thought no better of themselves than they did of the negroes."

For several hours the rebels met no resistance, but by morning they began to find homes deserted and they realized that a warning had been spread. Raising the militia proved difficult, however, for many whites were attending a camp meeting in North Carolina. The final home visited by the rebels, just about noontime, was that of Mrs. Rebecca Vaughan. She was killed, along with her niece, Eliza, her younger son, Arthur, and their overseer. Her older son, George, had fallen victim to the band when they had encountered him earlier. The Vaughan house lay close to the highway leading to the county seat, and Turner revealed later that "here I determined on starting for Jerusalem." Presumably his goal was the local armory, where weapons, powder, and shot were stored in abundance.

As they rode toward Jerusalem, they came to the entrace of James Parker's farm, three miles from the town. Turner sent a band of slaves to gather recruits on Parker's farm, but the slaves, discovering Parker's cellar of apple brandy, did not return quickly. As Turner went to rally them, a detachment of militia rode into view. Here, in Parker's cornfield, the first armed confrontation took place between the rebels and their masters. Although there were no fatalities on either side, the whites, better armed and organized, proved too much for the slaves, who were thrown into confusion by the encounter and dispersed. Nat Turner realized that the road to Jerusalem was effectively barred. With his force reduced in number and much harder to manage, he resolved to try a crossing of the Nottaiway River, which lay between him and Jerusalem, but a quick reconnaissance showed it to be well guarded.

For all practical purposes, the rebellion was now over, but Turner did not abandon hope. Gathering the remnants of his force, he turned south, seeking recruits. However, when it became evident that the countryside was now alarmed, he turned north again, crossed the path he had followed, and holed up for the night.

Meanwhile news of the revolt spread beyond Southampton County as express riders carried the alarm up to Petersburg and from there to the capitol in Richmond. Governor John Floyd, fearing a statewide uprising, alerted the militia and sent cavalry, infantry, and artillery units to the stricken county. Federal troops from Fortress Monroe were also on the way, and other volunteers and militia outfits were marching from neighboring counties in Virginia and North Carolina. Soon over three thousand armed whites were in Southampton County, and hundreds more were mobilizing.

During the night, a number of the new recruits fled Turner's band; by the morning, only twenty men were left. These set out for Dr. Simon Blunt's farm to get volunteers, not knowing they were riding into an ambush. Some reports state that Blunt armed his slaves and that they helped resist the rebels, but it appears that it was the whites, barricaded in the house, who opened fire at point-blank range, killing one or more insurgents and capturing several others, among them Hark Travis. Turner led a handful of the faithful, still hoping to gather reinforcements. But the militia overtook the little band, and, in a final skirmish, killed Will and scattered the rest. Turner escaped to the vicinity of the Travis farm and hid in a hole under some fence rails.

By Tuesday evening, August 24, the rebellion was over. Somewhere around sixty whites—more than half of them women and children—had been killed, although as one Virginian noted with evident surprise, "not one female was violated." Of the victims only one, Margaret Whitehead, was killed by Turner himself. Between sixty and eighty slaves had joined the rebels, along with at least four free blacks, one of whom, Bill Artis, in order to avoid execution or sale into slavery, walked into the woods, placed his hat on a stake, and shot himself.

On Tuesday evening and Wednesday morning, a massacre of blacks of Southampton began as armed whites prowled the woods and swamps in search of fugitive rebels and alleged collaborators. They chased the blacks down with howling dogs, killing those who resisted. Within a week nearly all of the bona fide rebels, except Turner, had been either executed or imprisoned, but not before white vigilantes and some militiamen had perpetrated barbarities on scores of innocent blacks. Vigilantes rounded up Negroes and decapitated them, while a militia unit from North Carolina beheaded several blacks and placed their skulls on poles, where they remained for days. Everywhere whites took blacks from their shacks and tortured, shot, and burned them to death and then mutilated their corpses. How many blacks were killed is unknown, but it seems that nearly two hundred black people lost their lives in the reign of terror of several weeks that followed Turner's two-day uprising. There would have been many more had not the militia commander of Southampton County disbanded and sent home the militia and the artillery and infantry units, issuing a proclamation that any further acts of "inhuman butchery" would be dealt with according to the Articles of War.

On Wednesday, August 31, the court at Southampton County convened to try the rebels. By this time, almost all had been captured except the "great bandit chieftain," as newspapers called Nat Turner. For more than two months, Turner managed to elude a large-scale manhunt. Rewards totaling $1,100 were placed on his head. The announcement of a reward of $500 for Turner's capture by Governor John Floyd included the following description:

Nat is between 30 and 35 years old, 5 feet 6 or 8 inches high, weighs between 150 and 160 pounds, rather bright complexion, but not a mulatto, broad shoulders, large flat nose, large eyes, broad flat feet, rather knock-kneed, walks brisk and active, hair on top of the head very thin, no beard, except on the upper lip and the top of the chin, a scar on one of his temples, also on the back of his neck, a large knot on one of his bones of right arm, near the waist, produced by a blow.

On October 31, Benjamin Phipps discovered Turner in a hideout near Cabin Pond, where the rebellion had begun, and took him to Jerusalem at gunpoint. He was locked in the same wooden jail where the other captured rebels had been incarcerated. It was here that Thomas Gray, an elderly Jerusalem lawyer and slaveholder, came the next day to interrogate Turner as he lay in his cell "clothed with rags and covered with chains." Over a period of three days, Turner dictated his *Confessions* about the genesis and execution of the revolt, recounting his religious visions and insisting he was a prophet of God. At the end Gray asked: "Do you not find yourself mistaken now?" " Was not Christ crucified? Turner replied."

On November 5, Nat Turner came to trial in Jerusalem. The court quickly found him guilty of committing insurrection and sentenced him to hang. He went to his execution six days later with dignity and composure, refusing an invitation to make a final statement to the large crowd that had gathered to watch him hang.

In addition to Turner, the county court tried some forty-eight blacks on various charges of conspiracy, insurrection, and treason. Five of those arraigned were free blacks. In all, eighteen blacks—including one woman—were convicted and hanged. Twelve others were transported out of the state. The heirs of Turner's owners were awarded $375 in compensation by the court.

Turner's body was turned over to surgeons for dissection, and, according to oral tradition, souvenir purses were made of his skin.

REACTION TO THE REBELLION

Nat Turner's revolt sparked a panic that spread as far north as Delaware and as far south as Louisiana and Alabama. Dozens of communities were seized with hysteria as rumors flew that thousands of slaves had risen and that the entire South would soon be ablaze. In early October, there was a widely circulated report of a slave army of three thousand landing in Seaford, Delaware. Messengers ran through the towns and counties of the state shouting that the slave army had killed whites and was preparing to march inland for the purpose of destruction. The report proved to be utterly false, but so widely was it believed that many fearful whites hid in the woods for weeks. As one North Carolina paper versified:

> The flying rumors gather'd as they roll'd,
> Scarce any tale was sooner heard than told,
> And all who told it added something new.
> And all who heard it, made enlargements too:
> In every ear it spread, on every tongue it grew.

In November, President Andrew Jackson proposed an increase in the standing army to fifteen thousand to protect the South from further slave rebellion, but this did little to allay the fears.

It would be difficult to exaggerate the effect of Turner's revolt on rekindling the fears that ran deep in the Southern psyche. One reader wrote to the *Richmond Enquirer:* "There it is, the dark and growing evil at our doors. . . . What is to be done? Oh! My God. I do not know, but something must be done." Another contemporary in Richmond wondered if the Turner rebellion might not "excite those to insurrection that never thought of such a thing before." Still another raised the question, "If the slaves in that county would murder the whites, why are they not ready to do it in any *other county* in the state?" More simply, another Virginian observed: "A Nat Turner might be in any family."

During the panic, southerners turned in wrath toward preventing a recurrence of the insurrection. Vigilante committees were hurriedly formed to terrorize blacks, and state legislatures met in emergency sessions to pass laws that would further inhibit the freedom of slaves, discourage manumission, and restrict the rights of free blacks. An example of the Nat Turner backlash was the extension of the 1819 Virginia law to declare illegal every assembly of free or slave Negroes for the purpose of teaching them to read and write. The statute also had a chilling effect on the free blacks' ability to purchase books.

Virginians prided themselves on their "lenient" treatment of their slaves, compared with the more brutal conditions of the lower South. But the Turner revolt had not occurred in Mississippi or Alabama. "No one had dreamed of any such event happening in any part of Virginia," said one newspaper, and if it were to occur anywhere, surely it would not be in Southampton, an area of small farms in which the typical slaveholder owned only three or four blacks and overseers were almost unheard of. How, then, could it have happened?

Once the panic had subsided, Virginians turned their attention to seeking out the causes of the rebellion. Not surprisingly, they blamed "outside agitators." The leading target was William Lloyd Garrison, whose militant abolitionist weekly, the *Liberator,* had begun publication in Boston a few months earlier. Also blamed was David Walker, the free black tailor in Boston, whose revolutionary *Appeal* had been published in 1829. But there is no evidence that Turner ever saw a copy of either the *Liberator* or Walker's *Appeal.*

Some Virginians dared to argue that slavery itself was responsible for inspiring Nat Turner. Indeed the most striking outcome of the Turner uprising was a debate unique in Southern history. For the last time, Virginians openly discussed the possibility of ending slavery. There is an enduring myth in historical literature that Nat Turner killed a budding abolitionist movement in Virginia and closed off debate on slavery. In reality, the remarkable debates of January and February 1832 in the Virginia legislature could not have occurred without him. As one Richmond newspaper observed, "Nat Turner, and the blood of his innocent victims have conquered the silence of fifty years."

The Virginia debates ended with the defeat of antislavery resolutions. When confonted with an event that cried out for reassessment of the assumptions upon which the entire institution was based, the slaveowners opted instead for tightening the system of control. "We have," one Virginia lawmaker affirmed, "closed every avenue by which light might enter their minds. If you could extinguish the capacity to see the light, our work would be completed; they would then be on the level with the beasts of the field, and we should be safe."

Black abolitionists kept Turner's memory alive during the 1840s and 1850s. In the late 1850s, J. Sella Martin's sermons on Turner drew large crowds in Boston. By now, the name of "Old Prophet Nat" was an important element in the black oral tradition. In the slave community, blacks sang of the leader of the rebellion:

> You might be rich as cream,
> And drive you a coach and four horse team;
> But you can't keep the world from moving around,
> And Nat Turner from the gaining ground.
>
> You might be reader and writer too,
> And wiser than old Solomon the Jew;

> But you can't keep the world from moving around,
> And Nat Turner from the gaining ground.
>
> And your name might be Caesar sure,
> And got you cannon can shoot a mile or more;
> But you can't keep the world from moving around,
> And Nat Turner from the gaining ground.

WILLIAM STYRON'S *CONFESSIONS OF NAT TURNER*

Black abolitionist William Wells Brown wrote in 1863 of Nat Turner that "his looks, his sermons, his acts and heroism live in the hearts of his race on every cotton, sugar and rice plantation at the South." According to Brown, some blacks believed that Turner would return and lead a new fight for freedom. George Washington Williams, the pioneer black historian, wrote in the 1880s that "the image of Nat Turner is carved in the fleshy tablets of our million hearts. His history has been kept from the colored people at the South but the women handed the tradition to their children."

Among some Americans, Nat Turner figured as a symbol and folk hero in fiction, poetry, and drama. Even though she did not approve of the violence in the revolt, Harriet Beecher Stowe, in her novel *Dred*, which she published in 1856, used what little was known of Turner in shaping her principal character. In the main, however, among white Americans, Nat Turner, if known at all, was viewed as an insane if shadowy figure. Then in 1967, William Styron's novel, *The Confessions of Nat Turner*, became an instant best-seller, was awarded the Pulitzer Prize for fiction, and made the name of Nat Turner almost a household word. The novel won instant acclaim among most white historians but aroused considerable anger in the black and progressive white communities. Although seemingly based on Turner's confession, as given to Thomas Gray, the novel portrayed Turner as a celibate bachelor afflicted with masturbation fantasies about Margaret Whitehead, a psychosexual supposition unsupported by any known evidence. Styron also violated the historical record in many other details. He defended himself (and was so defended by many white historians) by claiming the rights of the imaginative artist for whom facts are less important than the re-creation of a larger reality. Notwithstanding all this, the author and his defenders insisted that, in the main, the novel reflected historical accuracy.

The attacks on Styron's historical accuracy were brought to public attention by Herbert Aptheker, author of a study on the Turner revolt, and in a volume edited by John H. Clarke, *William Styron's Nat Turner: Ten Black Writers Respond*. Nearly all the reviewers who had originally praised Styron rejected Aptheker's criticism and characterized most of the essays by the black writers as mere diatribes, filled with inaccuracies, and as attempting to create a mythic Nat

Turner. Even when it became clear that much of the evidence available in newspaper files and county records contradicted the truth of many of Styron's statements, many white scholars were still reluctant to deny the novelist artistic license. Then in 1971, Henry Irving Tragle's collection of source material on the Turner revolt was published by the University of Massachusetts Press. With a wealth of contemporary documents, Tragle's volume demonstrated conclusively the distortions and falsifications in Styron's Pulitzer Prize-winning book.

In one of his many interviews explaining his novel, Styron asserted that a visit to Southampton County showed that although the name of Nat Turner sometimes struck a responsive chord, no one with whom he talked could give him reliable information; even physical evidence of the event had been forgotten or destroyed. But Tragle retraced Turner's march over old maps and older fields and ridges. He uncovered nine of the victim's houses and a half a dozen other sites, and he also talked with a number of black and white citizens in the present-day neighborhood of the revolt. For whites, the rebellion lives on and is referred to as "the Insurrection." For blacks, however, much more was involved. "I believe it possible to say with certainty," Tragle wrote, "that Nat Turner exists as a folk-hero to several generations of black men and women who have lived in Southampton County since 1831."

Most scholars today relegate Styron's *The Confessions of Nat Turner* exclusively to the realm of fiction with no significance as a historical presentation of Nat Turner or the events surrounding his revolt.

MORE CONSPIRACIES AND REVOLTS

Reports of revolutionary activity among slaves surfaced every few months after Nat Turner's revolt. Some were bona fide conspiracies; others appeared to involve authenticated stories of proposed insurrections, and many were the product of white hysteria. In the first category was a major insurrection planned in 1845 by a forty-year-old Louisiana slave foreman, Uncle Isaac, with the aid of thirty others. The plot encompassed an area in which there were about forty thousand slaves, but it was betrayed by a slave. Isaac told his owner his reason for planning the revolt:

I was a slave. My wife and children were slaves. If equal with others before God, they should be equal before men. I saw my young masters learning, holding what they made, and making what they could. But Master, my race could make nothing, holding nothing. What they did they did for others, not for themselves. And they had to do it whether they wished it or not; for they were slaves. Master, this is not loving our neighbor, or doing to others as we would have them do to us.

Isaac assured his master of his determination to have carried through the insurrection had the plot not been disclosed.

Master, we were betrayed, but I tell you now, if we had succeeded, I should have slain old master and mistress and you first, to show my people that I could sacrifice my love, as I ordered them to sacrifice their hates, to have justice—justice for them—justice for mine—justice for all. I could not kill any human creature without being so. But, Master, God *here* [pointing to his heart] told me then, as he tells me *now*, that I was right.

The slave foreman refused to name any of his comrades. Just before being hung, he besought his companions to die like men and with honor. His final words were: "I will die a free man."

That same year, a slave outbreak occurred in Maryland. In July 1845, a group of about seventy-five slaves, from St. Mary's, Charles, and Prince George's counties, several of them armed, "set out in marching order for the free State of Pennsylvania." Fifty miles from their goal, the militia and other armed whites caught up with the rebels, wounded several, and captured all of them. One slave leader was hanged, and most of the others were sold out of Maryland by their masters. A free black was found guilty of complicity in the affair and sentenced to forty years' imprisonment.

Three years later, in August 1848, a similar break for freedom was made by about seventy-five slaves in Fayette County, Kentucky. Led by a young white college student, Patrick Doyle, and armed with guns and crude weapons, they set out for the Ohio River and liberty. Nearly all of the rebels, including Doyle, were captured. Three of the slave leaders were hanged, and Doyle was sentenced to twenty years in prison.

Both before and after the presidential election of 1856, an immense slave insurrection panic gripped the Southern states. The white fear began in Texas in September, and by December, budding slave rebellions were being reported in Louisiana, Mississippi, Alabama, Arkansas, Missouri, Maryland, Virginia, South Carolina, Georgia, Florida, Kentucky, and Tennessee. It was in the last two states that the insurrectionary fears reached their height. Under torture, confessions were extracted from slave laborers in the Cumberland Iron Works in which they reported a plot to murder all the whites at the rolling mill, attack the town of Clarksville, Tennessee, rob the bank, kill the whites there, burn the town, and then cut their way to a free state. Other slaves at forges in Kentucky and Tennessee were said to be planning to rise on Christmas night, kill the white men and children at the forges, seize the white women as their wives, and then link up with the rebels from the Cumberland rolling mill.

Whippings, shootings, and lynchings of slaves followed the discovery of the supposed revolutionary plots of Tennessee and Kentucky slave ironworkers. Whether the brutal actions suppressed a real threat of a slave insurrection or one that existed only in the panic-stricken minds of white Southerners is a matter of dispute. Some scholars are convinced that white hysteria rather than a black plot was responsible for the bloody panic in the Cumberland iron district.

There is no question, however, about the authenticity of two slave rebellions at sea in this period, and both were successful. Although only one involved blacks enslaved in the United States, both were connected with this country. The first occurred aboard the *Amistad*, a Spanish slaver, carrying fifty-three blacks (secured in Africa) from Havana to another port in Cuba in 1839 when the slaves mutinied and killed the captain and crew. Two years later, the Africans returned to their native land. I have discussed this famous slave uprising in volume 1 and will deal with it further below in discussing the antislavery movement in which it became a cause célèbre.

In October 1841, the brig *Creole* set sail from Hampton Roads, Virginia, for New Orleans with 8 crew members, 5 sailors, a cargo of tobacco, 6 white passengers, and 135 slaves destined to be sold in the lower South. On the night of November 7, 19 of the slaves, led by Madison Washington—a fugitive from Virginia who had returned from Canada to rescue his wife, had been captured, and was being returned to bondage—rose up, killed a slave dealer on board, wounded the captain, cowed the passengers, and took control of the *Creole*. Two of the blacks in the revolt were seriously wounded and one of them later died.

The mutineers then forced the white man overseeing the slaves to sail the ship to Nassau, New Providence. The mutineers knew that an American schooner, the *Hermosa*, had been shipwrecked the year before near Nassau, and the English wreckers had taken the slaves on the ship to the British island, where officials set them free.

The *Creole* arrived at Nassau on November 9. The nineteen mutineers placed themselves at the mercy of British authorities, but on the insistence of the American consul, all of the blacks were kept on board to prevent their escape. However, soon fifty boats filled with black islanders approached the *Creole* and threatened to free the blacks aboard if the authorities did not release them. The American consul fought to get the British governor to send the nineteen mutineers to the United States to stand trial, but he was rebuffed, and, convinced that if they did not do so, the black islanders would, British officials released all the slaves on the *Creole*. They were now free men.

In the United States, the southerners, fearing that the successful revolt on the *Creole* would stimulate other uprisings and seriously affect the operation of the domestic slave trade, insisted that the former slaves be extradited and indemnity be obtained by their owners. Although the blacks were never extradited, an Anglo-American claims commission in 1855 awarded $110,330 to the owners of the liberated slaves on the ground that the brig had been on a lawful voyage and had the right to expect shelter from a friendly power when "unavoidable necessity" drove it into Nassau.

When the *Creole* was returned to the United States, five of the blacks who had hidden in the hold were on it. But while the majority of the slaves on board the *Creole* had refused to take part in the mutiny, when freedom became certain in Nassau, they remained in the British island as free men, dispelling the view that nearly all slaves were content and preferred slavery to freedom.

In 1854, twelve slaves escaped by boat from Key West to Andros Island in the Bahama Islands. The group of men, women, and children traveled in a small, open boat, which they had stolen from the lighthouse keeper at Key West. A free Negro, familiar with the waters in and around the West Indies, piloted them to the Bahamas.

The means by which blacks resisted slavery varied greatly. On the simplest and most widespread level, slaves engaged in day-to-day resistance, manifested in breaking tools, feigning illness, doing shoddy work, stealing, and leaving plantations for a few days. More serious, as far as the masters were concerned, were arson, poisoning, and assaults on owners and overseers. Then, too there was permanent escape from slavery, usually to the North or Canada. Finally, there were slave conspiracies and rebellions.

Some scholars have added another category: religion. They insist that in a very real sense, religion could be an act of rebelliousness, an assertion of slave independence, which sometimes required outright defiance of the master's command. "The religious meetings in the quarters, groves, and 'hush harbors,'" Albert J. Raboteau argues, "were themselves frequently acts of rebellion against the proscriptions of the master." This view has not yet met with universal approval, but it has demonstrated that slave rebelliousness should not be thought of exclusively in terms of such acts as arson, sabotage, flight, and revolt.

One question has been raised with increasing frequency in recent years: Why were there far fewer and smaller slave revolts in the United States than in the Caribbean islands and in Latin America? Many historians have attributed the difference to a number of factors, the most important being the possibilities of success. The odds against a successful uprising in the United States were overwhelming. The smaller proportion of blacks in the total population in the United States, the relatively early ending of the African slave trade, and the large military force manned by the white population in defense of slavery made the prospects for rebellion bleak indeed.

In the most recent attempt to answer the question, Eugene D. Genovese agrees with this analysis and criticizes those who argue that slaves in the United States were simply more docile than those in Brazil, Jamaica, or Saint Domingue, which became the black republic of Haiti. It is arrogant, he notes, for historians to expect oppressed people to revolt when they were fully aware of the impossibility of victory and of the terrible consequences of defeat. He quotes a rebel slave recruit in Missouri as explaining: "I've seen Marse Newton and Marse John Ramsay shoot too often to believe they can't kill a nigger."

In developing his thesis, Genovese offers a tentative list of eight factors conducive to slave revolt "without regard for the presumed importance of one relative to another": (1) blacks greatly outnumbering whites; (2) relatively large slaveholding units; (3) suitable geographical terrain; (4) African-born slaves more numerous than New World-born ("creole") slaves; (5) absentee ownership; (6) conflict within the ruling class; (7) economic distress and famine, and (8) "the social structure of the slaveholding regime permitted the emergence of an autonomous black leadership." "The list," Genovese adds, "may be extended, refined, and subdivided."

A number of these factors have already been emphasized by historians in explaining the reason why the United States was less likely to experience large slave revolts than in other slave societies of the Western Hemisphere. Genovese, too, points out that in Jamaica, blacks outnumbered whites ten to one, while in the American South whites constituted a majority in every state except South Carolina and Mississippi. Even in these two states, blacks comprised less than 60 percent of the population. In addition, plantation units in the South were far smaller than those in the West Indies and Brazil. Southern slaves had little access to mountainous retreats, although they were able to get to the Great Dismal Swamp in eastern Virginia and North Carolina. Absentee ownership was far more common in the Caribbean islands than in most of the Southern states.

Though hardly as extensive as in other slave societies of the New World, slave rebellions in the United States were still the ultimate form of resistance. They also acted as a stimulus to day-to-day resistance. Among the letters that poured into Governor Floyd's office in September and October 1831 were reports of an unusual ''degree of impudence in the deportment of our slaves'' in the aftermath of the Southampton uprising. The conspiracies and revolts forced the issue of slavery into the arena of open debate and gave evidence to the country that the slaves did not accept the system. Viewed in perspective, slave revolts were anything but futile. In the short run, Vesey's plot and Turner's revolt may have failed, but they focused the nation's attention upon the status of blacks and thus helped spur the formation of the antislavery movement. They profoundly affected the subsequent development of the entire struggle against slavery.

In September 1851 *DeBow's Review*, the periodical published in the South, in the interest and enlightenment of slaveowners, carried an article by Dr. Samuel Cartwright, professor at the University of Lousiana, entitled ''Diseases and Peculiarities of the Negro Race.'' Cartwright announced that he had found the secret cause of slave resistance, to be two diseases ''peculiar to negroes.'' To one he gave the Latin name ''Dysaesthesia Aethopica . . . called ''Rascality' by overseers.'' This was the illness that caused slaves to steal, break machinery, and sabotage production in other ways. The second disease he named ''Drapetomania, or The Disease Causing negroes to Run Away.'' Cartwright derived his medical term from the Greek word meaning ''runaway slave'' and another meaning ''mad'' or ''crazy.'' The disease was unknown to our medical authorities, said Dr. Cartwright, but it was these diseases peculiar to the Negro, and not plantation conditions, that led slaves to resist by running away or other methods.

The subject of resistance is complex. Measuring slave discontent by the yardstick of militant rebellion is completely inadequate. There were relatively few outright rebellions—not because the slaves accepted their lot but because they realistically appraised the superiority of white America in arms, technology, and organization. But slave opposition went beyond the attempts at slave revolts and revealed an unceasing and varied conflict between slave and master. Resistance was possible on the plantation because slaves were part of an underground community and culture whose values sustained all forms of opposition and activity that might weaken and possibly undermine slavery. The slave system in the United States was able to absorb virtually all kinds of internal resistance, and the slaves' activities did not undermine Southern society, but they did enable blacks to survive and maintain their psychological and cultural independence from white society.

8

Free Blacks in the Antebellum South

In 1860, there were 4 million slaves and a little over 488,000 free Negroes in the United States. It is becoming increasingly clear to historians, however, that free black men and women were important far beyond their numbers. This is reflected in the increasing number of book-length studies published within the last two decades on free blacks.

In volume 1, I dealt with the free blacks from 1790 to 1820, a period during which the free Negro population increased from 59,446 to 233,504, the result of a combination of a natural increase from birth and a number of other factors, most important of which were the abolition of slavery in the North and the liberalization of manumission laws in the upper South. (Both were largely a product of the libertarian idealism of the American Revolution.) Among other factors influencing the growth of the free black population were flights from bondage, successful freedom suits, emancipation for military service, and self-purchase.

By 1820, several significant factors were already in evidence. Although almost twenty thousand slaves remained in the North and in the new states of the Northwest, various forms of long-term indentureships enacted to evade the anti-slavery provisions of the Northwest Ordinance, still flourished. The fate of slavery had been sealed and the number of free Negroes, augmented by natural increase and by fugitives from the South, continued to grow. In 1860, about a quarter of a million blacks, slightly less than half of the nation's free Negroes, lived in the North.

In the ensuing discussion of free blacks in the antebellum South, we shall deal with fifteen states and the District of Columbia. Delaware, Kentucky, Maryland, Missouri, North Carolina, Tennessee, Virginia, and the District of Columbia made up the upper South. Alabama, Arkansas, Florida, Georgia, Louisiana, Mississippi, South Carolina, and Texas constituted the lower South.

In the years between 1790 and 1810, the number of free blacks mushroomed in the South. Although the number in the upper South continued to grow, restrictions on manumissions and the tightening of procedures to limit runaways, adopted by frightened slaveholders, slowed the growth. Free Negroes in the upper South numbered 114,070 in 1820 and 224,963 in 1860.

In the lower South, the free black population increased from 20,153 in 1820 to 36,955 in 1860. Louisiana's free black community was the largest in the Deep South, outnumbering the combined free Negro population of Mississippi, Alabama, Georgia, and South Carolina by almost 3,000. In 1860, there were 18,647 free Negroes in Lousiana, 9,914 in South Carolina, 3,500 in Georgia, 2,690 in Alabama, and 773 in Mississippi, down from 1,366 in 1850.

The lower South had been barely touched by the rise in sentiment for manumission stimulated by the rhetoric of the American Revolution. If slaveowners there liberated any slaves, it was usually their own illicit progeny. The growth of the free black population was the product of a natural increase in an existing population, augmented by light-skinned refugees from black revolutions in the West Indies and by Creole residents of the Lousiana and Florida purchases.

Free blacks made up roughly 4 percent of the South's Negro population after the revolution and 8 percent by 1820. By 1860, the proportion had fallen to 6.2 percent, or 262,000 free persons. In contrast to the white and slave populations, there were many more free black women than men in the South. Most of the black women lived in the cities, where it appears that their close relations with whites more often led to manumission than was the case with black men.

RESTRICTIONS ON FREEDOM ROUTES

Manumission and freedom suits had been the primary routes to freedom for slaves of the South during the post-Revolutionary decades. By the mid-1830s, however, hostile judges had eliminated the earlier rules of freedom suits in which blacks born of free Negro women and illegally enslaved could obtain freedom. Thus, judges reversed the older policy of allowing hearsay evidence in freedom suits. By this time, too, most Southern states required slaveowners to get judicial or legislative permission to free their slaves and demanded that newly liberated bondsmen leave the state upon receiving their freedom. Those few states that still allowed slaveowners to emancipate their slaves also stipulated that manumitted blacks must either migrate or risk being forcibly deported or reenslaved. Legislators further discouraged emancipation by requiring masters to remove freed Negroes and by making those manumitted liable to seizure for unpaid debts even after emancipation. By the 1850s, all but three of the Southern states prohibited manumission altogether. The exceptions—Delaware, Missouri, and Arkansas—still allowed masters to liberate their slaves and permitted manumitted blacks to remain in the state.

States were not the only governing bodies to act in these matters. In 1840 local authorities in Raleigh, North Carolina, passed a law declaring free Negroes illegal immigrants and ordered them to leave unless they received exemption from the North Carolina legislature.

Actually, despite the restrictions, masters still continued to manumit individual slaves. Unfortunately many blacks thus freed were old and unable to support themselves. The truth is that masters found it profitable to unload elderly, enfeebled slaves. *Niles' Weekly Register* of January 16, 1830, noted "the unpleasant and oppressive fact that the aged and infirm and *wornout* negroes from all parts of the state are turned to Baltimore, to live if they can, or die, if they must." Thirty years later, the situation had not changed. "Old negroes like old horses are often turned loose to go where they wish," the *Richmond Daily Dispatch* acknowledged on May 29, 1858.

The decline in the free Negroes' rate of increase in the South made escaping to freedom in Southern cities more difficult for the slaves. When manumission was widespread, fugitives could easily find refuge in the cities where they were assimilated by the growing free Negro population. But by the 1830s, whites were able to identify most of the free blacks and more readily to capture slaves who tried to pass as free. Still, a few slaves continued to find a new life as free men in Southern cities. A few more gained their freedom as a reward for revealing conspiracies among their fellow bondsmen. South Carolina legislators freed the slaves who revealed Denmark Vesey's conspiracy of 1822, and in St. Charles Parish, Louisiana, the police jury agreed in 1829 to emancipate "Jenny and her son" because the slave mother had disclosed a plot "of the negroes against the whites."

SELF-PURCHASE IN THE ANTEBELLUM SOUTH

Some slaves were still able to purchase their freedom and even that of relatives and friends. Self-purchase was never easy, even under the best of conditions, and it became increasingly difficult as the antebellum period advanced. One reason was that ten Southern states prohibited slaves from hiring their own time, the principal way in which slaves could earn money. Had these laws been strictly enforced, there would have been no self-purchase movement. But self-hiring did continue, despite prohibitory laws, especially in the cities and particularly in the case of slaves who were skilled artisans.

The ways in which a slave obtained money for buying freedom varied widely; one of the most unusual methods was that used by George Moses Horton. He sold love lyrics to the students of the University of North Carolina for from twenty-five to fifty cents a poem. The poems were in the form of the acrostic— that is, a poem in which the initial letters of succeeding lines form a word or words. But Horton also wrote serious antislavery poetry, and in 1829 a volume of his poems, *The Hope of Liberty,* was published in Raleigh. The opening verses of one of the poems in the volume, "On Liberty and Slavery," went:

> Alas! and am I born for this,
>   To wear this slavish chain?
> Deprived of all created bliss,
>   Through hardship, toil and pain!

In a passionate outcry Horton appealed:

> Bid Slavery hide her haggard face
> And Barbarism fly;
> I scorn to see the sad disgrace
> In which enslaved I lie.

In 1845 Horton published his second book, *The Poetical Works of George M. Horton, The Colored Bard of North Carolina*. He had hoped that with the proceeds of his books he could purchase his freedom, but it was to take years before Horton gained his freedom, and it did not come through self-purchase. When the Northern troops occupied Raleigh in 1865, Horton escaped to their lines and became a freeman. In that same year his third work, *Naked Genius*, was published in Raleigh.

Some slaves earned money by performing arduous jobs after their regular work was done. Others, hired out by their masters (or hiring themselves out), were permitted to retain all money above a certain figure as an incentive for faithful performance of their duties. In all cases, hard work, persistence, energy, and determination were required. A study of cases of self-purchase reveals, first, that most of the slaves who were able to buy their freedom had some special skill or trade; and second, that the majority of them came from cities. In the countryside, there were few chances of earning the money necessary for slaves to buy their way out of bondage, even if their owner had granted permission. Skilled slaves in the cities were in a better position to earn money and thus purchase their family.

The actual act of self-purchase was effected either through direct negotiation between the slave and the master or through an intermediary, white or black. (Slaves were sometimes owned by several persons, so that the money paid by the bondsman in purchasing his freedom had to be divided among these various owners.) In some cases the sale was in cash; in others the transaction was on an installment basis. In attempting to negotiate directly for his freedom, the slave was dependent on his master's goodwill. The generally accepted legal theory held that a slave, being chattel property, was incapable of making a contract of any kind. Three states did, however, recognize in law the right of a slave to contract for his freedom—Delaware, Lousiana, and Tennessee. Theoretically, too, the slave had no right to accumulate property. Hence, the slaveowner might promise to let the slave buy his freedom but then, after getting the purchase money, sell him to someone else. In one case, a slave was resold three times after having each time paid the sum agreed upon as the purchase price. There are also cases of slaves who bought their freedom only to be reenslaved by the master's heirs or creditors.

In self-protection, a slave seeking self-purchase tried to have some third person buy and manumit him, using money furnished by the slave himself. This was much safer than direct negotiation, since the slave selected as his intermediary someone on whom he could rely. Often sympathetic white men served as intermediaries. Joseph Friedman, a Jewish merchant, agreed by prearrangement with slave Peter Still to purchase him for $500, after which Still would continue working in order to reimburse his new owner and purchase his own freedom. This was done. The slave gave his new master about $200 that he had saved and henceforth was permitted to work entirely for his own benefit. After paying the remaining $300, he was given a receipt, together with a handwritten certificate of freedom, and he left for Cincinnati.

More often a free Negro acted as intermediary. Jane Minor once bought a mother and five children for $1,500 and manumitted them on the same day. John Berry Meachum, a former slave, purchased his own freedom, bought his family, and over the years purchased twenty slaves, all of whom he encouraged to work out their freedom on easy terms.

The purchasing of the freedom of members of one's immediate family occurred frequently. In one week in March, 1834, Theodore D. Weld, the noted abolitionist, visited more than thirty Negro families in Cincinnati. He found that

some members of more than half these families were still in bondage, and the father, mother and children were struggling to lay up money to purchase their freedom. I found one man who had just finished paying for his wife and five children. Another man and wife had bought themselves some years ago, and have been working night and day to purchase their children; they had just redeemed the last and had paid for themselves and children 1,400 dollars! Another woman had recently paid the last installment of the purchase money for her husband. She had purchased him by taking in washing late at night after going out and performing as help at hard labor.

Of 2,500 blacks in Cincinnati at this time, 1,129 had been in slavery and of these, 476 had purchased their freedom at a total cost of $215,000. Some blacks devoted their entire lives to the purchasing and liberating of others, for during the 1840s and 1850s the amounts needed to purchase slaves rose enormously. Owners who permitted slaves to purchase their freedom usually stipulated that the blacks pay their market price. In the late antebellum years, a skilled slave could rarely hire himself out for more than $200 a year, out of which he had to pay his master and support himself. At the same time, slaves were selling for between $1,000 and $3,000. Little wonder that even skilled slaves found purchasing their freedom or that of a loved one a long, difficult task.

Increasingly blacks needed assistance to free their families. Some raised the required sums by public appeals and lecture tours throughout the North and West. Noah Davis, a shoemaker of Fredericksburg, Virginia, who had succeeded in buying himself, set out to liberate his wife and five children. He accomplished this not only by twelve years of hard labor at his craft but also by appearances before public gatherings in Philadelphia, New York, and Boston. Similarly,

Peter Still, having purchased his own liberty, bought the freedom of his wife and three children at a total cost of $5,500 through three years of hard work and with the aid of the proceeds of addresses delivered throughout New England, New York, and Pennsylvania. Lunsford Lane of North Carolina obtained his freedom and that of his wife and seven children at a cost of $3,500 through his own work and mass subscriptions obtained in Massachusetts and Ohio. In November 1855, the *Cleveland Leader* carried the following notice: "The Rev. George Brents, formerly a slave in Paducah, Ky., is the father of 7 children, and is now in the city seeking means to liberate his son, Anderson; Anderson's master has agreed to take $1,100. In other cities he's raised $260." A few months earlier the *Boston Commonwealth* notified its readers: "Edward Brown, a colored man of highly respectable appearance, is in this city, endeavoring to obtain money for the purchase of eight children who are now in slavery in Virginia." He had already purchased his wife and two of his children. For the eight remaining in slavery, $5,000 was being demanded, of which sum Brown had raised about $2,300. Bostonians were asked to contribute to the redemption fund and were assured by a number of distinguished whites that they had studied the documents and had no doubt about the "truth of his [Brown's] representations" that he was raising funds to purchase his children from slavery. As Martin Luther King, Jr., wrote in 1964:

"Help me buy my mother" or "Help me buy my child" brought the deep torture of black people's souls into stark focus for many whites for whom the horrors of slavery had been emotionally remote.

FEAR OF FREE BLACKS

In most parts of the South, the free Negro was hated and feared. By his very existence, a free Negro was a living reproach to the slave system, a system that could justify itself only on the premise that the Negro was incapable of freedom. Slaveowners believed that free blacks, by exerting an evil influence over their slaves, encouraged them to be unruly and to run away, even to revolt. "There is an identity of interest between the slave and the free person of color," a group of Charleston citizens declared, "whilst there is none between the latter class and the whites." This identity was sustained by many elements: "they are associated by color, connected marriages, and friendships. Many of the free Negroes have parents, brothers, sisters and children who are slaves." In case of any insurrection, they warned, "they would have every inducement to join it." "They are a plague and pest in the community," the *New Orleans Daily Picayune* declared, because they brought "the elements of mischief to the slave population." The *Daily Delta* in the same city argued that "the intercourse of free negroes with slaves is just as mischievous as letting loose abolitionists among them. . . . If they do not render the slave insubordinate, they make him vicious.'' A Norfolk County citizens' meeting on November 2, 1852, described free blacks as ''that bane of society'' and a ''serious evil'' of growing importance. Free Negroes, the participants said, caused ''great injury to our slaves, whose daily avocations bring them more or less under the degrading influence of this miserable species of our inhabitants.'' The citizens endorsed a resolution urging the legislature to ''adopt some speedy and salutary redress whereby we may get rid of our free Negro population.'' Similar meetings in other parts of the state resulted in similar resolutions, and a bill for the removal of all free blacks from the entire state was introduced into the Virginia legislature in Jaunary 1853. Although the bill did not become law, its introduction demonstrates the fear of free blacks in the state.

A St. Louis police report touched on another aspect of white objection to free blacks, declaring: ''It is the saucy and insolent air of the free negroes which is most dangerous to the slave population.'' Yet even if the free Negro was timid rather than ''saucy and insolent'' and remained totally aloof from any attempt to incite slaves or assist them to escape bondage, he would still be ''deemed subversive in the white mind.'' His very existence was enough to threaten the foundations on which slavery rested. The *Charleston Mercury* declared:

The presence of the free negro in the midst of our slaves, even if he should not attempt to sow broadcast the seeds of disaffection in the slave towards the master, will of itself, in spite of all our exertions to the contrary, engender, in the latter, a spirit of disquietude and impatience of control. Think you, that the slave as he looks up on the free negro, privileged to visit at pleasure our muster-fields and villages, to loiter and saunter about and beguile the six days appointed to labour, in fishing, hunting, and the like, will not crave to do likewise? Ah! indeed; the slave as he rests his eye upon the privileged gentry—these free negroes—who betake themselves when and where they please, becomes restless in performing his master's business—he wants to be a free man, and strut about ''as large as life.'' He curses in his heart the very thought that he has to go and come at his master's bidding, while another whose skin is as black as his, is permitted, as a free man, to spend his time, as though he was a descendant of the Anglo-Saxon race.

The Charleston editor greatly exaggerated the freedom enjoyed by the free blacks of his state, but the point he made was endorsed in a memorial of Charleston citizens. ''The superior condition of the free persons of color,'' they argued, ''excites discontent among our slaves, who continually have before their eyes, persons of the same color, many of whom they have known in slavery and with all of whom they associate on terms of equality.'' The slave saw these blacks ''freed from the control of the masters, working where they please, going whither they please, and spending money how they please.'' He thus became ''dissatisfied'' and ''pants after liberty.''

A Mississippi slaveowner argued that by merely enjoying ''rights which belong not to the slave,'' the free blacks exerted ''a most pernicious influence on the slave population wherever it can be felt.'' The *Jackson Semi-Weekly Mississippian* carried this point to its logical conclusion when it editorialized: ''A *free* negro is an anomaly—a violation of the unerring laws of nature—a stigma upon the wise and benevolent system of Southern labor—a contradiction of the Bible. The status of slavery is the only one for which the African is adapted, and a great wrong is done him when he is removed to a higher and more responsible sphere.'' The editorial was only one of many in the antebellum South that insisted that emancipation would be ''a positive curse'' to the slaves, ''depriving them of a guardianship essential to their happiness.''

The Sixth United States Census of 1840, the first federal census that attempted to enumerate mentally diseased and defective persons, appeared to confirm this argument. The census showed that the rate of ''insanity and idiocy'' among Negroes was eleven times higher in the North than in the South. The evidence of black madness in the slave states was only one in 1,558 compared to one in 162.4 in the free states. The ratio of insanity between Negroes and whites in the North was six to one, whereas it was three to five in the South. And the discrepancy appeared to widen with the geographical latitude. While one out of every 14 Negroes in Maine was a ''madman,'' only one out of 4,310 was so affected in Louisiana.

The slaveowners eagerly seized upon these figures as scientific confirmation of the theory that only bondage allowed blacks to lead a normal and useful life. John C. Calhoun spoke for them when he said: ''Here is proof of the necessity of slavery. The African is incapable of self-care and sinks into lunacy under the burden of freedom. It is a mercy to give him the guardianship and protection from mental death.'' In due time, Dr. Edward Jarvis, a Massachusetts physician and specialist in mental disorders, who had a passion for statistics (he later served as president of the American Statistical Association for thirty-one years), exposed the census figures as ''fallacious,'' charging that they included figures for mentally deranged blacks in hundreds of Northern towns that had no Negro inhabitants at all. Demands for correction of the census, including a petition from New York blacks, brought an official investigation by William A. Weaver, a southerner who had been superintendent of the 1840 census. To nobody's surprise, Weaver concluded that the errors had not been committed, and so the figures remained in the government books, cited again and again to justify slavery and the dangers of freedom for blacks. Thus, they appeared in the *Texas Almanac for 1858*, which then argued that they offered further proof that after a Negro had been ''civilized and Christianized in slavery and then freed, he invariably relapses more or less rapidly into ignorance and barbarism. Three generations as a free man found him, in his offspring, a confirmed barbarian.''

RESTRICTIONS ON FREE BLACKS

In all but one Southern state, the law presumed ''a negro *prima facie* a slave.'' In Louisiana alone, the presumption was that a person of color was not necessarily a slave, and it was the obligation of the whites to prove otherwise. In 1845, the Supreme Court of Louisiana declared: "It has been the settled doctrine here that persons of color are presumed to be free . . . and the burden of proof is on him who claims the colored person as a slave."

But everywhere else in the South, color created the presumption that a person was a slave, and the burden of proof of freedom, either by certificate of freedom or by other means, rested on the black. In most states, the free Negro had to register with a town clerk and give evidence of his nonservile status. (This requirement created a serious problem for many free blacks who had been manumitted by masters who had sent them out on their own without papers.) If the proof was satisfactory, the free black would receive certified identification papers showing the name, color, stature, and any distinguishing features or scars of the recipient. It had to be renewed every year if the free black lived in a city and every three years in rural areas. In either case, there was a fee to pay each time. Usually the fee was one dollar, but some states in the 1830s increased it to three dollars.

The certificate had to be carried at all times and could be inspected by any suspicious white. The free Negro who could not produce his registered paper faced the danger of being judged a fugitive and resold into bondage. If he failed to register, he could be fined and sold into servitude in default of payment. *Niles' Weekly Register* of September 8, 1821, noted that Baltimore newspapers frequently carried advertisements inserted by sheriffs in which blacks who claimed that they were free but had no certificate were being held in prison and if not soon claimed by an owner, would be sold for the fees, which went to the sheriff. "A *free* black," the article concluded, "may be imprisoned here, and sold for a term of years to pay the charges for keeping him confined, etc."

North Carolina required not only possession of a certificate but the wearing of a shoulder patch with the word *free* on it. In Washington, D.C., a free black was required to show the mayor not only proof of freedom but a certificate signed by at least three respectable white citizens stating that he was of good character. All persons lacking evidence of freedom were liable to arrest and imprisonment as runaway slaves.

If a white man in Mississippi employed a Negro who claimed to be free but who could not produce his certificate, the employer was subject to a fine of ten dollars. A captain or master of a steamboat or other river craft who employed an alleged free Negro who did not have the required certificate rendered himself liable to a $1,000 fine and, in addition, to a possible prison sentence of from six months to a year. This was based on the assumption that the Negro was a slave posing as a free black in order to escape to freedom.

Southern law also deprived free blacks of almost all rights associated with being white. Their right to move about freely was legally prohibited. In the courtroom, they could neither serve on juries nor give testimony against whites, though Negroes or mulattoes, slave or free, were competent witnesses in cases against free blacks. In some states, free blacks were denied a trial by jury. If convicted of a crime, they were liable to punishment more severe than that imposed on white men, and they could even be sold into slavery. They were prohibited from keeping guns and ammunition, burdened with special taxes, barred from certain trades, and deprived of the right to participate in politics. Their rights of assembly were also proscribed. In many parts of the South, evening activities were subject to a curfew, and meetings of benevolent societies and churches frequently required the presence of a respectable white person or were forbidden altogether. In Maryland a free Negro was allowed to have only one dog, and then only if he obtained an annual license from the justice of the peace, a requirement not imposed upon whites.

In addition to restrictions imposed by state legislatures, free blacks were subject to those imposed by city ordinances. These usually dealt with slaves and free blacks in a single section. An 1832 Baltimore ordinance dealing with Negro discipline read: "Such free negro or mulatto shall be subject to the same punishment, and be liable in every respect to the same treatment and penalty as slaves" and "be guilty of, and convicted of, any offense for which slaves are now punishable."

The corporation of the District of Columbia, which had been authorized by Congress in 1812 "to prescribe the terms and conditions upon which free Negroes and mulattoes and others who can show no visible means of support may reside in the city," proceeded, with congressional approval, to prohibit free blacks from having a dance, ball, or even a gathering of persons at their homes without first obtaining permission from the mayor or the justice of the peace. Violators were to be fined up to $10, and in the event of inability to pay, imprisoned for up to ninety days at labor. In 1821, again with congressional approval, the same corporation prohibited free blacks from playing cards, dice, or "any other game of an immoral tendency," imposing the same fine and punishment in the event of failure to pay as in the 1812 law. A ten o'clock curfew for free blacks, except for those with a pass from a justice of the peace or for those going to and from a house of worship, was put into force; free Negroes entering the district to reside had to post a bond of $500 "for his or her (and every member of his or her existing family) good and orderly conduct." Moreover, free Negroes were forbidden to obtain licenses for any economic activity except to huckster, or drive carts, hackney carriages, or wagons, and they were prohibited by special legislation from selling or bartering liquors, wine, ale, beer, cider, and any fermented liquors, and from keeping "any tavern . . . shop . . . refectory or eating house of any kind."

The impositions upon free blacks in the nation's capital reached their climax in an 1829 ordinance, also passed with congressional approval, which prohibited free Negroes from frequenting the capitol square. The penalty for violating the ordinance was a fine not to exceed twenty dollars or thirty days in the workhouse.

The courts in the nation's capital offered no protection to the black community when it challenged the restrictive legislation. In *Costin* v. *Washington*, decided in October 1821, the circuit court of Washington ruled that "the power given by the Congress to the Corporation, to prescribe the terms under condition upon which free negroes and mulattoes may reside in the City, is not repugnant to the Constitution.'' In other words, thirty-six years before the *Dred Scott* decision, blacks in the nation's capital had no rights that whites were bound to respect.

The erosion of the rights of free blacks is illustrated also in the actions of the constitutional conventions of Tennessee in 1834 and of North Carolina in 1835, both of which disfranchised the free Negro. North Carolina had granted the suffrage to free blacks who were taxpayers or fifty-acre freeholders, and Tennessee had also allowed property-holding free Negroes to vote. But by inserting the word *white* in the suffrage clause of the state constitutions, both disfranchised even wealthy free Negroes, while allowing all white men to vote.

With the changes in these two state constitutions, the free Negro could not vote anywhere in the South. Even in Delaware, which claimed to be the most advanced in its treatment of free blacks, the free Negro was deprived of the franchise and accorded only a limited number of civil rights, notably the right to hold, buy, and sell property. But not only was he robbed of the right to vote in Delaware; he was not even allowed to attend political rallies.

Life for free blacks in the South was indeed precarious. It is true that there was a difference between laws passed and executed, and, in fact, there are many instances of laws restricting the freedom of free blacks not being enforced. Nonetheless, the free Negro lived in constant fear that they might be enforced and that, in addition to police officials, white vigilante groups would crack down on him. At any time, any white person could demand proof of a free Negro's status, and even if his papers were in order, he was subject to humiliation and scorn. He lived with the constant danger that some unscrupulous white person would steal his registration certificate and sell him into slavery as a fugitive. Throughout the South, moreover, he faced the prospect of being sold into terms of servitude for unpaid fines and jail fees, and in Maryland and Delaware, free Negro criminals could be auctioned into long terms of virtual slavery.

In spite of all this, there was no black ghetto in the antebellum South, and free blacks usually could be found in almost every section of Southern cities, living closely to whites of every nationality. Nevertheless, by the time of the Civil War, segregation had extended to almost every corner of Southern life. Free Negroes were systematically excluded from accommodations and social activities throughout the South and were relegated to separate and usually second-class quarters in the public facilities to which they were admitted. Restaurants, saloons, and taverns were segregated by local custom and management policies. Hotels were off-limits to Negroes, but exceptions were made for the personal attendants of white guests. Free Negroes, no matter how wealthy, were segregated in hospitals, theaters, parks, railroad cars, and omnibuses. None of the libraries in the South admitted Negroes, nor did any of the local clubs, local chapters of national fraternal organizations, or any of the trade unions admit blacks to membership. Blacks and whites were physically separated in penitentiaries, and when Virginia eased the restriction, protests caused the state to solve the problem by leasing black convicts to canal and railroad companies by the year.

New Orleans free blacks had a social, economic, and legal position far superior to that of free Negroes in most other areas of the South. They attained unusual wealth and refinement and filled a wide range of occupations. The wealthy *gens* or *hommes de couleur libres,* as the French called them, went to great lengths to emulate higher-class white society. They had fine homes and carriages, imported their clothing, usually employed servants or owned domestic slaves, and sent their children to European schools.

Yet despite their wealth and education, the free people of color of New Orleans were segregated in public places. Theaters and public exhibitions were legally segregated by an ordinance adopted in June 1816 that forbade "any white persons to occupy any of the places set apart for the free people of color; and the latter are likewise forbidden to occupy any of those reserved for white persons." Actually the edict merely ratified a long-standing policy of management, for most exhibition halls and theaters had for many years segregated their customers, allocating rear sections or galleries, known as "nigger heavens," to their black patrons. When streetcars were introduced in New Orleans in 1820, those that did not exclude blacks altogether segregated them. A car carrying a yellow star was set aside for Negroes; in fact, the yellow star rapidly became the symbol of segregation in New Orleans. In keeping with this idea, the New Orleans City Council not only separated black and white convicts but also ordered blacks "to wear different clothes than do the whites."

Because of the fear of slave rebellions, free blacks were prevented by law from entertaining or visiting slaves. Late in 1822, South Carolina, thoroughly frightened by the Denmark Vesey conspiracy, passed a law forbidding free black seamen to leave their vessels while in port. Black cooks, stewards, mariners, and any other blacks on such vessels were "to be seized and confined to jail, until said vessel is ready to sail." At that time, either the seaman or his captain was required to pay the cost of the detention; should either fail to do so, "such free negroes or persons of color shall be deemed and taken as absolute slaves, and sold." During the years that followed, several other slave states passed similar laws, and Southern port towns from Charleston to New Orleans imprisoned free black seamen at their own expense until the ship took sail. This constituted a serious breach of federal law in the case of black citizens from the North and produced a storm of controversy until the Civil War. On several occasions, black subjects of Great Britain were detained, producing scandalous international incidents, with potentially serious repercussions.

ECONOMIC STATUS OF FREE BLACKS

Economically the free Negro in the South occupied both a difficult and a unique position. Free blacks who lived in the countryside earned their living working as farm hands and casual laborers. A small minority, however, became property owners. In rural Virginia, the value of free-Negro-owned land more than doubled between 1830 and 1860. But most free blacks in rural areas earned a meager living in subsistence farming or occasional labor. "By any standards, Delaware's rural free Negro population lived in abject poverty in 1860," James Ogden notes. "Free Negroes generally did not own land, and usually were dependent on their white neighbors for existence." In North Carolina, a few free blacks amassed considerable amounts of property, but the great majority owned no property.

In Louisiana, free Negroes were able to acquire wealth without much interference, and in 1860, the New Orleans free black population was worth an estimated $15 million, mostly in real estate. Aristide Mury inherited an entire city block on Canal and Old Levee streets from his French father. More remarkable was the case of Thorny Lafon, whose speculations enabled him to leave an estate worth almost $500,000.

Unlike white craftsmen, free Negroes in the cities were subject to special taxation and laws proscribing them from the most profitable occupations and enterprises. Free Negro mechanics had to pay high licensing fees to work in Charleston and Savannah, free Negro masons in Georgia had to have their work approved by whites, and free black butchers were barred from the city market in Memphis.

In the upper South urban free blacks worked as factory hands, teamsters, common laborers, washerwomen, and domestics. In Richmond, fully half of the adult free Negro men labored in tobacco factories, paper mills, and iron foundries in 1860. Approximately 20 percent worked as waiters, whitewashers, or stevedores or did a variety of menial jobs as day laborers.

The absence of white immigrant artisans in the South and the general shortage of workers in the cities forced Southern communities to depend on free black craftsmen. Despite repeated efforts of white workers to drive them out of trades, the needs of the community prevailed, and the free black was an indispensable part of the Southern skilled labor force, especially in the lower South. In Charleston, three-quarters of the free Negro men worked at skilled trades in 1860. Free black artisans, in fact, controlled a large share of the work in some prominent trades and dominated others. Fully a quarter of the city's carpenters, nearly 40 percent of the tailors, and 75 percent of the millwrights were free Negroes, although free blacks composed only 15 percent of the free male work force.

In both Richmond and Charleston, many important trades had no free Negro members. Had it not been for the considerable skill required in most of the trades in which they were prominent, free Negroes might not have been represented in those occupations either.

The situation in New Orleans was somewhat different. In 1860, only one-tenth of the free colored population of New Orleans was classified as common laborers. The free Negroes dominated such trades as carpentry, masonry, bricklaying, barbering, tailoring, cigarmaking, and shoemaking. Many were coopers, carmen, house painters, or clerks, and several became well-to-do home builders. The ratio of skilled to unskilled jobs among free Negroes was higher than that among Irish and German immigrants.

Throughout the South, free Negroes monopolized jobs in the service trades as caterers, stable owners, bathhouse keepers, coachmen, tailors, butchers, and barbers. After an occupation became black and was referred to as "nigger work," it was shunned by whites. Included in this category were jobs requiring hard and heavy labor, but there were also skilled occupations that required craftsmanship of the highest order and furnished steady work and good wages.

Although free blacks were able to occupy an important, if limited, place as skilled craftsmen in a number of Southern states, and, equally important, were able to train their sons to become skilled craftsmen, the majority of free black men were unskilled laborers—hod carriers, porters, and longshoremen—and the women worked at such menial, servile occupations as cooks, washerwomen, housekeepers, servants, and occasionally nurses and midwives.

Skilled free blacks did not receive wages comparable to those of whites doing the same work, and Negro common labor fared even worse. Poverty forced many to accept whatever pay was offered, to work two or three jobs to earn a living, and to send their wives and children out to work to make ends meet. Some free blacks in Baltimore hired themselves out for as little as ten cents a day, and they and many of their fellow free black workers would have agreed with *Niles' Weekly Register* when it declared on April 16, 1825, that "free blacks in Baltimore are less abundantly supplied with the necessaries and comforts of life than slaves."

For decades, white workingmen had sought to eliminate free black artisans and mechanics from the trades. But the general shortage of skilled workers and the increasing cost of white or slave workers gave the skilled free black a relatively secure place in the Southern economy, bringing with it steady work at fairly good wages. During the 1850s, the influx of Irish and German workers into the Southern cities changed this picture. These immigrants did not object to unskilled work, even that referred to derogatorily as "nigger work," and soon they began to displace the Negro. At the same time, in cities like Baltimore suffering a declining economy, native whites began to drive blacks from skilled and semiskilled jobs as well.

A case in point involved the black ship caulkers, men who practiced the skilled craft of sealing the seams of newly built wooden ships with hot tar in order to waterproof them. In Baltimore shipyards, free Negroes and some slaves had monopolized the caulking trade for years. But beginning in 1858, Irish and German immigrants began a concerted effort to drive the blacks out of the caulking trade. When petitions to legislative bodies failed to achieve this objective, the whites resorted to violence. Riots between black and white caulkers began to occur in the summer of 1858. To defend themselves and protect an occupation that had always belonged to them and was in danger of being taken away, the blacks formed the Association of Black Caulkers. Their white rivals then formed their own society of caulkers. We do not know much about the black association, but according to the Baltimore press, it set wages and insisted on black foremen. However, it went out of existence when a local court ordered both societies of caulkers to dissolve. The white society refused and even forced the owner of the leading shipyard to hire whites in place of blacks, conceding a few Negroes the right to work only after they obtained a permit from the president of the white society.

Blacks continued to constitute a majority of the caulkers in Baltimore, but they were often attacked and beaten by whites, and a number left the city in search of safer employment. On July 5, 1858, the *Baltimore Sun* reported: "So great is the fear excited in the minds of the colored caulkers by the frequent attacks made upon them that a number have deserted the city and sought labor in other seaboard cities."

The partial success of the campaign of white workers against black caulkers, produced by economic competition and exacerbated by racism, inspired white workers in other trades to drive out blacks. An examination of twenty-five leading Negro occupations in Baltimore in 1850 and 1860 reveals that there were losses in eighteen of them, four minor gains, and only two major gains (oystermen and brickmakers). In general, there was a total increase of 38.8 percent in Negro labor from 1850 to 1860. The increase in brickmaking can be explained by the large amount of construction taking place in Baltimore at the time.

EDUCATION FOR FREE BLACKS

Although African churches in several Southern states had educational programs for free blacks and even some white churches provided opportunities for them to learn to read and write, it became increasingly difficult for Negroes to do so. The opposition to African schools that had been building in the South since the turn of the century reached frenzied proportions after Denmark Vesey's conspiracy of 1821, especially after it was alleged that Vesey had learned to read and write at just such a school; it rose even higher after Nat Turner's rebellion ten years later. Laws prohibiting the instruction of blacks, free or slave, were passed by Southern states and cities. As a result, in a number of Southern states, African schools were unable to exist openly. In some cases, however, they did continue secretly. Indeed, had it not been for the African schools and the limited programs occasionally offered by white churches, black children in most parts of the upper South would have received no education at all. They were denied the opportunity to enter those public schools that existed, and even schools that accepted only fee-paying students refused to admit black children.

In the lower South, where African churches were not numerous and African schools consequently were few in number, schools for black children tended to be independent organizations supported by wealthy free blacks. The children of free people of color in New Orleans, excluded from the white private schools since early in the eighteenth century, were also denied admission to the new public school system that developed in the city in the 1840s. Without the assistance of an African church, the free Negroes instituted and supported a large number of private schools, most of them French-language academies, endowed by wealthy free Negro philanthropists. A number of black children in the Gulf port cities were sent abroad to finish their schooling.

Members of New Orleans' free Negro population were relatively well educated for the period. In 1850, close to 80 percent of New Orleans' 9,961 free Negroes were literate, and 1,008 of their children attended school. The literacy of the Crescent City's free Negro population rose to 90 percent in 1860. In Baltimore in 1850, on the other hand, only 40 percent of the 25,442 free Negroes were literate.

The situation in Maryland was much better than that in Virginia. The 1804–1805 session of the Virginia legislature, in codifying the laws dealing with slaves and free blacks, ended the practice of requiring some degree of education for black apprentices and stated, ''It shall not be lawful for the overseers of the poor who may hereafter bind out any black or mulatto orphan, to require the master or mistress to teach such orphan reading, writing, or arithmetic.'' Other restrictions followed, such as the law of 1831 labeling as ''an unlawful assembly'' any meeting of free Negroes for the purpose of ''teaching them reading or writing.'' In 1838, the Virginia legislature provided that any free black, ''whether infant or adult,'' who went outside the state for the purpose of gaining an education could not return. If ''infants'' returned, they would be bound out as apprentices until they reached the age of twenty-one; if adults, they would be shipped out of the state.

The criminal code of 1848 restated the prohibition against slaves or free blacks assembling with any white person for the purpose of learning to read or write. Any white engaged in teaching blacks would suffer a maximum of six months in jail and a fine not to exceed $100. The criminal code of 1860 repeated these prohibitions and penalties.

In 1847, the Missouri General Assembly made educating blacks in the state illegal. ''No person,'' the act read, ''shall keep any school for the instruction of negroes or mulattoes, reading or writing, in this state.'' Persons indicted and convicted under the law were required to pay a fine or face a maximum of six months in jail, or both. But in Missouri, blacks continued to teach free Negroes in defiance of the law, with some help from whites. Reverend John Berry Meachum, a skilled former slave who had purchased his freedom from his Virginia master and settled in Missouri in 1815, continued to conduct his school for free blacks with white teachers in the basement of the African Baptist Church. When the church school was closed by law enforcement authorities, Meachum transferred it to a steamboat, which he built, on the Mississippi. The black students traveled from the riverbank to the boat in skiffs, and no one interfered with them since the river was not within state jurisdiction. Reverend Meachum's ''School for Freedom,'' as it came to be known, taught hundreds of blacks in defiance of the 1847 law, and teachers came from the East to St. Louis to assist with its work. Nevertheless, although blacks paid a school tax in St. Louis, their money was used solely for the education of white children. No public school was open to blacks in antebellum Missouri.

When Reverend Meachum's school in the basement of the church was closed, a white teacher from England was arrested and accused of causing trouble by teaching blacks reading, writing, and "figuring." Lawyers hired by Meachum were able to free the teacher, and he was never prosecuted.

PERSECUTION OF MARGARET DOUGLASS

Margaret Douglass, a poor white seamstress in Norfolk, Virginia, was not so fortunate. Mrs. Douglass, a widow, and her daughter, Rosa, worshipped, along with many of the city leaders, at Christ Episcopal Church, which had a Sunday school in its assembly room where black children received instruction in Christian principles. The church also provided lessons in reading, gave the children primers or spelling books, and encouraged them to study during the week. The teachers in this Sunday school were the wives and daughters of Norfolk's leading citizens, and Mrs. Douglass assumed that free black children could legally attend classes in reading.

One day, Mrs. Douglass met James Robinson, a free black barber, whose boys attended the Christ Episcopal's Sunday school and who, though himself illiterate, was desirous of furnishing an education on a regular basis to his two sons and three daughters, something they could not obtain once a week at the white church's Sunday school. Mrs. Douglass volunteered the services of her daughter, Rosa, as a teacher and told the barber to send his children to her home. Before agreeing to have her daughter instruct the Robinson children, Mrs. Douglass made sure that all members of the family were free, "as I knew that the laws of the Southern states did not permit the slaves to be educated."

For a month, the Robinson children studied with Rosa and made excellent progress. Mother and daughter then decided to open a school for free blacks, and on June 1, 1852, the school, with tuition set at three dollars per quarter, opened. Through the Robinson family, the Douglasses made contact with other free blacks of Norfolk and invited them to send their children to the school. Immediately the Douglasses received more applicants than they could handle, since Robinson was scarcely alone in his desire for literacy for his children.

The school opened with an enrollment of twenty-five boys and girls. Early in the morning of May 9, 1853, eleven months later, Constable James Cherry, a police officer, arrived at the front door. He had come, he told Mrs. Douglass, at the mayor's order. Together they went up the stairs to the schoolroom, where the pupils were gathered around their teacher. Mrs. Douglass wrote later:

Never will I forget the frightened state of those children, and the countenance of their young teacher. My daughter sat paralyzed, covering her face with her hands, and it was some time before I could restore order in the room. Some were crying, some exclaiming "Oh my! oh my!" and some clinging around me in their terror.

The constable had orders to take the children to the mayor's office, and to do this he called another policeman who had been stationed at the back door. The two police officers wrote down the names of the children and of their parents, while Mrs. Douglass protested that they were all free black children, born of free parents, and that nearly all of them attended Christ Sunday school. "It makes no difference, madam," Constable Cherry replied, "it is a violation of the law to teach any person of color to read or write, slave or free, and an act punishable by imprisonment in the penitentiary." Mrs. Douglass answered: "Very well . . . if they send me to the penitentiary, it will be in a good cause, and not a disgraceful one."

All set off for the mayor's office, with the children walking two by two, one officer in front and one behind, "each with a great club in his hands." At city hall, Mayor Simon S. Stubbs paid no attention to Mrs. Douglass' statement that she had not known that it was against the law to teach free black children and that her pupils all attended Christ Church Sunday school. Instead he read from the statutes of Virginia the law forbidding instruction of people of color, slave or free, and providing a maximum penalty of a hundred dollars' fine and a six months' prison term. Her case was to be brought to the grand jury for presentment to the city's circuit court.

In July 1853, Mrs. Douglass received a summons to appear at the November term of the Norfolk Circuit Court to answer the charge made by the grand jury that she and Rosa "did . . . unlawfully assemble with diverse negroes, for the purpose of instructing them to read and to write, contrary to the Act of the General Assembly . . . and against the peace and dignity of the Commonwealth of Virginia." Lacking money to pay a lawyer, Mrs. Douglass resolved to plead her own case. In her defense, she called as witnesses three members of the Christ Church, all influential citizens. When one of the witnesses, a lawyer who was also president of the Exchange Bank, said of Christ Church's Sunday school that "he did not know that the law prohibited religious and moral instruction to negroes," Mrs. Douglass retorted: "If you, sir, who are engaged in the practice of law, did not know it, how could it be expected that I should." She was able to prove that she had been doing in her school what had been done for years in another Norfolk school and that if she was guilty of violating the law, she had "abundant precedents among the aristocracy of the city."

In her address to the jury, Mrs. Douglass refused to plead guilty. On the contrary, she took pride in her work. She did not go as far as to condemn slavery, but she dared to attack the Southern treatment of blacks in general and free blacks in particular. She asked the jury to remember her ignorance of the law, her good intentions, and "the abundant examples set before me by your most worthy and pious citizens." Surely they must see, she said, that she had no designs against "the peace and dignity of your Commonwealth." If she went to prison, she would go secure in the knowledge of her innocence. She had disobeyed none of

God's laws but only "one of the most inhuman and unjust laws that ever disgraced the statute book of a civilized community."

On the third day of its deliberations, the jury found Mrs. Douglass guilty but set the fine at one dollar and recommended that the judge not send her to prison. Judge Baker, however, ignored the recommendation. In his lengthy opinion, he ignored the fact that Mrs. Douglass had never engaged in the instruction of slaves and discussed at length the "great blessings" that Christianity had brought to the slave population of the South. Then he argued that Mrs. Douglass' "pertinacity and zeal . . . in behalf of the negroes" indicated that her action was "the settled and deliberate purpose of her mind, regardless of consequences, however dangerous to the peace." Therefore, as an example to all others and "in vindication of the policy and justness of our laws," he sentenced Mrs. Douglass to a month in jail.

Mrs. Douglass served the entire month. In February 1854, she collected her few possessions and moved with Rosa to Philadelphia, where she might live "happy in the consciousness that it is here no crime to teach a poor little child, of any color, to read the word of God."

Myrtilla Miner, another white woman, was more successful than Mrs. Douglass in providing education for free blacks—in this case, Negro girls in Washington, D.C. The public school system had been established in the district December 5, 1804, but from its inception, it was maintained for white children only. No provisions were made for the public education of black children, even though Negroes paid taxes for the maintenance of the schools. Schooling for them was furnished by the black churches' Sabbath schools and by private schools, usually organized by blacks themselves. One of these was the Union Seminary, with John F. Cook, a former slave, as headmaster, which in 1835 included a male and female department. The first seminary for colored girls in the district was established in 1837 and was administered by Maria Becraft, a black woman who had been educated in the district's private schools.

In 1851, Myrtilla Miner founded a school for colored girls in the district, with herself and an assistant as the teachers. The mayor condemned the seminary for raising the expectations of blacks beyond their possibilities in the society, and white street boys tormented the students. But when Miner's enemies invaded her schoolroom, threatening her with violence, they failed to intimidate her. According to a report of the United States Commission of Education, published later, she "laughed them to shame; and when they threatened to burn her [school] house, she told them they could not stop her in that way, as another house, better than the old, would immediately rise from its ashes." In 1860, the school was set on fire but was saved from total destruction.

Years later, Frederick Douglass paid tribute to Myrtilla Miner. He recalled that when Miner came to him in Rochester, stopping at the office of his paper *The North Star* to inform him

that she was then on her way to the city of Washington to establish a school for the Education of colored girls . . . I was amazed and looked to see if the lady was in earnest and meant what she said. . . . My feelings were those of mingled joy and sadness. Here I thought is another enterprise—wild, dangerous, desperate and impracticable, and destined only to bring failure and suffering. Yet I was deeply moved with admiration by the heroic purpose of the delicate and fragile person who stood . . . before me. . . . She advocated the feasibility of her enterprise and I (timid and faithless) opposed it in all earnestness. She said she knew the South. She had lived among Slaveholders. She had even taught slaves to read in Mississippi and she was not afraid of violence in the District of Columbia. To me the proposition was reckless almost to the point of madness. . . . The fate of Prudence Crandall in Connecticut and the then recent case of Mrs. Douglass at Norfolk was before me, and my own experience in attempting to teach a Sunday School in St. Michaels' came before me. Her resolution was taken and was not to be changed nor shaken, and the result I need not say has justified her determination.

The ''result'' was that in spite of constant attacks, the school grew, and in 1871 was joined with Howard University. In 1879, as the Miner Normal School (now Miner Teachers' College) it became part of the public school system of the District of Columbia.

BLACK CHURCHES

Despite efforts to reduce them to the level of the slaves, free blacks managed to survive and grow in numbers. They married, had children, enjoyed something of a normal family life, owned property, had the right to their earnings, and even enjoyed a measure of independence. Locked out of virtually every aspect of Southern society and fully segregated where they were permitted entry, free blacks created their own communities in which they established their own churches, benevolent societies, fraternal groups, literary organizations, schools, and business enterprises. The increasing number of free Negroes in the cities provided a small but growing market for black entrepreneurs. Most of these black enterprises were small cookshops and groceries, which usually doubled as saloons and gambling houses where free Negroes, slaves, and sometimes even whites gathered.

The most important institution in the Southern free black community, and the one that gave the free Negro the most relief from his often hostile environment, was the African church. Racial practices in the white churches eventually led blacks to form separate churches (see volume 1). It took some time, however, for the African church to grow in the South. When white Southerners learned that Nat Turner had been a preacher, they developed an almost irrational fear of independent black religious practices, which in turn resulted in a series of laws prohibiting them. The Virginia state legislature in 1832 provided ''that no slave, free negro or mulatto shall preach, or hold any meeting for religious purposes either day or night.'' Black persons disobeying this law could be punished by receiving not more than thirty-nine lashes. Further:

Slaves and free negroes who attend any religious meeting conducted by any slave or free negro preacher, ordained or otherwise, and slaves who attend any preaching at night, although conducted by a white minister, without the permission of the master, shall also be punished by stripes and may for that person be apprehended by any person without any written or other precept.

In the rural areas of the South, whites continued to view independent black churches with intense suspicion, and planters refused to permit the establishment of African churches. In the cities, too, forebodings about blacks coming together in their churches and "hatching plots against their masters" led some town authorities to close black churches. But white urban ministers of many denominations combatted such efforts, and at times, white churchmen circumvented city restrictions by placing black churches under their nominal sponsorship. The First African Church, Baptist, was founded in Richmond in 1842, and to avoid violations, the congregation held meetings only in the daytime in the presence of whites. Thirty black leaders, "men of discretion," held monthly meetings to conduct the church's affairs, with the white preacher in attendance.

By the 1840s, black Baptist congregations had begun to show real strength in Southern cities, with sizable memberships in all-black congregations in Baltimore, Mobile, Louisville, Lexington, Manchester, Norfolk, Petersburg, Augusta, Charleston, and Beaufort. Many of these churches had large rural memberships, which came to worship in the city. A few, particularly those in Virginia cities, had large numbers of free black members, but most were heavily slave dominated. Many congregations owned their own buildings, and most of them paid for their own preachers. Since thousands of black Baptists needed ministers to perform sacraments, white Baptists kept ordaining and licensing black preachers even when laws decreed otherwise.

By 1844, Methodist membership among Southern blacks totaled 92,000, and the African Methodist Episcopal church was well established in a number of cities of the upper South. There were, however, only a few black Presbyterians, Episcopalians, and Catholics. While the Roman Catholic church went further than any other denomination in permitting interracial contact during religious services, it failed to attract many blacks. When given a choice, blacks almost always chose to join the popular churches—the Methodists and Baptists. There were few opportunities for black Presbyterians, Episcopalians, or Catholics, which required a trained, educated clergy, to hold positions of responsibility in their churches, whereas in the Methodist and Baptist churches, lay preaching was common. Despite legislation designed to prevent it, free blacks were ordained as full Methodist and Baptist preachers in the South.

The number of African churches increased rapidly during the 1840s and 1850s. In 1860, Baltimore had fifteen African churches representing five different denominations, while Louisville had nine African churches, Savannah, five, Nashville, St. Louis, and Norfolk, four each, Memphis and Mobile, two each, and Raleigh, one. As these statistics indicate, there were few African churches in the lower South, where it appears that wealthier free blacks were able to enter white churches and therefore were less inclined to form their own religious institutions.

Wherever they were established, African churches quickly became the center of nearly all activities that concerned the free Negroes. Throughout the South, the African church was a center for education, a provider of social insurance through mutual aid activity, and a place where blacks might escape, if even temporarily, from the rigors of "rampant racism." The church strengthened family life by urging blacks to solemnize their marriages in religious services. Since many free blacks were married and buried in the same church, the religious institution also strengthened the ties that bound the black community together. African churches supported schools and fraternal associations, church choruses presented concerts, and church auxiliaries sponsored fairs, picnics, and banquets. "Not surprisingly," Ira Berlin observes, "ministers became the most important element in the black leadership class. More than this, the church gave free Negro communities a sense of unity and common purpose. It bred a sense of group identity and solidarity, which in turn fostered pride and self-respect and nurtured the belief that free Negroes could control their own destiny."

African churches in the South often taught reading and writing. While not all had Sunday schools—none of the four black churches in Norfolk did—most did and also supported day schools, where black children attended classes free or at a minimal charge. Many of the African churches established during the 1840s and 1850s included schoolrooms as part of their buildings, and, in addition to the usual Sabbath and primary schools, a few of the African Methodist and African Baptist churches sponsored secondary schools. Although they were often required to function secretly because of legislative restrictions, the African schools, assisted by their parent churches, emerged as among the most important institutions in the free black community.

BLACK SOCIAL, FRATERNAL, AND BENEVOLENT ORGANIZATIONS

Free Negroes in the South established a wide variety of social, fraternal, and benevolent organizations. Neither the local private clubs nor the local chapters of national fraternal organizations admitted Negroes to membership, so free blacks in the South who sought club membership and were able to pay for the privilege early formed large numbers of lodges and benevolent societies of their own. The Brown Fellowship Society, established in 1790 by wealthy, light-skinned, free Negroes in Charleston, became a symbol of mulatto exclusiveness. It was an elite benevolent association, open only to free-born men. Other free Negroes in Charleston formed their own fraternal societies. A group of successful free blacks in that city, after being barred from the exclusive Brown Fellowship

Society, organized the Humane Brotherhood and limited its membership to "Free Dark Men."

The black fraternal associations purchased burial plots and headstones; furnished weekly "sick dues" to disabled members and provided them with an income while they could not work; and furnished pensions for the elderly and for the widows and children of deceased members. Some of the associations established schools for orphan children or apprenticed the children of deceased members to successful free black tradesmen. Although most of the benevolent societies were for black men, as early as 1828, the Colored Female Roman Catholic Beneficial Society was organized in Washington, D.C. It specifically stated in its rules that membership was restricted to free colored women and the descendants of free colored men. Members were chosen by ballot; a fifty-cent entrance fee was required for membership, and monthly dues of twelve and one half cents were paid. Benefits of one dollar per week for up to six months were provided, and members with eighteen months' membership in the society were entitled to free burial. It is interesting to note that the organization was Roman Catholic, for while black Catholics had almost no opportunities for leadership, black women did play important roles within the Catholic structure in taking care of orphans and providing schooling for blacks.

In addition to insuring members against disaster, providing companionship for the disabled, and furnishing pensions and annuities to elderly members or their survivors, black fraternal societies also sponsored protective measures to guard free blacks against the ever-present danger of kidnapping. Baltimore had two such societies to guard against this practice. The Baltimore Society for Relief in Case of Seizure was organized by blacks, and the Baltimore Society for the Protection of Free People of Colour was formed by sympathetic whites, most of them antislavery, who, however, assured the slaveowners that "whatever may be their individual sentiments in relation to the policy or justice of slavery, it is *not* among the objects contemplated for this organization, to promote the abolition of legal slavery or to interfere with the legal rights which are exercised over slaves." But, they went on,

it is a matter of public notoriety, that a shameful traffic is carried on, in the person of many of these unhappy people, who, possessing a right to freedom and the precious enjoyment of liberty, are deprived of these inestimable privileges and entrapped into a state of slavery by theft, fraudulent purchase, and variety of other treacherous artifices.

The society met regularly for the purpose of devising "some method of preventing the numerous instances of kidnapping of free blacks which are constantly occurring in the vicinity of this city and other parts of the country."

Since few of the benevolent societies applied for state charters, most of them met clandestinely. Although it is difficult to determine how many such societies existed in the antebellum South, in 1838, Baltimore had at least forty benevolent societies ranging from workingmen's and literary associations to temperance and religious societies. Many free blacks belonged to more than one organization.

The emergence and proliferation of secret societies aroused great alarm in the South. One white citizen of Norfolk believed that secret societies were the real cause of trouble with blacks. He posed a series of questions:

Who supported these secret societies that are banded together as associations for ''Nursing the sick and burying the dead?'' . . . Is it known to you that these members of these societies . . . have secret signs and passwords? Is this lawful? Is it not contrary to the spirit, if not the letter of the statute? Is it not to the last degree imprudent to permit these large assemblages of men and women? With or without signs and passwords! When is it to end? Look to it, if you would avoid a bloody issue.

The *Norfolk American Beacon* took up the alarm and insisted that the black societies should be investigated, and, if allowed to continue, ''they should be compelled to have a white person or persons among their managers.'' ''It is time,'' the paper concluded, ''that the South should take some action. Forbearance has ceased to be a virtue.'' The *Richmond Enquirer* joined the attack on the black societies, and the Richmond police arrested several ''Union Travellers'' for meeting illegally, but nothing further was done about it.

A small elite of wealthy free blacks tended to remain aloof from the rest of their people. Most, however, mingled in churches and fraternal and benevolent societies without regard to differences based on income, education, religion, occupation, or complexion, and often without distinction between freemen and bondsmen. In fact, it was among the slaves that many free Negroes felt most at home. It was not at all unusual for slaves and free blacks to join together in matrimony. Slaveowners often frowned on these marriages, fearing that free blacks would help their slave spouses to escape, and, if the free black was a woman, deprive them of the services of the children, since the status of the mother determined that of the offspring. These objections, however, did not prevent such marriages from taking place.

Free blacks also helped slaves to freedom with forged passes, loans of money, and even by purchasing and liberating them. For their part, slaves showed their appreciation by feeding and clothing their free black companions from the masters' kitchens and supply centers. Slave millers were accused of feeding free Negroes in the neighborhood with supplies of flour, and a group of Virginia slaveholders declared: ''these slave millers are a sort of communication between our slaves and the free persons of colour, by which we believe much injuries done to our best interests.''

There were limits, however, to the degree to which free blacks were prepared to aid the bondsmen. Although they did help slaves escape and there are the cases like those of Denmark Vesey, a free Negro, the six free blacks in the Nat Turner revolt, and the free black post riders who carried messages for Gabriel Prosser to slaves in outlying parts of Virginia, these examples of free blacks involved in slave rebellions are few. As a result of their uncertain status in society, free blacks in the South seem to have been extremely cautious. In 1853, when Richmond blacks petitioned the mayor for the right to establish a Baptist African church, they promised to abide by any restrictions imposed by the city government, such as prior approval of teachers or preachers by the mayor and clearance with him of night meetings or "assemblages for Baptizing." Like all other free blacks in the South, they felt they had to be careful if they were to protect the few rights they had.

DETERIORATION OF THE STATUS OF FREE BLACKS

The decade of the 1850s witnessed a deterioration of the rights of free blacks. In Louisiana, where until the 1850s there had been few legal restrictions other than denial of suffrage and of the benefits of the free school law, the legislature now prohibited nonresident free Negroes from entering the state, made it mandatory for any slave freed in the state to leave it, and effectively closed the door to manumission. In the same period, most of the free Negroes' schools were closed, and the state legislature prohibited the incorporation of any new religious, charitable, scientific, or literary societies composed of free blacks. Free Negroes were forbidden to operate coffee houses, billiard halls, or liquor stores or to work as riverboat captains. Finally, in 1859, the legislature decided to encourage "free people of African descent to select their masters and become slaves for life."

The parishes and cities added their own restrictions. New Orleans prohibited free blacks from shooting off firecrackers, playing cards or dominoes, or holding dances with slaves. Further, the city prohibited any assembly of Negroes, slave or free.

The fact that free Negroes continued to enjoy many of the legal guarantees and privileges of whites made it difficult to enforce the laws. Free Negroes were tried in the same courts and under the same formalities as whites, and Louisiana was unique in the South in that free Negroes were accorded the right of habeas corpus. Further, their testimony was valid in cases against whites, and like the latter, the testimony of slaves was inadmissible against them (except in cases of insurrection). The Louisiana Supreme Court declared in 1850 that free Negroes were "such persons as courts and juries would not hesitate to believe under oath and moreover are entitled to the protection of our laws." Six years later, the same court affirmed that "in the eyes of Louisiana law, there is all the difference between a free man of color and a slave, that there is between a white man and a slave." Nevertheless, repressive laws had a serious psychological impact, which was exacerbated by the vicious attacks against free Negroes in the press and by the nightly rides of vigilante groups seeking out "uppity" free Negroes for punishment. All these had a harmful effect on New Orleans' free Negro population, and they were afforded only partial relief by the insulation provided by the free black community. As a result, emigration from Louisiana got underway. The free Negro population in the city of 11,906 in 1830 rose to a peak of 19,226 in 1840, but the growing hostility to free Negroes in the ensuing years caused the population to drop abruptly to about 10,000 in 1850, where it remained until 1860.

The principal destinations of those leaving Louisiana were France, Haiti, and the northern United States, with a handful going to Liberia, Mexico, or California. Many of these who left were the leaders of the free black community. Artists and intellectuals like Victor Sejour, Edmund Dedé, Eugene Marberg, Richard Lambert, Nelson Debroses, Joseph Rousseau, Pierre Dalcour, and Camille Thierry found life in Europe more tolerable than in Louisiana, then in the throes of a rising anti-free-Negro movement.

So too did Norbert Rillieux, son of a Frenchman by a New Orleans quadroon, whose invention transformed the sugar-making industry by hastening the process of sugar refining. Rillieux's father, an engineer, sent Norbert to school in Paris where he became an instructor at L'Ecole Centrale. When French manufacturers rejected his vacuum pan for evaporating syrup in the manufacture of sugar, he returned to New Orleans. During the decade 1845–1855, his machinery was widely installed, but, finding life in New Orleans at this time more and more difficult for men of color, he returned to France. In his later years he had the satisfaction of seeing his machinery installed in about 150 factories in Europe. Rillieux's evaporation device forms the basis of the modern sugar-refining industry and also is the process used for making glue, gelatin, soap, and condensed milk. A plaque in the Louisiana State Museum in New Orleans honors Rillieux. Its inscription reads:

> To honor and commemorate
>   Norbert Rillieux
> born at New Orleans, La.,
>   March 18, 1806
> and died at Paris, France,
>   October 9, 1894.
> Inventor of Multiple Evaporation
>   and its Application
> into the Sugar Industry. This
> tablet was dedicated in 1934 by
> Corporations representing the Sugar Industry
>   all over the World.

Not a word in the plaque mentions why Rillieux went into exile.

Florida also experienced an exodus of part of its free Negro population in the face of an intensification of restrictions on them. When the United States acquired the Floridas from Spain, it had to treat the free Negroes with special consideration in recognition of the fact that under Spanish law, they had enjoyed a measure of equality with whites. Unlike other Florida free Negroes, those who had resided in the state before 1821 were allowed to carry firearms and occasionally to sit on juries with whites. As late as 1847, the Florida legislature exempted these free Negroes from the requirement that every free black had to choose and establish a white person as legal guardian to supervise his or her affairs.

In 1856, the Florida legislature removed the exemption excluding the free Negroes who had resided in the state before 1821 and penalized all free blacks who had not established guardianship by imposing a fine of $10 or more and subjecting them to a jail sentence and court costs if the fine was not paid. The act also prohibited any white person from trading with any free Negro without the consent of the black's guardian, who had to be a white person of "good reputation." The penalty for failure to comply with this clause was a fine of from $100 to $500.

Several months later, the *Pensacola Gazette* carried a story about a group of free Negroes, known as Creoles because they had lived under the Spanish, who had gone into voluntary exile to Tampico, Mexico. It continued:

On Tuesday last, thirty-five colored persons took their departure from this city for Tampico, and in a few days the balance who are still remaining will also leave for the same place. It was a painful sight to see them parting from friends and their native country to seek homes in a foreign land. They take with them the sympathy of all our citizens on account of the causes which have lead them to leave us, and also our best wishes for their future happiness and prosperity in their new home.

The "causes" that led to the departure of the Pensacola free blacks did not leave with them. In 1858, the Florida General Assembly "permitted" free Negroes within the state to select their own masters and become slaves. The act also stipulated that "upon the complaint of any white person against a free Negro who appeared to be idle or to have any dissolute habits," the free black was to be arrested and kept in the county jail until the judge heard his case. If the Negro was judged guilty, he was to be sold at public auction to the highest bidder.

In Texas, too, the state legislature took steps to restrict further the rights of free blacks. In 1857, the legislature revised the penalties for criminal acts committed by free Negroes. Instead of prison terms as theretofore, capital offenses for slaves were to be capital offenses for free Negroes, punishable by death. Other crimes were to be punished with lashes or with labor on public works for not more than twelve months. In 1860, the last legislature of Texas to meet before its secession from the Union passed a law barring whites from participating in card games or other types of gambling with either slaves or free Negroes.

That same year, a group of free Negroes from Arkansas reached Ohio. In a pitiful appeal, they informed the citizens of the state that they had left their homes because of the enactment of a law by the Arkansas legislature requiring them either to depart or remain in an enslaved condition:

Today we are exiles, driven from the homes of our childhood, the scenes of our youth, and the burial-places of our friends. We are exiles; not that our hands have been stained with guilt or our lives accused of crime. Our fault, in a land of Bibles and Churches, of baptisms and prayers, is, that in our veins flows the blood of an outcast race; a race oppressed by power and proscribed by prejudice; a race cradled in wrong and nurtured in oppression.

In the very depths of winter we have left a genial climate of sunny skies, to be homeless strangers in the regions of the icy North. Some of the exiles have left children who were very dear; but to stay with them was to involve ourselves in a lifetime of slavery. Some left dear companions, they were enslaved, and we had no other alternative than slavery or exile. We were weak; our oppressors are strong. We were feeble, scattered, helpless; they, being powerful, placed before us slavery or banishment. We chose the latter. Poverty, trials and all the cares incident to a life of freedom are better, far better than slavery.

In the end, the free Negro's position in the Southern economy—the fear on the part of the Southern whites that they would lose an important part of their labor force as hundreds of free blacks headed north or left for Africa, Canada, and Latin America—along with the intimate relations that existed between light-skinned free Negroes and whites in a number of states, especially in the lower South—caused the Southern whites to draw back from forcing free Negroes to choose between leaving the South and being sold into slavery. But the fact that Southern states did attempt to expel all free Negroes from their borders and to force those who stayed behind to be sold into slavery indicated the precarious position of the free black in the South. Although Ira Berlin has made a distinction between the upper and lower South in their treatment of free blacks, he himself has pointed out that by the beginning of the nineteenth century, the "legal foundation of white control" was in place and that, as the century advanced, laws affecting free blacks became uniform throughout the entire South. "By 1860, despite regional variations in racial ideology," he acknowledges, "the free Negro's legal status was strikingly similar in every Southern state."

9

Free Blacks in the Antebellum North I

July 4, 1827, was a truly memorable day in the history of New York. In addition to the grand celebration held in commemoration of the nation's independence, it also marked the day when all men and women still held as slaves in the state were to be free. "No more shall the accursed name of slave be attached to us," rejoiced William Hamilton, leader of New York City's black community, as he addressed a celebrating gathering from the pulpit of the African Zion Church.

Throughout the North—those states that either made provision for emancipation following the American Revolution or entered the Union as free states—slavery was ended. But the legacy of that experience was still to haunt the Negro in virtually every aspect of his daily life. Blacks were usually proscribed from political rights, excluded from hotels, restaurants, and public transportation, and segregated in hospitals, theaters, and cemeteries. They faced a double standard of justice; police regularly arrested Negroes for crimes that whites committed with impunity. Once a Negro came to trial, he found it hard to retain an attorney to defend him, and there were no blacks on the jury that was to decide his fate. If convicted, Negroes received larger fines, longer jail sentences, and fewer pardons than whites. Not surprisingly, there was an exceptionally large number of blacks in the prisons. All over the North, blacks lived in a world segregated by law and custom. As William Chambers, an English traveler, summed up the situation on the eve of the Civil War: "We see, in effect, two nations—one white and another black—growing up together within the same political circle, but never mingling on a principle of equality."

SEGREGATION AND EXCLUSION: EAST AND WEST

Before the Civil War, Philadelphia with its 22,185 free blacks had a larger proportion of Negroes in its population than any other Northern city. New York

City, with 12,574, was second, and Boston, with 2,261 free blacks, was third. The national census of 1860 revealed that Boston's Negroes made up one-seventy-seventh of its population and New York's, one-sixty-third of the population. Philadelphia's Negroes comprised one-twenty-fourth of its population. Southern-born blacks made up almost one-third of the Negroes in Philadelphia and more than a quarter of those in Boston.

Philadelphia also had the notorious distinction of being the Northern city most hated by black Americans. Frederick Douglass frequently heaped scorn upon the city "for the insult and degradation offered to the colored citizens of Philadelphia." Following a visit to the city, Douglass wrote indignantly:

There is not perhaps anywhere to be found a city in which prejudice against color is more rampant than in Philadelphia. Hence all the incidents of caste are to be seen there in perfection. It has its white schools and colored schools, its white churches and its colored churches, its white Christianity and its colored Christianity, its white concerts and its colored concerts, its white literary institutions and its colored literary institutions . . . and the line is everywhere tightly drawn between them. Colored persons, no matter how well dressed or well behaved, ladies or gentlemen, rich or poor, are not even permitted to ride on any of the many railways through that Christian city. Halls are rented with the express understanding that no person of color shall be allowed to enter, either to attend a concert or listen to a lecture. The whole aspect of city usage at this point is mean, contemptible and barbarous.

As Douglass noted, every aspect of Philadelphia society found the Negro separate and excluded. While visiting the city's House of Refuge for Children in 1831, Alexis de Tocqueville was surprised to see not a single black child there. When questioned, the director explained that "it would be degrading to the white children to associate with beings given up to public scorn."

In September 1845, an exhibition of wax statuary representing the "Last Supper" and the "Trial and Crucifixion of the Savior" opened in Philadelphia's Assembly Buildings. The sponsors published an advertisement in the *Public Ledger* informing the "colored people of the community" that they could visit the exhibition on one day of the week, which was set aside for them "especially." Philadelphia's blacks responded with a resolution adopted at a large meeting held at the Brick Wesley Church, calling the offer "an insult to the colored people of this city, and one which no colored man can accept without consenting to his own degradation."

In 1853, the son of Robert Purvis, a leading member of the Philadelphia black community, accompanied by two young women "of education and refinement and of African descent," visited the exhibition of the Franklin Institute. They purchased tickets and were admitted without objection. But once in the hall, they were expelled by a policeman who acted "on the strength of an order of the Managers." Purvis prosecuted the policeman who committed the outrage before an alderman, who quickly dismissed the case. The experience convinced many black Philadelphians that they should avoid the Franklin Institute in order to be spared insult and mortification. Indeed, Sarah Forten, daughter of James Forten, Philadelphia's black sail manufacturer and pioneer advocate of Negro equality, informed her friend Angelina Grimké that her family seldom went to public places unless they were open to all and therefore did not have to suffer the mortification that usually followed.

Inequalities before the law existed in the Northeast, but they were far more pervasive in the Old Northwest and in the newer states beyond the Mississippi River. Ohio, the first midwestern state to be organized, set the pattern for the region. John Malvin, a Negro freeman born in Virginia, emigrated north to Ohio in 1827. "I thought upon coming to a free state like Ohio," he wrote, "that I would find every door open to receive me, but from the treatment I received by the people generally, I found it little better than in Virginia. . . . I found every door closed against the colored man in a free State, except the jails and penitentiaries, the doors of which were thrown wide open to receive them."

The Ohio constitution of 1802 deprived the Negro of the ballot, excluded him from public office, and prohibited him from testifying against white men in court. In succeeding years, the rights of Negroes were restricted even further by that state's black laws. The first of these, passed in 1804, provided that no Negro could reside in Ohio without a court certificate declaring him to be a freeman and not an escaped slave. Negroes entering a country had to register with the county clerk. If a white man hired a Negro without such a certificate, the employer could be fined fifty cents for each day the Negro was employed. In 1807, a more stringent set of regulations required all blacks who entered the state to post a $500 bond "to pay for their support in case of want." Since few, if any, Negro immigrants had that much money, the law, if enforced, would have prohibited immigration completely. Another section of the law put into statutory form the constitutional prohibition of Negro testimony in cases involving white men. In 1803, Negroes were barred from the state militia, and in 1831, they were effectively excluded from juries by a law limiting jury service to those with the "qualifications of electors." Negroes were also excluded from state poorhouses, insane asylums, and other public institutions.

The force of these laws was greatly moderated by lax administration. If they had been vigorously enforced, virtually no blacks could have entered Ohio. Yet by 1849, the year of the repeal of the black laws, almost 25,000 blacks were living in the state. Nevertheless, even though some of the black laws were flouted, their very presence on the statute books served as a silent threat—and, as we shall see, much more than that. Although black emigrants continued to pour into Ohio, some, like the runaway slave who wrote the following, went on farther:

> Farewell, Ohio!
> I cannot stop in thee.
> I'll travel on to Canada
> Where colored men are free.

Some of the black laws were consistently enforced, especially the law that prohibited Negro court testimony. Of all the black laws, this was one of the most onerous, for without the protection of the courts, no Ohio Negro could be secure in his life or property. Thieves could break into their homes with impunity. This is just what happened in Cincinnati in 1834, and even though one of the thieves confessed, they could not be convicted since the court had no proof, other than the inadmissible testimony of the victimized Negroes, that the property had been stolen. In a more extreme case, a public, daylight murder of a Negro by a white man went unpunished since only blacks were available as witnesses.

In addition to the legal restrictions embodied in the black laws, an unwritten code of segregation further confined the daily lives and opportunities of Ohio blacks. Churches and theaters either barred Negroes entirely or shunted them off to a separate gallery. No hotel or restaurant would serve a colored man in its dining room, generally insisting that he take his meals in the kitchen, although sometimes a colored servant might be allowed to eat with his master. Blacks were not allowed to ride a stagecoach if any white passenger objected.

In 1813 Illinois ordered every incoming free Negro to leave the territory under a penalty of thirty-nine lashes repeated every fourteen days until he left. Still later as a state, Illinois added the provision that it was a misdemeanor for a Negro to enter the state to set up a permanent residence. If he did, he could be fined and, if unable to pay the fine, could be sold at public auction into temporary slavery to persons paying the fines. Indiana barred Negroes altogether by the state constitution of 1851, a constitution approved by a popular vote of more than five to one.

On Sunday morning, November 13, 1842, the entire area surrounding the courthouse square in downtown Chicago was plastered with handbills advertising "A Man for Sale." The handbill announced that on Monday morning, a Negro would be sold at auction in front of the city jail. The handbills had been printed and distributed by two leaders of the Chicago antislavery movement. One was Zabina Eastman, editor of the abolitionist *Western Citizen,* the other was his aide, a young law student, Calvin De Wolfe.

These two men sought to break down the provision in the Illinois black law whereby any Negro in the state who could not prove his freedom must be apprehended and held until his master claimed him, and the Chicago city ordinance, which held that any person who had spent a term in jail and was penniless when his term expired was liable to be sold at auction in order to pay for his board and keep in the city jailhouse.

A few weeks before this event, a black by the name of Edwin Heathcock, who was known as a good workman and an active member of the AME church, had unwittingly offended his employer. The employer had Heathcock arrested and thrown into jail. He also charged that the Negro did not have "free papers" and was not by rights entitled to live as a free man in Illinois. As a result Heathcock was advertised for sale in Chicago papers. At first he was represented as a runaway slave with the traditional woodcut showing a bareheaded, barefoot

Negro striding along with a bundle over his shoulder on a stick. Then he was described as an indigent vagrant who must be sold at auction, this being the law in Chicago.

The auction was held, and when no one entered a bid, the sheriff declared, "Gentlemen, this is not a pleasant job. Don't blame me, but the law. I am required by the law to do it. If I cannot get bids for this man I must return him to jail and continue the sale at another time."

Finally the threat of putting the Negro back into the jail, led to a bid of twenty-five cents. No further bid was made, and the Negro was struck off to Mahlon D. Ogden, an abolitionist. Ogden took out of his pocket a silver quarter, handed it to the sheriff, and then said to the Negro, "Edwin Heathcock, I have bought you. I have given a quarter for you; you are my slave! Now, then, go where you please. You are free."

Michigan, Iowa, and Wisconsin followed the pattern set by Ohio, Illinois, and Indiana in excluding free blacks, demonstrating the truth of Alexis de Tocqueville's observation in 1835 that "the prejudice of race appears to be stronger in the states which have abolished slavery than in those states where it still exists, and nowhere is it so important as in those states where servitude never has been known." All told, the six states of the Midwest never had a black population in the antebellum era exceeding 1 percent of the total.

The laws developed in the Midwest with respect to the black population became the models for new territories farther westward as midwesterners followed the frontier to the Pacific. As Eugene H. Berwanger notes in his scholarly study of prejudice against the Negro in the "ever shifting regions which became free states or territories by 1860," "these pioneers pushed westward with an increased determination to keep the Negro, free or slave, out of the new lands." Before 1848, when California was still part of Mexico, its residents are said to have accepted Negroes as equal individuals and intermarried with them. But the situation quickly changed with the arrival of great numbers of Americans the following year. Delegates to the constitutional convention of California in 1849 voted without opposition to adopt the same constitutional restrictions on free Negroes in their fundamental laws that were found in the Midwest. A measure excluding free Negroes entirely from the territory was defeated only because of fear that this would delay congressional action on statehood. Slavery was declared illegal in the 1849 state consitution, although several attempts were made in the state legislature to allow slavery to establish itself in California through the back door. Although these efforts failed, the state legislature swiftly barred blacks from testifying against whites in court and from intermarriage with whites, and local authorities segregated them. In 1857, the state prison director shipped black inmates of the prison to New Orleans, where they were sold into slavery. In 1858, San Francisco's public schools were segregated, and black children were expelled from the schools they attended.

The law that black Californians hated most was the one that prohibited anyone with one-eighth or more "Negro blood" from giving legal testimony. Thus, under California law no black could testify in court against a white man, and as in the case of Ohio and other states with a similar restriction, whites could attack, steal from, and even kill blacks almost with impunity. Even whites were adversely affected by the provision, for there were times when whites needed Negro testimony. As one black California noted:

I may see the assassin plunge the dagger to the vitals of my neighbor. . . . I may overhear the robber or incendiary plotting the injury or utter ruin of my fellow-citizen. . . . The robbery may follow, the conflagration may do its work, and the author of the evil may go unpunished because only a colored man saw the act or heard the plot. Under these circumstances who are not really injured and and lose by the law? . . . Is it not evident that the white citizen is an equal sufferer with us? When will the people of this state learn that justice to the colored man is justice to themselves?

Most blacks who came to California were bent on striking it rich as miners during the gold rush of 1849. Others came just to earn a living. Mifflin Westar Gibbs belonged in the latter category. On borrowed money, he had traveled steerage class from Philadelphia to San Francisco, where he worked at everything from carpentry to shining shoes. After a few years he went into partnership with Peter Lester and opened a boot shop. They soon became two of San Francisco's most successful black merchants.

In San Francisco, blacks owned $5 million worth of property, and were taxed accordingly; they also paid a poll tax. But when they tried to vote, they were driven from the polls. Gibbs and Lester protested this practice by refusing to pay the poll tax in 1857. Their goods were promptly seized and put up for auction to pay the tax. Fortunately, in this instance, the story had a happy ending. A sympathetic white southerner persuaded the other people at the auction to give the goods a "terrible letting alone." Since no one bid on them, the goods were returned. But black Californians still were deprived of the right to vote.

By 1850 there were only 207 Negroes in Oregon and Washington. One reason for the small black population was that the Pacific Northwest duplicated the laws and customs of the Old Northwest and indeed was settled mostly from that region. In 1849 the territorial legislature of Oregon excluded Negroes entirely and ordered those already there to leave within thirty days. In August 1851, Theophilus Magruder, a white resident of Oregon City, swore out a complaint against Jacob Vanderpool, a Negro, before Justice Nelson of the territorial court. Justice Nelson issued a warrant ordering Vanderpool to leave the territory within the specified thirty days.

The success of the action against Vanderpool led to a similar complaint against George Francis, a black merchant, and his wife, both of whom were arrested. Francis' brother, Abner H. Francis, a native of New Jersey who had accompanied the arrested couple to Oregon Territory, wrote to Frederick Douglass: "And what do you suppose was the crime? That he was a Negro and that one of the laws forbids any colored person who had a preponderance of African blood from settling in the territory." The two were called before Justice O. C. Pratt on September 11, 1851, and the judge gave them four months to leave the territory. "Thus you see . . . that even in the so-called free territory of Oregon, the colored American is driven out like a beast in the forest," Francis ended his letter to Douglass.

His brother and sister-in-law refused to leave, however, and a petition was forwarded to the legislature requesting either the repeal of the 1849 act or a special act exempting Francis and his wife from its operation. Despite the failure of the legislature to act, Francis remained in business in Portland for some years, apparently without further molestation. But the possibility of being forced to leave remained with him. Nor was this all. The territorial legislature of Oregon subjected Negroes who refused to leave to periodic floggings and then replaced it with apprenticeship to white men.

The black laws of Oregon Territory included a clause prohibiting blacks from giving testimony or swearing an oath. "Look for a moment at the detestable principle here involved," Francis wrote to Frederick Douglass in 1855. "Outrages, insults, or abuse, many be practiced upon me, and I have no oath to defend myself."

The constitutional convention for Oregon statehood in 1857 continued all of the territorial restrictions upon Negroes and rapidly approved laws excluding blacks from the militia and the polls. A popular referendum rejected slavery by a majority of 5,000 but approved exclusion of free Negroes from the state by a majority of 7,500 (8,641 to 1,081). Congress admitted Oregon in 1857, the only free state with a Negro exclusion clause in its original constitution ever admitted. "Oregon is a land for the white man," said the *Oregon Weekly Times*. "Refusing the toleration of Negroes in our midst as slaves, we rightly and for yet stronger reasons, prohibit them from coming among us as free Negro vagabonds." A San Francisco newspaper hailed this approach and urged Californians to emulate Oregon and expressly bar Negroes from entering the state: "It is much better to keep them away than to let them come, and deprive them of all civil rights and the power of defending themselves as is done in this state."

It is clear that so far as blacks were concerned, there was little truth in Frederick Jackson Turner's thesis that the frontier experience was a major source and an ever-rejuvenating stimulus of the democratic impulse in American life.

NEGRO GHETTOES

A few of the more wealthy Negroes found it possible to live in white neighborhoods in Northern cities, but in general, the hostility of white landlords and tenants restricted the Negro to specific districts. Already in the nineteenth century, the fear of depreciated property was raised as an argument to justify excluding Negroes from white neighborhoods. In 1834, New Haven residents complained that the movement of blacks into previously white neighborhoods had devalued real estate from 20 to 50 percent, while in Indiana in 1850, petitions protested that the proposed establishment of a Negro tract would reduce the value of nearby white-owned lots by at least 50 percent.

Not all Northern cities were segregated. Cleveland, for example, showed "no evidence of the existence of well-defined ghettoes before 1890," and in both Cleveland and Detroit, blacks and poor immigrants shared neighborhoods. But by 1860, Boston, with its "Nigger Hill," was the most segregated city in the country, and Pittsburgh, with its "Hayti," and Cincinnati, with its "Little Africa," came close to duplicating Boston. In New York City, the Negro ghetto was limited to a few blocks, "but it was still a ghetto." Several thousand Negroes were scattered throughout Philadelphia as domestic servants in white families. but the bulk of the city's blacks lived in a ghetto on the south side of the city, with the poorest Negroes crowded in an area bounded by Pine, Fitzwater, Fifth, and Tenth streets.

While most whites criticized the Negro slums in the pre-Civil War North, some profited from them. In most of the Northern cities, whites owned the wooden shacks and shanties in the Negro ghetto. The white landlords, moreover, made few, if any, improvements, contenting themselves with the argument that Negroes lived that way naturally.

Restricted in their choice of a home, blacks were forced to accept whatever accommodations were offered to them. For many, conditions were appalling. While in New York City in 1842 during his grand American tour, Charles Dickens visited some lower-class Negro homes in Five Points and described them as "leprous houses," "hideous tenements," and "cramped hutches." He observed that the rooms were dingy, dark, and surrounded by alleys "paved with mud knee-deep." "Where dogs would howl to lie," Dickens wrote, "women, and men and boys slink off to sleep, forcing the dislodged rats to move away in quest of better lodgings."

A Southern observer described poor Negroes in Philadelphia as creatures living in a state of wretchedness. He found black people dressed in rags and covered with dirt, living in cellars without furniture or heat. Although the Southern observer was naturally biased against free Negroes, reports of Pennsylvanians show that the description was fairly accurate. A study in 1837 revealed that many Philadelphia blacks were living in cellars and shanties where some froze to death during the winter. In 1846 an investigation group of Quakers was shocked by the "dismal abodes of human wretchedness" they uncovered in the Philadelphia Negro slum:

We followed through a dirty passage so narrow, a stout man would have found it tight work to have threaded it. Looking before us, the yard seemed unusually dark. This we found was occasioned by a long range of two story pens, with a projecting boarded walk above the lower tier, for the inhabitants of the second story to get to the doors of their apartments. This covered nearly all the narrow yard, and served to exclude light from the dwellings below. We looked in every one of these dismal abodes of human wretchedness. Here were dark, damp holes, six feet square, without a bed in any of them, and generally without furniture, occupied by one or two families; apartments where privacy of any kind was unknown—where comfort never appeared. . . . Disagreeable odours of many kinds were ever arising; and with no ventilation but the open door, and the foot square hole in the front of the pen, we could scarcely think that life could be supported, when winter compelled them to have fire in charcoal furnaces. . . . Some of these six by six holes, had six and even eight persons in them, but more generally two to four. . . . It is not in the power of language to convey an adequate impression of the scene of this property.

Although the housing and general living conditions for the poor throughout Northern cities were appalling, the worst conditions existed in the Negro ghettoes. Not surprisingly the incidence of disease among free blacks in the North was in direct proportion to their exposure to their living quarters. The Philadelphia study of 1846 disclosed that practically all Negro infants in the ghetto died shortly after birth. In his analysis of health conditions among New York City's black population in 1842, the city inspector pointed out that "in the damp, dark and chilly cellars, fevers, rheumatism, contagious and inflammatory disorders, affection of the lungs, skin and eyes, and numerous others, are rife, and too often successfully combat the skill of the physician and the benevolence of strangers." In the summer and autumn of 1820, a bilious typhus fever, known as Banker-Street fever, swept New York City. In an analysis published the following year, Dr. John Pennel pointed out that of the 443 blacks living in the district who were better lodged, "only 101 were sick of this disease," while out of 119 living in unwholesome cellars, "*nearly one-half were taken down with the disease*, and that nearly one-half died at their places of dwelling."

Tuberculosis exacted a terrible toll on white lives in New York City; it had an even worse impact on blacks. In 1857, the city inspector reported that 1,078 natives and 1,734 immigrants died of tuberculosis, but that the disease was nearly twice as fatal to blacks as to whites.

JIM CROW TRANSPORTATION

In 1828 Thomas Rice, a successful black-face comedian, toured the West. While in Louisville, Kentucky, he heard an old black general handyman singing:

> Step first upon yo' heel
> An' den upon yo' toe,
> An' ebry time you turns around
> You jump Jim Crow.
> Next fall upon yo' knees
> Then jump up and bow low
> An' ebry time you turn around
> You jump Jim Crow.

Rice took down the words and built a song-and-dance routine that formed the core of a new large-scale production. As "Jim Crow," he would shuffle across the stage dressed in ill-fitting, patched clothes, wearing shoes with toes protruding, and sporting a silly grin on his cork-oiled face. Rice presented his act as part of a minstrel show and launched the Jim Crow mania, which spread throughout the country wherever the black-face minstrel sang his song. The stereotype of the Negro as childlike and simpleminded became associated with "Jim Crow" and, combined with the popular pseudoscientific attitudes toward blacks, it further burdened the black community. In 1841, Massachusetts railroad officials first used the phrase "Jim Crow" to designate a passenger car for the exclusive use of Negroes, up to now called the "dirt car." Subsequently Negroes encountered "Jim Crow" practices everywhere, although in its most precise application, the term referred to segregation in public conveyances. William Lloyd Garrison wrote: "If a person is found guilty of wearing a colored skin, he becomes a victim of plunder and must crawl into the 'Jim Crow' car or dirty car, so called."

"The conduct of officers of steamboats and packets to coloured people has been cruel in the extreme," wrote the editors of *Freedom's Journal,* the first black paper, in 1827. Charles Lenox Remond reported that during a boat trip from Boston to New York City, he was confined to the deck. This was the practice irrespective of climate, and Remond recalled that on one occasion, he nearly froze to death. The wife of Reverend T. S. Wright was less fortunate. In traveling from Philadelphia to New York, she was compelled to stay on the deck of the steamboat, even though the weather was wet and cold. Pleas to the captain that she was not well and the offer to pay double the usual cost of a cabin accommodation proved fruitless. Shortly after the boat docked, Mrs. Wright died of pneumonia.

Traveling on any form of public conveyance, not merely steamboats, could be a frustrating and humiliating experience for blacks. The public stages either refused to admit them or forced them to stand or ride outside. Since discrimination made few distinctions of social or economic class, blacks who had achieved considerable wealth and standing in the community might just as easily be faced with humiliation and treated as brutally as the most common laborer. Thomas Downing, one of the wealthiest blacks in New York City, whose oyster house was patronized by whites, was beaten by agents of the Harlem Railroad when he attempted to ride on that line.

Within the space of a few days, Frederick Douglass was turned away from a menagerie on the Boston Common, a lyceum and revival meeting in New Bedford, an eating house in Boston, and an omnibus to Weymouth, Massachusetts. He had been forcibly ejected from public trains several times because he refused to take a place in the "negro car." On one occasion, he purchased a first-class ticket on the Eastern Railroad from Boston to his home in Lynn, Massachusetts. He subsequently refused to leave the first-class car to take seats in the Jim Crow accommodations, as provided in the regulations of the railroad company, and the conductor and several others forced him out with great difficulty. "They however found me much attached to my seat," Douglass recounted, "and in moving me I tore away two or three of the surrounding ones, on which I held with a firm grasp, and did the car no service in other respects.'' He caused so much confusion and difficulty that the railroad superintendent ordered all passenger trains to bypass Lynn, much to the consternation of its residents.

The street railway situation especially tormented Northern blacks. They could choose not to attend a concert or a public lecture to avoid being humiliated. It was possible for them to send their children to separate schools, even though they were inferior, and hope they would obtain the rudiments of an education. But how could they get from one place to another in cities, visit friends and relatives, even get to work at the servile jobs open to blacks, without using the public transportation facilities? How could black ministers tend to the needs of their congregation when they could not use these facilities to visit them? In a letter to the editor of the *New York Evangelist* in 1853, Reverend James William Charles Pennington, a prominent New York clergyman and pastor of the Shiloan Presbyterian Congregation Church of that city, wrote:

You are aware that I am pastor of the Presbyterian church on the corner of Prince and Marion streets, in this city. My congregation extends from No. 1 Pearl Street to 65th Street, and from Hoboken to Brooklyn and Williamsburgh; so that in the discharge of my pastoral duties, I am constantly called to different points and from one extremity to the other of this distant field. And yet sir, according to the usage in this community, I cannot avail myself of the use of any of the lines of omnibuses or any part of the multiplying lines of railways in the city.

As Reverend Pennington noted, it was ''usage'' or custom, and not any specific legal ordinance, that barred black admittance. Increasingly in Northern cities, signs like the following greeted blacks when they attempted to ride the public transportation facilities: ''The proprietors wish it to be understood that PEOPLE of COLOR are *not* permitted to enter, EXCEPT WHEN IN ATTENDANCE UPON CHILDREN AND FAMILIES.''

In the spring of 1853, the *New York Tribune* carried a letter from a white correspondent under the heading, ''Brutality of Negrophobia.'' The writer related ''an incident in free, republican, independent America.'' He had entered the Fourth Avenue car, and when the car reached Canal Street, a man standing near him asked the conductor if he knew that a woman inside, ''closely veiled . . . was a colored woman.'' ''She was as well dressed as anyone in the car, but her skin being dark the Conductor said she must not ride there. Therefore the cars were stopped, and she obliged to get out.'' When asked why he did this, the conductor replied that ''his orders were preremptory from the Directors, to permit no colored person to ride in the cars—and if he did so he should lose his situation.''

On the afternoon of Sunday, July 16, 1854, Elizabeth Jenkins, a teacher in the public schools of New York City, sat down in a Third Avenue streetcar on her way to the First Colored Congregational Church, where she was the organist. The car was stopped, and the young black teacher was brutally assaulted and dragged off by the conductor. The injuries she sustained not only prevented her from attending the church but kept her from working at her public school for over a month.

That same year, William Wells Brown visited Philadelphia on his return from Europe. He and two British friends hailed an omnibus on Chestnut Street. The white men were furnished with seats, but Brown was told, "We don't allow niggers in here." "The omnibuses of Paris, Edinburgh, Glasgow, and Liverpool had stopped to take me up . . . ," Brown wrote angrily, "but what mattered that? My face was not white, my hair was not straight, and therefore, I must be excluded from a seat in a third-rate American omnibus."

Brown's experience forecast what was to follow after streetcars replaced the omnibuses. On January 20, 1858, the first streetcar line in Philadelphia was open to the public. Within the next two years, eighteen more street railway companies were in operation, and Mayor Alexander Henry proudly announced that no "public improvement has ever promised more general benefit to the community." But black Philadelphians could not share the mayor's joy. Of the city's nineteen streetcar and suburban railroad companies, eleven refused to admit Negroes to their cars. The other eight reluctantly allowed them to ride but required them to stand on the front platform of the horsecar with the driver, even when the cars were empty and it was raining or snowing. The only exception to the exclusion rule was for Negro nurses who were riding with white children in their care. In many parts of Philadelphia, blacks seeking transportation had to walk or hire an expensive carriage.

On June 16, 1859, George W. Goins entered a car of the Spruce and Pine Street Company without the conductor's noticing him. However, when he did note that Goins was black, the conductor requested that he either ride on the front platform or leave the car, since company rules did not permit Negroes to ride inside. When Goins refused to leave his seat, the conductor and a white passenger threw him from the car. Goins sued both the conductor and the passenger for damages. In 1861, the Philadelphia district court decided that the rule requiring blacks to ride on the front platform was legal and that the conductor was correct in his action. Judge Hare, the presiding judge, added that the court was not concerned with whether the discriminatory rule was wise.

Undaunted by the unfavorable court decision, another Negro passenger brought an action for damages against a conductor who ejected him from a car. The court again rejected the complaint and upheld the right of companies to exclude Negroes. The same Judge Hare pointed to the fact that Negroes were excluded "in our theatres, our schools, our lecture-rooms, our churches, and in fine, in all places where men congregate in public or private, for the transaction of business in common, or for enjoyment." It was too much to expect that a race "long civilized" would desire to travel in the company of those "emerging from the shades of barbarism." He concluded: "In the belief then, that the regulation [excluding Negroes] now before us is a wise one, or if not wise, will work its own cure best when least molested, we enter judgment for the defendant." The

Philadelphia Female Anti-Slavery Society branded the decision "an illustration of the hypocrisy of a people calling themselves democratic and Christian," but the companies, now twice reinforced by the court, continued their practices unchanged.

ANTIBLACK RIOTS

Lack of security for person and property alike was a problem for blacks in every Northern city. In 1819, three white women stoned a black woman to death in Philadelphia. In 1825, several white men entered a black church in the city and threw pepper into the stove, creating a panic during which several worshippers were trampled. There were also numerous reports in the Philadelphia press of Negroes' being beaten on the city streets, such as the following in April 1837:

We learn that, on Sunday evening last, a respectable colored young woman, who has been for several years employed in the family of B. H. Yarnell, was knocked down in Chestnut Street, as she was going to church, by some scoundrel who has not yet been identified. She lay for some time senseless, and was very seriously injured—one eye being since entirely closed from the swelling occasioned by the blow that she received.

Another similar outrage was perpetrated upon a colored girl, in the lower part of the city, the same evening, probably by the same audacious villain, or villains. It is said that she was so severely injured that her recovery is doubtful.

Sympathetic whites urged that an example be set by punishing some of these ruffians, "or the lives of peaceable colored people will no longer be safe among us." But nothing was done, and the attacks on blacks continued.

In Providence, Rhode Island, it was a common sight for blacks to be molested on the streets. At the city's "Scamps Corner," rows of white men stretched along the doorways regularly knocked off the hats of black men and pulled off women's shawls. In the first decade of the nineteenth century, Prince Hall complained about the "daily insults met in the streets of Boston." By mid-century the situation was much the same.

Between 1820 and 1850, major riots against black people occurred throughout the North. From Providence to Pittsburgh, New York City to Cincinnati, mob outbreaks were common. These riots, of course, were not confined to anti-Negro elements. Between 1812 and 1849 there were 207 major and minor riots in the United States, but blacks were the special targets of a large number of these outbursts. In each case, white mobs burned and looted Negro churches, meeting halls, and homes and clubbed, stoned, and sometimes murdered blacks. A three-day riot in Cincinnati in 1829 forced a thousand black people to seek refuge in Canada. Rioters in New York in 1834 destroyed Peter Williams' church, an African school, and a dozen homes where blacks lived. In Providence in 1831, a violent riot broke out in the settlement known as Hardscrabble, where many

Negroes lived. Angered because blacks dared to defend themselves from attack, a white mob, led by a dozen sailors, raged through the district, tearing down houses occupied by Negroes, "first pulling down the chimneys, and then with a firehook and plenty of axes and iron bars tearing down the buildings and rolling them into the street." "The whole street," wrote a bystander, "was full of spectators, a great many of whom were cheering the mob every time a house fell." The riot continued for three days and was finally quelled by the state militia. Ten men were arrested for their part in the Hardscrabble riot, but all were acquitted at their trial.

Philadelphia was the scene of bloody anti-Negro riots in 1820, 1829, 1834, 1835, 1838, 1842, and 1849. In 1834, the city had "a full-scale race riot" as a mob of several hundred men and boys, armed with clubs, marched to an area where Negroes were known to gather. Upon reaching their destination, the whites engaged in street fighting with blacks. The mob then tore down several buildings owned by blacks and assaulted some innocent people before the police dispersed them. The following evening, a crowd of whites assembled and proceeded to wreck a Negro church and several black homes. These attacks appeard to have been planned in advance since white homes were identified by lights in certain windows. The rioters gathered in another section of the city and wrecked a black church. In the three days of rioting, from August 12 to August 15, the mob destroyed two churches and thirty-one houses, killing one and severely injuring many blacks.

The worst of Philadelphia's race riots took place in 1842. On August 1, Philadelphia blacks gathered at the hall of the Moyamensing Temperance Society on Lombard and Seventh streets to begin a parade in celebration of Jamaican Emancipation Day. The twelve hundred marchers, carrying banners, had barely reached the public market stalls in Southwark's Third Ward, the home of many unskilled Irish workers, when a white mob, "spurred on by the enemies of temperance," began pelting the paraders with fruit, vegetables, bricks, and paving stones, and tore up their banners. The blacks broke ranks and retreated toward the Negro ghetto pursued by mobs who roamed the area attacking houses and assaulting blacks in the street. The violence subsided in the late afternoon as crowds of small gangs confined their activities to beating with sticks, staves, and iron bars any Negro who appeared on the streets.

That same afternoon, a few blacks fired muskets from the Negro quarter, wounding three Irish boys and reigniting the hostilities. The Irish responded with looting and arson, and by nightfall, a mutual aid building and a black Presbyterian church had fallen to the torches. Firemen were called, but they refused to do their duty because they feared the mob.

The next morning, fighting flared anew when Irish dock workers, "armed with shillalahs and clubs," assaulted blacks reporting to work on the Schuylkill docks. But many blacks had packed up their possessions and either fled the city or sought refuge from attack at the central police stations. A sheriff's posse of sixty arrived to quell the disturbance, but the Irish drove it into the city and resumed their attack on the blacks. The mayor then ordered seven companies of militia out for duty, and the troops finally dispersed the rioters.

Some Philadelphians raised the argument in defense of the mob that white bystanders had been angered by a flag "showing a colored man breaking his chain and depicting the rising sun of freedom." Supposedly some mobsters had misread the scene as "a Negro triumphing over the massacre of whites at St. Domingo." Leaders of the city's black community heatedly disputed this version of the riot's origin, pointing out that neither of the procession's two banners contained anything "calculated to give offence to a just or reasonable mind." The allegedly offensive banner was exhibited in the mayor's court for all to see. The inscription read:

> How grand in age, how fair in truth
> Are holy Friendship, Love, and Truth.
> Young Men's Vigilant Association
> of Philadelphia
> Instituted, July 23, 1841.

The riots in Philadelphia caused repeated flights of blacks from the city. Those who remained tended to concentrate their places of residence for protection, since little was done to defend them from further attacks. Philadelphia's black ghetto was a shantytown on the south side of the city, which now straddled the municipal boundaries of Philadelphia, Moyamensing, and Southwark. As a result, when a riot exploded in one part of the ghetto, the watchmen and constables took advantage of the confused boundaries to drag their feet in responding. Moreover, since it was the voting white majority rather than the disfranchised black minority that kept the constabulary in office, the elected constables were slow in coming to the aid of the rioters' victims. Constables were paid for the time they spent delivering warrants, serving papers, and collecting debts, rather than for keeping the peace. They received a small per diem stipend for each day on official riot duty, plus expenses, and they felt that this hardly compensated them for the risks involved.

Not only did blacks receive no protection in the riots, but they were actually held responsible for their taking place. A town meeting of Philadelphia citizens after the 1834 riot blamed blacks for being too forward in their conduct and advised Negroes with influence in the black community to "impress upon their younger brethren, the necessity as well as the propriety, of behaving themselves inoffensively, and with civility at all times, and upon all occasions, taking care, even as they pass along the streets, or assemble together, not to be obtrusive, thus giving birth to angry feelings and fostering prejudice and evil dispositions." After the 1842 riot, the authorities, yielding to the pressure of white citizens living in the vicinity of the Negro temperance hall on Lombard and Seventh streets, declared the building a fire hazard and ordered it to be destroyed brick by brick. George Sidney Fisher, a white Philadelphian, characterized this bitterly in his diary as "a greater outrage than the riot itself."

In the 1842 riot, Robert Purvis' dwelling had been one of the mob's targets. During the first day, he had sat on the inside staircase facing the front door, armed with a pistol and prepared to shoot the first intruder. The mob swirled about outside, but two fires in the neighborhood diverted their attention. On the next day, Purvis was saved when Father Patrick Moriarity, a Catholic priest, rebuked the mob. When Sheriff Lewis Morris called to say he could no longer guarantee his safety, Purvis retreated to his country home in Bucks County, and after the riot, he moved to Byberry, choosing to forfeit residence in the city of Philadelphia for the next thirty years. Before he quit the City of Brotherly Love, however, he poured out his feelings in a letter to Henry C. Wright, a white abolitionist who had asked about what Purvis called "the most ferocious and bloody-spirited mobs that ever cursed a Christian (?) community."

I know not where I should begin, nor how or when to end in a detail of the wantonness, brutality, and murderous spirit of the actors in the late riots, nor of the apathy and *inhumanity* of the *whole* community—in regard to the matter—Press, church, magistrates, clergymen and Devils are against us. The measure of our sufferings is full. . . .

From the most painful and minute investigation in the feelings, views, and acts of the community—in regard to us—I am convinced of our utter and complete nothingness in public estimation. I feel that my life and those tendrils of my heart, dearer than life to me, would find no change in death, but a *glorious* riddance of a life weighed down and cursed by a despotism whose sway makes Hell on earth—we the *tormented,* our persecutors the *tormentors*.

But I must stop. I am sick—miserably sick. Every thing around me is as dark as the grave. Here and there the bright countenance of a true friend is to be seen. Save *that,* nothing redeeming, nothing hopeful. Despair black as the face of death hangs over us— and the bloody *will* of the community to destroy us.

DISFRANCHISING THE BLACK VOTER

The denial of black voting rights and the resulting lack of political power was a major reason for Purvis' (and other blacks') feeling "of our utter and complete nothingness in public estimation." While it may have exaggerated, the *New York Tribune* was not far off the mark when it observed on September 7, 1850: "Only let it be understood that more voters can be obtained by Negrophilism than by Negrophobia, and Fred Douglass will be called to address a Ratifying convention in Tammany Hall, with two or three of Africa's noblest sons for Vice-President."

In the decade after the war of 1812, many Northern states went through a period of suffrage reform. Generally they democratized the franchise by removing property qualifications for male voters over the age of twenty-one. Simultaneously, however, there was another impulse, which aimed at disfranchising black voters. In its 1818 state constitution, Connecticut denied the vote to all black men who had not previously exercised it while expanding the right to vote for white men. Rhode Island still restricted the franchise, but it altered its suffrage law in 1822 so that only white male adults were eligible to be "freemen," and only freemen could vote. Even the number of white males who could become freemen was limited, but it was now impossible for any blacks to meet the qualification.

The Middle Atlantic states were even more vigorous against Negro suffrage. In New Jersey, the decision to restrict the ballot to whites came as early as 1807 through legislative enactment. While the 1844 convention debated the question of suffrage at some length, it ignored the Negro, and two petitions from blacks seeking the privilege of voting were filed without comment. The convention incorporated "white only" suffrage into the new constitution.

The New York State Constitution of 1777 included no provision for racial exclusion, and prior to the 1821 constitution, males who met the property qualification could vote. An 1814 law required the Negro to prove that he was free in order to vote, but with that proof, he could exercise the franchise. In 1821, a state constitutional convention was convened. One of its avowed aims was to extend the suffrage to workingmen by sweeping away property qualifications for suffrage. But many of the delegates who sought to broaden the suffrage to benefit poor whites now sought to eliminate black suffrage entirely. Among other arguments they advanced was the fact that since many Negroes had been born in slavery, they were filled with the spirit of dependence and consequently would vote according to the wishes of their employers, enabling rich men to control their votes, which would foster an aristocracy.

The attempt to restrict the vote to whites was defeated. But as finally adopted on October 8, 1821, article II, section 8 of the new constitution eliminated property qualifications for whites but kept them for blacks. In order to exercise the suffrage, blacks were required to possess a freehold estate of $250 "over and above all debts and encumbrances charged thereon." They were also required to have three years' residence in the state and to have paid taxes. Whites could qualify for the suffrage after one year's residence and the payment of taxes or by rendering either highway or military service.

The effect of the $250 requirement was to exclude most blacks from voting. Of the 12,559 blacks in New York City in 1825, only 68 were qualified to vote. In 1835, with an estimated Negro population of 15,061, a mere 84 could exercise this right, and in 1855, only 100 of the 11,840 blacks in New York City could cast ballots.

From 1780 until 1838, Pennsylvania's blacks exercised the franchise to some small extent. Pennsylvania's 1790 constitution enfranchised all men, but the local communities were given the power to discriminate so that in Allegheny, Bucks, Dauphin, Cumberland, York, Juniata, and Westmoreland counties, black men voted, while in Philadelphia, apparently, they did not. Blacks were deleted from the tax assessment in Philadelphia, thereby barring them from paying taxes to qualify for suffrage.

In 1837, in the case of *Hobles* v. *Fogg,* the Pennsylvania Supreme Court ruled unanimously that the framers of the state constitution had not intended the word *freeman* in the suffrage article to include blacks. Hence, Negroes were not entitled to vote under the existing state frame of government. The Reform Convention of 1838 called to write a new Pennsylvania constitution completed the work initiated by the state supreme court. On January 17, 1838, Benjamin Martin moved to insert the word *white* before the word *freemen* in the third article. A number of delegates argued that the motion to disfranchise blacks was a violation of Christian morality, but the opponents of Negro suffrage made it clear that they did not want to be jostled at the polls by Negroes; they did not care to sit in the same jury box, at the same constitutional convention, or to share with Negro men the social privileges of the militia. This would lead, they claimed, to amalgamation and the ultimate degradation of the white race. Suffrage was not only the entering wedge, but, as one delegate insisted, it was "amalgamation to the fullest extent." It would lead to a situation in which blacks would be allowed to be justices of the peace and judges in the courts and able to litigate white rights and properties. Finally, they argued that if the convention decided against restricting the suffrage to the white sector of the population, there would be a huge influx of blacks from states where they were deprived of the right to vote, and blacks would soon assume political control of Pennsylvania.

When the vote was taken, seventy-seven delegates voted in favor of the amendment and forty-five opposed it. After the word *white* had been inserted into the constitution, there was a move in the convention to spell out certain conditions under which blacks might eventually vote, but the attempt failed.

Since the law required the voters of the state to ratify the proposed constitutional amendments, blacks took action to prevent disfranchisement from going into effect. Three appeals from blacks in the state were addressed to the people of Pennsylvania and the legislature: *Memorial of the Free Citizens of Color in Pittsburg; The Appeal of Forty Thousand Citizens, Threatened with Disenfranchisement, to the People of Pennsylvania;* and *Memorial to the Honorable the Delegates of the People of Pennsylvania in Convention at Philadelphia Assembled.*

The *Appeal* of the forty thousand citizens, written by Robert Purvis and approved at a public mass meeting at the First African Presbyterian Church, pleaded:

We appeal to you from the decision of the "Reform Convention," which has stripped us of a right peaceably enjoyed during forty-seven years under the constitution. . . . To all her citizens the right of suffrage is valuable in proportion as she is free; but surely, there are none who can so ill afford to spare it as ourselves.

The *Memorial* addressed to the convention orginated at a mass meeting of blacks held at the Bethel AME Church, drafted by Peter Gardiner and Frederick Hinton, listed ten reasons why the proposed black disfranchisement should be defeated. The ninth reason read:

One of the difficulties which most embarrasses the condition of the people of color is the existing, and popular prejudice against the complexion which it has pleased God to give them. It is this which meets us everywhere and throws stupendous obstacles in our way; which excludes so many from Schools, and from opportunities of learning useful trades. Your memorialists therefore submit where in the exercise of that paternal regard, which your honorable body we are persuaded cherishes for the welfare of the humblest citizens, you can consent to give to a prejudice, of such wicked and malignant influence, the additional strength it will derive from the influence your high example and station.

The *Memorial* was considered so radical a statement that the convention members twice denied attempts to print it. But even when printed and distributed among the voters, the *Memorial* and *Appeal* were without avail. On October 9, 1838, the constitutional changes were approved by a vote of 113,971 to 112,759. Under the Pennsylvania Constitution of 1838, poor white males who had previously been disfranchised due to their inability to pay the required taxes were now enfranchised. But all black males, regardless of their income, status, or education, were disfranchised.

Pennsylvania was the last state to disfranchise Negroes who had actually voted in the state. The list included Delaware, 1792; Kentucky, 1799; Maryland, 1801; New Jersey, 1807; Connecticut, 1818; New York ($250 freehold restriction), 1821; Tennessee, 1834; North Carolina, 1835, and Pennsylvania, 1838.

It will be noted that no western state is on this list, for reason: these states never allowed blacks to vote. The Ohio, Indiana, Illinois, Michigan, and Iowa constitutions prohibited blacks from voting, or permitted the legislature to do so, or presented the problem to an electorate which, in every state, decided against the Negro. (A leading white Indiana citizen even proposed to disfranchise all who voted for Negro suffrage in a suggested referendum.) Wisconsin tried the referendum method also, and after one rejection, a slim majority of a meager total vote authorized Negro suffrage. However, the authorities simply disregarded the vote until a state supreme court decision seventeen years later announced that it must be obeyed.

Thus, one by one, between 1807 and 1847, all but five states disfranchised the Negro. The exceptions were Maine, Rhode Island, New Hampshire, Vermont, and Massachusetts. In Rhode Island, which had also disfranchised the Negro, the prohibition was repealed in 1842, and it became the only state to do so before the Civil War.

10

Free Blacks in the Antebellum North II

EARNING A LIVING

The main problem for free black men and women in the North was earning a living. At one time, the free black worker had occupied an important economic position; it is quite likely that in a number of Northern cities between 1790 and 1820, a large proportion, perhaps most, of the skilled craftsmen were black. Of course, most of them received less money than white artisans for the same work, but they at least found employment in their trades. The reason was that from 1776 to 1815, immigration from Europe declined, leaving openings for free black artisans. But with the end of the Napoleonic Wars in 1815, immigration to the United States started to flow once again, and immigrants from Europe, many with skills acquired in their native lands, flocked to this country, and settled in its Northern cities. Industrial development also attracted native Americans from the farms to the city, where they soon acquired the skills necessary to meet the demand for labor.

After 1820, the combination of immigration and the hostility of white workingmen prevented many blacks who possessed skills from using them and kept most younger Negroes from gaining apprenticeships and learning a trade. Prior to 1826, blacks were not welcomed in Cincinnati, but so long as they posed no threat to white workingmen and provided cheap labor when white labor was scarce, they were at least tolerated. But after that, white immigrants, determined to get rid of black competition for jobs, pressured the municipal trustees to act. In 1829, the trustees decided to enforce the state's stringent black laws. They gave blacks sixty days to post the required $500 bond as security against becoming wards of the community or leave the city. When authorities hesitated to carry out their threat, whites resorted to mob action. For three days and nights, blacks were assaulted on the streets and in their homes. As a result of the 1829 riot, between 1,000 and 1,200 blacks fled the city, hundreds migrating to Canada, and it was difficult for a Negro to find any job other than those menial tasks regarded as unfit for white men.

Niles' Weekly Register of August 30, 1834, carried the following item on its front page:

Though gatherings of large numbers of people at Philadelphia to commit acts of violence, had ceased after the third night—many excesses subsequently took place, and colored persons, when engaged in their usual avocations, were repeatedly assailed and maltreated, especially on the *Schuylkill* front of the city. Parties of white men have insisted that no blacks shall be employed in certain departments of labor.

A committee of Philadelphia citizens that investigated the riot condemned the mob but found fault with employers for providing blacks with work, thereby consigning whites to idleness and poverty. Not surprisingly, it declared, "Many of the most active of the rioters" were "white laborers anxious for employment." Obviously, black workers were not entitled to "employment." Encouraged by the report, white workers publicly denounced those who continued to employ blacks, and those who did not dismiss Negroes had their places of business burned or sacked.

Once they had replaced blacks as skilled workers, white mechanics and craftsmen in all Northern cities refused to accept blacks as apprentices or to work alongside them. Fugitive slaves who had been skilled workers on plantations found their trades useless when they came North. The day after he arrived in New Bedford as a fugitive from slavery, Frederick Douglass sought work as a caulker—and made an important discovery. No one would hire him because white workers refused to work with Negroes and made it clear that if he were employed, "every white man would leave the ship in her unfinished condition." Douglass put aside his caulking clothes and went in search of whatever work came his way. But he pointed out several years later:

Those who ask why we don't learn trades or do something to make ourselves respectable, do not seem to know the difficulties under which the negro labors from day to day. When I was a slave in the South, and the property of Capt. Auld, I earned for that dear man about $9 a week, at my trade, as a caulker, as well as if my skin were as white as his. But the moment I landed in New Bedford, eleven years ago, and asked for employment, I was told by an anti-slavery ship-builder there, who had a vessel on the stocks to be caulked, that if he should even venture to send me on that ship, every white man would leave him, and he could not get her ready for sea. Go where I would, I could not get employment at my trade. My case was the case of hundreds of fugitives.

Henry Boyd, an ex-slave who tried to find work in Cincinnati as a carpenter, had a similar experience. "On coming to this city," a committee investigating the condition of Cincinnati's blacks reported, "he was refused work by every man to whom he applied. At last he found a shop, carried on by an Englishman, who agreed to employ him, but on entering the shop, the workmen threw down their tools, and declared that he should leave or they would. 'They would never work with a nigger.' The unfortunate youth was accordingly dismissed.'' The committee noted that this was the common experience of all black artisans. Once when a Negro was hired by a Cincinnati firm, the white workers walked off the job and remained on strike until he was fired.

The result of this process was that by the 1830s, few blacks in the North were being employed as artisans and fewer still were receiving training as apprentices. In the fall of 1827, co-editor Reverend Samuel E. Cornish sent a report to *Freedom's Journal* from Boston in which he expressed his regret at having to inform the readers that very few members of the black population in the Bay City were mechanics and that those who were found it impossible to obtain work at their trades or to train their children as apprentices. An analysis of the economic status of Boston's blacks in 1831 confirmed Cornish's evaluation. Among the nearly two thousand Negroes in the city, "It does not appear that there is among them, one merchant, broker, physician, lawyer, blacksmith, shipwright, tinman, caulker, and graver, rigger, sail-maker, coppersmith, silversmith, brass-founder, mason, cooper, painter, glazier, printer, bookbinder, cabinetmaker, truck man, baker, or stonecutter, or any trader in any article except clothes." Three-quarters of the blacks in Boston were semiskilled or unskilled workers, mostly day laborers and seamen.

In most of the Northern cities by that time, the majority of blacks were confined to menial labor largely disdained by whites, with only a sprinkling of coachmen, waiters, barbers, carpenters, masons, and plasterers. They had no "honorable employment," the *New York Observer* reported in its 1825 survey of the economic status of free blacks in the North. A survey of "The Colored Population of the United States" in 1830 concluded that "at the north, where slavery is not tolerated, people of color are generally confined to a few callings, most of them considered servile." In 1833, a French traveler wrote that there was not a single trade in New York City in which blacks were allowed to work with whites.

In general, blacks found themselves restricted to occupations in the service and unskilled sectors of the local economy and denied access to better-paying jobs in the skilled trades and in manufacturing. In some cities, the process of eliminating blacks from the skilled trades occurred later than in others. In 1838, the colored mechanics of Pittsburgh were employed as "carpenters, blacksmiths, stonemasons, boot and shoe makers, plasterers, painters, tanners and curriers, coppersmiths, and shipwrights." Ten years later, most of these blacks had been driven out of the trades by white immigrants from other states or from Europe.

Providence blacks were unable to find employment in the rising textile industries and were forced to do work as draymen, carting raw cotton from the docks to the mills. In the years between 1825 and 1830, Philadelphia was viewed as the industrial center of America, and its recognition as such was based in part on its variety of manufactures. There were more than one hundred warping mills, producing over 81,000 yards of cloth daily. A heavy cloth known as "Philadelphia goods'' was in demand throughout the country. Canvas, fine carpets, fine china, glassware, various kinds of iron goods, and steam engines were manufactured in great quantities. But blacks were so totally excluded from the industrial sector of Philadelphia's economy that they are never mentioned in any contemporary accounts of the work force. In 1847, less than 0.5 percent of the black male force was employed in Philadelphia's factories. This was at a time when thousands of Irish immigrants were engaged in factory work.

In 1838, a survey of the free people of color of Philadelphia by the Pennsylvania Society for Promoting the Abolition of Slavery revealed that blacks were engaged in eighty-eight different occupations, representing almost all the trades pursued by whites. Yet the report conceded that the greater part of the black workers were ''engaged in the most menial services and severest labors'' and that it was becoming ''difficult for them to find places for their sons as apprentices to learn mechanical trades.''

Actually, the number of occupations in which blacks in Philadelphia were engaged continued to increase, and by 1847, it had grown to nearly 226 different occupations. But five of them accounted for 70 percent of the entire male force: laborers (38 percent), porters (11.5 percent), waiters (11.5 percent), seamen (5 percent), and caterers (4 percent). Another 10 percent were employed in miscellaneous laboring capacities.

Eight of every ten black working men were unskilled laborers. Another 16 percent worked as skilled artisans, but fully one-half of this group were barbers and shoemakers; the other skilled craftsmen were scattered among building construction (3.2 percent), home furnishing (1.3 percent), leather goods (1.2 percent), and metalwork (1.2 percent). Less than 0.5 percent of blacks found employment in the developing factory system. The remaining 4 percent of the labor force were listed as white-collar professionals but were mainly proprietors who sold food or second-hand clothing.

The occupational structure for black females was even more restricted than that for males. More than eight of every ten women were employed in day-work activities (as differentiated from those who lived and worked in white households) as domestic servants: ''washers'' (52 percent), ''day-workers'' (22 percent), and miscellaneous domestics (6 percent). Fourteen percent were seamstresses, and they accounted for all of the skilled workers among the female labor force. Finally, about 5 percent were engaged in white-collar work, which, as in the case of males, meant vending capacities in clothing and food selling categories.

The majority of Philadelphia Negroes were poverty-stricken, unskilled workers, relegated to menial labor and sporadic employment. Of 3,358 black men in 1849, 1,581 were listed as laborers, and of 4,249 women, 1,970 were listed as washerwomen.

In a report published in 1859, sponsored again by the Pennsylvania Society for Promoting the Abolition of Slavery, forty-one trades in which blacks were engaged in Philadelphia were listed for the first time. Added to those previously mentioned, they provided, at first glance, an imposing picture, but there was a cautionary note, which told the real story: "Less than two-thirds of those who have trades follow them. A few of the remainder pursue other avocations from choice, but the greater number are compelled to abandon their trades on account of the unrelenting prejudice against their color." More than two-thirds of black Philadelphians who had trades were not able to follow them because of racism.

Pushed out of the skilled trades, black men were forced to attempt to earn a living through manual work as laborers, dockworkers, teamsters, and so forth. Their skills were limited, the work was sporadic, and the pay pitifully low. The bleak situation, moreover, worsened. The arrival of nearly 5 million white immigrants shortly before the Civil War posed an alarming threat to the black workers' already meager employment opportunities.

In 1845, potato rot destroyed great portions of Ireland's vital food crop, and the 1846 repeal of the English Corn Law brought to an end Ireland's favorable position in the British trade system. The disastrous economic conditions caused a mass migration, most of it to America. Before the tide of emigration abated in the mid-1860s, 2.5 million Irishmen had landed on American soil. The number of Irish entering Boston increased from 443 in 1836 to a high of 65,556 in 1846.

These immigrants often reached the United States without funds, shelter, or job prospects. Many had been poor farmers in Ireland and had few skills useful in an urban environment. They became the chief economic competitors of blacks. Positions traditionally open to blacks, such as those of house servant, cook, waiter, porter, longshoreman, and laborer, were often filled instead by immigrants.

"P.O.," a perceptive analyst of the Moyamensing area in Philadelphia, which housed Irish weavers and unskilled laborers, among them numerous blacks, wrote that by 1849 the Irish had driven the blacks from the Schuylkill docks: "Where a few years ago one saw none but blacks, we now see nothing but Irish." The black longshoremen who at one time dominated the waterfront labor market in Philadelphia were ousted in large part by physical force. During the 1842 antitemperance riots in the Negro ghetto, attacks against blacks spread to the Schuylkill wharves, where black and Irish coalheavers had been engaged in a struggle for control over day labor unloading the barges, arriving from western Pennsylvania. It was at the Schuylkill docks that a sheriff's posse, sent to rescue some black coalheavers before they were trapped and burned alive in a warehouse, was dispersed by an angry crowd of Irishmen and chased to the edge of the black ghetto on the other side of the city.

In other cities, too, the waterfront was the setting for economic competition and hostility between blacks and Irish, and it was exacerbated when employers, playing one race against the other, hired black workmen as strikebreakers. But blacks were being eliminated not only from waterfront jobs. Many of them were deprived of employment in other unskilled occupations. "Every hour," Frederick Douglass lamented, "sees the black man elbowed out of employment by some newly-arrived immigrant whose hunger and whose color are thought to give him a better title to the place.'' In November 1851, the *African Repository* noted that in New York (and in other Eastern cities), it was no longer possible to see the Negro ''work upon buildings, and rarely is he allowed to drive a cart or public conveyance. White men will not work with him.'' In 1857, a group of sixty Irishmen engaged as laborers on a large building being erected on Duane Street in New York City quit work when the foreman employed a Negro to wheel dirt from beneath the building.

New York City not only refused to grant licenses to black cartmen, but refused all requests for porters' licenses. The city justified the actions as taken out of ''*mercy* to the colored man,'' since if licenses were granted, ''it would bring them into collision with the white men of the same calling, and they would get their horses and carts 'dumped' into the docks, and themselves abused and beaten.'' The idea that the city should protect its black citizens from such abuse never crossed the minds of the authorities.

In 1846, a visitor to New York City asked: ''Who may find a dray or a cart or a hack driven by a colored man?'' In truth, no one could. The same observer noted that blacks in the city had ''sunken much lower than they were a few years ago and are compelled to pursue none but the meanest avocations.'' The federal census of 1850 lent weight to this sad conclusion. Of those blacks gainfully employed in New York City, nearly three-quarters were servants, laborers, and other unskilled or occasional workers. Of a total of 3,337 individuals listed, 1,144 were laborers, 808 servants, 207 sweepers and scavengers, and 434 seamen, while 2 were general mechanics, 1 a blacksmith, 12 carpenters, and 2 hatters. In the service trades 122 were barbers, 107 coachmen, and 12 carpenters.

The number of black seamen is not surprising. Probably half of the native-born American seamen who manned the crews of American vessels in 1850 were men of color. Among other things, sailing offered a hope of escape for those who sought to flee the bonds of slavery. Runaway slaves usually made for a port and attempted to hire onto a vessel leaving for other countries. While intolerable conditions on board vessels induced many whites to jump ship, the black runaway slaves had no choice but to stay, and this made them attractive to shipowners as a labor force. The captains of ships did not delve too deeply into the backgrounds of blacks who wanted to become crew members, nor did they heed the admonitions included in an increasingly large number of advertisements for runaway blacks that all vessels were forbidden to carry them.

With decreasing opportunities for employment in the cities of the North, free black men also sought work as seamen despite the terrible exploitation of these workers. At sea, the sailor was ''wholly at the mercy of tyrant captains and brutal officers.'' But on board ships, black sailors experienced a somewhat different life from that on American soil. The atmosphere was freer, and in many cases racism was relatively absent as white and black seamen worked, ate, and slept together.

While the number of black seamen increased, their numbers as longshoremen and railroad workers, hodcarriers, and even porters and bootblacks decreased as they were displaced by immigrants, especially the Irish. Negro women began losing positions as maids, cooks, and washerwomen. The only trades in which blacks maintained a precarious hold during the last two decades before the Civil War were those of barber and hairdresser, coachman, and waiter. But during the 1850s, the number of foreign-born barbers and hairdressers increased at a fast pace. "A few years ago," Frederick Douglass wrote in alarm in 1853, "a *white* barber would have been a curiosity—now their poles stand on every street." With immigrants moving into barbering, black barbers in several Northern cities were gradually restricted to a black clientele. The same process was underway among coachmen and waiters, positions previously dominated by blacks. "Employments and callings, formerly monopolized by us, are no longer," Douglass wrote in 1853, summing up the situation.

Although they also faced competition from the Irish, black women still were able to take in washing, and this remained their chief form of employment. Others took positions as domestic servants in wealthy households. In Boston, well over half of the black married women and perhaps as many as three-quarters of the unmarried women and teenage girls were gainfully employed, drawing wages either in cash, produce, or room and board. This pattern of employment existed in other Northern cities as well and made women an extremely important part of the financial life of the black community. Often when men could find either no jobs at all or only seasonal or erratic employment, their wives' more continuous employment was critical for the maintenance of the household. Carter G. Woodson and Lorenzo B. Greene, in their study of Negroes as wage earners, stated that "without a doubt many a Negro family in the free states would have been reduced to utter destitution had it not been for the labor of the mother as a washerwoman."

From the cradle to the grave, the white worker, whether native born or foreign born, was taught to regard the Negro as an inferior. In a society in which racial prejudice was all but universal, it is hardly surprising that he refused to work with a black craftsman or laborer, believed that no black should receive the same wages and conditions as a white worker, and excluded blacks from his union. To work with a Negro in the same shop or even to travel with him in the same streetcar meant a loss of social status. John Campbell, a Philadelphia typesetter, spoke for many white workers in his book *Negromania,* published in 1851:

Will the white race ever agree that the blacks should stand beside us on election day, upon the rostrum, in the ranks of the army, in our places of amusement, in places of public worship, ride in the same coaches, railway cars, or steamships? Never! never! nor is it natural or just that this kind of equality should exist. God never intended it.

"Free Negro wage-earners were members of the labor force before the Civil War," writes Philip Taft in his *Organized Labor in American History.* But from the time the first trade unions were formed by white workers in the 1790s to the Civil War, no free Negro wage earner, North or South, was a member. To be sure, several unions, such as the printers, hotel waiters, shoemakers, and tailors, excluded white women as well. But no union allowed a black worker—skilled or unskilled, male or female—to join its ranks.

Any gesture by white trade unionists to help black workers was forcefully rebuked by their fellow unionists. An investigation of conditions of free Negroes in Cincinnati turned up the information that in 1830 the president of the local Mechanical Association, an early trade union, "was publicly tried by the Society for the crime of assisting a colored young man to learn a trade. Such was the feeling among the mechanics that no colored boy could learn a trade, or colored journeyman find employment." The short-lived Industrial Congress—a national organization of reformers and workingmen—did admit Negro delegates to an 1851 convention, but the Mechanics' Assembly of Philadelphia so resented the admission of blacks that it voted to sever all ties with the Industrial Congress.

In at least one instance before the Civil War, white workers sought to improve relations with blacks in their trade. Negro waiters in New York were successful in 1853 in forcing their employers to pay $16 a month at the same time that white waiters received $12. In this exceptional situation, the whites held a meeting to form the Waiters' Protective Union and to force equalization of their wages. The whites invited the leader of the black waiters to attend the meeting. The *New York Herald* of March 31, 1853, reported that "Mr. Hickman (colored) . . . said the colored men were the pioneers of the movement and would not work for less than eighteen dollars a month." The paper quoted the black waiter as saying, to the cheers of the whites: "I advise you to strike upon the 15th of April for $18 a month; and if the landlords do not give it, then you turn out, and be assured that we will never turn in in your places." Again the whites cheered and thanked the blacks. But no effort was made to open the union to blacks or to set up further cooperation between white and black waiters.

BLACKS AND PUBLIC SCHOOLS

"We must educate, we must educate, . . . if we wish to rise from our present condition," was a constant refrain in the black community. In the North, education for blacks during the antebellum period was better than in the South. But blacks in the North faced the same barriers of segregation and discrimination in education that prevented them from making progress in other phases of society.

Prudence Crandall, a schoolteacher of Quaker parentage and antislavery convictions, established a private academy for girls at Canterbury, Connecticut, in 1831. In 1833 when her school had become recognized as one of the best in the state, she admitted a Negro girl as a student and incurred the opposition of almost all the parents of her students, who threatened to withdraw their daughters from the school. When she decided to limit future enrollment to "young ladies of color," the reaction this time took the form of filling her well with refuse, forbidding her to enter church, attacking her house, and breaking the windows.

The town petitioned the state to enact a law prohibiting private schools for nonresident colored persons. The legislature passed the law and Miss Crandall was arrested and imprisoned under the law and was finally convicted. The case was carried to the state supreme court, and her conviction was reversed on a technicality in July 1834. During the appeal she was the object of further attacks, and finally her house was set on fire and badly damaged. This convinced her that she could never succeed in continuing her school. Following her marriage to Reverend Calvin Philleo, she moved to Illinois.

It was to the public schools, however, that most black parents looked for the education of their children. But here, too, they found the situation discouraging.

Public school admission practices varied in New England. In Maine, blacks were generally accepted, and in Connecticut, they were generally excluded. Massachusetts did not legally segregate the state's educational system, leaving it for each city to decide its own policy. Nearly all segregated their schools. Boston, however, did not, but few black children attended before 1800. Those who did were subjected to discrimination, mistreatment, and public ridicule from white students and teachers alike. As a result, in 1787 and again in 1796, blacks, led by Prince Hall, petitioned the Massachusetts legislature and the selectmen of Boston for the establishment of a separate black public school.

Failing in this, blacks organized the private African School in 1798. Initially students met in the home of Primus Hall, Prince Hall's son. By 1806, classes taught by Elisha Sylvester, a white schoolteacher, were meeting regularly in the basement of the African Baptist Church. The African School grew until the Boston School Committee decided in 1812 to place it within its own jurisdiction. From that time on, the school became an integral part of the Boston educational system, and soon the school committee began assigning nearly all blacks applying for instruction to the colored facility on Beacon Hill, or, as whites began to call it, "Nigger Hill."

In 1815, Prince Saunders, one of the early black teachers at the school, convinced Abiel Smith, a white merchant, to make a contribution to black education. When he died in 1815, Smith willed a portion of his estate to be used exclusively for the education of Boston's blacks. The African School took the name of its white benefactor, and from that time on was known as the Smith School. By 1820, the city was providing $200 annually for the education of black children. This amount, plus a twelve-and-one half-cent tuition charge per week per child paid by parents, sustained the school. Two of the school's best-known teachers were blacks: Thomas Paul, Jr., and John Browne Russwurm, a graduate of Bowdoin College and one of the first black college graduates in the United States. Russwurm taught at the Smith School for three years, until 1824, when he received word that he had been accepted by Bowdoin College.

In 1820, the Boston School Committee gave its official sanction to segregated schools in the city by opening the first all-black primary school entirely under the committee's auspices. In 1831, the city established another public black primary school, and, including the older Smith School, there were now three such schools. Although the city had accepted some financial responsibility for black education, black children, as a rule, received an inadequate education. The Law of the Public Schools specifically stated that "in every town containing fifty families or households, there shall be kept one school for instruction of children in Orthology, Reading, Writing [and] English Grammar." But over the protests of black Bostonians, the school committee barred "the colored children from learning grammar," ruling that only white children would be taught grammar. The inaccessibility of the black schools was another source of complaint of black parents. Indeed, one family living in East Boston was compelled to send their children to school by ferry. In addition to these problems, many teachers in black schools were inadequately educated and trained.

Before Pennsylvania passed a public school law, poor children who attended private schools were reimbursed through the use of tax funds. But although blacks paid taxes, their children received no education. The Pennsylvania School Laws of 1802, 1804, 1809, 1812, and 1818 contained no special provisions for Negro education. Legally, according to these laws, the Negro was entitled to free schooling, but no Negro children received public funds for their education—even though their parents were required to pay taxes into the public school fund.

The inability of blacks to obtain tax monies for education during this early period set a precedent that hindered later efforts to gain admission to public schools. Public education began in Philadelphia in 1818, but it was not until 1822 that the first school for the "free instruction of children of indigent coloured people" was established. The school was opened on September 6, 1822, with Henry A. Cooper utilizing the Lancastrian system to teach 199 pupils. (Under the Lancastrian system of instruction, emphasis was upon systematic drill and repetition.) One reason for the opening of the school was the popular belief that the Lancastrian system was a deterrent to crime and other social vices. And so after three years of public education, blacks were admitted on a segregated basis to a Philadelphia public school.

By the end of 1823, 237 boys and girls were enrolled in the school, but they were housed in rooms that had been converted for school purposes. The facilities in the school were so poor compared to those provided for white children that Philadelphia blacks complained that not many of the graduates were "fitted to take a respectable stand in society," because of the unequal treatment they received. In 1827, two black Philadelphia women assailed the unequal treatment and criticized the caliber of teachers assigned to blacks:

. . . We cannot believe that almost anyone is qualified to keep a school for our children. Enemies may declaim upon their dullness and stupidity, but we would respectfully inquire, have they not had dull and stupid instructors, who, if placed in any other than a coloured school, would hardly be considered earning their salt; but we must be silent, as any one who possesses a few qualifications is, in general estimation, fit to keep a school for us. . . . Conscious of the unequal advantages enjoyed by our children, we feel indignant against those who are continually vituperating us for the ignorance and degradation of our people.

As criticism of the educational facilities for blacks mounted, the controllers built a new school for white pupils and moved the black children from their inadequate school rooms to the Lombard Street school, abandoned by the whites. This initiated the practice in the Philadelphia school system of giving black children the older school facilities while reserving the newer structures for white children. Again, although by 1838, every public school in Philadelphia for whites had numerous assistant teachers to aid in breaking the school into classes, the Lombard Street school had one teacher for 199 boys and two teachers for 251 girls.

The first public Infant School opened in 1832 for white children between the ages of four and six, but no similar institution was begun for blacks until 1841. In 1837, a public high school was established for white pupils, but blacks were not accepted for admission, so they were forced to terminate their public education at the grammar school level.

In 1829, 14 percent of the total public school population was black. By 1839, that figure had slipped to 3 percent, although the overall Negro population in Philadelphia had increased from 15,000 to 20,000. Philadelphia's whites pointed to these distressing figures as indicating a lack of interest on the part of the city's black population in education. But they rarely mentioned the obvious fact that the segregated schools were inferior, housed in older buildings, and characterized by poor and insufficient staffing, continual teacher turnover, and a disregard for the potential of the students. Small wonder that black students had little inducement to attend.

Despite all this, Pennsylvania was determined to maintain a segregated school system. In 1854, the general assembly settled the issue with a law that required all school districts with twenty or more school-age black children to provide separate facilities for their education. Black separate schools were required to stay open only four months a year. As in the case of disfranchisement, the blacks' protests were of no avail. Not surprisingly, as we shall see in chapter 11 on the free black community in the North, black Philadelphians directed much attention to the formation of their own educational institutions.

Before 1846, the New York State legislature failed to establish entrance requirements for the state's district schools, allowing the various communities to decide the question themselves. Those communities with Negro populations usually chose to segregate: New York City in 1787, Rochester in 1834, Lockport in 1835, and Buffalo in 1842. In Rochester, the initiative for separate schools came from the blacks. Abuses suffered in the common schools motivated thirty-two Rochester blacks in 1830 to petition the state legislature for a separate school for their children. They stated in part:

Under the present organization our schools are open to all children and yet it is obvious that in this state the literary and moral interests of the colored scholar can hardly prosper. He is reproached with his color, he is tainted with his origin; and if permitted to mingle with others in the joyous pastimes of youth, it is a favor, not a right. Thus the law which may declare him free is a dead letter. His energies are confined, his mind is in chains, and he is a slave.

The petition was granted, and the first African school in western New York opened in 1834.

An 1846 school act in New York made the district schools free to all children between the ages of five and twenty-one. Since this law conflicted with the segregated conditions in the state's larger communities, the authorities resolved the conflict by not enforcing the law. Beginning in 1853, the legislature enacted laws that moved against the spirit of the 1846 school law. In that year, Buffalo's Common Council petitioned the legislature for a new charter to make the common schools free to white children and require the establishment of a separate Negro school. This petition, the first such request since the 1846 law, was granted on April 13, 1853. This, in turn, served as a precedent for similar legislation, which applied to the entire state. In 1856, the legislature permitted every city or town in the state to establish a school for Negro children, and six years later it granted to the school authorities of incorporated cities and villages the power to separate the schools for white and Negro children. Thus, segregation became the general policy of New York State.

The first organized attempt in New York City to found an institution dedicated specifically to the education of black youth was initiated by the New York Society for Promoting the Manumission of Slaves, which established the African Free School in 1787. Although the majority of the students contributed to the maintenance of the school, the resources of the Manumission Society and the contributions of parents proved insufficient to meet the school's needs. Accordingly, a state law of March 12, 1813, provided that the African Free School should be one of the institutions to receive a portion of the school funds allotted to the city and county of New York.

With this provision for its support, the school underwent a phenomenal growth. In June 1833, African School No. 7 was opened. Those who attended the African schools were taught map drawing, astronomy, logarithms, and navigation in addition to the standard subjects. The ability of Negro students to master these subjects was illustrated in public examinations given by specialists in the various fields, which most of the Negro students passed, with a number scoring impressively.

In 1830, 620 pupils, male and female, attended the African schools. But many Negro children were too poor to come to school at all. Some lacked proper clothing. Others, forced to work at very young ages, remained in school only long enough to "attain knowledge of mere monosyllable spelling and reading."

To help provide children with clothing so that they would not be ashamed to attend school, black women organized the African Dorcas Association. The association's object was stated to be "to procure by donations, second hand clothing, hats, shoes, etc., for the poor children, who are found or may be found so destitute as to be unable to attend school." It was largely due to the labors of this association of New York black women that many black children were able to attend school. Nevertheless, about half of the Negro youngsters in New York City in the pre-Civil War era had no formal education.

Another problem with the African schools was that the trustees of the New York Manumission Society adopted a policy of paying white teachers higher salaries than blacks, without regard to the qualifications and competence of the individuals. A French traveler, reporting on a visit to these schools, noted that "a man of color, of name of Hughes, receives but 500 dollars a year; while a white man, whose name it would be invidious to mention, as he is acknowledged to be inferior to the other in every respect, has 600, for performing the same duties in a school of the same class." However, a correspondent in *Freedom's Journal* sharply criticized the caliber of a number of the teachers in the African School, regardless of their salaries:

We are so skeptical that we cannot believe that almost *anyone* is qualified to keep school for our children. Enemies may declaim upon their dullness and stupidity; but we respectfully enquire have they not had dull and stupid instructors, who if placed in any but a coloured school would hardly be considered as earning their salt.

But even worse was to come. In 1834, the African Free Schools were taken over by the Public School Society of New York and later became part of that city's public school system under its new name of "Colored Free Schools." With the change in the status of the African Free Schools, the quality appears to have declined precipitously. Carter G. Woodson noted that "the schools lost in efficiency," and attendance "startlingly dropped." Some improvement occurred when the Colored Free Schools of the Public School Society were taken over by the board of education in 1853. Efforts were made to erect school houses for black children, and in the next few years, several new grammar schools were built. Black teachers were hired, and a normal school for the training of Negro school teachers was built.

The annual report of the board of education for 1853 conceded that the legal requirement that all black children be segregated in separate schools, regardless of where they lived, forced many of these children to walk long distances to get to school, and that in periods of antiblack riots, Negro parents were afraid to send their children away from home to walk these long distances through dangerous streets. But the report emphasized that the Negro population "shows a desire to enjoy school advantages quite equal to that of the white population, and in view of their social position, is not only highly creditable to them, but may serve to remove the erroneous idea that they are indifferent to the benefit of education."

In spite of this optimistic observation, the fact is that Negro education in New York City was in a state of neglect as compared with the rest of the population. The New York Society for the Promotion of Education Among Colored Children, founded in 1846 by black New Yorkers, reported in 1855 that there were 3,000 black children in the city as compared with 159,000 whites. Proportionately, nearly 25 percent more black children than white attended the public schools. Yet the board of education extended $1.6 million for white schools and only $1,000 for the black ones.

The same report gave a detailed picture of the different black schools in the city. Public School No. 2 on Laurens Street was over twenty years old and was located in "one of the lowest and filthiest neighborhoods, and hence, although it has competent teachers in the male and female departments, and a separate primary department, the attendance has always been slender, and will be until the school is removed to a neighborhood where children may be sent without danger to their morals." The story was the same for School No. 5, located at 19 Thomas Street, in "a most degraded neighborhood, full of filth and vice; yet the attendance of this school, and the excellence of its teachers, earn for it the need of a new site and building." The cellar of School House No. 6 was always flooded with four feet of water:

From a comparison of these school-houses with the splendid, almost palatial edifices, with manifold comfort, conveniences, and elegances which make up the school-houses for white children in the city of New York, it is evident that the colored children are painfully neglected, and positively degraded. Pent up in filthy neighborhoods, in old dilapidated buildings, they are held down to low associations and gloomy surroundings.

In 1859, the *New York Tribune* conducted its own investigation of the schools for black children in New York City, after which it reported:

The school houses for the whites are in situations where the price of rents is high, and on the buildings themselves no expenditure is spared to make them commodious and elegant. . . . The schools for the blacks, on the contrary, are nearly all, if not all, old buildings, generally in filthy and degraded neighborhoods, dark, damp, small, and cheerless, safe neither for the morals nor the health of those who are compelled to go to them, if they go anywhere, and calculated to repel than to attract them.

Outside of New York City, too, blacks were provided with inferior or discarded school facilities. Local boards usually forced blacks to attend a single school, even when their residences were scattered throughout the city. This hardship placed the average school attendance of black students far below that of white pupils. Buffalo Superintendent V. M. Rice wrote of the plight of black students in his 1854 report:

It excites one's pity to see them in cold stormy weather often thinly clad, wending their way over a wearisome distance. Anyone possessing humane impulses, can but regret that, with all the other burdens, which power and prejudice heaps upon this people, their children, when so young, are doomed to suffer so much in striving to gain a little light to make their gloomy pathway through life less tedious.

Rice expressed concern for the lives of black students: "There are some who live at a comparatively greater distance that at great risk of health, if not at the price of life, attend this school." But nothing changed.

The disparity of funds appropriated for white and black schools operated throughout New York State. In the year ending September 30, 1858, New York State spent $3,792,948.79 on schools. Of this, only $10,730 went to Negro schools. In 1859, Negro schools received $24,364 out of $3,664,617.57 spent. Thus, in two years, the state spent 0.47 percent of its school money on schools for black children at a time when Negroes made up 1.3 percent of the population.

Since blacks paid "their full share of the general and therefore the school taxes," the gross disparity in the funding and upkeep of their schools was especially galling. But as the editor of the *Anglo-African* pointed out, since blacks in New York were practically disenfranchised, "the members of the Board of Education feel themselves little, if at all responsible to the colored voters."

In the town of Plainfield, New Jersey, the public school was supported by a tax levied upon the inhabitants without any distinction of color. In 1848, the black children, whose parents paid their proportion of the tax, were placed in a basement by themselves and were visited by a teacher a few times a day. The parents of the black children did nothing until the basement became so cold without any heat that they withdrew them. On August 24, 1849, the *New Jersey Freemen* reported: "We know not how things are managed there now, but according to our latest information which was two or three months since, the colored children were by the united exertions of the Teacher and Trustees, entirely excluded from the school. Thus colored people are taxed to educate the white children of Plainfield."

In several western states, black children were virtually excluded from the public schools. Illinois did not even provide for their education until 1860 and Indiana not until after the Civil War. Michigan authorized Negro schools in Detroit in 1841, providing that when the school fund money was exhausted, the parents would have to bear the burden.

Prior to 1848, Ohio did not recognize the right of its black children to be educated at public expense. In 1844, the Reverend Hiram S. Gilmore of Cincinnati opened the Cincinnati High School for "those whom legislative neglect had exposed to ignorance and vice." It was the first school of its kind established for the education of the free black youths of the city and its surrounding area. Beginning with about twenty pupils, by 1847 it had increased to close to two hundred. Although tuition was charged, between one-fourth and one-third of the students had the expenses of their tuition defrayed by charity.

The 1848 Ohio school law authorized blacks to establish and manage schools with property taxes paid by themselves. Since the admission of black children to white schools could be blocked by formal complaint from any taxpayer or parent in a district, few schools were integrated. When the black laws were repealed in 1849, the school law was altered. The new provisions required that townships, towns, and cities where blacks were not admitted to white schools establish one or more segregated districts. Male black taxpayers were permitted to elect directors to manage their schools. Black property owners were guaranteed that taxes collected from them would be used exclusively to support black schools.

But there was no guarantee that blacks living in districts with few Negro residents would receive adequate funds for the support of separate schools. In fact, Cincinnati's school authorities, with the support of city officials, mounted a challenge against the law's constitutionality and refused, meanwhile, to turn over the money that was necessary for the maintenance of the black public school. But the Ohio Supreme Court ruled that the school was entitled to the $2,177.67 collected from black property owners. Peter H. Clark, a graduate of the private Cincinnati High School, had taught at the black public school without pay until the issue was decided by the court and then donated his $105 salary to help defray the black community's legal expenses.

In 1853, the Ohio General Assembly placed the management of black schools under the control of regular school boards. Shortly after the white board took control in Cincinnati, Peter H. Clark was dismissed on the charge of being an atheist. Actually, the real reason was his support of the black community in the court case. Meanwhile, students were attending the segregated school under wretched conditions. Girls met in a rented house that trustees described as "a perfect *rat-hole!*" The rooms were low, long, and dark, with little or no ventilation in summer and intense cold in winter because of numerous "air-holes." The house where boys met was "not fit for school purposes" and was located "in one of the lowest, most depraved and the most belligerent Irish . . . [sections] of the city."

Blacks outside Cincinnati found it extremely difficult to establish separate schools with the funds provided. The Columbus superintendent reported that a black school with seventy-five students organized under the 1849 law had to be discontinued because adequate classrooms were not available. This was true elsewhere in the state as well. In 1853, the state commissioner of education reported a total of twenty-two black schools in Ohio, enrolling 702 students out of 6,862 school-age children.

Only in Cleveland was the picture bright. There it was judged inexpedient to establish "a separate school for colored children." Although several white parents proposed that black children be seated in a separate room, the idea was rejected by the board of trustees. Cleveland alone of the cities in Ohio provided integrated education.

In November 1859, the Ohio Supreme Court handed down a decision in which it maintained that "colored youth . . . are not, as of right, entitled to admission [to white schools] . . . under the act . . . of 1853." The court's ruling had the effect of maintaining the segregated educational pattern.

"If we expect to see the influence of prejudice decrease and ourselves respected, it must be by the blessings of an enlightened education," a Negro National Convention resolved in 1832. In 1847, another Negro National Convention concluded that public school education was a failure for blacks. If a Northern city public school accepted Negroes at all, it most often put them into separate and inferior schools. The result?

The education of colored youth, up to this time, has been shamefully limited. In very deed it has not reached the dignity and elevation of education. It has been rudimental notings and superficial glancing. To comprehensiveness it has never yet made any pretensions, to profundity, not the most distant approach.

BLACKS AND COLLEGES

It has long been assumed that John Browne Russwurm was the first black college graduate in the United States. Although there is hearsay evidence that Alexander Lucious Twilight who graduated from Middlebury College, Vermont, in August 1823 was a Negro, the hard evidence indicates that the distinction of being the first black college graduate belongs to Edward Jones, who graduated from Amherst College on August 23, 1826. Since Russwurm did not graduate from Bowdoin College until September 6, 1826, he was the second black college graduate.

Edward Jones enrolled at Amherst College in 1822, the second year of its existence. He came from Charleston, South Carolina, where his father, a free black, was a hotelkeeper and caterer. In 1830, Jones was granted an honorary master of arts degree by Trinity College, and in 1841, he became principal of Fourah Bay Christian Institution in the British colony of Sierra Leone.

John Browne Russwurm was born in Port Antonia, Jamaica, on October 1, 1799, of a black mother and a white father, who was an English merchant in the West Indies. At the age of eight he was sent to school in Quebec, and when, a few years later, the elder Russwurm moved into the district of Maine, he brought his son with him. When Mr. Russwurm married a white widow who already had three children, the new Mrs. Russwurm took John into the family. After the senior Russwurm's death, Mrs. Russwurm remarried but continued to treat the young lad from Jamaica as her own son. Russwurm taught at the Smith School for black children in Boston for three years; he entered Bowdoin College in the fall of 1824 and graduated two years later.

While Edward Jones' graduation from Amherst went unnoticed, Russwurm's aroused some interest in the press. He delivered a commencement address entitled "The Condition and Prospects of Haiti," in which he defended the black revolution in the West Indies, noting that the suffering of whites during the long revolutionary struggle was nothing compared with the brutal system the slaves were determined to end. ("The cruelties inflicted by the French on the children of Hayti have exceeded the crimes of Cortes and the Pizarros.") He closed with the prediction that Haiti would yet win full recognition among the family of nations.

An extract from the speech was published in the *Portland Eastern Argus* of September 12, 1826, and was reprinted two days later in the *Boston Courier* and somewhat later in the *Philanthropist* and the *Genius of Universal Emancipation,* both antislavery journals. The last, published in Baltimore by Benjamin Lundy with the assistance of William Lloyd Garrison, headed the extract, "African Eloquence." The *Eastern Argus* also published the following report of the commencement:

One circumstance was particularly interesting and we believe it was a perfect novelty in the history of our Colleges. Among the young gentlemen who received the honors of the College, and who had parts assigned to them, was a Mr. Russwurm, a person of African descent. He came on the stage under an evident feeling of embarrassment, but finding the sympathies of the audience in his favor, he recovered his courage as he proceeded. He pronounced his part in a full and manly tone of voice, accompanied with appropriate gestures, and it was received by the audience with hearty applause. Altogether it was one of the most interesting performances of the day. His subject was happily selected. It was the condition and prospects of *Hayti.* Believing our readers would feel an interest in a literary performance so novel under all its circumstances, we have obtained the extracts which we subjoin. It is but just to add that Russwurm has conducted with great propriety during the whole course of his college life, and has always had the esteem of his classmates. He intends, as we are informed, to settle in Hayti. He will carry with him the best wishes of all his acquaintances for his happiness and success in life.

Six months before his graduation, Russwurm wrote to a relative in Tennessee: "If not particularly invited by the Haytian Govt., then I shall study Medicine in Boston, previous to an emigration to Hayti." Russwurm had attended anatomy lectures at Bowdoin's Medical School. However, he neither attended medical school nor emigrated to Haiti. Instead, he moved to New York and became the co-editor of *Freedom's Journal,* the first black paper.

In 1835, the National Negro Convention reported that at least five colleges admitted blacks on equal terms with whites. They were: Oneida Institute in Whitesboro, New York, Mount Pleasant in Amherst, Massachusetts, Hayes Academy in Canaan, New Hampshire, and Oberlin and Western Reserve in Ohio. The two colleges from which the first blacks had graduated—Amherst and Bowdoin—were not on the list. In the early 1830s, William C. Munro, a young black minister in Portland, Maine, applied to Bowdoin, Amherst, and Dartmouth but reported that he was either rejected or "was offered admittance only on such degrading terms, as no one who had any sense of the rights of man would accept."

One of the institutions listed by the 1835 National Negro Convention soon ceased to exist. That same year three Negro youths, Alexander Crummell, Henry Highland Garnet, and Thomas S. Sidney, traveled from New York City to enroll in the Hayes Academy opened by abolitionists in Canaan, New Hampshire. They soon discovered that they were the equals of any of the eighty or so white students already enrolled, but they were not to remain long in Canaan. On August 10, 1835, three hundred citizens of Canaan and other towns in the vicinity, enraged by the presence of three Negroes in the area, hitched ninety yoke of oxen to the school building and dragged it into a swamp a few hundred yards down the road, nearly destroying it in the process. Senator Isaac Hill of New Hampshire rose on the Senate floor and proudly described the action of his constituents who "had simply thwarted an invidious abolitionist scheme to mingle negro and white." The following year Crummell, Garnet, and Sidney entered the Oneida Institute at Whitesboro, New York, founded in 1833 by Beriah Green, a Presbyterian minister and abolitionist.

When Oberlin College was founded in 1833, it became the first American college to develop a policy of admission for two formerly despised groups in higher education: women and blacks. It began by admitting women. In 1835, its leaders decided to accept students of all races, but the college never enrolled many Negroes. Between 1840 and 1860 they made up 4 to 5 percent of the student body, including George B. Vashon, son of the wealthy Pittsburgh barber, and John Vashon, the first Negro to be graduated from Oberlin College, earning his degree in 1844, and a master's degree five years later. Oberlin's black graduates were William H. Day, the editor of Cleveland's first Negro paper, the *Aliened American*, and John Mercer Langston, the first elected black officeholder in Ohio, and later Congressman from Virginia. John A. Copeland, Jr., also an Oberlin student, was hanged with John Brown at Harpers Ferry.

Thomas Paul, Jr., of Boston entered Dartmouth College in 1838, but he was refused admittance into the college's literary society because of his color.

In spite of the few colleges that admitted blacks, Negro aspirants in general found the barriers to admission almost insurmountable. In part, this was because of inadequate preparation and limited finances, but mainly it was because of prejudice. In August 1849, John M. Langston graduated from Oberlin with high honors. Having decided to become a lawyer, he sought a place where he might pursue professional study. Many advised him to choose another career; others suggested that he migrate to the British West Indies where he could study and practice law. But Langston sought admission to J. W. Fowler's law school in Ballston Spa, New York. The school's board of trustees and faculty voted unanimously "against his admission, because of his color." Fowler suggested that a personal interview at Ballston Spa might alter this decision, carefully adding that nothing could be guaranteed. When Langston met with the school's representatives, he was told that the original decision would not be altered because his admission might cost the institution financial support. Fowler offered to allow Langston to "edge" into the school by passing "as a Frenchman or a Spaniard hailing from the West India Islands, Central or South America." Langston, "moved by a deep sense of the humiliation of his manhood," refused the offer. "I am a colored American," he replied passionately, "and I shall not prove false to myself, nor neglect the obligation I owe to the negro race."

Langston studied law under the guidance of a lawyer and was admitted to the bar in 1854. He defended his first client that year in Brownhelm Township, Lorain County, Ohio, and in the spring of 1855, John Mercer Langston became the first black American elected to public office in the United States when he won the post of township clerk in Brownhelm. In winning the election, Langston ran sixty votes ahead of the Liberty party ticket on which he had been nominated, even though he and his wife were the only blacks in the township.

David Jones Peck was the first Negro graduate of an American medical school, earning his degree from Rush Medical College in Chicago in 1848. But Peck set no real precedent. James P. Barnett was expelled from the College of Physicians in New York in 1851 because of his race, this in spite of the fact that his two-year record was outstanding. On May 25, 1852, William G. Allen, a black professor at New York Central College in McGrawville, New York, wrote to Gerrit Smith, the wealthy Syracuse abolitionist:

I have received intelligence from New York City that there are quite a number of colored men there desirous of obtaining a medical education. Some of these young men have already spent some time with distinguished physicians in the City, but on application to Medical Colleges for the purpose of attending lectures found admittance there denied them. One who had attended one term in Maine found on going the second time that the doors were closed against him.

Dr. Commodore F. Buckner served as physician to Cincinnati's black community for several decades after 1849. As an adolescent, Buckner worked on a river steamer, then as a hotel cook, and finally as a boatman on the Whitewater Canal. This last position offered him considerable free time, which he occupied in reading medical books. But prejudice against him because of his color was so strong "that no college dare receive him as a regular student." He attended medical school lectures only as a special student and received no degree. His training came from independent reading and private tutoring.

Even when a college admitted a few blacks, student and teacher prejudice made it impossible for most to continue. Charles B. Ray and Amos G. Beman entered Wesleyan College in Connecticut, but some of the Southern students objected so strenuously to their presence and, with the support of other students, made life so miserable for the two blacks that they finally left. Two blacks were successful in 1850 in breaking through Harvard University's policy of not admitting Negro students and were enrolled in the medical school. But student and faculty protest was so severe and continuous that both were forced to withdraw after one semester.

BLACK COLLEGES

Two black institutions of higher learning were established during the antebellum period: Ashmun Institute (later Lincoln University) in Pennsylvania (1854) and Wilberforce University in Ohio (1855). Although discrimination did play a part in the establishment of Ashmun Institute, its founding did not grow primarily out of the problems of black Americans but rather was a response to the needs of Protestant foreign missionary activity, especially in Africa. James Ralston Amos, a Negro Methodist Episcopal preacher who lived on a farm in Chester County, near Oxford, Pennsylvania, sought to further his training for the ministry and began taking instruction under the leading religious luminary of the area, Reverend John Miller Dickey, pastor of the Oxford Presbytery church. When Amos expressed a desire to further his education, Dickey arranged for his admission to a Presbyterian school in Philadelphia. But Amos was soon forced to withdraw because of the racial prejudice of the students, who threatened violence if he continued there. Dickey then appealed to his former teacher at Princeton Theological Seminary for Amos to study there. Although Princeton seminary had had black students since 1826, Charles Hodge, Dickey's former teacher, felt that Amos was not qualified. Finally, Dickey succeeded in enrolling Amos in a Presbyterian school in Philadelphia, where he was permitted to remain.

Opposed to the existence of slavery, Dickey was the leader behind the rescue of Elizabeth and Rachel Parker, two sisters who had been stolen by slave catchers from Maryland. He was an ardent colonizationist and the manager of the Chester County Colonization Society, a branch of the American Colonization Society, founded in 1816 to send free blacks in the United States to Africa and which created Liberia in 1824 for this purpose. There was a general conviction among colonizationists that the success of their program necessitated that prospective settlers receive some kind of education. Dickey accepted this premise, but he also gave it a second dimension. Many missionaries in the early 1800s referred to Africa as the "White Man's Grave," owing to the high mortality rate among those sent there to serve. While officiating at the ordination of a young white missionary who was about to assume a post in Africa, the idea of a school to train blacks for the purpose came to Dickey. Because blacks, he believed, were "better fitted for the deadly climate," he visualized an institution that would not only provide "pre-colonization education" but would also develop an "intellectual elite" of "divinely ordained" individuals who would "extend the Kingdom of God to Africa." The frustrations that he encountered in trying to enroll Amos seem to have reinforced his determination to develop such an institution.

The purpose of the school, Dickey pointed out in a sermon he preached in the Oxford Presbyterian Church in 1853, was to prepare black men in the United

States to spread the gospel among Africans. Since it had proved impractical to train blacks in white institutions, a separate school of higher learning for Negroes was the only practical solution.

In June 1853, the general assembly of the Presbyterian church approved the plan and called for "the establishment of a high school for the care and benefit of the free colored population of this country . . . with the understanding that it shall be wholly under the supervision of the Presbyterian Synod within whose bounds it may be located, thus securing such education as shall promote the usefulness and happiness of this class of people." In October 1853, the New Castle Presbytery endorsed the project and appointed a committee to secure a charter from the state of Pennsylvania, which would ensure the presbytery's control over the institution, and to raise the necessary funds for the opening of the school. The school was to be called "THE ASHMUN INSTITUTE, for the scientific, classical, and theological education of colored youth of the male sex."

In keeping with the colonizationist views of its founders, the school was named after Jehudi Ashmun of Baltimore, a minister of the Congregational church who was the agent of the American Colonization Society in Liberia between 1822 and 1828. During that time, he helped the floundering colony to become established, nursing the struggling group of transplanted blacks along until it became "an independent, self-governing and prosperous community." Stricken with malaria in 1828, Ashmun left Liberia for the United States and arrived in New Haven, where he died two weeks later at the age of thirty-five.

Since no one in Oxford except for Dickey wanted the school located in the town or even nearby, land was purchased four miles to the east of Oxford. Part of the property belonged to the estate of Emory Hinson, a former free black in the Oxford area, who had migrated to upper Canada, where he had died. Plans were then laid for securing a charter from the state legislature and raising funds for the new institution. The charter was signed into law on April 29, 1854, by Governor William Bigler, marking the establishment of the first black college in American history.

After months of appeals and journeying by board members from pulpit to pulpit, enough money trickled in to enable the project to get underway. By the fall of 1856, the buildings were nearing completion. On October 8, 1856, the Reverend John Pym Carter of the presbytery of Baltimore was elected principal and teacher. At his installation on the last day of 1856, Carter outlined his views on the new institution's policies. He stressed the impetus that colonization had provided for the school's founding and affirmed that the "chief influence of the Institute will be to cooperate in the noble cause of African education, missions, and colonization." Its purpose, he said, would be to prepare black men to fulfill their destiny in Africa, and he gave the following assurance to those who feared that the institute might become a center of antislavery agitation:

With respect to the principles which will guide us in the conduct of the institution, we wish it to be distinctly understood that we shall recognize and respect the legalized institutions of our united country. It is not, therefore, our purpose to interfere in any way with the claims of masters to their slaves; nor to preach a crusade against the institution of domestic slavery, as it exists at the South; nor to render the establishment of a hotbed of fanaticism, to cultivate the passions of one race against the other; but, while it will be our earnest and constant endeavor to promote, between the two races, every feeling of kindness, and respect, we shall zealously guard against offending a single prejudice which keeps these races distinct.

Classroom instruction began in the Ashmun Institute the next morning, January 1, 1857. President Carter, the sole teacher, had two students: James Ralston Amos, whose educational problems in 1852 had spurred the project, and his brother, Thomas H. Amos. They were joined in the fall of 1857 by a third student, Amistead Miller. The three were graduated in 1859 and left for Liberia to carry on missionary work in Africa.

By 1860, there were ten students, one of whom, Christian A. Fleetwood, wrote that the course of study

covered the useful English branches, with the addition of Theology, Metaphysics, Greek and Latin. All of the students excepting myself were preparing for the ministry and followed the curriculum. I was taking a business course preparatory to an expected mercantile life in Liberia, and so substituted Bookkeeping, French and Spanish for Theology, Greek and Latin, but had to do my turn at all of the English branches, Arithmetic, Algebra, Grammar, Geography, History, and Elementary Philosophy would about cover it. . . .

I was the only student to leave the Institute in June, 1860, and so was appointed "Valedictorian of the class of 1860." I can only recall one idea in my address which was a prophecy, that the voice of the Negro would be heard in the halls of Congress. This most improbable (at that time) happening occurred in so few years after, that it was fixed in my memory.

Wilberforce University, the second black college, owed its existence to the efforts of several black leaders of the AME church. In 1847, Bishop Daniel A. Payne and other church leaders purchased 172 acres of land twelve miles west of Columbus, Ohio, and established Union Seminary, the embryo of Wilberforce University. Later several AME ministers became interested in improving the condition of and furnishing educational facilities for Ohio's 25,000 blacks. The Cincinnati Conference of the Methodist Episcopal church on September 28, 1853, appointed a committee to report on "what can best be done to promote the welfare of the colored people among us." This committee's report, submitted on August 9, 1854, recommended a plan to establish a literary institute for the training of black teachers. After discussion, the conference adopted the recommendation.

Taiwana Springs, Ohio, offered an ideal location for the new institution, and the Methodist Episcopal church purchased fifty-two acres and several houses in the area. From the outset, the AME church and the Methodist Episcopal church, North, cooperated in naming the institution, and it was decided to call it Wilberforce University, in honor of William Wilberforce, the zealous British antislav-ery and anti-slave-trade activist. Later, the Union Seminary at Columbus merged with Wilberforce under a new charter. The college was now the sole property of the AME church, which had purchased it from the Methodist Episcopal church for $10,000. Bishop Payne became its president.

11

The Free Black Community in the Antebellum North

Northern free blacks for the most part were considered "not slaves, but . . . pariahs, debarred from every fellowship save with their own despised race, scorned by the lowest white ruffian." "They are free, certainly," a contemporary noted, "but they are also degraded, the target of the offscum and the off-scouring of the very dregs of society." Given this situation, it was inevitable that free blacks in the North would establish their own community.

Each city in the antebellum North with a sizable black population developed a separate black community and a separate subculture, both of which were active and viable.

THE BLACK CHURCH IN THE NORTH

"As among our people generally," wrote Martin R. Delany to Frederick Douglass in 1849, "the church is the Alpha and Omega of all things." Except in a few cities of the North, such as Cleveland, where blacks worshipped in integrated communities, the black church became the focal point and gathering place for a city's blacks, and the subculture's leadership came predominantly from the clergy.

The independent black church arose primarily as a response to the discrimination blacks faced in white churches (see volume 1). Even when Negroes were permitted to attend the same churches as whites, they were usually seated either in separate pews in the back of the church or upstairs in a gallery especially set aside for colored persons; they also usually received communion after whites. The movement for an independent black church began in Philadelphia's St. George's Methodist Episcopal Church, when white officials attempted to segregate black members in a separate gallery. On April 17, 1787, Richard Allen and Absalom Jones organized the Free African Society, from which two black con-

234

gregations emerged. Jones took the lead in establishing St. Thomas' Episcopal Church of Philadelphia, which was associated with the white Protestant Episcopal denominations. St. Thomas' Church was accepted on the condition that its members would not take part in the general church government. Not until 1864 did the black church receive recognition on the basis of equality, but its congregation, made up of cultured and wealthy blacks, was always small. In 1795, it numbered only 427, and by 1860, it had declined to 105.

Richard Allen and his followers organized the Bethel Church in Philadelphia, which began with weekly gatherings in Allen's blacksmith shop. In 1794, with the aid of a few whites, they were able to build a church. It was dedicated by the white Methodist bishop and later became known as the Bethel African Methodist Episcopal Church. ("Bethel," from the Hebrew *beth'El,* means "house of God.") In 1816, Allen and fifteen other delegates organized the African Methodist Episcopal church with Allen as bishop. By 1820, the church had 4,000 members in Philadelphia alone. The AME Church continued to grow, and by 1846 it had 296 churches in fourteen states and Canada, with 17,375 lay members presided over by 3 bishops, 48 deacons, and 62 elders. Members of the AME church were at various times called "Allenites," and their churches the "Bethel Churches," after the name given the first church in Philadelphia. When Bishop Allen died in 1831, he was succeeded by his assistant, the Reverend Morris Brown.

On August 11, 1820, the African Methodist Episcopal Zion Church was founded as an autonomous all-black church in New York, and the following year, Peter Varick was elected as its bishop. In 1839, the church had a membership in the city of between twelve hundred and two thousand, and ten years later, the *National Anti-Slavery Standard* noted that Zion was considered to be "the largest and wealthiest church of the coloured people in this city—perhaps in the country." Although on a national basis, the AME church considerably outstripped Zion in membership and churches, the latter remained the largest of the individual congregations in New York's black community. In 1848, Frederick Douglass reported that AME Bethel Church in Philadelphia was the "largest church in this Union, and from two to three thousand worship there every Sabbath," but he also observed that Zion Church in New York City "exerts considerable influence over the next largest colored denomination of the country." Slight differences in church government and probable rivalry for leadership prevented the unification of these groups.

African Baptist churches were established in Petersburg, Richmond, and Williamsburg, Virginia, in other Southern cities, and in Boston, Philadelphia, and New York. Although organized as separate organizations in the North, the black Baptist churches remained affiliated with the white Baptists. In 1836, the Providence Baptist Association of Ohio became the first independent Afro-American Baptist conference in the country. Although local and state conferences organized the Western Colored Baptist Convention in 1853, no national organization was formed until the 1890s.

By 1837, Philadelphia had four Baptist churches with seven hundred members. New York's Abyssinian Baptist Church, organized in 1809, struggled for several years without any steady pastor. It also suffered many financial difficulties, and, on one occasion, the building in which the congregation worshipped was sold at auction. But the church continued to progress, and by 1850, it could support a membership of 450 communicants, with Reverend Sampson White as pastor.

Zion Baptist Church was an offshoot of the Abyssinian Baptist congregation. Formed in 1832 with only sixteen members, mostly female, its pulpit was occupied by various preachers, both white and black. A permanent pastor was finally obtained in 1843, and three years later, Zion was able to boast a membership of 446.

The only black Baptist church in New England, the Free Will Baptist Church, was formed in Providence, and it became the largest of the Negro religious groups. Providence also had an African Methodist Episcopal Zion church, established in 1837, and an African Methodist Episcopal church, launched a year later. The fourth and smallest of the black churches in Providence was Christ Church, with Alexander Crummell, a recent arrival from New York, as pastor.

Although the independent black churches no longer had to deal with the problems caused by the prejudice of the white churches and clergy, this was not true of those that remained within the larger white denominations. They still had to fight to abolish the "nigger heaven" in the upper church galleries where the black members were seated. Black ministers still had to struggle for equal treatment. Although he was a member of the presbytery of New York, the Reverend Samuel E. Cornish never attended a general assembly of that body, despite the rule that every member in turn was to be a delegate. In a stinging indictment of his fellow Presbyterians, Cornish wrote that for ten or fifteen years, he and his fellow black Presbyterian, Reverend Theodore S. Wright, "have been passed by, and neglected by the brethren. Never exchanged pulpits with, never appointed to any ecclesiastical delegation, nor to fill any vacancy. No, nor never invited to a pulpit neither in the city nor out of the city; so far as the country is connected with our Presbytery." He continued:

The brethren, when they take a journey either for health or business, will sooner close their churches, than to admit a colored brother to their pulpits. And they have so taught their people, that if a colored minister happens to be present, whatever his piety and talents, when their pulpit is unoccupied, they will rather dismiss without preaching and go to their homes than to invite him to officiate or receive the word of life from his lips.

All this was in spite of the fact that black Presbyterian ministers were formally trained and had carefully studied theology. However, the same could not be said of many of the other antebellum black ministers. Daniel Alexander Payne, who served as AME bishop from 1852 to 1896, declared that the first four bishops of the church did not have even a common school education. While whites often expressed contempt over this fact, they failed to understand that religious activities in black churches were essentially different from those in white churches. Black ministers spoke before a people oppressed by a hostile society, and it was their emotional appeal, rather than presentation geared to the fine points of theology, that influenced their listeners. And some whites conceded that the lack of educational attainment was not necessarily a disadvantage. In an article entitled "A Colored Female Preacher," the *National Anti-Slavery Standard* reported in May 1843 that "last Sabbath afternoon we had the pleasure of listening to a very touching discourse from a colored woman, in the Sixth Street Methodist colored church of New York City. She was once a slave, and is a fine specimen of natural oratory. In propriety, energy, and grace of action, she beats any teacher of elocution we ever heard."

The black churches became centers of social intercourse in a manner foreign to white churches. They spawned beneficial societies, black schools, and a number of other agencies that sought to promote the welfare of the black masses. No other institution disseminated news or information among blacks as quickly as the church. Since blacks were not generally served by labor unions or occupational benevolent associations, the church took on much of this type of activity. The only formal employment aid center established for blacks in antebellum Boston was founded by a black minister.

Black ministers could usually relate to the needs and concerns of the laboring members of their congregations, since they themselves were personally familiar with many of the problems of poverty and discrimination that affected the lives of all blacks, especially the poorer ones. So many members of Leonard A. Grimes' church in Boston were fugitives from slavery that the church was commonly called the "fugitive church."

The black church served as a community service center, an educational center, and an assembly hall for protest meetings. Shiloh in New York City could accommodate sixteen hundred people in its building at Prince and Marion streets and was considered "eminently suited as a meeting hall" in a city where blacks could not ordinarily hire such halls. The church was also a social welfare agency, seeking to maintain the viability and integrity of the black family unit by encouraging parents to bring up their children under a strict moral regimen and to impress upon them the necessity of keeping their young in school.

Believing that "knowledge is power," the black church developed its own schools. Nineteen black Philadelphia churches offered Sabbath school education taught by blacks, and in 1856, 1,882 blacks attended these schools. Conducted on Sundays, these schools mainly emphasized the memorizing of the Scriptures. However, the libraries established on the church grounds offered poor children of the black community one of their few contacts with a variety of reading materials. The Sabbath schools were either free or low in cost, but they had the disadvantage of being staffed by church members whose emphasis was on religion rather than on education.

The church also furnished a cultural center for the black community. Musical concerts and dramatic productions were held on its premises, which served as both practice center and concert hall for musical performances. The buildings were the meeting centers for all sorts of religious and secular societies. They signified the emergence of economic cooperation in the black community. W.E.B. Du Bois has pointed out that "it was the Negro's desire to purchase his own house of worship that began a pooling of their meager economic resources."

The role of the black minister, like that of the church, was of necessity diverse. "The preacher's function," Carter G. Woodson noted, "was not limited to pulpit reading and soul saving. He was a walking encyclopedia, the friend of the unfortunate, the social welfare organizer, and the interpreter of the signs of the times." Some ministers were better known for their organizational work than for their work in their churches.

Among their other activities, black ministers were involved in education, and many taught evening classes for adults. Samuel E. Cornish served as a traveling agent for the African Free Schools of New York to encourage attendance. Other ministers who also served in this capacity were Benjamin Paul, William Miller, and Peter Williams, Jr. When the African Dorcas Association was organized to provide clothing for the children attending the schools of the New York Manumission Society, the ministers of the African churches comprised the committee.

Black ministers were an important force in the development of Philadelphia's Institute for Colored Youth, one of the nation's outstanding black schools. Begun by a group of Quakers as a farm school in 1842, the institute moved to the city ten years later at the urging of Philadelphia's black ministers, led by William T. Catto. Among the subjects to be taught at the institute's new facilities were philosophy, physiology, Latin and Greek, classical literature, and advanced mathematics, including trigonometry. On the advice of the black ministers, Haitian-born Charles L. Reason, a professor of mathematics at New York Central College, was hired and placed in charge of implementing this new curriculum. When Reason resigned his post in 1855, the black ministers helped select black teacher Ebenezer Don Carlos Bassett to succeed him. A graduate with high honors from Birmingham Academy and Connecticut Normal School, Bassett had taught in the public grammar schools of New Haven and taken graduate courses at Yale University.

Once admitted to the Institute for Colored Youth, students were issued books and library privileges without charge. The institute's reading room and library contained over two thousand volumes. All six teachers were black, three of them graduates of the institute. Sarah Mapps Douglass, from a prominent Negro Quaker family in Philadelphia and for many years a teacher, was in charge of the Preparatory Department of the Institute for Colored Youth, and lectured in physiology and hygiene.

Although black ministers paid tribute to the Quaker gift of education, they openly resented the paternalistic view of many Quakers that Negroes were childlike and had to be looked after and told what to do. Such condescending treatment of blacks in Quaker-financed schools, they believed, did little to aid in the development of black pride.

Some black ministers found that their congregations were either too small or too poor to provide them with a salary or to support them in their old age. But in general, they were supported by the black community. In this respect, black ministers were more independent of white society than other blacks. They could speak out on controversial subjects like slavery and civil rights with some immunity from a white backlash. In this respect, too, black ministers in Northern cities were more fortunate than those in the South, where their activities were curbed by the white society. But even the Northern black minister had to be cautious, for the power of that white society could make itself felt in riots in which black churches were often the first targets.

The church was thus the most important institution in the Northern black community. It was a place of worship, a social and cultural center, a political meeting place, a hiding place for fugitives, a training ground for potential community leaders, and one of the few places where blacks could express their true feelings. "It has been in the church," wrote black sociologist E. Franklin Frazier, "that the Negro has found a meaning for his existence and it was the church that enlisted his deepest loyalties."

BLACK MUTUAL AID AND BENEVOLENT SOCIETIES

Despite their widespread poverty, blacks could not expect help from the mushrooming array of evangelical Christian or immigrant-aid societies, since most of these served only either white denominations or the nationalities that financed them. Black beneficial associations arose to help meet this problem. Although their privileges and benefits were limited to members and their immediate families, the aid societies performed invaluable roles in caring for those blacks who were sick, homeless, and destitute.

The first society with a goal of mutual aid was the Free African Society of Philadelphia, founded in 1787 and out of which grew Bethel, the original AME church. The society taxed its members a shilling a month in order to make funds available to the needy, "provided this necessity is not brought on them by their imprudence." The society also pledged itself to provide school or apprenticeships for the children of deceased members.

The first organization among Philadelphia blacks exclusively devoted to mutual aid was established in 1795. Other mutual aid organizations followed rapidly, and by 1815, there were eighty such organizations with 7,448 members. The growth continued, and by 1855, Philadelphia's blacks had 108 mutual benefit societies with 9,762 members, an annual income of $29,600, and permanent investments totaling $28,365. Participating members paid dues ranging from $3 to $5 a year, collected weekly or monthly.

The societies apparently worked efficiently. Edward Needles' study of blacks undertaken for the Pennsylvania Abolition Society revealed that the number of blacks receiving aid in the almshouses had decreased between 1837 and 1847 because of the work of these benevolent associations.

The New York African Society was formed in 1817 "to raise a fund to be appropriated exclusively to the support of such of its members as shall by reason of sickness and infirmity be incapable of attending their usual vocation of employment and also towards the relief of the widows and orphans of deceased members." The society grew rapidly. In 1852, its yearly income from rents and properties amounted to $2,000, while its membership dues for that year totaled $197.25.

The African Clarkson Association, incorporated in 1829, was another mutual aid society formed in New York. It was founded as a "charitable society of African descent to afford mutual means of education to the members thereof and relief to their families in case of sickness and death." Members had to be between the ages of twenty-one and forty and pay dues of twenty-five cents per month. Sick benefit payments of $2 per week were provided for three months to members with one year's standing. Widows were granted $20 per year in addition to a $15 burial allowance.

The Abyssinian Benevolent Daughters of Estes Association in New York City was patterned closely after the men's mutual aid societies. Those between the ages of sixteen and fifty were eligible for membership, but the society excluded "any person addicted to insobriety or having a plurality of husbands." Dues were seventy-five cents quarterly. Included in the benefits to the members was a $2 weekly sick benefit payment for six months, "provided the sickness is not the result of immoral conduct." Benefits were also provided in case of the incapacity of members' husbands, but specifically barred was any allowance in case of pregnancy.

When the city of Boston refused in a number of instances to care for those Negroes who were too poor or too sickly to take care of themselves, a group of forty-two blacks came together in 1796 and formed the African Humane Society. Although poor, they paid a twenty-five cent membership fee and contributed what they could to help the sick, pay the funeral expenses of those Negroes whose families could not afford it, and provide aid for widows and children who could not otherwise care for themselves. In their constitution, the members made it clear that they were only a benevolent organization, and that "behaving ourselves . . . we take no one into the society who shall commit any injustice or outrage against the laws of their country."

Other Boston benevolent associations exercised a different form of selectivity in deciding who should be members. While the African Society of Boston set its initiation fee at twenty-five cents and required another twenty-five cents in monthly dues, the dues had to be paid for one full year before any benefits were provided to the member. This financial requirement probably made membership in the society difficult for all but the economically stable.

Although most benevolent associations confined themselves to meeting the need for which they had been organized, some also engaged in social and ceremonial activities. Members of the African Society of Salem, Massachusetts, often appeared with musical instruments at weddings and funerals and paraded on the anniversaries of the abolition of slavery in the British West Indies. Karl Bernhard, a foreign visitor to New York, described the formal dress parade of the Wilberforce Philanthropic Society of New York, organized in 1812, when "during a quarter of an hour scarcely any but black faces were to be seen on Broadway." The imminent passage of the New York State law abolishing slavery was the occasion for this "great procession of well-dressed Negroes on October 26, 1826 parading through the streets two by two preceded by music and a flag." Bernhard noted, too, that one member "solemnly bore a large sky blue box containing the fund raised by weekly subscription for the purpose of assisting sick and unfortunate blacks while alongside stood the treasurer of the society carrying a large golden key. . . . The rest of the officers wore ribands of several colours and badges like the officers of free Masons, while Marshals with large staves walked outside of the procession."

African Dorcas Associations were formed in many cities and towns by black women. Like their biblical namesake who gave clothing to the poor, the groups provided hats, shoes, and coats to needy blacks, especially school children. The Harrisburg (Pennsylvania) Dorcas Society stipulated that none of its food, clothing, or fuel was to go "to drunkards, kidnappers, betrayers or base idle persons." The African Dorcas Association in New York City was formed by women connected with the African Free School (assisted by black ministers) for the purpose of "providing and making garments for the destitute," especially children who could not attend school for lack of clothing. In 1829, the group reported that it had clothed forty-nine boys and twenty-five girls during the year and had distributed a total of 232 garments, including shoes and hats.

An important benevolent enterprise of the period was the Colored Orphans Asylum in New York City. In 1833, two black women made plans for establishing a home for black children. The public was urged to contribute funds, and $2,000 was collected. In 1836, a board of twenty-two lady managers was elected, with an advisory committee of five men. A constitution was adopted, and the organization was launched under the title of the "Association for the Benefit of Colored Orphans." The society's object was "to provide and maintain a place of Refuge for colored orphans, where they shall be boarded, clothed, and suitably educated until of an age to be bound out or apprenticed." While full orphans would receive preference, half-orphans would also be admitted.

After unsuccessfully trying to induce property owners to lease an empty dwelling, a small building was acquired on Twelfth Street, near Sixth Avenue, for the sum of $9,000. The association progressed so rapidly that by 1843, it was financially strong enough to move into new headquarters on Fifth Avenue. Indeed, so effective was the work of the Colored Orphans Asylum that it attracted both municipal and state support. By February 1851, the asylum had received 524 children. Most of them at the time of their admittance were young—half under eight years of age. They remained at the institution until the age of twelve, when they were apprenticed in the country. Half-orphans' parents paid a small amount for board and could receive custody of their children at the age of twelve, provided they could prove their ability to take care of them.

The Society for the Relief of Worthy Aged, Indigent Colored Persons in New York City, more popularly known as the Colored Home, was another organization formed by the black community to ameliorate the conditions of needy blacks. Incorporated by the state legislature in 1845, the society made arrangements with the commissioner of the alms house to receive at a very low rate all aged black paupers in the city, reserving the right to reject such applicants as the resident physician should pronounce medically unfit for the Colored Home. By 1852, the twelfth year of its operation, the Colored Home was accommodating upwards of two hundred persons at its building on Sixty-fifth Street, between Avenue A and First Avenue.

The Colored Seamen's Home in New York City represented another type of black benevolent enterprise. In 1837, the American Seamen's Friend Society, a Protestant missionary organization, established a home for sailors in the city. Two years later, the society approached William P. Powell, a former black seaman active in New York's black community, with the proposal that he start a home for black seamen, some two thousand of whom sailed regularly from the port of New York City. The need was desperate. If conditions were horrible for white seamen, they were doubly so for black sailors. For paltry wages—$10 a month for long voyages for ordinary seamen—they experienced extreme personal danger and the ''unbearable brutality of master and mate.'' Many were ''despoiled of their clothing by shipmates, and sometimes by the officers'' while at sea. Destitute and homeless, many black sailors were denied admission into the alms house or the Sailors Snug House. Most were at the mercy of rum-selling boardinghouses, where they could quickly be robbed of their wages.

With the financial assistance of the American Seamen's Friend Society, Powell launched the Colored Seamen's Home in mid-1839 at 70 John Street. While most boarders paid for their stay, no ''destitute black sailors'' were turned away, and all received board and clothing. To accommodate an increasing number of seamen, a three-story brick building was acquired at 230 Pearl Street in 1849. In that year, Powell reported that the annual average number of boarders was 400, and that since its founding, about 4,175 had been cared for. While the American Seamen's Friend Society was the principal source of outside financial support for the Colored Seamen's Home, Powell provided additional funds out of his own pocket, and on the tenth anniversary of its founding, it was reported that ''in a pecuniary point of view, it [the home] had been to him a source of considerable loss.''

For black seamen, boardinghouses were more than residences. They performed the function of fraternal organizations and social clubs as well. For those without families, boardinghouses provided companionship and mutual support. They were sometimes small communities offering recreation, social contact, and even protection for their residents. After a visit in February 1848, Frederick Douglass praised Powell's Colored Seamen's Home as "an *Oasis* in the desert, when compared with many houses where seamen usually congregate." The banner of temperance floated conspicuously throughout the establishment, and an excellent library and other reading room facilities were available. At meal times and on every other occasion, Powell led discussions of the issues confronting blacks. Douglass himself had escaped from slavery with the aid of a black seaman who was his height and who had lent him his sailor's suit and a sailor's "protection," and he was very much impressed with the discussions held at Powell's home concerning slavery and the need for conducting a continuous struggle against it.

During the Civil War the Colored Seamen's Home became the headquarters of the American Seamen's Protective Association, a pioneer union of Negro workers and the first seamen's organization in the United States. Even before the Civil War, black workers tried to unite for protection and alleviation of their conditions. But such societies as the New York African Society for Mutual Relief, founded in 1808; the Coachmen's Benevolent Society and the Humane Mechanics, organized in Philadelphia in the 1820s; and the Stewards' and Cooks' Marine Benevolent Society, established in New York in the 1830s, resembled fraternal lodges more than trade unions, emphasizing "the need to relieve the distressed, and soften the forms of poverty, by timely aid to the afflicted."

Another type of organization among black workers before the Civil War was the American League of Colored Laborers, organized in New York City in July 1850, with Samuel Ringgold Ward as president and Frederick Douglass as vice-president. Its main object was to promote unity among mechanics, foster training in agriculture, industrial arts, and commerce, and to assist member mechanics in setting up in business for themselves. Clearly the league was interested in industrial education rather than trade union activity; moreover, its orientation was toward the self-employed artisan.

BLACK FRATERNAL SOCIETIES

Among the most important organizations in the black community were secret societies, such as the Masons and Odd Fellows. Both movements resulted from the discrimination practiced by whites. Freemasonry among blacks developed after the Revolutionary War, when Prince Hall, a Methodist minister who had served with the colonial army in the American Revolution, and fourteen other Boston blacks received a charter from the Grand Lodge of England, after American Masons had denied the group a charter. Organized as African Lodge No. 459 with Hall as master, and later renamed the Prince Hall Lodge, the African Lodge grew in size and influence, and its program of education and community service was notable. Weekly sick dues were provided for members unable to work, and loans were made to members and their families.

By 1797, the movement had spread to Philadelphia and Rhode Island, by 1812 to New York, and by 1825 to Washington and Maryland. In those states, too, the lodge's programs complemented those of the mutual aid societies and the black church. In 1832, another Grand Lodge of black Masons was established by a dissident group in Philadelphia known as the Hiram Grand Lodge of the State of Pennsylvania. In 1847, the Prince Hall Lodge of Massachusetts joined with the two Pennsylvania lodges to form the National Grand Lodge of Colored Masons. Although they were united among themselves, the black Free Masons still did not achieve legitimacy in the eyes of white Free Masons.

The Odd Fellows movement had a similar history. In 1842, blacks in New York and Philadelphia were denied admission to the international order because of race. The Grand Lodge of New York made it plain that only "free white males of good moral character" were eligible, causing the *Ram's Horn*, a black paper, to comment that "strange as it seems the very persons who had been prating of obligations to their fellow men and of sympathy and suffering, who had inscribed on their banners that beautiful triad—'Friendship, Love and Truth'—now felt their dignity in danger and most incourteously refused their request." The black groups sent Peter Ogden, a New York black, to England to make application to the parent body. Ogden was initiated as a member of the Victorian Lodge in Liverpool, achieved high honors in the society, and returned to the United States with authority to establish a branch in New York. In 1843, the Philomethan Lodge of the Odd Fellows, the first lodge of which blacks could become members, was chartered. Within five years, twenty-four lodges had been established with a combined membership of almost two thousand.

The fraternal groups presented large musical festivals and dances several times during the year. Especially famous was the "Soiree Musicale" sponsored by the Odd Fellows of Boston during the 1840s. Organization members marched in full regalia to the hall, already crowded with party goers. Entertainment for the evening included vocal and instrumental presentations, followed by dancing.

In September 1856 a convention of the Colored Odd Fellows of New York, Baltimore, Philadelphia, Boston, and Washington, D.C., was held in New York City. The procession of the black Odd Fellows moved up Fifth Avenue, Seventeenth Street, Fourth Avenue, Bowery, Chatham, and Nassau streets, and back up to the Broadway Tabernacle where the chair was taken by the Grand Master, David B. Bornsen of Philadelphia. In the evening, a grand promenade concert was held at the Crystal Palace, which was brilliantly illuminated for the occasion. The *New York Tribune* commented:

Upon the whole, this demonstration showed that our colored people North, who are so frequently represented as lazy, poor, and miserable, are rather thrifty, brotherly, respectable, and independent. . . . It was a turnout creditable to itself and to our city, and pleasant to look upon.

Delegates representing Colored Free Masons from five states convened at the Columbus (Ohio) AME church in June 1857, heard speeches, passed resolutions, and treated the citizens to a parade complete with brass band in full regalia.

These conferences and local meetings were important to blacks who were excluded from white cultural institutions. They provided socialization and programs for economic advancement and mutual relief and gave their members a feeling of prestige. All blacks experienced a sense of pride in the public demonstrations.

BLACK SELF-IMPROVEMENT SOCIETIES

Barred in nearly all Northern cities from using libraries, attending lectures, or participating in debates with whites outside of the ranks of abolitionists, blacks formed their own self-improvement societies. In the late 1820s and early 1830s, literary clubs, debating groups, and library companies sprang up in every urban community of the North with a sizable black population. Boston had its Debating Club, in which eighteen or twenty members met once every two weeks for the extemporaneous discussion of current subjects. Philadelphia had its Library for Colored People, with over one thousand volumes and at which young black men spent two and three evenings a week debating moral and literary questions. Pittsburgh had its Theban Literary Society, Albany its Union Society for the Improvement of the Colored People in Morals, Education and Mechanic Arts, and Troy, New York, its Mental and Moral Improvement Association. In 1831, the Female Literary Association was formed in Philadelphia and was followed a year later by the Afric-American Female Intelligence Society in Boston. The latter was both a literary and mutual aid organization. Maria W. Stewart, the first black woman lecturer and one of the first women of any color to speak in public, delivered an address before the Afric-American Female Intelligence Society in 1832, the same year it was founded.

One of the most celebrated of these societies was the Phoenix Literary Society of New York City. Founded in 1833, it included Christopher Rush, Thomas L. Jennings, Theodore S. Wright, and Peter Vogelsang, and the white Arthur Tappan. The board was composed of both whites and blacks, but it was Tappan, the wealthy philanthropist and abolitionist, who remained the society's chief financial backer. Its aim was indeed ambitious, since it sought to accomplish the following objectives:

To visit every family in the ward, and make a register of every colored person in it—their name, sex, age, occupation, if they read, write, and cipher—to invite them, old and young, and of both sexes, to become members of this society, and to make quarterly payments according to their ability—to get the children out to infant, Sabbath, and week schools, and induce the adults also to attend school and church on the Sabbath—to encourage the women to form Dorcas societies to help clothe poor children of color if they will attend school, the clothes to be loaned, and to be taken away from them if they neglect their schools; and impress on their parents the importance of having the children punctual and regular in their attendance at school—to establish mental feasts, and also lyceums for speaking and for lectures on the sciences, and to form moral societies—to seek out young men of talent, and good moral character, that they may be assisted to obtain a liberal education—to report to the board all mechanics who are skillful and capable of conducting their trades and with respectable farmers for lads of good moral character—giving a preference to those who have learned to read, write and cipher—and in every way to endeavor to promote the happiness of the people of color, by encouraging them to improve their minds, and to abstain from every vicious and demoralizing practice.

The Phoenix Society normally held its gatherings at New York City's famous Broadway Tabernacle. There literary presentations were often given by its members, but the society did not limit itself to literary exercises. It established the School for Colored People, which met three times a week also at the Broadway Tabernacle. Tuition was $3 per quarter, and instruction was offered in reading, writing and geography. The school operated for two years and then suffered a sharp decline. By 1839, the Phoenix Society itself had passed out of existence.

The literary society that outlived all the others and exerted the greatest influence in the New York black community was the Philomathean Literary Society. Founded in 1829 for the purpose of "devoting itself to the improvement of literature and useful knowledge," it met regularly on Tuesday evenings in its own hall on Duane Street. At its gatherings, debates and recitations were presented, along with select readings on moral and scientific subjects.

Membership was limited to those with a "good moral character and the desire to improve the mind," and its roster of members included such distinguished black leaders as Dr. James McCune Smith, the physician and civil rights activist, and Philip Bell, owner of the *Colored American,* who was also active in the New York African Society for Mutual Relief. Members of the society read original essays and poetry, held debates, and attended lectures on scientific and literary subjects. The 1841 program, for example, included lectures on "Music—Its Practical Influence in Society," "Geography," "The Philosophy of Phrenology," "Duty of Young Men," "Touissaint L'Ouverture," and "Patriots of the American Revolution." Of the fourteen men scheduled for lectures in 1841, almost half were black, including Reverend Samuel E. Cornish, whose lecture was "The Incipient Measures to a Right Understanding of the Laws that Govern Mind and Matter," Dr. James McCune Smith on "Circulation of the Blood," and Alexander Crummell on "Oratory—Interspersed with Recitations." At the time, the Philomatheans owned a library of over eight-hundred books and still expanding.

"Among no people in proportion to their means and advantages is the pursuit

of knowledge more honored than among the colored inhabitants of Philadelphia,'' wrote ''A Southerner'' in 1841. On March 20, 1828, William Whipper, a prominent Philadelphia black, gathered a group of his people together for
the purpose of the ''Improvement of Colored People in the Neighborhood of
Philadelphia.'' Whipper noted the limited educational opportunities for blacks in
the city and felt ''bound to open an institution to which they may repair and
qualify themselves for future usefulness.'' A ''Reading Room'' was established
at the African Methodist church on Lombard Street, and weekly meetings afforded members the opportunity to discuss ideas gained from the reading of
books.

Founded in 1833, the Philadelphia Library Company of Colored Persons emu-
lated the white library company that had been started by Benjamin Franklin. By
1841, it had a hundred members and six hundred books. There was a fee of one
dollar to join and monthly dues of twenty-five cents. The Rush Library and
Debating Society (1836), the Demosthenian Institute (1837), and the Moral
Reform Society (1837) followed. In 1837, there were five lyceums and debating
clubs in Philadelphia maintained by black men and women, with a combined
membership of 260. Philadelphia also had the only self-improvement society
made up of members of both sexes—the Gilbert Lyceum, founded in 1841, with
Jacob C. White as president and Grace Douglass as treasurer. But Philadelphia's
black women, not satisfied with the single opportunity, also formed four of their
own self-improvement societies. The first was the Female Literary Society of
Philadelphia, followed in the 1830s by the Minerva Literary Society and the
Edgeworth Society. The last of the antebellum women's societies was the Sarah
M. Douglass Literary Circle formed in September 1859, named in honor of the
teacher of Philadelphia's black young women.

The most noted of the antebellum Philadelphia black literary societies was the
Banneker Institute, named after the black scientist Benjamin Banneker. Founded
in 1854, it was composed primarily of young black men. The institute had a
library of 450 books by 1860, by which time its lectures and discussions were
well known in the city. The schedule of speakers and topics for 1855 and 1856
included Sarah M. Douglass, on ''Anatomy,'' Isaiah C. Wears and Miss A. M.
Shadd, on ''Canada,'' Robert Campbell, on ''Chemistry of the Atmosphere,''
Reverend Jeremiah Asher, on ''Does the Bible Sanction Slavery?'' and Professor Pliny E. Chase, on ''Mental Physiology.'' In 1859, lectures were given on
such diverse subjects as music, mathematics, and Napoleon III.

The Debating Society of the Banneker Institute met in the evening in the
building of the Institute for Colored Youth to discuss both scholarly matters and
events of the day. On February 2, 1859, the debate was on the question ''Has
Slavery Been Beneficial to the African Race?'' Another subject debated at the
institute was ''Has Africa Any Claims Upon Us as a People?'' Fortunately, John
C. White, Jr., the Banneker Institute's secretary, kept careful minutes of its
meetings and debates for many years, and these and other records have been
preserved by the Historical Society of Pennsylvania.

In 1858, an effort was made to include the Banneker Institute in the white debating societies' city-wide organization. A petition was submitted to the National Literary Congress asking that the Banneker Institute be considered for membership. Congress delegates visited the meetings of the black group ''in order to ascertain if it were a *bona fide Literary Society*.'' These men reported back to the Congress that the organization was purely of literary character and recommended that it ''admit the Banneker Institute as a member of the Literary Congress.'' In the end, however, the proposal was rejected because of the color of the institute's members.

Throughout its existence, the Banneker Institute gave its black members opportunities to debate and discuss the current issues of the day and to read on a wide variety of subjects. It provided a practical training ground for young black men. The discussions were not solely academic. The members of the institute regularly sent memorials to the Pennsylvania legislature calling for repeal of laws discriminating against blacks.

Most of the antebellum black literary societies, like all of the fraternal and many of the mutual aid societies, were for men only. Yet in many of the social groups in the black community, men and women worked together. Significantly, too, the black-sponsored Adelphic Union Library Association of Boston, when it broadened its program to include lectures on various topics of educational and current interest, invited women to speak before them. Indeed, the association opened its meetings to all, regardless of color or sex.

Unlike groups like the Brown Fellows of Charleston, most of the Northern urban black societies did not represent an economic or social elite. There was certainly a disproportionate number of small businessmen, professionals, and skilled workers among the membership, but unskilled black workers were not totally excluded. (They would have been discouraged, however, by the practice of the Boston Adelphic Union Library Association of charging fifty cents for each lecture or seventy-five cents for the seasonal series.) There was no evidence of color distinction in any of the Northern societies.

The existence of black self-improvement societies appeared to some to be, in itself, an effective refutation of the charge of Negro inferiority. A black New Yorker put it strongly (if somewhat naively) in the *Colored American* of March 11, 1837:

Mr. Editor—It is certainly gratifying to know that there is in existence, in this city, a number of associations, male and female, devoted to the mental and literary improvement of our people. Their establishment has been procured by the spirited efforts of individuals, who have deeply at heart, whatever concerns the interest of the oppressed; and for years have been diffusing among us their benign influences. I care not how many societies, whose objects are moral and mental improvement are raised up. They will do good among us. They will tend to clear us from the charge of indolence, or indifference, to our own welfare which has been heaped upon us. These societies will be productive of the happiest, and most beneficial results, and will not fail to win the approbation of the wise and good of every community. If academic privileges are withheld, they prove a readiness in us to avail ourselves of every means of improvement which lies within our reach. They show, too, that we are not a people given to revelry and licentiousness as we have been basely misrepresented, but that the leisure hours of many are devoted to thought and literary advancement.

Both the benevolent and literary societies reflected a deepening concern on the part of the black community, or at least of some in the community, for the mental and moral uplift of the people. But the major uplift organization in the black community was devoted to destroying the influence of "demon rum." Black leaders were deeply committed to the temperance cause as a solution to the major problems of poor Negroes, including child neglect. They insisted that poverty was in part due to intemperance and that no progress could be made toward solving the situation of those living in squalor until they swore to refrain from drinking.

BLACK TEMPERANCE SOCIETIES

Although some of the mutual aid and other improvement bodies frequently sponsored temperance, blacks were urged to sustain the cause of temperance by the "formation of societies for its promotion." The response was immediate, and local temperance societies sprang up in cities all over the North, at whose meetings blacks took the "cold water pledge." In 1837, there were four black temperance organizations in Philadelphia, and the number appears to have grown to about ten in 1842. During the 1840s, nearly one-fourth of Cincinnati's entire black population belonged to temperance societies. Pressure within the community prohibited blacks from openly selling alcoholic beverages. In 1834, William Whipper operated a "Free Labor and Temperance Grocery" in Philadelphia, and when he married Harriet L. L. Smith in Columbia, Pennsylvania, in 1836, the wedding omitted both wine and the products of slave labor. Lemonade was the standard drink at social gatherings among the black upper class in Philadelphia. James Forten, one of Philadelphia's leading black businessmen, refused to hire any worker who was not a teetotaler to work at his sail-manufacturing establishment.

The Temperance Society of the People of Color of New Haven, founded in 1829, was the pioneer local black organization, and the Connecticut State Temperance Society of Colored People, organized in 1836, was the first such statewide organization. Others followed, including the Grand Lodge of the Order of Colored Sons of Temperance, formed on January 1, 1850, at Cincinnati.

The various black temperance groups maintained a steady stream of circulars, lectures, and newspaper articles to curb habitual drinking, which they claimed would "destroy us and all we hold dear." But the black temperance crusade was long on planning and passing resolutions and short on performance. Little action was taken to attract lower-class blacks, laborers, sailors, and other unskilled workers who required the most aid, and the societies were mainly made up of those most committed to the middle-class values that temperance represented. Although temperance meetings were held regularly, the participants were inactive between programs. Prejudice also plagued the temperance movement. In 1850, the national division of the Temperance Society excluded blacks from membership. In general, white temperance societies did not provide the blacks with much-needed cooperation. Yet despite shortcomings, the temperance movement among black Americans was at least as effective as that among whites.

We lack data as to the precise number of societies formed by blacks in the North during the antebellum period. One student has estimated that at least fifty were launched between 1800 and 1860 in New York City alone, and we know that in Philadelphia, there were several hundred societies during these same years. Many, to be sure, were weak and short-lived, such as the American League of Colored Laborers, organized in New York City in July 1850 with Samuel Ringgold Ward as president and Frederick Douglass as vice-president. Its main objectives, as we have seen, were to promote unity among mechanics, foster training in agriculture, industrial arts, and commerce, and assist members in establishing businesses for themselves. But it seems to have gone out of existence directly after it was organized. Other societies, however, flourished and grew into significant organizations. Mutual aid and self-improvement societies, Masonic Lodges, Odd Fellows, and temperance movements, founded and controlled by blacks, provided a sanctuary where no one was insulted because of complexion. The church, the lodge, and the society provided for common social needs and brought people together for praying, singing, dancing, talking, and learning in an environment free of the repressions and persecutions of the dominant white society.

THE BLACK PRESS: *FREEDOM'S JOURNAL* AND *RIGHTS FOR ALL*

"We wish to plead our cause. Too long have others spoken for us." These words are from *Freedom's Journal*, the first black newspaper in the United States. The launching of *Freedom's Journal* resulted from a variety of circumstances. The New York City press regularly featured continuous tirades against blacks, and by 1827, leaders of the black community had decided that the only effective answer lay in the launching of a black newspaper. Early that year, at a meeting in the home of Boston Crummell, they put up the funds for a black-owned paper and selected two young blacks to launch and continue the journal. Reverend Samuel E. Cornish was chosen senior editor and John Browne Russwurm, recently graduated from Bowdoin College, junior editor.

Samuel E. Cornish was born free in about 1795 in Delaware and was raised in Philadelphia and New York City. After graduating from a Free African School, he studied for the Presbyterian ministry. In 1819, he was judged by the presbytery of Philadelphia to have received "a respectable literary education" and to be "of good moral character," and he was licensed as a probationary minister. He was later ordained by the New York Presbytery, and in 1824 he became the first pastor of the First Colored Presbyterian Church of New York City, serving in that capacity until 1818.

Russwurm, it will be recalled, had planned to move to Haiti or attend medical school in Boston after his graduation from Bowdoin College. Instead, he moved to New York City, and his presence there as well as the availability of Cornish must have been a major factor in the move to launch *Freedom's Journal.*

Describing themselves as editors and proprietors, Cornish and Russwurm issued and distributed a prospectus announcing the forthcoming publication of a paper to be called *Freedom's Journal.* Appealing for subscribers, they wrote:

Daily slandered, we think that there ought to be some channel of communication between us and the public through which a single voice may be heard, *in defense of five hundred thousand free people of colour.* For often has injustice been heaped upon us when our only defense was an appeal to the *Almighty;* but we believe that the time has now arrived, when the calumnies of our enemies should be refuted by forcible arguments.

The census of 1830 listed only 319,599 free Negroes in the United States. But *Freedom's Journal* always referred to 500,000. Undoubtedly the editors, like other blacks of the period, were aware that many escaped slaves hid from the census takers.

Upon receiving the prospectus, blacks in several communities began drumming up support. Toward the end of February 1827, several leading blacks in Boston met and passed resolutions that "there is reason to believe that great good work will result to the People of Colour by the publication of 'FREEDOM'S JOURNAL.'" They urged that Boston's black citizens give it their utmost support and patronage in order to secure its success.

The first issue of *Freedom's Journal,* appearing on March 16, 1827, had sixteen pages, including an editorial page with the heading "To Our Patrons." It opened with the historic words quoted at the opening of this section: "We wish to plead our own cause. Too long have others spoken for us." It stressed the "interesting fact" that "no publication as yet" had been devoted "exclusively" to the "improvement" of the hundreds of thousands of free people of color in the United States and that, therefore, this "large body of our citizens have no public channel" through which to voice their grievances. *Freedom's Journal* proposed to fill this vacuum, though, at the same time, the editors "would not be unmindful of our brethren who are still in the iron fetters of bondage." The opening editorial also took a stand in favor of civil rights in general and the ballot in particular. "The civil rights of a people being of the greatest value," it stressed, "it shall ever be our duty to vindicate our brethren, when oppressed; and to lay the case before the public. We shall also urge upon our brethren . . . the expediency of using their elective franchise; and of making an independent use of the same. We wish them not to become tools of party."

The editors pledged to print "everything that relates to Africa" and to devote space to "News from Hayti." They guaranteed that "we shall never insert any news whatever of a doubtful nature concerning that island," whose citizens had "erected the standard of liberty," and were determined to maintain their independence "in the face of the universe." Finally, the editors declared that it was their

earnest wish to make our Journal a medium of intercourse between our brethren in the different states of this great confederacy; that through its columns an expression of our sentiments, on many interesting subjects which concern us, may be offered to the public: that plans which apparently are beneficial may be candidly discussed and properly weighed: if worthy, receive our cordial approbation; if not, our marked disapprobation.

Besides the prospectus, the opening editorial, and the testimonial of good-wishers, the first issue contained the first installment of the "Memoirs" of Paul Cuffe, the black sea captain, ship owner, and philanthropist; a report on the "Unconstitutional seizure and imprisonment of free men of color in the South"; articles on the "Common Schools of New York," "The Church and the Auction Block," "Chinese Fashions," "The Egg Trade," and "On Choosing a Wife by Proxy"; an antislavery article reprinted from the *New York Christian Advocate*; a poem about the capture and enslavement of an African chief; "A True Story," an essay on "The Effect of Sight upon a Person Born Blind"; and entertainment and variety departments. Also included in the paper were notices of marriages, deaths, and court trials. Commercial advertisements were printed on the last page. The paper was to be published every Friday at 5 Varick Street in Manhattan and would sell for three dollars a year. Already, readers were informed, *Freedom's Journal* had authorized agents in Portland, Maine; Boston and Salem, Massachusetts; Providence, Rhode Island; New London, Connecticut; Philadelphia and Columbia, Pennsylvania; Albany, New York; Newark, Princeton, and New Brunswick, New Jersey; Baltimore; and Washington, D.C.

As part of a campaign against wholesale detractors of black people, *Freedom's Journal* ran a series of articles designed to educate both blacks and whites to some of the notable accomplishments of blacks in various parts of the world. Five articles appeared on the history of Haiti, highlighting the virtues of the black-run government after the island's successful revolution against French control and the establishment of the first black republic in 1804. At about the same time, the paper carried a three-installment piece on Touissaint L'Ouverture, the brilliant black general who had led the black revolution and ruled the island until he was tricked into departing for France, where he died in prison. Other articles dealt with Antony Williams Arno, an African philosophy teacher in Europe, Olaudah Equiano, an African who wrote an autobiography of his life in Africa and America, Richard Allen, Benjamin Banneker, James Derham, black doctor, Paul Cuffe, shipowner and pioneer African colonizationist, and quite often, the female poet, Phillis Wheatley. "Anything relating to Phillis Wheatley, who by her writings has reflected honour upon our name and character, and demonstrated to an unbelieving world that genius dwells not alone in 'skins of whitish hue,' " it declared in its January 23, 1828, issue, "will not surely be deemed uninteresting by the readers of *Freedom's Journal*." Writing in the issue of November 2, 1827, from Boston, Samuel E. Cornish commented: "To our shame I write it, '*our Poetess*' lies buried in the Northern-Burying-Ground, without a stone to mark the spot, where repose African genius and worth." He urged a nationwide drive by blacks to erect a monument in her honor—"let us evince to the world that we are not insensible to the fame and renown which her writings have conferred upon us—*that we are proud of them*."

The paper published poems by Phillis Wheatley and other blacks, including those by George M. Horton, the slave-poet of Chapel Hill, North Carolina. Emphasizing the "black is beautiful" theme, it carried the following poem by a black in its issue of June 8, 1827:

The Black Beauty
Written from Solomon's Songs.

"Black, I am, oh! daughters fair,"
But my beauty is most rare;
Black, indeed, appears my skin,
Beauteous, comely, all within:
Black, when by affliction press'd
Beauteous, when in Christ I rest;
Black, by sin's defiling flood.
Beauteous, wash'd in Jesus' blood:
Black, I am in mine own eyes,
Beauteous, in my Lord's I rise;
Black I am to men 'tis true;
Beauteous, in the angel's view:
Black, if Jesus frowns awhile,
Beauteous, when I see him smile;
Black, while in the tomb I lie,
Beauteous, when I mount the sky!

In the issue of August 10, 1827, a black woman, who signed herself "Matilda," spoke out in favor of "women's rights" in general and, in particular, for the rights of Negro women who, she pointed out, did not possess "the advantages with those of our sex, whose skins are not coloured like our own, but we can improve what little we have, and make our one talent produce two-fold." The editors welcomed "Matilda's" criticism that they did not pay enough attention to this question, and she wrote several articles for the paper on the role that young black women should play in the freedom struggle.

Every measure designed to limit the freedom of free blacks was reported in *Freedom's Journal* and editorially condemned. In its November 16, 1827, issue, the paper carried the text of the new ordinance adopted in Washington, D.C., requiring blacks to furnish "satisfactory evidence of their title to freedom" or face imprisonment "as an absconding slave." The editorial comment went:

We cannot see by what rules of equity, the free man of colour, in the pursuit of his lawful business, should be incarcerated in prison, called upon to prove his freedom, and in case of refusal, sold as an absconding slave. In common with other citizens, we have rights which are dear to us: and we shall never sit patiently, and see them trampled upon, without raising our feeble voice, and entering our protest against the unconstitutionality of all laws which tend towards curtailing them in the least degree.

The exclusion of blacks from the skilled trades by employers and white workers and the need for them to settle for work as common laborers came under frequent attack. "Such is the present state of things," declared *Freedom's Journal*, "that whatever qualifications our sons may possess, if we offer them to a respectable mechanic, we are met with the unreasonable reply, that my apprentices are not willing to work with coloured boys." The black paper firmly insisted that this pattern could be changed if employers would stop allowing hiring policy to be determined by their white journeymen and apprentices and would themselves take a firm stand against racial exclusion: "Let good men discountenance the evil." But the *Journal* failed to note that it was employers who often were responsible for the evil.

To the oft-repeated charge that the "jails and penitentiaries are crowded with coloured convicts," *Freedom's Journal* replied:

The coloured man's offence, three times out of four, grows out of the circumstances of his condition, while the white man's, most generally, is premeditated and vicious. Therefore, if more of our people, in proportion, have unhappily become the tenants of jails and penitentiaries, it does not prove them more subject to crime, or their characters more debased. . . . The white man possesses all the advantages, to education and competency, while the coloured man has scarcely any.

Freedom's Journal did not neglect the evils of slavery. In its fourth number (April 27, 1827), it struck a significant note, observing: "It is no use to wait until the negroes are fit to be freemen. Nothing but freedom will fit a man to be free. No other condition will draw forth the energies of his mind." It made its position clear in editorials like the following: "We abominate slavery, and all its advocates. We consider it as the most iniquitous system ever set in operation; which must sooner or later meet its due reward." When the editor of the *New York Evening Post* praised slavery both in the West Indies and in the Southern United States, *Freedom's Journal* lashed out:

For this absurd attempt, we can make but one apology; that is, of old age. The many years he the editor has been permitted to enjoy the goodness of Providence, perhaps, have impaired his mind, and left it without much of its former fruitfulness, without sufficient vigour to guide its decisions. This is the most charitable view we can take of such an effort. . . . The only rewards we can promise him, are the patronage of the South, and what is still more important the *eulogies* of the *Enquirer*.

The *New York Morning Enquirer* was a leader in the repeated scurrilous attacks upon New York's black community, which had led to the launching of *Freedom's Journal*.

Although it fulfilled the role as a paper of protest, *Freedom's Journal* devoted most of its pages to serving the developing black urban community. As Frederick Cooper points out: "It gave extensive coverage to the activities of black mutual relief, literary, temperance and fraternal societies, announcing their meetings, encouraging people to attend, and reporting what happened."

Cornish had originally accepted editorial responsibility for six months. When his term came to an end with the issue of September 14, 1827, he was succeeded by the junior editor, John Browne Russwurm. Immediately there was a noticeable decline in the quality and amount of editorial material. More serious was the fact that the Bowdoin graduate did an about-face on colonization to Africa.

From the outset, *Freedom's Journal* had waged a campaign against the American Colonization Society, and this had brought down upon it the bitter opposition of champions of colonization. Reverend Dr. Samuel Miller of Princeton, New Jersey, a fervent colonizationist, denounced the black weekly as "exerting an unfavourable influence upon the coloured population of New Jersey, and unworthy of the support of the wise and good among them." Then, late in January 1829, evidently under severe financial pressure, Russwurm wrote to James Gurley, secretary of the American Colonization Society, that he stood ready to take a staff position in Liberia. In February he announced his support of the "return to Africa movement" and started to feature articles in favor of colonization and the Colonization Society.

To the dismay of many blacks, Russwurm came out in the issue of March 7, 1829, in defense of a law recently passed in Ohio requiring free blacks to leave the state if they could not post a $500 bond guaranteeing good behavior. Russwurm put the reason succinctly: "Our rightful place is in Africa." In the issue of March 28, 1829, he announced that he was severing his connection with *Freedom's Journal*, and, convinced that blacks would never achieve "the rights and privileges of citizens" in the United States, he was leaving for Liberia.

Russwurm was well rewarded by the American Colonization Society for his advocacy. Awarded a master's degree by Bowdoin, he was sent to Liberia as superintendent of schools in 1831, became editor of the *Liberia Herald*, and five years later was made governor of the Maryland colony of Cape Palmas.

Russwurm was forced to resign his editorship after he had endorsed the American Colonization Society. Cornish resumed his former role and tried to undo the damage caused by Russwurm's defection. In May 1829, backed by a group of black stockholders, including the influential Thomas Jennings and Peter Williams, Cornish issued the first number of *Rights of All* and pledged that "this Paper will more especially be devoted to the rights and interests of the colored population.'' Although the paper continued to stress the same issues as *Freedom's Journal* had under Cornish's original editorship, it dealt especially with the new crisis facing free blacks in Ohio: enforced migration as a result of the state law and the riots by white laborers in Cincinnati designed to force blacks to leave more quickly. Under the heading, ''Barbarism in Ohio,'' Cornish labeled the $500 bond act ''unparalleled for illegality and barbarism in the history of the world.'' As for Cincinnati, he recommended ''all the outlaws of foreign countries to go there, and as an inducement we are authorized to inform them that the mob rules there four evenings out of five. . . . 'Hail Columbia, happy land.' ''

Cornish kept the paper alive for a number of issues, but financial problems forced him to suspend publication. By the fourth number, his income was only $36 with which to meet expenses of over $200. Many of the former subscribers to *Freedom's Journal,* disgusted with the issues under Russwurm's editorship, were evidently unwilling to subscribe to its successor at the $2 annual subscription price.

Thus came to an end the first journalistic venture of black Americans, the ''first to be owned, operated, published and edited by and for black people.'' Until its last period, *Freedom's Journal,* as Boston blacks declared at a meeting in its support, was ''a powerful auxiliary'' in the struggle of black Americans for freedom and equality—not in Africa but in the United States.

THE BLACK PRESS: OTHER BLACK PAPERS

After the demise of *Rights of All* there was a lapse of only a few years before another black newspaper appeared. During 1831 and 1832, John G. Stewart edited a paper in Albany, New York, entitled the *African Sentinel and Journal of Liberty,* but it quickly passed from the scene. In the mid-1830s, Philip A. Bell of New York began publishing the *Struggler,* but it, too, lasted only a few issues. In January 1837, the *Weekly Advocate,* edited by Reverend Samuel Cornish, came into existence in New York City, and in March of that same year, it was renamed the *Colored American.* As the editor explained: ''We are *Americans* . . . colored Americans, brethren—and let it be our aim to make the title *Colored American* as honorable and as much respected before the world as *white* Americans or any others.''

While it paid attention to slavery, the *Colored American* made it clear from the outset that it believed that racism in the North was the main problem that should be attacked and that it was a mistake to focus attention exclusively on slavery in the South. Hence, although the paper devoted much space to the struggle against slavery, it concentrated on Northern racial prejudice, which brought daily humiliation to free black people, deprived them of schooling, apprenticeships, jobs, and the vote, and segregated them in every aspect of society from the church to the lyceum. Fight back, Cornish editorialized: ''Brethren, be careful never to go into the prescribed Negro pews. Stand in the aisles, and rather worship God upon your feet, than become a party to your own degradation. You must shame your oppressors, and wear down prejudice, to this holy policy.''

From the beginning, the *Colored American* encountered severe financial difficulties. Cornish served virtually without salary, and Philip A. Bell, the proprietor, obtained no income to offset his investment. "The Editor has not received *one cent,* nor asked for any pecuniary consideration as yet; and the Proprietor—worse still—is in debt,'' Cornish informed the readers in mid-June 1837. Efforts to improve the paper's financial condition were fruitless. Cornish left it in May 1839, and between November 1839 and March 1840, it suspended publication. Charles B. Ray, who was to become editor when the *Colored American* reappeared, kept the paper alive until March 13, 1841, when it was forced to suspend permanently.

In August 1838, David Ruggles, secretary of the New York Vigilance Committee, published the *Mirror of Liberty* in New York, first as a quarterly and then as a monthly magazine devoted to the welfare of the free Negro. Its publication came to an end in September 1841.

In April 1838 Benjamin Roberts began publishing the *Anti-Slavery Herald* in Boston, with the hope of making it the voice of the city's black community, in spite of William Lloyd Garrison's insistence that his *Liberator* fulfilled that purpose. Determined to have the *Herald* printed and edited solely by Negroes, Roberts had to purchase and set up his own printing press and then teach his employees how to run it. This proved costly, and the paper appeared only sporadically from April to October when Roberts announced he would have to stop publication until the first of the year. But Boston's only pre-Civil War Negro newspaper never appeared again.

The 1840s brought a substantial increase in the number of black publications. In Albany, New York, in 1842, Stephen Myers edited the *Elevator*. The *National Watchman*, with which William G. Allen was associated, was circulated from Troy, New York, beginning in the latter part of 1842 and lasting until 1847. The *Clarion* was published by the Reverend Henry Highland Garnet in Troy, but it was short-lived. The *People's Press* was edited in New York City by Thomas Hamilton during 1843. In the same year, Martin Robinson Delany edited the *Mystery* in Pittsburgh. The *Ram's Horn,* edited in New York City by William Hodges, was published in January 1847 and expired eighteen months later. In 1853, William H. Day provided Ohio blacks with their first newspaper, the *Aliened American*. It was soon discontinued because of economic difficulties. Day tried again in 1855 with the *People's Exposition*, but it too soon failed. Still another short-lived black paper was the *Pacific Appeal*, published in San Francisco and edited by Mifflin W. Gibbs and J. H. Townsend.

That these papers lacked stability is hardly surprising. Their circulation was usually small, with their subscription lists confined for the most part to the city in which the journal was published. Black papers faced great difficulties: there were few Negro merchants and professional men who bought advertising; the Negro people were too poor to make substantial contributions to requests for funds; and not many white people were interested in black journals. Constantly needing financial assistance, nearly all of the journals expired after a valiant battle to exist.

The following announcement in the *Ram's Horn* of November 1, 1847, marked the beginning of a new era in black journalism:

FREDERICK DOUGLASS AND HIS PAPER
PROSPECTS FOR AN ANTI-SLAVERY PAPER TO BE ENTITLED—THE NORTH
STAR.

Frederick Douglass proposed to publish in Rochester, New York, a weekly anti-slavery paper with the above title. The object of *The North Star* will be to attack slavery in all its forms and aspects; advocate Universal Emancipation; exact the standard of public morality; promote the moral and intellectual improvement of the colored people; and to hasten the day of freedom to our three million enslaved fellow-countrymen.

The paper will be printed on a double medium sheet, at $2.00 per annum, paid in advance, and $2.50 if payment be delayed over six months.

Frederick Douglass was born in February 1817, somewhere in Tuckahoo, Talbot County, on the Eastern Shore of Maryland, the son of an unknown white father and Harriet Bailey, a slave. As a child he suffered much from both a lack of nourishing food and the cold, and he grew to detest slavery. He saw slaves brutally whipped; worked from sunrise to sunset six days a week; was fed insufficient amounts of pork or fish and low-quality meal; and was sheltered in dirty, crowded, uncomfortable quarters in which the clay floors were their only beds.

Douglass' mother was hired out to a farmer twelve miles away, and to see her son, she would walk the distance after a day of labor in the field and then return to the farm to begin another day of labor at dawn. These visits ceased during Douglass' seventh year, when she died. He was not even allowed to attend her funeral.

A major turning point in Douglass' life occurred in 1825 when his mistress, Mrs. Thomas Auld, at his request, began teaching him to read. In a short time, he had mastered the alphabet and was learning to spell words of three and four letters.

At this point, Mrs. Auld informed her husband of her efforts to teach Douglass to read and of her pupil's mental agility. Astounded at his wife's naiveté, Auld ordered her to discontinue the instruction, explaining in Douglass' presence that education would spoil even the best of ''niggers'' by making them unmanageable, discontented, and determined to run away. The lessons ceased, but Douglass was impressed by Auld's assertion that education and freedom were somehow related. He resolved to learn to read and write, despite his master's stern opposition and without Mrs. Auld's aid—indeed, over her objections. To accomplish this purpose, he made the streets of Baltimore, where he now worked as a slave, his school and used his white playmates as teachers. Out of his pocket would come the leaves of books he had raked "from the mud and filth of the gutter," a copy of his Webster's spelling book, and a slice of bread to pay for his lessons.

By the time he was twelve or thirteen, Douglass had learned to read and had turned his attention to writing. While working in the Baltimore shipyards, he watched the carpenters label the prepared pieces of timber with letters indicating the part of the ship for which they were designed, and he practiced drawing these letters in his spare time. Then using the fences as his copybooks and blackboards and chalk as his pen and ink, he learned to write.

A second major turning point in Douglass' life as a slave occurred when he fought back against the cruel "slave-breaker," Edward Covey. "The battle with Mr. Covey," he wrote in his autobiography published in 1845, "was the turning-point in my career as a slave. It . . . revived within me a sense of my own manhood. . . . It was a glorious resurrection, from the tomb of slavery to the heaven of freedom. My long-crushed spirit rose, cowardice departed, bold defiance took its place. . . . I now resolved that, however long I might remain a slave in form, the day had passed forever when I could be a slave in fact."

From the summer of 1836 to the summer of 1838, Douglass worked in the Baltimore shipyards, first as an apprentice, then as a skilled caulker. In the evenings, after a day's work in the shipyards, Douglass extended his education. He met free blacks who were well versed in literature, geography, and arithmetic, and he sought to learn from them. As a slave, he was not able to join any of the forty benevolent institutions established by the free blacks of Baltimore, but he was permitted, by special dispensation, to become a member of the East Baltimore Improvement Society. There he took a prominent part in debates and there, too, he met Anna Murray, who afterward became his wife. Anna was one of twelve children of slave parents and the first of their five children born in freedom, escaping by one month the fate of her older brothers and sisters born in slavery.

On Monday, September 3, 1838, Douglass bade farewell to slavery. From a black seaman friend who was his height, he borrowed a sailor's suit and a sailor's "protection," a paper listing the physical features of its owner who, as a free American sailor, could move about the country. (The suit was later returned to its owner by mail.) In the late afternoon of September 3, Douglass arrived in Philadelphia and then went on to New York City, where he was joined by Anna Murray. On September 15, twelve days after his escape, they were married by the Reverend James W. C. Pennington, who had fled from a Maryland master ten years earlier. Two days later, they were on their way to New Bedford, Massachusetts, where Douglass believed that his skill as a caulker would secure him a livelihood. However, white racism prevented him from working at his trade, and for three years Douglass led a hand-to-mouth existence as a day laborer. In 1841, following the discovery that he possessed a talent for the public platform, he became an abolitionist lecturer. He had changed his name from Bailey to Douglass soon after his arrival in New Bedford, the name *Douglass* having been suggested to him by a black with whom he stayed for a while and who was an admirer of the Douglass in Sir Walter Scott's *Lady of the Lake*.

While he was on an antislavery tour of England in 1846, a group of British antislavery women, led by Ellen and Anna Richardson of Newcastle, raised $711.96 to purchase his emancipation from his master in Maryland, so that on his return to the United States, Douglass was legally free. A group of British antislavery women also raised $2,175 to enable Douglass to purchase a printing press and establish his own paper. Julia Griffiths, the daughter of a close friend of William Wilberforce, the British abolitionist, organized the campaign for Douglass' paper and furnished him with a "valuable collection of books, pamphlets, tracts and pictures" to use as editor.

The first issue of the *North Star* came off the press on December 3, 1847, its masthead proclaiming the slogan: "Right is of No Sex—Truth is of No Color—God is the Father of us All, and we are all Brethren." The editors were Frederick Douglass and Martin R. Delany, who had just resigned the editorship of the *Pittsburgh Mystery*. William C. Nell, like Douglass a self-taught Negro, was listed as publisher.

The weekly paper, edited by a former slave who had never gone to school, became the best-known, most influential, and longest-lasting black paper of the antebellum and Civil War era. The paper changed its name to *Frederick Douglass' Paper* in 1851 and in 1859 to *Douglass' Monthly*. It remained in existence from December 1847 to May 1863, when Douglass suspended publication to help raise black troops for the Union Army.

Had it not been for Julia Griffiths, Douglass' paper would not have been able to maintain its unbroken existence for almost sixteen years. There were many occasions when it was on the verge of suspending publication and surely would have done so without her aid. For example, when she learned in the spring of 1848 that the *North Star* was in financial trouble, she wound up her affairs in England and came to Rochester with her sister to help put the journal back on its feet. "She came to my relief," Douglass wrote later, "when my paper had nearly absorbed my means, and I was heavily in debt, and when I had mortgaged my house to raise money to meet current expenses; and in a single year, by her energetic and effective management, enabled me to extend the circulation of my paper from 2,000 to 4,000 copies." In a single year, too, she paid off a debt of between seven hundred and eight hundred dollars.

With the assistance of the Rochester Ladies' Anti-Slavery Society, of which she was secretary, Griffiths organized fairs, published gift books, and conducted numerous other activities on behalf of Douglass' paper. When paying tribute to those who had enabled him to continue as an editor, Douglass noted that "we are indebted to none more than to the ever active and zealous friend of the slave, Miss Julia Griffiths."

In format and typography, Douglass' paper was typical of nearly all of the other black papers published before the Civil War. It consisted of four pages of seven columns each. The first page usually featured the full text of speeches or sermons. Foreign reports also rated a front-page position, as did reports of local, statewide, and national antislavery meetings or black conventions. The second page was filled with editorial matter, which sometimes poured over onto the next page. The third page contained reports of meetings, notices of activities to come, and letters to the editor. The fourth was generally devoted to clips from other sources, poetry, installments of novels running serially, book reviews or "literary notices," announcements of antislavery tracts, advertisements of pills, "all sorts of horse medicines," and ointments.

In the first number of the *North Star*, Douglass pledged: "Giving no quarter to slavery at the South, it will hold no truce with oppressors at the North. While it shall boldly advocate emancipation for our enslaved brethren, it will omit no opportunity to gain for the nominally free complete enfranchisement." Douglass continually stressed in his editorials that the free Negro and the slave were chained together and must rise and fall together. "To strengthen prejudice against the *free*," he argued, "is to rivet the fetter more firmly on the slave population. Only show that the free colored man is low, worthless, and degraded, and a warrant for enslaving him is readily acknowledged." The free black, he maintained, must not resign himself to a position of inferiority in American society. Both for his own sake and for the sake of his brothers in chains, he must allow no feeling of fright or disillusionment to stand in the way of his self-improvement. The strongest argument for emancipation was a Negro proving by endeavor and achievement that he was as good as the white man. The white man and the Negro were equals, and the white man was superior only when he outstripped the Negro in improving himself; the Negro was inferior only when he proved himself incapable of accomplishing what his white brother had accomplished. It must no longer be white lawyer and black wood sawyer, white editor and black street cleaner, white intelligent and black ignorant, "but we must take our stand side by side with our fellow countrymen, in all the trades, arts, professions, and callings of the day."

The longest-lasting black paper founded in the antebellum era was the *Christian Recorder*, the official organ of the African Methodist Episcopal church. It began publication in Philadelphia in 1854 and continued until 1901. Like other black journals, the *Christian Recorder* was a weekly. The *Anglo-African Magazine*, a monthly published in New York City by Thomas Hamilton, appeared in January 1859. Its ambitious and varied aims were listed in its prospectus:

To present a clear and concise statement of the condition, the past history, and the coming prospects of the Colored population of the United States, free and enslaved.

To afford scope for the rapidly rising talent of Colored men in their special and general literature.

To examine the population movements of the Colored people.

To present a reliable statement of their religious condition, of their moral, and economic statistics.

To present a statement of their educational conditions and movements.

Of their legal conditions and status in the several States.

To examine into the basis on which rest their claims for citizenship of the several States, and of the United States.

To present an elaborate account of the various books, pamphlets, and newspapers written or edited by Colored men.

To present the biographies of noteworthy Colored men throughout the world.

In addition to the information on these subjects there was a special reason, according to the prospectus, why blacks should support the new magazine:

On the condition and prospects of *free* Colored men, by common consent, rest, in a great degree, the condition and prospects of enslaved Colored men. Hence, besides the intrinsic interest which attaches itself to a magazine of such scope and information, the end of all who wish to advance the great cause of Immediate Emancipation is earnestly solicited for its support.

For twenty-five cents a copy or one dollar a year, the reader of the *Anglo-African Magazine* was introduced to the views of some of the leading black intellectuals of the era—Dr. James McCune Smith, Frances Ellen Watkins, Martin R. Delany, William C. Nell, J.W.C. Pennington, Edward Blyden, Thomas Holly, Daniel A. Payne, George T. Downing, George B. Vashon, John B. Vashon, John Mercer Langston, J. Sella Martin, Amos Garry Beman, Charles L. Reason, and Frederick Douglass. The breadth of the articles is apparent in some of the titles: "The Attraction of Planets" by Martin R. Delany; "The German Invasion" by James McCune Smith; "The Educational Wants of the Free Colored People" by M. H. Freeman; and "A Review of Slavery and the Slave Trade" by J.W.C. Pennington.

The magazine ceased publication with the issue of April 1860. It was succeeded by the *Anglo-African*, a weekly newspaper, edited by Robert Hamilton, whose brother had published the magazine. It survived for five years until 1865.

"Circumstances make it absolutely necessary that we should have a press of our own," declared the State Convention of Colored Freemen of Pennsylvania in 1841. "It is just as absurd to imagine that we can become intelligent and enterprising by others speaking and writing for us, as that we can become fat by their eating and drinking for us." A black press did come into existence in the North during the antebellum period. In his *Condition, Elevation, Emigration and Destiny of the Colored People of the United States, Politically Considered,* published in 1852, Martin R. Delany listed "twenty odd newspapers" published by blacks in the previous twenty years. Others have added to the list so that over thirty black papers are known to have come into existence before the Civil War. While copies of most of them have not been found and many existed only briefly, it seems clear that the black press did voice the concerns of black people in the North and contributed substantially to the creation of a viable black community. There may be some question as to whether Samuel E. Cornish or Frederick Douglass was the outstanding Negro journalist of the pre-Civil War period, but there is no doubt that both rank high in the history of American journalism.

12

The Free Black Elite

"Is it not astonishing," declared Frederick Douglass in the 1850s,

that, while we are plowing, planting, and reaping, using all kinds of mechanical tools, erecting houses, constructing bridges, building ships, working in metal of brass, iron, copper, silver and gold; that while we are reading, writing, and cyphering, acting as clerks, merchants, and secretaries, having among us lawyers, doctors, ministers, poets, editors, orators, and teachers; that while we are engaged in all manner of enterprises common to other men—digging gold in California, capturing whale in the Pacific, feeding sheep and cattle on the hillside, living, moving, acting, thinking, planning, living in families as husbands, wives, and children, and above all, confessing and worshipping the Christian God, and looking hopefully for life and immortality beyond the grave—*we are called upon to prove that we are men?*

In this chapter we will discuss several of the activities of free blacks mentioned above, but before so doing let us note one not mentioned in Douglass' list. These were the black mountain men who helped open the American West.

BLACK TRAILBLAZERS

James P. Beckwourth, son of a white southerner and a slave mother, became a mountain legend in the upper Missouri country. From the stories told about him and from the tall tales he related in his ghost-written autobiography, Beckwourth came to be called the "Black Kit Carson." As a young man, Beckwourth accompanied William H. Ashley on the latter's fur trading trek up the Missouri in 1823. Later he became an adopted Crow with the name of "Bloody Arm." He became their leading war chief, and married several Indian women. He eventually was elected first counselor of the Crow Nation, later succeeding to the position of chief with the name of *Nan-kup-bah-pah,* which meant "Medicine Calf."

By 1845 Beckwourth had traveled over much of the American West. He discovered Beckwourth's Pass, a green valley in the region of the Sierra Nevada Mountains. In 1842 he became the first man to settle the site of what eventually became the city of Pueblo, Colorado. Beckwourth was famed for knowing the Rockies better than the Indians did.

Edward Rose, a Negro Cherokee, was the guide for Jedediah Smith when he rediscovered the South Pass in present Colorado in 1824. Originally discovered in 1812 by Robert Stuart of the American Fur Company, the South Pass was a wagon route through the rugged Rocky Mountains. The rediscovery of the pass opened up a great highway of overland emigration to California, the main artery for the transcontinental traffic of fur traders, explorers, and emigrants. The South Pass became a major link of the Oregon Trail, the great causeway westward.

Another Negro who helped open the American West was Jacob Dobson. Dobson accompanied the famous explorer-soldier John C. Frémont on his three expeditions that charted the Great Plains to the Pacific Ocean between 1842 and 1845, during which time the Oregon Trail was surveyed.

BLACK MEN OF WEALTH

Although the vast majority of free blacks in the North and West were poor, a minority managed to accumulate a fairly considerable amount of wealth. Some of them gained this through inheritance. The wealthiest black person in antebellum Boston was a servant, Aran Morris, with $40,000 in personal property. It is assumed that he accumulated his wealth from white benefactors, who probably left it to him in a will as a reward to a devoted and faithful employee.

From a start in service trades like hairdressing, wig making, and catering in Salem, Massachusetts, John Remond built a wholesale-retail trade in provisions, both standard and exotic. A dealer in old wines and cordials, he also offered oysters, spices and pickled nuts, casks of hams, and leg of bacon, which he advertised for local family use and for "shipping to any market." He became a prosperous businessman and left his son Charles Lenox Remond enough to enable him to devote himself exclusively to the antislavery movement and the struggle for black equality.

Born a slave in 1811 in Lexington, Kentucky, Lewis Hayden taught himself to read by deciphering discarded newspapers and a Bible. With the assistance of Calvin Fairbank, a white student at Oberlin, and his fiancée, Hayden and his wife, a fellow slave, escaped from bondage. After a stay in Canada and Detroit, Hayden moved to Boston, and in 1849 founded a custom and ready-made clothing business, which became the second largest establishment in the city owned by a black man.

In an article, "Character and Condition of the Colored People of Cincinnati," published in the *North Star* in 1850, Frederick Douglass cited Henry Boyd, Samuel T. Wilcox, and William W. Watson as outstanding examples of their race who rose "by the force of their own genius, from small beginnings, [through] hard labor and unwearied application to their business."

Henry Boyd was born in Kentucky in 1802, and when he migrated to Ohio in 1826 as a skilled cabinetmaker, he was denied employment because he was black. After working briefly as a stevedore, Boyd formed a partnership with a white carpenter, a relationship that, even if unsatisfactory socially, did enable the black man to acquire capital. In 1836, Boyd went into business for himself making bedsteads and did so well that in 1842 he erected a building in Cincinnati on the corner of Broadway and Eighth streets, installed steam-powered machines, and produced all kinds of furniture. By 1856, his concern occupied buildings on both sides of the street, and Boyd was reportedly worth $40,000. He employed as many as fifty-two men, including blacks, native whites, Irish, Scots, English, and French. A series of fires and his inability to obtain adequate insurance forced him to abandon the business in 1859.

Samuel T. Wilcox also began humbly and accumulated a sizable fortune. As a cabin boy on an Ohio River packet, he won the favor of his employers and was promoted to a steward. He was able to use his position to conduct a personal trading business between Cincinnati and New Orleans, and by 1850 he had accumulated $25,000. Determined to show "that colored people could do something besides being barbers," Wilcox opened an exclusive grocery store on the corner of Broadway and Fifth streets in Cincinnati, selling the best liquors, the finest hams, canned and dried fruits, and the most expensive soaps. Skillfully using his old river connections, he built up an extensive fancy goods business with the packet lines, catering also to Cincinnati's wealthy class. Wilcox built his wholesale and retail grocery business to the point where he was doing $140,000 in business a year. By 1859, he had accumulated $59,000 in property, additional capital in banks, and $1,000 worth of stock in the Kentucky Trust Company. His extravagant habits caused him to sell half of his business, and it succumbed to the panic of 1857, but Wilcox remained wealthy.

In 1831, William W. Watson's brother-in-law borrowed $750 to purchase Watson's freedom. After arriving in Cincinnati, he worked as a barber in his brother-in-law's shop until he was financially able to enter business for himself. Rather than opening just another barber shop, however, he called himself a hairdresser and owner of a "finely arranged bathing establishment." He quickly prospered as the city's elite flocked to the new establishment. After repaying the debt that had secured his freedom, Watson purchased that of his mother, brothers, and sisters.

Robert Gordon was another Cincinnati black capitalist. He arrived in the city in 1847 with $15,000 that he had managed to accumulate while still in bondage and invested a portion of his capital in the coal business. Gordon built docks on the river, purchased coal only in large quantities, and owned his own wagons, bypassing unnecessary middlemen. He survived a price war waged by white coal dealers, who attempted to drive him out of business, and became one of the city's leading entrepreneurs. He remained in the coal business until his retirement in

1865. During the Civil War, he invested heavily in government bonds and used the profits to acquire real estate.

Stephen Smith, the remarkably successful lumber and coal merchant, was one of the leading black capitalists of the mid-nineteenth century, if not the leading one. Smith operated his business in Columbia, Pennsylvania, until 1842, when he took up residence in Philadelphia and left the management to his new associate, William Whipper. In 1849, Martin R. Delany visited the enterprise and found a stock of several thousand bushels of coal, 2¼ million feet of lumber, and twenty-two railway cars. The partners jointly owned $9,000 worth of stock in the Columbia bank. Whipper also owned a substantial house on Front Street in Columbia, and by 1860, he owned five properties within the borough, as well as other holdings in Lancaster County and Philadelphia, valued at $23,800. For his part, Smith owned fifty-two "good brick houses" in Philadelphia, besides several in Lancaster and Columbia. Delany called Smith "decidedly the most wealthy colored man in the United States" but did not specify his exact wealth. Since Thomy Lafon, the tycoon of New Orleans, was worth $50,000 at his death, Smith must have been extremely wealthy.

Delany also visited Henry Scott's pickling business in New York City and found it to be one of the most successful enterprises in that field. Its operation was confined principally to supplying sea-going vessels. "There has been many a purser," Delany wrote, "who cashed and filed in his office the bill of Henry Scott, without ever dreaming of his being a colored man."

Thomas B. Downing, a well-known caterer, was for thirty years the proprietor of a first-class restaurant near the corner of Wall and Broad streets in New York City. One of the leading black entrepreneurs of the period, Downing was said to have made "three fortunes." His son, George T. Downing, moved to Rhode Island in 1850, where he owned a catering business in Providence and several summer hotels in Newport.

Born free in North Carolina, John Jones moved to Chicago in 1845. After educating himself, he became a prosperous tailor and the owner of valuable property in downtown Chicago.

These men were exceptions. The most common business establishments run by blacks were grocery stores, boardinghouses, and dry goods stores, and their customers were usually members of the black community. Since the services of the financial communities in the North were not generally available to blacks, the small businesses operated by black entrepreneurs had to provide credit to their customers, but they themselves could get no credit from the banks. In the hope of helping to solve this problem, Dr. James McCune Smith of New York proposed the establishment in March 1851 of a mutual savings bank. In his report on the "Social Conditions of the Colored Race," with which he unveiled this scheme, Smith outlined a plan whereby all the bank's depositors would have the power to buy and sell real estate, to discount paper, to lend money on bonds and mortgages, and to deal in merchandise. Nothing came of Smith's proposal, however.

A study of black ownership of real and personal property in New York City reveals that there were indeed those who made considerable gains. In 1837, the *Colored American* reported that blacks had from $50,000 to $80,000 in the city's savings banks. Fifteen years later, it was estimated that $755,000 had been invested by blacks in businesses conducted by themselves, and that apart from business enterprises, blacks held $733,000 in real estate. By 1857, the taxed real estate in the city owned by blacks had risen to $1.4 million; their personal estate came to $710,000; and money they deposited in savings banks amounted to $1.21 million. Commenting on this economic progress, James Freeman Clarke wrote in 1859:

Twenty years ago, when this population was three-fourths of what it is now, the property was less than half of what it is now. The only colored beggars seen in New York are those who ask for money to help them buy their wives, their sons, or their daughters.

Only a small portion of the black population actually benefited from these economic advances. The great mass of black families experienced no substantial improvement in their lot; indeed their condition steadily deteriorated. As Robert Ernst points out in his study of the economic status of New York City Negroes, "wages failed to keep pace with rising rents and the prices of provisions, while in depression years, as in 1857, unemployment swelled the relief rolls."

On the eve of the Civil War, the per-capita property of Boston blacks was only $91 compared with the per-capita wealth of the entire population of Boston of $872. Even the Irish, only recently arrived in the city, had a per-capita wealth of $131.

BLACK TEACHERS, DOCTORS, AND LAWYERS

The 1842 directory of Salem, Massachusetts, listed no black doctors, ministers, lawyers, or teachers, and even the teacher of the African school was a white man. In the larger cities of the North, there were black professionals, though their number was miniscule. In Boston, for example, their percentage of the city's total work force ranged from less than 1 percent in 1830 to about 2 percent in 1860. In the New York State census of 1855, fifty black professional men were listed, half of them teachers and clergymen. There were also fifteen Negro musicians, five physicians, a dentist, a lawyer, and an artist.

Among the black professionals was William Allen, the first black college professor in the United States. A graduate of Oneida Institute, he studied law in Boston before becoming co-editor of the *National Watchman*, published weekly in Troy, New York. He taught Greek and German at Central College in McGrawville, New York, until 1853. After his marriage to a white student, he and his wife were forced to leave the country. In England, where he continued to teach, he wrote *The American Prejudice against Color*, an account of the mob attack that drove the Allens from their homeland.

John Isom Gaines, for whom, in later years, Gaines High School in Cincinnati was named, had acquired economic independence as a supplier of provisions for the steamboats. Between 1849 and 1853, he was a member of Cincinnati's black school board, and in the capacity of board clerk, he influenced the financing of existing schools and sought to upgrade the quality of instruction. His work was interrupted by his unexpected death at the age of thirty-eight. In 1859, when Cincinnati's blacks erected a monument at his grave site, they commemorated his service as an educator rather than his success as a businessman.

Peter H. Clark was another leader in the field of education. Educated in Cincinnati's private schools and at Oberlin College, Clark became a teacher of black students in his home town during the 1850s and an administrator after the Civil War. After regular school hours, Clark held special classes for advanced students in an attempt to provide blacks with qualified instructors. Clark's energy and ability made him one of the most prominent figures in education among black Americans.

The first university-trained black doctor in the United States was Dr. James McCune Smith. He was born in New York City in 1813, the son of a slave emancipated by the Emancipation Act of the State of New York and of a slave woman who had bought her freedom. Smith was educated in the African Free School and entered the University of Glasgow in 1832, receiving the B.A. degree in 1835, the M.A. in 1836, and the M.D. in 1837. Following a short period in the clinics of Paris, he returned to New York City, where he practiced medicine until his death in 1874. His advertisement, which appeared regularly in the *Colored American* and *Frederick Douglass' Paper*, read: "Dr. James McCune Smith may be consulted at his office 93 Broadway from 7 till 10 A.M., from 2 till 4, and from 8 till 10 P.M. House, Reade Street, two doors from Greenwich." Smith also ran an apothecary establishment, as did Philip A. White, another black doctor. William C. Nell described both as "practical men" who "conduct their business, preparing medicines, etc., etc., with as much readiness and skill as any other disciple of Galen and Hippocrates."

Dr. Smith was the author of a series of scientific pamphlets, including *Influence of Climate on Longevity, with Special Reference to Life Insurance*, published in 1846. His most famous lecture was entitled, "On the Fourteenth Query of Thomas Jefferson's *Notes on Virginia*," in which the black doctor demolished Jefferson's widely quoted claim that "the blacks, whether originally a distinct race, or made distinct by time and circumstances, are inferior to the whites in the endowments of both body and mind." It was published in the *Anglo-African Magazine* of August 1859.

Under the heading, "Colored Physicians," the *New York Tribune* in 1853 carried the news that John V. De Grasse of New York City and Thomas J. White of Brooklyn (then a separate city), students of Bowdoin Medical College, had received the M.D. degree, "notwithstanding the doors of the Medical College of this city being barred against them." With diplomas in their hand, they were ready "to go to work in the respective cities. They are young men of intelligence and moral worth."

The facts of the story of Dr. James Still make all of Horatio Alger's later attempts to trace the upward mobility of poor urchins seem pallid in comparison. He was born in Indian Mills, New Jersey, in 1812, one of eighteen children of Levin and Charity Still, both former Maryland slaves. His father sawed wood for a living and counted any day a good one on which he had food enough for his family's supper. James became a wood chopper and plough boy, but he was determined to become a doctor.

When Still was about three-and-one-half years old, a doctor came to the family's cabin to vaccinate the children, and in the process, he also "injected" young James with a dose of medical ambition. As a small boy, he had received about twelve weeks of education, so that at nineteen, he could neither write nor do basic arithmetic. His father then put him out as an indentured farm worker. As part of the arrangement, he received one month's schooling each winter. His lifetime schooling totaled six months, but this did not lessen his desire to be a doctor.

When he was released from indenture on April 19, 1833, with a new suit and $9.50 in cash, Still found that "two 12½-cent cotton handkerchiefs were sufficient to hold my worldly goods." He walked to Philadelphia and got a job in a glue factory. With some of his earnings, he bought three books on medical botany and anatomy. This was all the medical literature he read. The rest he learned by studying roots and herbs and by intuition.

James settled in Medford, New Jersey, where he built a cabin and worked at hard labor to support a wife and young daughter. He confined his medical work strictly to members of his immediate family until a desperate neighbor, learning about him, insisted on his providing help for his daughter. Still quickly cured her of scrofula, whereupon another man in intense pain demanded help and was made well in a few days. Those who were healed told those who were sick, and an informal practice began to grow slowly.

Still shunned the accepted medical practices of the day—bleeding, violent purgatives, blistering, and administering mercury and arsenic medicines—and also opposed most surgery. Instead he dispensed his own "vegetable medicines." Although he was scorned by the medical establishment as a quack, his neighbors, mostly whites, rallied to his support and hailed him as a humane and skillful practitioner who had discovered that nature had "written truth and science in every root of the forest and every leaf that grows."

Still's practice grew, and he became a prosperous landowner. By the time he died in 1885, he was the third largest property owner in Medford Township. On that day, he still had fifty patients to whom he was attending.

While James Still never received a medical degree, one black doctor obtained two. He was Louis Charles Roudanez, born on June 12, 1823, in Saint James Parish, Louisiana, the son of Louis Roudanez, a French merchant, and Aimée

Potens, a *femme de couleur libre*. While still a youth, Roudanez was sent by his parents to New Orleans, where he received the beginnings of an education and, afterward, some practical business experience in a notions store. During the depression of the 1840s, he invested a few hundred dollars he had saved in deflated municipal bonds. When the economy returned to normal, he sold the securities for far more than he had paid for them, acquiring a small fortune. Having achieved financial independence, he decided to travel to France to study medicine.

Arriving in Paris in 1846 at the age of twenty-one, Roudanez studied at the University of Paris' Faculty of Medicine under the famous expatriate American doctor, Philippe Record. After seven years of instruction, Roudanez was graduated in 1853 with honors. Upon leaving Europe, he was advised by French friends not to return to New Orleans, and he decided to settle in the North. Instead of beginning medical practice, he went to Dartmouth College in New Hampshire and began to study for another medical degree. After four years, he acquired a degree there in 1857. That same year, he left for New Orleans and quickly developed a large, lucrative practice, including among his patients some of the "best families" in the city. Soon he was one of the leaders of the free colored elite.

Dr. John Sweet Rock of Philadelphia and Boston was a doctor in two separate fields—dentistry and medicine—and a lawyer besides. Rock was born in Salem, New Jersey, in 1825, and he early showed an interest in reading books, which his parents, who were poor, encouraged. In 1844, he became a teacher, but after spending six hours teaching each day, he tutored private pupils for two hours and read medical books from the library of two local physicians for an additional eight hours. Upon being denied admission to medical schools because of his color, he turned to the study of dentistry under the tutelage of a doctor who admired his mental ability. In 1850, he opened hs own dentist's office in Philadelphia and was soon so adept at making dentures that he was awarded a silver medal by the profession.

While successfully practicing dentistry, Rock resumed his medical study, gaining entrance into American Medical College, from which he graduated with a medical degree in 1852. The next year, he decided that life was more agreeable in Boston's more "liberal atmosphere," and he moved to that city, where he not only practiced medicine and dentistry but also became an effective lecturer in the cause of both temperance and antislavery.

Long hours of study and overwork took its tool, and in 1858, Rock left for France for surgical treatment. He returned the following year with his health improved, but he still felt he was not strong enough to practice medicine adequately. So in 1860, Rock began the study of a third profession—law. He was admitted to the Massachusetts bar in 1861 and established law offices on Tremont Street in Boston. In 1865, John S. Rock became the first black man admitted to practice law before the United States Supreme Court.

Rock was not the first black lawyer. That honor appears to belong to Macon B.

Allen, who was admitted to the bar in June 1844 from the office of Samuel Fessenden in Portland, Maine, after an examination. Allen moved to Boston where, on the motion of Samuel E. Sewall, he was admitted to practice for the April 1845 term of the Common Pleas.

Robert Morris of Salem, Massachusetts, became the country's second black lawyer. After spending the first thirteen years of his life in Salem, Morris went to work as a "table boy" for the wealthy white King family in Boston. While in their employ, he met the wife of Boston attorney, Ellis Gray Loring, who soon hired him as a servant. So impressed were the Lorings with Morris' quick wit and intelligence that when the white youth who worked in Loring's law office as "copyer" gave up the position, Morris was given the job. He performed so well that he became Loring's law clerk and student.

Morris passed the law examination and was admitted to the bar in Boston in February 1847. In his first case, a suit brought by a black man against a white man for "services rendered," the opposing attorney treated Morris with disrespect in a private session held before the formal court appearance. When the case came to court, the room was filled with black spectators. Later Morris recalled the scene:

There was something in the courtroom that morning that made me feel like a giant. The courtroom was filled with colored people, and I could see, expressed on the faces of every one of them, a wish that I might win the first case that had ever been tried before a jury by a colored attorney in this country. At last my case was called; I went to work and tried it for all it was worth; and until the evidence was all in, the argument on both sides made, the judge's charge concluded, and the case given to the jury, I spared no pains to win. The jury after being out a short time returned, and when the foreman in reply to the clerk answered that the jury had found for the plaintiff [Morris' client] my heart bounded up and my people in the courtroom acted as if they would shout for joy.

In the *Liberator* of April 30, 1831, a correspondent wrote that if a black man ever became a lawyer in Boston, "he will never handle a white man's fee, whatever his talents." But Robert Morris proved him wrong. He quickly gained a reputation as an effective defender of the poor, both black and white; and, indeed, many of his clients were Irish. He was appointed a justice of the peace, but during the late 1850s, when he sought to move out of Boston's black community, he encountered the same racism that poor blacks faced. In 1858, Morris signed an agreement with a builder to purchase an estate with a fine mansion on the lands of the Cary Improvement Company in Chelsea, a suburb of Boston. While negotiating for the purchase, Morris informed the builder that some persons would probably object to his purchase of the mansion as a residence, believing that it might depreciate the value of their property, and that he did not wish to make the purchase if it would injure the sale of the builder's other property adjoining the estate. The builder replied that he built houses and reconstructed them to make money, that Morris' money was as good as anybody's else, and that if the Cary Improvement Company should refuse to approve the contract, he would do no more work for them. The contract was signed, and certain alterations were made in the house to suit Morris' wishes. When news of the purchase became public, some of the neighbors became excited, and two in particular threatened that if Morris moved in, they would ''sell out or . . . let their houses to Irish tenants.'' The company thereupon refused to honor the contract, and when Morris protested, one of the company directors told the black lawyer and justice of the peace that he did not think Morris should ''push'' himself ''into the vicinity or neighborhood of persons'' who did not wish to have him as a neighbor. Morris replied: ''if we moved whenever someone objected to our presence in a community, it might be somewhat difficult to find a resting place anywhere.'' But the company stood firm, the builder did not, and Morris had to give up the estate.

Not all black professional men could afford mansions. During the years 1856 and 1857, Dr. James McCune Smith of New York City was reported to have taxable real property worth $13,200, but he was listed as having no personal property. Dr. John S. Rock of Boston was reported to have no taxable property and only $500 in personal property.

BLACK ARTISTS

The publication of Oliver W. Larkin's *Art and Life in America* in 1949 is considered a landmark, not only in American art history, but in the teaching of American art as well. Nevertheless, Larkin's Pulitzer-Prize-winning book does not contain the word *black* in its long index, except as part of the title of three pictures. Nor does ''Negro artists,'' ''Negro art,'' or ''Negro influence.'' (The term *Negro craftsman* receives four brief references.) Of the Afro-American artists of the nineteenth century, only one (Henry O. Tanner, 1859-1927, who arrived at his mature style just prior to 1900) rates a short paragraph. Three are accorded a single sentence each.

Among the first of the black Americans to become known as an artist was the truly remarkable painter Joshua Johnston, a freeman who lived in Baltimore or its environs from about 1796 to 1824, moving from one prominent white family to another as a portrait painter. His discoverer, Dr. J. Hall Pleasants, described Johnston as ''a Negro painter of considerable ability with a style peculiarly his own.'' Johnston produced about twenty-one portraits, all of white subjects, and most of them leading citizens of Baltimore, in whose museums several of Johnston's works still hang. His ''Portrait of a Clerie'' is Johnston's only known work of a Negro subject.

Joshua Johnston was more fortunate than those black artists who followed him. If it was hard for a white to be an artist in the United States during the antebellum years, one can imagine the discouragement that confronted a black bent on becoming one. Even though many white American artists had to leave

America to win recognition, with the establishment of the Pennsylvania Academy in 1805 and the New York Drawing Society (later named the National Academy of Design) in 1830, they were able to study in this country. Black artists, however, still had no opportunity for such study in America at any formal school, and association with white artists at a level of genuine integration in the art circles then in existence was not possible. Yet a trip abroad was difficult at best. It required advance contacts and money, self-confidence, and an assurance that the venture would bear fruit.

Still there were those who presevered. Robert Douglass was one of them. Educated in a Quaker school in Philadelphia, he learned painting. In the July 20, 1833, issue of the *Emancipator,* there is a tribute to Douglass as a portrait painter whose paintings were judged to be comparable to that of the best artists then working in the country. The brother of Sarah H. Douglass, the noted black female educator in Philadelphia, Robert was able, partly through her connections, to develop a friendship with Thomas Sully, Philadelphia's outstanding portrait artist of the day and president of the Pennsylvania Academy. In 1838, Robert applied for a passport to visit England in order to secure further instruction in portrait painting. He was refused a passport by the secretary of state who contended that by the new constitution of Pennsylvania, Negroes were not citizens and therefore not entitled to passports. Actually he had already sailed for England by the time the passport was refused, carrying with him recommendations from Sully to friends abroad. He worked at the British Museum and the National Galleries of London. He was back in the United States by 1842. His prints sold widely in New York and Philadelphia, and his portraits of abolitionists were widely praised.

Douglass freely shared his knowledge of the arts with other blacks. The work of David B. Bowser, one of his followers, consisted mainly of landscapes, which he contributed to exhibitions of black craftsmen and mechanics held to familiarize the populations of various cities with the capacities of the Negro people. In April 1851 the Colored American Institute for the Promotion of the Mechanic Arts and Sciences held one such exhibition, which included one of Bowser's paintings along with articles such as sofas, stoves, stoneware, and embroidery. A review in the *New York Herald* of April 6, 1852, praised Bowser's work, which was included in an exhibition in that city. Although a few of his paintings (including portraits of Abraham Lincoln) and ephemeral designs have been found, nothing remains of the work of his teacher, Robert Douglass, to document the impressive notices about him that appeared in the antislavery press of his day.

Patrick Reason was apprenticed through the efforts of abolitionists to a white engraver and became a gifted portraitist and engraver at midcentury. Reason recorded the features of James Williams, Benjamin Tappan, Henry Bibb, De Witt Clinton, and Granville Sharp, the British abolitionist. He was an accomplished technician whose work was deeply rooted in the tradition of realism. Indeed Reason introduced a new note of realism in his depiction of the life of slaves. One of his engravings, done in a stipple technique, presents a female slave forced to a kneeling position with chains hanging from her wrists and carried the words, "Am I not a woman and a sister?" Such an appeal was new to American art.

Under the leadership of Bishop Daniel A. Payne, the African Methodist Episcopal church sponsored exhibitions and prizes for paintings and drawings. A. B. Wilson won a prize for a lithograph depicting the Reverend John Cornish delivering a sermon, his face firmly expressing unswerving conviction, and below it were the words: "And as for pharoah's host, he overthrew them."

Perhaps the ablest pre-Civil War painter was Robert S. Duncanson, son of a Canadian Scotsman and a mulatto woman, who was born in Cincinnati in 1821. He first gained notice in that city in 1843, and his education was furthered when he was sent abroad to study by the Anti-Slavery League. The *Cincinnati Gazette* reported that Duncanson's motive for leaving the United States was his desire to find a place where his color did not prevent his association with other artists.

After having won fame as a landscape artist in Europe, Duncanson returned to the United States in 1854. He became one of the best exponents of the Midwest school of romantic realism, which was an offshoot of the Hudson River school of landscape painting. Duncanson's "Shylock and Jessica," "The Ruins of Carthage," and "Trials of Shakespeare" were all widely praised and were considered to have placed him among the nation's foremost painters. His most famous landscape, "Blue Hole, Little Miami River," now hangs in the Cincinnati Art Museum. Duncanson was also a distinguished painter of portraits, which decorated many of the wealthiest homes in Cincinnati. Unusually versatile for his time, Duncanson also enjoyed noteworthy success as a mural painter and as a painter of landscapes.

Edwin M. Bannister was born in the province of New Brunswick, Canada, in 1828, orphaned at an early age, and reared by a white lawyer. He began sketching as a child, and in the 1850s he went to Boston for training. He was ostracized by white artists and took odd jobs before opening his own hairdressing salon, in the rear of which he worked at his art. Finally, after a fortuitous marriage to a wealthy business woman, Bannister was able to convert his salon to a studio, and he won prominence as an artist. His reputation was further solidified when he won a competition at the Philadelphia Centennial Exposition of 1876. But when Bannister stepped forward to claim the award, the judges, surprised by the appearance of a black artist, hurriedly met to reconsider the choice. However, the other contestants stood resolutely by their black rival, and the award was granted.

Edmonia Lewis, born of a Negro father and a Chippewa Indian mother, was orphaned at an early age and brought up first by Indian kinsmen and then at an orphanage until she was sent by a group of abolitionists to Oberlin College. While at Oberlin, she began to work in sculpture, and William Lloyd Garrison brought her to the attention of the Boston sculptor, Edmund Brackett, who trained her until she went to Rome in her early twenties for further instruction. There she became a favorite of the expatriate American art community. Two of her works—the sculpture, "Death of Cleopatra" and the monument of Richard

Allen—were displayed at the Centennial Exposition of 1876 in Philadelphia, with funds raised by the African Methodist Episcopal church. Her most famous work, "Forever Free," was done in 1867 for the Harriet Hung mausoleum at Mount Auburn Cemetery in Cambridge, Massachusetts, and depicts a free Negro couple triumphantly displaying their broken shackles. Lewis created many figures of American Indians and Negroes, as well as the busts of famous abolitionists.

Black artists in the period before the Civil War were almost entirely confined to the North. In Louisiana, however, a number of *gens de couleur* were active as artists. Eugene and Daniel Warburg were sculptors, and Alexander Pickell and Julien Hudson were painters. Eugene Warburg spent many years in France, Belgium, Italy, and England, but his remembrance of his people is reflected in a series of bas-reliefs illustrating episodes in Harriet Beecher Stowe's *Uncle Tom's Cabin*. The series was purchased by the Duchess of Sutherland in England. Two of Julien Hudson's portraits are owned by the Louisiana State Museum: one a self-portrait, the other a portrait of Colonel Jean Michel Fortier, commander of the corps of free Negroes in the 1815 battle of New Orleans.

The 1850s witnessed the development of a new art form, the daguerreotype photographic process, which furnished competition to portrait artists. Businessmen and professionals who wanted to leave their likenesses to posterity patronized the daguerreotype galleries. A number of blacks, including Philadelphia artist Robert Douglass, Jr., earned both reputations and financial reward in this new art form. J. Presley Ball was called Cincinnati's "principal daguerreotypist." His gallery was described as "very large, finely skylighted, and handsomely furnished" and was "literally crowded from morning until evening with ladies, gentlemen, and children." "Few go to Cincinnati," Martin Delany noted, "without paying the deguerrean gallery of Mr. Ball a visit." When the gallery was destroyed by a tornado in May 1860, threatening the operation with financial disaster, many white families supplied funds to rebuild and reequip it.

In 1867, a Boston newspaper observed that "the Negro seems to have an appreciation for art, while being manifestly unable to produce it." While the work of black artists before the Civil War includes a great deal that is mediocre—as does those of white artists—we have seen enough to prove the wrongness of this observation. The portraits of Joshua Johnston reveal skill, while the more sophisticated and accomplished paintings of Robert S. Duncanson and Edward Mitchell Bannister and the sculpture of Edmonia Lewis rank with those of the other leading artists of the era. They merit a permanent place in any history of American art.

BLACK COMPOSERS, MUSICIANS, AND SINGERS

Standard reference books on American music, while paying great attention to Negro music (spirituals, ragtime, and jazz), have practically nothing to say about the black musicians of the nineteenth century. Even W.S.B. Mathew's enormous book on American musicians, which appeared in the 1880s and lists important American performers, shies away from the American Negro.

The earliest black composer in the United States is thought to have been Newport Gardner (1746-1826), a singing master of Newport, Rhode Island, and a writer of sacred music, but the most celebrated composer of the antebellum period was Francis Johnson of Philadelphia (1792-1844), who was at the head of a Philadelphia circle that included William Appo, Aaron J. R. Connor, Isaac Hazzard, James Hemmenway, and others. These men began their careers as leaders of military bands and dance orchestras and therefore found it expedient to write their own arrangements of the operatic tunes they played for society cotillions. As their careers developed, they were called upon to produce musical soirées and ''sacred music concerts''; accordingly, they began to write overtures, variations, vocal and choral pieces, and compositions for solo instruments and ensembles. Soon the public demanded easy arrangements of the most popular of these pieces, suitable for performance in home parlors, and a considerable amount of music written by these black composers was published.

If Philadelphia held sway as the musical center of black America in the midnineteenth century, it had a close rival in New Orleans. There the importance given to the cultivation of the arts served to encourage the development of talents among men of all colors; lessons could be obtained from European musicians associated with the theater and opera, and sons of the wealthy (natural as well as legitimate) were sent to the Paris Conservatoire. Chief among those of color who won recognition for their compositional skills were Edmund Dedé, Lucien Lambert, Joseph White, Basile Barés, E. V. McCarty, and Samuel Snaer.

Black composers in cities other than Philadelphia and New Orleans who were highly regarded included Henry F. Williams and Frederick Lewis of Boston, Justin Holland of Cleveland, William Brady of New York, Robert Murray of Baltimore, and T. W. Portelwaite of St. Louis. There were some who maintained that ''Blind Tom'' Bethune, the Georgia-born slave who became a phenomenal pianist, was also a talented composer.

Scholars who have examined the available music of these early black composers find, as Eileen Southern puts it, ''a high level of musicianship, skillful compositional craftsmanship, a good knowledge of instrumental techniques and timbres and an over-all style which embraces the classic and romantic tradition.'' Few seem to have been concerned with writing music that reflected an interest in their African heritage. Francis Johnson came closest in his ''Recognition March on the Independence of Hayti'' (c. 1825), but the music itself contains no Haitian elements. Until the time of the Civil War, black composers wrote in the same styles and used the same forms and techniques as did white composers.

According to the United States census returns of 1850, twenty-four black men in New York were listed as professional musicians, more than in any other city in the nation. There were indeed a number of important black musicians in the antebellum period both in and outside of New York. There was the Luca family, a singing group from Connecticut, who attracted wide attention in the 1850s.

There was Justin Holland, born in 1819, who studied piano and flute but switched to guitar and became America's foremost guitar virtuoso. He transcribed hundreds of baroque and classical pieces for his instruments, and in 1874 he published *Holland's Comprehensive Method,* the standard text on guitar playing. There was also the Lambert family. Richard, the father of seven children, taught music in New Orleans. His son, Lucien, born in 1828, was a pianist, composer, and teacher who went to the Paris Conservatoire for his training. On his return to New Orleans, discouraged by the color bar, he finally settled in Brazil.

Then there was the lyric soprano, Elizabeth Taylor Greenfield, who was known in her day as the "Black Swan." She was born in slavery in 1809 in Natchez, Mississippi, but was brought to Philadelphia as a baby by Mrs. Greenfield, a Quaker woman, who reared her and whose friends gave her elementary instruction in singing (despite the general Quaker opposition to music). By 1851, she was singing in public. She concertized throughout the North and in Canada and was compared with Jenny Lind. Critics pointed to a range that extended over three octaves, "reaching from the sonorous bass to a baritone to a few notes even above Jenny Lind's highest." " 'The Black Swan,' " Martin R. Delany, black journalist, novelist, and emigrationist, reported in 1852, "is singing to fine fashionable houses, and bids fare to stand unrivalled in the world of song." Already, according to Delany, "she ranks second to no vocalist in the world."

In 1853, Miss Greenfield went to England where she gave a command performance at Buckingham Palace for Queen Victoria. She was heard by Harriet Beecher Stowe, whose diary gives an account of her concert at Stafford House. The singer, she wrote, was "rapturously" received, after which the conductor-composer Sir George Smart "took her to the piano and tried her voice by skips, striking notes here and there at random, without connection, from D in alto to A first space in the bass clef. She followed with unerring precision."

Miss Greenfield often accompanied herself on the piano during her recitals, and this, too, won praise from critics. The *London Advertiser* pointed out that her talent was "a convincing argument against the assertion so often made that the negro race is incapable of intellectual culture of a high standard."

She left England in 1854, returned to Philadelphia, and began a brief concert tour of Northern cities, during which she received rave reviews. The critic for the *Cincinnati Daily Times* (who called her the "Sable Swan") noted that while her natural key "approaches nearer a mezzo-soprano than anything else . . . she sings in baritone, alto and tenor at will." In one song, she "manifested a perfect baritone—such as we have never heard from any other woman—and in the second part resumed her middle soprano, showing by contrast the greatness of her vocal scope." Still, he reported, the hall was only "moderately" filled, and this appears to have been the usual case. White audiences would not fill an auditorium to hear a black singer, no matter how remarkable were the reviews. As one Philadelphia critic put it: "She wants only a white skin in order to make a sensation in the musical world."

Elizabeth Greenfield left concertizing for teaching. When the phonograph records of voices of great black singers were issued in the United States in 1921, they were called the "Black Swan" records.

BLACK ACTORS

From 1821 to 1828, New York City blacks maintained their own theater, the African Grove, where ballets and plays were presented with black actors, and where, ironically, a special gallery was reserved for white spectators. The principal actor in the African Company was James Hewlett, who both sang and performed the leading roles in Shakespeare's *Othello* and *Richard the Third,* and is regarded to be "the first of the Negro tragedians." But the white spectators who came to laugh at blacks who dared to play Shakespeare became obstreperous over what they called the "spectacle" of *Richard the Third* being performed "by a fellow as black as the ace of spades." They became so riotous that the police closed the theater in 1828.

Before the African Grove Theater was closed down, Ira Aldridge, a youngster attending the African Free School, made an early stage appearance there. He was then noted mostly for his singing of "Negro songs," but he was soon to be acclaimed throughout Europe for his Othello, Macbeth, Lear, and Shylock.

Born in either Baltimore or New York City, probably on July 24, 1807, Aldridge became attracted to the stage during his childhood and obtained a job at the Chatham Theater where, behind the scenes, he could watch the actors and observe the delivery of their lines. After his performances at the African Grove Theater, his father interrupted his stage career and sent him to Scotland to further his education. He matriculated at the University of Glasgow and won several prizes for scholarship and a medal for Latin composition.

But the call of the boards was too much for him, and he went to London eventually to play the part of Othello at the Royal Theater. (After the closing of the African Grove Theater, James Hewlett had left for London and also performed at the same theater to enthusiastic audiences.) There Aldridge's rise to fame and stardom began. April 10, 1833 signified an event of great importance to the black actor, for on this date, he played Othello for the first time in the celebrated Covent Garden Theater. It was while playing the part of the Moor in Dublin (and this after some delay, since the manager was reluctant at first to hire a Negro for the role) that Aldridge came to the attention of Edward Kean, the greatest of the Shakespearean actors, who engaged him at once to play Othello to Kean's Iago. The two became great friends, touring England and the Continent together.

Writing to a French theater manager in 1854, Aldridge listed some of his triumphs:

For three years I have toured the principal cities of Germany, Austria, Hungary, where my representations have been crowned with the greatest success. It is unheard of that a person of African nationality should play dramatic roles. The success I have had in the greatest theaters of Germany has increased my desire to make an attempt in the French capital.

His Majesty, the King of Prussia, has condescended to honor me with the Large Gold Medal for Art and Sciences, the Emperor of Austria with the Medal of Ferdinand, and Switzerland with the White Cross.

My intention is to come to France with a troupe of English players to give the following: *Othello, Macbeth, King Lear, Richard III, The Merchant of Venice.*

In a letter to Dr. James McCune Smith of New York, Aldridge noted that his performances of these roles in Russia had met with "an unparalleled success." After several performances, he was presented with a picture of Shakespeare bearing the eloquent inscription: "To Ira Aldridge from the Russian Actors— Your Wisdom, Talent and Noble Effort have revealed the Great Shakespeare to us. We will never forget Othello, Shylock, and King Lear."

In June 1857, the reports of Aldridge's European triumphs caused the *New York Sunday Atlas* to remind its readers that Aldridge had once performed in their city and that the theater in which he had acted had been closed as a result of white rioters. It expressed its doubts over whether Aldridge's triumphs had changed anything as far as white New Yorkers were concerned:

We can crowd three or four theaters every night to witness white men with blackened faces, indulging in Ethiopian eccentricities; but if a real Simon-pure native of Africa was to show his face in contiguity to that of Miss Heron, or Mrs. Hoey, or any other of our favorite, fair performers, good Heavens! Wouldn't there be a row! The sacrilegious darkey would be torn to pieces on the spot, or burned alive in front of the City Hall.

Ira Aldridge never performed again in the United States. He died in Lodz, Poland, on August 7, 1867, and was given a solemn state funeral.

More than seventy years were to pass after the closing of the African Grove Theater by city authorities in 1828 before Negroes again appeared on a stage in New York City in a show produced, directed, and performed by themselves.

BLACK AUTHORS

Even though they belonged to a people largely denied formal education, a surprising number of black men and women published books during the antebellum years. Slave narratives sold widely both in the United States and abroad. They varied greatly in quality and originality. Some, like those of Frederick Douglass, William Wells Brown, James W. C. Pennington, Samuel Ringgold Ward, and Jermain Loguen, were written by the fugitives themselves. Some were ghosted, some were dictated to whites by the former slave, such as the narrative of Solomon Northup, and still others, like the narratives of Lunsford Lane, Sojourner Truth, and Harriet Tubman, were set down in the third person by whites.

The most famous of the antebellum slave autobiographies were Frederick Douglass' *Narrative,* published in 1845; William Wells Brown's *Narrative,* published two years later; Josiah Henson's *Life*; and Solomon Northup's *Twelve Years a Slave.* All slave narratives were immensely popular. Brown's account went through four editions the first year it was in print; that of Solomon Northup sold 27,000 copies in its first two years; and that of Josiah Henson sold more than 100,000 copies. Many of the narratives were translated into French, Dutch, German, and Russian.

While all of the slave narratives provide clear evidence of how blacks reacted to slavery, several are especially important in what they tell us about slavery from the viewpoint of the slave. Henry Bibb and James Pennington tell much about the sexual exploitation of black women; Solomon Northup shows how Northern free blacks were kidnapped and enslaved; Moses Roper, Henry Watson, John Anderson, and Charles Ball record the hard labor, continuous hunger, and repeated floggings that many slaves experienced; Josiah Henson described in detail the agonizing effects on the slave mother of separation from her children; and Jermain Loguen, Frederick Douglass, and Austin Steward demonstrated how the blacks retaliated against their owners by fighting back and even killing them. All of the narratives furnish valuable information on life in the quarters where slaves developed a community of their own, the family relationship, respect for elders, and the enduring culture, part of which were folktales, spirituals, and a religion different from that of their masters.

During these same years, poets George M. Horton, James W. Whitfield, and Frances E. W. Harper published their own works, and William C. Nell, the first black to write the history of his race, published *Colored Americans in the Wars of 1776 and 1812* (1851), and *The Colored Patriots of the American Revolution* (1855). A self-taught historian, Nell collected the stories of blacks who had fought in these wars. His books are still a useful source.

Several black writers published works in different forms. Frederick Douglass published two autobiographies (*Narrative of the Life of Frederick Douglass* in 1845 and *My Bondage and My Freedom* in 1855) and ''The Heroic Slave,'' a short story about Madison Washington, the rebel leader of the slave uprising on the *Creole,* which appeared in 1853. Martin R. Delany published *The Condition, Elevation, Emigration and Destiny of the Colored People of the United States Politically Considered,* in 1852, and the novel, *Blake, or Huts of America,* in the years 1859–1862.

The most prolific and varied black author was William Wells Brown. It is a matter of record that although he could neither read nor write until he was twenty-one years old, Brown, who was born in or about 1815, published the following works before the Civil War:

1847—*Narrative of the Life of William Wells Brown,* published by the Massachusetts Anti-Slavery Society.

1848—*The Anti-Slavery Harp: A Selection of Songs for Anti-Slavery Meetings,* published in Boston.

1852—*Three Years in Europe*, published in London.
1853—*Clotel; Or The President's Daughter, A Narrative of Slave Life in the United States*, a novel, published in London.
1855—*Sketches of Places and People Abroad*, published in London.
1858—*The Escape, or a Leap to Freedom*, a play, published in Boston.
1860–1861—*Miralda; or, the Beautiful Quadroon*, a revised version of *Clotel; Or The President's Daughter*.

James Whitfield was born in Boston in 1830 and moved to Buffalo, New York, when he was a young man, earning his living as a barber. In 1853, his *America, and Other Poems* was published, and its success enabled Whitfield to give up his work as a barber. He devoted himself to the public platform and advocated the cause of emigration as the solution to the problems of black Americans. His view of his native land is expressed vividly in the opening lines of his poem, "America":

> America, it is to thee,
> Thou boasted land of liberty,—
> Thou land of blood, and crime, and wrong.
> It is to thee my native land,
> From which has issued many a band
> To tear the black man from his soil,
> And force him here to delve and toil;
> Chained on your blood-bemoistened sod,
> Cringing beneath a tyrant's rod,
> Stripped of those rights which Nature's God
>   Bequeathed to all the human race,
> Bound to a petty tyrant's nod,
>   Because he wears a paler face.
>
> Almighty God! thy aid impart,
> And fire anew each faltering heart,
> And strengthen every patriot's hand,
> Who aims to save our native land. . . .
> We pray, and never meant to cease,
>   Till weak old age and fiery youth
> In freedom's cause their voices raise,
> And burst the bonds of every slave;
> Till, north and south, and east and west,
> The wrongs we bear shall be redressed.

Frances Ellen Watkins Harper, the second black woman poet and the most popular American Negro poet of her time, was born in Baltimore in 1825 of free parents. She was educated in that city, and in 1850, she moved to Ohio and taught domestic science at Union Seminary in Columbia. In 1853, she went to Little York, Pennsylvania, to work with the Underground Railroad. A year later, she was engaged as a full-time lecturer by the Anti-Slavery Society of Maine.

Her first book, *Poems on Various Subjects,* was published the same year. Her books of antislavery and religious verse sold widely, and *Poems on Various Subjects* went into several editions. The poem, ''The Slave Auction,'' was widely reprinted:

> The sale began—young girls were there,
>   Defenceless in their wretchedness,
> Whose stifled sobs of deep despair
>   Revealed their anguish and distress.
>
> And mothers stood with streaming eyes,
>   And as their dearest children sold;
> Unheeded rose their bitter cries,
>   While tyrants bartered them for gold.
>
> And woman, with her love and truth—
>   For these in sable forms may dwell—
> Gaz'd on the husband of her youth,
>   With anguish none may paint or tell.
>
> And men, whose sole crime was their hue,
>   The impress of their Maker's hand,
> And frail and shrinking children, took,
>   Were gathered in that mournful band.
>
> Ye who have laid your love to rest,
>   And wept above their lifeless clay,
> Know not the anguish of that breast,
>   Whose lov'd are rudely torn away.
>
> Ye may not know how desolate
>   Are bosoms rudely forced to part,
> And how a dull and heavy weight
>   Will press the life-drops from the heart.

William Wells Brown was born in Lexington, Kentucky, the son of a mulatto slave mother and a father who was a slaveholder. When he was about twelve years old, he became the caretaker, companion, and servant of the small son of his master's brother. Unfortunately for William, his master's nephew was also named William, so to avoid confusion the young slave's name was changed to Sandford. This taught him a bitter lesson; that a slave had absolutely nothing that was inviolate—not even his name—if a white person had any use for it. When he was about nineteen years old, William became a fugitive slave, and with the assistance of a Quaker, Wells Brown, whose name he adopted, he escaped to the North. Finding employment on a boat on Lake Erie and later becoming a steward on that boat, he immediately launched his career of service to his fellows in bondage by helping a fugitive get to Canada. Making his home in Buffalo, New York, he then organized a vigilance group, whose main function was to supply food, clothing, information, money, and whatever else was needed by the fugitives to help them on their way to freedom. During this time, he spent the winter months in an evening school and availed himself of private instruction.

In 1843, Brown was employed as an agent by the Western New York Anti-Slavery Society and became a lecturer for that organization. In 1847, he transferred to the Massachusetts Anti-Slavery Society. While living in Massachusetts, he studied medicine and later practiced that profession in Cambridge. But he also found time for writing books.

From the beginning of his career as an antislavery agent in 1843, Brown decided that in order to win and hold the attention of possible converts to the antislavery cause, he must vary the form in which he made his appeals. Within thirteen years, he had presented his arguments against slavery by means of autobiography, songs, fiction, and drama. When Brown compiled *The Anti-Slavery Harp,* he included a poem that had appeared in the *Edinburgh Magazine,* which dealt with Thomas Jefferson's alleged offspring, whose mother was Sally Hemmings, the beautiful quadroon slave girl who had accompanied Jefferson's youngest daughter to Paris in 1787 and who was said to have become his concubine. In the poem, one of Jefferson's mulatto daughters is sold as a slave, and the poet exclaims in horror:

> The daughter of Jefferson is sold for a slave!
> The child of a freeman for dollars and francs!
> The roar of applause, when your orators rave,
> Is lost in the sound of her chain, as it clanks.

Brown did not forget the poem. When *Clotel; Or The President's Daughter,* the first novel written by an American Negro, was published in London in November 1853, the heroine was immediately thought to be Jefferson's daughter. Indeed, Brown did use reports concerning Jefferson's fathering and selling one of his mulatto children at auction to arouse the reader's attention and hatred of slavery. In the process of telling the Jefferson story, based only on such reports as he could obtain, Brown also struck at various aspects of the ''peculiar institution.'' Thus, he wrote:

The bells of thirty churches were calling the people to the different places of worship. Crowds were seen wending their way to the houses of God; one followed by a negro boy carrying his master's Bible; another followed by her maid-servant holding the mistress' fan. . . . The next day, all these staunch Christians were at the slave pens, picking over slaves as if they were cattle.

From November 30, 1860, through March 16, 1861, the *Weekly Anglo-African* of New York City published (in weekly installments) Brown's novel *Miral-*

da; or, the Beautiful Quadroon, a revised version of *Clotel.* In 1864, the novel was published in book form under the title, *Clotelle: A Tale of the Southern States.* This time Clotelle was made the daughter of an American senator. The American edition, issued in a dime-novel series, "Redpath's Books for the Campfire," was read widely in the Union Army.

William Wells Brown was also the first black dramatist. His first drama, entitled *Experience, Or How to Give a Northern Man a Backbone,* consisted of three acts divided, respectively, into two, five, and two scenes, the last of which ended with a "Grand Political Finale." The plot told of how a white Boston doctor of divinity, hostile to antislavery, was transformed into an abolitionist by being kidnapped and sold into slavery, from which he was released after a time. On his return home to Boston, he repented having previously condoned slavery and avowed his hatred of the institution. To prove his transformation, he resolved to help a fugitive slave escape to Canada.

Experience was never published. Between May 27, 1856, and May 20, 1857, Brown read his drama before numerous audiences in New England, New York, Ohio, and Pennsylvania. The readings met with widespread approval, and Brown then completed another drama—*The Escape, or, A Leap for Freedom. A Drama, in Five Acts.* Sometime in 1858, *Escape* was published in Boston. Like *Experience,* it was never produced as a play but was presented by Brown himself as a dramatic reading. The plot of the play revolves about the difficulty created in the domestic circle of a slaveowner and his wife's justified jealousy of a slave girl and her attempt to remove her from the household. But unwilling to part with her, Dr. Gaines secreted the slave girl in a cabin in the mountains. There he offered her all sorts of worldly goods in exchange for her "honor." She refuses, and in a style derived from the eighteenth-century comedy of manners, she cries out:

Sir, I am your slave; you can do as you please with the avails of my labor, but you shall never tempt me to swerve from the paths of virtue. Let me warn you, if you compass my ruin, a woman's bitterest curse will be laid upon your haid . . . a curse that shall embody itself in the ghastly form of the woman whose chastity you will have outraged. Command me to bury myself in younder stream and I will obey you. But I beseech you not to commit a double crime, outrage a woman, and make her false to her husband.

Dr. Gaines then determines to get rid of Glen, the girl's husband, by selling him down the river. Brown conceived of the situation as an excellent example of the limitless power a master had over a slave and often used for the most immoral pursuits. He portrays Dr. Gaines throughout as a slave speculator of the worst order, who buys and sells slaves as he might deal in stocks and bonds. When he sells Black Sam, who is married to Hannah, who loves her husband dearly, he casually orders her to "jump the broomstick" with an obnoxious house servant. For the pious Hannah, this act symbolizing marriage was frightful. She had been married to her husband by a Christian preacher. Not only was she being forced to give up her husband and commit a sin by remarrying, but that second marriage was to be consecrated by a heathen tradition. Small wonder that reports of Brown's dramatic reading stressed the fact that at this point in the play, audiences openly wept.

Brown stated that the play's background was drawn from his own "experience of eighteen years at the South." However, he conceded in the preface that "the play abounds in defects but as I was born in slavery and never had a day's schooling in my life, I owe the public no apology for error."

Martin Robinson Delany was born a free person in Charleston, Virginia (now in West Virginia) on May 6, 1812, one of five children of Samuel and Pati Delany. Both of his grandfathers were native Africans, and both had been tribal chieftains. Both had also been captured during wars and sold into slavery. When Delany was a child, the state of Virginia forbade free blacks as well as slaves an education. However, a Yankee peddler passing through Charleston surreptitiously sold Mrs. Delany the *New York Primer and Spelling-book*, a famous reader of the day. The peddler lingered long enough to give Martin one lesson; subsequently all of the Delany children learned to read and write from that primer. When the family moved to Chambersburg, Pennsylvania, the children were at last permitted to go to school.

At an early age, Delany left the Chambersburg school to take a job. But in 1831, when he was nineteen, he set out on foot for Pittsburgh where he hoped to continue his education. He found work as a barber and studied at night at a school run by Reverend Lewis Woodson, a black Methodist minister who had recently moved to Pittsburgh from Ohio. With the tutelage and encouragement of two doctors, Delany in time became a doctor's assistant, performing such services as cupping, bleeding, and leeching. Later he also became proficient in dental care, and in 1839, he traveled through several states as a dentist. Upon his return to Pittsburgh, he started a weekly newspaper, the *Mystery,* which he edited from 1843 to 1847.

On March 15, 1843, Delany married Catherine Richards, the daughter of Charles Richards, owner of some of Pittsburgh's best property. Delany and his wife had eleven children, whom they named after important figures in black history, including Touissaint L'Ouverture and Alexandre Dumas, the black French novelist. One was named Ramses Placido, the first name being that of an Egyptian pharaoh and the second that of the Cuban poet and revolutionary martyr.

In the middle of 1847, Delany sold his interest in the *Mystery*, and from December 1847 through June 1849 was assistant editor of the *North Star*, Frederick Douglass' paper. He then returned to Pittsburgh, determined to pursue formal medical studies. After being rejected by three schools, he was admitted to Harvard Medical School. He attended Harvard for one sixteen-week term in 1851–1852 but was not permitted to complete the course of studies because his white fellow students objected to his presence. The faculty then voted to dismiss Delany and two other black students at the end of the winter course of lectures, after which Delany returned to Pittsburgh, where he practiced medicine.

In 1852, Delany published at his own expense *The Condition, Elevation, Emigration, and Destiny of the Colored People of the United States, Politically Considered*, a remarkable source of information about the antebellum free black population of the North. One sentence in the appendix is the most quoted of the work: "We are a nation within a nation; as the Poles in Russia, the Hungarians in Austria; the Welsh, Irish and Scotch in the British dominions." It was in this privately published book that Delany first formulated his theory of black nationalism.

Delany's novel, *Blake, or The Huts of America*, appeared in serial, but fragmentary form, from January until July 1859 in the *Anglo-African Magazine*. Although the editors introduced the novel with the statement that it contained "some 80 chapters and about 600 pages," only twenty-six chapters were published. The entire novel appeared in the *Weekly Anglo-African* in consecutive weekly installments from November 26, 1861, until some time in May 1862. Even in fragmentary form, *Blake*'s publication marked the first novel to be published in the United States by a black American. (It has been claimed that *Our Nig*, a novel by H. E. Wilson, was by the black woman Harriet E. Wilson of Boston, and that when it was published in 1859 it became not only the first novel published by a black person in this country, but also the first by a black woman, as well. But the evidence for this claim is still not convincing.)

The novel is about Henrico Blacus, later to be known as Blake, a black West Indian stolen from his home and brought as a slave (renamed Henry Holland) to the Red River region of Louisiana. There he marries another slave, Maggie, who had been fathered by her owner, Colonel Stephen Franks. After Maggie is sold to the wife of a Northern judge, who takes her to Cuba, Henry escapes from the Franks plantation and moves throughout the South, spreading his plan for a unified rebellion to overthrow slavery.

> From plantation to plantation did he go, sowing the seeds of future devastation and ruin to the master, and redemption to the slave, an antecedent more terrible in its anticipation, than the warning voice of the destroying Angel, on commanding the slaughter of the first born of Egypt. Himself careworn, distressed and hungry, who just being supplied with nourishment for the system, Henry went forth a welcome messenger, casting his bread upon turbid waters of oppression, in hopes of finding it after many days.

Henry then returns to the Franks plantation and aids several slaves to escape. This ends the first part of the novel. The second part begins with Henry sailing for Cuba as a servant of an American traveling group. He finds Maggie and buys her freedom. He now emerges as Blake and becomes general of a black insurrectionary force in Cuba. With the constant aid and poetic encouragement of Placido (the pen name of Gabriel de la Concepción Valdes, a free-born Cuban mulatto poet who was executed as a rebel by the Spaniards in 1844), Blake plans the overthrow of the Cuban government and the repulsion of Americans intent upon annexing the island to the United States for the expansion of slavery.

We do not know how Delany concluded his novel, since the last four chapters have not been found. But even in its uncompleted form, the novel is a remarkable work. Delany avoids the sentimentality of the tragic mulatto theme and focuses throughout on the political and social issues of the 1850s: slavery as an institution, Cuba as the prime target of Southern expansionists, the practicability of a militant slave revolution, and the psychological liberation possible through collective action. At one point in the narrative, after his wife Maggie has been sold, other slaves try to console Henry with appeals to religion. He rejects the plea:

I'm tired looking the other side! I want a hope this side of the vale of tears. I want something on this earth as well as a promise of things in another world. I and my wife have been both robbed of our liberty and you want me to be satisfied with a hope of heaven. I won't do any such thing; I have waited long enough on heavenly promises; I'll wait no longer. I—''

As Henry passes from plantation to plantation, confiding his secrets for the organization of a great slave rebellion, all who hear him acknowledge that somehow light has dawned in their lives: And Delany comments:

Light, of necessity had to be imparted to the darkened region of the obscure intellects of the slaves, to arouse them from their benighted condition to one of moral responsibility, to make them sensible that liberty was legitimately and essentially theirs, without which there was no distinction between them and the brute. Following as a necessary consequence would be the destruction of oppression and ignorance.

Some black writers were prolific and appeared often in print even if not in book form. William J. Wilson, a boot maker and shoemaker by trade, wrote a regular column for *Frederick Douglass' Paper* under the pen name Ethiop. He also contributed poems and satirical essays to the *Anglo-African Magazine* and editorials to the *Weekly Anglo-African*.

Black men of wealth who had close business associations with the white community were viewed with reservations by many in the black community. Some of this was fully justified, for many black businessmen openly identified with whites, were extremely solicitous of white opinion, adopted white standards as their own, and reconciled themselves to a world of white domination. But even the most prosperous and well-established members of the free black community never fully escaped the stigma that whites attached to their color, and they soon learned that most whites failed to distinguish between rich and poor, or literate and illiterate Negroes: a black was a black. Apart from ties of blood, kinship, and common origin, white racism bound all free blacks together. Wealth provided no insulation from racial prejudice.

Black men of wealth made their contributions to the black community by helping to finance the construction of churches and schools and by supporting black conventions to which they were often delegates. Some went further and delivered public lectures denouncing slavery and racism, but few were as active as black professionals. Although Dr. James McCune Smith was a noted doctor and surgeon, his fame rested largely on his activities in the struggle of the black community of New York for equality and in his battle against slavery. Both Smith and Dr. John S. Rock made use of the lecture platform to challenge the racist conception that Negroes were inferior to whites. Lewis Hayden's custom and ready-made clothing store provided garments for fugitive slaves while the profits were used to feed runaway slaves while they were in Boston.

B. P. Burr, a watercolorist in Philadelphia, was an active abolitionist and a member of the committee that organized the "Appeal of the Forty Thousand" in opposition to the disfranchisement of Negroes in Pennsylvania. The "Appeal," it will be remembered, was written by Robert Purvis, a vigorous opponent of slavery until the adoption of the Thirteenth Amendment and a fighter against discrimination against his people until his death in 1898.

Robert J. Douglass, Jr., the Philadelphia artist, was a militant abolitionist and wrote frequently for the *North Star* and the *National Anti-Slavery Standard*. He was one of the founders of the Pennsylvania Augustine Society for the Education of People of Color in 1818 and a member of the committee to appeal for funds to establish a normal school for Negroes.

Peter H. Clark's ability was not confined to education alone. He launched his own newspaper, the *Herald of Freedom,* in Cincinnati, but it did not last out 1855, the year in which it was founded. He also served as correspondent for *Frederick Douglass' Paper*, became involved in efforts to aid fugitive slaves, and participated actively in the black convention movement, where his natural talents placed him among the leaders.

One black professional who came under sharp attack in the black community was the "Black Swan." Elizabeth Greenfield was angrily dubbed the "Black Raven" by Frederick Douglass after she consented to perform before an audience in New York City from which "colored persons" were excluded. Stunned by the criticism, in which a number of other leading blacks joined, Greenfield voiced "regret" that the management of the Metropolitan Hall had "debarred" people of her color, although she noted coolly that "it was expressly stated in the agreement for the use of the hall, that such be the case." However, she added: "I will with pleasure sing for the benefit of any charity that will elevate the condition of my colored brethren."

She did sing to help raise funds to purchase the freedom of slaves and for the benefit of the Abyssinian Baptist Church—but the criticism continued. Even though blacks were no longer excluded from her concerts, her white managers insisted on appending the following note to notices advertising her concerts: "The gallery will be appropriated exclusively to colored people." One infuriated black wrote from Cincinnati: "Miss Greenfield sang to an audience under circumstances so humiliating as to cause us to regret her coming here."

Elizabeth Greenfield was not the only one guilty of such practices, but they were not typical of most blacks who appeared in public. The vast majority hated the racial prejudice that they saw around them and spoke out strongly against it and against the human bondage under which their people suffered.

13

The Colonization Controversy

In volume 1, I discussed the origins and early history of the American Colonization Society, which was formed in 1816 for the purpose of "colonizing (with
their consent) the free people of color, residing in our country, in Africa, or such
other place as Congress shall deem most expedient." In August 1822, representatives of the society purchased land from African chiefs near the British colony
of Sierra Leone. When the Colonization Society recommended the establishment
of a colony on the land, President James Monroe interpreted the Slave Trade Act
passed by Congress as authorizing him to assist the colonizationists, and he made
available a navy brig, a navy schooner, navy surgeons, and supplies to assist the
venture. In 1824, the name *Liberia*, "land of freedom," was given to the colony
in West Africa, and the major town, originally called Christopolis, was renamed
Monrovia to honor the American president.

GROWTH AND IDEOLOGY OF THE AMERICAN
COLONIZATION SOCIETY

The early American blacks who made the crossing to Africa to settle in Liberia
had to face fever, full-scale assaults by nearby tribal warriors who feared their
encroachment, and other dangers. While their struggle for survival continued,
the American Colonization Society conducted a drive to recruit American blacks
for its colony and for funds to finance the colonization venture. To assist the
campaign, the society's periodical, the *African Repository*, began regular publication in 1825 under editor Ralph Gurley, who was also the society's secretary.

From the start, the motives behind the colonization drive were mixed. Some
backers supported it out of the humanitarian feeling that free Negroes were
prevented from receiving a fair chance to compete in American society because
of overwhelming white prejudice. Hence, the reasoning went, they would be

better off among their own kind in Africa. Others saw colonization as a means of gradually bringing an end to slavery by making it possible for a slaveowner to manumit his slaves, a step prohibited by law in most Southern states unless the owner, at the same time, arranged for emigration from the state. Still others viewed colonization as a channel for draining off freed blacks, whom they considered an "undesirable, even dangerous" element. The Negroes sent to the colony would civilize and Christianize Africa, while at the same time ridding the United States of a group of people considered totally undesirable. (The contradiction inherent in a plan for the redemption of Africa through the medium of "undesirables" was never explained.) Others, unconcerned with moral and humane considerations, visualized the movement as opening a vast and valuable trade with the African continent, with Liberia serving as a commercial station, while helping to undermine the persistent, though outlawed, transatlantic slave trade.

Between 1818 and 1830, the African Colonization Society received the approval of the national conventions of the Presbyterian, Methodist, Baptist, and Dutch Reformed churches, as well as of regional conferences of Congregationalists, Quakers, and Episcopalians. In the period from 1826 to 1832, the legislatures of Virginia, Maryland, Tennessee, Ohio, New Jersey, Connecticut, Rhode Island, Indiana, Vermont, Kentucky, Pennsylvania, Massachusetts, New York, and Delaware all gave their approval to the society. By 1835, it had penetrated every region of the United States—there were seventeen state societies, twelve local auxiliaries, and numerous affiliates—and it was endorsed by eminent public and private figures and supported by both state and private donations. The list of members and contributors published in the *African Repository* indicates its widespread support. It included Thomas Jefferson, James Madison, James Monroe, Henry Clay, and Daniel Webster and such antislavery figures as Benjamin Lundy (who also served as lecturer for the American Colonization Society and as vice-president of the Kentucky Colonization Society), Arthur Tappan and Gerrit Smith (both of whom gave large donations to the society), and William Lloyd Garrison, who even subscribed for life membership. In fact, the American Colonization Society functioned as a kind of halfway house for many who became abolitionists in the 1830s.

As the society grew, other colonies were established in Africa for blacks from the United States. The Maryland Colonization Society, breaking off from the national organization, won a grant from the state legislature of $10,000 a year for ten years to finance its own colonizing scheme. In 1832, it sent a ship with 144 colonists to Liberia, and, two years later, it established its own colony at Cape Palmas, some three hundred miles down the coast from Monrovia, where a small settlement named "Maryland in Liberia" was developed.

Others followed suit. The Philadelphia Society, in collaboration with the New York Society, bought its own ship for transporting settlers. In 1835, it established its own colony along the St. Johns River, led by men devoted to the Quaker principles of peace and temperance. In the first year, the colony was almost wiped out by a native attack. The Mississippi Society, too, launched its own colony under the name "Mississippi in Liberia," 130 miles southeast of Monrovia. Encountering many problems, it barely managed to survive.

The ideas of the Colonization Society were particularly attractive to those southerners who favored emancipation but who were discouraged by the growing hostility to any proposal for ending slavery. In fact, Southern emancipationists concocted a grand design in which colonization would become the spur to end slavery throughout the South through a step-by-step process. By removing emancipated Negroes, they argued, masters would become more willing to free their slaves. White laborers would quickly replace blacks and provide more efficient—hence cheaper—labor and further speed the eradication of the "peculiar institution." Over the years, by means of manumission and deportation, emancipation would come to Maryland, and this, in turn, would influence other border states to follow suit. Once the institution had been ended in the upper South, the process would begin in the lower South.

Such a grandiose vision had the effect of practically putting an end to whatever organized abolitionism there was in the South, most of which moved into the colonization camp. In addition, white artisans and laborers in the South, who stood to benefit from the elimination of Negro competition, became enthusiastic advocates of colonization and made regular contributions to the work of its societies. At the same time, however, the emphasis on colonization as the first step leading to the eventual abolition of slavery, even in the Deep South, was responsible for the fact that the Colonization Society met with anything but enthusiastic support in the lower South. Despite the existence of "Mississippi in Liberia," slaveowners in the lower South were suspicious of the movement, and to overcome this feeling, colonizationists emphasized the benefits slaveholders would reap once they ousted the free blacks. The threat of insurrection would be removed, and there would no longer be any refuge for fugitive slaves. Slaves who were suspected of being potential leaders of uprisings could be manumitted and deported, thereby again lessening the dangers of revolts. Thus, deportation would strengthen slavery by freeing the South of a subversive group. Moreover, the colonizationists assured the slaveowners that they were opposed to any interference with the "rights of a master in his slave," that the society had never "in a solitary instance" addressed itself to the slave, and that it "would view the interference of Congress on this subject as unconstitutional as a flagrant and unjustifiable usurpation of the rights of the slaveholding States."

Eventually the colonizationists barred any discussion of slavery. The Maryland Society instructed its agents "to avoid everything relating to the question of slavery, [their] duties being connected with *Colonization* only." Still, the American Colonization Society was never able to convince many slaveowners, particularly in the lower South, that the organization was not a front for abolitionists or that colonization did not infringe upon the right of the master to his slaves as property. Nor did the colonizationists' emphasis on the danger of slave insurrections and the need to remove potential rebels impress these slaveowners. After

Nat Turner's insurrection, the states of the upper South "opened their treasuries to state colonization societies," but the agents of the society who came to the lower South had difficulty raising any funds, and sometimes they had to flee to escape violence. "Although a few auxiliary societies were eventually established," Ira Berlin notes, "colonization had few friends in the Lower South."

The Colonization Society discovered this fact when it sought to obtain additional federal funds. Launching a drive for such federal aid, Gurley and other society spokesmen argued that private and state funds were not sufficient to achieve the object of colonizing free Negroes and that only Congress could supply sufficient "national means" to solve a national problem. In 1825, Thomas Jefferson seconded the move, urging that proceeds from federal land sales be used to support colonization. Seven state legislatures passed resolutions endorsing this proposal, but members of Congress from the lower South, responding to the fears expressed by the region's planters that this would only strengthen "abolitionists who wanted to wreak havoc in the South," objected. In February 1827, Robert Y. Hayne of South Carolina declared in Congress that "the spirit which lurks beneath their [the colonizationists'] fair professions is hostile to the peace and best interests of the Southern states; and not the less so, because it comes clothed in the garb of friendship, and with professions of peace and good will." In December 1827, Congress rejected financial assistance to the society, resolving that it had no "power in any way to patronize a direct appropriation" for its benefit.

But the champions of colonization did not give up. In 1833, Henry Clay, a long-time colonization advocate and soon to head the society, pushed through Congress a bill to distribute to the states federal surplus funds from land sales to be used for education, internal improvements, or colonization as each state chose. But President Andrew Jackson, himself a slaveowner, doomed the society's efforts by vetoing its so-called distribution bill.

Blocked from federal aid, the society won support from other quarters. More and more, it began to come from white Americans who looked upon colonization as a means of ridding their communities of an unwanted Negro population. In the North, those who supported colonization were especially desirous of preventing their states from becoming dumping grounds for penniless blacks from the South, whom they regarded as inherently incapable of moral and intellectual development and as destined to become either a future source of lawlessness and crime or public charges. In the South, supporters of the society regarded the free Negro as an "intolerable nuisance" because his presence among slaves was a constant cause of insubordination and discontent. Moreover, they looked upon the free black as an ally of the slave and as one who was always ready to join him in "any mischievous design." Finally, they believed that the two races were totally "irreconcilable" and that the animosities between them would, unless the blacks were ultimately removed, lead to a wholesale war of extermination. However, as we have seen, these views did not make much headway among slaveowners in the lower South, who feared the "emancipationist implications" of colonization more than they did the free blacks and who, in some cases, believing the free Negro to be useful as an intermediary between slaves and masters, did not wish to see them deported to Africa.

North and South, the supporters of the society were convinced that the free Negro was a source of evil to the whites, and they were determined to rid the country of an unwanted population, or, as they termed it, a "dangerous element in American society." Although the society asserted that it was motivated by concern for Negroes, it was inevitable that it would use anti-Negro sentiments to attract the support of the white population. Many of its arguments fostered the doctrine of racial inferiority of the Negro. Basically the society was interested in the improvement of the Negro's status only in order to prepare him to emigrate to Africa. Of Negroes in this country, it frankly declared: "The moral, intellectual and political improvement of people of color within the United States are objects foreign to the powers of this Society." Basic to the existence of the society was the assumption that because of inherent racial inferiority—the handiwork of both God and nature—Negroes could never be integrated into the American body politic, no matter how much education they acquired, and therefore should leave America. Robert Goodloe Harper, one of the founders of the society, was brutally frank: "You may manumit the slave, but you cannot make him a white man; he still remains a negro or a mulatto." The society itself said, equally bluntly: "*Causes beyond the control of the human will* must prevent their [blacks'] ever rising to equality with the whites. . . . This is not the fault of the colored man, *nor of the white man*, nor of Christianity; but it is AN ORDINATION OF PROVIDENCE, *and no more to be changed than the laws of nature.*"

The *African Repository* and the official publications of the state and local colonization societies were replete with aspersions on the character, morals, and intelligence of free blacks. Expressions such as "corrupt," "debased," "depraved," "degraded," "vicious," "thriftless," "wretched," "destitute," "dangerous," and "thieving," appeared regularly in their pages. So, too, did articles and speeches emphasizing that there was no future for this "species of humanity" in America. "No merit, no services, no talents can elevate them to a level with the whites," was a typical comment.

ATTITUDE OF FREE BLACKS TOWARD THE AMERICAN COLONIZATION SOCIETY

In the discussion of the American Colonization Society in volume 1, I noted the fact that some free blacks were ready to emigrate to Liberia because of the miserable circumstances in which they lived, even though they were free, and their belief that they never would achieve equality in the United States. Reverend Daniel Coker, a teacher-preacher of Baltimore's free Negro community, who had helped to organize the African Methodist Episcopal church, declined appointment as a bishop in order to go to Africa. Similarly, despite his success as a minister of the Baptist church in Virginia and as a founder of the Richmond African Missionary Society, Lott Cary left for Liberia. When asked why he was willing to give up a promising career in the United States, he replied: "I am an African, and in this country, however meritorious my conduct and respectable my character, I cannot receive the credit due either. I wish to go to a country where I shall be estimated by my merits, not by my complexion."

Reverend William Cornish of Bethel Church in Baltimore presided at a meeting at the church in December 1826 that supported colonization. The Baltimore blacks argued that their situation was not unlike the one that the Puritans had faced in England. "We would remind you," they resolved in a message to the white community, "of the time when you were in a situation similar to ours, and when your forefathers were driven by religious persecution to a distant and inhospitable shore. We are not so persecuted; but we, too, leave our homes, and seek a distant and inhospitable shore."

But more representative black thinking was opposed to the American Colonization Society. The opposition began soon after the society's founding in 1816 and grew in intensity in the years that followed. On four separate occasions between 1817 and 1819, Philadelphia Negroes spoke out against colonization to Africa. The first was a meeting at Bethel Church late in January 1817 at which three thousand Philadelphia Negro men, virtually the entire black adult male population of the city, firmly and unequivocally rejected the idea of colonization and condemned the founders of the Colonization Society for "the unmerited stigma attempted to be cast up on the free people of color . . . 'that they are a dangerous and useless part of the community.'" As chairman of the great meeting, James Forten introduced the resolutions, which went on to explain the reasons for their opposition to the society's program: first, since blacks had been brought to this country not by their own choice but had, nonetheless, become "the first successful cultivators of the wilds of America, we their descendants feel ourselves entitled to participate in the blessings of her luxuriant soil, which their blood and sweat manured"; second, they believed that the deportation of free blacks would result in permanent bondage for those who remained as slaves, to whom they felt strong ties of affection; and third, they regarded exile in "the savage wilds of Africa," without the benefit of government and education, as a "return to perpetual bondage." The resolutions were adopted "without one dissenting voice."

As the African Colonization Society made clear its plans for transporting free people of color to Africa, a wave of protest swept through free black communities of the North. Even Richmond's free Negroes took a cautious step against the society's removal policy. They agreed that in principle, colonization might benefit many blacks, but they expressed the desire to be colonized in a remote part of this continent rather than being "exiled to a foreign country." In the North, the free blacks were much more outspoken in their opposition. Inherent in this was a deep feeling of loyalty to and responsibility for their brethren in slavery. Free blacks in the North pointed out that their removal from America would strengthen slavery by expelling its most active adversaries. They made it clear, too, that they viewed the Colonization Society as a racist organization seeking to degrade and separate their race.

By the early 1820s, the anticolonization sentiment appeared so well defined among free blacks that the issue was viewed as dead so far as black communities in the North were concerned. Yet on August 17, 1827, *Freedom's Journal* carried a dispatch from Samuel E. Cornish in New Haven that noted that wherever he went and to whomever he talked to in the black community, "as usual the conversation turned on African colonization."

What accounts for the revival of interest in the subject of African colonization in the late 1820s? For one thing, as we have seen, conditions for free blacks in the North grew worse during that decade as immigration from Europe, held back by the Napoleonic Wars, resumed and increasingly pushed black mechanics out of the skilled positions they had once occupied. There was often a direct relationship between a free black's desire to leave the country and his inability to find satisfactory employment in the labor market. In Liberia, they were promised new opportunities for employment, and it is interesting to note that a great many of those who contacted the colonization societies were free black craftsmen who hoped that emigration would provide them with better opportunities in their trades. A letter received by the American Colonization Society in 1828 asked if the society would "bear the expenses of about thirty or forty persons passage," most of whom were "mechanics and all of whom are very anxious to go." Another group of petitioners seeking information about LIberia consisted of "industrious and intelligent mechanics—men who expect to labor for a livelihood and who are prepared also to endure privations."

Then too, the decade was marked by an increasing use of violence to drive blacks out of Northern communities. Whites in the City of Brotherly Love burned Negro homes in 1820 in an attempt to force blacks to leave Philadelphia. In 1822, the black community of Rhode Island suffered a cruel blow when the general assembly explicitly denied the suffrage to any black, and hard on the heels of this racist legislation came the first anti-Negro riot in Providence—the Hardscrabble riot. It occurred in October 1824 in Hardscrabble, a northern suburb of the town "populated principally by blacks who located themselves on that quarter to avoid . . . their hostile neighbors." Groups of white sailors invaded Hardscrabble and, in the course of walking about, deliberately tried to force Negroes off the sidewalks. A brawl ensued in which the invaders were routed. The next morning, signs appeared throughout Providence calling upon whites to assemble the following evening and teach the blacks to respect men with a "superior skin color." Four hundred to five hundred people responded—a mixture of rowdies and respectable citizens—and in the course of a few hours, they leveled Hardscrabble.

Except for one or two editorials that blamed the Hardscrabble black inhabitants for having brought the tragedy upon themselves, the Providence press ignored the incident. But the black community was not unmoved by the two blows it had received in so short a period. In January 1826, the only group of

Rhode Island blacks ever to emigrate to Africa left for Liberia under the aegis of the American Colonization Society. They were led by Newport Gardner, then seventy-five years old. After purchasing his freedom, Gardner had become a music teacher in Newport and rapidly emerged as a leader of the black community. In 1780, he had been instrumental in the formation of the African Benevolent Society; he had been prominent in the organization of the African Union Society in 1808, which had as its primary purpose the establishment and maintenance of a school for black children; and he was, in addition, an active church member and deacon of the Congregational church. Gardner was, in fact, in every respect, an example of a black who had achieved success in America—rising from slavery to eminence in his community. But the Hardscrabble riot, coming on top of the loss of suffrage, had shattered his confidence in America, and fourteen months later, he left his comfortable home in Newport and departed for Africa. Gardner's statement on leaving for Liberia reflected his despair over the future of his race in the United States, a feeling shared by not a few blacks. "I go," he said, "to set an example, for the youth of my race. I go to encourage the young. They can never be elevated here. I have tried it for sixty years . . . it is in vain." The black emigrants from Rhode Island arrived in Liberia on February 6, 1826. They soon fell victim to fever, and in less than a year, more than half the number had died.

In the United States, Gardner's parting statement was widely publicized by the American Colonization Society. But a real publicity campaign got underway in 1828 over the return of Abd al-Rahman to Africa. The sixty-four-year-old Abd al-Rahman was a slave in Natchez, Mississippi, where he was known as the Prince. He claimed to be the son of the king of Futa Jallon (in present-day Guinea), saying he was a Muslim, and had spent five years at school in Timbuktu, where he learned reading, writing, arithmetic, geography, astronomy, and the Koran. All this he set down in a letter in Arabic, which was sent to the State Department in Washington. Eventually President John Quincy Adams and Secretary of State Henry Clay agreed to buy Abd al-Rahman's freedom and send him home to Africa so that he might fulfill his wish to die in his own country. The Prince's owner agreed to give him his freedom and to sell his wife for $200. A subscription drive quickly netted the necessary funds to buy her. But when Abd al-Rahman raised the question of trying to purchase his five children and eight grandchildren from slavery, his owner put his foot down.

In the spring of 1828, Abd al-Rahman and his wife, carrying their manumission papers, arrived in Washington. At that point, it became clear that the Prince was not from Morocco, as had originally been thought, and since the United States had no relations with the kingdom in Africa from which he did come, Clay suggested that the African Colonization Society, of which he was a vice-president, send Abd al-Rahman and his wife to Liberia. The society agreed, but only if the Prince would go on a money-raising tour for the society and agree to live in Liberia after he arrived. The society promised that if he did go on the tour, it would buy freedom for his whole family.

Abd al-Rahman spoke in Baltimore, Philadelphia, Providence, New Bedford,

Boston, Springfield, Windsor, Hartford, New Haven, and New York. All told, about $4,000 was raised, but it was estimated that nearly $10,000 would be needed to persuade their owner to sell the Prince's five children and eight grandchildren. In February 1829, Abd ah-Rahman sailed with his wife for Liberia aboard the *Harriet*, with 160 other emigrants. Within weeks after his arrival in Liberia—just over forty years after he had been snatched from Africa by slave traders and shipped to America—Abd al-Rahman died of malarial fever.

The American Colonization Society did obtain publicity from the Prince's tour, which focused attention on its campaign to settle Liberia with free blacks. But it does not seem to have made many converts among the free Negroes. At a public dinner held in honor of Abd al-Rahman in Boston's African Masonic Hall, a song written for the occasion was sung, the opening verse of which went:

> All hail to the chief from old Africa's shore,
> Who forty years' bondage has had to deplore
> Huzza for the chieftain—huzza for the chief;
> Huzza for the chief from old Africa's shore.

While Boston blacks prayed for the Prince's successful return to Africa, they made it clear that they intended to stay in America and battle for both the freedom of their brethren in slavery and their own equal rights. "Liberty and Equality" was the theme of the chief toast of the evening, tendered by Thomas Dalton, president of the Massachusetts General Colored Association.

Soon, however, the African Colonization Society achieved its most important victory in its efforts to convince blacks to emigrate. *Freedom's Journal* became the first and only black newspaper in the United States to announce its endorsement of the society and its support of African emigration. Both Samuel E. Cornish and John Browne Russwurm, editors of the black weekly, had opposed colonization at first, lamenting the vast sums being spent on that enterprise and suggesting that they could better be used in educating the black population. But Russwurm's attitude toward colonization changed as he became increasingly convinced that there was no future for blacks in America. "If the slaves of our country with one accord were delivered from bondage," he asked, "can they be elevated to an equality with the whites? Can they while in this country be divested of the odium of inferior and degraded caste?" The answer, he maintained, was, "No!"

On February 14, 1829, Russwurm announced his conversion to the doctrine of colonization, which he had initially opposed: "We have always said that when convinced of an error we would hasten to acknowledge it. That time has now arrived. The change which has taken place has not been the hasty conclusion of a moment; we have pondered much on this interesting subject, and read every article in our reach both for and against the Society." The conclusion? "Our right place is in Africa." When attacked for inconsistency, he replied that it was "a mere waste of words to talk of ever enjoying citizenship in this country; it is utterly impossible in the nature of things; all therefore who pant for these, must cast their eyes elsewhere.''

In December 1826, a group of Baltimore Negroes expressed their approval of the Colonization Society. Philadelphia's black leaders immediately called a mass meeting and drafted a "Remonstrance" charging their brothers to the South with aiding the common enemy. One can therefore imagine the feelings unleashed by Russwurm's announcement. Enraged black leaders forced Russwurm to resign as editor of *Freedom's Journal* and accused him of having been bought by the "Hydra-headed monster," as many free blacks dubbed the Colonization Society. In vain, Russwurm protested his sincerity and insisted that his decision was based on his conviction "that all efforts here, to improve the mass of coloured persons must prove abortive; and this conclusion we adopt from the evidence of our own eyes." Russwurm was even burned in effigy when he announced he was accepting a post from the Maryland Colonization Society. He migrated to Liberia where he revived the *Liberia Herald* and later became governor of Maryland in Liberia. While he was in Liberia, black leaders in this country continued to condemn him as a "Judas," but the Colonization Society viewed his conversion as a great victory.

Although emigration to Liberia received a spurt from Russwurm's conversion, it was overshadowed by the mounting opposition to colonization within the black community. In 1832, William Lloyd Garrison, who only three years earlier had become a "life member" of the American Colonization Society, published a treatise, *Thoughts on African Colonization*, which was one of the strongest denunciations of African colonization to that time, calling its advocates apologists for slavery and slaveholders and the "disparager[s] of free blacks." In the section on the "Sentiments of the People of Color," Garrison featured statements by black leaders and from mass Negro anticolonization meetings. In the year 1831 alone, such meetings were recorded in fifteen cities and eight states and the District of Columbia.

In the declarations of black leaders and the resolutions and addresses at the mass meetings, several basic arguments against African colonization were advanced. One was that the Colonization Society was part of a conspiracy to rivet the chains more firmly on the slave, which it would accomplish, first, by enabling slaveholders to exile disruptive slaves, leaving the more submissive bondsmen in bondage, and second, by making life so miserable for free blacks that they would be forced to emigrate and abandon their brothers and sisters in bondage. Another argument was that as native-born Americans who had fought and died to establish the American nation in the American Revolution and to defend it in the War of 1812, blacks had a right not only to be allowed to remain in the United States but to receive the full protection of its laws and the full benefits granted to all its citizens. Linked to this argument was the fact that white immigrant groups were welcomed in this country while Negroes were being asked to leave. "See the thousands of foreigners emigrating to America every year," observed Bishop Richard Allen, "and if there be ground sufficient for them to cultivate, and bread for them to eat; why would they wish to send the *first tillers* of the land away?'' Peter Williams, Jr., rector of New York's St. Philip's Protestant Church, made the point more forcefully:

We are natives of this country, we ask only to be treated as well as *foreigners*. Not a few of our fathers suffered and bled to purchase its independence, we ask only to be treated as well as those who fought against it. We have toiled to cultivate it and raise it to its present prosperous condition; we ask only to share equal privileges with those who come from distant lands, to enjoy the fruits of our labor.

Similarly, James Forten declared early in 1831:

We ask not their compassion and aid in assisting us to emigrate to Africa, we are contented to remain in the land that gave us birth, and which many of us fought to form, and many of our Fathers fought and died for, during the war which established our Independence. . . . All this appears to be forgotten now, and the descendants of these Men, to whom we are indebted for the part they took in the struggle for Independence, are intended to be removed to a distant and inhospitable country.

"Here in America we were born," the blacks of Pittsburgh declared in 1831, and "here we will live by the help of the Almighty—and here we will die, and let our bones lie with our fathers."

Another argument raised by free blacks was that the formation of local colonization societies was often followed by an intensification of racism. In Ohio, the colonization societies formed in 1826 immediately began a campaign to promote the removal of the "degraded" and "impoverished" blacks who were beginning to "infest" the state. Stiffer enforcement of the black laws was demanded, and a harsh spirit of intolerance and even persecution of blacks now appeared. The local colonization society was an important force behind the tragic Cincinnati race riot of 1829. A "Poor Colored Man" expressed his thoughts on such developments in verse:

> We say that—
> Men who ask "our lives to stake,"
>   In Afric's clime to roam,
> Disclose their friendship like a snake,
>   By biting us *at home*.

The view that Africa was an uncivilized continent, unsuitable for settlement by black as well as white Americans, was another argument advanced against colonization. Although, in part, this represented an acceptance of the stereotype of the African continent held by most whites, it was bolstered by the reports from Liberia that described the deaths of emigrants from fever. These supported the feeling that black Americans would not fare well in such a tropical climate. At their anticolonization meetings, however, blacks made it clear that not only were they not opposed to missionary work in Africa, but they strongly favored it and that they were interested in developing both cultural ties and commerce with the African people. What they were opposed to were the methods and motives of the Colonization Society's missionary work. The black citizens of Brooklyn, New York, in the "Address" adopted at a huge rally in 1831 put it plainly:

We are much in favor of Christianizing Africa, but not according to the plan of the Colonization Society, to purchase their lands of them; with a few paltry guns, beads, etc., and then establish forts and garrisons, to protect traders and traffickers, without, perhaps, once naming the religion of Jesus to them.

In this and other addresses of anticolonization meetings, blacks pointed to several developments in Liberia that justified this condemnation of the Colonization Society. They noted that a number of emigrants sent by the society had gone to Africa as representatives of United States trading companies, while others became Liberian representatives of American commercial firms. Again, the sharp trading practices of many colonists who had turned to local trade, bartering cloth, rum, and beads with native tribes for ivory, cam wood, and palm oil, had aroused resentment among the African people. Finally, they noted that reports were already trickling back to the United States of a basic conflict between the American blacks and the indigenous people, who resented the complete power held by the black settlers.

Still another anticolonization argument was that the Colonization Society's professed aim "to colonize colored people on the Coast of Africa, with their OWN CONSENT" was being proved false by events. Not only were society agents "*scheming, begging, threatening* and *beguiling* our people in THAT CONSENT," but in Maryland, the society had engineered the enactment of legislation that provided for forcible deportation of free blacks. Under the Maryland plan, county clerks had to report all manumissions to the board of managers, who instructed the Colonization Society to remove the emancipated slaves to Africa or wherever else the society deemed suitable. Newly freed Negroes who wanted to remain in the state could choose reenslavement or appeal to a county orphan's court to remain. Emancipated Negroes unwilling to be reenslaved or to migrate to Africa and unable to obtain court permission to remain were to be forcibly deported.

The Maryland plan, which the Colonization Society hoped would be adopted by other states, tore the mask off the society and turned even Baltimore's free blacks, who had formerly been favorable to the organization, against it. A Maryland colonizationist reported in 1832 that "the prejudices of the coloured people in Baltimore" against the society "are strong, and that distributing literature among them would be to throw it away." At a mass meeting in 1831, Baltimore's free blacks served notice that they had no intention of leaving. "We considered that land in which we were born our only 'true and appropriate home,'" they announced, "and when we desire to remove we will apprise the public of the same in due season."

So hostile were Baltimore's free blacks to the society that they were even accused of following colonization agents into the rural areas to dissuade Negroes who might be induced to emigrate. Would-be emigrants were told that they were "traitors to their race" and that "every emigrant to Africa diminished by one the numerical force" that was needed to obtain "for the colored people . . . 'their rights.' "

Colonizationists also frequently complained that even slaves who had been manumitted with the understanding that they would emigrate refused to depart. In 1829, a Virginia colonizationist found thirty-four slaves who had been freed by a provision in their master's will for their emigration to Africa but who had remained despite the threat of reenslavement. "I have tried every means in my power to get these people to go to Liberia," he reported. "But they are so connected, husbands, wives and children, that they cannot be induced to go."

Repeatedly, too, colonizationists found that potential emigrants vanished. "Our slaves ought not to remain in Norfolk more than a few days," warned a Virginia colonizationist, "for although they may not consent to go to Africa, yet most of them would rather make their escape to New York or Philadelphia and would embrace any opportunity for doing it." Despite close supervision, few vessels left for Africa with full contingents of emigrants.

Responding to the charge that he alone was responsible for turning blacks against the Colonization Society, William Lloyd Garrison wrote that this not only greatly overrated his influence but ignored the fact that it was free black opposition to the society that was instrumental in his own conversion to anticolonization: "From the organization of the American Colonization Society, down to the present time [1832], free people of color have publicly and repeatedly expressed their opposition to it. They indignantly reject every overture for their repatriation." This is not entirely true. At a time when most blacks rejected African settlement, there was talk of emigration to Haiti. In 1824, the Colonization Society, realizing that even blacks whom it had been able to convince that their future lay in emigration but were hesitant to return to Africa and the struggling settlement of Liberia, entered into correspondence with President Boyer of Haiti to provide information for those who might opt for the West Indian island. Boyer assured the immigrants of a welcome and assistance when they arrived. "Those who come," he wrote, "being children of Africa, shall be Haytians as soon as they put their feet upon the soil of Hayti."

That same year, Colonel Jonathan Granville, an agent for Haitian emigration, spoke to the black community of New York and invited blacks to emigrate to Haiti but only if they preferred "industry and reputation to calumny and contempt. But if accustomed to the mark of ignominy, if they persevere in dragging on a shameful existence, let them remain; let them drink deep of the cup of dishonor, but may their feet never contaminate our shores." Reverend Thomas Paul, pastor of Boston's African Baptist Church, impressed by a report of Granville's speech, invited him to talk to the black community of Boston on Haitian emigration, and he was quoted in the *Columbian Centinel* of July 3, 1824, as saying: "The time, I trust, is not far distant, when all wise and good men will use their influence to place the free coloured people of the United States upon the delightful island of Hayti.''

Few free blacks actually did emigrate to Haiti. More did to Canada, and there was wide support for Canadian emigration.

Let the champions of colonization ''endeavor to remove prejudice,'' James Forten demanded. Only by eliminating white prejudice and washing ''from the stars and stripes one of the blackest spots that ever cursed the globe,'' declared Baltimore free blacks, could colonizationists prove their friendship. Samuel Cornish put it best: ''It is race prejudice not the negro which must go.''

LIBERIA AS UTOPIA

Neither the small number of emigrants nor the hostility of most free blacks to African emigration weakened the determination of the American Colonization Society to carry out its program. On the contrary, it stepped up its propaganda campaign to encourage emigration to Africa and to counteract the unfavorable opinions being spread on this subject in the black community. The society distributed an address ''to the colored people of the United States,'' drawn up by a committee of the ''citizens of Monrovia,'' in which reference was made to the circulation among free blacks in the United States of ''many misrepresentations . . . of a nature slanderous to us, and, in their effects, injurious to *them*.'' The address gave as the reason for the decision of the ''citizens of Monrovia'' to leave the United States the desire for ''liberty, in the sober, simple, but complete sense of the word. . . . We did not enjoy that freedom in our native country; and, from causes which, as respects ourselves, we shall soon forget forever, we were certain it was not attainable for ourselves or our children.'' In contrast to the situation that had confronted them as mechanics in the United States, in Liberia, they asserted, they were profitably employed: ''Mechanics, of nearly every trade, are carrying on their various occupations; their wages were high; and a large number would be sure of constant and profitable employment.''

Soon spokesmen for the Colonization Society were projecting Liberia as a black utopia. Reverend John T. Matthias offered a glowing account in his report to the New York Colonization Society:

The colored man in this country is incomparably happier than in America, whether he is there a slave or freeman. The climate here is better for him; the soil is better and the road to wealth and respectability is open before him. This is the spot for the colored man. . . . We have no fogs, and there is little variation in the temperature. It is now Christmas, and when you in New York are suffering from the cold, the country around us is dressed in the richest garb, and this will be the case during the year.

In an effort to persuade other blacks to go, a number of black emigrants to Liberia returned to the United States and traveled widely as agents of the Colonization Society. They reported that the Liberian colony was getting its feet on solid ground; there were 2,500 black American residents in 1838, along with a slightly smaller number of rescued Africans, and an estimated 28,000 tribes people. With twenty-eight trading firms and eight ships operating regularly, Liberia exported $250,000 worth of goods and received $150,000 of imports. Truly a black utopia was emerging.

Nothing, however, was said of the tension between the native Africans and the black emigrants to Liberia, but Reverend Robert Sawyer, who was appointed by the Presbyterian Board of Foreign Missions as a missionary to Liberia, was not so reticent. In his letters to the Presbyterian board, he reported that the colonists felt superior to the natives: "The most wealthy Planter of the Southern States does not make a greater distinction between himself and his slaves than the Colonist makes or supposed to exist between himself and the native. I have heard the natives ridiculing this same feeling. 'Well' said a shrewd native man, 'they [the colonists] call us negro and black men,' and with a laugh, he exclaimed, 'what are they?' '' Another sneeringly said, '' 'Why, they think themselves white men.' '' To his amazement, Sawyer found that the blacks from the United States were opposed to educating the native population.

The glowing reports of progress and prosperity communicated to blacks in the United States did little to alter black opposition to African emigration or to the Colonization Society. At each local, state, and national meeting representing a cross-section of the black community in the North, free Negroes continued to pass resolutions against emigration and the society. Some meetings, like that in Cincinnati, resolved that "every freeman of color" who should emigrate to Africa or should advocate such action was to be considered an "enemy to humanity and a traitor to his brother."

EMIGRATION TO TRINIDAD

In addition, much to the Colonization Society's dismay, in the late 1830s, an active colonization venture began that threatened to direct potential black emigrants away from Africa. With the end of slavery in the British West Indies in 1835, the sugar planters there were eager to recruit black Americans as laborers. Their former slaves were deserting the plantations by the thousands, many in order to avoid the stigma of slavery and others to become freeholders. With the labor situation in such a state of uncertainty, the planters began looking around for a substitute form of controlled labor, and the free black population of the United States was looked upon as potential replacement laborers for the sugar estates.

In November 1838, the Legislative Council of Trinidad passed an ordinance to facilitate emigration to the island by guaranteeing immediate employment to those who came. Attracted by this prospect, several hundred blacks from the United States arrived in Trinidad in 1839. Recruiting agents representing Trinidad addressed black meetings in New York, Philadelphia, and Boston, hoping for a mass exodus. So strong did the "Trinidad fever" appear to be that the *Colored American* warned blacks to be careful lest they be victimized. "Brethren beware," it entitled several editorials on this theme.

Late in 1840, a group of 160 "colored persons" sailed from Philadelphia for Trinidad. This was the high point of the campaign. The next year, only 29 black Americans officially entered Trinidad, a significant drop from the previous year. In 1843, there were none.

So desperate had the Trinidad planters become for black laborers from the United States that they had not even bothered to determine if the immigrants from urban centers were suited for sugar cane work. The result was that shortly after they started to work in the cane fields, they left for urban-type jobs. When these were filled, they returned home. Others returned directly from the cane fields with reports of broken promises and agreements by planters and complaints that they were overworked, underfed, and treated like slaves.

The American Colonization Society used the Trinidad experience to push emigration to Liberia. The society argued that blacks could never hope to rise in the British West Indies to a social equality with their European employers, "whereas in Africa, they would be among equals." While British law now declared a black man to be a free citizen, "it is not to be expected that the planters . . . will receive the American colored laborers as their equals. . . . He has a master not an employer . . . a white man who cares only for his labor, not for his elevation. Schools may be provided for colored children, but the white planters can have no interest in encouraging their education; it is the cultivation of his land which he seeks and not the cultivation of the minds of those who till it." Only by emigrating to a country where "they can be the owners of the soil, and conductors of their own government," could "our free colored people" achieve true elevation and independence. Such a place was Liberia.

REJUVENATION OF COLONIZATION ACTIVITIES

On July 3, 1847, a constitutional convention met at Monrovia and approved a national constitution. On July 26, the convention announced that "we the People . . . hereby solemnly associate and constitute ourselves a Free and Sovereign and Independent State by the name of the Republic of Liberia." The great national seal of the infant black republic portrayed a dove, a sailing ship before a rising sun, together with a palm tree, plow, and spade under the national motto, "The love of liberty brought us here." The nation's flag bore six red and five white stripes, symbolizing the eleven signers of the Liberian Declaration of Independence, and a blue corner square with one white star representing Africa with Liberia "lighting its way." In October 1847, elections were held in which the voters, all black settlers from the United States, ratified the constitution and formally elected Joseph Jenkins Roberts president of Liberia. The black republic's first president had left Petersburg, Virginia, in 1829 at the age of nineteen, accompanied by his mother and two brothers, whom he had persuaded to join him.

The independent republic of Liberia was recognized by most of the great powers, with the exception of the United States. Unwilling to allow black ambassadors in Washington from Liberia (as from Haiti), the United States delayed recognition of both Liberia and Haiti until 1862.

With Liberia an independent nation, the American Colonization Society was relieved of a great financial responsibility and was able to concentrate on the actual transporting of emigrants. More funds were channeled into propaganda activities and increasing the number of agents. With Southern courts increasingly upholding the legality of manumission by will in which freedom was contingent on removal from the state and in which the society was often authorized to receive the slaves, the society began to function more effectively all over the South. Moreover, judging from the number of letters written by Southern free blacks to the society, the new campaign brought results in this quarter too. Although semiliterate, the writers made their sentiments clear. "I have made up my mind," wrote Peter Butler in 1848 from Virginia, "and wish to inform you that I wish to go to Liberia. So as I may injoy the Right of a man. I have tried a great many places in these United States and I find that none of them is the home for the Culerd man and So I . . . wish to be and Emigrant for the land of my auntsestors." A Savannah free black asked the Colonization Society to "sind ous a vessel in April or May" so that his group could quickly find a place in the new Liberian republic. He assured the society that the group "will be yousfoull Citizen to that young Republic Some of them Ear men of worth among them Ear mecinist, talors, Engeniers, masians Black smiths, farmers and ministers." M. D. Artist, a free black in Missouri, while skeptical about the climate and the economic possibilities of the republic of Liberia, was convinced that it alone held out hope for himself and his people. He wrote in 1848:

My doctrine is that our people must emigrate from . . . this land of oppression. . . . I believe that the man of Color must go Seak and obtain a home a peace of earth that he can call his own. He must till that peace of earth with his own hands and water it with the sweat of his brow. He must plant the tree of liberty, and built a temple, Sacred to Religion and Justice. Then Shall the forest blossom like a rose.

While it appears that the new propaganda campaign of the Colonization Society had some effect in the South, it did not carry much weight among free blacks in the North, except for Ohio. The appeals of David Christy, the Colonization Society's new agent for the state, are an excellent example of the Colonization Society's propaganda in the late 1840s. Christy began by warning Ohio blacks that their economic future was hopeless since the continued influx of European immigrants would remove them from even menial jobs. Their civil and political future was equally bleak. They had two ways of achieving full citizenship. They could achieve "a change in the State Constitution" or they could emigrate to the republic of Liberia where only "colored men . . . [were] recognized as citizens." The first alternative was a mirage, for it would take nothing less than "a revolution for public sentiment" to effect constitutional change of that magnitude in Ohio. Thus, the only real alternative was emigration to Liberia.

Ohio blacks had a special place set aside for them in Africa, for a portion of new territory acquired by Liberia was named "Ohio in Africa" and was reserved for blacks from Ohio, Indiana, and Illinois. John McMicken, son of the founder of the University of Cincinnati, offered to finance any Ohio blacks who decided to resettle in "Ohio in Africa." Meeting on March 5, 1850, a group of Cincinnati blacks gathered to discuss the merits of emigration to "Ohio in Africa." They resolved that while blacks remained in America, they could "not hope for respect much less equality" because "the antagonism of races . . . [was] too strong for any such a consummation." The failure of the state legislature in 1849 to repeal the black laws was sufficient proof of this conclusion. But while the majority of the meeting favored emigration, they believed it wise to send agents first to investigate actual conditions in Africa.

Peter H. Clark, Cincinnati's black educator, and two black Oberlin students were chosen to visit Africa and report on the prospects for "Ohio in Africa." When he reached New Orleans, however, Clark refused to embark on the dirty lumber schooner that had been chartered by the Colonization Society to carry him, the students, and 119 emigrants to Africa. Clark returned to Cincinnati, but the others did leave. Before sailing from the Gulf of Mexico, smallpox erupted and the ship put in at Charleston, South Carolina, for medical help. There all blacks not stricken with the disease were jailed for illegally entering the state. Three months later, they were freed and sailed for Africa. Within six months after arriving in Africa, 90 percent of the passengers had died of various diseases. This disaster brought an end to "Ohio in Africa."

COLONIZATION REJECTED

The rejuvenation of colonizationist activities after Liberia's independence was only temporary. By the beginning of the 1850s, the membership of and support for the American Colonization Society again declined. Once again, the majority of the free blacks had made it clear that they would not leave the United States "peaceably or forcibly" and that they planned to concentrate on the struggle on behalf of their brothers and sisters entrapped by slavery in the South, and to achieve equality for the "nominally free" at home. Frederick Douglass voiced the dominant feeling in the black community:

We do not mean to go to Liberia. Our minds are made up to live here if we can, or die here if we must; so every attempt to remove us, will be, as it ought to be, labor lost. Here we are, and here we shall remain. While our brethren are in bondage on these shores, it is idle to think of inducing any considerable number of free colored people to quit this for a foreign land.

For over two hundred and twenty-eight years has the colored man toiled over the soil of America, under the burning sun and a driver's lash—plowing, planting, reaping, that white men might roll in ease, their hands unhardened by labor, and their brows un-moistened by the waters of genial toil; and now that the moral sense of mankind is beginning to revolt at this system of treachery and cruel wrong, and is demanding its overthrow, the mean and cowardly oppressor is meditating plans to expel the colored man entirely from the country. Shame upon the guilty wretches that dare propose, and all that countenance such a proposition. We live here—have lived here—have a right to live here, and mean to live here.

During the 1850s, there was a rebirth of the colonization spirit in a number of Northern black communities, which we will examine in the next volume. Meanwhile, let us turn our attention to the united action taken by blacks through national, state, and local conventions to achieve justice and equality in American society.

14

The Convention Movement

THE FIRST NATIONAL NEGRO CONVENTION

"Barbarism in America," was the heading on Reverend Samuel E. Cornish's editorial in *Rights of All* on the Cincinnati riots which, for three days beginning on August 22, 1829, terrorized the city's Negro population and caused many of its victims to seek asylum in Canada. "Are there no Christians, no philanthropists, no patriots, no ambassadors of Jesus Christ in Ohio?" he fairly wept. In Congress, Senator Thomas Hart Benton of Missouri gave the answer: there were none. Comparing the expulsion of the black population of Cincinnati to the "expulsion of the Moors from Spain and the Huguenots from France," Benton noted that "not one word of objection," "not one voice had been raised in protest," not even from the white abolitionists, the so-called "friends of the black." They, too, were "all silent, all hushed."

But the free blacks in the North refused to be silent or hushed. Meeting in the Coloured Wesley Methodist Church on February 16, 1830, Philadelphia's blacks announced their sympathy for their kinsmen who had been forced to leave their country, "one whose republican constitution declares, '*that all men are born free and equal.*'" They affirmed their determination to continue to protest: "While the laws of this country permit the freedom of expression, and cease to muzzle the press, we will cheerfully vindicate the cause of our oppressed people."

In Baltimore, the Cincinnati riots convinced sixteen-year-old free black Hezekiel Grice of "the hopelessness of contending against oppression in the United States"; the only hope of survival was for his people to follow the Ohio black population to Canada. He was, however, unwilling to make such a proposal on his own; he felt the decision should be made by a representative gathering of leaders of black communities. In the spring of 1830, Grice began a correspondence with prominent Negro leaders, requesting their opinion on the need for a convention to decide whether blacks should emigrate as a body or remain in this country.

The response was slow in coming, but by August, the leaders of black communities in New York and Philadelphia had approved Grice's proposal. Then, after obtaining the consent of the Philadelphia black community, a committee, headed by AME Bishop Richard Allen, issued a call for a convention to be held in that city on September 14, 1830.

Twenty-three delegates and seventeen honorary members—forty in all—from Pennsylvania, New Jersey, New York, Connecticut, Rhode Island, Ohio, Maryland, Delaware, and Virginia, all elected by local black organizations, gathered at Bethel Church on September 15. They met in secret session for five days, fearing that white mobs might break up the gathering, and then held public sessions from September 20 through September 24. Among "the forty immortals of our Valhalla," as John W. Cromwell, a black historian of the early National Negro Convention movement, called the participants in the historical gathering at Bethel Church, were Bishop Richard Allen, Hezekiel Grice, William S. Whipper, Frederick C. Hinton, James Cornish, Junius C. Morel, and John Bowers, all Philadelphia militants; Austin A. Steward, a runaway slave turned grocer in New York; and Abraham D. Shadd, leader of the Wilmington black community. Earlier, Bishop Allen had allowed Marena Lee, a black woman evangelist, to preach at his church. But the idea that a black woman should be represented at a gathering to decide the question as to whether her people should emigrate or stay in America did not seem to occur to either the bishop or any of the other delegates. The first National Negro Convention was an all-male affair.

Bishop Allen was chosen president, and the convention proceeded to organize the "American Society of Free People of Colour for improving their condition in the United States; for purchasing lands; and for the establishment of a settlement in the Province of Canada." This was the parent organization and was to be composed of such persons of color who paid not less than twenty-five cents on entering and eighteen and three-quarter cents quarterly (seventy-five cents a year) thereafter. Auxiliaries were to be established in every community and were to be contacted regularly by a committee of correspondence elected by the parent body.

An "Address to the Free People of Colour of these United States" was issued by the convention. It opened:

Impressed with a firm and settled conviction, and more especially being taught by that inestimable and invaluable instrument, namely, the Declaration of Independence, that all men are born free and equal, and consequently are endowed with unalienable rights, among which are the enjoyments of life, liberty, and the pursuit of happiness;

Viewing these as incontrovertible facts, we have been led to the following conclusions; that our forlorn and deplorable situation earnestly and loudly demands of us to devise and pursue all legal means for the speedy elevation of ourselves and brethren to the scale and standing of men.

Various means had been resorted to in pursuit of this objective, the address continued, the most prominent being those of the American Colonization Society. While not doubting "the sincerity of many friends" engaged in that cause, it did not meet with the convention's approval. However "great the debt the United States may owe to injured Africa," it was not possible for black Americans to repay it: "We who have been born and nurtured on this soil, we, whose habits, manners, and customs are the same in common with other Americans, can never consent to take our lives in our hands, and be the bearers of the redress offered by that Society to that much afflicted country." Still the fact remained that "in the nineteenth century of our Christian era," laws had been enacted in several states "to compel an unprotected and harmless portion of our brethren, to leave their homes and seek an asylum in foreign climes." No means thus having yet been devised for their relief, the convention reached the conclusion that the formation of a settlement in upper Canada "would be of a great advantage to the people of color." It would, in fact, be especially advisable for all blacks with large families who desired to see their children "happy and respected" to emigrate to Canada and locate themselves in a land where the laws and prejudices of society would "have no effect in retarding their advancement to the summit of civil and religious improvement."

Perhaps the most significant achievement of the 1830 convention was the recommendation for the formation of a parent society, to be called the American Society of Free Persons of Labor, with auxiliaries in different towns and cities. In the five years following 1830, a series of conventions met annually. Sixteen delegates met in Philadelphia in June 1831; twenty-nine delegates met again in Philadelphia in June 1832; fifty-six delegates convened in Philadelphia in June 1833; forty delegates from seven states met in New York City in June 1834; and the 1835 convention met in June in Philadelphia. In addition to discussing and adopting programs for the security and elevation of the Negro people, the convention founded a series of organizations, known as Phoenix Societies, in the urban areas of the North. Under the direction of Reverend Christopher Rush, Reverend Theodore S. Wright, and Reverend Peter Williams, Jr., these local societies made proposals to improve the moral welfare of the Negroes and to instruct them in literature and the mechanical arts.

OTHER CONVENTIONS OF THE 1830s

Four main issues dominated the annual conventions between 1831 and 1836. First was the question of aiding emigration to Canada. After intense controversy in 1832, the convention resolved in 1833 "that there is not now, and probably never will be actual necessity for a large emigration of the present race of free colored people." It was recommended that the brethren devote their thoughts and energies to their improvement in their native land, "rejecting all plans of colonization anywhere." Thus the stand taken by the first convention was reversed, and the majority of the delegates opposed emigration, holding to the view that blacks should insist on their full rights as Americans.

In a related vein, the conventions repeatedly voiced their firm opposition to the American Colonization Society's program for emigration to Liberia. A third proposal called for the establishment of a manual training college for blacks. The 1831 convention supported a plan for such an institution and elected Samuel Cornish as agent to collect the necessary funds, while auxiliary committees to assist him were set up in the important centers of free blacks.

New Haven was chosen for the site, and plans for the college, with a board of trustees consisting of a majority of Negroes, were drawn up. Arthur Tappan purchased several acres of land in the southern part of New Haven with the intention of presenting it to the Negro Convention for the school campus, but so much opposition arose from the townspeople that on September 8, 1831, the mayor issued an order prohibiting the proposed school within the city limits. On September 10, the "best citizens" of New Haven, led by the mayor and a number of Yale professors and students, staged riots before the homes of supporters of the college. Many blacks wished to proceed in the face of this hostility, but some timid white abolitionists withdrew their support, and the project was abandoned.

The fourth major concern of the early convention movement was directed toward securing the elevation of the free black population through moral reform. The chief theoretician and spokesman for this principle was William Whipper, a black businessman and temperance leader of Philadelphia and Columbia, Pennsylvania. At the 1834 National Negro Convention, Whipper, as chairman of a special committee appointed to prepare a "declaration of sentiments," elaborated his views on elevation through moral reform. Observing how the "descendants of an *ancestry* once enrolled in the history of fame" had been reduced to degradation by slavery and prejudice, he looked to "the agency of divine truth and the spirit of American liberty" for the ultimate redemption of his people. "We therefore declare to the world," he went on, "that our object is to extend the principles of universal peace and good will to all mankind, by promoting sound morality, by the influence of education, temperance, economy, and all those virtues that alone can render man acceptable in the eyes of God or the civilized world." Not only was this statement accepted by the convention, but after adopting a constitution for "the National Convention of the People of Colour," the delegates resolved to "recommend the establishment of Societies on the principle of *Moral Reform,* as set forth in the declaration of sentiment."

When the 1835 convention met, Whipper and his allies (led by the Philadelphia contingent) assumed complete control. After some heated debate, it was resolved to form a "National Moral Reform Society," and Whipper was named chairman of the committee to prepare its constitution. That document created the American Moral Reform Society, which was to be open to any person who pledged to sustain the general principles of moral reform, especially those of education, temperance, economy, and universal liberty. The society was to meet annually in Philadelphia. The 1835 convention accepted the constitution and then unanimously recommended the formation of auxiliary societies, which were to send delegates to the society's annual meeting and contribute at least $5 yearly to promote its objects. It also suggested that the society's principles be promulgated through its own press.

Other actions of the 1835 National Negro Convention reflected the triumph of the moral reformers. Resolutions were adopted urging temperance, calling on the black churches to support the cause of moral reform, and praising the Christian forbearance of blacks who had been subjected to mob violence in 1834. Then, after some animated discussion, the convention unanimously adopted a resolution introduced by Whipper: "That we recommend as far as possible to our people to abandon the use of the word 'colored' when either speaking or writing concerning themselves; and especially the title of African from their institutions, the marbles of churches, etc."

Finally, the convention authorized the reprinting of the declaration of sentiments approved a year earlier, together with an address to the American people that set forth the program and goals of the American Moral Reform Society. Written by Whipper, it emphasized that all men were equal under God, but that black men in America had been reduced to degradation by slavery and prejudice. However, it maintained, fidelity to natural laws and human rights and to the laws of universal love would bring about the end of all complexional distinctions. The rallying points for such a general effort at moral reform would be education, temperance, economy, and universal liberty. By practicing these virtues, the free black population would be elevated and objections to immediate emancipation would be nullified. Meanwhile the oppressed must bear their burdens with Christian fortitude: "If we but fully rest ourselves on the dignity of human nature, and maintain a bold enduring front against all opposition, the monster, prejudice, will fall humbly at our feet."

Before it adjourned, the 1835 convention voted to meet next in New York City on the first Monday in June 1836. But a series of dissensions that had been brewing since 1831 prevented the 1836 meeting from taking place. Indeed, there were no more meetings of the national convention for several years. Throughout the early conventions, there had been rivalry and disagreements between the New York and Philadelphia contingents. The New Yorkers, convinced of the inability to achieve equality for blacks in existing institutions, favored continuing the establishment of separate schools and churches for the Negro people. This was opposed by a group of Philadelphia blacks under the influence of Robert Purvis, William Whipper, and James Forten, Sr., who refused to recognize any special needs and problems of the Negro people that required separate organizations and who called for their immediate and complete integration into American life. These Philadelphia blacks were strongly influenced by the doctrines advanced by William Lloyd Garrison, and the strong influence of Garrisonian principles was evident in their support for nonviolence and their opposition to separate black schools, churches, and other institutions.

AMERICAN MORAL REFORM SOCIETY

With the Philadelphia blacks devoting their attention almost exclusively to their favorite project, the American Moral Reform Society (AMRS), the national convention movement vanished. Between 1836 and 1841, the AMRS met annually. In September 1838, its official organ, the *National Reformer*, with William Whipper as editor, made its appearance.

But the moral reform cause never really caught on among Northern free blacks. Whatever prospects it may have had were critically damaged when a major controversy erupted at its 1837 meeting over the use of the term *colored*. The agenda committee reported a series of seven resolutions, the first of which recommended that the ''free people of colour'' form societies to provide educational opportunities for their youth. For three days, debate raged over this resolution, with Whipper and his allies contending that it represented degradation and discrimination and, further, that the society should consider the needs of the white as well as the colored community. Defenders of the resolution argued that colored men should first take care of their own needs through their own agencies.

When the reference to ''people of colour'' was eliminated from the resolution, many blacks in the North were infuriated. The Reverend Samuel E. Cornish, editor of the *Colored American,* voiced their rage when he accused Whipper and his allies of being ''confused in their views'' and of refusing to identify with their own people, while the society they headed was ''but an existence of weakness, scattering its feeble efforts to the winds.'' For the next several months, the columns of the *Colored American* were dominated by the exchanges between Whipper and his critics. Cornish repeatedly argued that ''he that would better the condition and elevation of the character of colored men, in this country, must consider the peculiarity of their position and adopt his measures accordingly.'' But Whipper insisted that all moral principles were universal in their application and embraced all men without distinction of color. ''To confine our Society *now*, within the precincts of complexional domains,'' he insisted, ''would be to render it ridiculous, by destroying its moral bearing on universal principles, and its nationality in measures.''

The American Moral Reform Society went doggedly ahead, but its authority within the black community had been seriously weakened by the debate. Its supporters were largely restricted to Philadelphia and its environs. In December 1839, the *National Reformer* made its last appearance.

Although it was actually expiring by the time of its 1839 meeting, the American Moral Reform Society amended its constitution to admit persons without regard to sex. But the 1840 meeting, despite an invitation to all friends of universal reform without regard to complexion or sex, attracted only five delegates, all from Philadelphia. At its sixth annual meeting in August 1841, the American Moral Reform Society quietly expired.

The American Moral Reform Society failed to gain the support of the overwhelming majority of black leaders, who remained convinced that black people must form their own organizations to serve their own immediate needs. Its failure was also the result of the emergence in the late 1830s and early 1840s of a number of younger black men who broke with the older leaders and their counsel of caution in the struggle for racial freedom. The younger group—Henry Highland Garnet, Samuel Ringgold Ward, Jermain Loguen, James McCune Smith, and later Frederick Douglass—challenged the society's assumption that cooperation with whites was the best route to black achievement. They argued in favor of all-black conventions and organizations, not to separate blacks from American society, but rather to ensure a meaningful black presence in that society.

Significantly, in the final number of the *National Reformer*, William Whipper conceded that the Moral Reform Society's views had little support in the black community. "We have been advocates of the doctrine that we must be 'elevated' before we could expect to enjoy the privileges of American citizenship." He continued. "We now utterly discard it, and ask pardon for our former errors." The Declaration of Independence and the laws of God made all men equal, and it was not lack of "elevation," Whipper conceded, but "complexion" that deprived the man of color of equal treatment. Religious, moral, and intellectual elevation would not secure full political privileges for his people—" because we are *black*." As for whites: "All we ask of them is that they take their 'feet from off our necks,' that we may stand free and erect like themselves."

REVIVAL OF THE NEGRO NATIONAL CONVENTIONS

Even before the collapse of the American Moral Reform Society, a demand arose for the holding of a new National Negro Convention, and toward this end, committees of correspondence and local and regional bodies were established. After a lapse of seven years, the convention reconvened in Buffalo in 1843. Forty-eight delegates were present. Thirty-six of them were from New York State; nine other states, including Virginia, North Carolina, and Georgia, were represented. Amos Gerry Beman, a New Haven clergyman, was elected president, and Frederick Douglass served as one of the vice-presidents. But the outstanding figure at the convention was Henry Highland Garnet, pastor of the Liberty Street Presbyterian Church in Troy, New York, whose famous proposal calling for support of a slave uprising to overthrow bondage was debated for several days before being narrowly defeated. The convention voted to send capable black speakers into Northern communities to inform whites and Negroes about "the claims, disabilities, sentiments, and wishes of the colored people," to impress the free Negroes with the importance of education, of improvements in science and literature, and of applying themselves to the mechanical arts. The convention also went on record in favor of the circulation of petitions to Congress for the abolition of slavery in the territories and opposing the annexation of Texas.

Meeting in Troy, New York, in 1847, the National Colored Convention was attended by sixty-eight delegates from nine states, including forty-six from New York and fourteen from Massachusetts. A report was adopted on the best means of abolishing slavery and destroying caste in the United States. It endorsed "a faithful, earnest, and persevering enforcement of the great principles of justice and morality, religion, and humanity" as the means of achieving this twin objective. The delegates also voted to establish a national Negro press, "wholly controlled by colored men . . . towards which the strong and the weak amongst us would look with confidence and hope."

Nothing came of the plan to establish a national Negro press, but the National Convention movement continued. In September 1848, between sixty and seventy delegates met in Cleveland, representing a cross-section of the free black people—printers, carpenters, blacksmiths, shoemakers, engineers, dentists, gunsmiths, editors, tailors, merchants, wheelwrights, painters, farmers, physicians, plasterers, masons, clergymen, barbers, hairdressers, coopers, livery stable keepers, bathhouse keepers, and grocers. Committees were appointed in different states to organize vigilant groups "so as to enable them to measure arms with assailants without and invaders within." At the suggestion of Frederick Douglass, a resolution was amended to read that the word *persons* used in the resolution as a designation of delegates be understood "to include *women*."

For five years after the Cleveland convention, the National Convention movement lay dormant, victim of basic differences as to the best way to end slavery, disputes among various religious sects, and numerous petty jealousies and feuds, all of which prevented the adoption of a coordinated program that would present the viewpoint of the Negro people to the nation. Furthermore, the absence of a functioning organization between conventions resulted in a failure of the delegates to implement the work during the intervening period. Nor was there a national body in existence with sufficient authority to call meetings of the Negro people to take action on the vital issues of the day. Even the conventions themselves were brought into being by groups of individuals acting solely on their own initiative. Consequently the movement lacked both continuity and authority.

Following the passage of the Fugitive Slave Act of 1850, many Negroes were too terrified to attend public gatherings. Any black who was unable to produce satisfactory proof of his freedom was in danger of being returned to slavery. Hundreds of Negro families from Ohio, Pennsylvania, and New York fled to Canada, abandoning their homes and work.

THE 1853 ROCHESTER CONVENTION AND ITS AFTERMATH

The intensity of the drive against the Negro population in the North compelled the revival of the national convention. In July 1853, 140 delegates from nine states gathered in Rochester, New York, in what was the most important of all the National Negro Conventions. Reverend J.W.C. Pennington was elected president, and the vice-presidents included Frederick Douglass, William C. Nell, and John B. Vashon. Douglass was also the chairman of the Committee on Declaration of Sentiments and drew up the "Address of the Colored Convention to the People of the United States." This remarkable document set forth the basic demands of the Negro people for justice and equality.

The address demanded that "the doors of the school-house, the work-shop, the church, the college, shall be thrown open as freely to our children as to the children of other members of the community"; that "the white and black may stand upon an equal footing before the laws of the land"; that "colored men shall not be either by custom or enactment excluded from the jury-box"; that "the complete and unrestricted right of suffrage, which is essential to the dignity even of the white man, be extended to the Free Colored Man also"; and that laws "flagrantly unjust to the man of color . . . ought to be repealed." These demands were justified on the principle that the Negro people were American citizens, "asserting their rights on their own native soil."

Realizing that this claim of citizenship was denied by the national government, the address presented a masterly historical analysis to buttress the argument, quoting extensively from state constitutional conventions, from congressional debates, and from Andrew Jackson's proclamation to the free colored inhabitants of Louisiana during the Battle of New Orleans. It concluded:

The case is made out. We and you stand up on the same broad national basis. Whether at home or abroad, we and you owe equal allegiance to the same government—have a right to look for protection on the same ground. We have been born and raised on the same soil; we have been animated by, and have displayed the same patriotic impulses; we have acknowledged and performed the same duty; we have fought and bled in the same battles; we have gained and gloried in the same victories; and we are equally entitled to the blessings resulting therefrom.

"No nobler paper was ever put forth by any body of men," commented the reporter of the *New York Tribune*.

One of the most controversial issues before the Rochester convention was the question of founding a manual labor college for colored youth. A number of delegates, led by Charles L. Remond and George T. Downing, were hostile to the proposal, arguing that the establishment of such a school was too costly a project, since the majority of blacks could not participate, and that it would be a capitulation to segregation. Frederick Douglass, Dr. James McCune Smith, and James W. C. Pennington led the battle for the industrial college. They argued that it would produce skilled workers and that the presence of an "industrious, enterprising, upright, thrifty and intelligent free black population would be a killing refutation of slavery." Since the college would be open to all students regardless of color, it could hardly be considered a segregated institution. The majority of the delegates concurred with the arguments in favor of the industrial college and voted to sponsor the institution.

To implement the convention's program and provide for its functioning before the next national meeting, the Rochester convention organized the National Council of the Colored People, consisting of two members from each of ten Northern states. Aided by state councils, the popularly elected members of which were to have direct control of local affairs, the National Council set up four committees: the Committee on a Manual Training School, which was to procure funds, select the location, and establish the school, complete with dormitories and a farm; the Committee on Business Relationship, which was to establish a large-scale employment office; the Committee on Publication, which was to compile records, statistics, and the history of every phase of Negro life, a collection that was to be made available to the public; and the Committee of Protective Union, which was to establish a kind of cooperative at which Negroes could buy and sell staples.

Thoroughly satisfied with their work, the delegates left Rochester imbued with a determination to translate their deliberations into action. They had reason to feel elated. The convention had received favorable comments from a large section of the press. A citizen of Rochester wrote a glowing letter to the *New York Tribune* describing his reactions to the sessions:

Throughout, it has been conducted by colored men, and their debates as well as proceedings generally have been equal to any of the white men who have heretofore espoused their cause as abolitionists or philanthropists of any kind. . . . I have never heard more chaste and refined dictum from any class of men, neither have I seen better oratorical powers displayed. . . . I have never seen delegates come in cleaner apparel, and more dignified manner than have the colored men.

Inspired by the great success of the Rochester convention, dozens of local and regional Negro people's conventions were held throughout the North during the closing months of 1853. Numerous mass meetings were held in churches and schools to endorse the proceedings at Rochester, and many leaders of the National Convention visited black leaders to help them establish local groups. Unfortunately, most of the plans laid down at Rochester and ratified at local conventions never got beyond the paper stage. At the first meeting of the National Council in January 1854, not enough delegates were present to constitute a quorum. The second and the last meeting, in Cleveland, was disrupted by factional disputes shortly after it got underway.

A combination of factors was responsible for the failure to carry out the program of the 1853 convention. Although defeated at Rochester, the colonizationists increased their efforts to convince the Negro people that emigration was the only solution to their problems. Shortly after the Rochester convention, a call was issued for a convention to be held in Cleveland on August 24, 1854, to discuss the emigration question. (We will discuss the emigration convention in our next volume.) The endless debates and factional disputes before and after the emigration convention created confusion among black leaders and diverted attention from the problem of implementing the programs of the National Convention.

Little progress was made in the campaign to establish a manual labor college. As chairman of the committee to establish the school, Frederick Douglass drew up a detailed plan for the institution, which was to be known as the American Industrial School. It was to be located within one hundred miles of Erie, Pennsylvania, on a site of at least two hundred acres of land, one hundred and fifty of which would be used as a farm for agricultural instruction. Teachers would be selected and students admitted to the school "without reference to sex or complexion," and special efforts were to be made "to aid in providing for the female sex, methods and means of enjoying an independent and honorable livelihood." For every course in literature, there would be a course in handicrafts. Each student would occupy half his time while at school working either at some handicraft or on the farm, and all handicrafts produced would be sold at a market within easy access of the school.

It was an ambitious program and one that anticipated the curriculum and organization of most of the manual labor schools established after the Civil War. But its fulfillment hinged upon the raising of a foundation fund of thirty thousand dollars to launch the institution. Initially, supporters attempted the sale of stock at ten dollars per share, but this was not successful, mainly because black supporters could not generally afford to purchase stock and white abolitionists, especially Garrisonians, were opposed to a separate black school and were not appeased by the plan calling for an integrated institution. The project's doom was sealed in 1854 when Harriet Beecher Stowe, author of *Uncle Tom's Cabin*, reconsidered her early enthusiasm for the school and refused to finance it. By June 1855, two years after the Rochester convention, only a small amount of money had been collected, and the project had to be abandoned.

The collapse of the program for the elevation of free blacks outlined at the Rochester Convention practically spelled the end of the antebellum National Negro Convention movement. On October 16, 1855, 124 delegates representing six states and Canada met in Philadelphia and conferred for three days. After a heated debate on the subject of the manual labor school question, the plan for such an institution was rejected as being designed to separate further the black youth from the population, and a substitute plan was adopted calling for the establishment of industrial associations in communities with large black populations. The associations were to correspond and cooperate with one another and hold a national convention in October 1857.

Despite the spirited discussion, the delegates had few illusions concerning the possibility of continuing the National Convention. When they left Franklin Hall on October 18, 1855, the majority knew that they had participated in the last National Convention for years to come.

BLACK STATE CONVENTIONS

The idea of meeting in conventions spread to the state level as well. As far as it is known, the Convention of the Colored Inhabitants of the State of New York in

August 1840 was the first statewide gathering of blacks in the United States. Assembled for the specific purpose of agitating for the right of suffrage, it was reported to have attracted a large audience, with sessions ranging in size from 40 to 140 delegates and supporters. Between 1840 and the outbreak of the Civil War, various state conventions were held. Nine were held in New York (in August 1840, August 1841, September 1844, September 1845, August 1850, July 1854, January 1855, September 1855, and September 1858); two in Pennsylvania (in August 1841 and December 1848); two in Indiana (in January 1842 and August 1851); one in Michigan (in October 1843); nine in Ohio (in August 1843, September 1844, January 1849, January 1850, January 1851, January 1852, January 1856, January 1857, and November 1858); one in New Jersey (in August 1849); two in Connecticut (in September 1849 and September 1854); two in Illinois (in October 1853 and November 1856); two in Massachusetts (in January 1854 and August 1858); and three in California (in November 1855, December 1856, and October 1857). There was one regional convention, with delegates from Massachusetts, Rhode Island, Connecticut, Maine, New York, New Jersey, Pennsylvania, Illinois, and Canada, called the New England Colored Citizens Convention, which met in Boston in August 1859. The only one held in the South before the Civil War was the Maryland Free Colored People's Convention, which met in Baltimore in July 1852.

There are similarities between the national and state conventions. Like the former, the latter were concerned with the twin struggle against slavery and for equality for the free black community. Virtually all the state conventions, however, had as their main objective the general improvement of the Negro people within their respective localities. Among the many-sided issues around which they revolved were colonization, the battle to obtain the suffrage, education, abolitionism, and the struggle for equality. Other issues, too, received a hearing, such as the establishment of farms and manual labor schools, support for black organizations (such as the church and literary and benevolent institutions), and the need for a black press. Economic concerns loomed large on the agenda of the state conventions, and the issue of overcoming limitations on economic opportunities for blacks in the North was frequently discussed. But the overwhelming theme, reaffirmed again and again, was the demand for basic American rights. "These rights," declared the 1857 Ohio State Convention of Colored Men, "are not created by *Constitutions*, nor are they uncreated by *Constitutions*. Their existence is not dependent upon the curl of a man's hair, the projection of his lips, the color of his skin, or the clime in which he had his birth. They are a constituent element of manhood—whether that man be encased in ebony or livery."

In all of the state conventions outside of Massachusetts where blacks could vote, the demand for the suffrage was a key issue. In the Midwest and Far West, the main issue was often the repeal of the notorious black laws, which placed proscriptions upon the Negro people in nearly every aspect of their daily life. Although the Ohio black laws had been largely repealed in 1849, the 1857 State

Convention of the Colored Men of Ohio called upon the state legislature "not only to repeal *all* of the remaining Black Laws of this state, but to strike out the word WHITE from the Constitution wherever it occurs." The issue of equal testimony in courts was the major issue in the two conventions held in California before the Civil War. In its address, the First Convention of Colored Citizens of the State of California, held in 1855, pointed out to the state legislature: "You have enacted a law, excluding our testimony in the courts of justice of this state, in cases of proceedings wherein white persons are parties; thus openly encouraging and countenancing the vicious and dishonest to take advantage of us."

The State Convention of Colored Citizens of the State of Illinois, held in 1856, set up a State Repeal Association to achieve repeal of the state's black laws. The preamble read: "We the people of the State of Illinois, are cursed by the blighting influence of oppression, as displayed in the inequality of its laws, in depriving us of the rights of oath and franchise. And whereas, we believe these laws to be morally wrong and impolitic; therefore, we deem it our duty to organize associations to employ all lawful and honorable means for the repeal of the Black Laws of the State, and for the final accession of our political rights." The association announced that it would recruit members—dues were set at twenty-five cents per month—and would seek to gain rights for blacks in Illinois through public meetings, lectures, and petitions, "thereby producing such a change in public opinion as shall induce the voters of the commonwealth when presented therewith, and [the] Legislature, when petitioned, to grant them."

Every state convention condemned the caste system and discrimination against free blacks in the North. The New England Colored Citizens Convention of 1859 put it best:

This prejudice pervades every grade and contaminates every portion of society with its pestilential effluvia; that there has not been exemplified, in the treatment we have received in the evangelical church, any evidence of vital piety; that the prejudice against our color finds admission in the habitations of rich and poor, the noble and ignoble, the peasant and the peer, the philosopher and divine; it hovers over the courts of judicature; it visits periodically the pulpit and executive chair; it resides in the merchant's palace and the yeoman's cot; it is depicted upon the lawyer's physiognomy, the politician's and the poet's brain, and the itinerant scribbler's closet is its welcome habitation. It is the barrier to our elevation, and has a crushing and blighting influence upon the hopes and happiness of the rising generation; and we will never cease our denunciations against it, while our race is the victim of its unhallowed and debasing effects.

The state conventions of this period generally followed the same format. A call would be issued; delegates would respond from various parts of the states, the most numerous from the large urban areas; the conventions would begin with an opening address; and resolutions touching upon a broad range of black concerns would then be introduced and vigorously debated. Education for their children, for example, appeared frequently as a question that blacks were earnestly asked to support. Resolutions were also frequently introduced calling attention to the need to support or read newspapers, especially those organs, whether white or black, that championed their cause. Other resolutions dealing with slavery and antislavery, colonization, and the evils of intemperance and vice figured in the proceedings of most of these conventions.

Following the presentation and approval of resolutions, the official address of the convention, setting forth its claims and sentiments, was sent forth to the general public. It was not unusual to have at least three such addresses: one directed to the state legislature, another to the white people of the state, and a third to the blacks. For keen analyses of the issues outlined and for breadth of research and argument, these addresses are among the outstanding political documents of the period. Some were unusually long and repetitive at times, but most presented their arguments in a clear, detailed, and masterly fashion. Together with the addresses of the National Negro Conventions, these documents of the black state conventions, with their arguments in support of black rights, compare favorably with the major legal and constitutional treatises in American history.

In addition to national and state conventions, free blacks of the North gathered in numerous local conventions. Generally these meetings dealt with local issues, such as the organization of temperance and benevolent societies. But it was at such local meetings that blacks first condemned the American Colonization Society and later the Fugitive Slave Act of 1850. From these local meetings, moreover, there emerged new leaders who later rose to state or national prominence.

SIGNIFICANCE OF THE NEGRO CONVENTION MOVEMENT

Factional disputes, divided leadership, conflicting programs, personal jealousies, and a lack of finances were among the major reasons for the failure of the Negro Convention movement to maintain a stable existence. Yet even though only a small number of blacks took part in the movement, it was of great significance for the Negro people. The auxiliary conventions, directed by officers of the national convention, were able to improve conditions for Negro people living in Northern rural sections and remote villages. Throughout all Northern cities, the local black meetings organized benevolent societies to provide essentials for needy persons, to create mutual insurance funds for their members, and to provide teachers and social workers for the communities. Sponsoring itinerant speakers, the national convention emphasized the importance of rudimentary education and advanced study in arts and sciences even where public education facilities were restricted. Particularly did the convention movement address itself to the courage and self-reliance of the Negro people to counteract the propaganda of white newspapers and speakers. It urged Negroes to apply themselves to trades and respectable daily tasks. At the same time, the convention exposed merchants and industrialists, including white abolitionist employers, who refused to hire Negro help or insisted on placing them only as porters. The convention's opposition to emigration was influential in dooming the colonization movement to failure. The efforts and accomplishments of the convention elicited the frank praise of incredulous whites and did more than any other instrument to refute the widespread theory of Negro inferiority.

The national convention and its state and local auxiliary societies created a feeling of confidence and self-reliance among the Negro people. It was to these groups that the free black turned to voice his opinions, for the convention movement at national, state, and local levels served as the voice of Northern blacks from 1830 to the Civil War. These organizations belonged to the free blacks themselves; they spoke, wrote, and petitioned not as individuals but as members of the Convention of American Negroes. The convention brought Northern Negroes together as no other body did and provided them with an opportunity to develop the techniques, leadership, and program for political, social, and economic equality. They helped to unite the black communities in conducting an organized struggle to attain equal rights.

15

The Battle for Equality

Through their newspapers, conventions, and meetings, free blacks in the North raised their voices in protest against racial oppression, something their brothers in the South, even though more advanced economically, did not dare to do. Equally important, they were able to organize and, through such organization, seek to end some of the worst aspects of this oppression. When, in Boston in 1826, black tailors and clothing shop proprietors David Walker, Thomas Dalton, William C. Nell, and James Barbadoes founded the Massachusetts General Colored Association to work for equal rights, they signaled the fact that despised and degraded as free blacks were in the North, they still enjoyed a degree of liberty unknown in the slaveholding South. How they exercised that right and with what results we now consider.

THE TWIN BATTLE IN MASSACHUSETTS

From 1838 to 1843, Massachusetts became the battleground for two major efforts to eliminate racist practices: one to rid the Massachusetts law, on the statute books since 1705 (and revised in 1786), forbidding marriages of blacks and whites, and the other to force railroads within the state to stop running Jim Crow cars. Although the drive against the antimiscegenation law was the first of the twin battles, it was stalled in the legislature and did not move ahead until after the Jim Crow car issue was resolved. When in 1839, 736 white women from Lynn, Massachusetts, petitioned the legislature for an end to all statutory proscriptions against the Negroes of the state, it was ridiculed as a petition "for the PRIVILEGE of marrying black husbands." However, in 1840, the legislature named a committee to look into the question of repealing the 1786 law.

The committee's majority called the law "the last relic of the old slave code of Massachusetts" and favored its repeal. The senate actually passed the repeal bill, but the house of representatives decided it needed more time and, in a close vote, it postponed action for another year. Before that, however, the issue of discriminatory treatment accorded Negroes on public conveyances became the main concern. It became particularly important when many blacks began actively protesting by purposely sitting in cars set aside for whites, acts that frequently led to violence and even bloodshed. Boston's black community was enraged when David Ruggles, the popular editor of the *Mirror of Liberty* and secretary of the New York Vigilance Committee, was beaten by the captain of the New Bedford-Nantucket steamboat for complaining after he had been refused the purchase of a $2 ticket, which would have entitled him to all the privileges of the boat. Soon after this incident, Ruggles was assaulted on the New Bedford & Taunton Railroad for not taking a seat in the car set aside for blacks. He was dragged out by the railroad superintendent and several others, his clothing being torn in the process, and was thrown off the train.

Ruggles sued the New Bedford & Taunton line but lost his case, the judge ruling that the railroad could assign seats at its discretion. A few weeks later, Frederick Douglass and John A. Collins, the white general agent of the Massachusetts Anti-Slavery Society, took seats side by side in a car of the Eastern Railroad. When the conductor ordered Douglass to move into the Jim Crow car, Collins and several of the other white passengers objected. The conductor recruited four or five men, and they seized Douglass and carried him into the car for blacks. In the process, Collins was injured and Douglass had his clothing torn.

Nor were black women and children spared. Mary Newhall Green, secretary of the Lynn Anti-Slavery Society, boarded an Eastern car with her husband and baby. Because they would not sit in the all-Negro car, they were forcibly thrown off the train. The baby was injured, and the husband, who had sought to defend his family, was badly beaten.

The executives of the Eastern Railroad replied to the bitter protests engendered by this incident that they intended to continue to exercise the "right to tell people where they will ride, as tavern keepers have the right to tell people where they will sleep." This only further enraged the Massachusetts blacks.

In February 1842, both Wendell Phillips, the white abolitionist, and Charles Lenox Remond, the first black in Massachusetts history to appear before a state legislative committee, addressed the committee of the house of representatives considering a bill calling for equal traveling rights. In his address, Remond conceded that there was a "marked difference" between social and civil rights and that "we all claim the privilege of selecting our society and associates," but that in the matter of civil rights, "one man has not the prerogative to define rights for others." "The grievances of which we complain," he told the committee, "are not imaginary, but real—not local, but universal, not occasional, but continual, everyday matter-of-fact things—and have become, to the disgrace of our common country a matter of history."

Although Remond helped convince the committee members to file a report unanimously approving the bill, the legislature failed to act. At a meeting held in February 1843, black Bostonians spoke out vigorously in favor of ridding the state's statute books of laws that made color distinctions, including the racial intermarriage law, which "we rejoice to believe . . . will soon be wiped away." This marked one of the few times that blacks had publicly participated in the campaign to remove the ban against racial intermarriage. Up to then, the campaign had been largely conducted by white Boston abolitionists, but when opponents of repeal indicated that Boston blacks were in favor of the existing law, a new organization was set up, called, the Colored Citizens of Boston, to push for repeal. At its opening meeting, the blacks present denounced all attempts to persuade the public that they were opposed to the efforts of their white allies to erase all laws that made color distinctions from the Massachusetts statute books.

Early in March 1843, after a twelve-year campaign, the 1786 marriage law was repealed by both houses of the legislature and signed by Governor Marcus Morton. "It is a most signal victory over prejudice and the spirit of caste," William Lloyd Garrison noted happily. However, the legislature failed to pass any law outlawing discrimination on the state railroads, but continued protest and rising public support forced the railroad companies to integrate their trains. At the end of 1843, the Eastern line finally opened its passenger cars to blacks and whites alike. In January 1844, the Massachusetts Anti-Slavery Society observed: "We are happy to have reason to believe that . . . no distinctions any longer exist upon any of the Railways of Massachusetts." Thus, with the support of white allies, Massachusetts blacks had been able to win two important victories against racial oppression.

THE BATTLES FOR EQUAL EDUCATION: MASSACHUSETTS

While he was hailing the victories that ended the segregated seating practices on Massachusetts trains and repealed the law banning interracial marriage, Charles Lenox Remond told audiences throughout the state that he longed "to see the day when it would no longer be possible . . . to point to . . . pro-slavery colored schools [in Massachusetts]." It was to take another twelve years before this vision to be was realized and for Massachusets to become the first and only state to outlaw separate public schools for blacks before the Civil War.

It was no easy achievement, and it required persistent agitation. But as a meeting of the colored citizens of Boston at the Belknap Street Church, March 24, 1851, announced:

We have waged eternal war against exclusive schools, on account of their hindrance to our rights; and we believe them injurious in all communities where *men*, without distinction of color, are equal before the laws. In Massachusetts, according to the Constitution and the laws, the colored man is acknowledged equal. As this is the fact, we wish, as law-loving and law-abiding citizens of this Commonwealth, to enjoy perfectly and unqualifiedly all the rights and privileges we are entitled to. We wish to have the blessings of common schools distributed without partiality—EQUAL. These are our desires; and for the fulfilment of the same we shall continue to pray, until the fact is established, that in Massachusetts, *all men live in full enjoyment of their rights.*

Salem blacks initiated the agitation for equal rights in Massachusetts in May 1830 when a black girl passed the entrance examination to East High School but was refused admission. With the help of a legal opinion stating that she had as much right to attend as any white child, she was responsible for integrating the school two months later. But when three years later, 176 whites protested against the admission of black girls to the East School, the school committee compromised by establishing an African grammar school with William Dodge, the city's best teacher, as instructor. But even a good teacher could not overcome the effects of discrimination, and blacks demanded integration. When their pleas were rejected by the school committee, a boycott followed, and daily attendance at the colored school dropped from sixty to seventeen. In December 1843, blacks petitioned the school committee urging abolition of the separate and inferior school. Finally, in March 1844, prodded by Mayor Stephen Phillips, an abolitionist, and by black parents, the school committee acted to discontinue the African school and admit blacks to district schools.

Charlotte Forten, daughter of Philadelphia's James Forten, was one of the graduates of Salem's integrated public schools. She went on to state normal school, and after graduation, she was appointed by the Salem school committee to be an assistant in the Eppes Grammar School, where she taught until ill health forced her to resign in 1858. Upon her resignation, the *Salem Register* commented:

She was graciously received by the parents of the district and soon endeared herself to the pupils (white) under her charge. From the beginning, her connection with the school has been of the happiest and most useful character, disturbed, we believe, by no unpleasant circumstance. . . . We are happy to record this instance of the success of this lady as a teacher in our public schools. We do not mention it so much to praise Miss Forten as to give credit to the community and to the school committee which sanctioned this experiment. It is honorable to our city, and to the school committee which appointed her.

In February 1842, the blacks of Nantucket met in a local church and complained of the segregated school system, calling it a "wound of some years standing." All they asked for was equal school rights: "we contend not for . . . any rights and privileges that are not common to the rest of the members of this community." Two years later, when abolitionists were elected to all three school committee positions, blacks petitioned to have their children admitted to the grammar schools. The committee agreed, and the African school became an integrated district school, but one attended mostly by blacks who lived some distance from the other schools. Actually the committee's action was only temporary, and the following year the school committee was replaced by men who voted to resegregate the entire system. But after two years of a black boycott of the African school, the integrationists were again victorious, although by a small margin. This time the school committee voted to close the African school and to assign blacks to the city schools. Finally a new school committee reopened a black primary school, but with the provision that if blacks so desired, they could attend city schools.

By 1845, Lowell, New Bedford, and Worcester, as well as Salem and Nantucket, had integrated their schools, and nearly all reported that the advantages of integration far exceeded their most optimistic predictions. Testifying in 1846 before Boston's school committee, a black graduate of Salem's integrated schools commented on what was "perhaps the most gratifying result of Salem's integration victory." "The colored children generally," he reported, "were treated by the white children as equals and companions in all respects; that the white children invited the colored children to their parties and the colored children invited the white children." The school committee was not impressed, however, and Boston continued to relegate blacks to segregated schools. But a tremendous campaign was underway to alter the existing structure and compel Boston to follow the communities that had already integrated their schools.

The leader of the campaign was William Cooper Nell, black writer and self-taught historian, and a loyal supporter of William Lloyd Garrison. Nell determined to fight against segregation in Boston's schools as early as 1829 when, as a boy, he attended the Belknap Street school for black children. Following an examination of the students in the presence of Boston's mayor, Harrison Gray Otis, and another civic leader, Samuel T. Armstrong, Nell and two others were chosen to receive the highest award of merit, the Franklin medal. Instead of the medals, however, they were each given an order on a certain book store in Boston for a biography of Benjamin Franklin. Several white students who had excelled in a similar examination and were chosen to receive awards were invited to a dinner at Faneuil Hall where they were feted, extolled, and presented with the awards.

Nell learned beforehand of the dinner and arranged with one of the waiters to be present by assisting with the serving of the food. He was recognized by Armstrong, who whispered to him, "You ought to be here with the other boys." As Nell related the story many years afterward, he was tempted to reply, "If you think so, why have you not taken steps to bring it about?" but instead he kept quiet. Many years later, he reminisced: "The impression created in my mind by this day's experience deepened into a solemn vow that, God helping me, I would do my best to hasten the day when the color of the skin would be no barrier to equal school rights."

Nell's boyhood resolution was realized in the 1840s and 1850s as petitions, mass meetings, newspaper articles, and other forms of public expression aroused the citizens of Boston to the evils of segregation in the public schools. The agitation received its greatest support from the abolitionist movement. William Lloyd Garrison, Wendell Phillips, Francis Jackson, and Henry W. Williams joined Nell in signing a petition requesting that the city government eliminate segregation and grant equal rights to black school children. The request was rejected. In the ensuing years, this petition was followed by many others, largely instigated by Nell and bearing thousands of signatures of prominent individuals demanding the elimination of segregation. In 1844, seventy residents of "Nigger Hill" sent a petition to the school committee in which they told the body that in Salem, where "the whites and colored children attend the same schools . . . some of the colored youth were among the best scholars. The colored children were well treated and well taught." Again the school committee rejected the petition. The petitions were supplemented by mass meetings, articles in Boston's newspapers, and picketing of the Smith school for black children to persuade parents to refuse to send their children to classes. Blacks boycotted the separate school, and attendance dropped by some 80 percent.

Faced with this constant agitation, the Boston School Committee appointed a committee to investigate the problem. The majority report, submitted on June 15, 1846, upheld segregation, but the minority report by abolitionists Edmund Jackson and H. I. Bowditch urged the abolition of segregated schools. "Our common schools . . . are common to all," they began. Having investigated conditions throughout Massachusetts, they had learned that "this city is now we believe the only place in the commonwealth, where any distinction whatever exists with respect to color in the common schools. . . . It is to be hoped that the philosophy or *morals* which slavery teaches may not be established as our guide. . . . From a childhood which shares the same bench and sports, there can hardly arise a manhood of aristocratic prejudice, or separate castes and classes." The minority report insisted that "our constitution and laws" had repudiated "all distinctions" based on "race or any other ground." The school committee, however, voted fifty-nine to sixteen to retain segregation and announced boldly that "the continuance of the separate schools for colored children is not only legal and just, but is best adapted to promote the education of that part of our population."

Not only did this adverse ruling fail to stem the agitation, but it was encouraged by Judge Richard Fletcher's opinion against the Salem School Committee. Fletcher said that exclusive colored schools were a disadvantage to the Negro and ruled that "colored children are lawfully entitled to the benefits of the free schools, and are not bound to accept an equivalent." Shortly after this opinion was made public, Benjamin F. Roberts, a black printer, brought suit against the city of Boston. Roberts had tried on four separate occasions to enroll his five-year-old daughter, Sarah, in the white schools, and on each occasion, she had been refused admittance by the school committee on the grounds of color. What particularly annoyed Sarah's father was the fact that his daughter had to pass five different white primary schools on the way to her own colored school. Upon being informed that his child would, upon request, be admitted to the colored school, Roberts refused to make such a request. To test the constitutionality of the school committee's power to enforce segregation, Roberts, with the help of Nell and other Boston blacks, brought suit in Sarah's name under the 1845 Massachusetts statute providing that "any child, unlawfully excluded from public school instruction in this Commonwealth, shall recover damages . . . against the city or town by which such public instruction is supported."

Charles Sumner, a bitter foe of slavery and an ardent supporter of equal rights for blacks, acted as Roberts' counsel and was assisted by Salem-born Robert Morris, the first Negro to pass the bar in Massachusetts and the second to practice law in the state. The case was finally brought before the supreme judicial court of Massachusetts. Chief Justice Lemuel Shaw, the preeminent state jurist of his day, and three other justices heard the arguments of the attorneys representing Roberts and the city of Boston. The latter was Peleg W. Chandler, Massachusetts' foremost expert on municipal law.

After observing that various parts of the Massachusetts constitution condemned inequality and discrimination in civil and political institutions, Sumner argued that the state legislature, in establishing public schools, had made no provision for separate schools in their educational system. He showed that the Supreme Judicial Court had never countenanced any discrimination in the administration of the public schools. On the contrary, the court had decided that "the schools required by the statute are to be maintained for the benefit of the whole town, . . . to give all the inhabitants equal privileges for the education of their children."

Basic to Sumner's argument was the principle that "Caste and Equality are contradictory. . . . Where Caste is there cannot be Equality; where Equality is there cannot be Caste." He went on:

A separate school, though well endowed, would not secure to them that precise Equality which they would enjoy in the Common Schools. The Jews in Rome are confined to a particular district called the Ghetto, and in Frankfort to a district known as the Jewish Quarter. It is possible that their accommodations are as good as they would be able to occupy, if left free to choose throughout Rome and Frankfort; but this compulsory segregation from the mass of citizens is of itself an inequality which we condemn. It is a vestige of ancient tolerance directed against a despised people. It is of the same character with the separate schools in Boston.

Much of what Sumner said anticipated the U.S. Supreme Court's historic decision of May 17, 1954, which was based on the premise that separate but equal school facilities do not provide equality. He concluded his presentation with these eloquent words:

The bodies of men may be unequal in beauty or strength; these mortal blocks of flesh may differ, as do these wordly garments; these intellectual faculties may vary, as do the opportunities of action and the advantages of position, but amidst all unessential differences, there is an essential agreement and equality. . . . They [Negroes] must be equal in the sight of all just institutions.

The case presented for Boston simply asserted that it was the right of the school committee under the law to make all arrangements necessary for organizing the schools. If the committee could separate schools by sex, grade, and ability, then it could separate students because of race.

The *Boston Post* warned of tragic consequences if the court ruled in favor of Roberts. "If . . . the Smith School is abolished," it editorialized, "there will be serious trouble in the western wards of the city . . . all because a parcel of *rabid enthusiasts*, pretending to be friends of the colored people, chose to meddle with matters that did not concern them, and with a system which was working . . . in all love and harmony."

The *Post* need not have worried. Justice Shaw, writing the unanimous opinion of the court, rejected Sumner's argument and upheld the school committee and the system of segregation. Shaw claimed that plaintiff Roberts had access to a school "as well conducted in all respects . . . as the other primary schools." Since the school committee had decided "that the good of both classes of schools will be best promoted by maintaining the separate primary schools for colored and for white children," the decision of the committee must "be deemed conclusive."

Justice Shaw's opinion provided the constitutional basis for the separate but equal doctrine of racial segregation. It was used in the 1896 eight-to-one decision of the U.S. Supreme Court in *Plessy* v. *Ferguson*, affirming the separate-but-equal doctrine under the due-process clause of the Fourteenth Amendment. It remained as such justification until overruled in the 1954 *Brown* v. *Topeka Board of Education* decision, which eliminated segregated public schools in the United States.

Despite the judicial defeat, the campaign to integrate the schools of Boston continued as before, with petitions, picketing, mass meetings, and boycotts of the Smith School. The campaign, however, had to face the determined efforts of black separatists to maintain the black public school. The leader of this group was Thomas Paul Smith, nephew of Reverend Thomas Paul, founder in 1804 of the first black Baptist church and a firm believer in the idea that a black child would fare better in his own school, "cheered on by the unanimous shout of encouragement of all his fellows with no jeers or unkindness to make heavy his heart." "Shall we . . . abolish our institutions because the whites won't admit us to theirs?" he asked, and replied: "I say never! for so doing, we rashly destroy the means for all future happiness and improvement."

Smith set about trying to get the school committee to appoint Thomas Paul, his cousin and son of the Reverend Paul, as master of the Smith School. A graduate of Dartmouth College, Paul had been head of a black school in Albany, New York, and Smith believed that if a black principal was placed at the head of the Smith School, the black community would be satisfied, and separate education for black children could continue. The school committee, anxious to break the back of the boycott of the Smith School, also believed that the appointment of a distinguished black educator as principal would cause many parents to support segregated education.

Most Boston blacks, however, opposed the attempt to appoint a black principal, suspecting that it was a device to derail the integration campaign. The black majority resolved at a meeting that "in our battle for freedom, the influence of all colored men and women is indispensable. . . . We want no *neutrals* among us. Those colored persons who are not for us in this trying hour must be counted in the ranks of those who would deprive us of our heaven-decreed rights." Some, like Nell, Benjamin Roberts, and Robert Morris, even charged Thomas Paul Smith with being paid by white foes of school integration to lobby for Thomas Paul's appointment as master of the Smith School.

Smith denied the charge, and to strengthen his cause, contacted Dr. James McCune Smith of New York City, asking his opinion of the advantages of having black teachers and a black principal. The New York physician informed Thomas Paul Smith that black teachers had much more success than whites with black children, "in spite of the balance of power and monied influence which white trustees fling into the scale of the latter." He felt, too, that Paul "would make a better, more brilliant and useful teacher than any white man living. . . . To have manly colored scholars, we must have manly and accomplished colored teachers." Delighted to have such a response from so staunch an integrationist as James McCune Smith, Thomas Paul Smith forwarded the letter to the Boston School Committee.

But in his correspondence with Dr. Smith, Thomas Paul Smith had neglected to mention the controversy taking place in Boston over segregated schools, nor had he pointed out how crucially important the Paul appointment had become in the struggle between those who wanted to close down the Smith School and those who wished to keep it open. When Dr. Smith learned of these facts, he sent a letter to the blacks fighting for school integration, pointing out that

the question as to the relative merits of mixed and separate schools was not raised by Mr. T. Paul Smith; nor was my reply to that gentleman written with the remotest view to such a question. . . . It has ever been my solemn conviction, that separate organizations of all kinds, based upon the color of the skin, keep alive prejudice against color; and that no organizations do this more effectually than colored schools.

That settled the question of whether to send black children to the Smith School with or without a black principal. The boycott not only continued but Boston blacks sent their children to attend two protest schools held at the homes of black citizens. Others transported their offspring to integrated schools in nearby towns, while still others even moved from Boston to communities with integrated school systems. Meanwhile petitions were circulated by a new organization, the Committee for Equal School Rights, calling upon the school committee to integrate the public schools of Boston. A petition was also submitted to the Harvard Board of Overseers calling upon it to open the undergraduate school and the schools of theology, law, and medicine "to all persons, without distinction of color." Like the petitions to the school committee, this one made little headway.

At this point, Boston blacks and their white allies decided to change their tactics, launching a campaign to lobby for a state law forbidding segregated schools. In February 1855, William C. Nell, assisted by thirteen agents in ten Massachusetts towns, secured 1,700 signatures on a petition demanding the outlawing of racial discrimination in public school admissions. Following an intensive investigation of the effects of integration in other Massachusetts cities and towns, with Nell furnishing valuable information, the legislature's Committee on Education submitted a report favoring a bill requiring an end to using race as a criterion for school admission. The heart of the legislation lay in its first section, which proposed that

in determining the qualifications of scholars to be admitted into any public school, or any district school in this Commonwealth, no distinction shall be made on account of the race, color, or religious opinions of the applicant or scholar.

Within a few weeks, the bill had passed both Massachusetts houses, and it was signed into law by Governor Henry Gardner on April 28, 1855, to take effect the following September.

When word of the legislation reached New York City, the pro-Southern *Herald* fairly wept: "Now the blood of the Winthrops, the Otises, the Lymans, the Endicotts, and the Eliots, is . . . to be amalgamated with the Sambos, the Catos, and the Pompeys. The North is to be Africanized. Amalgamation has commenced. . . . God save the Commonwealth of Massachusetts."

Actually segregation continued for the remainder of the school year, but throughout the summer of 1855, Nell and his friends organized a new boycott of the Smith School for the fall and persuaded black parents to keep their children out of it. By the September opening, there were so few pupils in the primary and grammar schools—seven in the former and none in the latter—that the Boston School Committee cited insufficient attendance in terminating the educational program at both schools.

The joy felt by the black people of Boston, as September 3, 1855, the opening day of school approached, was best described by Nell, who witnessed a Negro boy passing by the Smith School on September 2. "Raising his hand," observed Nell, "he exultingly exclaimed to his companions, 'Good-bye forever, colored school! Tomorrow we are like other Boston boys.'" The introduction of black children into white schools was completed with little trouble in any part of the city. The *Boston Telegraph* reported that it "was accomplished, with general good feeling on the part of both the teachers and the white children."

At a meeting in the vestry of the Baptist church, the black assemblage adopted a resolution thanking the legislature for its action, and affirming that "to attest our appreciation of the passage of the anti-colored school act, we, the colored parents of Boston, do hereby pledge ourselves to have our children punctually at school, and neat in their dress, and in all other ways will aid their instructors in the task which has been assigned them.'' In December, an interracial celebration was held at the Southac Street Church for the purpose of presenting a testimonial to Nell ''for his disinterested and untiring exertions procuring the opening of the public schools of the city to all children and youth within its limits, irrespective of complexional differences.'' The highlight of the evening was the presentation of a gold watch to Nell, on the back of which was inscribed:

A Tribute to
William C. Nell
From the Colored Citizens
of Boston,
For his untiring efforts
in behalf of
Equal School Rights
Dec. 17, 1855

After the presentation, Nell delivered an address in which he expressed his gratitude for the gift but noted that he was made even happier by the ''healthful glee of boys and girls of all colors and races in these temples of learning, so justly a theme of pride to every citizen.''

THE BATTLE FOR EQUAL EDUCATION: ROCHESTER, NEW YORK

Although the battle for equal education in Rochester, New York, was by no means as difficult or extensive as that waged in Boston, it was the outstanding one in New York State during the antebellum period. There, Frederick Douglass played somewhat the same role that William C. Nell had assumed in the Boston struggle. Douglass had moved to Rochester late in 1847 to begin publishing the *North Star*. He immediately became involved in a controversy over school segregation. The Rochester Board of Education refused to allow his children to enter Public School 15 near his home and insisted that they travel to the other side of the city to attend the school established for black children only. Although Rochester's blacks had sought the establishment of a separate school, Douglass refused to accept the segregated system of education. ''If we yield to this encroachment,'' he explained in his paper, ''perhaps the next demand will require us to live in a certain part of the city. Our children are to go to a particular school—colored people are to attend their own meeting, and it may by and by follow that we are to occupy a given place in the town.''

In August 1858, Douglass arranged to have his daughter attend Seward Seminary, a school for girls in Rochester. He was very pleased when he learned that the principal was an abolitionist, and he left for a visit to Cleveland happy in the thought that his child "was about to enjoy advantages for improving her mind and fitting her for a useful and honorable life." It is not difficult to imagine his rage when he discovered on his return that Rosetta had been isolated in a room by herself and was being taught separately. He promptly protested to the principal "against the cruelty and injustice of treating my child as a criminal on account of her color." The principal replied that the school trustees had objected to the admission of a black girl and that to overcome their prejudices by gradual stages, she had hit upon the idea of having the child taught separately until such time as she could be admitted to the regular classes.

Upon Douglass' protest, the principal agreed to submit the question of Rosetta's status to the pupils, asking them, "How many of you are willing to have this colored child be with you?" All of the children held up their hands. When the question was put to their parents, only one objected, but Rosetta was still asked to leave the school. Douglass had in fact already decided to withdraw his daughter from the seminary, and after announcing publicly that *"in no emergency"* would he send any child of his to a segregated school, he sent his daughter to a private institution in Albany for about three years; in 1851, he secured the services of a governess for her and his other children. Meanwhile he worked with other citizens of Rochester to abolish the separate school system, which he called "the question of questions for the colored people of this place."

Douglass' contention that school desegregation was more important than any other public desegregation was based on his belief that the mixing of white and black children at the public school level was essential if racism was to be eradicated. "Colored children," he pointed out, "find themselves excluded from white schools, and they early learn that their complexion is the cause of their exclusion. The consequence is, they are induced to undervalue themselves, and to look up on white children as their oppressors." On the other hand, "with equal school rights . . . colored children . . . come into contact on equal terms with white children and youth, three hundred days in the year and from six to ten hours each day. And these children, in a few years, become the people of the state."

The agitation for integrated public schools in Rochester started to bear fruit when separate schools for black children became an uneconomical operation because of the high per-capita cost. On July 7, 1856, the Rochester Board of Education moved "in favor of closing the colored school for the present term." With this action, twenty-four years of colored schools in Rochester came to an end, for while the board never formally integrated the schools, the separate schools for blacks remained closed. In any case, Rochester was far ahead of all other cities in New York State. New York City's public schools were not legally desegregated until 1884.

THE BATTLE FOR EQUAL EDUCATION: RHODE ISLAND

After Massachusetts had legally abolished segregated public school education in 1855, black leaders in Rhode Island began a major campaign to integrate that state's public school system. By 1859, most of the towns in the state admitted blacks to mixed schools, but Providence, Newport, and Bristol, which had the largest Negro populations, still kept their public schools segregated. Black leaders stepped up the fight for the total abolition of segregated schools in the state. In this campaign, they obtained the support of several white Protestant ministers and long-time antislavery fighters, including Elizabeth Chase, Edward Harris, and Rowland Hazard.

George Henry, James Jefferson, and especially George T. Downing were leaders of the Rhode Island black community in the battle against segregated schools. In addition to taking care of his real estate and restaurant interests, Downing was active in all phases of the struggle for equality in Rhode Island. He was the guiding spirit of the Committee on Behalf of the Colored People of Rhode Island, which spearheaded the drive for integrated schools. The main argument of the integrationists was that segregated education was, by definition, inferior education. The physical plants of the black schools, compared to those of the white schools, were dilapidated; the curriculum was weaker; the teachers were inferior; and the administration was understaffed. But even if the buildings, teachers, and curricula were equal to those of the white schools, the Negro's education would still remain inferior. Many black children did not attend school regularly since they lived too far from the separate schools. More important, segregated schools reduced the Negro to a state of inferiority, and because of the caste system, he came to believe in that inferiority and ceased striving to improve himself. Caste schools thus had a disastrous psychological effect on the Negro. The integrationists posed the question as to how a white man would feel if his child was forced "to go one or two miles distant to a small, uncommodious caste-marked building? Would he not feel, that there was daily building up in the minds of his little ones a feeling of degradation, a consciousness of mean position, or depressing of all noble motive?"

The segregationists relied heavily on the argument that integration would ruin the public school system. Whites and blacks, they insisted, would be in conflict, and the white parents would enroll their children in private schools. The integrationists, the *Providence Journal* charged, "would see our public schools quite broken up, and our means of public education quite destroyed, rather than that one little nigger boy should be compelled to attend the school that has been assigned to him."

The integrationists emphatically denied that there would be a mass white exodus from public schools because a few blacks were admitted. They pointed out that it had not happened in either Boston or in Rhode Island communities that had integrated their schools. Far from weakening the school system, they maintained, integration would improve it, since money would no longer be wasted on costly duplication and the funds thus saved could be used to improve the schools.

On May 30, 1859, the Special Committee on Colored Schools of the Rhode Island Legislature submitted a majority report favoring the abolition of all segregated schools that remained in the state. It based its recommendation on three key arguments: (1) that the state's constitution made no distinction on account of color; (2) that in admitting blacks to citizenship under the Constitution, Rhode Island guaranteed them the full enjoyment of every civil right and privilege that that instrument secured to each and every other citizen; and (3) that the constitution called for promoting public schools to achieve the education of the entire population, citizens and strangers, and if this was the privilege of the stranger, it was surely the right of the citizen—"a right which cannot be withheld, limited or abridged, without manifest injustice." The report concluded: "It is plain to the Committee that every citizen stands equal before the law, and that his children are entitled to equal privileges of education in the schools of his district, without respect to race, color or condition."

In publishing the report, the *Liberator* voiced the hope that "its adoption is certain," but it was not to be. The Rhode Island legislature rejected the committee's recommendation. None of the efforts of integrationists, black and white, to secure legislation abolishing segregated schools in Providence, Newport, and Bristol were able to produce a victory before the Civil War.

Before leaving the subject of public school integration before the Civil War, it should be noted that the value of an education, segregated or integrated, to a young black was limited by the fact that no matter how well he or she was educated, they were limited to jobs for "beggarly paid menials." If the Negro students managed to complete a public school education, whether in an integrated or a segregated school, they entered a hostile world, which refused to recognize or employ their talents. "After a boy had spent five or six years in the school," observed a New York teacher, "and . . . is spoken of in terms of high approbation by respectable visitors, . . . he leaves school, with every avenue closed against him which is open to the white boy for honorable and respectable rank in society, doomed to encounter as much prejudice and contempt, as if he were not only destitute of that education . . . but as if he were *incapable* of receiving it."

THE BATTLE FOR EQUAL SUFFRAGE: NEW YORK

Blacks in New York were denied the franchise under the provisions of the state constitution of 1821 unless they owned property valued at $250. No such requirement was imposed upon whites. Up to 1821, most blacks had exercised the vote; the effect of the new requirement was to exclude the majority of the free Negro population from exercising this right.

In 1837, the first of a series of petitions signed by New York blacks urged the legislature to revise the state's constitution and extend the right of voting to all male citizens "on the same terms, *without distinction of color*." Other petitions asked for the "abolition of an odious distinction, which, while it acknowledges them as citizens, denies them the right which all others possess as attached to that honorable appellation."

When the legislature proved unresponsive, New York's blacks met in a state convention in August 1840 for the specific purpose of agitating for the right of suffrage. In its address, the convention informed New Yorkers:

We base our claim upon the possession of the common and yet exalted faculties of manhood. . . . WE ARE MEN. 1. Those sympathies which find their natural channel, and legitimate and healthy exercise in civil and political relations, have the same being and nature in us that they have in the rest of the human family. 2. Those yearnings and longings for the exercise of political prerogatives, that are the product of the adaptedness of man's social nature to political arrangements, strive with irrepressible potency within us, from the fact of our disfranchised condition, a prevalent and unreasonable state of caste, and the operation of laws and statutes not proceeding from, yet operating upon us. 3. Those indignities and wrongs which naturally become the portion of a disfranchised class, and gather accumulated potency from an increase and intenseness of proscription, naturally and legitimately revert to us.

The convention voted to place continued reliance upon petitioning the legislature, and for this purpose a Central Committee and County Committees were established. The County Committees were to circulate petitions and forward them to the Central Committee, which, in turn, would forward them to the appropriate legislative committee in Albany. Since the legislature was scheduled to convene on January 2, 1841, it was imperative that the committees act swiftly and that the petitions be signed speedily. Before adjourning, the convention appealed to New York blacks to take decisive action with all possible speed:

Colored men of New York! Are you willing that your people should longer constitute the proscribed class? Are you willing ever to be deprived of one of the dearest rights of free men? Are you willing to remain quietly and inactively, political slaves? Are you willing to leave your children to better public inheritance than to be among the disfranchised—the politically oppressed?

Let every man in the state arouse himself. Let every city and town and village bestir itself to action . . . to obtain the name of every man to a petition to be presented by the State Central Committee to the legislature, until all traces of proscription are stricken from the statute book. Let petitions be scattered in every quarter. Let every man send in his remonstrance.

The *Colored American* added its own plea: "*Brethren, one and all, sign the petition.* And you who cannot write your name, get some one to do it for you. Secure also the names of your friends, your white friends. SIGN THE PETITION."

At least four different types of petitions were circulated, all calling upon the legislature to amend the state constitution so "that the Elective Franchise may be extended to us on the same terms as enjoyed by other citizens." A total of 2,806 signatures for the entire state was obtained, with 1,700 names coming from New York City. The number of signatures impressed at least some of the legislators, and they were further impressed when Henry Highland Garnet testified before the Judiciary Committee of the state assembly in mid-February 1841, arguing in favor of the claim of black New Yorkers for the vote. Garnet pointed out "the unsoundness of the policy that oppresses and degrades any of the citizens of the commonwealth."

Shortly afterward, the Judiciary Committee proposed an amendment to the state constitution that would have given suffrage to all male persons, regardless of color, who could read and write the English language and who were residents in the state for at least six months prior to an election. But the state legislature rejected the amendment. An angry *Herkimer Journal* blasted the legislature in an editorial entitled "Political Oppression in New York":

Most people believe that slavery was abolished in the State of New York many years ago, and that the colored people now residing in the State are now FREE. Is this so? Is the black man really free in the Empire State? No! Though nominally free, he is still borne down, crushed, enslaved, by a cruel and relentless prejudice, that prevents his children from receiving the advantages of education, learning trades, and becoming useful and respectable citizens. Nay, reader, look into the constitution of this State, and see the poor black man, though born and bred in your own town, denied the right to vote, unless he is owner of $250 worth of real estate!

The right to vote is accorded to every description of *white* citizens (save in certain cases of crime), no matter how ignorant, worthless, or degraded they may become; yet it is refused to nearly all our *blacks*, no matter how enlightened, virtuous, or useful they may be. Is this right? Is it honest? Is it decent? No—it is an outrage upon humanity, and a disgrace to the State!

But no serious discussion of the suffrage question occurred until 1846, when the state convened a new constitutional convention, which remained in session from June 1 to October 9. On September 30, the first draft of article II, section 1 of the revised constitution was reported out of committee. It began: "Every *white* male citizen of the age of twenty-one," and went on to specify the requirements for the "*white* male citizen" to vote. Immediately, several delegates, pointing out that this marked a further limitation on the rights of black citizens, moved to strike out the word *white* as a requirement for the franchise. They were answered by the arguments that if blacks were given the ballot, "our republic would soon be degraded to a level with those of Mexico and South America," that if the Negro received the vote, he would have to be admitted "to an equal seat with us in the jury box, and to hold office," and that in a close election between whites, the black vote could decide the outcome. "We want no masters, and, least of all, no negro masters, to reign over us," they insisted.

After considerable debate, the convention voted to keep the property requirement for black suffrage. It did, however, submit a separate amendment calling for
equal suffrage, with the provision that if adopted by the people, it could become
part of the suffrage article of the new constitution. In line with this, ballots were
printed with the following choice:

> Equal suffrage to colored persons? Yea.
> Equal suffrage to colored persons? No.

With the leading papers in the state urging a ''no'' vote, it was not easy for
blacks to influence the outcome. Indeed when Willis A. Hodges wrote to the
New York Sun answering its arguments against black suffrage, he was told he
would have his letter published on payment of fifteen dollars. When it was
published on these terms, Hodges found that it not only had been edited but had
been placed in the advertisements column. When he complained, he was told:
''The *Sun* shines for all white men, and not for colored men,'' and that if he
wished to advocate equal suffrage for blacks, he would have to publish his own
paper. He did; with his friend, Thomas Van Rensselaer, he published the *Ram's
Horn* and kept it in existence for eighteen months.

The new constitution was approved by the voters on November 3, 1846, by a
vote of 221,528 to 96,436, but the proposed amendment granting equal suffrage
to blacks was rejected—85,306 to 223,834.

The defeat was a bitter blow to New York blacks. Many were now so discouraged that they decided that it was hopeless to agitate any further. It was not
until a decade later that the struggle was renewed, and even then it was not
possible to overcome the feeling in the black community that agitating for equal
suffrage would be a waste of time and energy. In September 1855, a convention
of blacks meeting in Troy resolved ''to give the ear of our Legislature, and our
fellow citizens generally, no peace until they shall wipe from the statute book the
anti-Republican discrimination against us.'' To press the issue, the convention
established the New York State Suffrage Association, headed by Frederick
Douglass, but little was accomplished. As the *Weekly Anglo-African* noted, the
battle for equal suffrage had been ''left to the labors of a few zealous colored
men.'' Yet this was to be expected, ''because the masses labored under the
depression of hope deferred.''

Still, the labor of the ''few zealous colored men'' did finally rouse New York
blacks from inactivity. With James McCune Smith in charge, the Suffrage Association launched a campaign to place the issue of the franchise high on the black
agenda. By the summer of 1860, there were forty-eight local suffrage clubs in
New York City, eighteen in Brooklyn, and about twenty in the rest of the state.
The activities of these clubs were partially responsible for the fact that in September 1860, the state legislature once again presented the issue of equal suffrage to
the voters for their approval or rejection.

The black suffrage clubs hurled themselves into the campaign for voter approval of equal suffrage. The New York City and County Suffrage Committee of Colored Citizens published *The Suffrage Question in Relation to Colored Voters*, which was widely distributed; in a twelve-week tour of the state on behalf of unrestricted suffrage, Douglass alone distributed twenty-five thousand copies of the tract.

As the blacks intensified their activities on behalf of the measure, which would place Negro citizens on an equal footing with others in the exercise of the right of suffrage, the press whipped up a hysteria over the consequences of a victory for the black efforts. The *Brooklyn Daily Times* warned:

Give the Negroes an unlimited suffrage, and the logical and inevitable result is a Negro alderman, a Negro representative on the county ticket, and so forth.

. . . If [the black] Alderman officiates in places of civil honor, with his badge and staff of office, can you deny him the entree to your semi-public assemblies—can you keep him from meeting even the ladies of your family, on many semi-public occasions, as a social equal?

. . . It needs no prophetic eye to foresee that ere long, the countless millions of Asiatic barbarians, Chinese and Japanese—will overflow the narrow limits in which these fecund hordes have been confined—and spread through the Pacific states, all over this continent. Gladly will the negro voters of this State welcome these allies. The unrestricted franchise which we are now asked to extend to negroes, may be a fearful weapon when turned against us.

When the ballots were counted, it was clear that white New Yorkers had once again emphatically rejected equal suffrage for blacks. The vote was 337,984 against to 197,503 for. Interestingly, the increases in the votes for and against equality of suffrage between 1846 and 1860 were within two thousand of each— an increase of 113,648 against and of 112,097 for.

Thus, despite three decades of agitation and organization, blacks in New York did not gain equal suffrage rights before the Civil War. Indeed, the property qualification applying to blacks only was not abrogated until the ratification in 1870 of the Fifteenth Amendment to the federal Constitution.

THE BATTLE FOR EQUAL SUFFRAGE: PENNSYLVANIA

After their total disfranchisement in 1838 with the adoption of the state constitution granting the right to vote only to white males, blacks in Pennsylvania began the struggle to regain the franchise. They kept the suffrage issue alive through local meetings, state conventions, and petitions to the legislature urging elimination of the white-only clause. During the period from 1839 to 1851, Pennsylvania blacks sent eighty-one separate petitions to the general assembly requesting that body to restore to them the right of suffrage. In addition, two state conventions—one in 1841 and the other in 1848—issued addresses to the white citizens appealing for support for the petitions:

It is impolitic for the state thus to restrict any portion of her inhabitants, because it degrades them, and in so far detracts from the honor and respectability of the state. It deprives them of one of the most powerful stimulants to a virtuous and upright life; paralyzes their efforts to attain wealth and respectability; and thus lessens the general wealth paid into the state treasury. It is oppressive, because we are required to pay the same homage and obedience to the laws as other citizens, and the same taxes, and are yet denied the same equivalent. It also deprives us of political defence. Our worst adversaries may be a candidate for an office, the salary of which is in part made up of taxes paid out of our own pockets, and yet we have not the power of casting a single vote to prevent his triumph. It tears away the bulwark, the very citidel of our liberties, and leaves us exposed on every side. It is wrong, because it inflicts punishment upon the innocent. The elective franchise is the highest privilege known to republicans; it is the foundation and only safeguard of all political rights; and to deprive one of it, is to inflict the highest political punishment.

In 1848, blacks organized the Citizens Union of the Commonwealth of Pennsylvania and vowed to use every means available to regain the franchise and to maintain constant pressure upon state officials until the suffrage was restored, but nothing seemed to work for the black cause. A few friendly representatives and senators introduced legislation in Harrisburg to amend the constitution to enfranchise blacks in 1845 and 1855, but their efforts were futile. The apathy of the legislators caused Philadelphia blacks to take the unusual step of sending a petition to Congress. The *Memorial of Thirty Thousand Disfranchised Citizens of Philadelphia to the Honorable Senate and House of Representatives* made it clear to white Americans that if they expected the allegiance of its black citizens, they would have to provide them with protection and equal rights. The memorial noted that since 1838, Pennsylvania blacks had sent petitions to the state authorities to regain their suffrage rights, but all in vain. It cited the fourth article of the Articles of Confederation to prove their right to the franchise. This article provided that the free inhabitants of the land of each of the states (excluding paupers, vagabonds, and fugitives from justice) should be entitled to all privileges and immunities of free citizens in the several states. Since Negroes of Pennsylvania did not come under any of the excepted categories, they, too, should have the right to vote, but because of prejudice and expediency, they had been deprived of that right. To be sure, whites argued that this was done to prevent corruption of the political process by inferior blacks, but the petitioners pointed out that there was no inherent inferiority among races. The memorial concluded with an appeal for immediate action to bring justice to America.

This appeal, like those sent to the Pennsylvania legislature, fell upon deaf ears. And as in New York, the lack of response from the legislature produced a feeling of discouragement among many blacks in Pennsylvania. Interest in the issue declined to the point that two public meetings on equal suffrage in Philadelphia during the winter of 1856–1857 drew audiences of about forty persons each. For the time being, at least, the suffrage issue was dead. Blacks could only comfort themselves with the observation of the *Pennsylvania Freeman* that their struggle for equal suffrage at least had taught the white population that "their victims are not satisfied with degradation, that they know their rights and are resolved to secure them." But as in the case of New York, it was not until the ratification of the Fifteenth Amendment in 1870 that Pennsylvania blacks gained equal suffrage.

This was also the case in Connecticut. As early as 1838, an amendment extending the vote to the Negro was suggested but rejected by the legislature. With the election of Roger S. Baldwin as governor by the antislavery votes, the issue was revived, and the matter was brought to public vote in 1846. Through a committee of Amos Beman, Joseph Brown, and James Pennington, and under the direction of the state Negro Temperance Society, the blacks issued an appeal to the voters:

We are your fellow-citizens—native born, and with you we must live and die. You have an interest then, whether you feel it or not, in our welfare; in our being intelligent, virtuous; and good citizens. We cannot be ignorant, vicious and degraded without injury to yourselves. It is for your good as well as our own that we should be attached to the Government and have confidence in the equity of its laws, and in the justice of the administration. But the surest way to degrade us, is to disfranchise us, the most direct way to make us bad citizens is to treat us as aliens. . . .

We appeal to you in the sacred name of justice. We appeal to you as Christians and ask you in the name of Christians. Is it Christ-like to treat the heir of a common salvation this invidiously?

We ask it in the name of all our people who are striving with all the energy and devotion in their power, to promote their Moral, Intellectual, Social and Religious elevations.

The hopes of the Negroes were dashed. The voters refused enfranchisement. Blacks in Connecticut did not obtain the right to vote until the state ratified the Fifteenth Amendment.

THE BATTLE FOR EQUAL SUFFRAGE: RHODE ISLAND

Efforts of blacks to regain the vote in New Jersey were also without success, but they did achieve victory in Rhode Island. What discrimination took away in 1822, when Rhode Island altered its franchise law so that only white male adults were eligible to be "freemen," and thus to vote, the black community won back in 1842.

By 1840, Rhode Island was the only state that still confined the franchise to property owners ("freemen"). The frame of government was the colonial charter granted in 1663, and the property owners tenaciously resisted efforts to expand the suffrage. As Rhode Island became more industrialized after the War of 1812, a growing propertyless population agitated for the vote. Workingmen leaders such as Seth Luther, a housewright and militant advocate of social reform, and William Tillinghast, a barber, led the efforts of the laboring class.

They were joined by sympathetic freeholders, the most famous of whom was Thomas Wilson Dorr. A graduate of Harvard College, he practiced law in Providence and represented the city in the Rhode Island General Assembly from 1834 to 1837. Dorr was an abolitionist, and in leading the movement for manhood suffrage, he also supported equal rights at the ballot box for blacks. But the majority of those in the suffrage movement were advocates of a white-only franchise, and Dorr did little to overcome this attitude. In 1841, the advocates of suffrage reform called an extralegal convention to write a constitution for the state. Black leaders tried to unite with the movement and influence it to act on their behalf, but anti-Negro prejudice was too strong. When the People's Convention met in early October, it proposed to liberalize the franchise for all white males, including the foreign born, but excluded the Negro. Before the suffrage provision was voted upon, Alexander Crummell led a committee of blacks to present a remonstrance to the delegates urging them not to ignore the Negro. The five black petitioners protested that exclusion on account of color was unwarranted, antirepublican, and destructive in its effects. They argued that the United States had been founded on the principle that all men were created free and equal, that exclusion violated that principle, and that what made this doubly shameful was that it was on the Declaration of Independence that "the People's Constitution" was based:

. . . We appeal to that great written Charter of American liberty—the declaration of independence—in support of our protestation. We believe that "all men are created free and equal"; and we affirm, that no tinge of the skin can possibly invalidate that cardinal doctrine of our country's liberty, or make nugatory or partial the political privilege which, as deductions, may proceed from it.

Disfranchisement, the black petitioners argued, caused a sense of inferiority and lessened the sense of individual worth: "Surely, it must sicken the soul, and eat out the heart of any people." They warned that discrimination on the basis of color could easily set the pattern for future exclusions on the basis of equally irrelevant distinctions, for "the annals of nations clearly teach that there is always danger in departing from clearly defined and universal truths, and resorting to unjustifiable and invidious penalties." They concluded: "By all humane feeling, by all regard for principle, we entreat, do not commit this great wrong to us."

The petition had little effect. After limited debate, the convention voted forty-six to eighteen to retain the white provision in the suffrage clause and then submitted the new constitution to the vote of the people of Rhode Island. Blacks immediately protested vigorously against their exclusion from the suffrage, both to Thomas Dorr and to the Rhode Island Anti-Slavery Society. Dorr ignored the protest, but the other Rhode Island abolitionists did not. Although they had participated in the struggle for wider extension of the limited franchise, they now felt betrayed, and the executive committee of the Rhode Island Anti-Slavery

Society issued a circular calling on all abolitionists "to make a combined and vigorous effort against the proposed Constitution."

Frederick Douglass and five other leading antislavery speakers, including Abby Kelly, came into the state to hold rallies against the constitution. Their meetings were broken up by white mobs, but they persisted, and Douglass was appointed by the Anti-Slavery Society to carry the protest against the white clause to the Suffrage Convention when it reconvened in January 1842 to count the vote on the revised constitution. The count revealed that the abolitionist and black effort had had little impact: the People's Constitution was approved by a vote of 13,944 to 52, the largest number of votes cast in any Rhode Island election up to this time.

Although the ties between the suffragists and blacks were now completely severed, some connections had developed between the conservative freeholders and the blacks. In fact, the conservatives chided the Suffrage party on the issue of votes for blacks. While the conservatives at first were also opposed to extending the suffrage to blacks—they excluded the Negro from the convention they held to write a state constitution and left the issue of black suffrage to the discretion of the legislature—in the end, they did take a stand opposite to that of the Suffrage party. Calling themselves the Law and Order party, the conservatives championed Negro suffrage and made it possible for the new constitution to include blacks in its suffrage provision. They did so for a variety of reasons, but a major one was their fear of lower-class, foreign-born, Catholic (French-Canadian and Irish) workers who were entering New England in increasing numbers. Forced to expand the franchise but concerned by the influx of these potential Catholic voters, the old-stock Protestant conservative freeholders sought allies against the foreign born. The black community gladly grasped the opportunity. As Frederick Douglass later explained: "We cared nothing for the Dorr Party on the one hand, nor the 'law and order' party on the other. What we wanted, and what we labored to obtain was a constitution free from the narrow, selfish, and senseless limitation of the word *white*." Given the assurance of black support against the rising tide of the foreign born, the conservatives promised to incorporate Negro suffrage into the new constitution.

By the time the Law and Order constitutional convention met in September 1842, the conservatives had an additional reason for granting blacks the franchise. For when Thomas Wilson Dorr headed an armed force in an attempt to seize the government and institute the reform constitution, with its provision for suffrage only for whites, Providence's black community rallied to support the existing government. Nearly two hundred blacks volunteered and became part of the Providence Home Guard, helping to patrol the streets. The Law and Order party repaid blacks for their support in the Dorr war with the franchise. Delegates at the convention in September 1842 voted forty-five to fifteen to drop *white* from the suffrage clause. With blacks voting unanimously for the new constitution, it was approved in November 1842 by a margin of 7,024 to 51.

The Dorrites were enraged, and, holding the blacks responsible for Dorr's defeat, threatened to mob any Negro who dared to vote. Even some white abolitionists criticized blacks for supporting the conservatives. But this criticism ignored the fact that the black community had tried to side with the Suffrage party and that it was only after they had been turned away that they cast their votes for the party that promised them the vote and delivered on that promise.

Meanwhile, although elected governor of the state by the dissident, pro-suffrage forces in 1842, Dorr was forced to flee the state twice. On returning in 1843, he was arrested and sentenced by the Rhode Island Supreme Court in 1844 to imprisonment at hard labor and solitary confinement for life. Less than a year before his death, the General Assembly of Rhode Island repealed, reversed, and annulled the judgment of the court, but it did not touch the right of blacks to vote.

The fact that blacks regained the vote in Rhode Island in 1842 while efforts to achieve this objective elsewhere in the North failed was largely the result of the particular situation in Rhode Island. There the real struggle was over the question of universal white manhood suffrage, an issue essentially settled elsewhere. In this particular period, a section of the white population was more fearful of the vote of white, foreign-born Catholics than of blacks. Although blacks took advantage of this situation, their reenfranchisement would not have occurred without an active effort on their own part.

THE MILITIA ISSUE

In every Northern state where they were disfranchised or their right to vote limited, blacks battled to regain the suffrage. They drafted documents that affirmed their right to vote and appealed to both the legislatures and white electorates to end their exclusion from the ballot box. Except in Rhode Island, the results were negative. One reason for that failure was political. Each of the major parties feared that the black vote would help the opposition. But there was a more fundamental explanation: most whites feared that enlarging civil rights would mean contact on a level of social equality, and this, they vowed, they would never accept.

In no area was this more explicitly stated that in the action of state legislatures limiting membership in the militias to white male citizens. While other restrictions on blacks were removed, efforts to strike the word *white* from militia laws failed. In 1851, when William C. Nell's book dealing with the Negro's role in the War for Independence and the War of 1812 was published, it enabled blacks to remind the white community that Afro-Americans had fought for independence from Lexington and Concord to Yorktown and had helped Captain Oliver H. Perry defeat the British on Lake Erie and General Andrew Jackson win the Battle of New Orleans in the War of 1812. But it made no difference. State legislatures continued to refuse to allow blacks to enroll in the militia.

In February 1852, Robert Morris and William J. Watkins appeared before the Military Committee of the Massachusetts legislature and presented petitions signed by sixty-five Negroes asking for a charter to form an independent military corps, and pointed to past military exploits by Negroes. The appeal brought no result. When Watkins' speech was published as a pamphlet, he wrote in the preface that he was not "a man of war. . . . These pages are a vindication of our Rights as Citizens, not a discourse upon our Duty as Christians. A military Hero is not his *beau idea* of a Christian, but *vice versa*."

It was because they believed that the issue of equality was deeply involved that Boston blacks organized their own militia company without receiving prior sanction from the state. When the state refused to furnish them with arms, the blacks raised the necessary money to purchase weapons and uniforms. In November 1857, a company of the Negro militia, armed and uniformed, paraded through the streets of Boston. They were pelted with rocks and bags filled with flour by white groups lined up on the sidewalks. By the time they reached the Boston Common, the militiamen were being besieged from all sides. Finally, several of the black militiamen left the column and "charged bayonets on the rowdies, who fled like cowards before a desperate foe." The members of the company then marched down to their armory, turned in their equipment, and went home. This ended the first and last public parade of a Negro militia company in Boston before the Civil War.

During the campaign on the militia issue, William J. Watkins asked a pertinent question: "Why is it that we colored people are thus treated? In the days of the Revolution, our fathers stood side by side with your fathers, and perilled alike their lives for a common liberty. Yet now, when we petition for the right to be enrolled in the military companies of the State of Massachusetts, we are told that our complexion is 'unconstitutional.'" The same answer had been given to every other demand raised by blacks in the long battle for equality. Surveying that battle, Frederick Douglass conceded on the eve of the Civil War that compared with the efforts that went into the campaign, the results might seem slight. There was an occasional partial victory, as in California, where, although the right of Negroes to testify against white persons in court was not established until the Civil War, a few judges in San Francisco began in 1858 to receive black testimony. As a result several old Negro women were able to obtain justice against white men who had beaten them. But only in two states and one city were there real victories—three in Massachusetts (transportation, intermarriage, and education), one in Rhode Island (suffrage), and one in Rochester (education). "It will be a long time before we gain all our rights," Douglass wrote in 1848, in drafting "An Address to the Colored People of the United States." That, he was convinced, would come only with the deliverance of the millions held in slavery: "It is more than a mere figure of speech to say, that we are as a people, chained together. We are one people—one in general complexion, one in common degradation, one in popular estimation. As one rises, all must rise, and as one falls all must fall." For their own sake, as well as for the millions in bondage, free blacks had to take a leading role in the struggle to end slavery.

16

"A Firebell in the Night"

ANTISLAVERY AFTER THE WAR OF 1812

The Presbyterian General Assembly met in Philadelphia from May 18 to May 30, 1815, a time when Americans were congratulating each other over the triumphant end of the war against England and were getting down to the business of rebuilding trade, commerce, and the other economic activities suspended during the embargo and war years. The assembly was primarily concerned about taking advantage of the impending economic revival to secure funds for a theological seminary at Princeton, and the commissioners were in no mood to consider such disturbing issues as slavery.

But present at that Philadelphia meeting was a man representing the Lexington (Virginia) Presbytery who had other ideas. He was George Bourne, who had come from England only eleven years earlier and who had settled in Virginia as minister in a presbytery many of whose members were slaveowners. While others in the church ignored this, Bourne could not. He came to know what slavery was and found it abhorrent and totally at variance with every principle of conduct embodied in moral law. He refused to allow slaveholders in his own church and went to the 181st General Assembly prepared to raise the question as to whether members of the church who retained slaves could be Christians. When the chairman of the business committee, a Virginia neighbor of Bourne, refused to permit the question to be introduced, Bourne raised it from the floor and went on to describe the "horrors of slavery." He delivered a scorching indictment of men who held human beings of a different color in bondage and even included in his denunciation ministers and members of the church.

The assembly was unmoved, however, and contented itself with the innocuous recommendation to all members of the church to provide religious instruction, at least for the young slaves, in preparation for the day "when God in his providence may open a door for their emancipation." Denouncing the action of the

348

assembly as "deceptive and two-faced," Bourne threw caution to the winds, wrote a treatise against slavery, and then had it published in Philadelphia in 1816 in a limited edition under the title, *The Book and Slavery Irreconcilable*. In that work, Bourne condemned slavery as "an abomination in the sight of God," declaring that a rational being could never be property and that a legislature could never legalize slavery "without the most diabolical impiety." Slavery, he asserted, annulled "every principle of justice, decency, order, rectitude and religion." "The Gospel," Bourne continued, "unequivocally declares that to enslave a man is the highest kind of theft . . . to divest man of his rational characteristics is the most diabolical impiety . . . and to prolong human existence in agony, the mind bereft of consolation and the body needful of support, is a concatenation of crime indescribable." He concluded from all this that the slaveholder could not be "a genuine disciple" of Jesus Christ.

Little of this was new in antislavery literature in this country. What was new was the fact that Bourne dispensed entirely with the idea that American slavery was simply an evil foisted upon this country by the British and inherited from colonial days, and also with the idea that since slaves were ignorant and obviously unfit for freedom, the institution would have to be continued until blacks were fully civilized. Bourne denounced slavery as a personal, not an inherited, sin and one that required personal and immediate repentance and restitution. In short, he insisted that the sin of slavery could be expiated only by the immediate emancipation of its victims.

The publication of *The Book and Slavery Irreconcilable* struck the first important blow for unconditional and immediate emancipation. However, it was not until fifteen years later, when William Lloyd Garrison read Bourne's book and popularized its ideas in his *Liberator*, that the principle assumed a dominant importance in the antislavery struggle. Bourne's book became a major influence on Garrison's thought. "The more we read it," he said, "the higher does our admiration of its author rise." In 1816, when Bourne's book was published, not only was immediate emancipation far from the thoughts of the abolitionists but even the drive for gradual emancipation had lost its impetus in the South. In vain, antislavery southerners warned that God's judgment would come in the form of slave insurrections and urged that "*something must be done* to appease the kindling wrath of outraged humanity and violated justice, ere the fate of ancient Egypt or of modern St. Domingo shall be ours." Southerners refused to heed these warnings, and Southern antislavery societies fell into decline as their members retreated in the face of the bitter attacks that held them responsible for instigating the slaves to revolt.

The thesis that the South was well on its way to emancipating the slaves without the intervention of the militant Northern abolitionism of the late 1820s has little relationship to reality. This is not to say that antislavery did not continue to make itself felt to some extent in the South. George Bourne did advocate immediate emancipation in Virginia, and Charles Osborn, a Quaker, joined with several other Quakers early in 1815 to establish the Tennessee Society for Promoting the Manumission of Slaves, later called the Manumission Society of Tennessee. In August 1817, Osborn launched the earliest antislavery newspaper, the *Philanthropist,* in Tennessee, in which he urged the "irrevocable system of gradual but complete abolition of slavery." In 1816, James Jones, president of the Manumission Society of Tennessee, revealed a plan to attack slavery by persuading Congress to legislate against the interstate domestic slave trade as it had previously outlawed the international slave trade.

The pressure of opposition to their views forced nearly all antislavery advocates to emigrate from the South. Bourne felt this shortly after the publication of his antislavery treatise; he was suspended by the presbytery of Lexington, which brought him before the general assembly of the Presbyterian church "as a setter forth of strange and unacceptable doctrines, offensive to the churches of that region." In 1818, the action of the presbytery was sustained by the general assembly, which passed a resolution declaring "the Appeal of Mr. Bourne to be dismissed; and that the decision of the Presbytery of Lexington declaring him deposed from the Gospel ministry be, and it is hereby confirmed." Soon afterward, Bourne was forced to leave Virginia to escape the wrath of the slaveowners.

The departure of the antislavery adherents, especially the Quakers, from the South left only remnants of the forces opposed to slavery. Most of them retreated from their antislavery principles and concentrated instead on removing the Negro from American society, on the ground that the "degraded, inferior free blacks" could never be incorporated as citizens, a principle symbolized by the American Colonization Society.

The Southern emancipationists did spread their ideas to the regions of the West to which they emigrated. In the Quaker-dominated communities of eastern Ohio, there was a committed abolition movement, led by Charles Osborn and Benjamin Lundy and composed mainly of Southern antislavery Quakers who had emigrated to the Northwest. (Although born in New Jersey, Lundy, a Quaker, grew to hate slavery while working at the saddler's trade in Virginia.) This movement, organized in 1816 as the Union Humane Society, openly denounced slavery, advocated gradual emancipation, agitated for repeal of the black laws "and other legal impediments which obstruct people of colour in the enjoyment of civil rights," and opposed any schemes for colonizing freed blacks abroad. What was rare for the time was that the Union Humane Society recognized that race prejudice and slavery were related evils.

In 1818, the American Convention for Promoting the Abolition of Slavery, a loose federation of antislavery societies, which gathered annually in Philadelphia to exchange information, changed its name to the American Convention for the Abolition of Slavery and Improving the Condition of the African Race. That same year, the Union Humane Society applied for admission to the American Convention and, upon being accepted, participated in a vigorous debate on colonization. The UHS took the position that colonizationists were guilty of acute race prejudice and that their plan was basically a slaveholders' conspiracy to transport all free blacks from the United States. Its vigorous opposition helped influence the final decision of the 1818 Convention to oppose colonization.

But while the American Convention constituted a semblance of a national antislavery society, the only one in existence, and was, unlike many of the local antislavery societies, opposed to colonization, it was virtually lifeless. The high hopes that had buoyed the spirits of the movement that slavery would fade away had been proved false. On the contrary, as David Brion Davis notes in *The Problem of Slavery in the Age of Revolution, 1770–1823*, the "peculiar institution" had demonstrated remarkable vitality and resilience. The victory of gradual emancipation in the North had to be balanced by the vigorous resurgence of slavery throughout the South.

Emancipation was still the ultimate goal of the American Convention, but it did not establish any hard and fast rule as to how or when it should be obtained. "The best method is still a question," it reported. "We cannot expect a speedy accomplishment of that event." The gradualists who made up the American Convention believed in orderly change and reason, but they were unable to convince the slaveowners, who spurned the most cautious proposals for gradual emancipation. Lacking a focus as well as numbers, the antislavery movement was an ineffectual force. It had succeeded in keeping slavery out of the Old Northwest, but a generation of abolitionists had accomplished nothing in the South, and many had fallen by the wayside. "Those actively engaged in the cause of the oppressed Africans are very small," lamented the original abolitionist organization, the Pennsylvania Society, in an 1817 address to the American Convention.

THE MISSOURI CONTROVERSY

Just when antislavery seemed about to expire, an event temporarily breathed new life into abolitionism. In the years following the War of 1812, thousands of settlers moved into the trans-Mississippi West, and a large number went into the Missouri Territory, part of the vast territory known as Louisiana, which had been purchased in 1803 from the French government. In 1810, Missouri's population had been 20,845. But by 1820, there were 10,222 slaves in the Missouri Territory, reflecting the rise of the Cotton Kingdom. An attempt was made by a few Southern antislavery emigrants to prohibit the perpetuation of slavery in Missouri, but they failed to arouse any support.

With its population increasing so rapidly, Missouri was raised in 1816 to the highest order of territorial government, and in 1817 the citizens of the area began petitioning Congress for statehood. The House of Representatives began its consideration of the proposed Missouri enabling act in February 1819. On February 13, the bill was introduced, and the debate had hardly begun when Congressman James Tallmadge of New York threw a bombshell into the proceedings by moving to prohibit the future introduction of slaves into the state of Missouri and to provide that "all children born within the Said State, after the admission thereof into the Union, shall be free at the age of twenty-five years." The Tallmadge amendment was patterned on the laws for the gradual emancipation of slaves passed by the New York State legislature in 1799.

According to the *Annals of Congress*, "this motion gave rise to an interesting and pretty wide debate." In view of the ferocity of the speeches and the frequency with which threats of disunion and civil war were hurled back and forth, that observation ranks as one of the great understatements in American history. Congressman Thomas W. Cobb of Georgia spoke openly of the secession of the Southern states and accused Tallmadge of having "kindled a fire which all the waters of the ocean cannot put out, which seas of blood can only extinguish." Congressman Colston of Virginia accused Tallmadge of stirring up slave insurrections and went on to charge that any member who encouraged blacks to regard slavery as wrong was "no better than Arbuthnot nor Arbrister, and deserves no better fate." (Arbuthnot and Arbrister were British citizens whom Andrew Jackson had arrested in Florida for stirring up the Indians, including the blacks among them, against the Americans, and had been tried by court-martial and summarily executed.)

Not in the least intimidated, Tallmadge shouted back that if the southerners extended slavery over the Western empire, "you prepare for its [the Union's] dissolution." As he spoke, a coffle of slaves passed by the door of the capitol, and pointing to the unhappy group, he declared: "The extension of the evil must now be prevented or the occasion is irrevocably lost, and the evil can never be contracted."

On February 15, 1819, after fewer than two days of debate, the Committee of the Whole incorporated the Tallmadge amendment into the Missouri bill by a vote of seventy-nine to sixty-seven. The following day, the House passed each of the two clauses of the amendment, the vote in both cases being almost strictly sectional, with those for the proposal coming entirely from the North. On February 17, the bill was read for the third time and promptly passed.

In the Senate, the bill was referred to a committee in charge of a memorial from the Alabama territory, and that body struck out the Tallmadge amendment. The Senate, after a "long and animated debate," sent the bill back to the House in that amended form. The House, by a majority of two, refused to concur and returned the measure to the Senate, which would not retreat from its position. Since the House remained equally stubborn, the Fifteenth Congress adjourned with the Missouri question unsettled.

The struggle over the extension of slavery was not confined to Missouri. On February 17, 1819, a bill to create the Arkansas Territory out of the southern portion of Missouri was taken up in the Committee of the Whole. At the time, the area contained a population of more than 14,000, of whom 12,579 were white and 1,617 slave. In the Committee of the Whole, John W. Taylor of Saratoga County, New York, proposed an amendment similar to the Tallmadge amendment. It provided for the prohibition of the further introduction of slavery into the

Arkansas Territory and that all children born of slaves within the territory "shall be free, but may be held to servitude until the age of twenty-five years." When the Committee of the Whole rejected the amendment and reported the bill to the House for action, Taylor immediately reintroduced his amendment from the floor. After three days of debate, the House moved to a vote. The result was an eighty-eight to eighty-eight deadlock, which left it up to Henry Clay, Speaker of the House, to decide whether the Territory of Arkansas should be slave or free. Clay threw his vote in favor of slavery. The Arkansas bill was passed by the House without the Taylor amendment and was sent to the Senate for its concurrence. There, another attempt was made to prevent the further introduction of slavery within the territory, but this amendment was defeated, nineteen to fourteen. On March 2, 1819, President James Monroe signed into law the bill creating the Territory of Arkansas, without any restriction on the then or future existence of slavery.

In the nine months between the adjournment of the Fifteenth Congress and the opening of the Sixteenth Congress on December 6, 1819, the slavery question became a public issue on an entirely new level. State legislatures sent memorials to Congress urging it to prevent the extension of slavery into the trans-Mississippi country; public meetings were held throughout the North at which dozens of resolutions were adopted; and still more memorials were sent to Congress protesting the admission of Missouri as a slave state.

The antislavery forces suddenly came alive, and in several Northern cities, the disheartened abolitionists abandoned their gloom and arranged mass meetings to protest slavery in Missouri and its admission to the Union. A mass meeting in Providence, Rhode Island, called by the all-but-defunct Abolition Society, was typical. The meeting unanimously adopted a resolution declaring that the nation would be endangered by the further extension of slavery and voted to submit a memorial to Congress expressing its opposition to the introduction of slavery into any state thereafter admitted to the Union. Special committees of antislavery societies were established to correspond with each other and to coordinate action on the Missouri crisis. In the *Philanthropist*, Elisha Bates, a Virginia Quaker, who had replaced Charles Osborn as editor in 1818, helped coordinate this movement and kept up a steady barrage against the entrance of Missouri into the Union as a slave state. The antislavery paper also published antiadmission petitions to Congress, including those circulated by the Union Humane Society in Ohio, which demanded the proscription of slavery in the territories and the gradual abolition of slavery where it already existed.

For the first time, large audiences began to gather at meetings sponsored by antislavery societies, and people who up to then would not have been seen in the company of "fanatical abolitionists" not only attended such gatherings but also voted for resolutions and signed memorials drawn up by antislavery adherents, denouncing slavery as "a great political as well as moral evil," declaring that the national government ought to "prevent the extension of such an evil," and defending the right of Congress to forbid slavery in Missouri and the admission of a slave state from the new lands of the Louisiana Purchase. To be sure, at a number of the public meetings, it was made clear that the opposition to the extension of slavery into new states like Missouri was based not only on moral and political objections to slavery as an institution but also on the belief that the introduction of a black population was "fraught with the most fearful consequences"—meaning that it was the sort of people who were slaves that was being objected to rather than the fact that they were slaves. But in any case, opposition to the extension of slavery was being forcefully expressed.

When Congress assembled on December 8, 1819, the first steps were taken that later led to the Missouri Compromise. On opening day, both Missouri and the recently established Territory of Maine sought admission as states. On January 3, 1820, before action could be taken on admitting Missouri, the Maine bill passed the House and was sent to the Senate. There it was assigned to the Committee on the Judiciary, and when it reappeared, it was coupled with a clause to admit Missouri without restriction. On February 18, the Senate added a compromise rider to the effect that slavery should be excluded in all territory north of the line 36° and 30', with the exception of Missouri. The House voted down the Senate compromise clause, and when the Senate refused to concede, a Committee of Conference was appointed.

During the next three months, while the conference committee held sessions, Congress was the scene of stormy debates during which the legal, constitutional, moral, economic, and political aspects of slavery and its extension were discussed from every possible angle. By prohibiting slavery in Missouri, Northern congressmen emphasized, Congress could be asserting that in the future, a human being, whatever his color, as Joshua Cushman of Massachusetts put it, "shall feel the force of these self-evident truths—*that God created all man-kind equal, and endowed them with certain inalienable rights amongst which are 'life, liberty, and the pursuit of happiness.'*" If Congress did not act now, a number of Northern congressmen inquired, when would it act? "An opportunity is now presented," cried Arthur Livermore of New Hampshire, "if not to diminish, at least to prevent the growth of a sin which sits heavily on the soul of every one of us. By embracing this opportunity we may retrieve the national character and, in some degree, our own." Turning directly to the Southern members of Congress, Taylor of New York predicted that their appetite for more territory for slavery would never be satisfied, despite avowals that the institution was an evil:

You must have the Floridas. Your ambition rises. You covet Cuba, and obtain it. You stretch your arms to the other islands in the Gulf of Mexico, and they become yours. Are the millions of slaves inhabiting these countries, too, to be incorporated into the Union and represented in Congress? Are the freemen of the old States to become the slaves of the representatives of foreign slaves? The majority may be in your hands. You may have the power to pass such laws, but beware how you use it.

Clearly the question of political power derived from the three-fifths clause of the Constitution, under which five slaves were to be counted as equivalent to three free persons in representation in the House of Representatives, was a key factor in the opposition to the admission of Missouri as a slave state. Yet the southerners were enraged by the speeches of Senator Rufus King of New York, who, while emphasizing this point, vigorously attacked slavery itself, arguing that all laws imposing such a condition upon any human being were absolutely void, because contrary to the law of nature, which is the law of God, by which he makes his way known to me, and is paramount to all human control.''

John Quincy Adams noted in his diary that ''the great slave-holders of the House gnawed their lips and clenched their fists as they heard him.'' James Madison condemned King's ''inflammatory conduct,'' and one southerner wrote that the New York senator's language would ''sound the tocsin of freedom to every negro of the South, and we may live to see the tragical events of Santo Domingo repeated in our own land.'' Since King's speeches were printed in the press and widely circulated in pamphlet form by a New York City committee organized to oppose the further extension of slavery, southerners had reason to worry that they would get into the hands of slaves and free blacks. This is precisely what did happen.

Southern congressmen and senators hit back with lengthy speeches defending both slavery and their right to extend the institution and insisted that Congress could not deny the right. If it did, they warned, the Union's days were numbered. As for slavery's being in conflict with the Declaration of Independence, a point repeatedly emphasized by antislavery spokesmen in both Senate and House during the whole Missouri controversy, that document was nothing but ''a fanfaronade of metaphysical abstractions,'' ''merely abstract aphorisms'' emanating from the ''speculative philosophy'' of Jefferson's ''young and ardent mind,'' and had no standing in American law. In any case, slavery was the only suitable condition for blacks and a vast improvement over the kind of life they would have experienced had they remained in Africa. Hence, those who sought to end the institution were really the ''greatest enemies of the blacks.''

THE MISSOURI COMPROMISE

As the debates continued and invectives and threats continued to be flung about without restraint, John Quincy Adams wrote in his diary that ''the flame now raging throughout the Union . . . threatens its dissolution.'' He considered the Missouri controversy to be ''a title page to a great tragic volume.'' Thomas Jefferson, in retirement in Monticello, also viewed the struggle with alarm. He wrote to John Holmes, a congressman from Massachusetts, that for some time he had paid little attention to public affairs, ''confident that they were in good hands. . . . But this momentous question, like a fire bell in the night, awakened and filled me with terror. I considered it at once as the knell of the Union.'' To a fellow Virginian, he confided: ''In the gloomiest moment of the revolutionary war, I never had any apprehension equal to what I feel from this source.''

In this situation, the Northern members of Congress retreated and demanded only that the ''further introduction'' of slaves into Missouri be prohibited. In other words, they were willing to accept Missouri as a slave state in 1820, on condition only that there be a ban on the further importation of slaves. The South, however, refused to accept even this moderate proposal. With the aid of a handful of northerners, just sufficient to provide a majority in both houses of Congress, and with Clay as Speaker of the House playing the dominant role, the southerners gained the admission of Missouri without any restriction on slavery. By the Missouri Compromise, Maine entered the Union as a free state, and Missouri was admitted with its legislature being allowed to adopt a constitution that did not prohibit slavery in the state, on the condition that in all other areas of the Louisiana Purchase north of 36° 30' (Missouri's southern boundary) slavery was to be excluded.

But the Missouri question had still not been settled. In 1820, Missouri held a constitutional convention, and although the antislavery forces conducted a vigorous campaign to elect delegates who would vote to restrict further introduction of the ''odious system,'' the antirestrictionists were overwhelmingly victorious. The constitutional convention then drew up a constitution for Missouri (adopted on July 19, 1820), which first forbade the legislature to interfere with slavery and then ordered the body to frame laws that would prevent free blacks and mulattoes from settling in the state. Although more than one Northern state had regulations discriminating against free blacks and some had measures to keep them from entering their states, the opponents of slavery extension seized upon the antiblack clause in the Missouri constitution to reopen the fight to keep the state out of the Union. When the Sixteenth Congress convened for its second session, it found itself confronted with the Missouri question for the third time.

The Senate, dominated by southerners, voted to admit Missouri with the understanding that it was already a state and that the clause excluding free blacks could no more be considered by Congress than it could deal with similar clauses in other slave states. The House, on the other hand, held that the clause abridged the ''privileges and immunities'' of citizens of the United States, thereby violating the federal Constitution, and that until the clause was eliminated, Missouri could not enter the Union. The third Missouri debates did not last long. Congress agreed to admit Missouri on ''the fundamental condition'' that the clause in its constitution excluding free blacks from the state would ''never be construed to authorize the passage of any law discriminating against the citizens of another state.'' On August 10, 1821, the Missouri controversy officially came to an end when President Monroe proclaimed the admission of the state.

While the South was enraged to see slavery dealt with by outsiders and was unhappy that the institution had been barred from such a large area, it swallowed the settlement as the best it could obtain at the time. On the other hand, many abolitionists claimed that the Missouri Compromise was a victory for slavery. To criticism from their antislavery constituents, Northern congressmen who voted for the compromise responded that they had had no choice, even though they shared their constituents' distaste over the extension of slavery. Congress, they maintained, would never have agreed to the admission of Maine and Missouri with a restriction on the latter. In any event, they argued, it was likely that Missouri would soon abolish slavery of its own accord. This "likelihood" took almost half a century and a bloody Civil War to come to fruition.

For the moment, however, the first major slavery controversy was over. The compromise that settled the controversy was, as Thomas Jefferson remarked, "a reprieve only, not a final sentence."

THE CLOSED SOUTHERN MIND

The stimulus given by the Missouri controversy to the antislavery movement encouraged a number of abolitionists to renew their efforts. In the spring of 1820, Elihu Embree, a Tennessee Quaker, began publishing the *Emancipator* in which he demanded the end of slavery. He continued publication, amid a rising tide of Southern hostility, until his death in December 1821. Since no one in Tennessee was willing to risk continuing the paper, its publication ceased.

Benjamin Lundy believed that the Missouri controversy—by revealing that slavery, far from dying of its own accord, was actually growing with menacing vigor—had stimulated awareness of the problem and made many people receptive to antislavery ideas. Hence, he was encouraged to begin publication in January 1821 in Mount Pleasant, Ohio, of a new paper, *Genius of Universal Emancipation*. After only a few issues, it was moved to Greenville, Tennessee.

It soon became apparent, however, that on the subject of slavery the Southern mind was closed. In 1822, an agent for the *Philanthropist* reported that he found "such an objection in the minds of slaveholders to read anything that may cast a ray of light upon the *principle* of slavery" that it would be a waste of paper to send any more copies of the antislavery journal for circulation among them:

I believe some years ago there was an openness in the minds of the people, in which they saw the iniquity of slavery, but I believe since the discussion of the Missouri question in Congress, the prejudices of slaveholders have increased against the advocates of liberty, and perhaps the mind, has become darkened under the determination not to yield to the convictions of truth in the light afforded.

He saw no course other than to leave the slaveowners alone for the time being in the hope that they might become weary of their oppressive system, "and when their strength is exhausted, [they] will sit down in the cool of the day to rest and reflect. Then possibly the avenues to the mind may be again open for instruction." It was a forlorn hope. The agent's letter was published on April 20, 1822.

A few weeks later came the large-scale slave conspiracy in Charleston led by Denmark Vesey, and the minds of the slaveowners closed even more tightly.

As we have seen, Denmark Vesey had carefully laid the groundwork for a slave insurrection in Charleston. He was betrayed by informers, and the alerted authorities quickly rounded up the conspirators. Thirty-seven were hanged. Despite its failure, Vesey's conspiracy contributed considerably to the fear among whites of a general servile war. The *Charleston Times* branded blacks "the Jacobins of the country . . . the anarchists and the domestic enemy; the common enemy of civilized society, and the barbarians who would, if they could, become the destroyers of our race." Dr. George Logan, a prominent Charleston physician, wrote that "a more painful degree of anxiety has never before been experienced here. Our Legislature now in session will adopt every measure suited to the crisis." Although ample punitive legislation was passed, including a more rigorous slave code, Charleston never freed itself from its fear syndrome.

As they searched for the causes of the Vesey conspiracy, the whites blamed it singly or collectively on the Haitian revolution, the influence of free blacks and slave artisans, the indulgence of urban slaves by naive masters, the speeches in Congress on the Missouri question, and the antislavery societies. The last became a special target of attack. A Charleston businessman warned those who "preach up emancipation": "Let them ponder (think deeply about) on the deeds of darkness and misery that would have taken place had this plot even in part succeeded."

To an increasing number of Americans, however, there was an alternative to the constant fears of insurrectionary plots, and that was gradually to do away with the institution that created them. With this in mind, the Ohio General Assembly proposed in 1824 that the federal government, with the consent of the slaveholding states, should pass a law providing "that all children of persons now held in slavery, born after the passage of such law, should be free at the age of twenty-one years," on condition that they then consent to be transported abroad to a foreign colony. The expenses of the project were to be borne by all the states of the Union, "upon the principle that the evil of slavery was a national one." This proposal was then forwarded to Ohio's representatives in Congress, as well as to all the other states for their consideration.

Eight Northern states approved of the Ohio proposal. But in the slaveholding states, it was not only rejected but vehemently denounced, and nothing came of it.

NULLIFICATION AND THE SLAVERY ISSUE

In his *Prelude to Civil War*, in which he explores how the Vesey plot affected South Carolina and national politics during the 1820s and 1830s, William W. Freehling has pointed out that although the antislavery crusade remained "relatively undeveloped" and a "distant threat" in the 1820s, South Carolina politicians responded "hysterically" and delivered fire-eating harangues at any mention of abolition. He also notes that having experienced their first and longest economic depression in 1820, and then, two years later, the slave conspiracy of Denmark Vesey, South Carolinians were prepared to take a firm stand in defense of the "peculiar institution," even if it might mean civil war. The nullification controversy of the late 1820s and early 1830s is usually viewed as a policy dispute in which South Carolina insisted that it would use its full power to prevent the operation of the tariff acts of 1828 and 1832 within its boundaries— in other words, that it would seek to nullify the acts. To counter this threat, the Force Act of March 2, 1833, gave President Andrew Jackson the power to use the armed forces of the nation to collect duties, seize ships and cargoes when duties were not paid, and suppress combinations of persons obstructing the enforcement of national life. But the Force Act was not applied, and the nullification controversy was settled by a compromise tariff.

As Freehling sees it, the nullification controversy was a struggle not merely against protective tariffs as such but against forces that the nullifiers believed would lead ultimately to the abolition of slavery. The slaveowners of South Carolina viewed any increase in congressional power as opening the door to action against slavery. While other Southern states were not prepared to follow South Carolina down the road to nullification, partly because they possessed less concentrated slave populations and were therefore less tense about slave revolts and less worried about abolitionists, the South as a whole was prepared to defend slavery by every means, including civil war. Thus, although Georgia refused to join South Carolina, its governor told the legislature that Georgians had to be wary, since very soon, "the United States Government, discarding the mask, will openly lend itself to a combination of fanatics for the destruction of everything valuable in the Southern economy." He entreated southerners "to stand by your arms." And even while he was rejecting nullification as a constitutional right, John Randolph of Virginia was lamenting that the "slave interest . . . has the knife at its throat in the hands of fanatics and rogues and fools, and we *must* and *shall* and *will* defend ourselves."

This view that the development of nullification sentiment was the result of paranoiac fears of South Carolinians about slavery and the antislavery threat has come under attack as being highly exaggerated. What cannot be denied, however, is that slavery had become central to almost every issue of the period. With the Missouri debates, the Denmark Vesey conspiracy, and the nullification controversy, the slavery question had been pushed to the center of the American stage. The "firebell in the night"—Jefferson's famed description of the debates leading to the Missouri Compromise—was never again to be silent.

DECLINE OF ABOLITION SOCIETIES

While the Missouri debates had stirred the antislavery societies after their years of inactivity, it was only a temporary revival. By January 1822, the Union Humane Society was defunct, and other antislavery organizations were either dead or in decline. The weak and shadowy American Convention of delegates from abolition societies never regained either its zeal or its membership. At the 1828 gathering, the convention conceded that its member societies were discouraged by the slight progress achieved by the cause in the South but urged them to "continue to press forward with increased energy to the goal they have set before them, the complete and final abolition of slavery within the United States." But the most the convention could do to help them was to recommend that the societies disseminate information on the evils of slavery and the text of laws for gradual emancipation adopted by Northern states, in the hope that this would persuade Southern legislatures to follow suit. Evidently the rejection of the Ohio plan of 1824 for gradual emancipation had taught the American Convention nothing.

Disenchanted by the lethargy of the American Convention, Benjamin Lundy still persisted in keeping up the fight. In 1824, he moved the *Genius of Universal Emancipation* to Baltimore, and while he called for gradual rather than immediate emancipation and was preoccupied with schemes to colonize free blacks, he condemned both slavery and the slaveowners. To those who warned him against "impolitic" discussion, he thundered: "Ours is the cause of Justice, it is the Cause of Heaven. No earthly consideration should interfere with it." But most antislavery advocates of the 1820s were convinced that only moderation could win over the slaveholders. Moreover, most of them were always inhibited by the fear of the consequences of releasing "uncivilized Negroes" on the white community. Hence, as far as they were concerned, colonization of blacks offered the best, indeed the only, means "of ridding our country of the great curse of slavery." They therefore pinned their hopes on the efforts of the American Colonization Society to found a Negro colony in Liberia. Furthermore, their plans to end slavery gradually always depended on the cooperation of the South, which was never forthcoming.

Nor could it be expected to be. Slavery represented a property interest amounting to billions of dollars, covering the whole plantation system and numerous Northern industrial and commercial activities that rested upon servile labor. Small wonder, then, that so many antislavery figures hesitated to antagonize this powerful economic and political alliance and were content to mouth pious expressions in favor of gradual emancipation.

Weakened by internal dissensions—which were aggravated by the fact that some of its members continued to hold slaves—and by its repeated failures, the American Convention by 1829 was at an organizational ebb. Only seven societies were represented at that year's gathering, and only two of these were from the South.

DAVID WALKER'S REVOLUTIONARY *APPEAL*

Few black voices were heard amid the sporadic attacks on slavery during the 1820s. The existing abolitionist societies refused to admit Negro abolitionists to membership, and blacks did not have their own papers in which to express their views. Late in the 1820s, however, this situation was changed, and an entirely new dimension was added to the antislavery movement. The dominant tradition in the movement was for gradual emancipation; it not only opposed immediate emancipation but insisted that slaves must take no action to change their status, relying instead on the goodwill of God to free all bondsmen in time. The few black antislavery spokespersons who addressed themselves to the subject of slavery also tended to support these views.

Freedom's Journal marked a partial break with this tradition. Soon after it was launched in March 1827, the first black paper not only denounced slavery but called for immediate emancipation and unconditional freedom. When Benjamin Lundy refused to support the principle of immediate emancipation, *Freedom's Journal* commented: "We shall only be throwing dirt in other's eyes, if we talk of anything short of this. It is just one simple thing and is to be taken so, as much as a declaration of war." However, the paper did not advocate slave rebellion. The slave was urged to be patient and wait for the day of freedom, the inevitability of which was both certain and near at hand, since the American people were bound to see the glaring inconsistencies at the heart of their Christian democracy. Meanwhile, the *Journal* cautioned that, although it was the slave's right to be protected by law, it was also his duty "to submit himself to his own master, so long as the laws of this country make him a slave."

On July 4, 1829, in Boston's Park Street Church, the twenty-four-year-old William Lloyd Garrison, a native of Newburyport, Massachusetts, delivered the first of his public addresses against slavery. A disciple of Benjamin Lundy, he called for gradual abolition and urged support for the American Colonization Society, pleading for the establishment of auxiliary societies "in every state, county and town." At the same time, Garrison warned the Boston colonizationists, who made up his audience, that a failure to act against slavery would produce a catastrophic race war. The time to conquer the slave monster, he proclaimed, was when it was still in its infancy, for in time it would go forth "a gigantic cannibal" in search of white men's blood: "A cry of horror, a cry of revenge, will go up to heaven in the darkness of midnight and re-echo from every cloud. Blood will flow like water—the blood of guilty men, and of innocent women and children."

In that same city later in that same year, a pamphlet was published that gave substance to Garrison's dire warning. At one stroke, its publication broke with both the gradualist orientation of the antislavery movement and the opposition to revolutionary action by the slaves to break their chains. Its author was David Walker. He was born in Wilmington, North Carolina, in 1785, the son of a Negro slave man and a free black woman. Under the law of North Carolina, as of other slave states, he was free. But Walker left the South when he was thirty years old because, as he was to write: "If I remain in this bloody land I will not live long. As true as God reigns, I will be avenged for the sorrows which my people have suffered. This is not the place for me—no, no. I must leave this part of the country. . . . Go I must."

In 1825, Walker made his way to Boston, where he opened a store selling new and used clothing. He taught himself to read, married, took up residence in the heart of the city's black section, and became active in the Boston-based Massachusetts General Colored Association, an organization founded in 1826 to oppose slavery and the restrictions on the civil rights of free Negroes. In a speech before the association, Walker answered those who saw no need for such an organization:

Do not two hundred and eighty years of very intolerable sufferings teach us the actual necessity of a general union among us? Do we not know indeed the horrid dilemma into which we are, and from which we must exert ourselves to be extricated? Shall we keep slumbering on, with our arms completely folded up, exclaiming every now and then, against our miseries, yet never do the least thing to ameliorate our condition, or that of posterity?

When Walker learned that *Freedom's Journal* was to be published, he greeted the news enthusiastically and served as one of its two Boston agents, helping to build up its circulation. By 1828, his business was sufficiently prosperous to enable him to advertise regularly in *Freedom's Journal* and for some six months in the Boston *Columbian Sentinel*. He was, however, subject to police harassment, and in 1828, he was indicted (along with two other black clothing dealers) and tried before the Boston Municipal Court on the charge of receiving stolen goods. It was a transparent effort on the part of white clothing dealers to drive their black competitors out of business. Two of the blacks, including Walker, were acquitted, and the charges against the other were dropped. But the experience intensified Walker's dissatisfaction with the situation facing blacks, even in the supposedly more liberal atmosphere of Boston.

Meanwhile, Walker had been working on a tract, which he published at his own expense in September 1829 under the title: *Walker's Appeal, in Four Articles; together with a Preamble, to the Coloured Citizens of the World, but in Particular and Very Expressly to those of the United States of America*. More commonly known as *David Walker's Appeal*, the seventy-six-page pamphlet covered many subjects of interest to blacks, including the crucial and controversial issue of colonization, a condemnation of Thomas Jefferson for his disparaging remarks about blacks, the political, social, educational, and economic subjugation of free blacks in American society, and a plea to free blacks to work together to overcome the obstacles white racism placed in the path when they sought to elevate themselves. Walker heaped scorn upon Jefferson's argument that it was not their condition but nature that had produced "black inferiority." Calling blacks "the *most wretched, degraded* and abject set of beings that ever *lived* since the world began," he demonstrated through scientific observation, environmentalism, and comparative analysis that the wretched condition of the Negro was caused by the ignorance and debasement in which he was held. Walker pointed out that the black uprising in Saint-Domingue, leading to the establishment of Haiti, proved that "a grovelling servile and abject submission to the lash of tyrants . . . are not the natural elements of the blacks." He accused Jefferson and the rest of white America of hypocrisy. "Compare your own language," he wrote, referring to the Declaration of Independence, "with the cruelties and murders inflicted by your cruel and unmerciful fathers and your-selves on our fathers and on us—men who have never given your fathers or you the least provocation!!!!"

So devastating was the blow that Walker delivered to African colonization that the section entitled, "Our Wretchedness in Consequence of the Colonization Plan," was distributed separately among free blacks in the North. He pointed out that while the slaveholding party that headed the American Colonization Society had always been "oppressors and murderers" of black people, Bishop Richard Allen and other "men who have the fear of God, and the welfare of their brethren at heart," were entirely opposed to colonization "and advise us to stay where we are." Whose advice, then, should blacks take? Walker answered with another question: "Will any of us leave our homes and go to Africa?" He answered:

Let no man of us budge one step, and let slave-holders come to beat us from our country. America is more our country, than it is the whites—we have enriched it with our blood and tears. The greatest riches in all America have arisen from our *blood and tears:*—and will they drive us from our property and homes, which we have earned with our *blood*? They must look sharp or this very thing will bring swift destruction upon them. The Americans have got so fat on our blood and groans that they have almost forgotten the God of armies. . . . Surely, the Americans must think that we are brutes as some of them have represented us to be. They think that we do not feel for our brethren, whom they are murdering by the inches, but they are dreadfully deceived.

All this reflected the new militant spirit among Northern Negroes, but it was another part of the pamphlet that threw the slaveowners into a frenzy—not so much because he indicted the slaveholders and exposed crimes against the Negroes as because he sounded a call to armed resistance. Yet while Walker proclaimed hatred for the whites, he offered friendship and forgiveness for those whites who repudiated their role as oppressors and accepted the Negro as a brother. He warned Americans that blacks "must and shall be free" and asked the slaveowners if they wished to risk having the slaves take their freedom by force. "Will it not be dreadful for you?" What a happy country this would be "if the whites will listen"! Should the slaveowners fail to respond by ending slavery immediately, the slaves had only one course to follow: to begin a bloody insurrection against their masters. While Walker cautioned against such action until the way was clear and even though he himself was deeply religious, he rejected the idea of waiting for heaven to redeem the slaves from their "cruel oppressors and murderers" and urged the slaves to revolt:

It is not to be understood here that I mean for us to wait until God shall take us by the hair of our heads and drag us out of abject wretchedness and slavery, nor do I mean to convey the idea for us to wait until our enemies shall make preparations, and call us to seize their preparations, take it away from them, and put everything before us to death, in order to gain our freedom which God has given us.

Walker appealed to the slaves to act, and

if you commence, make sure work—do not trifle, for they will not trifle with you—they want us for their slaves and think nothing of murdering us in order to subject us to that wretched condition—therefore, if there is an *attempt* made by us, kill or be killed. Now, I ask you, had you not rather be killed than to be a slave to a tyrant, who takes the life of your mother, wife, and dear little children? Look upon your mother, wife, and children, and answer God Almighty: and believe this, that is it no more harm for you to kill a man, who is trying to kill you, than it is for you to take a drink of water when thirsty; in fact, the man who will stand still and let another murder him, is worse than an infidel, and, if he has common sense, ought not to be pitied.

"Every dog must have its day," Walker wrote and prophesied that "the American's is coming to an end." He stressed that as long as slavery existed in America, no black would ever be accepted on an equal basis with any white man. For this reason, every free Negro had to support the overthrow of slavery immediately and by force, if necessary, including insurrections by the slaves themselves. But Walker was under no illusion that his people would automatically revolt. On the contrary, he indicted the Negroes for "abject servility," but he was confident that they would assert their manhood and that docility could be transformed into its opposite by effective argument. Hence the *Appeal*.

Clearly as George W. Forbes, a leader of the Boston black community early in the twentieth century, noted in an unpublished paper on Walker, everything said or written by blacks on slavery up to that time was "a mere zephyr, to a West Indian hurricane" compared to what was written by the Boston clothes dealer and community leader. One might add that the same was true of everything that had been said or written by nearly all antislavery whites. Indeed, it is now more and more acknowledged that Walker's pamphlet marked the real transition from the gradualist, passive antislavery era to that of militant abolition. ("With the appearance of the *Appeal*, a militant antislavery crusade was born," wrote Charles M. Wiltse in the introduction to a 1965 edition of the pamphlet.) The best tribute to it came two decades after it was published when Henry Highland Garnet, himself a pioneer militant black abolitionist, reprinted it at his own expense, explaining in the preface:

The work is valuable, because it is among the first, and was actually the boldest and most direct appeal in behalf of freedom, which was made in the early part of the Anti-Slavery Reformation. When the history of the emancipation of the bondmen of America shall be written, whatever name shall be placed first on the list of heroes, that of the author of the Appeal will not be second.

Free blacks immediately bought up the first edition of Walker's *Appeal*; a second rapidly followed, and a third came off the press in March 1830. Copies were sent South by Walker and other blacks, and free black sailors (and a few white seamen) carried the *Appeal* with them for distribution among slaves and free blacks wherever they could manage it. The slaveowners' response was immediate; the *Appeal* was banned everywhere below the Mason-Dixon line, and the warning was issued that any slave found with it could be killed.

The governors of both Georgia and Virginia and the mayor of Savannah wrote to Boston's mayor, Harrison Gray Otis, demanding Walker's arrest. Otis made it clear that he shared the southerners' fears; he deplored "this attempt to throw firebrands into your country" and assured the South that not only all white citizens but even the "decent portion" of Boston's blacks disapproved of the pamphlet. However, since the publication violated no law, he could do nothing about it. The *New England Palladium* conceded that there was, unfortunately, no law on the statute books that could be used to arrest Walker, but it went on to urge: "One should be enacted without delay."

The *Boston Daily Courier* went to the trouble of sending a reporter to visit Walker, and it then informed its readers that the "seditious pamphlet . . . cannot have been the work of that man. There are too many allusions to names and incidents in ancient and classical history scattered through the pamphlet to admit of such a belief. It has the appearance of being the work of an educated and well-read writer, endeavoring to conceal his real character, by affecting the style of an illiterate man, and endeavoring to keep down to the supposed level of the negro." This was the first of several articles questioning whether a black man could have written so informative and well organized a pamphlet.

But the South had no doubt about its authorship, and Walker was given fair warning that he would be a marked man if he tried to return to the region. Rewards were posted for his capture—$1,000 if he were brought back dead and ten times that if he were returned alive. The slaveholders were not able to make an example of Walker, but in Charleston, Edward Smith, a white steward on the brig *Columbo* of Boston, was fined $1,000 and sentenced to one year in prison for distributing copies of the *Appeal* to Negroes of that city.

WALKER AND GARRISON

In August 1829, responding to an invitation from Benjamin Lundy to come to work as his assistant so as to enable him to issue the antislavery journal on a weekly rather than a monthly basis, William Lloyd Garrison went to work in Baltimore helping to publish the *Genius of Universal Emancipation*. Soon the two men were in disagreement with one another. Lundy's antislavery views had been nurtured in the Old Northwest and upper South, where his attacks on slavery and the slaveowners were blunt and vehement but were still moderated by the fact that he felt he had to win over the slaveowners. Garrison was more emphatic in his approach; he began to write articles for the *Genius* that Lundy felt were more suited to Boston than Baltimore.

While in Baltimore, Garrison saw for the first time the peculiar institution in operation, for though Baltimore's slave population was relatively small—about 4,000 in a total population of 80,000—the daily sight of the horrors of the system deeply influenced Garrison. A month before his arrival in Baltimore, he had declared that complete and immediate emancipation was "not desirable" and a "wild . . . vision." But by the time he left the city, he was convinced that the need for an immediate end to slavery was urgent.

Garrison's conversations with members of Baltimore's free black community, which in 1830 numbered almost 15,000, also persuaded him to alter his opinions on colonization. The view of Baltimore's free blacks that colonization was actually a device to strengthen slavery further through the expulsion of potentially subversive blacks made Garrison see that his support of the movement was incorrect, and by the time he left the city, he had reached the conclusion that colonization was both "impotent" and "wrong."

From April 17 to June 5, 1830, Garrison was in jail because of his inability to pay the fine and costs imposed by the court in a criminal suit for libel committed by him as coeditor of the *Genius of Universal Emancipation.* In the November 13, 1829, issue of the paper, Garrison had revealed that Francis Todd, a prosperous merchant in Newburyport, Massachusetts, had recently transported seventy-five slaves from Baltimore to New Orleans under shocking conditions. The following week, Garrison had provided further details and suggested that people like Todd should be "SENTENCED TO SOLITARY CONFINEMENT FOR LIFE" and should ultimately "occupy the lowest *depths of perdition.*" Early in January Todd instituted a civil suit for libel against Garrison. Garrison was found guilty, and the court imposed a fine of $50 and costs (approximately $100 in all), far more than Garrison was capable of paying. He was imprisoned and remained in jail for seven weeks until he was released by New York antislavery philanthropist Arthur Tappan, who sent him, by way of Benjamin Lundy, a contribution of $100.

Garrison was with the *Genius of Universal Emancipation* for nearly a year when David Walker's pamphlet arrived in the mail. Although he was increasingly militant in his editorials in the *Genius* (which appeared under his own byline), even Garrison was astounded by the language of Walker's pamphlet. Both he and Lundy decided not to make any reference to it in the paper. However, Walker's vivid description of the slave's plight and his call for slave revolution continued to trouble Garrison, and when the South started to make a real issue of Walker's *Appeal,* he decided to comment on it. Reviewing the *Appeal* in the *Genius,* he began: "We have had this pamphlet on our table for some time past, and are not surprised by its effect upon our sensitive Southern brethren. It is written by a colored Bostonian and breathes the most impassioned and determined spirit." But he deplored its circulation, calling the pamphlet "a most injudicious publication," while conceding its author's "bravery and intelligence."

Walker's *Appeal* nevertheless influenced the tone of Garrison's editorials, which became more and more vehement in their attack on slavery and the slaveowners. Walker's call for an immediate end to slavery and his bitter denunciation of colonization also influenced Garrison's thinking.

On June 28, 1830, just three months short of his forty-fifth birthday, David Walker died suddenly (and to many blacks mysteriously) in Boston. Whether his death was caused by poison, as has frequently been charged, or due to natural causes, Walker's influence continued from beyond the grave. At an anniversary dinner attended by Boston's leading blacks in the fall of 1830, one of the spokespersons, Domingo Williams, offered a toast to David Walker and his *Appeal* and predicted that it would continue to advance freedom's cause until slavery was abolished.

At about the time of David Walker's death, William Lloyd Garrison decided to leave Baltimore. He had abandoned the path of gradualism and colonization, and he departed for Boston to plan the launching of a new journalistic venture of his own in which he would advance his new antislavery principles. In the first issue of this paper, which he called the *Liberator*, Garrison deprecated the "spirit" of Walker's pamphlet but admitted its power and influence on his thinking, calling it "one of the most remarkable productions of the age."

17

The Proslavery Argument

Perhaps no other source contributed more to racism in the United States in the three decades preceding the Civil War than did the Southern defenders of slavery. The beginnings of the nineteenth century witnessed the birth of John C. Calhoun's generation of southerners. They devoted themselves to bringing about the acceptance of as virulent a doctrine of racism as the world has known. The earlier generation of Thomas Jefferson had recognized the inconsistency between their slaveholding and the principles of the Declaration of Independence. Consequently, not a few of them, at least in theory, condemned slavery as an institution. Their successors among Southern political thinkers were also aware of this inconsistency, but they rejected the egalitarian political theory of the Enlightenment, in which society was viewed as a partnership of equals, and formulated a new one, based on the idea of inequality. As George M. Fredrickson points out, antebellum racial thought permitted white southerners to enjoy the ideals of the American Revolution while denying their applicability to the inferior blacks.

These racist ideas were not without precedent. The traditional belief is that the formulation of the proslavery argument, with all its racist paraphernalia, was a reaction to the rise of the new antislavery movement in the 1830s, led by William Lloyd Garrison. Actually, however, that period produced no sudden change in the attitude of the planter class. All that happened was a change in tactics from apologizing for a system considered evil in the abstract to defending it as a positive good. As I pointed out in volume 1, nearly all of the elements of the proslavery argument of the 1830s were present in Thomas Cooper's *Essay on the Constitution of the United States and the Questions That Have Arisen under It*, which was published in 1826. But where, before 1830, there had been only a trickle, now there was a flood.

Kenneth M. Stampp points out that the first challenge to the slaveowners, "forcing them to take a positive stand in the defense of slavery," came not from the North but from within the South. He cites *A Review of Debates in the*

Virginia Legislature of 1831 and 1832 by Thomas R. Dew, a professor of political economy at William and Mary College. Dew's expressed purpose in publishing the pamphlet defending slavery was to fight the abolitionists within his own state who had "opened this delicate question in a careless manner in the legislature" and almost brought about a vote in favor of abolition.

The Northern abolitionists were the targets of the next proslavery statement. In 1835, in a message to the South Carolina legislature demanding the outlawing of the abolitionists by Northern legislatures, Governor George McDuffie expressed the theory that slavery was a positive good. Only slavery, he argued, could keep the menial classes in their proper place and do away with the need for centralized government, despotic rulers, and orders of nobility, all of which were inimical to republican liberty. "Domestic slavery," he reasoned, "instead of being a political evil, is the cornerstone of our republican edifice."

A SCHOOL FOR "BARBARIANS"

Champions of the "positive good" theory defended the economic advantages of slavery, claiming that it transformed ignorant and inferior African savages into productive workers. "There is nothing but slavery which can destroy the habits of indolence and sloth, and eradicate the character of improvidence and carelessness, which mark the independent savage," Thomas R. Dew argued. Albert Taylor Bledsoe picked up the argument, and, after sketching the horrors of life in Africa, concluded that "no fact is plainer than that the blacks have been improved by their servitude in this country. We cannot possibly conceive indeed, how Divine Providence could have placed them in a better school of correction." William J. Grayson of South Carolina versified the same argument:

> Instructed thus, and in the only school
> Barbarians ever know—a master's rule,
> The negro learns each civilising art
> That softens and subdues the savage heart,
> Assumes the tone of those with whom he lives,
> Acquires the habit that refinement gives,
> And slowly learns, but surely, while a slave,
> The lessons that his country never gave. . . .
> No better mode can human wits discern,
> No happier system wealth or virtue find,
> To tame and elevate the Negro mind.

All proslavery writers argued that slavery was more than merely an economic system; it was primarily a social and humanitarian agency that turned a "wild and savage race of people into useful human beings." "Why are they better than their brethren in Africa?" asked Jefferson Davis. He answered: "Because they have passed through the school of slavery in the United States." It was the female slaves, moreover, who benefited most. Among "African savages," women were degraded. Slavery in the United States changed this:

Her faculties are developed; her gentle and softening influence is seen and felt; she assumes the high station for which nature has designed her, and happy in the hallowed affections of her own bosom, unweariedly exerted these powers so well adapted to the task of humanizing and blessing others.

THE PSEUDOSCIENTIFIC ARGUMENT

Although this phase of the proslavery argument indicated a belief in the ability of environment to bring about changes in a race, the Southern defenders of slavery really believed that this was unlikely to occur. During the antebellum period, the doctrine of Negro inferiority, already fixed in the American ideology as early as the seventeenth century, was dressed up in pseudoscientific garb and elevated to the position of a principal argument justifying slavery. "The Negro races stand at the lowest point in the scale of human beings, and we know no moral or physical agencies which can redeem them from their degradation," insisted Dr. Josiah Nott, an Alabama naturalist and the South's leading ethnologist, in 1851. "It is clear that they are incapable of self-government and that any attempt to improve their condition is warring against an immutable law of nature." Nott went even further in denigrating the Negro, writing that

the negro is a totally distinct and inferior animal and species of animal from the Caucasian; . . the negro is the connecting link between man and the brute creation; . . . the negro is intended by nature for a similar dependence upon the Caucasian man, in which only the ox, the ass, and the horse fulfill the intent of their creation.

The pseudoscientific justification of slavery argued that the races differed in tone, muscle, and in the proportionate size of the brain. The Negro's brain, it was claimed, was lighter in relation to his weight; his skin had an extra quantity of pigment; his vocal organs were incapable of pronouncing the white folks' language; and he had an animal odor. All this proved his inferiority. Slavery's boldest apologist, publicist J.D.B. DeBow, argued that "the physical differences between the two races" were so great "as to make what is wholesome and beneficial for the white man, as liberty, republic and free institutions, etc., not only unsuitable to the negro race, but actually poisonous to its happiness." It was therefore only fitting that he should be taken care of by white people, and slavery was the means by which this could be done. "It was a duty slaveowners owed to the civilized world," a duty, moreover, ordained by God himself. In the *Bible Defense of Slavery*, Reverend John Priest wrote: "The fact of their being created with a lower order of intellectuality than either of the other races, is evidence of the preordination of their fate as slaves on the earth, as no one but God could have done and determined this thing." And in *Slavery Ordained of God*, F. A. Ross wrote that the very enslavement of the Negro by the whites was proof itself that it was "divinely foreordained." James Henry Hammond concluded his proslavery defense on this note:

I think, then, I may selfly conclude and I firmly believe, that American slavery is not only not a sin, but especially commanded by God through Moses, and approved by Christ through his Apostles, and here I might close its defence, for what God ordains and Christ sanctifies, should surely command the respect and toleration of man.

Proslavery writers argued that law, custom, and the social pressure of the community provided the slaves with protection from any abuse of power. But they also admitted that there were times when these mechanisms might rely too heavily on the goodwill of the masters for their proper operation. Hence, they advanced the further argument that the economic interests of the master would themselves prevent the abuse of slaves. After all, masters would not kill, maim, overwork, or otherwise mistreat their slaves because to do so would be against their own self-interest. William John Grayson contended that slavery "is the only condition of society in which their [employers' and workers'] interests are combined and not in conflict." "Every plantation," John C. Calhoun wrote, "is a little community, with the master at its head, who concentrates in himself the united interests of capital and labor, of which he is the common representative."

Throughout this proslavery ideology, slaves were pictured as dependent parts of the master's family. The emphasis was upon the obligations of the master and the protections that such a relationship afforded to slaves. The slaves became integrated into the master's family, and the responsibility for providing for their welfare devolved upon him. The children, the aged, the sick, the disabled, and the unruly, were all the objects of his care. Cruelty was inadmissible. In short, the proslavery writers resolved the problem of any possible abuse of power in slavery by denying the presence of any conflicting interests between master and slaves.

And, the argument went on, the fact that the slaves were thoroughly contented with their lot proved conclusively that these various mechanisms actually operated to protect them. "There are few people," wrote William Gilmore Simms, "so very well satisfied with their condition as the negroes—so happy of mood, . . . and so generally healthy and cheerful." Another proslavery writer exclaimed: "There are few slaves we believe in the Southern country who would change their present condition, which is one of dependence, for all the advantages which freedom would bring."

And why should they? Only those blinded by abolitionist propaganda could fail to see that the slaves were happy because they were relieved of all responsibility for the care of both themselves and their offspring. From this point, it was no problem for the proslavery argument to advance to the proposition that slavery—properly defined—was not in fact "peculiar" to the South but rather a fundamental feature of the system of labor in states north of the Mason and Dixon line as well. The only difference lay in the treatment of the worker, and in this respect, the slave in the South was infinitely better off.

CHATTEL SLAVERY AND WAGE SLAVERY

In a powerful speech delivered in the United States Senate in 1850, John C. Calhoun put forth the assertion that slavery was not an evil but "a good—a positive good" and that southerners should no longer apologize for it. In every civilized society, he argued, the bearers of culture must live upon the labor of others. Inequality is indispensable to progress; all that differ are the modes of exploitation. The person who worked for wages, he contended, was more severely exploited than a chattel laborer. Moreover, in times of sickness, unemployment, and old age, he was committed to the mercies of either the streets or an almshouse. On the other hand, the slave not only suffered less exploitation for his labor but was the recipient of solicitous attention in sickness and old age. "Compare his condition," exclaimed Calhoun, "with the tenants of poorhouses in the more civilized portions of Europe—look at the sick and the old and infirm slave on the one hand, in the midst of his family and friends under the kind superintending care of his master and mistress, and compare it with the forlorn and wretched condition of the pauper in the poorhouse."

But it was George Fitzhugh of Virginia who most vigorously and consistently proclaimed the moral superiority of chattel slavery over wage slavery. In his essays published as *Sociology for the South* (1854) and *Cannibals All! or Slaves Without Masters* (1857), Fitzhugh claimed that slavery was a universal tendency and that plantation slavery was more humane than the industrial conscription of the supposedly "free" labor market. What Fitzhugh called "the White Slave Trade" (by which he meant the economic order of industrial England and the Northern United States) was, in his opinion, "far more cruel than the Black Slave Trade, because it exacts more of the slaves, and neither protects nor governs them."

Free society, Fitzhugh maintained, had failed. Free laborers were essentially slaves without the rights, privileges, or advantages of domestic slaves. The North was an oppressive society, an example of exploitative capitalism; the South had a more economically humane society. Did not modern industrial society, Fitzhugh asked, boast that the profits of free labor were greater than those extracted from slave labor? And didn't this mean that the employer of free labor paid less, directly or indirectly, to his employees? The so-called freedom of white workers was illusory. They were obliged to begin work as children; they were discarded when business was slack or when sickness, disability, or old age overtook them:

Shelterless, naked, and hungry, he the free worker is exposed to the bleak winds, the cold rains, and hot sun of heaven, with none that loves him, none that cares for him. His employer hates him because he asks high wages or joins strikes; his fellow laborer hates him because he competes with him for employment.

In contrast:

The negro slaves of the South are the happiest, and, in some ways, the freest people in the world. The children and the aged and infirm work not at all, and yet have all the comforts and necessaries of life provided for them. They love liberty, because they are oppressed neither by care nor labor.

The same comparison, and again emphatically in favor of the South, was drawn in William J. Grayson's poem, *The Hireling and the Slave*. In Grayson's idyllic picture, the South was portrayed as a contented region. The plantation slave was fed, clothed, and housed from the cradle to the grave. The "hireling" of Grayson's title, on the other hand, although paid wages, was truly a slave in desperate straits. Wage slavery ("Hirelingism") was a brutal system that forced men, women, and children into ill-paying, hopeless drudgery. "The most wretched feature in hireling labor," Grayson argued in his introduction, "is the isolated miserable creature who has no home, no work, no food, and in whom no one is particularly interested." But under Southern slavery, "there is no such thing . . . as a laborer for whom nobody cares or provides."

The lot of the hireling was insecurity, starvation, disease, and war. From these evils the slave was entirely free:

> And yet the life, so unassailed by care,
> So blessed with moderate work, with ample fare,
> With all the good the starving pauper needs,
> The happier slave on each plantation leads,
> Safe from harassing doubts and annual fears,
> He dreads no famine in unfruitful years;
> If harvest fail from inauspicious skies,
> The master's providence his food supplies;
> No paupers perish here for want of bread,
> Or lingering live, by foreign bounty fed.

In short, on Grayson's Southern plantation, "The slave escapes the perils of the poor."

The defense of slavery through a comparison between chattel slavery and wage slavery, especially as expounded by George Fitzhugh, led to an interesting conclusion, which went somewhat as follows: The proper organization of the work force was a task of immense and alarming urgency for the modern world. Under industrial capitalism, modern production techniques necessitated a submissive work force. Yet workers' conditions were so harsh that social harmony was being replaced by class conflict. The South had solved the problem through plantation slavery, in which social harmony predominated. In doing so, it had set a pattern for others to imitate. The propertied classes of the North and South had basically the same interests, and any attack upon existing labor relations in either section was an attack on both. In an article entitled "The Conservative Principle; or, Social Evils and Their Remedies," Fitzhugh wrote: "The greatest objection to confining the defence of slavery to the negro and giving up the general principle is that it cuts off conservatives of the South from alliance with conservatives of the North."

NORTHERN ECHOES

The basic purpose behind the various justifications of chattel slavery was to obscure the reality of plantation slavery in the era of the Cotton Kingdom. Yet it would be a mistake to regard the proslavery argument as having been advanced exclusively by Southerners. The views of Dr. Josiah Nott were paralleled by those of Louis Agassiz, a Harvard naturalist whose prestige and authority as dean of the American school of anthropology lent respectability to the pseudoscientific concept of the biological inferiority of the Negro. "The brain of the negro," Agassiz observed, "is that of the imperfect brain of a seven month's infant in the womb of the white." Therefore it was folly to talk of equality for the Negro. In contrast to those who saw promise and great value in many of the Negro characteristics, Agassiz, who had reviewed the history of the Negro in Africa and in the Western Hemisphere, concluded that he was "indolent, playful, sensual, imitative, subservient, good-natured, versatile, unsteady in . . . purpose, devoted, and affectionate."

The anthropolitical theory of Nott and Agassiz was in some ways an extension of *Crania Americana* by Dr. Samuel G. Morton of Philadelphia, which was published in 1839 and achieved immediate popularity. This book posited that different races displayed different head shapes and that cranial capacity and conformation, like color, were distinctive racial characteristics. According to Morton's theory, there were five races, each with its subfamilies, and they ranked in order of their cranial capacity as follows: Caucasian, Mongolian, Malayan, American (Indian), and Ethiopian. The book described the "chief physical and moral characteristics of each race." Then in 1844, Morton published his *Crania Aegyptiaca*, which portrayed what he called the great age of the races and noted that slavery was among the earliest of the social institutions of Egypt. The social position of Negroes had been the same in Egypt as it was to later become in the nineteenth century—that of servants and slaves—and this followed inevitably from their lower intelligence, which in turn was reflected in their cranial capacity.

There were also those in the North who not only accepted the "positive good" argument of the Southern defenders of slavery but advanced their own version of the thesis. William Gouge, a Philadelphia editor and economist, conceded that "the want of liberty is a great drawback in happiness" but quickly added that "the slave is free from care. He knows that when he grows old or becomes infirm, his master is bound to provide for his wants." Orestes Brownson, the New England intellectual, was convinced that Southern slavery had elevated, not degraded, the Negro. In a reply to a French author's criticism of American slavery, James Fenimore Cooper, the major literary figure in America of the 1830s, assured the critic that he had seen women "performing offices in France, in the polished city of Paris itself, far more laborious and onerous" than any he had ever witnessed among Negro women in America. "They are provided for in their age," Cooper stressed, "and are never seen crowding the approach to the altars, objects of misery and disgust, imploring alms and exhibiting their ailings and their wants." Charles Edwards Lester, a New York abolitionist, wrote at length after a visit to England to prove that Britain's "white wage slaves" were exploited far worse than the chattel slaves of the South. After visiting the South, James K. Paulding, a New Yorker who served as secretary of the navy in the Martin Van Buren administration, wrote in praise of the "peculiar institution":

All those who have visited the states in which slavery prevails, whatever may have been their previous impressions of the horrors of that condition, must have been struck with the uniform hilarity and cheerfulness which prevails among blacks. . . . In the meadows and harvest fields they lighten their labors by songs, the measures of which accord with the stroke of the cradle and scythe; and in whatever enjoyment they may be associated, they are always joking, quizzing, or bantering each other. The children enjoy a life of perfect ease. . . . The parents being freed from all anxiety or exertion for the present or future support of their offspring, are never beset by the gnawing cares of the free white man, whose whole life is one continuous effort to provide for himself and his children. The aged and infirm are also taken care of by the master. . . . None of them ever become wretched paupers . . . ; and if a philanthropist were to visit their quarters during one of their holy days, he might behold a picture of careless, thoughtless hilarity, which would neutralize much of his horror of that state, which in every age and nation of the world has been the lot of millions of human beings, of all shades and colours.

A similar view was expressed by Calvin Colton, another Northern exponent of the proslavery argument, who wrote: "It is commonly reported and believed, by disinterested visitants to the slave states of the Union, that, from all appearances, the slaves, as a body, are the happiest in the world." A native of Massachusetts, graduate of Yale College and Andover Theological Seminary, Presbyterian minister, and journalist, Colton was the author of numerous books and pamphlets that shared the Southern view of the Negro as infinitely inferior and best suited for slavery. While slavery was not without its "evil aspects," the institution did provide for humane treatment of a people so limited in innate ability as to be unfit for "freedom in its widest scope."

A number of northerners, even though they themselves did not approve of slavery, echoed the proslavery argument that chattel slavery was vastly superior for the worker to wage slavery, and that of the two, the wage system was a worse form of oppression. Seth Luther, the foremost labor agitator in the Jacksonian era, asserted that children born in Southern slavery did not work one-half the hours or perform one-quarter of the labor that white children did in the cotton mills of Massachusetts. George Henry Evans, editor of three labor papers published in New York City—the *Daily Sentinel,* the *Man,* and the *Working Man's Advocate*—wrote that there was more real suffering among the white workers of the North than among the slaves of the South. The poor Negro, he maintained, led the life of a farm horse, while the poor white worker, like a horse kept in a livery stable, was worked by everybody and cared for by nobody. Furthermore, the poor Negro had a master both in sickness and in health, while the poor white worker was a slave as long as he was able to toil and a pauper when he could toil no more. To free the Negro people for wage slavery would be a great disadvantage for them, since they would be exchanging their "surety of support in sickness and old age" for poverty and unemployment. All the real slaves in the United States insisted Theophilus Fiske, a Boston labor editor, had *"pale faces."*

It is thus clear that the new antislavery movement emerged and grew at a critical time in the struggle over slavery. Cotton was king, and every Southern institution—the schools, churches, and economic agencies—paid homage to the new monarch whose throne rested on the labor of millions of enslaved human beings. The inferiority of the Negro was "scientifically proved" a priori. The southerners devised and northerners borrowed the "positive good" theory, which proclaimed that slave labor was essential to the development and progress of the nation; that the Negro was destined, by all evidence, to be kept in a subordinate position; that slavery lifted a whole race of heathens to a Christian status and, in the process, civilized the barbarians and improved the white people because it afforded them leisure time for the development of culture and the arts; and that the peculiar institution had distinct advantages for the slaves, who were better fed, better clothed, and happier than either the free blacks or white workers in the North and England. In short, slavery was not only the logical but also the best possible institution for this "inferior" race of people.

18

American Historians and the Abolitionists

TRADITIONAL INTERPRETATION OF ABOLITIONISTS

It is difficult to find a more widely misunderstood and misrepresented group of radicals and reformers in American history than the "new abolitionists." (As used here, the term *new abolitionist* refers to ones who worked outspokenly for the immediate, complete, and uncompensated liberation of all American slaves.) In their day, these men and women were called "rapacious . . . misguided fanatics," "irresponsible revolutionaries," "nigger-lovers," "amalgamationists," "reckless incendiaries," and "dreaming philanthropists." It is true that they enjoyed a brief popularity that they rarely achieved thereafter in the writings of nationalist historians after the Civil War. But by the 1930s and 1940s, they were again being condemned—this time by historians, no less—as "religious fanatics," "zealots," "hotheads," "seditionists," "rabble-rousers," "madmen," "malcontents," "neurotics," "amalgamationists," agitators who were "full of humanitarian gabble." In the single work, *Lincoln and the Radicals*, T. Harry Williams described the abolitionists as "radical . . . zealous . . . fiery . . . scornful . . . revolutionary . . . [imbued by] a spirit of fanaticism . . . narrowly sectional . . . bitter . . . sputtering . . . fanatical . . . impractical . . . extreme."

In most historical works, the abolitionists were accused of lurid indictments that exaggerated the cruelties of slavery; of destroying a promising Southern antislavery movement and with it the chance for a peaceful transition from slavery to freedom; of launching reckless attacks against the slave system while offering no constructive program for its eradication; of being driven in their crusade by a fanatical hatred of the South; of being more concerned with their own desire for personal salvation than with the plight of the slave; of hypocrisy in urging a supposedly humanitarian crusade for the slave while doing nothing about the wretched conditions of the free Negro and the exploited white worker;

and above all, of having, through their demagogy, brought on a needless war that cost half a million American lives. In their two-volume history, *The Growth of the American Republic*, Samuel Eliot Morison and Henry Steele Commager condemned the abolitionists for having "closed every avenue to emancipation save Civil War. . . . Abolition came in spite of the Abolitionists rather than because of them, and in the worst way." In his work, *The Coming of the Civil War*, Avery Craven blames the abolitionists for fostering such hatred of the South that compromise became impossible and the Civil War inevitable. In fact, he maintains, had it not been for the abolitionists' agitation, slavery probably would have died peacefully before the end of the century.

Both in their own day and in the writings of latter-day historians, abolitionists were accused of failing to understand the historical process, oversimplifying human motivations, and ignoring the realities of institutional entrenchment. Southerners, these critics asserted, were not sinners, as the abolitionists claimed, but rather good men and women, caught in a difficult situation. They insisted that many Southern slaveholders were decent people who secretly regretted the deep injustices of slavery and treated their own slaves well. These good men were simply the tragic victims of a cruel and unjust fate. Furthermore, slavery was not nearly as bad as the abolitionists painted it. Then, too, many of the abolitionists were portrayed as equivocating when they were faced with the question of racial equality and of doing nothing to help Negroes economically while avoiding them socially. On this score alone, the slaveowners were said to be more humane in their approach to the blacks than the abolitionists.

Some scholars, in their attempt to discover why certain Americans embarked on an antislavery crusade in the 1830s, have attempted to probe the abolitionists' psyches and have satisfied themselves that their concern for the slave flowed from a decline in their own class status and, further, that they used their self-sacrificing commitment to the movement in order to expiate their own feelings of guilt. David Donald, for example, analyzed them as a displaced, socially and psychologically frustrated New England Federalist elite. In a similar vein, Stanley Elkins depicted them as intellectuals whose ideas had become "anti-institutionalized, individualized, abstract, and charged with guilt"—a guilt that became "unstable, hard to control, [and] often destructive." In Elkins' judgment, abolitionists of all descriptions were guilt-conscious, moral absolutists, blind to the functioning of institutions and hostile to the use of constructive political power. Elkins even offered what he called a "catalogue of preliminaries—a series of separate short-term reforms rather than root-and-branch abolition," which might have gradually achieved emancipation and averted the needless Civil War.

While not sharing Elkins' distaste for the antislavery men and women, John L. Thomas, David Brion Davis, and Ronald Walters found them guilty of anti-institutionalism. Hazel Wolf pictured them as wallowing in self-pity and glorying in their persecution in a manner typical of martyrdom. Even William H. Pease and Jane H. Pease, who represented a break from the traditional view of the antislavery crusaders, maintained that "many" of them "coveted to become martyrs."

THE TRADITIONAL VIEW OF WILLIAM LLOYD GARRISON

Wendell Phillips once remarked that William Lloyd Garrison's own contemporaries had heard him "styled a mere fanatic so long" that they had found it "impossible to judge him fairly." Despite a brief period of general admiration for Garrison following the Civil War, this view of him continued. Indeed, whatever attacks have been leveled against abolitionists in general in the writings of many American historians have been mild compared to the special opprobrium reserved for Garrison. (Two others who have shared this dubious distinction in historiography have been Charles Sumner and John Brown. Sumner has been portrayed as "doctrinaire," "fanatical," and "rabid," and John Brown was considered either a "madman" or a "fanatic," with the major emphasis placed on his "insanity.") Allan Nevins, in *Ordeal of the Union*, described Garrison as having an "arid, colorless, and narrow mind," and emphasized his intolerance, fanaticism, and unreasonableness, claiming that he turned "a stony ear" "to those who argued the danger to both races of loosing large numbers of slaves without preparation." Other historians have accused Garrison of having deliberately provoked mob attacks upon himself and his followers in order to win the support of responsible citizens.

For more than a generation, it has been the standard practice, even among proabolitionist historians, to minimize Garrison's importance and to deny his central role in the crusade against slavery. Dwight L. Dumond, for example, although an ardent champion of abolitionists as a group, denigrated Garrison as "insufferably arrogant" and "a man of distinctly narrow limitations" among the giants of the antislavery movement—one who "disrupted and demoralized the crusade" with his "romantic non-resistance" and his rejection of church and government alike as proslavery institutions.

Dumond was a student of Ulrich B. Phillips, the proslavery historian of slavery, in the latter's seminar at the University of Michigan. Gilbert Hobbes Barnes, another student of Phillips, regarded Garrison and his followers as "deadweights" exercising a negligible influence in the antislavery struggle. Barnes questioned the vitality of the New England antislavery movement, where Garrison's influence was greatest, and attributed this so-called legend to the fact that nearly all antislavery histories and biographies have been written by people from New England. Barnes, on the other hand, maintained that the major antislavery impulse originated in western New York in the 1820s, in the midst of a great religious revival, and spread into the Midwest. The real giant of the crusade, according to Barnes, was not Garrison in New England but Theodore D. Weld in the West.

In two biographies of Garrison published separately in 1963, John L. Thomas and Walter M. Merrill made him out to be both narrow and doctrinaire. Garrison and his circle, Thomas argued, were Christian anarchists, whose hatred of institutions was "deeper even than their aversion to slavery" and whose complete rejection of all institutions brought them close "to the brink of insanity." In Thomas' opinion, Garrison's greatest weakness lay not in the fact that he had precipitated a needless war but that he failed to endow it with a realistic moral purpose. Thus, when the North was finally ready to listen to him, "he had nothing to say." Slavery had been ended, their guilt feelings had been dissolved, and the problem was "solved." Although Merrill's biography is well researched and fully documented, he falls into the mold of most other historians in viewing the Garrisonians as ineffectual and psychotic.

Historians generally have contended that the Garrisonian abolitionists contributed little to the struggle after 1840, when a split occurred in the American Anti-Slavery Society, which they controlled. This interpretation sees Garrison presiding over a truncated society, bereft of members and lacking funds. According to these scholars, after the split the American Anti-Slavery Society was able to claim the allegiance of only a few itinerant agitators. Thus Dumond states that "when Garrison gained control of the American Anti-Slavery Society in 1840, it had outlived its usefulness and was little but a name." Leon Litwack goes even further and dismisses entirely the significance of Garrisonian abolitionism after 1840:

Nonresistance, the rejection of political action, disunion, and a proslavery interpretation of the Constitution did not strike many abolitionists in the 1840's and 1850's as being either suitable or realistic weapons with which to abolish southern bondage or northern proscription. Indeed the final triumph of Garrisonian objectives resulted almost entirely from the employment of strictly non-Garrisonian methods—political agitation and armed force.

A NEW LOOK AT THE ABOLITIONISTS

During the 1950s and 1960s, a vigorous rehabilitation got underway of the abolitionists in general and Garrison in particular. Scholars began to cast doubt upon the usual interpretations. Benjamin P. Thomas set the new tone in his 1950 biography of Theodore D. Weld, in which he complained that "it has too long been the fashion to scoff at them [the abolitionists], to write them off as harmless fanatics." A major factor in accelerating this revisionist approach was the civil rights movement that flourished during this period. Indeed, in his study of a decade (1959–1969) of historiography dealing with the abolitionists, Merton L. Dillon observed: "The modern Civil Rights movement made the program, tracts, and frame of mind of Abolitionists comprehensible to more persons that at any other time since 1865."

Louis Filler, in *The Crusade against Slavery, 1830–1860*, published in 1960, viewed abolitionism as the great reform in an era of reform and as an extension and application of the finest components in the religiopolitical structures of the Enlightenment. He emphasized its grass-roots character and the indispensable strength it drew from the sympathy and support given it by tens of thousands of "plain folk." Filler also corrected the exaggerated role attributed to Theodore Weld and the diminished contribution assigned to Garrison in the influential works of Dwight L. Dumond and Gilbert H. Barnes. Finally, his work showed a greater appreciation than usual of the decisive contributions made by Negroes themselves to the antislavery cause.

In 1962, Louis Ruchames accused antiabolitionist historians of having failed "to read the writings of those whose opinions they present" and of a "misreading of documents when confronted with facts that suggest the opposite of what they wish to prove." A major example of such distortion of history, Ruchames went on, was the tendency to deny Garrison's place in the antislavery movement. He sharply criticized Dumond and Barnes for having "found it necessary to tear down Garrison's reputation in order to establish Theodore Weld's" and for attempting to prove that Weld, not Garrison, "was the most important and effective abolition leader." Consistent with this point of view, Ruchames, in his collection of antislavery documents, published in 1963, placed Garrison at the center of the abolitionist movement. Certainly it is clear today that to deny Weld's preeminence as the central figure in the antislavery crusade by no means negates his greatness or the magnitude of his contribution to the movement. Benjamin Thomas, Weld's biographer, Louis Filler, and Louis Ruchames, among others, have pointed out that the Dumond-Barnes view is built on either insufficient evidence or no evidence at all.

A major contribution to this new look at the abolitionists was the anthology (made up largely of articles previously published in scholarly journals) edited by Martin R. Duberman and published in 1965 under the title, *The Antislavery Vanguard: New Essays on the Abolitionists*. In "Abolitionists and Psychology," Duberman pointed out that psychologists have demonstrated the uniqueness of each human personality and that we do not know enough about individual abolitionists to generalize about "the Abolitionist personality," as David Donald and Stanley Elkins, to name only two historians, had done. In the same vein, Bertram Wyatt-Brown noted that the individuality of the abolitionists "defies sociological pigeon-holing." A large number were clergymen; some were merchants; some were statesmen; and some were scholars, poets, aristocrats, workers, or farmers. In "Who Were the Abolitionists?" Betty Fladeland argues that by no means all of them had a martyr complex; they were mostly "earnest men led by God toward the accomplishment of good" and were conservatives in that they sought to preserve the basic freedoms of speech, press, and inquiry. Fladeland examined the extensive range of persons affiliated with the antislavery movement and concluded from their variety that there was no "typical" abolitionist who fit Donald's model. Similarly, in his article, "Who Was an Abolitionist?" Larry Gara pointed out that abolitionism could not be identified with any particular group or class but represented a wide spectrum of sentiment throughout the North.

In "Abolitionists and Freedom Riders: The Tactics of Agitation," Howard Zinn conceded that the abolitionists were "agitators, radicals, and extremists" but insisted that these were precisely the qualities needed to battle a system as brutal as slavery, which, he reminded his readers, Allan Nevins had called "the greatest misery, the greatest wrong, the greatest curse to white and black alike that America has ever known." When viewed against the background of this acknowledged brutality of slavery, Zinn observed, "How mild Garrison's words seem!"

In his article, "The Northern Response to Slavery," Martin Duberman saw the abolitionists as not notably eccentric but as possessing a humanitarian "sense of commitment and concern" in demanding the immediate abolition of the sin that was slavery. They were willing to risk both the nation's "present wealth and future power" in their demand that the evil be eradicated "root and branch," since they thought it "tragic to weigh human lives in the same scale with material possessions and abstractions of government."

The consensus of the Duberman volume was that, on the whole, the reforming zeal of the abolitionists was the expression of well-balanced minds, with a Christian optimism that was laced with a sense of humor, and a faith in God's benevolence and the ultimate perfectibility of man. In predicting that America was doomed unless it practiced the creed set forth in the Declaration of Independence that all men were created free and equal, they demonstrated a remarkable clarity of vision.

THE NEW VIEW OF GARRISON

The fact that this new look was carried over to Garrison as well is reflected in the publication by the Harvard University Press of his letters, edited by the late Louis Ruchames and Walter M. Merrill. These volumes, still incomplete, revealed that while Garrison may have been guilty of some egocentrism, he played a very important role in the crusade against slavery. Scholars began to make a new and more intensive study of Garrison's thinking on strategy and tactics, his uncompromising devotion to freedom of speech, thought, and behavior, his advocacy of humanitarian and democratic reforms, and his extraordinarily consistent logic. Truman Nelson, in his introduction to a selection of Garrison's editorials, entitled *Documents of Upheaval*, called him "one of the most seminal of American thinkers." Even in his biography of Lewis Tappan, the New York philanthropist and abolitionist, Bertram Wyatt-Brown credited Garrison with being the dean of abolitionism. Contrary to the view that Garrison was an extremist, Wyatt-Brown considered his ability to appeal to the moderates as his greatest contribution. In fact, Garrison's very respectability, according to Wyatt-

Brown, was an asset to the antislavery cause. Finally, the writer credited Garrison with a sophisticated version of ''anti-politics,'' based on his calculated appraisal of the power of minority action. ''From a theoretical point of view,'' he concluded, ''Tappan's conception of politics was as conventional and unimaginative as Garrison's was new and provocative.'' In like manner, James B. Stewart used the same adjectives in characterizing the ''Garrisonian political strategy'' of ''adhering to non-voting,'' and thereby remaining ''unfettered by formal political ties [and] advising voters on how to use their ballots in the interest of antislavery.''

I have my own reservations as to the merits of these arguments, but there is no doubt that they demonstrate the error of accusing Garrisonians of being apolitical merely because they shunned party labels. Moreover, regardless of their validity, they serve to underscore the fact that William Lloyd Garrison was beyond a doubt the most prominent figure in the American antislavery movement.

In 1969, Aileen S. Kraditor published *Means and Ends in American Abolitionism: Garrison and His Critics on Strategy and Tactics, 1834–1850*. Kraditor admitted that she had begun her work with ''a rather negative opinion'' of Garrison, derived mainly from reading the two recent biographies by John L. Thomas and Walter M. Merrill. Whatever respect they inspire for their subject, Kraditor noted, was ''more than balanced by the conviction that he was bullheaded, arrogant, vindictive, and incredibly blind to some obvious truths.'' As she delved deeper, however, she found that Garrison was not nearly as narrow and doctrinaire regarding certain issues as many of his critics have made him out to be. In his letters, she found him to be conciliatory, candidly unsure about some of his opinions, and desirous of encouraging discussion in his paper, the *Liberator*. She even found him to be occasionally witty ''at his own expense.'' And so, as she proceeded, she reported, the picture she had of Garrison began to dissolve. What she found most impressive was the ''logical consistency of his thought on all subjects.''

Kraditor conceded that Garrison had changed his opinions from time to time, but she held that ''the changes themselves represented a logical development.'' He viewed abolition as a radical rather than a reform movement because he felt that slavery and the racial dogmas that were used to justify it so thoroughly permeated American society and government, North and South, that the eradication of the institution and its ideological defenses (and Garrison considered the racism inherent in the latter as important as slavery itself) was a root-and-branch operation. On this score, he never equivocated. Nonetheless, Kraditor acknowledged that the Garrisonians ''were less radical than they imagined, for they had no profound understanding of the nature of power and the conditions for its overthrow.'' Kraditor argues that if politics is the art of the possible, then agitation is the art of the desirable. It is here that Garrison's strength lay.

Garrison's abolitionist opponents, Kraditor argued, were reformers, not radicals. They believed in both constitutional means and political strategy. They sought to be "realists" and to attract moderates rather than repel them by the raising of what they considered "extraneous" issues. They believed that American society, government, and institutions were fundamentally sound and that once the alien institution of slavery was removed, all would be well. Hence, they were appalled by Garrison's intransigent denunciation of the Constitution as "a covenant with death, and an agreement with hell," which "should be immediately annulled." They also deplored his demand for disunion, along with other assorted "extraneous demands," such as the dissolution of government, church, and party and the struggle for women's rights.

Garrison's view, Kraditor emphasized, was that American society was not only not fundamentally sound but thoroughly corrupt. Hence his urging to do away with it, root and branch. He would not trim his sails, he would not compromise, he would neither vote for corrupt politicians nor support corrupt governments and churches, and he would not temper his means for achieving his ends. As Kraditor put it: "The key to Garrison's ideology is perfectionism." He believed strongly in the perfectibility of man.

Kraditor attributed the split in the abolitionist ranks between 1837 and 1840 to basic differences over social philosophy. The "radicals" were those who believed, with Garrison, that America's immorality, with slavery the worst of its sins, required fundamental changes in the nation's "institutional structure and ideology." Opposed to them were the "conservative" abolitionists, or reformers, who saw "Northern society [as] fundamentally good" and who would abolish slavery as a deviation in order to preserve the North's "basically moral arrangements." Kraditor rejected the notion of many historians that the split in the abolitionist ranks was caused by a "personality conflict." She emphasized that it was differences in theory that led to a conflict over the proper means of agitation for abolition. She was convinced that history had, to a degree, vindicated Garrison. After all, she pointed out, it did require a revolution, a war, and a repudiation of the old Constitution, as well as some drastic revisions in other constitutions, to abolish slavery. She dismissed Elkins' support for gradualism, arguing that it was an impossible option for the abolitionists since "slavery was an integral part of the institutional structure of the nation as a whole." (Barrington Moore, Jr., was even more critical of Elkins. "In the circumstances of mid-nineteenth-century American society," Moore wrote of Elkins' "catalogue of preliminaries," "any peaceful solution, any victory of moderation, good sense, and democratic process would have to be a reactionary solution.") Kraditor concluded her study by speculating as to what might have happened if the abolition movement had "not weakened the moral focus of its propaganda and not accepted the compromises dictated by political expediency." She considered it altogether possible that if the Garrisonian approach to strategy and tactics had been universally accepted in the antislavery movement, slavery might have been abolished earlier.

A REVOLUTIONARY MOVEMENT

The Marxist historian, Herbert Aptheker, has argued that even those historians who had written favorably about the abolitionists had failed to grasp the revolutionary nature of the movement. Although Kraditor viewed the Garrisonians as radicals, she did not consider them revolutionaries. Both Fladeland and Wyatt-Brown, on the other hand, insisted that the Garrisonians were really conservatives. To most historians, including the revisionist scholars who had challenged the traditional interpretation of the abolitionists, the antislavery movement was essentially a reformist, philanthropic endeavor. Aptheker, however, saw the movement as a "revolutionary one," and all "new Abolitionists" as revolutionaries, since they sought the uncompensated, immediate liberation of millions of slaves. Thus, in seeking the elimination of slavery, they set as their goal the confiscation of $4 billion worth of private property, the ownership of which, added to the land worked by these slaves and the crops produced by their labor, formed the basis of the power of the slaveowning oligarchy. That oligarchy—the 350,000 slaveowners—represented the single most powerful vested interest in the nation, and they, together with their Northern commercial allies, controlled the government.

The abolitionist movement, Aptheker went on, was revolutionary "because it sought the overthrow of the ruling class—the ruling class not only in the South, but also in the nation as a whole." Furthermore, Aptheker viewed the battle to abolish slavery as "part of the whole history of the labor movement in this country and in the world," and part "of the liberation struggles of the especially oppressed peoples and nationalities of the earth."

BLACKS AND THE ANTISLAVERY MOVEMENT

The Abolitionists: Reformers or Fanatics, edited by Richard D. Curry and published in 1965, is a volume of readings on the abolitionist movement without a single essay devoted to the Negro himself—either to the specific conditions under which he lived or to his own participation in the antislavery struggle. This neglect was not atypical. While black historians like Carter G. Woodson, Charles H. Wesley, John Hope Franklin, and Benjamin Quarles, and white historians like Herbert Aptheker, Elizabeth Lawson, Henrietta Buckmaster, and several others, including myself, have long emphasized that the original dynamic force behind the antislavery crusade was the Negro people themselves, and that throughout the crusade, blacks were the staunchest and most clear-sighted members of the abolitionist movement, this view was generally ignored by most white historians writing on abolitionism. Although the dominant American historiography of the 1950s and early 1960s may have differed from the traditional viewpoint in its interpretation of the abolitionist movement, it too either ignored the role of the Negro people or presented them merely as objects of history. One feature of more recent works on the subject is their belated recognition of the important role played by black abolitionists.

A dispute continues, however, over the degree of racism in the white abolitionist movement. William H. Pease and Jane H. Pease have pointed out that many black abolitionists, no matter what faction of the movement they may have joined, almost always had a clearer sense of antislavery purpose than did their white colleagues. (In several works, they have also argued that racial prejudices were extremely influential within the abolitionist movement, and they have accused the white abolitionists of being slow to abandon their private prejudices and reluctant to afford the Negro the opportunity to become economically self-sufficient. They concluded that on this issue, temporizing, coupled with paternalism, were the hallmarks of white abolitionism.)

While conceding the existence of racism in white abolitionist ranks, Benjamin Quarles noted in his 1969 work, *Black Abolitionists,* that many white abolitionists were interested in the free blacks as well as the slaves and did fight against discrimination in the North as well as against bondage in the South. Blacks, moreover, understood this, and one of the fruits of the antislavery movement was a vast increase in black-white unity. "In 1830," Quarles pointed out, "a great majority of the 320,000 free Negroes were in the habit of regarding all whites as their enemies. The Abolitionists changed this stereotype."

James M. McPherson saw egalitarianism as central to the abolitionist movement. In such a soil, he argued, prejudice could hardly be said to have taken root, since the whole movement was predicated on the doctrine of universal liberty as set forth in the Declaration of Independence. Influenced as they were by the radical liberalism of the Enlightenment and by both transcendental thought and evangelical Protestantism, they were driven by the logic of their movement to defend the Negro's right to equality. Finally, Herbert Aptheker has repeatedly pointed out that the abolitionist movement achieved a unity of Negro and white men and women, from both North and South: "All the societies, all the committees, all the conventions—the entire warp and woof of the movement—represented a united battle of Negro and white people.

In the ensuing chapters, we shall have an opportunity to evaluate the validity of the various interpretations of the abolitionists and the antislavery movement. We begin with the launching of the *Liberator* on January 1, 1831, and as we conclude this prefatory discussion, it is worth reprinting the editorial, "The Liberator," by W.E.B. Du Bois, published in the *Crisis,* organ of the NAACP, on the occasion of the centennial of the appearance of Garrison's paper. We might also note that as early as 1909, Du Bois had published a biography of John Brown in which he challenged the prevailing view among historians that Brown was an insane fanatic who represented only evil. As presented by Du Bois,

Brown was an eccentric but always a genuinely moral and sane man, in whom the hatred of slavery began at an early age and continued to grow until it was the main force of his life: "John Brown worked not simply for Black Men—he worked with them; and he was a companion of their daily life, knew their faults and virtues, and felt, as few white Americans have felt, the bitter tragedy of their lot."

As for Garrison and the *Liberator:*

One hundred years ago, William Lloyd Garrison founded *The Liberator*. Many men and measures contributed to the emancipation of the Negro slave in America, but it must ever be the considered verdict of history that no one man and no one periodical did so much as William Lloyd Garrison's *Liberator*. Let us then with full hearts remember not simply the evil we have suffered in America but the great Americans who have toiled and sacrificed for our uplift and the emancipation of mankind.

19

The *Liberator* and the American Anti-Slavery Society

In 1832, the delegates to the National Negro Convention reversed that organization's stand favoring the expatriation of free black Americans to Canada and instead urged their brothers and sisters to remain in this country and renew the struggle to end slavery and achieve full equality. There is more to this reversal than meets the eye. Certainly it did not take place because the status of blacks had improved in the two years since 1830. On the contrary, violence directed against Negroes occurred in 1831 in Providence, Philadelphia, New Haven, and other cities. That same year, Nat Turner's insurrection resulted in the unleashing of a barrage of terror against slaves and free blacks alike. But 1831 also witnessed the rise of a new force that gave the delegates to the 1832 National Negro Convention the courage to believe that there was hope for their people—both slaves and free blacks.

One of the reasons for black despair in 1830 had been the fact that Negroes no longer seemed to have any allies in the white community. Not only was the white abolitionist movement breathing its last, but even white friends who had formerly spoken out vigorously against slavery—albeit not for immediate emancipation—and for equal citizenship rights for the free blacks were now all too frequently distinguished by their silence. Lundy, Gerrit Smith, the Tappan brothers, and William Lloyd Garrison were all still colonizationists, and black leaders viewed with sorrow as one after another of their white friends were "swept away by the waves of expatriation." Gerrit Smith, the wealthy New York antislavery philanthropist, had frequently supported African schools, but he had become so enamored of colonization that he informed the American Colonization Society that he was curtailing all his contributions to black education projects and transferring them to the society "to relieve our country of its black population."

The free blacks were thus left to fight practically alone against the rising tide of persecution, racism, and violence. Their leaders were convinced that by themselves they could not stem the tide and that emigration to Canada was the key to survival. The 1832 National Negro Convention, however, spoke of a new force that had come into being in white America since their last meeting. They spelled it out when they voted to recognize

Wm. Lloyd Garrison, the bold and uncompromising advocate of the rights of man, as an editor and advocate of the free colored population, an able and fearless declaimer against oppression, as a man, a true and faithful friend, possessing honesty, virtue, and piety. For his exertions rendered to us as a people—therefore we do *ourselves,* and in behalf of those we represent, present him our sincere thanks

LAUNCHING THE *LIBERATOR*

William Lloyd Garrison was born in 1805 in Newburyport, Massachusetts, of Nova Scotian immigrants to a mother who was a pious Baptist and a father who deserted his family when their son was three years old. He became a newspaper apprentice at thirteen and later edited newspapers in Newburyport, Boston, and Bennington, Vermont, voicing the views of the dying New England Federalist faction. Eventually he lost his faith in conservative institutions and became increasingly involved in both the movement to end slavery gradually and in African colonization. In 1827, he met Benjamin Lundy who persuaded Garrison to move to Baltimore in the fall of 1829 and join him in editing the *Genius of Universal Emancipation.*

Soon after his release from the Baltimore jail on June 5, 1830, Garrison announced his intention of publishing a new antislavery paper in Washington, D.C. However, when he learned that Lundy had moved the headquarters of the *Genius* to the nation's capital, Garrison quickly decided to establish his paper in Boston. Actually, he was not overly distressed by Lundy's preemption of Washington. He was more and more coming to the opinion that the antislavery movement had no future in the South; his experience in Baltimore had convinced him that Lundy was wrong in his belief that the majority of southerners were ready to listen to antislavery arguments and would, if they were educated about the evils of the system, soon put an end to the peculiar institution. Garrison left Baltimore convinced that if it was left to southerners, the end of slavery—either gradual or immediate—would never come. Nor was he under any illusion as to the welcome he would receive in the North. Referring to a recent tour he had made of the free states, he noted that he "found contempt more bitter, opposition more active, detraction more relentless, and apathy more frozen, than among the slaveowners themselves." But this served only to convince Garrison that a strong antislavery voice was needed in the North and that in that section, there at least existed the possibility of mobilizing public opinion against the institution. Eventually, through this means, he hoped, the South might be forced to abandon slavery.

On Saturday, January 1, 1831, in Boston, the twenty-six-year-old William Lloyd Garrison issued the first number of the *Liberator,* in which he announced his determination to attack the system of slavery until "every chain be broken, and every bondman set free." Its motto was: "Our country is the world—our countrymen are mankind." On the first page appeared Garrison's creed of no quarter for and no compromise with the institution of human slavery. His clarion call was for immediate emancipation:

Assenting to the "self-evident truth" maintained in the American Declaration of Independence, "that all men are created equal, and endowed by their Creator with certain inalienable rights—among which are life, liberty and the pursuit of happiness," I shall strenuously contend for the immediate enfranchisement of our slave population. In Park Street Church, on the Fourth of July, 1829, in an address on slavery, I unreflectingly assented to the popular but pernicious doctrine of *gradual* abolition. I seize this opportunity to make a full and unequivocal recantation.

Then followed the most famous of Garrison's passages:

I *will* be as harsh as truth, and as uncompromising as justice. On this subject I do not wish to think, or to speak or write, with moderation. No! No! Tell a man whose house is on fire to give a moderate alarm; tell him to moderately rescue his wife from the hands of a ravisher; tell the mother to moderately extricate her babe from the fire into which it has fallen;—but urge me not to use moderation in a cause like the present. I am in earnest—I will not equivocate—I will not excuse—I will not retreat a single inch—and I WILL BE HEARD.

From the outset, then, the *Liberator* demanded immediate, uncompensated, and unconditional emancipation for all the slaves.

When it first appeared, the *Liberator* was issued by Garrison and Isaac Knapp as partners, with the names of both appearing on its masthead as publishers. Garrison was also listed as editor and Stephen Foster as printer. The fact that the paper appeared at all was due largely to the encouragement and support of James Forten, the Philadelphia Negro sailmaker. In December 1830, Forten had sent Garrison fifty-four dollars, representing twenty-seven subscriptions solicited by him from his Negro friends in the city. In forwarding the funds, Forten expressed the hope that the paper would be "the means of exposing more and more the odious system of slavery and raising up friends to the oppressed and degraded people of colour throughout the Union." Two months later, Forten organized a mass meeting to stimulate additional interest in Garrison's paper. Although it had only been in existence for a month, Forten was jubilant over the effect the *Liberator* was having on the black community. "It has," he wrote, "stirred up a spirit in our young people that has been slumbering for years, and we shall produce writers able to vindicate our cause."

While Garrison was in jail in Baltimore for supposedly libeling Frances Todd, John Hilton, a hairdresser by profession, leader of Boston's Negro Masons, and an abolitionist since 1830, began trying to raise money to free the young white abolitionist. But before the drive could get off the ground, Arthur Tappan had

already arranged for Garrison's release. Hilton then turned his attention to helping Garrison issue his antislavery paper. However, many of Boston's blacks
withheld their support, largely because of Garrison's earlier approval of an
appeal for support of the American Colonization Society. By 1831, Garrison,
largely through the influence of free blacks, had changed his mind, and he
announced that it was the aim of his life to atone for his previous support of so
"ridiculous and unworthy" a movement as colonization. The *Liberator* was
scarcely six weeks old when Boston's black leaders sent a sizable donation to the
paper, affirming that "the descendants of Africa . . . are convinced of the
sincerity of your intentions, and are proud to claim you as their advocate. . . .
Go on, then, friend and patriot of our cause, and whatever aid we can render you,
shall be promptly tendered."

On June 2, 1832, Garrison published a 238-page pamphlet, *Thoughts on
Colonization*, which was arranged in two sections. In the first, he argued against
colonization, insisting that blacks should not be sent to a foreign land but should
instead be granted citizenship and equal rights in this country. He specifically
repudiated and condemned the program of the American Colonization Society.
The second part of the pamphlet consisted of testimony against colonization by
various black meetings and organizations. The effect of this powerful philippic
was to stimulate a series of resignations of influential Northern whites from the
Colonization Society and still further cement relations between Garrison and the
black community. As William C. Nell noted, Garrison's pamphlet fully "un-
masked the hydra-headed monster, colonization."

In the first issue of the *Liberator,* Garrison had appealed to free Negroes
everywhere for their support: "Your moral and intellectual elevation, the advancement of your rights, and the defence of your character, will be a leading
object of our paper." He acknowledged that the free blacks were struggling
against adversity, but he expressed the hope that "some patronage may be
given" and that "that little may save the life of 'The Liberator.' " Garrison was
not to be disappointed. By the end of 1831, the number of Negro subscribers to
the *Liberator* had increased to 400 out of a total of approximately 450. "The first
year," Garrison later recalled, "the *Liberator* was supported by the colored
people, and had not fifty white subscribers." In fact, throughout the *Liberator's*
early years of publication, fewer than one-fourth of its subscribers were white.
Moreover, according to Garrison, Negroes paid for their subscriptions more
promptly than whites, and there is no doubt that the paper would not have
survived without them. Little wonder, then, that Garrison viewed the *Liberator*
as belonging "emphatically to the people of color—it is their organ." The
Liberator Aiding Association, organized by Boston blacks and headed by John
T. Hilton, also regarded the paper as their spokesman, a view which made it
extremely difficult to establish a black newspaper in that city.

When the aristocratic Mayor Harrison Gray Otis of Boston received a protest
in 1831 from the governors of Georgia and Virginia about "an incendiary paper" published in Boston, he was genuinely surprised. He had not even heard of

Garrison's *Liberator*. His officers informed him "that they had ferreted out the paper and its editor; that his office was an obscure hole, his only visible auxiliary a Negro boy, and his supporters a very few insignificant persons of all colors." Mayor Otis assured the Southern governors that this "new fanaticism" would not obtain any supporters among "respectable" people. Before long, Otis was compelled to admit sadly: "In this, however, I was mistaken."

Beginning in 1831, the antislavery crusade burst forth with a new intensity and, within a few years, was to establish itself as one of the most profound revolutionary movements in the world's history. The slave rebellion in Virginia, led by Nat Turner in September 1831, was a portent of the sharply accelerating conflict between proslavery and antislavery forces. On October 21, 1831, James Forten, a militant Philadelphia Negro leader, predicted jubilantly that the Turner rebellion would strengthen the antislavery cause by "bringing the evils of slavery more prominently before the public. . . . Indeed, we live in stirring times, and every day brings news of some fresh effort for liberty, either at home or abroad—onward, onward, is indeed the watchword."

They were truly stirring times. A new society was developing west of the Alleghenies, placing its mark on the social and political life of the entire country. A young labor movement was rising in the East, protesting the hardships caused by a rapidly expanding industrial system. Ecclesiastical revolts and religious revivals were asserting man's innate goodness and capacity for self-improvement and were demonstrating a new interest in the weak and helpless—in temperance reform, prison reform, and, quite logically, in the conditions of the slave. It was an "age of great movements," which showed a "power to exalt a people," said William Ellery Channing, the New England liberal. "It was an era of sympathy with the suffering, and of devotion to the progress of the whole human race."

This was the great age of reform in American history, and many Americans spoke out for justice for all people who were mistreated or denied the common rights of humanity. This era witnessed Horace Mann's campaign for public schools and Dorothea Dix's fight for understanding and help for those in jails and insane asylums. It was the time when Samuel G. Howe was seeking to prove that the deaf, dumb, and blind could be educated, and Elizabeth Cady Stanton and Susan B. Anthony were battling for equal rights for women.

The revived antislavery movement was part of this effort to reestablish American democracy upon the principles of the Declaration of Independence. It was part of a great democratic and humanitarian impulse, for abolitionism sprang from a rich soil that gave us at the same time crusades for public education, women's rights, peace, temperance, and utopian socialism.

The publication of the *Liberator* marked a new phase in antislavery history and a major breakthrough in American antislavery thought. The old abolitionist movement, with its program of conciliation and persuasion, gave way to the new abolitionists, who were no longer interested in preparing for emancipation in the distant future. Instead they set out to slay the dragon of slavery immediately and unconditionally in order to fulfill "the law of God and the Declaration of Independence.'' The new movement also acquired a new locale for its activity. It no longer drew its members from the slaveholding and adjoining states; rather it shook New England, where societies had ceased to exist in 1793, and stirred Ohio, Indiana, Illinois, Michigan, and New York—in fact, the entire North.

REVIVALISM

"Nowhere in the nation were there so many reformers ripe for abolition doctrine as in New England,'' writes Gilbert Barnes. There, a rapidly expanding factory system was ushering in a new way of life and creating both new social relations and new problems. Unitarianism had opened the way for a shift away from the Calvinistic debasement of man to ''adoration of his goodness,'' dignity, and worth. But crime, hunger, evil, and greed still plagued the nation and were intensified by the complexities of the new industrial order. The newly awakened New England conscience sought an answer to all of these problems and found it in the individual himself. Within each man and woman, went the belief, there lived the secret voice of God, which, once heard, would enable the individual to transcend all evils in society and fulfill the good life. Beginning with a respect for human nature and a reverence for human liberty, the reformers set themselves to the task of reform.

The convert to revivalism considered slavery particularly sinful because of his new understanding of the nature of man. If man were inherently depraved and totally dependent on God for justification, he could not complain about his station in life. But since God had made every man a free moral agent, to enslave him was to deny him his moral responsibility. Therefore revivalism insisted that slavery was not only wrong but sinful. Moreover, revivalism preached that those who were saved had to act immediately to exterminate sin wherever it existed and demanded that some positive action must be taken to abolish the sin of slavery.

Garrison and others who applied the logic to the revival to slavery also regarded it as a sin. In calling for immediate emancipation, they were seeking both the immediate recognition of the sin of slavery and immediate repentance: ''The colonizationists had wanted to remove the Negro because he was dangerous. The immediate emancipationist thought that by removing the sinful shackles of slavery, he would remove the danger and confront the Negro as a man.''

The most powerful preacher of the revival was Charles Grandison Finney. Born in Warren, Connecticut, in 1792, he studied for admission to Yale but instead taught school for several years and later decided to enter the law. In 1821, he was converted and, responding to what he was convinced was a call to preach, he studied privately under Reverend George W. Gale and was licensed and ordained by the presbytery in 1824. Possessed of a magnificent voice and a dramatic delivery, Finney immediately entered on a career that was to mark him as one of the greatest evangelists in American history. He inaugurated ''protracted meetings'' that sometimes lasted for weeks; he organized his converts into ''holy bands''; he instituted the ''anxious seat'' in front of the congregation; and, to the horror of the local ministry, he permitted women to pray in public meetings.

Finney told his listeners: ''If we desire the happiness of others, their happiness will increase our own, according to the strength of our desires. If we desire their welfare as much as we do our own, we are made as happy by good, known to be conferred on them, as upon ourselves; and nothing but selfishness prevents our tasting the cup of every man's happiness and sharing equally with him in all his joys. . . . To be happy, then, you must be benevolent.'' Finney's contribution to the antislavery cause lay in the fact that he spread the view that slavery was a sin, not an evil. Men could reason that if slavery was only an evil, it could be tolerated and eliminated gradually; but if it was a sin, no Christian could tolerate it, even for a moment. While this would seem to place Finney in the camp of immediatism, it is worth noting that his solution for the evils of slavery was the ''personal reformation of the individual malefactor.''

Although he stood firmly for emancipation, throughout his ministry in New York City at both the Chatham Street Chapel and the Broadway Tabernacle, where Finney preached, Negroes were segregated and assigned to the upper galleries. When Lewis Tappan sought to arrange for a distinguished black man to serve on the Board of Trustees of the Chatham Chapel, Finney quickly vetoed the attempt. While blacks were accepted as members of the church, they were excluded from either voting or holding office.

THE ''LANE REBELS''

The impact of Finney's ideas was clearly evident in the famous debates at Lane Theological Seminary in Cincinnati. The Presbyterian seminary had been founded in 1830 after Arthur and Lewis Tappan had promised the trustees the income from thirty thousand dollars if Lyman Beecher, considered the foremost preacher of his day, accepted the presidency.

Arthur and Lewis Tappan, brothers from Northampton, Massachusetts, were brought up in a strict Calvinsit home. In 1826, Arthur founded what was to become a flourishing business in New York City importing silks. Lewis joined him in 1828 but later left to found the first major national credit rating agency— the Mercantile Agency, the forerunner to Dun and Bradstreet. The Tappans were reformers before they joined the antislavery movement. As devout Calvinists (Arthur accepted Lewis as a business partner only after the younger man agreed to depart from the Unitarianism he had embraced against the wishes of their pious mother), they worked through the American Tract Society and other agencies to create a regulated Christian society. Their concerns included stricter Sabbath observance, temperance, the evils of tobacco smoking, and prostitution.

After having displayed a moderate interest in the question of slavery through their involvement in the Colonization Society, the Tappans were brought fully into the struggle by Garrison. Arthur became an abolitionist first; then Lewis espoused the cause. Their friendship with Garrison began in 1830 when Arthur paid the fine that got Garrison out of a Baltimore jail and gave him some money to start the *Liberator*. Spurred on by Garrison, the Tappans resigned from the American Colonization Society in 1833. That same year, they helped establish the *Emancipator*, an antislavery newspaper, in New York. Reverend Finney helped to reinforce the conversion of the Tappan brothers to the antislavery cause and their defection from the Colonization Society.

While Finney's converts numbered in the thousands, none was to exert a greater influence than Theodore D. Weld. Weld had his first contact with the plight of blacks when, as a child of seven, he dared to take a seat besides a little Negro boy who was the butt of other children in the elementary school at Hampton, Connecticut. He was a twenty-two-year-old freshman at Hamilton College when he first heard Finney in 1825. At first, Weld was scornful of Finney's "new measures," but he later became his eager disciple and joined Finney's "Holy Band" as one of the most ardent and successful evangelists. In 1830, the Tappan brothers prevailed upon Finney to come to New York, where they built a tabernacle for him. Through Finney, Weld was brought to the attention of the Tappan brothers, and in 1831, he became their agent for the Society for Promoting Manual Labor in Literary Institutions. Weld encouraged the Tappans to finance the establishment of the Lane Theological Seminary, which he hoped might become the prototype for a manual labor and antislavery institution in the Midwest.

In 1832, Weld resigned his agency for the Manual Labor Society and enrolled at Lane Seminary. He was part of its first theological class, which had been largely recruited from the East, and particularly from the section of New York State where Finney's revivalism had flourished. Lane Seminary drew no color line. James Bradley, a native of the African Gold Coast who had purchased his own freedom, was a member of the first theological class admitted.

At first, none of the students at Lane Seminary except Weld (who by now was fully devoted to the antislavery cause) had any profound opinions about slavery. There was even a flourishing branch of the Colonization Society at the institution. With his attention focused on the students from the South, Weld challenged the colonizationists in the seminary to a series of debates scheduled for eighteen evenings. The first nine were devoted to a discussion as to whether slave states should immediately abolish slavery. Weld spoke for two hours on each of the first two evenings. William Allan, a slaveholding student from Alabama, then described the treatment of plantation slaves. Bradley, the African-born freeman, moved the audience to tears when he described how he had been captured as a child on the Gold Coast, smuggled into the United States in violation of the 1808 law abolishing the African slave trade, and endured various horrors until a kind master educated him and permitted him to purchase his freedom.

At the end of the first nine evenings, a vote was taken, and all but five students voted for immediate emancipation. The succeeding series of nine meetings considered the program and policies of the American Colonization Society. One Southern student, John P. Pierce, later recalled that he had been a convinced colonizationist and had even refused to attend some of the early meetings. By chance, he heard Weld speak against colonization, and years later, he wrote that this had been his "conversion"and that "Weld . . . was the means of opening my blind eyes." At the conclusion of the meetings, the Lane students voted against colonization almost unanimously and went on to organize an antislavery society.

Weld wrote to Lewis Tappan: "We believe that faith without *works* is dead. . . . We have formed a large and efficient organization for elevating the colored people of Cincinnati." The Lane students established libraries, lectures, and Bible classes for the free blacks of Cincinnati. When their first school opened in March 1834, so many Negroes enrolled that classes had to be conducted in shifts. Two of the Lane students, Augustus Wattles and Marius Robinson (the latter a Tennessean), withdrew from college to serve as teachers, intending to work one year and then be replaced by others. (Wattles boarded with a black family.) Arthur Tappan paid the expenses of four young women from New York who joined the teaching staff. Weld frequently taught in these classes and almost deserted his own white world for the slum ghettoes of the Cincinnati blacks:

If I ate in the City it was at their Tables. If I slept in the City it was in their homes. If I attended parties, it was *theirs*—Weddings—*theirs*—Funerals—*theirs*—Religious meetings—*theirs*—Sabbath schools—Bible classes—*theirs*. During the eighteen months I spent . . . I was with the colored people in their meetings by day and by night.

The Cincinnati black community, whose welfare they tried to improve, deeply appreciated the efforts of the Lane students. The white community, however, was infuriated by their contacts with blacks in a city where blacks had been confined to a distinctly second-class status and constantly threatened by riots, where trade unions combined to prevent their employment, except in the most menial occupations, where the law forbade their attendance at public schools, and where the courts were virtually closed to them. In addition, the city was the center for an important Southern trade, and local businessmen were concerned lest the activities of the Lane students lead to a boycott of their stores by enraged slaveowners.

The straw that broke the camel's back occurred when a Lane student was seen walking around Cincinnati with a black girl and addressing her as if she were white. Choosing a time when President Beecher was in the East raising funds—a tour from which, as trouble mounted, he refused to return, in spite of Weld's urging—the board of trustees (with only one negative vote) resolved that from then on, no student organization should be permitted unless it was connected with academic work and fulfilled the explicit preministerial training functions of the seminary. The board further forbade any public discussion of controversial subjects, including slavery, without prior approval. As a result, the students were ordered to disband their antislavery society. The penalty for violation of these rules was expulsion. In addition, the trustees dismissed Professor John Morgan, a native of Ireland and a graduate of Williams College, who had supported the students in the antislavery debate.

Under the leadership of Weld, fifty-three of the fifty-six students at the seminary signed a protest petition and withdrew from the institution. Two of the "Lane rebels," as they were thereafter called, enrolled at Auburn Seminary; four transferred to Yale, two to the Western Theological Seminary, and one to Miami. Four "confessed their error" and were reinstated. The remainder set up a school of their own, continuing their labors in the city's Negro community. Although beset by financial difficulties, which persisted in spite of some support from the Tappan brothers and the black community of Cincinnati, they resolved to carry on their work.

At about that same time, the Oberlin Collegiate Institute in Oberlin, Ohio, which had been founded in 1831, was having difficulty meeting its expenses. In 1834, the Oberlin trustees authorized their agent, John Jay Shipherd, to make a tour of various sections of the country for the purpose of collecting funds for the institution. When the Lane rebels withdrew from the seminary, Shipherd conferred with them, along with Weld. Together, they agreed on a program designed to win the support of the Tappan brothers for Oberlin. Charles G. Finney and John Morgan, the dismissed Lane professor, were to be invited to Oberlin as members of the faculty. Asa Mahan, the sole Lane trustee who had been friendly to the Lane rebels, was to be elected president of Oberlin; and the former Lane students would enroll at Oberlin if the trustees would guarantee them free speech on all reform issues and admit Negro students on equal terms with whites.

Shipherd and Mahan went to New York and explained the situation to Arthur Tappan. Delighted by the terms they had worked out, Tappan canvassed his wealthy friends for contributions to Oberlin and pledged thousands of dollars on his own account. He also persuaded Finney to join the Oberlin faculty.

Without delay, Shipherd conveyed both the conditions and Tappan's pledges to the Oberlin board. Much to his disappointment, they provoked a storm of opposition in the board, the faculty, the student body, and the local community. The opponents expressed the fear that the college would be "changed into a Negro school" and that "hundreds of Negroes would be flooding the school." A student poll showed thirty-two votes against the proposal and twenty-six for. The board voted unanimously to meet all the requirements except that of admitting Negroes. Thus, even with the very future of the college at stake, they would not admit blacks.

The question of admitting Negro students was proposed again, and this time the trustees divided evenly on the issue. John Keep, a Yale graduate and Congregationalist minister and president of the board of trustees, then cast the deciding vote for the admission of Negro students to the school, and they were able to join women, who had previously been admitted, as members of the Oberlin student body.

With all their conditions met, the forty Lane rebels entered the theological seminary. To be sure, there was no flood of Negro students; in fact, the first black graduate, George B. Vashon, did not earn his degree until 1844. But Oberlin did become a stronghold of abolitionist activities, as well as a school for all races. After graduation, the Lane rebels became some of the foremost antislavery lecturers. Moreover, from their experience in the Cincinnati Negro community, they also took the lead in urging the antislavery movement to participate directly in work among the free blacks.

NEW ENGLAND ANTI-SLAVERY SOCIETY

The growing worldwide sentiment against human bondage had already resulted in the abolition of slavery in all the countries of South America except Brazil. Mexico had put an end to slavery in 1829. The British parliamentary debate of 1830 on emancipation in the West Indies had placed the question on the front pages of American newspapers. It had also brought the issue of immediatism to the fore. The British movement to end slavery in the West Indies had a strong influence on the American antislavery efforts. In 1823, the British had formed the Society for the Mitigation and Gradual Abolition of Slavery throughout the British Dominions, better known as the Anti-Slavery Society. (By 1839, it was to become the British and Foreign Anti-Slavery Society.) The first British emancipation efforts were gradualist, as the name of the society formed in 1823 would suggest. But after a few years of experience that revealed the unwillingness of the colonial governments to heed the orders in council sent to them by the British Parliament—orders intended to improve the conditions of slaves and move gradually toward emancipation—the opinion in British antislavery ranks began to harden. Doubts were increasingly expressed about the adequacy of gradualism, since the colonial governments seemed unwilling to make even minor token moves in the desired direction. Since the colonial legislatures seemed immovable, the debate grew angrier and more heated. By 1826, the British Parliament was beginning to get some petitions calling for immediate emancipation. The colorful and significant debates in Parliament in 1830 were widely reported in American newspapers, including the eloquent and heated appeal of Lord Henry Brougham for the immediate abolition of slavery in the colonies.

Garrison early became attracted to British immediatism, and he maintained that the American antislavery forces should proclaim the same principle. He also advocated following the British example in forming antislavery societies, and by late 1831, he was organizing a small group into what was to be the first of many new antislavery societies in the United States and one of the first immediatist societies in the country. On January 6, 1832, the New England Anti-Slavery Society was officially founded, with Garrison as its secretary. The society's constitution stressed opposition to colonization, the improvement of the lot of the free blacks, and immediate emancipation. The name *antislavery* rather than *abolition* society was chosen in order to distinguish it from the previous organizations that had sought to eliminate slavery gradually, in the main favored colonization, and excluded blacks.

Garrison and more than seventy others met in the school room of the African Baptist Church in the Negro section of Boston to sign the society's constitution. Of the seventy-two signatories to the document, about "a quarter were those of colored men, some . . . barely able to write."

On November 21, 1832, the prospectus of the *Abolitionist,* the proposed monthly organ of the New England Anti-Slavery Society, was distributed in Boston. It was to be "exclusively devoted to subjects connected with the rights and happiness of the colored people, and its design will be to present to the community the true character of slavery and the American Slave Trade—to urge upon Patriots, Philanthropists and Christians the obligations they are under to their country, our fellow men, and their God, to break every yoke and set the oppressed free." The first issue of the *Abolitionist* carried the text of a resolution adopted by the New England Anti-Slavery Society inviting the Negroes "to form auxiliaries to this society." The first black association to respond to the invitation was the Massachusetts General Colored Association, which was established in 1832 with the chief objective of achieving the abolition of slavery. The Massachusetts Association informed the New England Anti-Slavery Society that it approved of the society's objectives and that it desired to become an auxiliary. It was accepted, and several members of the Colored Association—including Charles Lenox Remond, the Reverend Samuel Snowden, and John Hilton—were elected to high posts in the New England society. Within two years, the Colored Association disbanded, and a number of its members directly joined the New England Anti-Slavery Society.

FORMATION OF THE AMERICAN ANTI-SLAVERY SOCIETY

In the *Liberator* of March 9, 1833, the New England Anti-Slavery Society announced a planned mission to England by William Lloyd Garrison "for the purpose of procuring funds to aid in the establishment of the proposed MANUAL LABOR SCHOOL FOR COLORED YOUTH, and of disseminating in that country the truth in relation to American Slavery, and its ally, the American Colonization Society." But Garrison had no funds for the journey, and an appeal was issued to the "Friends of Emancipation" to pay his passage to England and his expenses there. Among the first to respond were the free blacks, and meetings to raise funds were held in Boston, Philadelphia, New York, Albany, Providence, Newark, and Brooklyn. At the Philadelphia meeting, presided over by James Forten, resolutions were unanimously adopted expressing approval of Garrison's mission and hailing the *Liberator*'s editor as "the friend of the colored population." A collection was taken up and a committee appointed "to solicit subscriptions to aid in defraying Mr. Garrison's expenses in England."

As a result of the meetings and other contributions, sufficient funds were raised to finance the trip. After being feted by several groups of Boston's blacks, Garrison sailed for England, landing in Liverpool on May 2, 1833. He arrived just as the British abolitionists were awaiting the passage by Parliament of the abolition bill, and by the time he left for the United States, Great Britain had freed the 800,000 slaves in its West Indies colonies.

Garrison had long felt the need for a national antislavery organization in the United States, and the success of the British abolitionists strengthened his belief that the time was ripe for such an organization. Arthur Tappan was also working to form a national antislavery group and was visiting many friends to urge them to organize opinion in this direction. But then an event occurred that cooled his enthusiasm. On October 2, 1833, the first meeting of the New York Anti-Slavery Society was scheduled to be held in Clinton Hall. But the trustees, anticipating violence, revoked their contract and refused the building to the group headed by Arthur Tappan. At the suggestion of Lewis Tappan, who was a trustee of Chatham Street Chapel, it was agreed to hold the meeting in that hall's lecture room. Oral notices were distributed, and about fifty "stout-hearted abolitionists" gathered at the hour of the meeting. A proslavery mob congregated near Tammany Hall, eager to attack the chapel. After Louis and Arthur Tappan passed through the crowd unnoticed, the meeting opened. A constitution was quickly adopted, Arthur Tappan was chosen president, and Lewis Tappan was named one of the board of managers. After the abolitionists had gone, the mob rushed in, and frustrated by the fact that the hall was empty, pounced upon a passing Negro, constituted itself a mock abolition meeting, placed the black man on the platform, called him Arthur Tappan, and demanded a speech. Thereupon the unknown Negro delivered the following heroic words:

I am called upon to make a speech. You doubtless know that I am a poor, ignorant man, not accustomed to make speeches. But I have heard of the Declaration of Independence and have read the Bible. The Declaration says all men are created equal, and the Bible says God had made us all of one blood. I think, therefore, we are entitled to good treatment, and it is wrong to hold men in slavery, and that—

At this point, the speaker was interrupted by a combination of shouts and blows.

Garrison, unrecognized, had watched the mob as it had vented its anger at failing to disrupt the founding meeting of the New York City Anti-Slavery Society.When the Tappans told him that, in view of the riot, they felt it would be best to postpone the plan for a national antislavery society, he rejected their advice. A new society must be founded, he insisted, while the British action abolishing slavery was still fresh in people's memory, and he succeeded in bringing about a convention for that purpose in Philadelphia in December 1833.

The question of delaying the formation of a national antislavery society was not the only difference that had arisen between Garrison and the New York abolitionists, led by the Tappan brothers. Another revolved around the meaning of immediatism. The constitution of the New York City Antislavery Society declared the organization as being for immediate, not gradual, emancipation. But the New York abolitionists were convinced that slavery could not be abolished immediately, since it had grown too strong and was too firmly entrenched in the nation's economy. They therefore insisted that the correct approach was to call for "immediate emancipation, gradually accomplished." To Garrison, this position merely amounted to playing with words and constituted a denial of principle. He insisted on immediate, unqualified emancipation—the doctrine he had laid down in the first issue of the *Liberator* in 1831—and it was his position that prevailed in Philadelphia.

From December 4 through 6, 1833, sixty delegates, including seven blacks, met in Philadelphia's Adelphia Hall and, in an atmosphere of deep hostility in the city, with angry crowds milling around the hall, formed the American Anti-Slavery Society. A struggle for power soon developed between Garrison and his New England associates on the one hand and Lewis Tappan and the New York group on the other. Since the New Yorkers were more numerous, the absent Arthur Tappan was elected president. Garrison accepted the office of secretary of foreign correspondence and wrote the society's Declaration of Sentiment, the most important document to come out of the convention and one of the great documents in American history.

In the declaration, Garrison noted that the American Anti-Slavery Society was meeting in the same city in which the Declaration of Independence was adopted, and he utilized the rhetoric of the original manifesto in the new document. This, he wrote, was logical, since the purpose of the new antislavery society was to erect the entire structure on the "cornerstone" upon which the men of the Revolution had "founded the Temple of Freedom." Without the abolition of slavery, he declared, the "achievement of our fathers is incomplete."

After looking back to 1776, the declaration announced that it was speaking for the millions held in bondage, the "one-sixth of our countrymen," who were

recognized by the law, and treated by their fellow-beings, as marketable commodities, in goods and chattels, as brute beasts; are plundered daily of the fruits of their toil, without redress—really enjoying no constitutional nor legal protection from licentious and murderous outrages upon their persons; are ruthlessly torn asunder the tender babe from the arms of its frantic mother—the heart-broken wife from the weeping husband—at the caprice or pleasure of irresponsible tyrants. For the crime of having a dark complexion, they suffer the pangs of hunger, the infliction of stripes, and the ignominy of brutal servitude. They are kept in heathenish darkness by laws expressly enacted to make their instruction a criminal offense. No man has a right to enslave or imbrute his brother—to hold him . . . as a piece of merchandise—to keep back his hire by fraud—or to brutalize his mind by denying him the means of intellectual, social, and moral impròvement.

At the same time, the declaration acknowledged the constitutional and legal guaranties surrounding slavery: "We fully and unanimously recognize the sovereignty of each State, to legislate exclusively on the subject of slavery which is tolerated within its limits; we concede that Congress, under the present national compact, has no right to interfere with any of the slave states in relation to this momentous subject.''

The constitution of the American Anti-Slavery Society stated as its objective the ''entire abolition of slavery in the United States.'' However, it set forth another purpose as well: to ''elevate the character and condition of the people of color, by encouraging their intellectual, moral and religious improvement, and by removing public prejudice, that thus they may, according to their intellectual and moral worth, share an equality with the whites of civil and religious privileges.'' The remainder of the sentence, which stressed the Garrisonian principle of nonviolence and nonresistance, went: ''but this Society will never, in any way, countenance the oppressed in vindicating their rights by resorting to physical force.''

The six black delegates to the founding convention of the American Anti-Slavery Society were James G. Barbadoes of Massachusetts, and James Mc-Crummell, Robert Purvis, James Forten, John B. Vashon, and Abraham D. Shadd of Pennsylvania. Among the sixty-two signers of the Declaration of Sentiments were three Negro delegates: Barbadoes, Purvis, and McCrummell. The declaration was written at McCrummell's home. The board of managers included Barbadoes, Purvis, McCrummell, Vashon, Shadd, and Peter Williams. Several blacks also served on the executive committee of twelve, which was chaired by Arthur Tappan. Thus, blacks assumed prominent roles in the first national antislavery society formed by the new abolitionists.

The society, founded for the purpose of bringing about the immediate abolition of slavery in the nation and improving the condition of the free Negro, immediately drew within its orbit a zealous group of men and women, both black and white. The procedure for entering the national organization was simple. Any society professing the principles of immediate emancipation as set forth in the Declaration of Sentiments of the national organization automatically became an auxiliary by submitting a copy of its constitution and a list of its officers.

With the organization of the American Anti-Slavery Society, the state bodies of Maine, New Hampshire, and Vermont withdrew from the New England society and formed their own local state organizations. What was left of the New England Society decided to limit its operations to Massachusetts. By 1834, therefore, it became a state society, and its name was changed from the New England to the Massachusetts Anti-Slavery Society.

FEMALE ANTISLAVERY SOCIETIES

On July 14, 1832, the *Liberator* proudly announced the formation of the first female antislavery society in Providence, Rhode Island. ''We trust it is the forerunner of a multitude of similar associations, not only in this but in every part of our country,'' Garrison wrote. It was followed the next year by a society in Salem, and by 1834, there were at least ten female antislavery societies in

Massachusetts (including one of black women), two in Maine, one in New Hampshire, and others in New York City and Philadelphia. Female societies also sprang up in the West, and the first antislavery organization in Michigan was a female society organized in Adrian in 1834. By the end of the decade there were female societies in every state in the North—with the largest number in Massachusetts—and by 1838, there were no fewer than 112 female societies—51 in Massachusetts alone. Included among them were female antislavery societies formed by black women in Rochester and New York City.

The constitution of the Boston Female Anti-Slavery Society forthrightly expressed the sentiment that inspired the women who formed these organizations: "Believing slavery to be a direct violation of God, and productive of a vast amount of misery and crime, and convinced that its abolition can only be effected by an acknowledgement of the justice and necessity of immediate emancipation . . . we hereby agree to form ourselves into a Society." The constitution of the Philadelphia Female Anti-Slavery Society coupled "slavery and prejudice against color" as being "contrary to the laws of God, and to the principles of our far-famed Declaration of Independence." It called not only for "immediate emancipation" but also "for the restoration of the people of color to their invaluable rights."

All of the female antislavery societies emphasized woman's responsibility to her suffering black sister in bondage and denounced "the operation of a system which annuls the marriage tie, destroys all parental and filial obligation, denies the right of the mother to call her slumbering babe her own, produces every species of licentiousness and sets at naught the laws of God and nature." Sometimes, this sentiment took a poetic turn:

> Think of the frantic mother
> Lamenting for her child
> Till falling lashes smother
> Her cries of anguish wild.
> Shall we behold unheeding
> Life's holiest feelings crushed?
> When woman's heart is bleeding
> Shall woman's voice be hushed?

In order to weaken the economy of the South and thereby hasten emancipation, the female antislavery societies renounced, wherever possible, the use of products made by slave labor. As a result, they sparked the growth of what was called the "free produce" movement. It started as an organization called the Society for the Encouragement of Free-Labour among some Philadelphia and Wilmington Quakers in 1827 and was created "to organize the cultivation of such articles by Freemen as are now produced by the labour of Slaves." Although the quantity contemplated was small, the society believed that "if promptly taken hold of, a beginning may be made which will result in extensive good." In December 1830, Philadelphia blacks, meeting in Richard Allen's church, formed a Free Produce Society, with a membership of 230 people pledged to abstain from the use of slave-produced commodities. In 1834, William Whipper briefly operated a "Free Labor and Temperance Grocery" in Philadelphia.

The movement did not really get underway until the American Free Produce Association was founded in 1838 with a special appeal to the female antislavery societies, whose interest in textiles and foodstuffs made their cooperation especially significant. The appeal went:

> Those sugars and syrups—you think them so nice.
> Were purchased for us with a horrible price.
> They were raised in a land where the labor of slaves
> Has borne many thousands away to their graves!

Free produce stores selling unbleached muslin, calicoes, twilled muslin, sugar, and rice—all untainted by slave labor—were set up in the large cities. Agents shopped for raw cotton produced by free labor and arranged with mill owners to have it manufactured. Advertisements in antislavery papers notified their readers:

FREE Labor Goods.

MANUFACTURED by the American Free Produce Association, and for sale at No. 31 North Fifth-street, Philadelphia.

A large and handsome assortment of Prints on hand.

FREE LABOR GROCERIES

I have just received, and shall keep constantly on hand, a good assortment of Brown and White Sugars, Molasses, Rice, and Coffee, all the products of *Free Labor*. Those in want of such goods are invited to purchase, and can be assured of the genuineness of the articles. 133 Main, corner of North street, Rochester. G. B. Stebbins

The American Anti-Slavery Society endorsed the free produce movement, and Lucretia Mott, a Quaker, worked indefatigably to gather support for the idea. Those abolitionists who favored the plan believed that an extensive boycott of slave-produced goods would accomplish three things: the individual crusader would achieve self-purification through noncooperation with the system; the slaveholder's conscience would be affected; and the economic coercion might hasten the end of slavery. These advocates pointed to the fact that after 800,000 Englishwomen had signed a pledge not to use slave-grown sugar, there was a penny-per-pound drop in price, which alarmed West Indian slaveowners and hastened the move for the abolition of slavery in the British colonies.

Most abolitionists, however, did not patronize the free labor stores, since their prices were high. The only New York City free labor store appealed: "The proprietor aims to sell as low as he can to continue the business. With double the patronage, prices could be somewhat reduced; probably every article could be sold as low as similar goods in the market." Also, the choice of patterns and colors was limited, and orders were not filled promptly. In the view of the nonsupporters, the entire boycott idea involved a self-denial for a purpose that many believed had no effect on slavery. A loyal minority of women, however, continued to carry their own "free sugar" wherever they went, in order not to partake of "the slaveholder's sin."

In March 1837, for the first time in American history, a national convention of antislavery females was called—"a new thing under the sun," as the *Liberator* joyfully called it. When 71 delegates and 107 corresponding members, nearly all from female antislavery societies, descended upon New York City in May 1837, the press greeted them with a combination of condescension and ridicule. "The spinster has thrown aside her distaff," the *New York Commercial Advertiser* jeered; "the blooming beauty her guitar; the young mother has left her baby to nestle alone in the cradle, and the kitchen maid her pots and pans to discuss weighty matters of state, to decide upon intricate questions of international policy and weigh with avoirdupois exactness, the balances of power."

The convention placed no restrictions on the basis of race or creed. Negro and white women, women of every religious denomination, came together, organized the National Anti-Slavery Convention of American Women, and worked out a program for a common goal. Numerous resolutions on all phases of the slavery question were passed, and pledges for funds for the printing of antislavery pamphlets were collected. The convention set up a Central Committee of six—two each from New York, Philadelphia, and Boston—for the purpose of correspondence on the best ways to combat slavery. Then the delegates departed to continue the work in their local female antislavery societies, and the first women's convention in America became history.

There were also young men's antislavery societies, which flourished in the larger towns, particularly in Massachusetts and New York. By 1838, thirty juvenile societies, the majority of them female, were operating in the North. Several were black, like the Garrison Independent Juvenile Society of Boston, led by William C. Nell. The American Anti-Slavery Society employed a special agent to spread antislavery propaganda among children. As the society's second annual report stated:

Every child understands the right and wrong about slavery, the moment the case is stated. It is only the wise and prudent, who have grown hoary in threading the images of expediency . . . that have so mystified and mixed up the subject, as to think that slaveholding is half right and half wrong. . . . "Away with it," says the unsophisticated child. "The man in chains is no less a brother because he is black."

ANTISLAVERY AGENTS

In the forceful Declaration of Sentiments adopted by the American Anti-Slavery Society at its founding convention, the delegates pledged:

> We shall organize anti-slavery societies, if possible, in every city, town, and village in our land.
> We shall send forth agents to lift up the voice of remonstrance, of warning, of entreaty and rebuke.
> We shall circulate unsparingly and extensively anti-slavery tracts and periodicals.

The struggle to carry out this pledge was waged with a fervor, persistence, and skill that have rarely been matched in our nation's history and that provide Americans with a rich legacy of agitational and organizational traditions. The abolitionists worked out a complete propaganda program. They circulated petitions by the thousands, which they showered on Congress and state legislatures; they appeared before legislative committees; they sent out traveling agents; they slipped printed handkerchiefs bearing antislavery slogans into bales designed for Southern markets; and they mailed pictures depicting the cruelties of slavery. They held antislavery meetings in every conceivable place from a stable loft to a church. Resolutions were passed, ardent speeches were made, and hymns were sung. Typical was the following stirring song written by Garrison:

> I am an Abolitionist
>   I glory in the name
> Though now by Slavery's minions hissed
>   And covered o'er with shame:
> It is a spell of light and power
>   The watchword of the free:
> Who spurns it in the trial-hour,
>   A craven soul is he!

The new abolitionist movement in the United States was part of a worldwide movement against the enslavement of the African peoples. It is not surprising, therefore, that the movement had international aspects and ties. Leaders of the American Anti-Slavery Society frequently went to England to consult abolitionists in that country and to raise support for the crusade in the United States. There were also visits by foreign antislavery men to the United States. In addition, there were common conventions and joint expressions of opposition to slavery.

The central features of abolitionist agitation were the use of lecturers, or traveling agents; the printing of newspapers and periodicals; and the publication of books, pamphlets, leaflets (broadsides), cartoons, poems, and songs.

"The National Society is now organized," Elizur Wright, Jr., wrote to Theodore D. Weld on the last day of 1833, "the question is whether it shall *live*. We want a number of faithful and mighty agents to whose persons the Society shall live and breathe and wax strong before the public. We must have men who will electrify the mass wherever they move—and they must move on no small scale." It was Weld, a master of all forms of agitation, and Wright, the organizational genius of the American Anti-Slavery Society, who developed to a high degree of effectiveness the system of agents who would travel from town to town, explaining the principles of abolitionism and forming local societies to carry on the work.

The society's agents had to be of good moral character, sincere, thoroughly steeped in the subject, and financially trustworthy. Wright wrote questioningly to Weld about one candidate: "Has he the efficiency, . . . the galvanism that can reanimate the dead as well as the steadfastness that can withstand the onset of the living?" Having met these qualifications, which might have required an investigation of a month or more, an agent would then begin his travels, "mobbed out of the big cities and pelted out of the little ones," jolting over primitive roads in hard coaches from day to day, speaking in barns, churches, taverns, schools, and private parlors—on the town common or in the nearest forest when nothing else could be obtained.

For the grueling work they performed, agents received wages of $416 a year, if single, plus expenses; those who had left a wife and family at home received $600 a year—when they were paid. The "Instruction to Agents" cautioned them to remember that "silver and gold are the Lord's" and to be frugal in their expenses. To implement this advice, Wright scanned each agent's monthly expense and work reports with a stern, economical eye.

These work reports convey simply and dramatically the sincerity, courage, and self-sacrificing devotion of the antislavery agents. Many traveled on foot, valise in hand, covering about fifty miles a day, eating and sleeping wherever they were invited, and frequently going hungry. Being mobbed was a common experience. Agents were stoned, pelted with garbage, and shouted at as they spoke nine or ten times a week to restless, noisy, and hostile audiences. Stephen S. Foster was so frequently a target for stones that he is described in James Russell Lowell's poem in these words:

> Hard by, as calm as summer even,
> Smiles the reviled and pelted Stephen;
> Who studied mineralogy
> Not with soft book upon the knee,
> But learned the properties of stones,
> By contact sharp of flesh and bones.

During the eighteen months of its existence, the American Anti-Slavery Society was able to afford only five traveling agents. They visited the important cities and towns of New England and New York. One of them, Henry B. Stanton, singlehandedly "abolitionized" Rhode Island by establishing the Rhode Island State Anti-Slavery Society. In 1835, Theodore Weld served as the society's great lecturing agent in Ohio, and his apostles were the Oberlin students—the Lane rebels who had seceded from Lane Seminary in Cincinnati over the slavery issue. In the course of eight months in 1835, Weld laid the foundation for the antislavery movement in Ohio. He pounded whole towns into submission with the insistence of his great voice, speaking five to fifteen times in a single village. Weld later went on to upstate New York while his disciples, the Lane rebels, took over the work in Ohio.

"THE SEVENTY"

Between 1834 and 1836, the officers of the American Anti-Slavery Society became increasingly aware of a direct relationship between the growth of antislavery sentiment in an area and the agency activity there. Those states that had received the greatest attention from agents had the largest number of auxiliary societies. The society's executive committee therefore voted to reduce its expenditures on publications and concentrated its resources on the employment and direction of additional lecturers who would spread the message of abolition and organize antislavery societies. The name given to the agents of 1836–1837 was "the Seventy," in accordance with the biblical precedent as set forth in Luke 10, which begins: "After these things the Lord appointed other seventy also, and sent them two and two before his face into every city and place, whither he himself would come."

The agents were called to New York from November 8 to 27, 1836, for instruction and orientation. Weld was in charge, and the speakers included himself, Garrison, and Stanton. Garrison, who stayed until the end, wrote:

The questions discussed were manifold—such as, What is slavery? What is immediate emancipation? Why don't you go to the South? The slaves, if emancipated would overrun the North. The consequences of emancipation to the South. Hebrew servitude. Compensation. Colonization. Prejudice. Treatment and condition of our free colored population. Gradualism, etc., etc. All the prominent objections to our cause were ingeniously presented, and, as conclusively shown to be futile.

The training sessions and the subsequent efforts of the agents represented a milestone in antislavery history. (The topics discussed at the sessions, moreover, revealed, as some recent historians have pointed out, that the abolitionists were keenly aware of the effect of bondage on the masters as well as slaves and of the impact of racism on all Americans.) While the number seventy was never attained and the panic of 1837 intervened before the end of the projected full year of effort, the sixty-five men and two women who did serve were able to double the number of antislavery societies in the nation, to win thousands of Americans to the support of their cause, to increase donations to the national society by 45 percent, and to induce churches, legislative bodies, and other groups to announce their opposition to the South's peculiar institution.

The two women among the famous seventy agents trained by Weld were Sarah and Angelina Grimké of South Carolina. They were members of a prominent slaveholding family; their father was a justice of the state's supreme court. They became Quakers as a result of a visit to Philadelphia, renounced slavery, and began to voice their criticism of the institution during the very decade when the new proslavery "positive good" theory was being developed. It was during this period that the sisters left the South for good—Sarah in 1821 for Philadelphia and Angelina following her in 1829. In 1835, they joined the antislavery movement, and Theodore Weld, whom Angelina married in 1838, trained them for service in the cause.

Frances Wright, the young Scottish woman who lectured in the United States in 1829 in behalf of free opportunities for women and the rights of labor, was the first woman to speak in public in this country. The first American-born woman to speak publicly was Maria W. Stewart, a black resident of Boston. The young widow moved from published prayers and meditations to the lecture platform, addressing the newly formed Afric-American Female Intelligence Society in 1832. At meetings of men and women, first announced and later reported in the *Liberator,* this dedicated Negro woman delivered four lectures in Boston in 1832 and 1833 urging the abolition of slavery, the advancement of blacks, and equality for women.

Months of lecturing as part of the seventy took the Grimké sisters beyond their adopted city of Philadelphia to antislavery meetings in the cities and towns of Massachusetts. The novelty of the Grimké sisters' public appearances, and particularly the excellence of Angelina's lecturing, attracted great crowds. The antislavery testimony of these aristocratic Southern women carried great weight with their audiences, for they "spoke as if they were part of a system—a penitent part." Beyond that, the Grimké sisters paved the way for other women antislavery agents. Abby Kelly, a descendent of Irish Quakers, was also recruited by Weld and became increasingly active as an agent for both the Massachusetts and American Anti-Slavery societies.

While four men of the seventy were designated to work with the free Negroes, none was black. In March 1835, the American Anti-Slavery Society's agency committee sought to employ Reverend Israel Monroe, a black, to promote the improvement of blacks in New York City, and in June of the same year, the committee tried to persuade another black, Theodore S. Wright, one of New York's leading Negro ministers, to accept a temporary assignment as an agent to promote the education and general improvement of free b;acks, but there is no record that either was engaged. In 1836, partly as a result of Weld's urging that it pay more attention to the free Negro, the society resolved to employ an agent, even if white, to "advance the great work of elevating the pecuniary, social, intellectual and moral condition of the free people of color." The executive committee employed John J. Miter and William Yates to work among the free blacks on the eastern side of the Appalachian Mountains, to encourage them to provide for the education of their children, to organize temperance societies, to establish and support a newspaper of their own, and to aid, as much as they could, their people still held in slavery. For the western side of the Allegheny Mountains, the society hired Augustus Wattles (one of the Lane rebels who had taught blacks in Cincinnati) to aid free Negroes, collect information about their condition of life, and encourage them to establish reform societies, purchase land, and become farmers. For similar work among the 10,000 to 15,000 blacks, all fugitives from slavery, who had sought refuge in upper Canada, the society appointed Hiram Wilson, another of the Lane rebels.

While the panic of 1837 cut short the plans to continue the work of the four agents among the free Negroes, during the period they were active, they were able to obtain the support of several Negro communities, help form antislavery societies among blacks, and furnish statistics on conditions of life among free blacks. Yates, for example, gathered material for a pamphlet, *Rights of Colored Men for Suffrage, Citizenship, and Trial by Jury* (1838). It was the first publication to present a detailed picture of black disfranchisement and to urge the right of the Negro to suffrage in the states that had deprived him of the right to vote.

Still, the fact that none of the four agents was black severely limited their influence among free Negroes. In 1838, Charles Lenox Remond, the first black antislavery agent, began his long career with the American Anti-Slavery Society. Soon there were so many black antislavery agents in the field that by 1839 the *Herald of Freedom,* the official organ of the New Hampshire Anti-Slavery Society, was able to report of the various antislavery societies: "They have [negro] men in action now to maintain the antislavery enterprise and to win their liberty and that of their enslaved brethren—if every white Abolitionist were drawn from the field."

ANTISLAVERY PAMPHLETS AND TRACTS

Weld's prodigious efforts during the campaign of the seventy, added to his taxing schedule of speaking from five to fifteen times in single towns, night after night, brought an end to his speaking days forever. He lost his voice, and only long afterward was he able to speak, even in normal conversation, without pain. He turned his talents to supervising the New York office and to writing and editing, at which he was equally masterful. He brought out two tracts that were probably more widely read than any others issued by the American Anti-Slavery Society: *Emancipation in the West Indies,* by James A. Thorne and Joseph A. Kimball, and his own *American Slavery As It Is: Testimony of a Thousand Witnesses.* Weld had decided to publish a factual, firsthand proof that emancipation from slavery would work. Thorne, a Lane rebel, Oberlin graduate, and Southern abolitionist, and Kimball, editor of the *Herald of Freedom,* were dispatched to the West Indies to gather facts about the results of the emancipation of the 800,000 slaves freed by parliamentary and colonial legislation. After an enormous job of putting their product into readable form and correcting their statistics—he was a stickler for accuracy—Weld published their book, *Emancipation in the West Indies,* and ran it through several editions, one of which alone totaled one hundred thousand copies. When bought in quantity, the book sold for twenty cents a copy, and it rapidly rose to the best-seller class.

Weld's own masterpiece, *American Slavery As It Is,* was written to provide a definitive answer to a favorite argument of the new "positive good" proslavery doctrine: that slaves had no cause for complaint since they were well provided for and treated with paternalistic kindness. "That old falsehood, that the slave is kindly treated," Weld declared, "shallow and stupid as it is, has lullabied to sleep four-fifths of the free north and west; but with God's blessing this sleep shall not be unto death." To collect material to prove his thesis, Weld prepared a form letter, which he sent to key figures in the antislavery movement, asking for the names and addresses of persons who, in the course of residence in the South, might have witnessed acts of cruelties inflicted upon slaves. Meanwhile, he himself scoured Southern newspapers and court proceedings to find such evidence, always making sure that nothing was included in his final product that was not accurate. Enough material was obtained to fill 210 double-columned pages in small print. After a rigid examination by the society's executive committee and by William Jay, a legal genius who had been converted to abolitionism, the pamphlet was published in 1839. Thousands of people all over the North and in England read the collection of evidence testifying that slaves were

overworked, underfed, have insufficient sleep, live in miserable huts, generally without floors, and with a single apartment in which both sexes are herded promiscuously; that their clothing serves neither the purposes of comfort nor common decency; that barbarous cruelties are inflicted upon them, such as terrible lacerations with the whip and paddle, fastening upon them iron collars, yokes, chains, horns and bells, branding them with hot irons, knocking out their teeth, maiming and killing them.

All this was based on Southern sources—advertisements in newspapers for fugitive slaves, a compilation of slave laws from various Southern states, court records, letters of slaveowners, and the testimony of reputable men who personally had witnessed the treatment of slaves. *American Slavery As It Is* sold in the hundreds of thousands of copies. It provided ammunition for agents in their debates in the field and became the source book for almost all British antislavery propaganda, whether on platforms or in pamphlets and books. Following his visit to the United States in 1842, Charles Dickens borrowed a good deal of Weld's book for his attacks on slavery in his widely read *American Notes.* According to Harriet Beecher Stowe, who was one of Weld's converts, *American Slavery As It Is* was the seed from which *Uncle Tom's Cabin* grew.

As we shall see below in chapter 22, "Black Abolitionists," there were important pamphlets written by blacks in the antislavery movement, especially by the fugitive slaves. Two important works were written by women. One was Angelina Grimké's *An Appeal to the Christian Women of the South,* which the

American Anti-Slavery Society published in 1837 and with which it flooded the Southern mails. "It was like a patch of blue sky breaking through that storm cloud to the antislavery cause," Elizur Wright, Jr., said later.Even more important was Lydia M. Child's *An Appeal in Favor of That Class Called Africans,* published in 1836. This 216-page book began with a brief history of Negro slavery and "its inevitable effect upon all concerned in it," and went on to depict clearly the horrors of the slave trade. To prove that slavery "presses heavily against the best interests of the state," Child quoted at length from a speech by Faulkner of Virginia in the famous debate of 1832 in that state, in which the latter had argued that the institution "banishes free white labor—it exterminates the mechanic—the artisan—the manufacturer. It deprives them of occupation."

A chapter on colonization, in which the American Colonization Society was denounced as being really interested in the slaveholder, was followed by two chapters dealing with the intellect and moral character of Negroes. These are prefaced with the statement: "I shall take some pains to prove that the present degraded condition of that unfortunate race is produced by artificial causes, not by laws of nature." To prove her argument, Child cited numerous individual examples of spirit, courage, and talent, beginning with "the famous Zhinga, the Negro queen of Angola, born in 1582," and including Phillis Wheatley, Touissaint L'Ouverture, and many others not as well known, from Jamaica, Brazil, England, and other parts of the world. The final chapter, discussing "prejudices against people of color and our duties in relation to this subject," traced the historical origin of prejudice and urged that truth alone was needed to dispel it. In like manner, the abolition of slavery would be brought about by "our almanacs and newspapers showing fairly both sides of the question," "by our preachers speaking of slavery as they do of other evils," by the influence of poets and orators, and by each individual making himself or herself a crusader for the cause. In keeping with her firm belief in the Garrisonian doctrine of moral suasion as the means of ending slavery, Child argued that the truth alone was enough to crush the system. Even the South was "well aware that the ugly edifice is built of rotten timbers and stands on slippery sands, if the loud voice of public opinion could be made to reverberate through the dreary chamber, the unsightly frame would fall, never to rise again."

In the preface of the *Appeal,* Lydia M. Child wrote: "I am fully aware of the task I have undertaken, but though I expect ridicule and censure, I do not fear them." She proved to be an accurate prophet. The book was immediately attacked. The Atheneum, Boston's most exclusive library, withdrew the card it had given her after the publication of her popular novel of colonial times, *Hobomok* (which, interestingly enough, ends with a happy marriage between a Puritan girl and an Indian). The sales of her other books fell off. Boston shut its doors to her socially, and her husband's law practice dwindled. But as she had written in her preface, she did not "fear" these consequences. On the contrary, when an angry letter from the South promised her a "warm reception and lodgings in the calaboose with as much 'nigger company' " as she desired, she wrote to a friend: "How could he know in his moral midnight that choosing to cast our lot with the lowest on the earth was the very way to enter into the companionship with the highest in heaven?"

Despite these attacks, the *Appeal* was widely read. Dr. William Ellery Channing, Charles Sumner, and Thomas Wentworth Higginson were influenced by it, and Wendell Phillips is said to have remarked on reading it, "I don't know but I shall be obliged to come out an abolitionist." He did, of course, come out, not only as an abolitionist but as one of the greatest.

In 1840, the American Anti-Slavery Society issued over 250,000 tracts and pamphlets in comparison to the 47,000 circulated two years before. They were sold under a system of distribution worked out by Theodore Weld and John Greenleaf Whittier in 1838. They made selected tracts for towns, villages, and school districts and had them boxed to sell for twenty, ten, and five dollars, respectively. The local societies readily bought them, and traveling agents distributed them as they moved about the North and West. A package might include "To Mothers in the Free States" by Mrs. E. D. Follen; "Colonization" by Rev. O. B. Frothingham; "The 'Ruin' of Jamaica" by R. Hildreth; "Influence of Slavery upon the White Population," by "A Former Resident of the Slave States"; and "Slavery and the North," by Charles C. Burleigh. Burleigh's antislavery tract had the important task of answering an argument widely disseminated in the North against the abolitionists: that emancipation would throw Northern workingmen into competition with an enormous supply of Negro labor and reduce Northern workers to the lowest level of wages. On the contrary, Burleigh argued,

Instead of sending up the southern blacks to compete with the working classes here, it would both keep them at home and draw back many who were driven hither by slavery, but would gladly return when they could do so and be free. Besides, it would much enlarge the market at the South, for the fruits of northern industry and enterprise. The southern laborers, when free and paid, would buy of us many comforts and conveniences not allowed them now;—cloths, hats, shoes, furniture, house-hold utensils, improved working-tools, a countless variety of northern manufacturers, and of foreign wares, imported through the North;—the demand for which would give new activity to our shops and mills and shipping, and steadier employment, and, most likely, higher wages, to all kinds of labor here. Three million new consumers of the wares we make and sell, would add greatly to the income of the North. New shops and factories built to meet their wants, would grow to villages and towns; and, employing many busy hands in every useful calling. . . . Slavery keeps from us all these benefits, and thus, in robbing southern labor, robs also northern.

Burleigh summarized one of the chief criticisms that antislavery theorists made against the Southern slave system: that the inability of the slave labor force to consume was the main barrier to economic growth in the South.

From its beginnings, abolitionism involved the editing and circulating of newspapers. Without reaching very large circulations, the abolitionist papers multiplied both in number and influence, and the latter was extended through quotations from them by other newspapers. In 1834, the *Liberator* had a weekly circulation of 2,300, with 75 percent of its subcribers Negroes. The weekly *Emancipator*, which was the society's official organ (the *Liberator* being the personal organ of Garrison) reached a circulation of 3,800 copies each issue. There were fourteen abolitionist papers—organs of the state antislavery societies—being published in 1839.

Besides newspapers, books, and pamphlets for adult readers, the American Anti-Slavery Society also published Jane Elizabeth Hitchcock's *The Young Abolitionist*, a children's guide to slavery and abolition, and a monthly magazine for children, the *Slave's Friend*, containing accounts of exciting escapes from slavery, as well as an "Anti-Slavery Alphabet" and "Alphabet of Slavery," which went in part:

> A is an Abolitionist
> A man who wants to free
> The wretched slave—and give to all
> An equal liberty.

* * *

> A is an African torn from his home,
> B is a Bloodhound to catch all that roam.
> C is the Cotton Plant Slaves pick and hoe.
> D is the Driver who makes their Blood flow.

ANTISLAVERY FAIRS

To maintain the antislavery press required constant and unremitting effort. Financial campiagns were undertaken, and special appeals were made regularly. Money would come in, sometimes in the form of handsome legacies, sometimes in the form of a bracelet, sometimes in the form of a sizable donation from wealthy merchants like the Tappan brothers. Most often, however, the finances came from shoemakers, factory girls, country parsons, college professors, poets, farmers, students—from men and women, Negro and white.

Perhaps the greatest contribution of the female antislavery societies, and certainly the one in which the greatest number of women were able to participate, was in the raising of funds necessary to carry on the antislavery work. The annual antislavery fair, sponsored by the female antislavery societies, became a vital source of funds for the cause. The fair was usually held the week before Christmas, so that people could buy their Christmas gifts and at the same time contribute to a cause dear to their consciences. All through the year, female societies and sewing circles sewed and knitted. European friends made annual contributions of money and articles. In 1841, Maria Weston Chapman, who organized the Boston fair for a period of twenty years, wrote to Lydia M. Child: "Petersburg, Paris, Geneva, Rome, London, Glasgow, all Ireland, the lovely city of the Cape, and the Haitian city of Santiago are all contributors." Friendly merchants made donations or sold articles at wholesale prices to the women. Among the articles offered at the 1840 Boston fair was "jewelry of friends who had renounced it for their own wearing for the sake of the cause" with the hope that the new wearers would learn to renounce it in the future.

The receipts from the Boston fair increased annually from $300 in 1834 to $5,270 in 1857, at which time a subscription list was subsituted for the fair. The Philadelphia Female Anti-Slavery Society was credited with raising $35,000 during the antislavery crusade. Large or small, the funds raised at the fairs were unquestionably, in the words of Garrison, a "source of life-sustaining energy" to the antislavery movement, not only financially but educationally as well. As a social function, the fair made many new friends for the slaves, enlisting the interest of men and women who were not prepared to make greater sacrifices.

The American Anti-Slavery Society and its auxiliary societies did not rely on the printed word alone. Some 40,000 copies of "pictorial representations of slavery and of emancipation . . . prepared by artists" were struck off every year. A steel engraving of "kneeling slaves" by the black artist Patrick Reason enjoyed a great vogue, as did the medallion bearing the motto, "Am I not a man and a brother?" Struck in 1787 by Josiah Wedgewood, the British master potter and abolitionist, it pictured a Negro in chains, with one knee on the ground and both hands lifted up to heaven. Its design was taken from the seal of the Committee for the Abolition of the Slave Trade, formed in Britain in May 1787.

Most of the antislavery societies were poor. The *Anti-Slavery Record* of the American Anti-Slavery Society notes for 1835 the following contributions: January, $11,000; April, $35,000; May, $13,000; July, $24,000; November, $9.25; December, $3.25. In several years, the monthly contributions were closer to those of November and December 1835 than to those of the other months. The Massachusetts Anti-Slavery Society collected approximately $6,000 annually, and most other state societies received only about $3,000. Yet despite their frequent lack of funds, the abolitionists carried their message into every area of American life. They kept the community astir; they made people think and talk. And as the campaign to reach all got underway, the ranks of the abolitionists steadily increased. There were 60 societies in 1835; 527 in 1836, including eight state societies; 1,006 in 1837; 1,350 in 1838; and 2,000 in 1840. Local societies, auxiliary to both the state and the national associations, mushroomed all over the North. There were almost 150 in Massachusetts alone before the end of the decade. It has been estimated that the societies averaged eighty members each, which would mean a total of close to 200,000 members in 1840, or almost a quarter of a million organized adult abolitionists just six years after the American Anti-Slavery Society began.

20

Civil Rights and Antislavery

In an 1836 letter "To the Women of Great Britain," Mary Parker, president of the Boston Female Anti-Slavery Society, wrote: "Scenes of outrage have become so common as to follow regularly upon the expression of our opinions. We are made to feel in our persons that the violation of the rights of the black man has made the rights of the white man insecure." Abolitionists were not alone in this feeling. The rapid growth of abolitionist sentiment during the 1830s was not merely the result of a thoroughgoing system of education. Many white Americans gradually began to see clearly that there was an identity between the struggle for Negro freedom and that for freedom of all people and that the democratic rights of all people were threatened by the same power that kept millions of slaves in chains. There was a growing conviction that the slaveholders and their Northern sympathizers were potential threats to the constitutional rights of all white Americans, and that to preserve their own civil liberties, they had to support the democratic rights of the abolitionists to fight slavery.

The new abolitionists, led by William Lloyd Garrison, believed that the entire nation had to be saved from the sin of slaveholding and that this could be done peacefully by moral suasion—that is, by convincing both the slaveholders and the nonslaveholders of their complicity in wrongdoing. Although they eschewed all violence and many believed in nonresistance, violence stalked their path. The New York Anti-Slavery Society was organized in 1832 while a determined mob raged outside the hall. Antislavery agents were stoned and their meetings broken up. Nor were the woman spared. Abby Kelly was frequently met by hails of mud and stones. Meeting halls and churches closed their doors to abolitionist speakers, and newspapers, North and South, reviled them as conspirators, incendiaries, and insurrectionists. They were called "enemies of the law of the land, the constitution of the government, the union of the states, the common courtesies of life, the precepts of religion, and the rights and lives of millions of our countrymen." Ely Moore of New York, who was elected as "labor's first Congressman'' in 1834, declared on the floor of Congress that abolitionism was allied to "blind, reckless, feverish fanaticism." According to Moore, "the wild, enthusiastic and impetuous spirit which . . . strewed the Plains of Palestine with the corpses of the crusades stood with lighted and uplifted torch, hard by the side of abolitionism ready to spread conflagration and death around the land." The very term *abolitionist* became a degrading epithet. As Charles Godfrey Leland recalled later:

There was hardly a soul whom I knew, except my mother, to whom an abolitionist was not simply the same thing as a disgraceful discreditable malefactor. Even my father, when angry with me one day, could think of nothing better than to tell me that I knew I was an abolitionist.

One Northern newspaper expressed regret that the abolitionists could not be banished "upon the same principle that dogs are muzzled in hot weather," and the *New York Courier and Enquirer* even denied the abolitionists the right to police protection, editorializing: "When they endeavor to disseminate opinions, which if generally imbibed, must infallibly destroy our National Union, and produce scenes of blood and carnage . . . the egis [*sic*] of the law indignantly withdraws its shelter from them." Senator James Buchanan of Pennsylvania, the future president of the United States, questioned the right of the abolitionists to claim the constitutional guarantes of free speech, assembly, and press. He conceded that "the right of free discussion certainly ought never to be surrendered" and then continued: "But a right is one thing and its abuse is another. It is certain we all have a right to discuss the question of slavery; but is it proper for us to organize ourselves into antislavery societies, and to exercise this right systematically, not for the purpose of doing good at home, for thank God! here slavery does not exist, but for that of spreading terror and alarm throughout the Southern states?"

In the South there was no longer even "a right to discuss the question of slavery." After 1830, freedom of speech and of the press on the slavery question did not exist in many Southern states. William W. Freehling has shown that in the South Carolina nullification controversy of 1832, some southerners sought to prevent widespread criticism of slavery by diverting attention from it to the tariff. Nearly every Southern state passed laws aimed at publications designed to encourage abolition, and a resolution introduced in the Georgia Senate on November 20, 1831, and signed into law on December 24, 1831, offered $500 to

any person or persons who shall arrest, bring to trial and prosecute to conviction, under the laws of this State, the editor and publisher of a certain paper called the *Liberator*, published in the town of Boston and State of Massachusetts; or who shall arrest, bring to trial and prosecute to conviction, under the laws of this State, any other person or persons who shall utter, publish or circulate within limits of this State said paper called the *Liberator*, or any other paper, circular, pamphlet, letter of address of a seditious character.

Because the original draft of the resolution did not specify the amount of the reward, Garrison sarcastically inserted the sum "$999888777,666555444, 333222111" when he reprinted the resolution in the *Liberator*.

Before the 1830s, some southerners tried to suppress any news of slave revolts and conspiracies. In 1800, after the Gabriel Prosser plot in Virginia had failed, Governor James Monroe warned President Thomas Jefferson that it was imperative that news of the incident not be made public. Twenty-two years later, the same policy was urged during the Denmark Vesey scare in South Carolina. But the same policy was not adopted with the Nat Turner revolt, which could be blamed on the new abolitionists; the fact that the uprising occurred only a few months after the appearance of the *Liberator* made it easy to convince many people that the antislavery paper was responsible for the slave revolt even though had Turner read the first issue of the *Liberator* (a paper he neither read nor saw), he would have come upon the following in a poem addressed by Garrison to the slaves:

> Not by the sword shall your deliverance be;
> Not by the shedding of your master's blood.

In a letter to the *Emancipator,* official organ of the American Anti-Slavery Society, Reverend Thomas Sydenham Witherspoon, a Presbyterian minister in Alabama, defended slavery and threatened any abolitionists who dared come South with lynching. This letter read in part:

I draw my warrant from the scriptures of the Old and New Testaments to hold the slave in bondage. The principle of holding the heathen in bondage is recognized by God. . . . When the tardy process of the law is too long in redressing our grievances, we of the South have adopted the summary remedy of Judge Lynch; and really, I think it one of the most wholesome and salutary remedies for the malady of Northern fanaticism that can be applied, and no doubt my worthy friend, the editor of the Emancipator and Human Rights, would feel the better of its enforcement, provided he had a Southern administrator. I go to the Bible for my warrant in all moral matters. . . . Let your emissaries, dare venture to cross the Potomac, and I cannot promise you that their fate will be less than Haman's. Then beware how you goad an insulted, but magnanimous people to deeds of desperation.

CAUSES OF ANTIABOLITIONIST VIOLENCE

As the abolitionist movement mushroomed, opposition to it mounted proportionately. This hostility had a variety of causes, and not all of them had the same effects on all classes and groups in Northern society. Nor is it possible to say that a monolithic Northern consensus opposed to abolitionism developed during the 1830s. Moreover, as Norman Ratner points out in a recent study of the subject, "anti-abolitionism was usually expressed in slogans and emotional appeals rather than in rational argument." Yet beneath the rhetoric associated with opponents of antislavery agitation, there were economic, social, and psychological factors, which were totally rational.

The threat of losing millions of dollars in slave property brought a furious response to the antislavery crusade from the slaveowners. "Our slave population at this time numbers about three millions of souls, estimated to be worth one thousand millions of dollars," declared a Mississippi slaveowner in the mid-1830s.

This is a vast amount of property which no five millions of people in the world will voluntarily give up for the sake of conscience. But as large as this amount is, it is only one item: The depreciation in the value of our land, and other property, as the result of abolition, would equal the value of the negroes—that is one thousand millions of dollars. In a word, the abolition of slavery in the South would impoverish every slave state in the Union with probably one or two exceptions. This we cannot and will not tolerate.

This was only part of the picture. Slavery was also important for the businessmen of the North. Right up to the outbreak of the Civil War, New York City dominated every phase of the cotton trade from plantation to market. The cotton factors of the South were either themselves New Yorkers or the agents of New York firms. The shipping vessels that carried the cotton either directly to England or coastwise to New York or New England were frequently owned by New Yorkers. New York companies handled the insurance of the cotton cargoes. The advances necessary for the planting of the new crop came from New York firms and banks. Finally, the domestic and imported merchandise used in the Cotton Kingdom came mainly from New York. Even goods manufactured in Newark, Hartford, Boston, and other eastern cities were sold to southerners in New York. Little wonder, then, that New York City was referred to as "the prolongation of the South" where "ten thousand cords of interests are linked with the Southern Slaveholder."

A handful of New York merchants, especially Arthur and Lewis Tappan, welcomed the new abolitionists and themselves became part of the antislavery movement. They contributed time and money to the cause, even after they had been threatened that they would "lose the benefit of the Southern trade." But they were the rare exceptions. The viewpoint of the vast majority of the merchants was expressed in a "card" inserted by New York firms in the newspapers assuring their customers that not only were they not abolitionists but they regarded "the agitation of the slave question, and the interference with the rights of Southern slave-holders as inexpedient, unjust and pregnant with evils." As for "interference with the rights" of antislavery men and women, not only did that not matter, but New York merchants would see to it that they could not be exercised. This attitude is well expressed by a partner in a large mercantile house in an 1835 conversation with Samuel J. May, a prominent abolitionist:

Mr. May, we are not such great fools as not to know that slavery is a great evil and a great wrong. But it was consented to by the founders of the Republic. It was provided for in the

Constitution of our Union. A great portion of the property of the Southerners is invested under its sanction; and the business of the North as well as of the South, has become adjusted to it. There are millions upon millions of dollars due from the Southerners to the merchants and mechanics of this city alone, the payment of which would be jeopardized by a rupture between the North and the South. We cannot afford, sir, to let you and your associates succeed in your endeavor to overthrow slavery. It is not a matter of principle with us. It is a matter of business necessity. We cannot afford to let you succeed. And I have called you out to let you know, and to let your fellow laborers know, that we do not mean to allow you to succeed. We mean, sir, to put you Abolitionists down—by fair means, if we can, by foul means, if we must.

What this New York businessman told an abolitionist was repeated, with variations, by his colleagues in Boston and Lowell, where there was a "triple entente between the 'Lords of the Lash,' the 'Lords of the Loom,' and the 'Lords of the Long Wharf.'"

Although the businessmen and other propertied elements were themselves part of the antiabolitionist mobs, they relied mainly on the lower classes to stop antislavery activity by "foul means." The spectre that emancipation would throw Northern workingmen into competition with an enormous supply of liberated black workers was repeatedly raised to arouse labor hostility to the abolitionists. Senator James Hubbard warned that the antislavery agitation would, if successful, fill the "rich valleys of New England with the free black population of the south, and there to compete with her free labor." Congressman Ely Moore was of the opinion that the real object of the antislavery crusade was to bring the Southern Negro into conflict with the Northern worker so that the moral and political character, the pride, power, and independence of the latter "would be gone forever." William Leggett, editor of the *New York Evening Post* (who was later converted to the antislavery cause), argued that the influx of a vast number of emancipated Negroes would not only throw the white workers out of employment but would depreciate the value of labor to an extent that would be fatal to their prosperity. He warned that if the emancipated slaves "cannot bring themselves up to the standard of the free labouring white man, they might pull the latter down to their own level, and thus lower the condition of the white laborer by association, if not by amalgamation."

These and other appeals to the Northern white workers were distributed in handbills and broadsides in working-class districts, along with attacks on the abolitionists for hypocritically seeking to divert attention from the "wretched" plight of the Northern laborer. Addressing a group of Boston mechanics at a meeting held near the office of the *Liberator,* labor editor Theophilus Fiske urged the abolitionists to forget about the black slaves in the South and "advocate and demand the immediate emancipation of the white slaves of the North." The next day the appeal was distributed widely in Boston in leaflets paid for by merchants engaged in the Southern trade. Such incidents led Lydia M. Child to insist that it was not the workers "who are to blame for the persecutions suffered by the abolitionists'' but rather that ''manufacturers who supply the South, merchants who trade with the South . . . are the ones who really promote the mobs.'' William Goodell also contended that mobs that attacked antislavery meetings and lecturers in the North were instigated, or at least passively approved of, by the ''higher class of society.'' Goodell went on to write: ''The aristocracy of a city or village, and its mobocracy, if not exactly identical, or even if exhibiting the strong contrasts of splendor, were found to be the inseparable ingredients, the *sine qua non* of a riot.'' The people making up the mob often became the unwitting tools of the upper classes. In a study of the antislavery constituency in Jacksonian New York City, John B. Jentz has demonstrated that the views of Child and Goodell were not without substance, and that the presence of artisans and other workingmen in the antislavery movement should qualify the generally accepted picture of ''the hostility of labor to abolition.''

In his study of Northern opposition to the antislavery movement in the 1830s, Norman Ratner concludes that racism was the primary motive. The belief in Negro inferiority, which was stressed by newspaper editors, essayists, and novelists, rendered the concept of black equality unacceptable to most white Americans, and they believed that social equality and amalgamation were the ultimate objective of the antislavery movement. This alone was enough to trigger antiabolitionist violence. On the other hand, in his study of opposition to abolitionism in the 1830s among men of the ''Jacksonian persuasion,'' Gerald S. Henig concludes that ''one factor does emerge paramount'': ''fear that outside interference with slavery in the South might possibly endanger the existence of the Union.'' Other factors were important, but whatever their ''specific field of interest,'' antiabolitionism among the Jacksonians ''was primarily a result of their view that the antislavery crusade possessed the potential to provoke a dissolution of the Union.''

Of course, as the New York merchant told Samuel J. May, in threatening to use ''foul means'' to put down the abolitionists, business interests ''would be jeopardized by a rupture between the North and the South.'' In any case, whatever the ''primary'' reason, there were plenty of cases of ''foul means.''

THE ''MOB YEARS''

In the summer of 1834, a mob, stirred up by the accusation in leading newspapers that abolitionists sanctioned interracial marriage, rioted in New York City. The mobsters broke into an integrated antislavery meeting at the Chatham Street Chapel. It then crashed into the home of Arthur Tappan, dragged out his furniture and bedding and tossed them into a bonfire, and damaged Tappan's store. It broke the windows of the home of a minister who had dared to defend the antislavery viewpoint from his pulpit, invaded St. Philip's African Episcopal Church on Center Street, destroying its organ, and in general, terrorized all blacks and whites known to be friendly to the antislavery movement. The mayor allowed the mob to wreak its riotous will for three days, after which it was belatedly dispersed by the militia.

The July riots in New York City were followed by two and a half years of violent opposition to the abolitionists, a period that Russell B. Nye has called the "mob years." In August 1834, the *Boston Commercial Gazette* called for indictment of Garrison and his associates as "public nuisances," offering the alternative of "a wholesome and salutary coat of tar and feathers." In September, George Thompson, the British antislavery leader whom Garrison had met in England in 1833 and persuaded to come to the United States to help the antislavery effort, received a rude welcome upon his arrival with his wife and children. Thompson wrote to Garrison from New York City that he had been "warmly greeted by the abolitionists of this city, but somewhat curiously received by the other dwellers in this commercial metropolis of the *freest empire* under the sun." The "curious" reception consisted of the banishing of the Thompson family from the Atlantic Hotel on the insistence of the other boarders, who met and passed resolutions deploring the presence of "foreign incendiaries" in the house and forced the management to ask Thompson and his family to look for lodgings elsewhere.

At first, Thompson's tour went well, and he drew good crowds as he spoke in Massachusetts, Maine, New Hampshire, and Rhode Island. Trouble began in October in Augusta, Maine, where windows were broken. Missiles were thrown in Concord, New Hampshire. In Lowell, the town hall in which he was speaking was surrounded by a mob who threw several missiles through the windows, barely missing Thompson's head. By December, all Boston halls had been closed to Thompson except for that of the New England Anti-Slavery Society and a few churches. Then in late February and early March 1835, Thompson spoke to big crowds in New York and Philadelphia without incident. The press of abolitionists to hear Thompson was so great in Philadelphia that the galleries in the Cherry Street Reformed Presbyterian Church where he lectured partially collapsed.

But this was only the calm before the storm. The summer of 1835 was more turbulent than that a year earlier. There was an anti-Negro riot in Philadelphia in mid-July. That same week, George Thompson was mobbed in New Hampshire. On July 29, prominent citizens of Charleston, South Carolina, broke into the post office and appropriated mail brought from New York. They sought out and discovered various papers and items of mail coming from the American Anti-Slavery Society. On the next night, the abolitionist mail was publicly burned, and effigies of Garrison, Arthur Tappan, and other "fanatics" were hanged and then burned. In early August, the citizens of Richmond met and issued a pronouncement: "The South has a constitutional right to its slave property in the States, the Territories, and the District of Columbia . . . the only way to preserve the Union is by suppression of the abolitionists." The South, it declared, would not tolerate "inflammatory" publications being sent into the region, and the postmaster-general in Washington was asked to prevent any future dispatching of abolitionist material to the South. The North was asked to show its sympathy for the South—"by works as well as by words."

During this period, Amos Dresser, one of the Lane rebels, was distributing antislavery newspapers and pamphlets in Kentucky and Tennessee, but not to "any person of color, bound or free," since all of the slave states were aroused by the discovery of quantities of abolitionist material in the Southern mails. On August 18, 1835, the mayor of Nashville had Dresser arrested and brought to trial before the "Committee of Vigilance and Safety" for having allegedly posted handbills in the city "inviting an insurrection of the slaves." The Vigilance Committee, which was "composed of a great portion of the respectable citizens of Nashville," including "most of the elders of the Presbyterian Church," found Dresser guilty of belonging to an Ohio abolitionist society and of distributing antislavery literature. It sentenced him to receive twenty lashes on the back and ordered him to leave the state within twenty-four hours.

When the mob broke into the South Carolina post office, absconded with, and then burned antislavery publications in an enormous bonfire, Charleston postmaster Alfred Huger sought the advice of Postmaster-General Amos Kendall, who, in turn, conferred with President Andrew Jackson. Although he was himself a slaveowner and a bitter foe of the abolitionists and even though he denounced "this wicked plan of exciting the negroes to insurrection and to massacre," President Jackson suggested that the mail be delivered. However, Kendall intimated strongly to Huger that if South Carolina censored the mails, Washington would not enforce the law. On August 4, Kendall announced the administration's official position: "We owe an obligation to the laws, but a higher one to the communities in which we live; and if the former be perverted to destroy the latter, it is patriotism to disregard them."

New York City postmaster Samuel L. Gouverneur immediately requested of Kendall the same arbitrary authority to detain circulation of abolitionist mailings. The latter responded affirmatively on August 22.

Throughout August and September, antiabolitionist meetings were held in Northern cities, and when the abolitionists tried to meet, their gatherings were attacked. William H. Seward recalled that "even in the capitol of Vermont, antislavery meetings held in the legislative halls were assailed, and in other portions of the State they were broken up. In Pennsylvania, twenty-five out of thirty meetings were interrupted." Small wonder that Garrison wrote an impassioned editorial entitled "Reign of Terror."

The situation in the vicinity of New York and Connecticut became so explosive that it was deemed unsafe for Thompson to speak in either New York City or New Haven. He, Garrison, and the Tappans were threatened with assassination. Lydia Maria Child wrote to a friend on August 15, 1835:

I am at Brooklyn, at the house of a very hospitable Englishman, a friend of Mr. Thompson's. I have not ventured into the city, nor does one of us dare to go to church today, so great is the excitement here. . . . 'Tis like the times of the French Revolution, when no man dared trust his neighbors. Private assassins from New Orleans are lurking at the corner of the streets to stab Arthur Tappan; and very large sums are offered for any one who will convey Mr. Thompson into the slave States. . . . He [Thompson] is almost a close prisoner in his chamber, his friends deeming him in imminent peril the moment it is ascertained where he is.

Thompson reached Boston on August 18. The clerk in the antislavery office wrote to his brother from that city that there were people ready to assassinate Thompson in daylight. Groups of white hoodlums were roaming the streets, looking for Negroes to beat up, and many homes of blacks were looted. Along with Thompson and Garrison, Negroes bore the brunt of the attacks during this infamous period in Boston's history. On September 10, a gallows, labeled for both Garrison and Thompson, was constructed in front of the house in which Thompson was to live.

On October 14, Thompson was scheduled to address the anniversary meeting of the founding of the Boston Female Anti-Slavery Society. The Boston press immediately swung into action. "When before in this city or any other did a benevolent society of ladies publicly invite an itinerant vagabond, a hired foreign incendiary, to insult their countrymen and fellow citizens, and to kindle flames of discord between different members of the Union?" the *Boston Courier* raged. Another paper called openly for violence: "Whether surrounded by females or not, he must meet the consequences his reckless and wicked conduct merits."

The Female Anti-Slavery Society rescheduled its meeting for October 21 and relocated it at the antislavery office. It was decided that Thompson would not attend the meeting, and this intelligence was reluctantly imparted by Garrison to the mayor of Boston when inquiry was made. The store owners in the area were anxious lest a mob damage their property and were pressuring the city government to prevent the meeting. The mayor let it be known that Thompson would not appear, hoping that would suffice to calm things. But the day of the meeting, signs appeared on the streets:

THOMPSON, THE ABOLITIONIST!!!

That infamous foreign scoundrel, Thompson, will hold forth this afternoon, at the Liberator office, No. 48 Washington Street. The present is a fair opportunity for the friends of the Union, to *snake Thompson out!* It will be a contest between the Abolitionists and the friends of the Union. A purse of $100 has been raised by a number of patriotic citizens to reward the individual who shall first lay violent hands on Thompson, so that he may be brought to the tar-kettle before dark. Friends of the Union, be vigilant. Boston, Wednesday, 12 o'clock.

Garrison also received a note warning him not to issue the *Liberator* anymore, or he would be tarred and feathered and would risk the loss of his life. Instead Garrison published the Thompson "inflammatory handbill" and asked: "Who are the incendiaries now?"

The women gathered for their meeting as announced, and Garrison appeared punctually to address them as he had been requested to do. But a crowd of disorderly young men was already in the hall, and the mayor ordered the women to leave since he could no longer guarantee their safety. "He saw fit to disperse us rather than the mob," stated Maria Weston Chapman, in protest against this violation of their right to assemble. As the women marched through the angry crowd, down the stairs, and into the street, two by two, a white woman taking the arms of a black "sister," they were shocked to see "the gentlemen of property and standing" lined up apparently ready to attack them.

Garrison had retired to his office, which was divided from the hall by only a board partition. Since the women were gone and it was obvious that Thompson was not available, interest centered on Garrison in his office. There were cries of "Lynch him!" The crowd demanded that the antislavery sign be taken down from the office and the mayor complied. However, this did not satisfy the crowd, which continued to howl for Garrison. He was persuaded by both his friends and the mayor to make his exit from a back window of the building; however, he was soon detected by the mob, seized, and led through the Boston streets with a rope around him. The mayor's forces finally rescued him from the mob and got him into the city hall. The city fathers then decided that Garrison's continued presence would endanger the building and that the abolitionist leader would be safe only in jail, where he was finally taken. The next morning, he inscribed an appropriate message about his imprisonment on the walls of his cell:

Wm. Lloyd Garrison was put into this cell on Wednesday afternoon, October 21, 1835, to save him from the violence of a "respectable and influential" mob, who sought to destroy him for preaching the abominable and dangerous doctrine, that "all men are created equal," and that all oppression is odious in the sight of God. "Hail, Columbia!" Cheers for the Autocrat of Russia and the Sultan of Turkey!

Reader, let this inscription remain till the last slave in this despotic land be loosed from his fetters.

On the day on which Garrison was nearly hanged, black John Hilton remained close by him as long as it appeared that he was in danger and left him only after the sheriff had locked him in the jail. In fact, during this entire period when it appeared that Garrison's life was in danger, a small group of Negroes followed him after dark in order to try to prevent harm from coming to him. John B. Vashon, a prosperous black barber and for many years Garrison's close friend (he was entertained in Garrison's home on the day of the mob attack), visited the imprisoned abolitionist the morning after the riot, and presented him with a new hat to replace the one destroyed by the mob.

On October 23, two days after he was mobbed, Garrison and his wife, Helen, who was pregnant with their first child, arrived in Brooklyn, Connecticut, at the home of his wife's family. He remained there, except for occasional trips to Boston, until the latter part of September, 1836, when he returned to the city permanently with his wife and their infant son. Only then was it decided that it was safe for Garrison to continue to live in Boston. Meanwhile all of the Boston papers and many city officials took the position that the real cause of the mob was the abolitionist insistence on holding meetings in spite of the hostile public sentiment.

On the same day that the mob disrupted the Boston Female Anti-Slavery Society meeting and Garrison narrowly escaped lynching, a Utica mob dispersed a convention called to form a New York State antislavery society. When Gerrit Smith, who in 1835 was a colonizationist rather than an abolitionist, witnessed the dispersal of the convention, he invited all of the delegates to convene at his estate in Peterboro, some twenty-five miles from Utica. A majority of them accepted the invitation, but on the roads of Peterboro, they "encountered logs deliberately placed to impede progress, and endured an occasional pelting by mud, eggs, clubs, and even stones." In its Third Annual Report, published in 1836, the American Anti-Slavery Society noted: "The 21st of October, 1835, will long be remembered for two mobs, from the infamy of which our country can recover only by a full repentance and the complete abolition of slavery."

The end of 1835 and the beginning of 1836 witnessed still further efforts to suppress the antislavery movement. It was considered unsafe for George Thompson to appear in public, and his visit to the United States came to an end on November 8. Even then he had to depart in secret. He was rowed out at night to the New Brunswick packet and had to leave his wife and children behind until they could rejoin him safely.

Later that month, the South Carolina legislature unanimously adopted resolutions "earnestly" requesting that the nonslaveholding states "promptly and effectually suppress all those associations, within their respective limits, purporting to be Abolition Societies, and that they . . . make it highly penal to print, publish and distribute newspapers, pamphlets, tracts, and pictorial representations calculated . . . to excite the slaves of the Southern States to insurrection and revolt." On December 7, in his annual message to Congress, President Jackson recommended passage of a law prohibiting circulation "through the mails in the Southern states of incendiary publications intended to instigate the slaves to insurrection." In response to Jackson's recommendation, Senator John C. Calhoun reported a bill "making it illegal for any deputy postmaster knowingly to receive and put in the mail any pamphlet, newspaper, handbill, or other printed paper, or pictorial representation, touching the subject of slavery, directed to any person or post office in those states where the laws prohibited their circulation." Although the bill was ultimately defeated in the Senate by a vote of fifteen to nineteen, "decisions for mail were finally placed in the hands of local postmasters. Abolitionists gave up their attempt to keep the mails free."

FREEDOM OF THE PRESS

On January 1, 1836, the first issue of the *Philanthropist,* an antislavery newspaper, was published in New Richmond, Ohio, under the editorship of James G.

Birney. The son of a wealthy Kentucky slaveowner, Birney became interested in colonization between 1826 and 1833 and served as a lecturer for the American Colonization Society and as vice-president of the Kentucky Colonization Society. An early advocate of gradual emancipation, Birney broke with the colonizationists in 1834 and came out in favor of immediate emancipation. That same year, he emancipated his six household slaves, and five years later, he freed twenty-one slaves inherited from his father. While Birney advocated immediate emancipation, he attempted to treat the subject of slavery with "candor and fairness and with a strict regard to the well-established principles of amicable discussion." Nevertheless, he began to encounter violent opposition in New Richmond, and in April 1836 he moved the *Philanthropist* to Cincinnati, where it soon became the official organ of the Ohio State Anti-Slavery Society, an organization of about twelve thousand Ohio abolitionists. On July 12, 1836, the office of Birney's printer, Achilles Pugh, was broken into by a riotous mob, the issue of the *Philanthropist* for that week was torn up, and the press was broken up and the smaller parts were stolen. Undaunted, the executive committee of the Ohio Anti-Slavery Society helped Pugh reassemble his press and guaranteed him that it would bear any further loss of his shop resulting from mob violence. Pugh agreed to continue publication of the *Philanthropist,* and Birney immediately published an editorial declaring that the attempt to silence the paper was an attack on the fundamental freedom of speech and press. However, his efforts were of no avail and aroused no interest among the city authorities. On July 30, the mob reassembled, completely destroyed the interior of the printer's shop, and threw the press into the river.

The following year, the *Alton Observer*, the official organ of the Illinois State Anti-Slavery Society, met a similar fate, but its editor, Elijah P. Lovejoy, was less fortunate. He was killed in the meleé while defending his press.

The son of a Presbyterian minister from Albion, Maine, and a graduate of Waterville (now Colby) College, Lovejoy had moved to St. Louis in 1827 to teach school and edit a Whig newspaper. Five years later, he returned to the East to study at Princeton Theological Seminary. Licensed to preach by the Philadelphia presbytery in 1833, Lovejoy went back to Missouri to edit the *St. Louis Observer*, a Presbyterian weekly, and to champion gradual emancipation, temperance, and anti-Catholicism. His difficulty as a crusader began in St. Louis. A mob had removed a Negro from jail and burned him. In the investigation that followed, the judge refused to indict any of the whites involved and blamed the mob action on Lovejoy's criticism of slavery. In 1836, Lovejoy moved his press up the Mississippi River to Alton, Illinois.

By March 1837, Lovejoy had been converted to immediate emancipation, joined the American Anti-Slavery Society, and announced his intention of organizing local and state abolitionist societies. The *Alton Observer,* Lovejoy's paper, became the most influential antislavery paper in Illinois. While it attracted many adherents, it also attracted enemies. Already troubled by a recent decline in the local economy, many of Alton's leading men were frankly alarmed at the prospect of their town's becoming a center for an organized antislavery movement, which they felt would lead, among other things, to a boycott of their businesses by southerners. Many prominent citizens organized to silence Lovejoy and his press.

Up to that point, Lovejoy had adhered faithfully to the declared nonviolence, nonresistance policy of the American Anti-Slavery Society and had regularly published the clause in the society's constitution reading: "never in any way [to] countenance the oppressed in vindicating their rights by resort to physical force." When a hostile Alton mob threatened to destroy his press and tar and feather the editor, Lovejoy appealed to the law to protect his property and his freedom of speech. But Alton's mayor said he did not have the necessary police to protect him, and Alton's leading citizens warned him to leave town. Mobs destroyed his press three times, dismantling it and throwing it into the river, and repeatedly invaded his house, driving his wife into hysterics. At this point, Lovejoy decided to abandon nonviolence and nonresistance and to protect himself and family; he brought guns into his home. "I have had inexpressible reluctance to resort to this method of defence," he wrote in a letter published in the *Liberator*. "But dear-bought experience has taught me, that there is at present no safety for me, and no defense in this place, either in the laws or the protecting aegis of public sentiment. . . . Every night when I lie down, it is with the settled conviction that there are those near me and around me who seek my life. I have resisted this conviction as long as I could, but it has been forced upon me."

In November 1837, Lovejoy's fourth press arrived, and he stored it for safety in a stone warehouse near the river. To guard it Lovejoy, with the permission of the mayor of Alton, armed himself and his friends, and they took turns staying inside the warehouse. On the night of November 7, 1837, the warehouse was attacked by a mob. Lovejoy was mortally wounded by rifle fire when he and another man rushed out of the stone warehouse to shoot a rioter attempting to set fire to the roof. He was thirty-five years old when he died. No one was punished for the murder.

Even while they were beginning to debate among themselves as to how to reconcile self-defense and nonresistance, the abolitionists enshrined Lovejoy as a martyr to their cause. Samuel J. May and the Grimké sisters publicly protested Lovejoy's act in arming to protect himself at the time he met his death, condemning it as a violation of the principle of nonviolence and nonresistance. However, they were a minority among the abolitionists, and the American Anti-Slavery Society refused to condemn Lovejoy's action.

Blacks had no such problem in assessing Lovejoy. On November 25, 1837, in a front-page editorial, surrounded by black borders, the *Colored American* announced gravely: "Elijah P. Lovejoy, that fearless advocate of the press, has fallen a victim of the fury of a mob, thirsting for his blood, because he dared to lift up his voice against the oppression of the poor slave." Mass meetings were held by blacks throughout the North to condemn the murder and to raise funds for Lovejoy's widow.

FREEDOM OF ASSEMBLY

"Fanueil Hall Refused," read a headline in the *Liberator* of December 3, 1837, under an announcement that a public meeting would be held "in the old Cradle of Liberty" by the citizens of Boston "to express their abhorrence of the recent tragedy at Alton, which resulted in the murder of the Rev. Elijah P. Lovejoy for attempting to maintain the liberty of the press." Beneath the notice of the refusal (in which Garrison attacked the Boston press and the mayor and aldermen as "accessories under the fact of the Alton murder"), was the announcement: "Faneuil Hall Granted." After widespread protests, permission had been granted to hold the meeting.

Increasingly, however, abolitionists were finding it difficult to obtain public halls in which to meet. Even churches, including those of the Quakers, closed their doors. In 1835, the Massachusetts Anti-Slavery Society was shut out of seven Boston churches, the Masonic Temple, and all but two of the city's public halls, including Faneuil Hall. The situation worsened the following year, when delegates were forced to gather in a small meeting room above the antislavery office at 46 Washington Street in Boston. By 1837, the society was reduced to assembling in a barn loft near the Marlboro Hotel (Garrison quipped that it placed the group "upon a *stable* foundation"). That same year, however, the society received permission for the first time to hold an evening session in the hall of the Massachusetts House of Representatives, commonly called the State House.

The Pennsylvania State Anti-Slavery Society (which had displaced the old Pennsylvania Abolition Society founded in 1775) was not so fortunate. In 1837, the society, unable to find a meeting place in Harrisburg, petitioned the House of Representatives for the use of its hall. It was refused. That same year, Philadelphia had three antislavery societies in addition to the state society: the Philadelphia Anti-Slavery Society, the Philadelphia Female Anti-Slavery Society, and the Philadelphia Young Men's Anti-Slavery Society. Not one of them could obtain a public meeting place in the city.

When all other meeting places were barred, a Negro church or hall was always available for abolitionists, but they were reluctant to make use of the facilities too often since it involved great danger for the blacks. In commenting on the fact that only the African church in Boston was open to the abolitionists, Wendell Phillips noted: "The Monday evening meeting I regretted to hold where we were compelled to as it left the colored people exposed all night to the remains of the mob."

To remedy this situation and provide office space for their societies and publications, Philadelphia abolitionists organized the Pennsylvania Hall Association in 1837 and decided to build a hall of their own. To effect this, a joint-stock company was formed and shares sold for twenty dollars apiece. The purchasers included many antislavery Quakers, "mechanics, working men, and (as in the case of almost every other good work), a number of females." Those not able to contribute cash were given shares in return for supplying materials and labor necessary for the construction. The forty thousand dollars needed to erect the building was quickly raised, and there were even good prospects of making a profit, once the hall was available for rent. The managers made it clear that the hall was not to be used for antislavery purposes alone. In fact, the building would be available "for any purpose not of an immoral character" so that "the citizens of Philadelphia should possess a room, wherein the principles of Liberty, and Equality of Civil Rights, could be freely discussed, and the evils of slavery fearlessly portrayed." Theodore Weld hailed the structure as the "Temple of Freedom," "the first and only one in a republic of fifteen millions, consecrated to Free Discussion and Equal Rights."

The doors of Pennsylvania Hall, located in the southeast corner of Sixth and Haines streets (between Cherry and Race), were opened on May 14, 1838, at ten in the morning. The Pennsylvania State Anti-Slavery Society planned four days of morning, afternoon, and evening sessions of speeches by well-known abolitionists. Garrison spoke on the second day, and he censured the board of managers because "not a single colored brother has occupied a seat upon your platform." "Why is this?" he asked. "It cannot be because there is no one present who, on the score of intellectual and moral worth, is entitled to such respectful treatment. Is it, then, the result of accident or design? I fear this exclusion may be traced to a wicked prejudice, or to a fear of giving public offense."

If it was the latter, it was not successful. That evening, anonymous placards were posted in various parts of the city stating that "a convention to effect the immediate emancipation of the slaves throughout the country is in session is this city, and it is the duty of citizens who entertain a proper respect for the Constitution of the Union and the right of property to interfere." The poster further called upon citizens to assemble at Pennsylvania Hall the next morning "and demand the immediate dispersion of said convention." However, nothing happened on the following day, although crowds gathered around the hall, some lured by reports that Negroes and whites were sitting together in the building and were walking, arm in arm, from the building. There were, in fact, Negroes as well as whites in the hall, and one Philadelphia newspaper commented bitterly that "blacks and whites were indiscriminately mingled."

On the evening of the third day—May 16—antislavery women held a meeting. Maria Weston Chapman, Angelina Grimké (who had just been married to Theodore Weld in a ceremony attended by Negroes as well as whites), Abby Kelly, and Philadelphia's leading abolitionist, Lucretia Mott, spoke to an overflowing audience. Women made up most of the audience, but men were also present in large numbers, and Negroes were scattered throughout the assemblage. Mott explained that the gathering was not an official session of the National Anti-Slavery Convention of American Women because many of its members considered it improper for women to address mixed audiences of both male and female persons. She expressed the hope that "such false notions of delicacy and propriety would not long obtain in this enlightened country."

Outside the hall, a crowd estimated at three thousand persons surrounded the building, and some began to hurl rocks and bricks through the windows. As Angelina Grimké Weld was speaking, "the tumult from without increased, and the brickbats fell thick and fast." The meeting broke up at ten o'clock and the audience filed out into the streets. The angry mob did not harm any of the women, but Negroes leaving the hall were reported to have been assaulted.

Despite the posters instructing the people to break up the meetings, the authorities had taken no precautions to defend the hall. On the following day, May 17, a hostile crowd again assembled in the streets. At mid-morning, the managers of the hall sent a committee to the mayor's office to request police protection. The latter said that any further meetings would lead to violence and advised the owners to cancel plans for such gatherings. If they refused to do this, he promised at least to appear at the hall and speak to the crowd. The managers also applied to the county sheriff for help, but he said it was the mayor's responsibility. They then urged the antislavery women not to allow Negroes to attend the meeting planned for that evening, but Lucretia Mott rejected the request. She urged all to attend and not to be deterred by a "little appearance of danger."

Mayor Swift did attempt to disperse the crowd outside Pennsylvania Hall that evening, but the mob refused. Soon after the mayor and his party left, a number of individuals forced open the hall's doors and began wrecking the interior. The rioters, many of them well dressed, now had Pennsylvania Hall in their hands. Young Samuel Yeager, of a respectable family, bounded to the top of the stairs leading to the auditorium and shouted, "Hurrah, boys, pull them down!" The auditorium was soon torn apart, and then the mob threw turpentine, tar, and other combustible materials on the piled-up furniture and window blinds and set them afire. Not content with igniting the broken furniture and blinds, the rioters started to rip out the gas lines that spread throughout the building.

By nine o'clock, with fifteen thousand spectators looking on, fire completely engulfed Pennsylvania Hall. Several of the numerous volunteer fire companies in the city came to the scene, but the firemen made no attempt to save the building, directing their efforts instead to the surrounding structures. Actually one company did attempt to put out the fire in the hall, but it was stopped when all the other companies turned their hoses on it. John Greenleaf Whittier, editor of the *Pennsylvania Freeman*, the state antislavery society's official organ, was able to save some of his papers by putting on a disguise and pretending to be a member of the invading mob. But Benjamin Lundy's belongings, including his clothing and his books and papers, were destroyed in the blaze. Three days after its official opening, the once-proud "temple of freedom" had become a smoking ruin.

In New York City's July 1834 riots, Irish workers do not seem to have been involved to any great extent in the attacks on Negroes and abolitionists, but in Philadelphia, the newspapers reported that shipwrights from the Delaware River docks, most of them Irish and hostile to the Negroes as job competitors, made up a large part of the mob. However, the leaders were "well-dressed" gentlemen, some of them Southern slaveowners who were visiting town and Southern medical students at the University of Pennsylvania.

The mob continued its rampage during the following days. The Shelter for Colored Orphans was put to the torch on May 18. The next day, the target of mob action was Bethel Church on Sixth and Lombard; the black church was damaged. Next in the path of violence was the *Philadelphia Public Ledger*, which suffered damage to its building because it had "aroused the citizenry [by] . . . an abusive article criticizing the Sheriff, Mayor, and Police for not preventing the destruction of Pennsylvania Hall."

There was much more sympathy in Philadelphia for the mob than for the *Public Ledger*. A report of the Committee on Police, after an investigation of the burning of Pennsylvania Hall, blamed the abolitionists for the mob action because they had advocated in the hall "doctrines repulsive to the moral sense of a large majority of our community." Specifically, the committee censured the abolitionists for encouraging practices "viewed by some as repugnant to the separation and distinction which it has pleased the great Author of nature to establish among the various races of man." It was reckless, the investigators charged, to have invited colored people to the proceedings in the hall and to have them "indiscriminately seated with the white." They considered it even more provocative that the abolitionists had exhibited "the unusual union of blacks and whites walking arm in arm" in the city streets. Thus, rather than being a "temple of freedom," the hall had been turned into a "temple of amalgamation" and, as such, had no right to continue to exist.

FREEDOM OF PETITION

The issue of civil liberties came to a head in the struggle over the right of petition. Except for a handful of radicals, few abolitionists in those early years believed that slavery could be eliminated constitutionally from the South by any authority other than the states themselves. Therefore, the constitution of the American Anti-Slavery Society and that of nearly every state society explicitly denied any intention of interfering with slavery in the states, where Congress did not have jurisdiction. But they did demand abolition in the District of Columbia and the territories, where Congress did have jurisdiction, and they also insisted that Congress had the power to abolish the domestic slave trade. A special target was slavery and the slave trade in the District of Columbia. The idea of buying and selling human beings and holding them in lifetime bondage in the nation's capitol was viewed as a national disgrace. As the *Anti-Slavery Examiner* put it,

"The District has become the great slave market of North America, and the port of Alexandria is the Guinea of our proud republic."

In 1828, a national petition campaign had forced the House of Representatives to vote on abolishing slavery in the District of Columbia, and while the proposal failed, the petitions continued. However, there were no further votes. When, late in 1831, John Quincy Adams, the former president and now Massachusetts congressman, introduced fifteen petitions from Pennsylvania Quakers seeking the abolition of slavery and the slave trade in the District of Columbia, all of the memorials were referred to the committee on the District of Columbia and were buried there.

Until late 1835 and early 1836, petitions continued to be referred to the committee on the District of Columbia and to be there ignored. But this was not enough to satisfy the slaveowners; and mere notice of the petitions filled them with fear and wrath. The ones introduced by John Quincy Adams had been published in the *Baltimore American,* and Frederick Douglass, then a slave, had read them in the paper, along with the speech Adams had delivered on the floor of Congress. Douglass read the newspaper story to his fellow slaves, and ten years later, in a speech in Lynn, Massachusetts, he said: "What joy and gladness it produced to know that so great, so good a man was pleading for us, and further, to know that there was a large and growing class of people in the north called abolitionists, who were moving for our freedom. This is known through all the south, and cherished with gratitude. It has increased the slaves' hope for liberty."

It also increased the slaveowners' fears, and in 1836, John C. Calhoun, their spokesperson, stood before the United States Senate and urged that all petitions calling for the abolition of slavery in the District of Columbia be tabled without discussion or referral to committee. "On the question of receiving," he cried out, "we must meet the enemy on the frontier; on the question of receiving, we must secure that important pass—it is our Thermopylae."

A similar measure in the House, introduced by Congressman James Henry Hammond, also of South Carolina, provoked a debate lasting over six weeks. Finally, the whole question was referred to a special committee headed by Henry Laurens Pinckney of South Carolina. The committee recommended that "all petitions relating to the subject of slavery or the abolition of slavery, shall, without being either printed or referred, be laid upon the table, and no further action whatever shall be had thereon." John Quincy Adams denounced the measure as "a direct violation of the Constitution of the United States, of the rules of this House, and of the rights of my constituents." When the measure was passed, Adams characterized the Northern members of Congress who had voted for it as "the Swiss guard of slavery fighting for pay."

After Congress adopted the gag rule, requiring immediate and permanent tabling of all antislavery memorials, the American Anti-Slavery Society began to circulate printed petitions among its local affiliates. In May 1837, the parent organization launched a national campaign that deluged Congress with over

400,000 petitions during the next twelve months. Many were introduced by John Quincy Adams and were immediately laid on the table. Session after session, when the day came for petitions, Adams was one of the first to be called, and he would sometimes occupy hours in presenting petitions, even though each was immediately laid on the table. One day, on behalf of a group of American citizens, he presented the Declaration of Independence, and because of its implicit antislavery sentiments, it too was tabled.

Amid cries of "Censure him! Censure him! Expel him! Expel him!"; amid accusations that the former president was a "traitor," "guilty of treason in fact," "deserving of a traitor's grave, a traitor's infamy"; amid suggestions from the *Charleston Mercury* that his actions "justified an immediate RESORT TO FORCE by the Southern delegation—Even on the Floor of Congress," Adams ("Old Eloquent") continued to present petitions and to link the issues of abolitionism and free speech in the fight to force Congress to consider these memorials. On March 30, 1840, Adams presented no fewer than 612 petitions, all laid on the table. That same year the gag rule was made a standing rule for the House.

In time, the hostile majority began to dwindle, until, on December 3, 1844, when John Quincy Adams was seventy years of age, his motion to abolish the gag rule was carried by 108 votes in favor against 80 opposed. From then until his death in 1848, Adams sat in the House of Representatives, where he opposed slavery and its extension.

CIVIL LIBERTIES AND ANTISLAVERY GROWTH

Speaking in Paisley, Scotland, on April 6, 1846, black abolitionist Frederick Douglass declared: "It is often asked, what have the abolitionists done?" He reminded the audience that "we had other things to do than merely to abolish slavery. It had so woven and interwoven itself with the religion and the politics of America, that abolitionists had an arduous and difficult path to pursue. . . . for the whole nation sprung up into an organised mob to crush the cry for freedom." But things had changed, Douglass pointed out:

In 1835, there was scarcely one of the press who dared to advocate our cause—now we have upwards of one hundred of them teeming with anti-slavery doctrines—now we can hold meetings with men standing round to protect us. In 1835, we could not get a hall, no one would hazard his property so far, except the old cradle of liberty, the Faneuil Hall. But now we can go into the very state-house itself, and there advocate our anti-slavery doctrines.

It was estimated that during 1835 and 1836, there were at least three hundred attacks on the abolitionists. These attacks, the *Boston Commercial Gazette* declared, arose "from the determination . . . to prevent free discussion on the subject of slavery," it being understood that "a free discussion on the subject leads at once to abolition, amalgamation, and immediate emancipation.'' When faced with such dangers, what mattered the legacy of freedom of speech, freedom of the press, freedom of assemblage, and freedom to petition Congress?

Perhaps the most disturbing feature of the attacks on abolitionists' civil rights was the near unanimity of the response in almost all the communities involved. Far from displaying remorse for the violence and destruction, most white citizens united in blaming the abolitionists for instigating them. "Fanatics provoke mobs," wrote the commander of the Pennsylvania militia in his diary. "Riots are the consequence, public sympathy is excited in favor of the rioters, because all the world condemn the fanatics . . . no one can be had to put down the riots and when the mobs have satiated their appetites for violence and outrage, order is restored by the exhaustion of the rioters." It was acknowledged in most contemporary newspapers that delay in calling out the police and the militia was the result of official and public sympathy with the rioters. "The mob," wrote William Ellery Channing, "have been too much the expression of public sentiment . . . because there is a willingness that the anti-slavery movement should be put down by force."

But Channing was confident that public opinion would change and that in the end persecution would help the cause. He urged the abolitionists not "to *recant* anything." Weld was of the same opinion. "Truth," he assured his colleagues, "has always been the gainer when men resort to bludgeons." Weld was confirmed in his belief when "almost daily letters" informed him that antislavery riots had helped rather than hurt the cause. Lewis Tappan left his damaged house on Rose Street, unrepaired after a mob attack, "a silent Anti-Slavery preacher," and many who came to see it were converted. "I remember," Schuyler Colfax, Republican Speaker of the House, told Tappan more than forty years later, "that it made me prejudiced, even then, against the institution of slavery."

When the *Philanthropist*'s press was thrown into the river by a Cincinnati mob, many who disclaimed abolitionism were ready to support the paper in its fight for the preservation of freedom of the press. Birney declared that the mob's action had won people to the cause by the thousands where there had been only ten before. Publication of the *Philanthropist* was resumed in 1836, and letters from all over the North urged Birney to maintain his firm stand. He assured the correspondents that he and others associated with the paper "shall still continue to maintain, and publicly to inculcate, the great principles of liberty incorporated in the constitution of our state and general governments."

Lovejoy himself had joined the issue of free speech and press. "Today a public meeting declares that you shall not discuss slavery," he wrote in his paper. "Tomorrow another meeting declares that it is against the peace of society that the principles of popery be discussed. . . . The next day a decree is issued against speaking against distilleries, dram shops, and drunkenness. And so to the end of the chapter. The truth is, my fellow citizens, if you give ground a single inch, there is no stopping place."

But it was Lovejoy's death that made the issue clear to many. After Lovejoy was killed, William Cullen Bryant, poet and editor of the *New York Evening Post,* wrote: "We regard this not as a question connected with the abolition of slavery in the South, but as a question vital to the liberties of the entire Union."

Lovejoy's murder led to what was probably the first antislavery meeting in Chicago. A number of citizens held a meeting in the upstairs hall of the Saloon Building and decided to organize against such outrages. They adopted a resolution denouncing the suppression of a free press and announced their intention to organize an antislavery society. And they invited Zabina Eastman to come up from Lowell, a small town about a hundred miles southwest of Chicago, to start an antislavery paper, the *Western Citizen.*

In *A Voice from America to England,* Calvin Colton, a Northern defender of slavery, praised those Philadelphians who participated in the burning of Pennsylvania Hall in 1838. They acted, he informed the British, out of "respect for the 'supreme law of the land,'" just as southerners who occasionally lynched abolitionists were motivated by a noble desire to protect society from those who imperiled "the peace and integrity of the American Union." Southerners also rejoiced in the burning of Pennsylvania Hall, and one rhapsodized: "To witness those beautiful spires of flame gave undoubted assurance to the heart of the Southern, that in his brethren of the North *he has friends who appreciate him.*" "We hail the event," exulted the *Richmond Compiler,* "as an index of the proper state of public sentiment on the subject of slavery." Indeed, members of the mob were hailed as patriots in the Southern press and their conduct deemed "worthy of Americans."

But many Northerners were becoming convinced that if "appreciation" required burning down of meeting halls, slavery was asking for more than they were willing to give. William Leggett switched from opposing to supporting the antislavery cause after the government's interference with the mail privileges of the antislavery journals, and the acting editor of the *New York Evening Post* and spokesman for the labor movement warned the workers that their journals would be next. During the campaign in Congress to deprive the abolitionists of the right to petition, the Philadelphia Trades' Union observed that the petitions of the abolitionists and those of the trade unions in behalf of the ten-hour day had received the same treatment. When the mayor of Philadelphia prevented Frances Wright from lecturing in that city on the subject of slavery, the *National Laborer* stated:

The people need not be surprised at this, when they remember that it is the same Mayor who demanded the enormous bail of $2,500 for the appearance of the Schuylkill labourers to answer the charge of riot, who were afterwards discharged because there was no crime found against them.

Undoubtedly the mob attacks frightened away supporters of the antislavery cause. Among blacks, however, there was only one desertion. Reverend Peter Williams, rector of St. Philip's Church in New York City, resigned his position as a manager of the American Anti-Slavery Society and a member of its executive committee, "by the advice of "Bishop Onderdonk of the Protestant Episcopal Church."

But the score was evened. During the New York City riots of 1834, blacks (not the rioters) were arrested and put in jail. While spending the night of July 7 in jail, Samuel Ringgold Ward made an "oath of allegiance to the antislavery cause." On his release, he became one of the most active of the black abolitionists.

The attacks actually brought many new recruits. Thus, Charles Sumner wrote: "We are becoming abolitionists at the North fast; the attempts to abridge freedom of discussion and the conduct of the South generally, have caused many to think favorably of immediate emancipation who have never before been inclined to it."

Not only were there new recruits, but a number were of special importance to the cause. William Jay, who had long advised the abolitionists in private but who had doubted the usefulness of organized societies, was converted by the 1834 riots in New York City. "We commenced the present struggle to obtain the freedom of the slave," he explained. "We are compelled to continue it to preserve our own." Jay became one of the leading legal advisers in the antislavery movement. After the burning of Pennsylvania Hall, conservative Quakers became more fearful of "the [American] Anti-Slavery Society and all its works." In 1839, the Philadelphia Yearly Meeting of Friends (Orthodox) urged its members to work for antislavery exclusively within the ranks of the Society of Friends. But Reverend William Henry Furness of the First Congregational Unitarian Church adopted an opposite course. Disturbed by the "words of hearty satisfaction and triumph over its ruins," he informed his Philadelphia congregation that he was joining the Pennsylvania Anti-Slavery Society and would now speak out publicly on the subject of slavery. He became a leading critic of the slave system.

Gerrit Smith, a New York philanthropist, was a member of the American Colonization Society and indifferent to the appeals of immediate emancipation until the mobbing of the antislavery convention that met in Utica, New York, in October 1835. He joined the American Anti-Slavery Society on November 12, and on November 24 he wrote to the secretary of the Colonization Society, announcing his withdrawal and explaining his adherence to the American Anti-Slavery Society. What was at stake now, Smith was convinced, was not simply the evils of slavery and the rightness and wrongness of abolitionism but the Bill of Rights itself.

John Quincy Adams was not an abolitionists before he became involved in the battle against the gag rule. When, in 1831, he introduced the fifteen petitions from Pennsylvania Quakers calling for the abolition of slavery and the slave trade in the District of Columbia, he said in his speech on the floor of Congress that he personally favored only abolishing the slave trade in the District of Columbia. He expressed opposition to the other demand, arguing that it "would lead to ill-will, to heart burning, to mutual hatred . . . without accomplishing anything else.'' But Adams came to see that slavery was an influence paralyzing free speech, and from that position he came to understand that slavery was an unjust and demoralizing system, ''a moral pestilence,'' ''the greatest evil now suffered by the race of man.'' In May 1836, he noted in his diary that opposition to slavery was the cause to which he would dedicate ''the last stage of life,'' adding: ''The cause is good and great.''

Adams hoped that the decision between slavery and emancipation would be made peaceably and settled without bloodshed, ''but it must come.'' So in 1841, Adams took on the *Amistad* case, serving as counsel for the fifty-three blacks who had been captured in Africa and brought to Havana, whence they were being shipped to Puerto Principle in Cuba, abroad the vessel *Amistad,* a Spanish schooner. Led by Joseph Cinqué (or Cinquez), the slaves revolted, killed the captain and the cook, and seized the vessel. They ordered the two spared Spaniards to take them to Africa, but instead they were brought into American waters, taken into custody by the United States revenue cutter *Washington,* and imprisoned in New London, Connecticut, on August 29, 1839. Charges of piracy and murder were laid against the Africans, and Spain claimed both them and the ship. While the blacks remained in prison, the *Amistad* case, with its international complications, went through a legal maze from court to court up to the Supreme Court of the United States, becoming, in the process, a national sensation, and Cinqué a hero in the fight against slavery. The abolitionists, especially Reverend Simeon S. Jocelyn, Joshua Leavitt, and Lewis Tappan, were prominent in their defense, but it was the elderly Adams who argued the case before the Supreme Court, urging their fredom on the basis of humanity.

The court, however, ruled in favor of the blacks on other grounds. Justice Story, writing for the majority, held that they were kidnapped Africans entitled to freedom because Spain had outlawed the African slave trade in 1820. In any case, the United States Supreme Court pronounced them free and ordered them returned to their native country. John Quincy Adams, ex-president, congressman, and abolitionist, was honored by his constituency for his role in the great struggle, as he continued to be for his defense of the right of petition in the battle against the gag rule.

On December 8, 1837, Wendell Phillips, the scion of a prominent Boston family, spoke out at a rally at Faneuil Hall that had been called to protest the killing of Elijah P. Lovejoy. Phillips' address was a reply to one by Attorney General John T. Austin, who had not been scheduled to speak but had unexpectedly taken the floor to condemn Lovejoy and the abolitionists and to praise those who had killed him, comparing them to the ''mob that managed the Boston Tea Party.'' Although this was not, as has usually been supposed, Phillips' first public speech or his initial antislavery address, it was one of the great addresses in American history and immediately put him in the front rank of abolitionist orators. The cause had gained a man who became abolition's leading white orator and who most resembled Garrison in the fierceness and mercilessness of his attack on slavery and racism.

So it was that in the very years of constant dangers and difficulties, "amidst insult and violence," to use William E. Channing's expression, the antislavery movement surged forward—in its membership, in the number of its local branches, which were being formed at the rate of approximately one a day, and in its broadening influence. Antislavery spokespersons agitated the civil liberties issue with an excitement and urgency that at times even took precedence over the demand for immediate emancipation. The *Liberator's* prospectus for 1836 made this clear: "The great question to be settled is not whether 2,500,000 slaves in our land shall be either immediately or gradually emancipated—or whether they shall be colonized abroad or retained in our midst—for that is now a subordinate point, but whether freedom is with us—THE PEOPLE OF THE UNITED STATES—a reality or a mockery."

But Garrison also saw the cause moving ahead in part precisely because more and more Americans understood the significance of the point raised in the prospectus. No wonder he exulted in an editorial in the *Liberator* on January 2, 1836:

Where now is . . . the American Colonization Society? Struggling in the agonies of dissolution! Look, now, at that powerful association, the American Anti-Slavery Society! Look at seven flourishing State Societies! Look at five hundred auxiliary societies, and see them multiplying daily! Look at the flood of our publications sweeping through the land. . . . See how many agents are in the field. . . . And the stream of sympathy still rolls on—its impetus is increasing—and must ere long sweep away the pollutions of slavery.

21

The Split in the Antislavery Movement

When Garrison reported in 1836 that the American Anti-Slavery Society's "impetus is increasing," he could not foretell that in four years the society would be rent asunder by the defection of the anti-Garrisonian abolitionists. There were strong personality issues in the split. Various charges were brought against Garrison personally. He was charged with having a "deliberate and well-matured design to make the anti-slavery organization subservient to the promotion of personal and sectarian views on the subjects of Women's Rights . . . Civil Government, the Church, the Ministry, and the Sabbath." Basically, however, the split was the result of genuine ideological differences.

MORAL SUASION, NONRESISTANCE, AND COME-OUTERISM

Abolitionists who began the new antislavery movement in 1833 believed that if they could convince the American people of the sinfulness of slavery, a universal sense of moral outrage would insist upon demolishing the system. It was for the indoctrination of public opinion that they painstakingly erected the federation of societies, turned their best minds to composing tracts, and sent out agents to convert the unbelievers. They felt it was not too much to hope that the southerner and even the slaveholder would see the light.

Garrison and his followers, in particular, placed major emphasis on the thesis that the way to get rid of slavery was to establish "in the hearts of men a deep and widespread conviction of the *brotherhood of the human race;* that God hath indeed made of one blood all nations of men for to dwell on all the face of the earth"; that fighting evil with evil was to be condemned; that the slave should be urged not to resist his torturer with carnal weapons, for that was sin; and that spiritual, not material, means were the only moral way to achieve good. The battle was not to be a wild crusade but a holy war, a sacred strife, waged not with earthly fire "but with weapons fresh from the armory of God . . . Prayer . . . Faith . . . and the word of God!" Said Wendell Phillips: "Those who cling to moral effort are the true champions in the fight. . . . We are working with God, and the times and the seasons are in His hands."

The 1833 Declaration of Sentiments of the American Anti-Slavery Society, written by Garrison, confined abolitionist activity to moral suasion and the nonviolent ending of slavery. The constitution of every other antislavery society contained the same principle: "Our very object precludes the idea of all resort to force. We have no force but the force of truth," was the way it was usually stated. Viewing moral suasion as the only legitimate form of antislavery action, the Pennsylvania Anti-Slavery Society confined its program almost entirely to propaganda. The American Anti-Slavery Society's *Particular Instruction to Agents* emphasized: "Insist principally on the SIN OF SLAVERY, because our main hope is in the consciences of men."

To be sure, the Garrisonians never rested on their moral weapons. The movement was always kept in vigorous operation. In spite of this, it became clear to many abolitionists that moral suasion alone would not free the slaves. It certainly would not convince the slaveowners to do so. James Henry Hammond, a rich slaveholder and leading South Carolina politician, made this clear in his response to the abolitionists: "Supposing that we were all convinced, and thought of Slavery precisely as you do, at what era of 'moral suasion' do you imagine you could prevail on us to give up a thousand millions of dollars in the value of our slaves, and a thousand millions of dollars more in the depreciation of our lands, in consequence of the want of laborers to cultivate them?"

THE CHURCH

An important cause of the antislavery split was a growing objection among abolitionists to what was called *come-outerism,* a principle deeply imbedded in Garrisonian thinking. Come-outer was the name originally applied to certain religious dissenters or reformers who separated themselves from an established organization. Come-outerism was applied specifically to those who advocated the idea that the churches were corrupt and, believing that it was man's duty to avoid evil, urged their members to leave them. Garrison believed that the clergy were mainly a group of "time-seekers" who never did enough for the antislavery movement and that the reluctance of the churches to take a forthright stand against slavery (by excluding slaveowners) proved their corruption. In fact, from the "first settlement of this country, by their countenance of, and participation in the system of American Slavery, and by throwing the shield of their sanction around that "complicated sin and sum of all villainies," the churches formed "the bulwark of American Slavery." Garrison urged antislavery men and women to "come out" of such churches by leaving them.

Garrison not only denounced the churches for forming "the bulwark of American Slavery," but he repudiated the divine inspiration of the Scriptures. It was harmful, he argued, to refer to the Bible as the Holy Book, inasmuch as nobody knew who had written it or when it had been written. A staunch antisabbitarian, he held as superstitution the setting aside the first day of the week for religious purposes, attributing the practice to the machinations of the "priestcraft for selfish ends."

WOMEN'S RIGHTS

When, in addition to these beliefs, Garrison also rejected the biblical injunction, "Let your women keep silent in the churches" and insisted that women should speak in public and should participate equally with men in the leadership of the antislavery societies, not a few abolitionists were shocked. Only a few antislavery men expressed their support for women who conducted antislavery activities by speaking in public and performing other such "unladylike" acts in behalf of the slave. And even they definitely opposed intertwining the cause with the women's rights question. Sarah Grimké wrote a series of articles proving that women's rights were bound up with the cause of human freedom, and her sister, Angelina, argued persuasively for linking the two when, speaking in behalf of twenty thousand women signers of an antislavery petition, she told the Massachusetts legislature: "American women have to do with slavery not only for moral and religious but political reasons. We are citizens of a Republic, and our honor, happiness, and well-being are bound up in its politics, government and laws." In speaking for the slave, women could not help but speak for themselves, or, as Sarah Grimké put it: "What then can woman do for the slave when she is herself under the feet of man and shamed into silence?"

But many ministers and large portions of the public continued to cite biblical authority to uphold the position that women should stay in the home and refrain from public activities. Most abolitionists believed that women should engage in antislavery activities but not as full-scale workers and only if confined to "conventional" roles. And many antislavery men and women were opposed to the cause's becoming entangled in the "woman question." John Greenleaf Whittier was very outspoken in such opposition. The poet and antislavery editor wrote to the Grimké sisters, praising their lectures as "powerful and practical assertions of the right and duty of woman to labor side by side with her brother for the welfare and redemption of the world." Why, then, was it necessary for them to raise the "controversial" issue of women's rights? To Whittier, this was tantamount to abandoning the slave. Weld was equally regretful. "Now can't you leave the lesser work to others," he wrote to the sisters, "who can do it better than you and devote soul and spirit to the greater work which you can do far better and to far better purpose than anybody else?" "Pro-slavery is chuckling," he concluded, "if they can divert you and cripple your influence on the subject of slavery."

Many women found themselves engaged in a double campaign—to free the slaves and to free themselves—and increasingly, Garrison, his *Liberator,* and his followers became the only supporters for their dual cause. From the beginning of the controversy, Garrison offered unqualified encouragement. "The cause of bleeding humanity," he contended, "is always legitimately, the cause of WOMAN." He deplored the failure of antislavery advocates to recognize women's right to equality. Since he believed an evil means could never bring about a just end, he refused to compromise on what he considered to be matters of principle. If the antislavery movement stood in defense of human freedom, how then could its advocates deny this freedom to women? Nor, he maintained, should women be backward in demanding their full right to equality. As early as July 14, 1832, he argued in the *Liberator* that the disposition of American women "to undervalue their own power, or through a misconception of duty, to excuse themselves from employing it," was an error in both logic and strategy.

Hence Garrison hailed the important contribution of women to the petition crusade. The *Liberator* on January 2, 1836, announced: "Honor to the Ladies! A very large proportion of our paper today is occupied with the report of an animated and important debate in Congress excited by the petition of ladies for the abolition of slavery in the District of Columbia."

Most Americans did not echo Garrison's tribute. In 1837, Congressman Caleb Cushing of Massachusetts presented 3,924 names from his district on a petition, all of which were of women. In a letter to the *North American Review,* he criticized the women for "interfering by petition in the political duties of society." Such preoccupation, he wrote, would cause them to sacrifice "all that delicacy and maternal tenderness which are among the highest charms of women." The *New York Commercial Advertiser* was even more hostile, recommending that those "females who so far forget the province of their sex as to perambulate the country" in order to collect antislavery petitions should be sent to the insane asylums.

But the women continued to sign petitions, and the women's Anti-Slavery Convention Report of 1837 noted that a hard-won signature "answers a threefold purpose. You not only gain the person's name but you excite inquiry into her mind and she will excite inquiry in others. Thus, the little circle imperceptibly widens." Reprinting the report, Garrison asked the antislavery foes of women's equality how they could maintain their position in the face of thousands upon thousands of petitions that women were forwarding to Congress on behalf of the slave. The *Liberator* gave the center of its front page to the following poem:

> And is not women's strength as mighty now
> As when it rescued Moses—roused the sons
> of Zabulon and Naphtali to arms

> Reversed the mandate of the Persian king
> And melted down the obstinate resolve
> Of Caius Marcius? Be it wielded then
> To serve the cause of justice.

And, it should be added, wielded not as an inferior, but as an equal.

POLITICAL ACTION

Perhaps the greatest difference between the Garrisonians and other abolitionists focused on political action. The Declaration of Sentiments of the American Anti-Slavery Society makes no mention of politics or voting. The constitution of the society declared that the organization would "endeavor to influence" Congress. However, the emphasis throughout was upon agitation and moral suasion rather than politics. But as Aileen Kraditor has pointed out, Garrison was willing to accept the right of the individual to participate in politics as long as his actions in no way aided the cause of slavery and as long as he supported only candidates opposed to slavery, regardless of party. Garrison summarized his views on voting in his *Address to the Abolitionists of Massachusetts*:

Do not stay away from the polls. Go and scatter your votes. This is the true way to make yourselves felt. Every scattering vote you cast counts against the candidates of the parties; and will serve as an effectual admonition to them to nominate the next time men whom you can conscientiously support.

However, Garrison opposed the formation of a separate political party on the grounds that it would be dangerous, if not fatal, to the cause. "If we were a political party," Garrison argued, "the struggle for places of power and emolument would render our motives suspect, even if it did not prove too strong a temptation to our integrity. If we were a distinct party, every member of it must vote for its candidates, however he might disagree with them on other points of public policy. Experience seems to show that under a free government, there cannot be at one time more than two powerful political parties."

Although without a party organization, there was little chance to elect abolitionists to national or state office, the candidates of the regular parties could be questioned about their attitude toward slavery. In the 1838 election, the executive committee of the American Anti-Slavery Society officially endorsed nominees who held acceptable views. Just before the November 1839 state elections in Massachusetts, Garrison printed an appeal to Boston's blacks to vote for Bradford Sumner as Suffolk County's congressional representative instead of "Abbott Lawrence [who] is not to be trusted. . . . Our colored friends may be supplied with genuine votes by calling at the Anti-Slavery office, 25 Cornhill."

At first, the controversy over political action was not over voting alone. It raged mainly over the question of whether abolitionists ought to form a political party. Some abolitionists found that the practice of questioning candidates was inadequate. This technique was predicated on the belief that antislavery men could hold the balance of power between the two parties or candidates, but what happened was that often neither candidate was worthy of support according to antislavery standards. Often, too, neither candidate would respond to questions, or one might answer unsatisfactorily and the other refuse to reply at all. Hence, many abolitionists came to feel that in such situations, the only way to register clear antislavery sentiment was to run candidates independently. From this position, it was but a short step to the advocacy of the formation of an antislavery political party.

But Garrison believed strongly that the creation of an abolitionist political party would be an impractical and divisive force within the movement and that with its formation, antislavery men would act not as "free moral agents" but as unrepentant "tools of party." Before long, Garrison even retreated from his early endorsement of voting. He studied the Constitution and concluded that in giving "solemn guarantees" to slavery, it was "a covenant with death, and an agreement with hell." He cited the clause that legalized the slave trade for a period of twenty years, the one allowing the slave masters to swell their representation in Congress through the three-fifths clause (which also proclaimed the slave three-fifths of a man), and the clause that pledged the use of the military power of the United States to put down slave rebellions and to enforce the fugitive slave law. These, he said, constituted a trinity of evil and branded the Constitution a compact of fatal compromises and the government of the United States an agency of the slaveowners and their allies. Consistent abolitionism was impossible under such a Constitution. Slavery was entrenched in the fundamental law of the nation; consequently, anyone who would defend and uphold the Constitution, as was implicit in the act of voting and holding office, participated in the guilt of the slaveholders. There was only one logical course to follow: to apply to the government of the United States the same policy followed with respect to the churches. As the Garrisonian "Declaration of Anti-Slavery Independence" put it: "such is the pro-slavery position of the organized Church and Government of the United States, that necessity constrains us to come out and separate ourselves from all Religious and Political fellowship with them." The Garrisonians kept on reiterating their claim that the only effective approach to abolition was for everyone to disavow the Constitution, that "covenant with death and agreement with Hell."

From denouncing the Constitution and the government, Garrison moved to denouncing the "blood-soaked" American Union. Although the issue of disunion did not gain prominence until 1844, when the *Liberator* adopted the slogan "No Union with Slaveholders," that position was foreshadowed as early as 1832 when he wrote: "There is much declaration about the sacredness of the compact which was formed between the free and slave states in the adoption of the Constitution. A sacred compact, forsooth! We pronounce it the most bloody and heaven-daring arrangement ever made by men for the continuance and protection of a system of the most atrocious villainy ever exhibited upon the earth.'' His implication was that abolitionists should do everything in their power to bring about the dissolution of the union and ''come out'' of the ''blood-soaked'' relationship between the North and South.

THE PASTORAL AND CLERICAL APPEALS

The conflict within the American Anti-Slavery Society came to a head at its annual meeting in May 1840, but trouble had been brewing for several years. In the summer of 1837, Garrison and the *Liberator* came under severe attack from the orthodox clergymen of Massachusetts, some of whom were abolitionists. The attacks were first caused during the speaking tour of the state by Sarah and Angelina Grimké, who had come in June 1837 at the invitation of the Massachusetts Anti-Slavery Society to present their antislavery message to the women of Massachusetts. They remained for almost a year, speaking to both female antislavery societies and church groups. Their original purpose was to speak only to women, but with the spread of their fame, men as well as women began to attend their meetings, thus breaking the prohibition against women publicly addressing mixed audiences of men and women. This aroused strong criticism among orthodox Congregational clergymen of the state and contributed toward evoking the July 28, 1837, ''Pastoral Letter of the General Association of Massachusetts to the Congregational Churches under their Care.'' Written for the most part by the Reverend Nehemiah Adams, the letter did not name names, but it did attack both Garrison and the Grimké sisters and insisted that ''agitating subjects'' should not ''be forced upon any church as matters for debate at the hazard of alienation and division,'' and also that allowing women to speak ''threatened female character with widespread and permanent injury—the vine usurps the role of the elm.''

But the Grimké sisters went on lecturing as before, and Garrison continued to support their activities. The attacks were continued in the ''clerical appeals.'' The Reverend Charles Fitch of the First Free Congregational Church led the initial attack, accusing the *Liberator* of ''rudeness harmful to abolition.'' Fitch and other clergymen, a number of whom had participated in the antislavery movement, also condemned Garrison's methods, his harsh language, the *Liberator*'s attacks upon individual churchmen for their proslavery or neutralist views on the issue of slavery, and Garrison's use of the *Liberator* for attacks upon the Sabbath and various church organizations. Garrison was even charged with having convinced many of Boston's Negroes to follow his ''ungodly ways'' and desert (''come-out'' of) the city's churches, especially those unfriendly to him. This view was further developed by the *New England Spectator*, the journalistic mouthpiece of the leaders of the ''clerical appeal.''

Garrison promptly struck back at the *Spectator* for its "unmanly . . . attack upon the editor of the *Liberator* and the colored population of Boston." The city's blacks immediately came to Garrison's defense. Led by John Hilton, they attacked both the clerics and the *Spectator*, explaining that in religious matters they had minds of their own and had never received any directions from Garrison. They also denounced the *Spectator* for its "offensive article . . . impeaching the moral and religious character of the colored citizens."

The *Colored American*, published in New York City, aroused the enmity of Boston's black population by refusing to publish their resolutions supporting Garrison. Samuel Cornish explained the refusal on the ground that he had not wanted to do anything that might lead to a wider split in abolitionist ranks. He insisted that blacks should not take sides in any contest between abolitionist groups because this would only create more dissension, and the real losers in the end would be the Negroes themselves. But Boston's blacks refused to be mollified. At a public meeting, they unanimously passed a resolution, offered by John Hilton, noting that "the treatment of the colored citizens of Boston by the editor of the *Colored American* is too unkind to merit, from them, any reply."

Not surprisingly, blacks turned out to be among Garrison's most fervent supporters in his battle with the churchmen. Indeed, he blasted the executive committee of the American Anti-Slavery Society for not coming to his support through its voice, the *Emancipator*. The committee members, in turn, urged him to cease burdening the antislavery cause with all these "extraneous issues" and said that the slavery issue was the most urgent and required exclusive concentration until it was resolved. In truth, by 1839, anti-Garrisonian feeling was beginning to run high among an increasing number of abolitionists. Garrison's tactics in fighting slavery were coming to be considered more destructive than helpful by a number of his former colleagues. In their view, he had completely alienated the churches from the antislavery cause by his vitriolic attacks, and he was alienating other segments of the community as well by championing women's rights, attacking the Constitution, and hinting at disunion as the solution to the problem of slavery. While they disagreed on a number of issues, these abolitionists were united in the belief that Garrison should somehow be dissociated, in the eyes of the public, from the antislavery movement.

THE FIRST SPLIT

On May 7, 1839, the American Anti-Slavery Society, at its annual convention, voted 180 to 140 to allow all persons present to be seated as members. One hundred and twenty members went on record as protesting the decision, stating that the right of women to speak, vote, and hold office was opposed to the recognized rules of propriety, was a breach of faith against those who joined the society believing it to be an organization of men, that at the convention held to organize the society, the women present did not sign the Declaration of Sentiments or enroll as members, and that this was a step to enlist the antislavery movement in a cause extraneous and foreign to its purpose.

Those in favor of women's participation, led by Garrison, stated that the constitution of the American Anti-Slavery Society made no distinction between men and women, but said, "All persons who consent to the principles" were to be admitted. The executive committee published a statement declaring that the action of the convention was not to be construed as committing the society to the principles of women's equality with men in public affairs. It became evident that there was a serious cleavage in the organization, even though Dwight L. Dumond believes, incorrectly, that the issue of women's rights was of minor importance in the splitting of the American Anti-Slavery Society.

Still, the American Anti-Slavery Society did not split in 1839. Rather, it was in Massachusetts that the first division occurred. In February 1839, the anti-Garrisonians in the Bay State founded the *Massachusetts Abolitionist* to vie with the *Liberator* for public support. Immediately the paper began attacking Garrison's "recklessness," arguing that "the opposition of Mr. Garrison to all organized churches, to the ministerial office, and to all regular civil government, will work disaster as far as it is encouraged."

In April, Amos Augustus Phelps, a former Garrison supporter, resigned from the Massachusetts Anti-Slavery Society because, he charged, it had "become a *woman's right, non-government Anti-Slavery Society*." Having failed in their effort to censure the Garrisonians at the annual meeting of the Massachusetts Anti-Slavery Society for their refusal to vote and for their willingness to permit the participation of women, all of these discontented elements seceded and formed a competing Massachusetts antislavery organization, called the Massachusetts Abolition Society, or "new organization." The Garrisonian Massachusetts Anti-Slavery Society was thenceforth known as the "old organization." The seceders announced that the old organization had perverted the movement "to purposes and objects not contemplated in our bond of union," attaching to it a cause (women's rights) "which is a millstone to sink in the depths of a bottomless ocean the hopes of enslaved millions." They also charged it with having abandoned the original doctrines and adopting instead the sectarian dogmas of a few individuals—the nonpolitical, no-government ideas of William Lloyd Garrison.

Although the Boston Female Society was also split on the issues that had led to the formation of the Massachusetts Abolition Society, a majority of the female antislavery societies in Massachusetts supported the old organization. They explained their position by affirming that Garrison "recognized the inherent right of all, without distinction of color, sect, sex or party." They passed resolutions heartily deploring the disunity within the antislavery ranks and proclaiming that the cause of freedom demanded the utmost unity.

These words had no effect. "The split is wide and can never be closed up."

Henry Stanton wrote from Boston to James Birney. And Lewis Tappan wrote in his journal:

I rejoice that a new society is formed in Massachusetts. Garrison and others have grown lukewarm on the anti-slavery subject and have loaded the cause with their no-government—woman's rights—non-resistant, etc. notions.

THE SPLIT IN THE AMERICAN ANTI-SLAVERY SOCIETY

During the remainder of 1839, the split developing in the antislavery movement widened over the trend toward the formation of an antislavery political party and the nomination of candidates for president and vice-president during the 1840 elections by such a party. In attacking the proposal, the Garrisonians now not only pointed to the proslavery nature of the American Constitution and government as being hostile to the cause of the slave but also urged that the abolitionists' recent experiences proved it. Congress had responded to the rising antislavery sentiment in the nation by simply legislating the censorship of abolitionist literature from the Southern mails and by refusing to consider antislavery petitions in the House of Representatives. On the other hand, the advocates of an antislavery political party contended that the ability of the abolitionists to prevent the enactment of the ban on antislavery mail proposed by President Jackson in 1835 indicated that it was already a successful political movement and that the controversy over the right of petition, by associating the cause with civil rights, had opened the way for the creation of an antislavery political party embodying abolitionist principles. In the *Emancipator* of May 2, 1839, James G. Birney argued that those whose consciences did not permit them to support a party should leave the American Anti-Slavery Society.

The conflict over antislavery political action came to a head in the period preceding the 1840 presidential election. On April 1, a convention was held in Albany, New York, by antislavery men who were favorably disposed toward the creation of an antislavery political party. It nominated James G. Birney and Thomas Earle of Pennsylvania. A second convention, held on May 13 and 14 in New York City, confirmed their nominations as candidates for president and vice-president of the newly formed Liberty party.

Garrison and his followers viewed these actions as a betrayal of the cause and a futile waste of antislavery energy. How could the Liberty party expect "to make an anti-slavery Congress of pro-slavery materials?" asked Henry C. Wright, a leading Garrisonian. "The nation must be abolitionized before an abolition Congress can be created." Why not, instead, lend all their energies to abolitionizing the nation? Then, of necessity, the fruits would appear in an antislavery Congress and government. This, of course, meant stepping up their moral suasion activities. But while the Garrisonians opposed the participation in government in general and the formation of an independent antislavery party in particular, they still favored the use of petitions and memorials to Congress. The advocates of independent antislavery political action, on the other hand, dismissed these techniques with the argument that only through the course they recommended could such activities prove meaningful.

The conflict reached its climax at the annual meeting of the American Anti-Slavery Society, held on May 12, 1840, in New York City's Fourth Free Church. Garrison's opponents attempted to capture the national society and oust Garrison from a position of power. Since every abolitionist present was to have a vote, Garrison chartered a steamer in Providence to take a boatload of his followers to New York to save the society from falling into the hands of his opponents. A rallying cry went out through the *Liberator*. The response was prompt: over four hundred delegates were prepared to "preserve [the] integrity of the anti-slavery movement." Persons of all ages, colors, and conditions, from veterans to new recruits, poured onto the steamer. They filled the berths and floors in the cabins and overflowed onto the deck.

When the group arrived at the convention, they made "clean work of everything with crushing unanimity," to use Garrison's words. Arthur Tappan had sent his letter of resignation, praying "that God may overrule the machinations of disorganizers among us, and save us from the disgrace I apprehend." Since he did not appear to preside, a close associate of his was elected to chair the meeting. By a vote of 557 to 451, Abby Kelly, the militant antislavery agent, was appointed to the business committee with Lewis Tappan and Amos Phelps. Tappan and Phelps then resigned from the committee and walked out of the convention, after which Lucretia Mott, Lydia Maria Child, and Maria Weston Chapman were put on the executive committee.

Garrison's opponents insisted that abolitionism must be divorced from no-government, nonresistance, theological heterodoxy, and equality of the sexes. Garrison's doctrines, they claimed, only weakened "the staff of accomplishment." Accordingly, Lewis Tappan invited all those opposed to the leadership of William Lloyd Garrison to meet in the basement of the church (where Garrison was then in control of the old society overhead) and organize a new society. About three hundred members of the American Anti-Slavery Society, including all the ministers present, accepted the invitation, and the American and Foreign Anti-Slavery Society was speedily organized, with Arthur Tappan as president, James G. Birney and Henry B. Stanton as secretaries, and Lewis Tappan as treasurer.

The new society's constitution, drafted in advance by Lewis Tappan, recognized the "rightfulness of government," urged political action as a duty, and declared that the admission of women to take part in its proceedings was an innovation "repugnant to the constitution of the society," "a firebrand in the anti-slavery meetings, and contrary to the usages of the civilized world." Its program naturally drew to the organization the more conservative members of the old society—those who "could not swallow Garrison." But it also attracted those who disagreed with Garrison's presentation of the Constitution as a pro-slavery document and with his opposition to the formation of an antislavery political party. For the most part, those who supported formation of the Liberty party also supported the new American and Foreign Anti-Slavery Society. The society published the *Liberty Almanac* to support the Liberty party. Its official organ, however, was the *Emancipator*, formerly the American Anti-Slavery Society's official newspaper. The American Anti-Slavery Society, for its part, created a new official organ, the *National Anti-Slavery Standard*, which began publication on June 11, 1840.

After the American and Foreign Anti-Slavery Society had been organized, Lewis Tappan explained to the absent Theodore Weld that the antislavery split was not solely the result of women voting, speaking, and being on committees and in offices. Nor, he went on, was it because of any opposition to women being members of the society. Rather, it was mostly because Garrison had "foisted upon the American Anti-Slavery Society the woman question, no government question, etc., and the bad spirit shown by the *Liberator*." He then explained the position of the anti-Garrisonians on the "woman question." Everyone had a right to be members of an antislavery society, but the business was to be handled by men. Women had a right to form societies for women only, and men had a right to form societies for men only. Men had formed the American Anti-Slavery Society and had the right to determine how it should be organized and run. Garrison was just trying "to make an experiment upon the public." He had said before that other reforms were "paramount" to the antislavery cause, and his activities were both causing the slave to be forgotten and alienating those who might otherwise cooperate with the abolitionists.

Lydia Maria Child answered the charge that the women's rights movement was "excess baggage" on the antislavery train by stating that it was an inevitable outcome of that struggle. Anyone with a reasonable amount of farsightedness, she declared, could see that "a struggle for advancement of any principle of freedom would inevitably tend to advance all free principles, for they are connected like a spiral line, which, if the top be put in motion, revolves even to the lowest point." In speaking for the slave, women could not avoid advancing their own cause, and Garrison was to be praised rather than censured for understanding the truth of this "principle of freedom" and encouraging women to implement it.

WORLD ANTI-SLAVERY CONVENTION

The finale of the woman question in the antislavery movement was enacted at the World Anti-Slavery Convention in London from June 12 through 23, 1840. The convention, unofficially sponsored by the British and Foreign Anti-Slavery Society, brought together 518 delegates from Continental Europe, the Caribbean, and the United States. The United States contributed the largest foreign delegation, and the Garrisonians, in defiance to the wishes of the convention's organizers, placed on their delegation women from female antislavery societies in Massachusetts and Pennsylvania. The delegates overwhelmingly defeated a motion offered by Wendell Phillips to seat the women, and they were forced to sit in the gallery without even being allowed to speak. The explanation given was that the admission of women was contrary to English usage and would offend the prejudices of some and shock the religious sentiment of others.

When he arrived after the convention had started, Garrison refused to present his credentials and instead sat with the excluded women. Charles Lenox Remond (who had been forced to cross the ocean in humiliating circumstances because of his color) joined Garrison in dramatizing the endorsement of women's rights by sharing their exile to the visitors' gallery. "I learned with much sorrow of the rejection of the female delegates," Remond wrote from London to a black friend in New York. "In the name of heaven, and in the name of the bleeding, dying slave, I ask if I shall scruple the propriety of female action. . . . I trust not."

When Garrison was welcomed back to Boston, he underscored the meaning of the action in which he and Remond had joined:

I cannot refrain from expressing my admiration of our friend, Charles Lenox Remond. Though a warmer welcome than ordinarily waits the white man was extended to him, as a man of color, he nobly refused to enter, where any of the advocates of human rights were thrust out. . . . The course pursued by the convention brought up before all Europe the question so important to the success of the anti-slavery enterprise, whether, in a moral cause, a woman may be a free moral agent.

Before leaving the World Anti-Slavery Convention, we should note that it was in London that Lucretia Mott and Elizabeth Cady Stanton, two of the excluded delegates, met and launched their dreams of another convention—a convention of American women, which would undertake the battle to eradicate precisely such discrimination and humiliation. This dream did not materialize until 1848, but in that year, these antislavery women, together with many other women and some men (Frederick Douglass among them), met in Seneca Falls, New York, and laid the foundation for the women's rights movement in America.

The presidential election of November 1840 witnessed the triumph of General William Henry Harrison, the Whig candidate, over Martin Van Buren, the Democratic candidate, with the Liberty party candidate, James G. Birney, receiving only 7,100 votes nationally. To Garrison, the ignominiously low vote for Birney seemed a total vindication of his opposition to the creation of an abolitionist political party on the ground that it was an impractical and divisive force within the abolitionist movement.

BLACKS AND THE ANTISLAVERY SPLIT

Black abolitionists also split on the same issues dividing white antislavery men and women. William C. Nell, Charles Lenox Remond, James G. Barbadoes, and

William P. Powell supported Garrison and continued to work inside the American Anti-Slavery Society, while Samuel E. Cornish, Christopher Rush (founder and second bishop of the African Episcopal Zion church), and Charles B. Ray, then an editor of the *Colored American,* became members of the first executive committee of the new American and Foreign Anti-Slavery Society. Henry Highland Garnet, too, was one of the founders of the new organization and a stump speaker for the Liberty party.

A resolution published in the *Liberator,* signed by a group of pro-Garrison Boston Negroes, concluded:

. . . of Mr. Garrison we can truly add, that we doubt not that the day will come, when many an emancipated slave will say of him, while weeping over his monument, ''This was my best friend and benefactor. I here bathe his tomb with the tears of that liberty, which his services and sufferings achieved for me.''

Resolved, That to slander Garrison, and pronounce him a hypocrite is certainly the most unkind and ungrateful expression that could ever escape the lips of any colored man, and in what we least expected to hear, after so much toil and suffering in our behalf; and we rejoice that such spirits are few and far between.

On the other side, Charles B. Ray wrote an interesting letter to Henry Stanton and James Birney, suggesting that Negro people might be feeling somewhat ''less warmth of feeling'' for Garrison because there were now so many efficient antislavery workers in addition to the editor of the *Liberator* and also because there was something left to be desired in the ''spirit with which Brother Garrison has conducted his own paper since the controversy commenced.''

Although Garrison was able to maintain his hold over Boston's black population, most blacks elsewhere were not so firm in their support. The rivalry between those who supported Garrison and those who opposed him was to become a major feature of black American society in the North during the two decades before the Civil War.

22

Black Abolitionists

For many years, the words *abolitionists* and *abolitionism* almost automatically conjured up the image of whites helping blacks to break the bonds of slavery. Too many people felt that, in the words of Charles H. Wesley, "Negroes contributed nothing of importance towards the abolition movement and the accomplishment of their own freedom." As if to give added credence to this notion, historians have traditionally dated the militant antislavery movement, with its demand for immediate emancipation, from 1831, when William Lloyd Garrison began to publish the *Liberator*. But this view ignores many important and exclusively black efforts to put an end to slavery that preceded this admittedly important event.

Almost four years before the *Liberator* appeared, *Freedom's Journal*, launched under the editorship of two blacks, criticized Lundy's and Garrison's advocacy of gradual emancipation, calling instead for the immediate abolition of slavery. The *Journal's* agents spread this doctrine among blacks in New England, New York, Pennsylvania, Maryland, the District of Columbia, and even in Virginia and North Carolina. Two years before the *Liberator* began publication, David Walker, one of the Boston agents for *Freedom's Journal*, issued his famous *Appeal* and initiated the period of militant abolitionism, urging immediate emancipation and calling upon the slaves to rise up to achieve that end.

Blacks were also the first to oppose colonization, and it was this black opposition that convinced leading white abolitionists to abandon advocacy of colonization as a path to emancipation. Fully half of Garrison's *Thoughts on African Colonization* was made up of opposition expressed by the Negro people. Elizur Wright, Jr., the brilliant organizer of antislavery propaganda, said in 1834: "If the honor of originating American Anti-Slavery as a plan of operations opposed to expatriation were now the matter in question, a strong claim might be urged in favor of some of our colored friends."

To this we can add the succession of Negro conventions, various self-improvement movements, and the black church, which both influenced and were influenced by the new abolitionism. The leadership of the black church and of many of the organizations that promoted black reform invariably included black abolitionists.

BLACK-WHITE JOINT ACTIVITY

The launching and continued publication of the *Liberator* was made possible by the encouragement, financial aid, and continued subscriptions of blacks. James Forten alone made up the financial losses of the paper for a considerable period, and, as Garrison himself reported, free blacks constituted the great majority of subscribers during its early years. But blacks contributed as well to other aspects of the abolitionist movement. James G. Barbadoes, William C. Nell, James T. Hilton, Philip Bell, James Forten, and other blacks were frequent participants in such ventures.

Blacks were among the major contributors to the gift books issued annually by several Female Anti-Slavery Societies. In *The Liberty Bell,* the annual gift book of the Boston Society (which Harvard undergraduates, in *Harvardiana,* labeled "poison in the shape of an annual," but which the *Liberator* termed a necessary article "in the parlor of every friend of the slave"), antislavery poetry and prose by blacks were regularly included. *Autographs for Freedom,* published by the Rochester Female Anti-Slavery Society, featured a number of black contributors. The first issue contained a biographical sketch of a Scottish abolitionist, John Murray, by James McCune Smith, and a sixty-seven-page short story by Frederick Douglass about Madison Washington, "The Heroic Slave," in which Douglass graphically described the slave rebellion aboard the domestic slave trader, *Creole.* In the second issue of *Autographs for Freedom,* there were five articles on every phase of the antislavery movement by black leaders Charles L. Reason, John M. Langston, William Wells Brown, James McCune Smith, and Frederick Douglass, as well as poems by Reason and George B. Vashon.

Black-white joint participation in the antislavery movement is also reflected in the movement's activities. The New England Anti-Slavery Society, founded in January 1, 1832, in a classroom of the African Baptist church in Boston's Negro ghetto, included blacks in its ranks from the outset; eighteen of the original seventy-two members were black. No fewer than nine prominent Philadelphia blacks—James McCrummell, Robert Purvis, John C. Bowers, Charles W. Gardiner, James Forten, William Dorsey, Charles Wise, James Cornish, and F. A. Hinton—participated in the organization of the Pennsylvania State Anti-Slavery Society. Six black women—Sarah Forten, Lydia White, Grace Douglass, Charlotte Forten, Hetty Burr, and Sarah M. Douglass—helped found the Philadelphia Female Anti-Slavery Society.

Susan Paul, daughter of Thomas Paul, held office in the Boston Female Anti-Slavery Society, and other black women were also active in similar organizations. Together with their white sisters, they participated in the antislavery fairs and bazaars that became annual fund-raising events in support of the antislavery campaign. They often saw to it that part of the funds raised were given to support black antislavery journals. Also together with their white sisters, they annually celebrated at picnics and jubilees the first of August, the anniversary of the West Indies' emancipation by the British in 1833. They joined together, too, in fasting on the Fourth of July "for the sin of slavery which is crying unto heaven for restitution."

Blacks were part of the organizational structure of the two national antislavery societies. Four of the original members of the board of managers of the American Anti-Slavery Society were blacks, and three were members of the executive committee. In the American and Foreign Anti-Slavery Society, five blacks were members of the executive committee.

INDEPENDENT BLACK ACTIVITY

For the most part, the goal of black abolitionism was integration and equality, not separation. Nevertheless, blacks also formed antislavery societies of their own—about fifty of them before the 1830s. While some, like the Massachusetts General Colored Association, a black antislavery group founded in Boston in 1826, did not reveal their purpose in their names, others, like the New York African Clarkson Association (1829), did demonstrate their antislavery motive in their names. (The names of William Wilberforce and Thomas Clarkson, leaders of the British antislavery movement, were given to quite a few of the early black antislavery societies.)

Even after the national antislavery organization was formed in the early 1830s, the trend toward independent black emancipationist organizations continued. Although many black abolitionists viewed these agencies as auxiliaries in the new antislavery movement, they met separately and existed independently of the integrated abolitionist organizations. Between 1834 and 1838, blacks formed their own antislavery societies in Rochester, Newark, Nantucket, Albany, Lexington (Ohio), Troy (Michigan), Middletown (Connecticut), Geneva (New York), New York City, and Philadelphia. Those in Philadelphia were called the Colored Free Produce Society and the Leavitt Anti-Slavery Society. In addition, the weekly newspapers owned, edited, and published by blacks paid special attention to the independent antislavery societies.

Not all blacks were active abolitionists or even openly identified themselves with the antislavery movement. In her sketch of the career of her abolitionist husband, Charles B. Ray of New York, Florence Ray disputed the view that activity in the cause of abolitionism was to be expected of a free black man or woman. She went on to explain that the mass of the Negroes (especially fugitive slaves) were so concerned with just surviving in the face of proscription, disfranchisement, and general oppression that it required extraordinary qualities for free blacks openly to espouse the cause of their enslaved brothers and sisters. Yet the fact is that blacks constituted a relatively high proportion of the abolitionist leadership. In New York State, for example, where Negroes accounted for less than 2 percent of the general population between 1830 and 1860, nine of the state's fifty most important abolitionist leaders were black. In his study, *The New York Abolitionists,* Gerald Sorin includes Theodore S. Wright, Henry Highland Garnet, Samuel E. Cornish, Charles B. Ray, and Frederick Douglass among New York's ten ranking abolitionist leaders.

CONTRIBUTIONS OF EX-SLAVES: THE NARRATIVES

Ex-slaves made an invaluable contribution to the antislavery cause. One of the most effective of the many attacks upon abolitionists was the charge that the majority of the Northern white antislavery agitators had never seen slavery as it really existed and therefore, did not know what they were talking about. One writer branded the whole galaxy of abolitionists as "a group of fanatics or zealots who never saw a slave in slavery." To be sure, Theodore Weld had provided antislavery agents with an arsenal of information to refute the "positive good" defense of slavery in his masterly *American Slavery As It Is,* but the abolitionists still needed concrete, irrefutable, and first-hand answers to the very persuasive arguments defending slavery that were coming from the South and that were echoed by Northern newspaper editors, politicians, novelists, and clergymen. As the flood of proslavery propaganda mounted in intensity, therefore, the antislavery movement was quick to recognize the potential value of having fugitive slaves paint a picture of slavery as "it really existed." Many fugitive slaves were encouraged to write or dictate their experiences in slavery. This was tempered, however, by the fear that divulging the escaped slave's name or verifiable facts about his or her slave past would open the door to kidnapping and return to bondage. Still, as Angelina Grimké wrote to Weld in 1838, "such narratives are greatly needed."

Slave narratives did appear depicting the essence of the institution of slavery better than any other works issued by the antislavery movement, and they flooded the bookstores. This type of writing usually required an editor, but William Wells Brown, Frederick Douglass, Henry Bibb, Samuel Ringgold Ward, and several other fugitive slaves prepared their own accounts for publication. As to be expected from writings produced from memory, there were inaccuracies, and southerners were quick to point to them as proof that the authors were imposters. But most of the slave narratives were authentic, and, as Larry Gara points out, "through reading many in the northern states obtained their only first-hand account of the peculiar institution as viewed by its victims." Josiah Henson's narrative so moved Harriet Beecher Stowe that in 1850 she visited and conversed with him in Boston and used the information contained in it effectively two years later in her *Uncle Tom's Cabin.*

The slave narratives sold well. The first edition of 6,000 copies of the life of James W. C. Pennington (the fugitive slave who earned the degree of doctor of divinity from Heidelberg University) was sold out within the year. Two years after publication, Solomon Northup's narrative had sold 27,000 copies. A total of 30,000 copies of Frederick Douglass' narrative had been published five years after it appeared in 1845 in the United States; editions had also appeared in England and Ireland and translations in French and German. Douglass' narrative was so popular that two versions were published before the Civil War: *Narrative of the Life of Frederick Douglass* and *My Bondage and My Freedom.* Referring to copies of Douglass' first reminiscences of slavery, a contemporary wrote: "They are scattered over the whole North, and all the theoretical arguments for or against slavery are feeble, compared with the accounts of living men of what they personally endured when under its dominion."

CONTRIBUTIONS OF EX-SLAVES: THE SPEAKERS

It was on the platform, however, that Douglass felt the former slaves could make their greatest contribution. He credited the printed word with effectiveness on some subjects but felt that "humanity, justice and liberty demanded the service of the human voice." Many white abolitionists agreed. In 1842 John A. Collins, an agent for the American Anti-Slavery Society, reported to William Lloyd Garrison:

The public have itching ears to hear a colored man speak, and particularly a *slave.* Multitudes will flock to hear one of this class speak. . . . It would be a good policy to employ a number of colored agents if suitable ones can be found.

Not all were "suitable" for the lecture platform. Many fugitive slaves could produce graphic illustrations from, and tell interesting stories about, their experience in slavery. But they spoke in a halting, stammering dialect, which weakened their hold on audiences. A reporter attending a lecture by Lewis Clarke, a fugitive, found "the uncouth awkwardness of his language had a sort of charm, like the circuitous expression, and stammering utterance of a foreign tongue, striving to speak the most familiar phrases. His mind was evidently full of ideas, which he was eager to express; but the medium was wanting." Another fugitive, when introduced to a meeting, "could not get the 'hang of the school-house' and sat down after a few remarks."

But there were very many fugitives who were more than "suitable"—Henry Bibb, Henry Highland Garnet, William Wells Brown, Sojourner Truth, Josiah Henson, Ellen and William Craft, Samuel Ringgold Ward, Henry "Box" Brown, Anthony Burns, and, of course, Frederick Douglass. People who paid little heed to the declarations of white abolitionists were moved by hearing these fugitives from slavery describe the institution. They and others like them spoke with the authority of experience. They could convey to white people, far removed from the environment of slavery, the atmosphere of chains, whips, blood-hounds, and "the pulse of the four million slaves and their desire for freedom." When white abolitionist speakers tried to deny that the slaves were content, they were told: "You know nothing of the condition of the slave; therefore, let him alone—he is happy in his present condition." But as one observer noted, "When one comes to them with his back scarred by the ruthless lash of the slave-driver, can they say, 'he knows nothing of slavery'?" These ex-slaves, after all, as one antislavery agent put it, were "graduates of the peculiar institution, with their 'diplomas' written on their backs."

But the ex-slave speakers did more than disprove the argument that slavery was a benevolent institution and that the slave was happy under it. They also helped undermine another basic proslavery argument: that the enslaved people were innately inferior, that their situation represented simply a practical application of natural forces, and that they could not take care of themselves and needed the paternalistic supervision of the slaveowners. Who could believe this after hearing ex-slaves describe the obstacles they had had to overcome to achieve freedom—after they heard, for example, Lunsford Lane tell of his experiences? Born a slave in Raleigh, North Carolina, Lane grew up as a house servant owned by Sherwood Haywood, who allowed him to begin to purchase his freedom. After Haywood's death, Lane hired his own time, ultimately saving the $1,000 necessary for self-purchase. Unable to make contracts while a slave, Lane per-suaded his wife's owner, Benjamin B. Smith, to purchase and then emancipate him. The latter, having failed to obtain permission to free Lane in North Carolina for "meritorious conduct," executed a deed of manumission in New York State in the early 1830s. Lane then returned to Raleigh and entered the tobacco trade. In Jaunary 1839, he contracted to purchase his wife and six children for $2,500, payable to Smith in five annual installments. The next year, local authorities declared Lane and other Raleigh free Negroes illegal immigrants and ordered them to leave the state. Unable to secure an exemption from the North Carolina legislature, Lane spent much of his time at abolitionist gatherings in New England soliciting the money to purchase his enslaved family. In April 1842, he returned to Raleigh to buy his relatives but was arrested for having delivered antislavery lectures in Massachusetts. Upon his release by the mayor, Lane narrowly escaped lynching at the hands of an enraged mob. He returned North with his wife, children, and aged mother and settled in Massachusetts, where he remained active in the antislavery cause. The story of his experiences told from the lecture platform (and also published in *The Narrative of Lunsford Lane*) served to convince many listeners and readers alike that the view that blacks were innately inferior and needed the care of slaveowners was a lie.

Like many other ex-slaves, Lane developed his speaking ability at a self-improvement society organized by blacks, which afforded opportunities to learn the fundamentals of public speaking. A white abolitionist who attended a session of one of these societies observed that in the discussions, "the colored people acquire the habit of thinking and speaking; a circumstances which may, in great measure, account for the self-possession of their manners, and the propriety and fluency of their language." Through self-education and continued effort, ex-slaves became as capable of expressing their ideas as many who had enjoyed a considerable amount of formal education. "Who are among our ablest speakers? Who are the best qualified to address the public mind on the subject of slavery?" William Lloyd Garrison asked, and he answered: "Your fugitive slaves—your Douglasses, Browns, and Bibbs—who are astonishing all with the cogency of their words and the power of their reasoning." Each of these men was a living refutation of the doctrine of racial inferiority, and they, along with other fugitives, did much to weaken (if not entirely destroy) the belief in black inferiority.

Prior to the Civil War, William Wells Brown had produced a travel book, a collection of antislavery songs, a novel, and a play. A reporter who heard this ex-slave hold his audience's attention for several hours wrote: "His dignity of manner, his propriety of expression were more than we expected to see in one who had spent the early part of his life as a slave." Of Henry Bibb, one who heard him speak, wrote: "This Henry Bibb is certainly no common man. His voice and enunciations are good—his language is chaste, very correct, and sometimes truly eloquent—his form and motions are easy and graceful—and he has that appearance of sincerity which seldom fails to win the heart." A report of Bibb's reading of his own narrative told of how "the audience was delighted with his address. They cheered, clapped, stamped, laughed, and wept, by turns, at his recital." Of Anthony Burns' lecture (which included an illustrated panorama with scenes showing the "degradation and horrors of American slavery"), one observer wrote: "His lecture cannot fail to kindle anew in the hearts of all a stronger opposition to that curse of all curses—American Slavery."

Like Burns, other ex-slaves used interesting devices to add color to their lectures. After his dramatic escape, Henry "Box" Brown spoke at numerous antislavery meetings, exhibiting the box used in his flight from slavery, along with a powerful diorama showing many scenes of Southern slave life, painted for him by Benjamin Roberts, a black artist from Boston.

Among ex-slaves, James W. C. Pennington, Samuel Ringgold Ward, Jermain Loguen, William Wells Brown, and Henry Bibb were rated as great orators. But no fugitive was a more effective speaker than Frederick Douglass. "The very look and bearing of Douglass are an irresistible logic against the oppression of his race," said James Russell Lowell, summing up a universal opinion of all who heard him speak. In fact, contemporary observers were so captivated by Douglass that they tended at times to ignore the contributions of lesser known blacks. Still, it cannot be denied that Frederick Douglass was truly unique.

FREDERICK DOUGLASS: ANTISLAVERY AGENT

Frederick Douglass escaped from slavery in Baltimore with the aid of a sailor's suit and a sailor's "protection" borrowed from a seafaring free black. In the late afternoon of September 3, 1838, Douglass arrived in Philadelphia; the next day he was in New York City, where he remained hidden for several days in the home of David Ruggles, the black secretary of the New York Vigilance Committee. Twelve days after his escape, he married Anna Murray, a free black woman with whom he had fallen in love while in Baltimore and who had come North to meet him. They were married by the Reverend James W. C. Pennington, who had himself fled from a Maryland master ten years earlier. Two days later, they were on their way to New Bedford, Massachusetts, where Ruggles believed Douglass' skill as a caulker would secure him a livelihood, a belief that proved to be unwarranted because of the racism prevalent in the city. In New Bedford, the couple stayed at the home of Mr. and Mrs. Nathan Johnson, a prosperous black family who helped many fugitive slaves become adjusted to freedom. It was Johnson who gave the name *Douglass* to his guest. While in New York, Frederick had dropped his two middle names (Augustus Washington), and changed *Bailey* to *Johnson*. Because there were a great number of New Bedford Negroes with that name, his benefactor, who had just finished reading Sir Walter Scott's *Lady of the Lake,* suggested the name by which he was soon to be known on both sides of the Atlantic.

Before he had left Baltimore, Douglass had already heard of the abolitionists and of their work to end slavery. He had received help from them en route to New Bedford, but he knew very little of their activities. Four months after arriving in New England, there came into his hands a copy of William Lloyd Garrison's *Liberator.* He was so deeply moved by the paper that, despite his poverty—he could only find menial work as a day laborer—he became a regular subscriber. Every week he read the journal avidly, studying its principles and philosophy. "The paper became my meat and my drink," he wrote six years later.

Douglass began to attend the abolitionist meetings held by the Negro people of New Bedford. On August 9, 1841, he attended the annual meeting of the Bristol Anti-Slavery Society, held in New Bedford, saw and heard Garrison for the first time, and entering into the discussion, made a marked impression on the abolitionist leader, who reported to the *Liberator* that at the meeting were "several talented young men from New Bedford, one of them formerly a slave whose addresses were listened to by large and attentive audiences with deep interest." The following day, with Garrison and forty other abolitionists, white and black, Douglass set sail on the steamboat *Telegraph* for an antislavery convention in Nantucket. The next morning, August 12, he was called upon to speak at the convention at Athenaeum Hall. Trembling and ill at ease, Douglass came forward to the platform and spoke with deep sincerity of his life as a slave, moving the entire audience with his eloquence. That evening, Douglass spoke again, and, as in the morning, the audience was deeply moved. In his report of the convention, the correspondent of the *National Anti-Slavery Standard* devoted special attention to the ex-slave from New Bedford:

One, recently from the house of bondage, spoke with great power. Flinty hearts were pierced, and cold ones melted by his eloquence. Our best pleaders for the slave held their breath for fear of interrupting him. Mr. Garrison said his speech would have done honor to

Patrick Henry. It seemed almost miraculous how he had been prepared to tell his story with so much power. . . .

Then Garrison arose, and burst forth into a more eloquent strain than I had ever heard before. He eulogized, as he deserved, the fugitive who had just spoken and anathematized the system that could crush to the earth such men.

Garrison asked the audience, "Have we been listening to a thing, a piece of property, or to a man?" The chant "A man! A man!" was raised by five hundred voices.

Before the convention adjourned, John A. Collins, then general agent of the Massachusetts Anti-Slavery Society, urged Douglass to become an active lecturer for the organization. Douglass, doubting his own ability, was reluctant to accept, but he finally agreed to work for the society for three months. He was to travel with white antislavery agents and, in addition to lecturing, was to solicit subscriptions for the *Liberator* and the *National Anti-Slavery Standard*. His salary was to be $450 a year.

During his first three months as a lecturer, Douglass usually traveled with John A. Collins, but they were joined at country-wide meetings by Garrison, Parker Pillsbury, Stephen S. Foster, Abby Kelly, and other leaders of the movement. The presence of these veterans failed to detract from the attention received by the new recruit. Over six feet tall, his presence was described by reporters as "bold," "manly," and "striking." On hearing him at a convention of the Plymouth Society on November 4, 1841, the editor of the *Hingham Patriot* was reminded of Spartacus, the gladiator:

He was very fluent in the use of language, choice and appropriate language, too; and talks as well, for all we could see, as men who have spent all their lives over books. He is forceful, keen and very sarcastic; and considering the poor advantages he must have had as a slave, he is certainly a remarkable man.

N. P. Rogers, editor of the *Herald of Freedom,* heard Douglass speak in Providence, Rhode Island, and wrote: "As a speaker he has few equals. It is not declamation—but oratory, power of debate. He has wit, argument, sarcasm, pathos—all that first-rate men show in their master efforts. His voice is highly melodious and rich, and his enunciation quite elegant, and yet he has been but two or three years out of the house of bondage." The reporter for the *Salem Register* made the same point after hearing Douglass in his city: "The most wonderful performance of the evening was the address of Frederick Douglass himself a slave only four years ago! His remarks and his manner created the most indescribable sensations in the minds of those unaccustomed to hear *freemen* of color speak in public, much more to regard a *slave* as capable of such an effort. He was a living, speaking, *startling* proof of the folly, absurdity and inconsistency (to say nothing worse) of slavery. Fluent, graceful, eloquent, shrewd, sarcastic, he was without making any allowance, a fine specimen of an orator." The writer then went on to class him, as an equal with "Everett or Webster."

In his early speeches, Douglass may have contributed little that was original or new, but he did give the movement a spark that it could not have otherwise obtained. By then, the speeches of most of the Garrisonians had pretty much fallen into a pattern, and everyone knew more or less what they would say. Each speech contained a fervent appeal for the slave, a denunciation of the slave system (with readings from *American Slavery As It Is*) and of the church and politicians supporting it, a condemnation of the Constitution as a proslavery document, and an appeal for separation from the South. Douglass too used this formula in his speeches (while chiefly describing his life as a slave), but he added variety and freshness. Like the other Garrisonians, he could denounce slavery and the slaveholders with invectives that were no less piercing, but he also injected humor into his speeches. He could thrill his listeners with an account of his battle with Edward Covey, the slave breaker, at the same time getting them to burst into laughter as he described the expression on the Negro tamer's face as he went down into the filth of the cowpen. He could bring shouts of appreciation from the audience as he portrayed his master, Mr. Auld, first being converted, the tears rolling down his cheeks as he worshipped God, then the same Mr. Auld, on the same day, dispersing a group of slaves who were assembled to worship the same God.

His keen sense of humor and his uncanny knack of mimickry were powerful weapons, and he used them devastatingly. At Faneuil Hall, the Cradle of Liberty, he enlivened a meeting one evening with "a very funny imitation of the way in which slaveholding clergymen would exhort their servants to obey their masters." He delivered this remarkable piece of mimickry time and again to the delight of his audiences and to the embarrassment of the Southern clergy. In a canting tone of voice, he would begin:

They the ministers would take a text—say this:—"Do unto others as you would have them do unto you." And this is how they would apply it. They would explain it to mean, "slaveholders, do unto *slaveholders* what you would have them do unto you:" and then looking impudently up the slave's gallery . . . looking up to the poor colored drivers and the rest, and spreading his hands gracefully abroad he says (*mimicking*), "And you too, my friends, have souls of infinite value—souls that will *labor diligently* to make your calling and election sure. Oh, receive unto your souls these words of the holy apostle—Servants, be obedient to your masters." (*Shouts of laughter and applause.*)

"Oh! if you wish to be happy in time, happy in eternity, you must be obedient to your masters; their interest is yours. God made one portion of men to do the working; and another to do the thinking; how good God is! Now you have no trouble or anxiety; but ah! you can't imagine how perplexing it is to your masters and mistresses to have so much thinking to do in your behalf! You cannot appreciate your blessings; you know not how happy a thing it is for you, that you were born of that portion of the human family which has the working, instead of the thinking to do! Oh! how grateful and obedient you ought to be to your masters! How beautiful are the arrangements of Providence! Look at your hard, horny hands—see how nicely they are adapted to the labor you have to perform! Look at our delicate fingers, so exactly fitted for our station, and see how manifest it is that God deigned us to be his thinkers, and you the workers—oh! the wisdom of God."

As reports from people who had heard Douglass poured into the *Liberator* and the *Anti-Slavery Standard,* it was clear that the antislavery movement had acquired an invaluable asset. Few of Douglass' contemporaries on the antislavery platform, white or black, had his range, versatility, and impact. Writing to Garrison from Northbridge, a veteran abolitionist summed up the opinion of all who heard him: "It has been my fortune to hear a great many anti-slavery lecturers, and many distinguished speakers on other subjects; but it has rarely been my lot to listen to one whose power over me was greater than Douglass, and not over *me* only, but all who heard him." Again and again whites who heard Douglass speak wrote that he was "evidence in his own person of the falsity of the notion that the coloured race are incapable of mental culture."

TRIALS OF BLACK ANTISLAVERY AGENTS

Although former slaves made a unique contribution to the antislavery crusade, their effect was reinforced by the abolitionist work of other able blacks who were born free. The list of these valiant fighters for freedom is legion, and we can mention only a few. Charles Lenox Remond, whom black historian Carter G. Woodson called "the ablest representative of the Negro race" in the antislavery movement prior to the appearance of Frederick Douglass, did yeoman work for the cause as an agent for the American Anti-Slavery Society. Remond was the first black abolitionist speaker to address large audiences. One can judge his popularity by the fact that when some members of the Lyceum in Lynn expressed opposition to his being invited to speak there in 1842, "a majority united in the formation of another institution . . . in order that they might hear his speech." That same year, Remond was chosen to address the Massachusetts House of Representatives in support of various petitions protesting segregated railroad accommodations in that state.

Robert Purvis, the prominent black leader of Philadelphia, was one of the outstanding leaders of the Garrisonian wing of the antislavery movement. He contributed funds to help launch the *Liberator* in 1831, became a charter member of the American Anti-Slavery Society at its founding convention in 1833, and served as president and vice-president of both the Pennsylvania State Anti-Slavery Society and the Philadelphia Vigilance Committee.

William C. Nell began his lengthy association with the *Liberator* in the early 1840s. In addition to operating the paper's Negro Employment Office, he wrote extensively on antislavery issues and on the struggle of free blacks for equality. Later he became publisher of Douglass' *North Star*, moved to Rochester, New York, and became active in New York State antislavery organizations.

Free black and ex-slave antislavery agents often traveled together, making a dual impact on white audiences. Often they received no salary and depended on a portion of whatever collections were taken after their lectures. A notice in the *National Anti-Slavery Standard* on May 7, 1843, informed the public that

William Wells Brown, agent for the Western New York Anti-Slavery Society, was beginning his lecture tour and that "while thus engaged, he is dependent for his sustenance on the aid of the philanthropist."

The life of a black antislavery agent was not all applause and praise. In some circles, they were not only considered part of the fraternity of "lunatics" and "miserable fanatics," represented by men like Garrison, Tappan, and Phillips, but they were blacks to boot—and what right had blacks to criticize *white* southerners? When Garrison, Remond, and Douglass spoke together in Buffalo, in 1847, the *Daily Courier* singled out the latter two for special attention because they were "blacks and although they were very good speakers, it seems remarkably impudent to hear them denounce the white population of the South, and dictate to the North what course should be pursued toward our Southern brethren."

All abolitionists needed special qualities of courage and determination to carry on their work in the face of intimidation and mob violence, but the black abolitionists were subjected to even more abuse and disdain than were their white colleagues. "Heartless and vulgar color prejudice" was the capsule description given to the reception accorded to the typical speaking tour reserved for black abolitionists. While white antislavery speakers could find accommodations on a railroad or steamboat or in a restaurant, hotel, or boardinghouse, the blacks were forced to face humiliating discrimination. They had to travel in dirty Jim Crow cars or on the decks of steamboats and to plan for overnight stays at the homes of sympathetic friends. Even that was not always possible. When William Wells Brown visited the town of Attica, New York, in the fall of 1843 as an agent of the Western New York Anti-Slavery Society, he was unable to find a tavern in the village that would lodge him for the night. Nor was there any home that would open its doors to him. As a last resort, he went back to the church in which he had lectured and spent the night there. Because it was extremely cold, he had to walk around in the building most of the night to keep from freezing.

The black antislavery agent was the first to be singled out by hoodlums who attacked antislavery speakers and broke up their meetings. Writing to Wendell Phillips from Philadelphia in April 1845, Charles L. Remond noted almost casually that "in most places" where he had been holding antislavery meetings and lecturing, "mobs, rumors of mobs have been the order of the day; but receiving personal injury in a single instance I will pass them without comment."

Frederick Douglass was mobbed so frequently that other Negroes would offer their bodies as shields. On the morning of September 16, 1845, in Pendleton, Madison County, Indiana, Douglass and his two white antislavery colleagues (William A. White and George Bradburn) were set upon by club-wielding rowdies who demolished the speaker's platform at their outdoor meeting and attacked its occupants. Douglass, who drew the mob's special wrath, was pursued and severely beaten by attackers who screamed, "Kill the nigger," "Kill the d——m nigger." "The leader of the mob," White wrote in a report to the

Liberator, ". . . struck him once with his club, and was raising it the second time to level a blow which must have been fatal had it fallen, but I, by dint of hard running, came up in time to throw myself upon him, and stop him in his murderous purpose."

The bleeding and unconscious Douglass was taken three miles by wagon to the farm of Mr. and Mrs. Neal Hardy, a Quaker couple, who treated his broken right hand and other injuries. Because the bones were not properly set, Douglass' hand never regained its "natural strength and dexterity." He never forgot the experience. Three years later, he wrote to White, it still "haunted" his dreams. He had gone "to bed thinking about Pendleton."

SOJOURNER TRUTH

Because they were women, Frances Ellen Watkins, Sarah P. Remond, and especially Sojourner Truth compelled unusual attention as black abolitionist speakers. And as black women on the lecture platform, they were able to personify the 2 million women bound in slavery. The three had different backgrounds. Frances Ellen Watkins was born in Baltimore of free parents, was educated at her uncle's school for colored children, moved to Ohio in 1850, and was engaged as a full-time lecturer in 1854 by the Anti-Slavery Society of Maine and in 1857 by the Pennsylvania State Anti-Slavery Society as lecturer and agent for Eastern Pennsylvania and New Jersey. While on the lecture platform, she sold her book, *Poems on Various Subjects,* and was considered one of the best antislavery lecturers on the circuit.

Sarah Parker Remond, sister of Charles Lenox Remond, was born in Salem, Massachusetts, in 1826, the daughter of John Remond, a prosperous black businessman, and was well educated. She joined the antislavery movement and, following in her brother's footsteps, spoke with him at meetings in upstate New York. She also shared the platform with Susan B. Anthony at antislavery conventions. She achieved renown principally as an antislavery speaker during the course of an 1858 lecture tour of Ireland and England.

Sojourner Truth was born a slave in New York in 1798 and freed on July 4, 1827, when the state liberated all its bondspeople. Thereafter she did domestic work, and following a period of religious revivalism, became an abolitionist, changing her name, Isabella, to Sojourner Truth. Although she remained illiterate all her life, she learned to use her quaint, broken manner of speech and became an eloquent advocate of antislavery, women's rights, and temperance.

Sojourner's deep voice raised some doubts as to whether she was a woman. Once after she had started to speak at a meeting in Indiana, a local physician shouted that she was an imposter and that, as her deep baritone voice indicated, she was really a man. He demanded that she bare her breasts to a committee of women to prove her sex. Before she could answer, he called for a vote by the audience as to whether she was male or female. By an overwhelming majority, the jeering crowd voted that Sojourner Truth was a man. Sojourner, infuriated, ripped open her dress and shouted above the tumult:

My breasts have suckled many a white baby when they should have been sucklin's my own. Some of those white babies is now grown men, and even though they have suckled my Negro breasts, they are far more manly than any of you. I show my breasts to the whole congregation. It ain't my shame but yours that I should do this. Here, then, see for yourselves!

Sojourner Truth considered herself a "Pilgrim of God," chosen to free her people from slavery. Her speeches were so eloquent and persuasive, in spite of their inelegance and lack of grammar, that she ranked behind only Frederick Douglass as the most powerful antislavery orator. Because of her effectiveness as a speaker, frequent efforts were made to silence her, and she was both stoned and beaten. But she persisted in her mission. Once when a mob milled around her and threatened to burn down any hall granted her, she shouted back at them in her low, powerful voice, "Then I will speak upon its ashes." When she arose to speak, she usually wore a satin banner with the words: "Proclaim liberty throughout the land and unto the inhabitants thereof."

BLACK ABOLITIONISTS AND WOMEN'S RIGHTS

In 1851, Sojourner Truth attended a women's rights convention held in Akron, Ohio. Everything seemed to be going wrong at the meeting. A number of ministers had invaded the hall, uninvited, and insisted on monopolizing the discussion, quoting biblical texts to the effect that women should confine their activities to childbearing, homemaking, and subservience to their husbands. Sojourner Truth sat listening through all this masculine abuse until one of the male speakers said that women need not be given any rights, since they were mentally inferior to men. At this point, she had had enough. She arose, marched to the speaker's audience, and told the startled audience:

Well, children, where there is so much racket there must be something out of kilter. I think that between the Negroes of the South and the women of the North, all talking about rights, the white man will be in a fix pretty soon. But what's all this here talking about?

That man over there says that women need to be helped into carriages and lifted over ditches, and have the best place everywhere. Nobody ever helps me into carriages, or over mud-puddles, or gives me any best place! And aren't I a woman? Look at my arm! I have ploughed, and planted, and gathered into barns, and no man could head me! And aren't I a woman? I could work as much and eat as much as a man—when I could get it—and bear the lash as well! And aren't I a woman? I have borne thirteen children, and seen them most all sold off to slavery, and when I cried out with my mother's grief, none but Jesus heard me! And aren't I a woman?

If the first woman God ever made was strong enough to turn the world upside down all alone, these women together ought to be able to turn it back, and get it right side up again! And now they are asking to do it, the men better let them.

The cheering was long and loud.

Sojourner Truth was not the only black abolitionist to champion women's rights. As James E. Oliver and Lois E. Horton have noted: "Although black women suffered from the sexist attitudes of their men as did most nineteenth-century women, black society was more tolerant of women in active roles as social protestors than was the society at large." Unlike many male white anti-slavery crusaders, black male abolitionists had no hesitation in having women play an active role in the movement. The Philadelphia Female Anti-Slavery Society's first presiding officer was a Negro and a man, Dr. James McCrummell. "None in the leadership forming the organization," observes Herbert Aptheker, "felt competent to preside at a public meeting, and the only man they could find courageous enough to associate himself with two such slandered causes as Aboli-tionism and the active participation of women in public affairs was this Dr. McCrummell." Speaking both for himself and his black abolitionist colleagues, William Wells Brown told a meeting of the Salem Female Anti-Slavery Society: "We are not those who would ask the men to help us and leave the women at home. We want all to help us. A million women are in Slavery, and as long as a single woman is in slavery, every woman in the community should raise her voice against that sin."

Many male black abolitionists had another reason to be " 'women's rights' men." They saw clearly that a number of the arguments used to justify the enslavement and persecution of black people were also employed to uphold male supremacy. They were helped in this realization by such newspapers as the *New York Herald,* a fervent defender of slavery and a bitter opponent of women's rights, which editorialized: "How did woman become subject to man, as she now is all over the world. By her nature, just as the negro is, and always will be, to the end of time, inferior to the white race."

Space does not permit a full discussion of the role of Negroes in the women's rights movement other than to indicate that it was considerable, particularly on the part of Frederick Douglass, whose paper, the *North Star,* from its first issue featured the slogan: "Right is of no sex."

While Douglass believed that the antislavery movement was doing much "for the elevation and improvement of women," he understood fully the need for an independent, organized movement to achieve equal rights for women. On July 14, 1848, the *North Star* carried the historic announcement:

A Convention to discuss the Social, Civil and Religious Condition and Rights of Women, will be held in the Wesleyan Church at Seneca Falls, New York, on Wednesday and Thursday, the 19th and 20th of July instant.

During the first day, the meetings will be exclusively for women, which all are earnest-ly invited to attend. The public generally are invited to be present on the second day, when

Lucretia Mott of Philadelphia, and others, both ladies and gentlemen, will address the Convention.

While other papers also carried news of the convention, the *North Star* was one of the very few that did not include editorials hurling ridicule and anathema at the sponsors.

A few days before the convention was scheduled to open, Elizabeth Cady Stanton, the driving force behind the meeting, joined with Lucretia Mott and others to draw up the Seneca Falls Declaration of Sentiments and Resolutions. They used the Declaration of Independence as a model:

We hold these truths to be self-evident; that all men and women are created equal. . . .

The history of mankind is the history of repeated injuries and usurpations on the part of man toward woman, having in the direct object the establishment of absolute tyranny over her. To prove this let the facts be submitted to a candid world.

They listed eighteen such facts and at the head of the list placed what they considered their main grievance: "He has never permitted her to exercise the inalienable right to the elective franchise."

With James Mott, Lucretia's husband, in the chair, the Declaration of Sentiments was read to the delegates and adopted unanimously. Eleven other resolutions, also adopted unanimously, set forth such demands as the right of women to personal and religious freedom; the right to testify in courts; equality in marriage and the right to their children; the right to own property and to claim their own wages; and the right to education and equality in trades and professions.

The twelfth resolution, however, did not have such an easy time being adopted. It read: "Resolved, That it was the duty of women of this country to secure to themselves their sacred right to the elective franchise." Even before the convention opened, Elizabeth Cady Stanton had been warned that the resolution on the franchise was too radical a step to propose. Lucretia Mott felt that the demand for the vote was too advanced for the times. "This will make us ridiculous," she cautioned. "We must go slowly."

But Stanton was determined to press the issue, and she looked about the convention for an ally. "I knew Frederick, from personal experience, was just the man for the work," she told an audience of suffragists years later. Hurrying to Douglass' side, Stanton read him the resolution, and, having been reassured that he would take the floor in her support, she determined to hold to her purpose.

When she introduced her daring proposal, the general sentiment appeared to be moving against the resolution, and it seemed that it would go down to defeat. It was at this critical juncture that Douglass asked for the floor and delivered an eloquent plea in behalf of woman's right to the elective franchise. The resolution was then put to a vote and carried by a small margin.

Years later, a tablet was erected commemorating the occasion:

On this spot stood the Wesleyan Chapel
Where the first Woman's Rights Convention
in the World's History was held July 19 and 20, 1848
Elizabeth Cady Stanton moved this resolution
which was seconded by Frederick Douglass
That it was the duty of the women of this country
to secure to themselves their sacred right
to the elective franchise.

On the occasion of the sixtieth anniversary of the Seneca Falls Convention in 1908, the black educator Mary Church Terrell extolled this "magnificant representative" of her race:

The incomparable Frederick Douglass did many things of which I as a member of that race which he served so faithfully and well am proud. But there is nothing he ever did in his long and brilliant career in which I take keener pleasure and greater pride than I do in his ardent advocacy of equal political rights for women and the effective service he rendered the cause of woman suffrage sixty years ago.

It is also worth noting that at the London World Anti-Slavery Convention, where the plan for the Seneca Falls gathering was born, another free black, Charles Lenox Remond, upheld the principles of equality for women. Eight years later, at Seneca Falls, the slave-born Frederick Douglass supported these same principles, including the very advanced concept of woman suffrage.

In the *North Star* on July 28, 1848, Douglass praised the action taken by the Seneca Falls convention and announced his support of "the grand movement for attaining the civil, social, political, and religious rights of women." He bade the women engaged in the crusade his "humble Godspeed" and pledged his active support. He was as good as his word. There were few women's rights conventions held before the Civil War at which Douglass was not a featured speaker and whose proceedings were not fully reported in his paper. Invariably, the notice would be accompanied by an editorial comment hailing the meeting and expressing the editor's hope that the proceedings "will have a powerful effect upon the public's mind." In 1853, when Douglass was considering a new name for his paper, he rejected the proposed title, the *Brotherhood,* because it "implied the exclusion of the sisterhood." He called it *Frederick Douglass' Paper,* and underneath the title were the words, "All Rights For All!" In her unpublished study, "The Woman's Rights Movement in New York State, 1848–1854," Helen T. Shea cites Douglass' paper as the most supportive journal in the state to the women's rights movement and as an indispensable source of information about its activities. In late 1855, Susan B. Anthony suggested to Gerrit Smith that he read Douglass' weekly for regular notices of women's rights gatherings.

Douglass learned much from the women with whom he associated at woman's rights conventions. At one time, he had entertained serious doubts about granting wives an equal right to share the disposition of property with their husbands, since "the husband labors hard" while the wife might not be gainfully employed for wages. But his discussions with Ernestine L. Rose, Elizabeth Cady Stanton, Abby Kelly Foster (by then married to Stephen S. Foster), Pauline Wright Davis, and other pioneers of the woman's rights movement convinced him that, even though wives were not paid for their domestic labors, their work was as important to the family as that of their husbands. Once convinced, he acted. He wrote the call for the 1853 women's rights convention in Rochester, New York, which demanded not only that women should be paid equally with men for their work but also that women, including married women, should have equal rights with men to the ownership and disposition of property. He urged all citizens of New York to sign a petition to the state legislature, drawn up by William H. Channing, calling for passage of a law which would "place Married Women on an equality with Married Men in regard to the holding, and division of real and personal property."

The women with whom he worked in the movement also gave Douglass a clearer understanding of the economic problems facing members of their sex. When he drew up a plan for an American industrial school for blacks to be established in Pennsylvania, he included a provision for females. He emphasized that "a prominent principle of conduct will be to aid in providing for the female sex, methods and means of enjoying an independent and honorable livelihood."

On one issue, however, Douglass refused to budge. He was critical of those women's rights leaders who addressed audiences from which blacks were barred. His particular target was Lucy Stone. Douglass often praised this abolitionist and veteran fighter for equal rights for women, but he criticized her for not having cancelled a lecture at Philadelphia's Music Hall when she discovered that blacks were to be excluded. Later he was more severe when he learned that Stone had invited Senator Stephen A. Douglas of Illinois, one of the architects of the Fugitive Slave Act of 1850 and author of the proslavery Kansas-Nebraska Act, to join the women who were to meet in Chicago in 1859 to publicize the women's rights cause. Throwing delicacy to the winds, Douglass bluntly accused her of willingness to advance women's rights on the back of "the defenceless slave woman" who suffered wrongs compared to which the injustices heaped upon other women were in an entirely different class. "Other women suffer certain wrongs," he reminded Lucy Stone and other women's rights leaders who pursued a similar policy, "but the wrongs peculiar to woman out of slavery, great and terrible as they are, are endured as well by the slave woman, who has also to bear the ten thousand wrongs of slavery in addition to the common wrongs of woman." He continued:

It is hard to be underpaid for labor faithfully performed; it is harder still not to be paid for labor at all. It is hard that woman should be limited in her means of education; it is harder still to be deprived of all means of education. It is hard for the widow only to receive the third part of the property of her deceased husband; it is harder still to be a chattel person to all intents and purposes.—It is hard only to enjoy a qualified right to one's children; but it is harder still for a woman to have no rights which white men are bound to respect.

Lucy Stone had her defenders, but they were all white. Blacks, including those who publicly supported the woman's rights movement, agreed with Douglass.

Nor did Douglass spare black women who collaborated with the racists. When Elizabeth Taylor Greenfield, the "Black Swan," who astounded the musical world in the United States and Europe during the early 1850s with her contralto voice, consented to perform before an audience from which "colored persons" were excluded, Douglass angrily dubbed her the "Black Raven."

Douglass' criticism of women, both black and white, who agreed to speak to segregated audiences was largely responsible for making the women's rights movement more sensitive to the issue of prejudice against black Americans.

BLACK ABOLITIONISTS ABROAD

Many abolitionists journeyed to England, Ireland, and Scotland to meet and consult with like-minded people in those countries in order to further the anti-slavery cause in the United States. In this respect, too, black abolitionists made a singular contribution.

Among those whom Benjamin Quarles has called "Ministers Without Portfolio," were such ex-slaves as James W. C. Pennington, Henry Highland Garnet, Samuel Ringgold Ward, Jermain W. Loguen, Josiah Henson, William Wells Brown, Frederick Douglass, William and Ellen Craft, and Henry "Box" Brown. Free-born Negro "Ministers Without Portfolio" included James McCune Smith, William G. Allen, William H. Day, William P. Powell, Martin R. Delany, Alexander Crummell, and Sarah P. Remond.

Most black abolitionists who went to Great Britain stayed for a few months or a year or two, delivering speeches on the antislavery lecture circuit, and, in the case of fugitive slaves, selling copies of their narratives. Some, however, remained and became part of the British antislavery movement. James McCune Smith, while still a student at Glasgow University, served as a committee member of the Glasgow Emancipation Society. The Reverend Alexander Crummell, who studied at Cambridge, was a lecturer for the British and Foreign Anti-Slavery Society. In the decade he spent in England, William P. Powell spoke regularly at meetings sponsored by the various antislavery societies.

In 1850, Henry Highland Garnet and James W. C. Pennington attended the World Peace Conference in Frankfurt, Germany, after which they helped set up an antislavery society in the German city. Both then went on an extensive speaking tour of Scotland. William Wells Brown spoke at a World Peace Conference in France in 1849, where he met Alexis de Tocqueville, author of *Democracy in America*. After the conference, Brown and the Crafts toured

England and Scotland for six months making speeches against slavery. Alexander Crummell was in London in 1851, along with Garnet, Henson, and Pennington, to attend the annual meeting of the British and Foreign Anti-Slavery Society. A few months later, Brown chaired a London public meeting celebrating West Indian emancipation, at which the audience included the historian, Thomas B. Macaulay, and the new British poet laureate, Alfred Tennyson.

While most black abolitionists went abroad either to proselytize against slavery in the United States or to seek an education in the British Isles, William P. Powell had still another reason. On July 31, 1851, *Frederick Douglass' Paper* carried the following announcement under the heading "The Shame of America":

Mr. William P. Powell of New York, an educated and highly respectable man, though of an unconstitutional color, intends to move to England with his large family to give his children a better chance than they have in this caste-ridden country.

In an interview, Powell explained that although he himself had been successful in the United States, this success had been "in spite of the obstacles which every day of my life have been thrown in my way because of my complexion." Since he had no way of knowing that his children would be blessed with equally good luck or that energy and enterprise would bring them success,

I have decided to remove to another country where my children will not, because of their color alone, be compelled to fight the battle of life at a disadvantage, which I too well know how to appreciate. I do not feel I would be discharging a parental duty by retaining them in a land which though theirs by birth, makes them alien to the protection of its laws and the benefit of its social relations.

Although he had the means to move to England with his wife and seven children, before leaving Powell chose to present claims to the New York legislature that had been denied him from his birth. He sent a petition to the legislature requesting assistance for the removal of his family to a new home. He set forth the facts that his grandmother had been a cook for the first Continental Congress and had thereby helped to form the glorious Union of the United States; that his father had been a slave in New York, and through his unpaid labor, had also contributed to the welfare of the nation; and that they had been entitled to receive the benefits of the Declaration of Independence but had been denied them because of their color, with the result that the contract embodied in the declaration guaranteeing to all "life, liberty and the pursuit of happiness" had been broken. Inasmuch as the New York legislature had taken favorable action to aid blacks "emigrating from this country to Liberia," Powell insisted that it make good what was owed to his grandmother and father by enabling him to give his own children "those opportunities for a livelihood and a respectable position in society, to which, as human beings, and as American citizens they are entitled, by making it possible to take them to the kingdom of Great Britain, where character and not color—capacity and not complexion, are the tests of merit."

Powell sent this petition to the member of the state legislature from his district, but that individual refused even to present it. "Had Mr. Powell asked permission to sell his children at auction to the highest bidder," commented the *National Anti-Slavery Standard,* "we have no doubt he would have gained a hearing, but a petition for aid to remove them where the buying and selling of their brethren would not consign them to contempt and degradation, was not deemed proper by his representative even to present to the Legislature."

In his parting letter to his associates in the antislavery movement, Powell urged them to be "true to principle, to be true to the slave." As for himself, he pledged to remain faithful while in England to those still "in the bondage of American slavery."

All of the black abolitionists made deep impressions in England, Ireland, and Scotland. They were popular figures, sought after by the antislavery societies as speakers, and their efforts contributed greatly to keeping alive interest in the American slave. In 1840, Charles Lenox Remond was appointed an American Anti-Slavery Society delegate to the World Anti-Slavery Convention in London. For more than a year following the convention, Remond journeyed through England and Ireland, addressing antislavery societies, establishing contact with numerous British leaders, winning praise for his effectiveness on the platform. "Our colored friend Remond," wrote Garrison who was also in England at the time, "is a great favorite in every circle." On his return to the United States eighteen months later, Remond brought with him the "Great Irish Address," a petition signed by sixty thousand Irishmen urging their Irish brethren in American to support abolition and black equality. But no one scored a triumph to equal that of Frederick Douglass.

Douglass' first visit to England was hastened by the publication of his *Narrative* in 1845. He had undertaken the task of putting down the facts about his slave past in order to answer the charge, precipitated by his oratorical skills and thoughtful analysis, that he had never been a slave. "Many persons in the audience," wrote a Philadelphia correspondent in the *Liberator* of August 30, 1844, "seemed unable to credit the statements which he gave of himself, and could not believe that he was actually a slave. How a man, only six years out of bondage, and who had never gone to school a day in his life, could speak with such eloquence—with such precision of language and power of thought—they were utterly at a loss to devise."

Publication of the *Narrative* effectively stilled the debate over Douglass' authenticity, but it increased fears that he would be recaptured and returned to the slavery. The knowledge that his life and liberty were now in jeopardy hastened Douglass' determination to visit Great Britain. He was already known in England as a result of the highly complimentary reviews of his *Narrative* in the British press and the accounts of both his speeches and the reactions to them that appeared in the *Liberator* and the *National Anti-Slavery Standard.* He was preceded in his visit by fulsome letters of introduction. Wendell Phillips spoke for all when he wrote that Douglass was "the most remarkable and by far the ablest colored man we have ever had here. Language, taste, fancy eloquence, vigor of thought, good sound common sense, and manliness are all his."

British audiences were quick to agree. "Oh, what a speech Frederick made!" Mary Brady wrote from Leeds to the *Liberator*. "It was indescribably beautiful, sublime, pathetic and powerful. Often the enthusiasm of the audience knew no bounds." Everywhere he spoke, Douglass' speeches evoked a similar response. Elizabeth Pease called him "a *living* contradiction . . . to that base opinion, which is so abhorrent to every human and Christian feeling, that the blacks are an inferior race." Similarly, Sarah Hilditch of Wrexham wrote that Douglass was "a living example of the capabilities of the slave, and though we do not expect *all* to be *equally* gifted, he proves that they *are not* what they have been misrepresented, mere chattels—with bodies primed for herculean labour, but without minds, without souls."

Even before Douglass arrived, the split that had occurred in the American Anti-Slavery Society had had its counterpart in British antislavery circles. The British and Foreign Anti-Slavery Society, organized in 1839, rejected Garrisonian antislavery and allied itself closely with the politically oriented American and Foreign Anti-Slavery Society. By the time Douglass arrived, British Garrisonians were losing the battle for influence and funds. But Douglass reversed this trend and put new life into the Garrisonian abolitionists. More important, he brought new converts to the cause of abolition. "Mr. Douglass is making a great impression in this country," Catherine Clarkson wrote in August 1846. "We have no pro-slavery party here, but too many seem to think that having paid £22,000,000 to redeem our own slaves, England has nothing more to do." By the time Douglass left England, this situation had been completely altered.

So impressed were British abolitionists with Douglass that in the fall of 1846 a group of them raised enough money to purchase his freedom from Hugh Auld, to whom his brother Thomas Auld had transferred ownership. His British friends turned over the manumission papers to Douglass, or as he put it, "They gave me myself." Upon his return from England, he told a welcome-home audience:

What a contrast is my presence with my former condition? Than a slave, now a free man; then degraded, now respected; then ignorant, despised, neglected, unknown, and unfriended, my name unheard of beyond the narrow limits of a republican slave plantation; now, my friends and benefactors, people of both hemispheres, to heaven the praise belongs!

Because she was a black woman abolitionist, throngs of British listeners awaited Sarah P. Remond's arrival in 1858. So unusual was the appearance of a "colored lady," reported the British press, that minutes after the doors to her lecture were opened, "a dense crowd filled every available seat." While Remond spoke out against slavery in general, she particularly stressed the plight of women enslaved, emphasizing both the "sufferings and indignities . . . perpetrated on her sisters in America" and the "immorality" and destruction of domestic happiness "amongst the families of slaveholders." The "fruits of licentiousness" were evident, she explained, in the 800,000 Southern mulattoes. "The female slave," she told a meeting sponsored by the Dublin Ladies' Anti-Slavery Society, was "the most deplorably and helplessly wretched of human sufferers." Most victimized of all who "drooped and writhed under the afflictions of the horrible system," the female slave had a special claim on the efforts of women everywhere.

The *London Morning Star*'s report on July 22, 1859, of a meeting in the Mellow Street School in the city is typical:

The place of meeting was densely crowded. Miss Remond was introduced by Mr. George Thompson, and delivered an address distinguished by much pathos and replete with statements of a deeply affecting character, more particularly descriptive of the degraded, brutalized, and defenceless condition of the enslaved women of America, on whose behalf the speaker made a powerful and touching appeal. The sentiments advanced by the feminine advocate of freedom were received with evident interest, warm sympathy and loud applause. Mr. Thompson moved a resolution to the effect: "That the system permitted to exist in the United States of America, which enslaved four millions of the human race, and subjected them under its influence to every conceivable wrong, personal and domestic, moral and spiritual, was at war with the natural rights of rational and responsible beings, with the commands of God and the precepts of Christianity; and that it was, therefore, the duty of every lover of freedom, and every friend of religion, to employ all legitimate means to extirpate the inhuman institution of chattel slavery from the face of the earth." . . .

After having been seconded by the Rev. W. H. Bonner, it was carried unanimously. Thanks having been voted to Miss Remond and the chairman, the meeting separated.

Black abolitionists in England did much to refute the argument, influential in British working-class circles, that the chattel slaves in the American South were far better off than the wage slaves in the British mines and factories, and that, therefore, the British abolitionists should concern themselves solely with problems at home. White abolitionists from the United States were unable to have much impact on British working-class opinion on this issue. While touring with Douglass in Sheffield, England, Garrison challenged the assertion that the conditions of slaves in America were more favorable than those of British laborers, but the audience was not impressed. However, Douglass followed and described, on the basis of his experience, what slavery was really like. He reminded the audience that the slave's "labour is not his own. If he works, it is that another may reap the profits of his toil . . . not for himself, not for the improvement and development of his facilities, but merely to administer to the ease and luxury of the slave-holders." The audience was deeply moved, and after a number of such speeches, British workers began to respond enthusiastically. "Working men,"

John W. Blassingame notes, "contributed their labor to prepare halls in which Douglass spoke, attended his lectures in significant numbers, sent anti-slavery petitions to the United States after hearing him, and sang ballads about him."

During his ten years in England, William P. Powell spoke frequently at meetings in working-class districts and hammered away at the theme that "the system of free and slave labor are as far [apart] as the Poles." Bad as conditions were in the mines and factories he had visited in England, the workers there

are not chattels, personal, subject to corporal punishment, ropes and chains, and separated, parents from their children, and husbands from their wives. But not so with the supposedly "sleek, comfortably clothed, well fed, fat and saucy southern slaves." Are there any laws forbidding corporal punishment of slaves for non-performance of tasks? Are there laws punishing with death the master, overseer, or driver, for murder, rape or *violence* committed daily upon the defenceless slaves? And yet we are supposed to believe that the American negro slaves are better off than the operatives in the cotton factories and coal mines of England!

British abolitionists reprinted Powell's attack on the defenders of chattel slavery and distributed it widely in labor circles.

Sarah P. Remond also devoted attention to this issue. She was confronted by it when Madame Lola Montez, an English dancer and former mistress of King Louis I of Bavaria, who had just visited the Southern states, told British audiences that the slaves were "idle and contented. They believed their own situation more favored than that of the white working class." Five days later, Remond replied. Speaking as a representative of 4 million in slavery and 400,000 "persons of colour nominally free," she rejected the statement that American slaves were content. Why then, she asked, would 40,000 of them have fled to Canada? As for the chattel slaves being better off than the white working class: "There was this immeasurable difference between the condition of the poorer English woman and that of the slave woman—that their persons were free and their progeny their own; while the slave woman was the victim of the heartless lust of her master, and the children whom she bore were his property."

British abolitionists were cheered by the fact that Remond's speeches on this theme were well received in industrial sections. When she spoke as an agent for the Leeds Young Men's Anti-Slavery Society in Yorkshire, her audiences were "principally composed of working men and factory operatives." The British *Anti-Slavery Advocate* saw it as a real blow to the proponents of the theory that wage slavery was worse than chattel slavery:

The enthusiasm and expressive sympathy manifested toward the slave, coupled with decided expression of abhorrence of slavery in every form, were sufficient evidence to refute the outrageous comparison which Americans are sometimes bold enough to allege—namely, that the working population of England are in a worse condition than the American slave. Such sentiments were resented with indignation and contempt.

On their return to the United States, black abolitionists met the chattel versus wage slavery issue head on. William Wells Brown would tell his antislavery audiences:

I have addressed large and influential meetings in Newcastle and the neighbouring towns, and the more I see and learn of the condition of the working class of England the more I am satisfied of the utter fallacy of the statements often made that their conditions approximate to that of the slaves in America. Whatever may be the disadvantages that the British peasant labours under he is free, and if he is not satisfied with his employer he can make choice of another. He has also the right to educate his children, and he is the equal of the most wealthy person before an English court of justice.

British workers and peasants may have felt, when they heard of this, that Brown was stretching the contrast too far. But there is no doubt about the fact that, educated to no small extent by the black visitors from the United States as to the real meaning of American slavery, British workers grew "strongly Northern in their sympathies." As Benjamin Quarles has noted, a force arose in England that would significantly influence events in favor of freedom during the Civil War.

Although David Brion Davis has popularized the idea in the first two volumes of his study of antislavery (*The Problem of Slavery in Western Culture* and *The Problem of Slavery in the Age of Revolution*), that British antislavery was essentially conservative, antagonistic to reforms in behalf of the working class, and attracted few in working-class circles, other recent studies have revealed that it actually had a strong working-class base, and was a force for reforming industrial conditions. The experience of the black abolitionists from the United States confirms the truth of the latter interpretation.

23

Black Abolitionists and the Underground Railroad

Black abolitionists battled slavery on two fronts—one public and the other secret. In the public phase of the struggle, they joined antislavery societies and, either with sympathetic whites or independently, petitioned, agitated, and kept the cause ever before the public. The second front in the war against slavery was private, underground, and unusually noninstitutionalized. This was the one that gave birth to the famed, legendary, and controversial Underground Railroad.

As we have seen, hundreds of slaves ran away from slavery each year. Some of the fugitives returned to their masters within a few days; others were tracked by bloodhounds, betrayed by informers, or captured by slave patrols. Some sought freedom in nearby Southern cities, where they could blend in with the free black population. Swamps and mountains offered some temporary asylum. An escapee from the Deep South or Southwest usually headed for Mexico.

A substantial number, however, escaped to the North, and their masters' efforts to recapture and return them to slavery met with ever-increasing resistance from antislavery men and women, both black and white. To protect the property rights of the slaveowners and enforce the ''person held to service or labor'' clause of the United States Constitution (article IV, section 2), Congress, in 1793, passed the Fugitive Slave Act. It gave slave masters or their agents the right, after escapees were seized, to take them before any federal, state, or county magistrate and secure a certificate granting their removal to the state from which they had fled. Not only was the fugitive denied the right to a trial by jury, but the simple oral testimony of the claimant was enough to secure a conviction. The law imposed a fine of five hundred dollars on anyone rescuing, harboring, or hindering the arrest of a fugitive.

It would seem that since the fugitives were denied the right to plead in their own defense, recovery should have been a fairly simple procedure, once they were located by their masters. But abolitionists, and especially black abolitionists, contrived to make such recovery difficult, if not impossible.

479

THE UNDERGROUND RAILROAD: FACT OR MYTH

The nature of fugitive aid has been a controversial issue in antebellum scholarship. Some have argued that most of the aid was rendered individually and spontaneously, while others maintain that there was an organized and effective Underground Railroad, with continually functioning vigilance committees, especially in New York, Philadelphia, and Boston. The most vigorous attack on the latter thesis was leveled by Larry Gara in his article, "The Myth of the Underground Railroad," and in his book, *The Liberty Line: The Legend of the Underground Railroad*. Gara called the "Underground Railroad legend" a "blend of fiction and fact," a "romance," which "inevitably led to exaggeration." Much of the aid provided for fleeing slaves, he asserted, "was rendered on a temporary and haphazard basis." In fact, he went on, most of the slaves who succeeded in escaping from bondage did so without much help of any sort, depending almost entirely either on their own resources or on assistance from individual free blacks. Such aid as they did receive was "mostly by chance and after they had succeeded in completing the most dangerous part of their journey." Even the most militant white abolitionists, said Gara, "declined to entice slaves from their bondage."

Gara is correct in noting that the antislavery movement neither unanimously nor consistently supported individual or organized fugitive slave assistance, that the free Negro's contribution in this work has been largely overlooked, and that a good part of the so-called Underground Railroad activity was not clandestine. But I believe that he errs in flatly rejecting the existence of an Underground Railroad and in minimizing the contribution of the antislavery movement to indivdual or organized fugitive slave assistance. In the process, he makes the further mistake of ignoring the significant contribution of black abolitionists to this important antislavery activity.

Levi Coffin, a Quaker, whose service on behalf of fugitive slaves over a period of thirty-five years resulted in gaining freedom for over two thousand bondspeople and earned for him the title of "president of the Underground Railroad," testified that when he left North Carolina and settled in Newport, Indiana, in 1826, he observed that "fugitives often passed through that place and generally stopped among the colored people." In 1837, James G. Birney made a similar observation while in Cincinnati. He learned that two fugitive slaves, a man and his wife, had recently passed through the city and that they had been cared for by Negro people. This, he remarked, was typical, since "such matters are almost uniformly managed by the colored people. I know nothing of them generally till they are past." In 1872, when he published his monumental *The Underground Railroad*, William Still, an important black official in the railroad, demonstrated the significance of the Northern free Negro's contribution to the fugitive slave.

Despite all this evidence, however, those historians who have acknowledged the existence of the Underground Railroad have consigned the free Negro to a minor role in the institution. While some blacks, like Frederick Douglass, Harriet Tubman, and Josiah Henson, are mentioned, the picture presented is basically one of white abolitionists, mainly Quakers, being responsible for providing aid to runaway slaves.

Fortunately, Charles H. Wesley and Herbert Aptheker, in their studies of the Negro in the abolitionist movement, have done much to correct this impression. Benjamin Quarles, in his article, "The Black Underground," originally published in the *Negro Digest* of February 1969 and later expanded into his book, *Black Abolitionists*, published the same year, demolished the myth that Northern free blacks did not play a significant role in fugitive aid. Quarles proved that blacks played a vital part in individual and institutional protection of the fugitive bondspeople and that they were the most significant element in the vigilance committees established to protect fugitive slaves and aid free Negroes. The directors of these committees in the two most important centers—Philadelphia and New York—were Negroes—William Still, David B. Ruggles, and Theodore S. Wright—while the corresponding secretary of the New York State Vigilance Committee was the black publisher, Charles B. Ray.

Yet these men constituted only a handful of the free blacks who were associated with fugitive aid. Because secrecy was crucial, few records of such activities (apart from Still's *The Underground Railroad*) have survived. Most of the information comes to us in the form of recollections recorded many years later. A majority of the participants in fugitive aid knew nothing of the Underground Railroad beyond their immediate neighborhoods. They fed and hid the fugitives, passed them along to the next station, and asked few questions.

As the new antislavery movement grew, the Underground Railroad grew with it, and workers on it numbered in the thousands. Prominent among them, as before, were blacks. In addition to those listed above, those who were particularly important included John W. Jones in Elmira, New York, David and Philip Rodrick in Williamsport, Pennsylvania, Stephen Meyers in Albany, Frederick Douglass in Rochester, Williams Wells Brown in Buffalo, Lewis Hayden, Peter Howard, and Robert Morris in Boston, J. W. Loguen in Syracuse, Martin R. Delany in Pittsburgh, George Baptist in Madison, Indiana (and later in Detroit), John Hatfield in Cincinnati, William Goodrich in York, Pennsylvania, Stephen Smith, William Whipper, and Thomas Bessick in Columbia, Pennsylvania, Daniel Ross and John Augusta in Newtown, Pennsylvania, Samuel Bond in Baltimore, and Sam Nixon in Norfolk.

THE UNDERGROUND RAILROAD: ROUTES, STATIONS, AND STATIONMASTERS

The Underground Railroad has been defined as a secretly organized activity on behalf of fugitive slaves and free Negroes. The origin of the term is obscure, but it appears to stem from southeastern Pennsylvania, whose citizens very early gained a reputation for helping fugitives. As far back as 1786, George Washington had written that one of his own slaves was in that area, "where it is not easy to apprehend them because there are a great number [of people there] who would rather facilitate the escape . . . than apprehend the runaway." Tradition has it, however, that it was a particular region in that area, the borough of Columbia, located on the Susquehanna River twenty miles north of the Maryland border, that gave birth to the name of the clandestine organization. Early in the nineteenth century, Columbia had attracted a considerable settlement of former slaves who had legally procured their freedom from their Virginia owners. In the succeeding decades, these blacks made their settlement a refuge for fugitives from slavery. According to the story, so many slaveholders lost their runaways around Columbia that they concluded "there must be an *underground railroad* out there."

This illegal and informal conspiracy, which hastened and shielded the escape of runaway slaves, used not only the name but also the language of railroading. The houses where aid and shelter were given were known as "stations"; those in charge of the "stations" were "stationmasters" or "agents"; those in charge of sending fugitives to "stations" were "brakemen"; and "conductors" guided the slaves from station to station. People who contributed money, clothing, and other financial support to the venture were "stockholders." The fugitives were designated as "valuable pieces of ebony," a "bale of Southern goods," or "prime articles"—in short, anything but slaves.

The passenger service on this clandestine railroad network was active from the 1830s to the Civil War, reaching its peak between 1850 and 1860, after the passage of the Fugitive Slave Act of 1850. Its unplanned and unscheduled nature, the secrecy surrounding it, and the lack of records make it impossible to map out the detailed routes on this railroad. But we know of several that were important, especially the one in Philadelphia, which was a veritable "Grand Central Station" on the line. Approaching the Quaker city were three much-used routes: one crossing the Susquehanna River above Havre de Grace, Maryland, and running northeast to Phoenixville; a second running through Baltimore, West Chester, and Phoenixville; and the third and most eastern, running through Delaware to Philadelphia, Lancaster, Chester, and Delaware counties had more lines per square mile than any other part of the Underground Railroad. But south-central and southwestern Pennsylvania also received many fugitives from Maryland and Virginia.

Located directly across the historic Mason and Dixon line from the slave state of Maryland, Lancaster and Chester counties were the main avenue of escape for slaves fleeing from locations in the Old South. According to Wilbur H. Siebert, who compiled a map of the routes of the Underground Railroad along which fugitives were hurried northward, these counties "became the field through which more routes were developed in proportion to its extent than any other area in the Northern States."

One of the most important routes ran northward along the west bank of the

Susquehanna, crossing into Lancaster County either at Peach Bottom or by the bridge from Wrightsville to Columbia. At Columbia, William Whipper, black businessman and moral reformer, was the stationmaster. He passed hundreds to the land of freedom, and from 1847 to 1860, he contributed one thousand dollars annually, both directly and indirectly, to the cause. On two occasions, Southern sympathizers tried to burn his lumber yard. "Much as I loved anti-slavery meetings," Whipper recalled, "I did not feel that I could afford to attend them, as my immediate duty was to the fleeing fugitive."

Stephen Smith ("Black Steve," as he was called) worked with Whipper in Columbia, both in business matters and in the operation of the Underground Railroad, until 1842, when he moved to Philadelphia and left his partner to manage their lumber operation. Smith continued to aid the Underground Railroad financially in both Columbia and Philadelphia, becoming one of the leading stockholders in Pennsylvania. He had a special reason for being active in this work: his mother, a runaway slave working in the home of General Boude in Columbia, was kidnapped and returned to slavery after he was born.

From Columbia fugitives were directed Westward to the home of Daniel Gibbons at Bird-in-Hand. Gibbons was one of the most active conductors in the system and reputedly handed over one thousand fugitives until his death in 1853. In the vicinity of Christiana, Pennsylvania, Lindley Coastes and Thomas Whitson were active conductors on the lines.

York was another railroad location in the southern part of Pennsylvania, which bordered on the slave state of Maryland. It was one of the first places to which fugitive slaves escaped, especially after the Pennsylvania legislature passed an act in 1832 to extend a road from York to the Maryland line. This road, which became known as the York-Baltimore Pike, was made to order for slaves escaping from Virginia and Maryland. One of the leading agents in the York area was William C. Goodridge, a black barber who had himself been a slave in Baltimore. His home and two other buildings he owned were stations on the Underground Railroad. Goodridge also owned thirteen railroad cars, which he used to send fugitives to William Still in Philadelphia and which became known as "Goodridge's York to Philadelphia Line."

Lewisburg in York County was the scene of an attempted kidnapping, which William Lloyd Garrison helped frustrate. A claimant and his assistant had seized a slave girl, and when Garrison, who was a guest at the nearby home of Joseph Wickersham, heard of the kidnapping, he and his host rushed to Lewisburg. Arm in arm, the two approached the kidnappers, gently grasped the arm of the slave girl, and the three walked away. The kidnappers stood by as if in a hypnotic trance and offered no resistance.

An important route of the Underground Railroad started in Philadelphia and passed through Harrisburg, Williamsport, Canton, and Alba, all in Pennsylvania, and then went through the New York towns and cities of Elmira, Watkins Glen, Canandaigua, Rochester, Buffalo, and Niagara Falls, finally ending in Saint Catherines, Ontario, Canada.

The Williamsport station was located in the "Nigger Hollow," the northern part of the town, where blacks lived. Runaways were usually secreted in the house of two blacks, David and Philip Rodrick, although other homes of blacks in the immediate neighborhood were used for the same purpose. Sometimes the fugitives reached Williamsport hidden in a canal boat, but more often they were on foot. Upon arrival, they were taken to a house in "Nigger Hollow," where they were kept in seclusion until an opportunity arose to take them over the hills to some convenient point on the Williamsport & Elmira Railroad, on which they were transported as "blind baggage" to Elmira. From all accounts, employees of the railroad were always willing to pass the "blind baggage" through without inspection and free of charge.

Elmira, New York, was one of the most important centers on the route. Between 1850 and 1860, more than a thousand fugitive slaves passed through the town on their way to Canada and freedom. The leading station was the home of John W. Jones, a fugitive slave who had settled in Elmira in 1844 and became chief stationmaster. Jones was in close contact with William Still, the famed stationmaster in Philadelphia, who regularly sent fugitives to his house. After recruiting several blacks (including his two brothers who were also fugitive slaves) and a number of whites, Jones established a program that provided food, clothing, and money for fugitives who would be stopping at his station. These included both fugitives on their way to Canada and others who chose to remain and settle in Elmira. Jones also obtained the cooperation of the baggagemen of the Northern Central Railroad to stow away the runaways on the baggage coaches.

On several occasions, Jones' home housed twenty to thirty runaways at a time, but usually groups of six or ten were cared for. On one occasion, Jones wrote:

FRIEND WM. STILL—All six came safe to this place. The two men came last night, about twelve o'clock; the man and the woman stopped at the depot, and went east on the next train about eighteen miles, and did not get back till tonight, so that the two went this morning, and the four went this evening.

> O, old master don't cry for me,
> For I am going to Canada where
> colored men are free.

P.S. What is the news in the city? Will you tell me how many you have sent over to Canada? I have nothing new to tell you. We are all in good health. I see there is a law passed in Maryland not to set any slaves free. They had better get the consent of the Underground Railroad before they passed such a thing. Good night from your friend.

John W. Jones.

Since Troy, New York, was located on the Hudson River, it was a natural way-station along the eastern route of the Underground Railroad. Reverend

Henry Highland Garnet operated the main station in this city, and he once claimed that he had personally sheltered 150 fugitives in a single year.

Rochester, New York, was the last major stop on the Underground. To this city the fugitive slaves came by railroad, by wagon, or on foot, exhausted from the harrowing weeks en route to freedom. By word-of-mouth direction, they found their way to the homes of the Posts, the Blosses, the Porters, and other white agents in the community. In the winter of 1847, Frederick Douglass' house on Alexander Street became an important station. By 1850, Douglass was the leader of the railroad in Rochester, superintending all the activities and maintaining contacts with agents in the rest of the state.

The first issue of the *North Star* carried the news that the editor was already involved in the operations of the Underground:

A SISTER RESCUED FROM SLAVERY

There has just left our office, an amiable, kind and intelligent looking young woman, about eighteen years of age, on her way from slavery.

News of the operation of the Underground in Rochester appeared in almost every issue. A typical entry read:

On Tuesday of this week, two likely boys, claimed as chattels personal in Kentucky by one Frederick Reason, passed through this city en route for Canada by the underground railroad. They left their home in Carter County, Ky., about six weeks ago; when they left Kentucky, they started for Cleveland, Ohio, being directed to that place by slaves who had themselves made the attempt to run away. In Cleveland they met with a person who knew the parents of one of them, who ran away some five years ago, and informed him that they lived somewhere on the St. Lawrence river. The boys resolved to hunt them up, and came to this place, on their way to Oswego, to cross the lake at that point. They were kindly cared for and sent on their way to Canada.

Horace McGuire, one of Douglass' newspaper employees, recalled that it was not unusual for him to find fugitives sitting on the office stairs in the early morning. As soon as Douglass arrived, he escorted the fugitives to the Posts' cellar, Edward C. Williams' sail loft, Lindley Moore's barn, William Bloss' woodshed, or Douglass' own attic. Throughout the day Douglass visited trusted sympathizers, passing the word that funds were needed to "ship a bale of Southern goods" and collecting money, food, and clothing. When night fell, the escaped slaves were usually sent on to Oswego or Lewiston. Some, too exhausted to travel, remained during the night, and were put aboard the morning train to Canada. "They usually tarry with us only during the night," Douglass wrote, "and are forwarded to Canada by the morning train. We give them supper, lodging, and breakfast; pay their expenses, and give them a half dollar over." On one occasion, Douglass had eleven fugitives at his house; "it was the largest group I ever had and it was difficult for me to give shelter, food and money for so many at once, but it had to be done so they could be moved on immediately to Canada.''

Douglass made another contribution to the Underground Railroad. Although his paper published reports of fugitives leaving from Rochester to Canada, he sharply criticized some of the abolitionists in the railroad for publicizing their activities too openly, and especially for encouraging fugitive slaves to reveal their methods of escape from the South. Douglass did not publicly divulge his avenue of escape until March 10, 1873, when, in a speech at the Philadelphia Academy of Music, he broke his long silence. When he published his *Narrative* in 1845, he explained this reticence by noting that the publication of escape methods would only stimulate the master

to greater watchfulness and enhance his power to capture his slaves. We owe something to the slaves south of the line as well as to those north of it; and in aiding the latter on their way to freedom, we should be careful to do nothing which would be likely to hinder the former from escaping from slavery. I would keep the merciless slaveholder profoundly ignorant of the means of flight adopted by the slave.

UNDERGROUND RAILROAD CONDUCTORS: NORTH

William Wells Brown became an active conductor of the Underground Railroad in Buffalo. Soon after he settled there in 1834, he began working on the lake steamers and immediately started to carry fugitive slaves to Canada by way of both Detroit and Buffalo. Between May and December 1842, as an officer of what might be called "the Lake Erie Division of the Underground Railroad," Brown carried sixty-nine fugitives to Canada. In one instance, according to his account, a young fugitive of very dark complexion was trailed by his claimant to the home of an abolitionist in Cleveland. For ten days, the home and all steamboats leaving from Cleveland were watched so closely that it seemed impossible for the fugitive to avoid recapture. Brown, however, secured the help of a painter, and "in an hour, by my direction, the black man was as white, and with as rosy cheeks, as any of the Anglo-Saxon race, and disguised in a dress of a woman, with a thick veil over her face." Thus disguised, the fugitive embarked on the steamer *North America* without being recognized by his claimant. With Brown's aid, the fugitive was carried to Buffalo and then on to Canada.

While it may appear that this episode is one of the so-called myths associated with the Underground Railroad, it is important to remember than in escaping slavery, fugitives assumed various disguises and often changed their appearance as they proceeded on their way to freedom. Many of the wives of Underground Railroad stationmasters had the responsibility of forming sewing circles to make disguises for the fugitives.

Brown made his home in Buffalo a station on the Underground Railroad. In her biography of her father, Josephine Brown recalled that because many fugitives passed through Buffalo en route to Canada, they frequently had "stopover passengers" to accommodate in their home. "As Niagara Falls was only twenty miles from Buffalo," she added, "slaveholders not infrequently passed through the latter place attended by one or more slave servants. Mr. Brown was always on the look-out for such, to inform them that they were free by the laws of New York, and to give the necessary aid."

In his *Narrative,* Brown described "one of the most fearful fights for human freedom that I ever witnessed." This battle, in the fall of 1836, began when a group of Buffalo antislavery men were informed that the Stanfords, a family of fugitive slaves (man, wife, and child) who had established a home in Saint Catherines, Ontario, Canada, had been kidnapped, and carried, bound and gagged, in a carriage to Hamberg, about eleven miles from Buffalo, where the party had stopped at an inn to change horses. The antislavery group numbered fifty, most of them black. Armed with pistols, knives, and clubs, they rescued the Stanfords and took them to the Black Rock Ferry to send them back to Saint Catherines. They were intercepted near the ferry by a sheriff's posse of sixty or seventy men, and a free-for-all fight between the two groups ensued. Amid the confusion, the Stanfords were put on a boat and rowed across the Niagara River to Canada. With their mission accomplished, about forty of the rescuers submitted to arrest by the sheriff's posse and were taken to Buffalo and imprisoned for the night. Twenty-five were found guilty of breaking the peace of the Sabbath and unlawful assembly and were fined five to fifty dollars. One black was so badly wounded in the fight that he died three months later.

William Wells Brown was not the only conductor who used the vessels on which they were employed as means of transporting fugitives to freedom. Elizabeth Barnes, who worked for a ship captain at Portsmouth, Virginia, hid slaves on vessels sailing for Boston and New Bedford. New Yorkers Edward Smith and Isaac Gansey of the schooner *Robert Centre* were charged by Virginia Governor Thomas W. Gilmer with having abducted slave Isaac, and $300 was offered for their delivery to the jailer at Norfolk.

By way of contrast, there was George L. Burroughs of Cairo, Illinois, who, as a sleeping-car porter on the train between Cairo and Chicago, was able to smuggle slaves to freedom.

UNDERGROUND RAILROAD CONDUCTORS: SOUTH— WHITES

The *Baltimore Sun* of June 29, 1850, carried a headline reading: "Lynch Law in Maryland—A Man and Woman Tarred and Feathered." The news report began: "The slave owners of Kent county, Md., have within a year or two, suffered heavy losses by running off of slaves, not less than sixty having escaped in 1848, and a large number since. These mysterious escapes created no little excitement." Two white persons, James I. Bowers and his wife, of Kent County, "well known to entertain strong antislavery sentiments," were charged with assisting the slaves to escape. When they were acquitted by the court because of insufficient evidence, a mob of slaveowners seized the couple in their home, tarred and feathered them, and drove them out of the community.

Other whites who aided, or were accused of aiding, slaves to escape suffered even worse treatment at the hands of the slaveowners and the courts. A few, like the couple tarred and feathered in Maryland, were southerners. Most, however, were Northern workers in the Underground Railroad who undertook the exceedingly dangerous activity of moving into the South and conducting slaves to freedom.

In 1836, Calvin Fairbank, a student at Oberlin, and Delia A. Webster, his fiancée, left Kentucky in a hack for Ohio. With them were the slaves Lewis Hayden, his wife, and their child. (Fairbank later recalled that when he asked Hayden, "Why do you want your freedom?" the slave replied, "Because I am a man.") The Haydens acted as servants or passed as white lady and gentleman, often veiled and cloaked; in times of danger, their child was hidden under the carriage seat. After they crossed the Ohio River, the Haydens were left at one of the Underground Railroad stations. (Ohio, with its long border adjoining the slave states, was a natural escape route and received a considerable fugitive traffic from its neighboring slave states.) Southern furor over the "invasion" by two northerners who had "conspired to steal a slave family" mounted while the Haydens rested near the Ohio River. When it was learned that slave catchers lay in wait along their anticipated flight to Oberlin, the flight course was changed to Sandusky, Ohio, where sympathetic Quakers hid and assisted the Haydens until they crossed the Canadian border.

In 1848 Calvin and Delia (now Mrs. Fairbank) were arrested and jailed in Lexington, Kentucky, for having helped the Haydens to escape. Delia Fairbank served several months in prison, and Calvin Fairbank remained in jail after she was released. Lewis Hayden, by now a clothing dealer in Boston, learned that for $650, his former owner was willing to sign a petition to pardon Fairbank. Within sixty days, he raised the money by public and private appeals. In August 1849, Fairbank was freed, but in 1851, he was again apprehended in Kentucky for the same offense of helping slaves to flee and again imprisoned. Fairbank appealed from jail to Frederick Douglass, explaining that "for want of money at present," he was unable to raise the $3,000 required for bail or even to hire a lawyer. "They expect pay," he wrote, adding: "Well friends, whatever comes, liberty, slavery, life, death, anything, I stand and shall stand for this faith in the living God that makes no law, knows no law, obeys no law for slavery. . . . I shall sit by the law that sits in the bosom of God, and develops itself in the harmony of nature, all countries, all rules, where all colors are alike, and all hearts are one."

"A truer friend of the American slave never lived," wrote Douglass in appealing for funds to help Fairbank. "No one who knows anything of his history, will doubt this." Money did begin to come in to Douglass' paper, but before the necessary amount could be raised, the state of Kentucky rushed through Fairbank's trial, found him guilty, and sentenced him to fifteen years' imprisonment.

Year after year, Fairbank languished in a Kentucky jail, enduring barbarous conditions. "I was flogged, sometimes bowed over a chair or some other object, often receiving seventy lashes four times a day, and at one time received 107 blows, particles of flesh being thrown upon the wall several feet away." Fairbank was finally released in 1864.

In the summer of 1844, abolitionist Jonathan Walker, a Harwick, Massachusetts, sea captain, carpenter, and mechanic, took four fugitive slaves aboard his ship in Pensacola, Florida, with the intention of transporting them to freedom in the Bahamas. The ship was intercepted on the Florida Gulf Coast, and Walker was captured and taken to Key West. Even though he was so weak from poor health that he had to be helped to get from the dock to the jail, he was put aboard a government boat where, with his hands and feet in irons, he was placed in the hold. There he remained, surrounded by rubbish and nearly suffocating from the steam of the boat. After seven days of this treatment, he was taken to the courthouse in Pensacola, where he was required to put up bail of $10,000. When he could not do so, he was put in a room by himself and chained by the ankle. Since he had no defense counsel, the judge appointed a lawyer to defend him.

Walker was indicted on four counts (one for helping, one for enticing slaves to escape, and two for stealing slaves) and was found guilty on all of them. He was sentenced to be branded with the letters "S.S" (for slave stealer) on the right hand, to remain in the pillory for one hour, to spend fifteen days in prison, and to pay a fine of $160.

Two days after the trial, the branding and standing in the pillory were carried out. Three men who were supposed to be owners of the slaves Walker had helped escape came to the prison and served three writs on Walker "for trespass and damage" in the amount of $106,000. In addition, they each spat on Walker as he was in the pillory and threw garbage and other foul objects at him.

The three indictments from the writs caused Walker to remain in jail from November 1844 to June 1845, when he was released because friends and sympathizers, including free blacks, collected the money to pay both his fines and his court costs. Walker reported that he was kept in chains during all but two and a half months of his imprisonment. In a letter thanking the blacks who had come to his aid, he wrote that even though he had only been upholding the principles embodied in the Declaration of Independence, the slave system had dealt with him as if he were a traitor.

The branding of Captain Walker was referred to by Frederick Douglass in a speech in Paisley, Scotland, during his British trip: "They branded him as a slave-stealer; but the abolitionists of the United States say they intend to make the letters read slave-saviour." The abolitionist poet John Greenleaf Whittier put the same thought in verse:

> Then lift that manly right hand, bold plowman of the wave.
> Its branded palm shall prophesy Salvation to the Slave.

John L. Brown, a native of South Carolina, was convicted in a local court in November 1833 of helping a slave woman to escape. For this, Judge John Belton O'Neall, one of antebellum South Carolina's leading jurists, sentenced Brown to death under a 1754 South Carolina law, which made it a capital offense for slaves or free people "to inveigle, steal, or carry away any slave." "You are to die—die a shameful, ignominious death, the death upon the gallows," O'Neall declared as he announced the sentence, at the same time angrily charging that the slave woman he had aided in escaping was his "mulatto mistress." The judge admonished Brown to "pray to God for his assistance."

Governor John L. Hammond commuted the death sentence to thirty-nine lashes on the grounds that the offender was youthful and the slave had been retrieved. Later he pardoned Brown altogether, but before he did, the death sentence had aroused tremendous indignation in the United States, and especially in Great Britain. Members of the House of Lords, including Lord Henry Peter Brougham, denounced the judgment, and British antislavery groups passed resolutions of shock and dismay. Abolitionist ministers sent a memorial signed by over thirteen hundred English clergymen condemning the sentence. Thomas Clarkson and Daniel O'Connell (the latter particularly indignant that a man with the Irish name of O'Neall should have acted so infamously) added their voices to the chorus of indignation. The closing words of a protest address from the Birmingham Anti-Slavery Committee to the citizens of the United States read:

Citizens of America!—You live under a government which professes to be democratic, and you tell us truly that liberty is the birthright of all men. Do justice to your principles. Give to every man his freedom, and then, and not till then, will the moral influence of America promote the cause of freedom in every part of the world.

These protests goaded Governor Hammond into writing a series of letters to Clarkson in defense of Southern slavery. Angered by the reproaches heaped upon him, O'Neall informed his critics that Brown's life would be spared and retreated from his earlier charge that the Negro woman Brown had helped escape "from his employer's service" had been Brown's "mistress." The judge also pointed out that Brown's conviction was based on a law that was nearly a century old and could scarcely be considered a reaction to the current "abolition folly." However, he went on, it would curb the "philanthropy" of those now inclined to steal slaves. O'Neall expressed the view that the Revolutionary forefathers would have had little consideration for those who helped slaves to escape and that "they would sooner, much sooner, have tied the noose, than cut it with their swords." However, he informed the protestors that he and his "brothers of the Court of Appeals" had recommended to the governor that Brown not be hanged but receive thirty-nine lashes on his bare back instead.

In closing, O'Neall asked if the editor of the *Emancipator and Weekly Chronicle* (a leading British critic of the sentence) would like to attend the whipping. If so, he was certain that Brown would then be glad "to accompany him to the

West, where he can soothe and cherish him as one of the 'young and ardent men' who *loved negro women,* and advised them to escape from slavery.''

John L. Brown of South Carolina was not the only John Brown who helped slaves escape. His more famous namesake of Harpers Ferry undertook this activity at the urging of a Missouri slave known merely as Jim. In December 1858, having just recovered from typhoid fever, he and a few comrades, led by Jim, went from Kansas into Missouri, freed ten slaves, killed one resisting slaveholder, and headed north. Although outlawed and pursued by posses and with a reward on his head offered by the president of the United States, John Brown led his band of men and women through Kansas, Nebraska, Iowa, Illinois, and Michigan into Canada where he left the ten blacks in March 1859.

Abolitionist Charles Turner Torrey was a Massachusetts Congregational minister whose activities in helping slaves escape ultimately brought him to incarceration and death in a Baltimore prison. Torrey was one of the leaders of the anti-Garrisonian faction in Massachusetts, an opponent of equal membership for women in the antislavery movement, and the first editor of the anti-Garrisonian *Massachusetts Abolitionist.* Although Garrison disliked him intensely, Torrey had gained the respect of many of Boston's blacks when he registered a complaint in the city's police court against ship captain Benjamin Higgins and his first mate, charging them with violating the laws of Massachusetts by refusing to free the slave, John Torrence, who had escaped to the schooner *Wellington* in May 1841 while it had been docked in New Bern, North Carolina. Torrence had been discovered only after the ship was already four days out to sea, and rather than return to New Bern immediately, Higgins and his mate decided to go on to Boston. Upon Torrey's complaint, they were arrested and brought to trial, but before the case could be decided, Captain Higgins took his vessel out of Boston harbor and set sail for New Bern, where Torrence was reenslaved. On top of this, the first mate (who was left behind) was acquitted by a grand jury when he was forced to stand trial alone.

Sparked by this event, a Vigilance Committee was established in Boston late in 1841 for the purpose of aiding fugitive slaves and protecting them from kidnapping. Torrey was one of the founders, but he did not confine his activities on behalf of slaves to work only in Boston. In 1843, he moved to Baltimore to engage in business and carry out his scheme for transporting fugitive slaves along a prearranged route to the free states. It was later disclosed that in the course of two years he helped about four hundred slaves from Maryland and Virginia to escape. He was arrested in Baltimore for this activity, with no hope of early release. While in prison awaiting trial, Torrey expressed gratitude for Garrison's support. He also revealed that his ideas on "the confounded woman question" were "materially modified, so far as it is connected with our cause."

After a trial distinguished by its indifference to the rights of the defendant, Torrey was convicted and sentenced to six years' hard labor in the state penitentiary. While in prison, both his mind and body deteriorated rapidly. An attempt was made in the United States and England to purchase Torrey's early release in order to save his life. The plan was to reimburse the Baltimore slaveowners whose slaves' escape Torrey had been found guilty specifically of aiding. Blacks in Philadelphia, New York, and Boston held public meetings to protest Torrey's imprisonment and raised funds for his release. But the governor of Maryland (whom Lewis Tappan described as standing "in such awe of his slave-holding constituents, that he is deaf to the claims of humanity") refused to negotiate the release. Finally, the offer of payment of money for the dying man's release was withdrawn. After serving slightly more than a year, Torrey died on May 9, 1846, of tuberculosis contracted in the Baltimore prison.

After Torrey's death it was disclosed that even if he had lived, the authorities of Virginia were ready to extradite him the moment his imprisonment in Maryland ended. The charges were that Torrey had aided in the escape of John Webb and his two children from Winchester, Virginia. Emily Webb, daughter of a "Virginia gentleman" by the name of Carr and a slave mother, had eventually purchased her freedom and then endeavored to buy the freedom of her husband and children. They were about to be sold to another slaveowner before she could raise sufficient funds. It was to prevent this that the desperate wife and mother had persuaded Torrey to intervene and help them escape. Torrey met John Webb and two of the children one night and drove them to freedom.

Torrey's body was carried to Boston, where he was honored at a public funeral as a martyr to the cause of freedom. (Garrison refused to become a member of the "General Committee of Arrangements for the Funeral of Rev. C. T. Torrey" but assured the committee that "I shall not suffer his cruel imprisonment and melancholy death to pass by without making them as efficacious as possible in hastening the downfall of the nefarious slave system.") The funeral address was delivered by the Reverend Joseph L. Lovejoy, the brother of the abolitionist martyr of Alton, Illinois. Torrey's letter from prison to a friend was read: "If I am a guilty man, I am a very guilty one; for I have aided nearly four hundred slaves to escape to freedom, the greater part of whom would probably, but for my exertion, have died in slavery."

In Northern black communities, Torrey's death evoked many expressions of grief, mingled with indignation. At Oberlin, blacks adopted a series of resolutions, drafted and read by William H. Day, tendering sympathy for Torrey's wife and children and condemning the governor of Maryland for not having pardoned him. Boston blacks, meeting in Zion Church, voted to erect a monument to Torrey and invited the cooperation of Negro people throughout New England. But the Torrey monument proposal met with little support from white abolitionists, and blacks could not, by themselves, raise the necessary funds. Garrison sealed the fate of the monument plan when he expressed the opinion that abolitionist money might be put to better use. Blacks continued to show their respect for Torrey by visiting and decorating his grave at Mt. Auburn cemetery in Cambridge, Massachusetts.

Angered by what had happened to Torrey, Boston's black lawyer, Robert Morris, became active in efforts to raise money to appeal the conviction of

Captain Daniel Drayton. In April 1848 the sloop *Pearl* was captured as it attempted to sail from the Potomac into Chesapeake Bay with seventy-seven slaves who were to be brought to New York. Daniel Drayton, captain of the sloop, and Sayres, its owner, were arrested and taken to a Washington jail. The trial that summer in Washington lasted for six weeks and resulted in Drayton's sentence to prison, while Sayres was forced to pay a fine of $10,000. Robert Morris succeeded in gaining Captain Drayton's release in April 1853 after he had spent four years in jail. Upon his release, Drayton was an honored guest in many black communities. But his health had been so severely affected by his imprisonment that he remained a very sick man. He grew more despondent with the passing years and finally committed suicide in New Bedford in 1857.

UNDERGROUND RAILROAD CONDUCTORS: SOUTH— BLACK (HARRIET TUBMAN)

If it took great courage for a white abolitionist to "carry the war into Africa," one can imagine what it required for a black abolitionist to risk being captured while helping slaves escape from the South. Yet the vast majority of conductors on the Underground Railroad who did go South to assist slaves escape were black. The list includes Josiah Henson, who made several trips back to Kentucky and, in all, led more than a hundred slaves to freedom. It includes Henry Bibb, who returned to the South six times to bring his wife and child out of slavery. He was finally captured and promised his freedom and that of his wife and child if he would tell the authorities the names of conductors and the locations of stations on the Underground Railroad. Bibb refused and was shipped to New Orleans, where he, his wife, and his child were put on the block for sale. But he escaped to Windsor, Canada, where he began publishing *Voice of the Fugitive,* which he later transferred to Detroit, where he also established a station of the Underground Railroad.

There was Leonard A. Grimes, born of free parents in Leesburg, Virginia, who became a hackman in Washington, D.C. Eventually he owned a number of horses and carriages, which he put at the service of the Underground Railroad. In one of his trips to Virginia, he was seized while transporting a free black man, his slave wife, and seven children in his hack in order that they might escape to Canada. Convicted, he was sentenced to two years in the state prison in Richmond. Upon his release, he returned to Washington but later moved North and became the minister of the Twelfth Baptist Church in Boston. Under his militant leadership, the church became an important station of the Underground Railroad, and Grimes was continuously involved in planning the escape of fugitives from federal authorities in Boston. When all else failed, Grimes and his congregation resorted to purchasing the freedom of individual slaves.

Free black Philadelphian Samuel D. Burris, born a slave in Delaware, was another conductor who went South. After several successful trips, the slaveowners were alerted for his next visit. He was caught and sold into slavery. Fortunately, his freedom was purchased by a member of the American Anti-Slavery Society.

The most renowned of these black conductors was Harriet Tubman. Born in Bucktown, a village of a few hundred persons in Dorchester County on Maryland's Eastern Shore, one of ten or eleven children, she became the property of a plantation owner who had so many slaves that he hired out those he did not need to other planters. Tubman was no more than five or six years old when she was put on household duties and was taking care of a baby; at nine, she was a nurse and general house worker. Before she entered her teens, she was doing field work, hauling wood, and splitting rails. She never got back to the housework she loathed during her slavery, and from the fields she gathered the great physical strength that stood her in good stead in later years.

Never humble or subservient, she was nearly killed in her early teens when she sought to protect another slave, and an overseer struck her in the head with a two-pound weight. The pressure on her brain caused spells of somnolence from which she suffered for the rest of her life. In about 1844, she married a free black, John Tubman, while she was still a slave on the plantation, which was now in the hands of the young heir of the plantation owner. In 1849, the young master died. Rumors spread among the slaves that they were either going to be sold off to the Deep South or sent off to chain gangs. After failing to persuade her fellow slaves to join her and unable to influence her husband to leave, she decided to make her break for freedom alone. With the help of several antislavery activists and her own resources and by following the north star at night, she at last crossed the line to free soil in Pennsylvania. She went on to Philadelphia and readily found many jobs in domestic work.

She was interested only in making enough money to finance the projects that had taken shape in her mind. She was also influenced by her deep sense of religion, the unremitting sacrifices of her black brothers and sisters in the abolitionist movement, and the white foes of slavery she had come to know. She became close to William Still, who helped fulfill her desire to become a conductor on the Underground Railroad.

Tubman did not let her illiteracy prevent her from communicating with her family. She dictated letters to friends, and when she received mail, it was read to her. By this process, she made plans for her first recorded trip back to the South. She returned to Baltimore in December 1850 and guided her sister and two children to freedom. What made this rescue particularly poignant was the fact that Tubman's sister was slated to be sold to a new master, which meant she would be separated from her husband, a free black. In order to prevent this, on the day of the sale, while the auctioneer was at dinner, her husband broke into the storage room where his wife and two children were being held and ferried them from Cambridge, Maryland, to Baltimore in a small boat. There Harriet Tubman was waiting to lead them to the North.

December 1851 found Tubman working her way back to the South to free her three brothers and three other slaves. She had sent a code letter to Jacob Jackson, a free black, in Dorchester County, Maryland, who took the responsibility of notifying her brothers. The letter contained a code passage with a biblical reference: "Read my letter to the old folks, and give my love to them, and tell my brothers to be always watching into prayer, and when the good old ship of Zion comes along, to be ready to step aboard." The postal authorities were suspicious—all mail to blacks was opened and read—and called Jackson in to explain what it meant. He read the letter and told the authorities he did not understand its contents and that it must have been sent to him by mistake. However, he immediately let the brothers know that their sister was on the way.

Harriet Tubman arrived just in time to keep her three brothers from being sold and sent to the Deep South. This had been scheduled to take place the next morning, but since it was Christmas, the sale was put off for twenty-four hours, giving Tubman time to plan for the escape. She told them to be ready by dark and that they would start for their father's place in Caroline County, some forty miles to the north. They arrived late Christmas Eve, tired and hungry. "Old Ben," Harriet Tubman's father, hid them in the fodder house and gave them food. It rained all Christmas Day, and they were unable to travel until late that evening. In the cold night, with little food, they set out, stopping at various stations on the way. One was in the home of Thomas Garrett, a Quaker businessman in Wilmington, Delaware, who spent most of his money to help buy food and clothes and pay the train fare for fugitive slaves and whose home was often guarded by Wilmington's free blacks who sacrificed their sleep in order to ensure that no harm came to the white Underground Railroad stationmaster. On December 29, 1851, Garrett wrote to J. Miller McKim of the Pennsylvania State Anti-Slavery Society and Philadelphia Vigilance Committee:

We made arrangements last night, and sent away Harriet Tubman, with five men and a woman to Allen Agnew's to be forwarded across the County to the city. Harriet and one of the men had worn their shoes off their feet, and I gave them two dollars to help fit them out, and directed a carriage to be hired at my expense, to take them out, but do not yet know the expense. I now have two more from the lowest County in Maryland, on the Peninsula, upwards of one hundred miles. I will try to get one of our trusty colored men to them tomorrow morning and you can pass them on.

Beginning with her first venture in 1850, Harriet Tubman is believed to have made at least nineteen trips back into slave country and is credited with helping more than three hundred slaves escape to freedom. There was great risk involved, but she developed a number of effective ruses. One was to use a horse and carriage, usually the master's, for the first stage of the escape journey. Negroes driving a horse and buggy were assumed to be on an errand for their master. Another device was to start the journey to freedom on a Saturday night so that she could be well on her way before the slaveowners had an opportunity the following Monday to advertise the escape of their slaves. She carried forged passes in case she was stopped by the slave patrols. Whenever she thought the party was in danger, she headed south instead of north. Babies were drugged with paregoric to keep them quiet, and she carried a gun to force the slaves to move when they were tired, saying, "You'll be free or die."

But she did have some narrow escapes. Once she was discovered by friends beneath a poster offering a reward for her capture. (By 1856, there was a price of $40,000 on her head in the South.) Since she could not read it, it meant nothing to her. Another time, hearing men reading a poster, she took out a book, not knowing whether it was right side up. It was enough to dispel the suspicions of the men because "the one we want can't read or write."

Her most memorable venture took place in June 1857 when she returned to the Eastern Shore, hired a wagon, and brought out her aged parents. The sensational rescue of the two seventy-year-old slaves gained mention even in John Bell Robinson's proslavery *Pictures of Slavery and Anti-Slavery*. Robinson raged against "this act of horror" in bringing "away from ease and comfortable homes two old slaves over seventy years of age. . . . I cannot conceive of a more wicked act towards parents. Confinement in the penitentiary for life would be inadequate to her crime, for stealing her old parents away from a warm climate altogether congenial to their nature, to a very cold one, and where there is nothing to depend on but their labor."

Tubman made her last trip in the service of the Underground Railroad in November 1860, bringing to freedom seven slaves: two men, two women, and three children. On December 1, 1860, Thomas Garrett wrote to William Still to let him know that "Harriet Tubman is again in these parts. She arrived last evening from one of her trips of mercy to God's poor." Station by station, Harriet Tubman brought her last party to freedom in Canada, remaining with them for several days at the home of Frederick Douglass, where she frequently brought her passengers, and to whom she expressed her pride that she had "never lost a single passenger." Years later, Douglass paid a moving tribute to the greatest conductor of the Underground Railroad:

The difference between us is very marked. Most of what I have done and suffered in the service of our cause has been in public and I have received much encouragement at every stop of the way. You, on the other hand, have labored in a private way. I have wrought in the day—you in the night. I have had the applause of the crowd and the satisfaction that comes of being approved by the multitude, while the most you have done has been witnessed by a few trembling, scarred and footsore bondmen and women, whom you have led out of the house of bondage and whose heartfelt "God Bless You" has been your only reward. Excepting John Brown—of sacred memory—I know of no one who has willingly encountered more perils and hardships to serve our enslaved people than you have.

It was this remarkable woman, whom the slaves called "Moses" and who in 1859 was described by Thomas Wentworth Higginson as "the greatest heroine of the age," who counseled and encouraged John Brown when he was formulating his plan for armed action against slavery.

VIGILANCE COMMITTEES: NEW YORK CITY

Many black and white abolitionists worked independently to aid fugitives, confining themselves to more informal efforts. But in the larger towns and cities of the North, vigilance committees were established. (Sometimes a vigilance committee was called a Slave Refuge Society or a Fugitive Aid Society.) Benjamin Quarles points out that the vigilance committees had numerous functions and aided the fugitives in a variety of ways:

Boarding and lodging them for a few days, purchasing clothing and medicine for them, providing them with small sums of money, informing them as to their legal rights and giving them legal protection from kidnappers. A primary function of the vigilance committee was to help a slave establish himself in a new location, to furnish him with letters of introduction, to help him find a job, and to give him guidance and protection while he was thus engaged in getting started.

While a number of the vigilance committees were integrated organizations, many were either all black or had a predominantly Negro membership, and nearly all were operated by Negroes. At the 1848 National Negro Convention in Cleveland, various local committees were appointed to organize vigilance committees in the black communities "so as to enable them to measure arms with assailants without and invaders within."

The first of the vigilance committees to be organized was the New York Committee of Vigilance, founded in November 1835 by a group of black and white "Friends of Human Rights" in New York City. The organization, with David B. Ruggles as its secretary and general agent, set down seven areas of concern:

1st. The arrival of persons (needing their aid and counsel) from the South and other parts.
2d. The arrival and departure of vessels, suspected as carrying slaves, or having persons on board claimed as slaves, or who were in danger of being kidnapped or sold.
3d. The arrival and proceedings of slave agents and kidnappers.
4th. The arrest of persons claimed as fugitive slaves.
5th. The abduction of persons by kidnappers.
6th. The recovery of persons detained in the South.
7th. The recovery of property due to colored people by wills, etc.

Of the seven objectives, the act of kidnapping received special attention. On one occasion, the committee alerted the black community with the following notice in the *Emancipator*: "Look out for kidnappers! We are informed that the notorious NASH has returned from the South, and is prowling about the city for more victims. Colored people should be on their guard. Let no white man into your house unless you know who he is, and what his business is. If he says he is an officer and has a warrant to arrest a fugitive slave, *don't let him in unless he shows a search warrant.* He has no right to go or stay in without one."

Much of the work of the New York committee lay in feeding and clothing runaways and sending them on to some points of safety outside of New York with money and letters of introduction to friends. A good deal of the committee's success in this and other activities can be credited to David Ruggles, its indefatigable black secretary. (One contemporary noted that Ruggles was "a General Marion sort of man for sleepless activity, sagacity, and talent.") Born of free parents in Norwich, Connecticut, he came to New York City in 1827 at the age of seventeen. He became a butter merchant, advertising that he sold only the products of free labor. Within a short time, he gave up his business to become a traveling agent for the *Emancipator,* the official organ of the American Anti-Slavery Society. When he was twenty-four, he opened a bookshop in New York City, from which he circulated antislavery publications. Since blacks were denied the use of libraries, he set up a reading room in his home. In 1835, his bookshop was burned to the ground by a proslavery mob. That same year, he became secretary of the New York Committee of Vigilance.

Ruggles estimated that during the five years he occupied this office, he helped more than six hundred slaves escape to freedom. He made it a practice to board arriving ships to see whether slaves were being smuggled in. On one occasion, he succeeded in bringing an indictment against a Frenchman from Guadaloupe who had clandestinely brought a slave to New York City. The *New York Express,* a leading pro-Southern organ in the city, denounced Ruggles for actions that tended to "embarrass trade" and urged the business community not to "put up with it."

Nevertheless, Ruggles persisted, tracking down illegal entries and exposing kidnappings, as well as helping fugitive slaves move on their way to Canada. In February 1839, he resigned as committee secretary and agent because of failing eyesight and a dispute over funds. An audit committee appointed to examine his accounts found that on several occasions, he had spent more money than he was supposed to and that he was indebted to the committee for $326.17. Ruggles, who had received a salary of four hundred dollars a year, felt secure in his own sense of honesty and vigorously denied the accusations. He was later fully exonerated.

With Ruggles' resignation, the New York Committee of Vigilance lost its driving spirit. Still, by 1842, it estimated that in its seven years of existence, it had helped 1,373 fugitives to freedom. The committee also won public acceptance of its campaign to win the right to a trial by jury for persons claimed as fugitives. A bill requiring such a guarantee was passed by the New York legislature and signed into law by Governor William H. Seward in 1841. A month later, the vigilance committee held a victory celebration at which Charles B. Ray, the black presiding officer, hailed the measure for sweeping clean from the statute books the last vestige of slavery in New York.

Before the new law could prove its effectiveness, however, it was nullified by the Supreme Court's decision in *Prigg* v. *Pennsylvania* (1841), giving Congress the exclusive right to enforce the Fugitive Slave Law and declaring state personal liberty laws invalid. In April 1843, the New York State Assembly voted to repeal the law requiring a trial by jury, but the action died there, and the law in question remained on the statute books, even though it could not be enforced.

VIGILANCE COMMITTEES: PHILADELPHIA

At the end of its first year of operation, the New York Committee of Vigilance reported that members of the black community in New York City had proved to be "efficient coadjutors. To them we have been principally indebted for funds, in them we find steady and uniform agents, and by their exertions, we trust this work will not only spread extensively in this city, but throughout the states." Robert Purvis in Philadelphia read this report, and having already become active in aiding fugitives—his house at Ninth and Lombard streets had a secret room, entered only by a trap door, for hiding runaway slaves—he persuaded a group of Philadelphians to join in forming a similar association in his city. In August 1837, the Vigilant Association of Philadelphia was organized by black and white abolitionists. Its stated object was: "To assist colored people in distress and for such other purposes as they shall think proper." To become a member, one had to pay a subscription fee of twenty-five cents and annual dues of seventy-five cents. It was to be managed by a Vigilance Committee, consisting of fifteen persons elected by the association, whose powers would be delegated to an active committee of four officers for day-to-day operations.

At its initial meeting, the association elected three black officers: James Mc-Crummell, president, Jacob C. White, secretary, and James Needham, treasurer. A few weeks later, it chose Charles Atkins, a black, to be the authorized agent to collect funds. As William D. Fergusson points out in his study of the organization: "Philadelphia's black community figured prominently in the formation of the Association."

The Vigilance Committee, an arm of the association, assisted destitute fugitives with board and room, clothing and medicine, and money. It informed them of their legal rights, gave them legal protection from kidnappers, and frequently persecuted individuals who attempted to abduct, sell, or violate the legal rights of free blacks. Runaways were helped to set up a permanent location or given temporary employment before departure along the Underground Railroad routes from Philadelphia to Canada. Many were sent to the Vigilance Committee in New York, with which the Philadelphia committee had a close working relationship.

The Female Vigilant Association of Philadelphia was launched in July 1838 as an auxiliary to the Vigilant Association. Its constitution pledged it to work in concert with the association and to assist it through fundraising and general support. Two of the Female Association's four officers—Elizabeth White, wife of Jacob C. White, and Sarah McCrummell, wife of James McCrummell—and four of the Female Vigilant Committee's seven members—Mary Bustill, Hetty

Reckless, Mary Proctor, wife of the Reverend Walter Proctor, and Elizabeth Colly, wife of Daniel Colly—were blacks.

In May 1839, Robert Purvis replaced James McCrummell as president, and Robert B. Ayres became secretary to allow Jacob C. White to devote more time to his job as agent of the Underground Railroad in Philadelphia, which was being operated by a committee of sixteen persons, most of them blacks. At this time, ten of the seventeen officers of the Vigilant Association of Philadelphia were blacks.

In 1842, another anti-Negro riot broke out in Philadelphia. When it was over, Robert Purvis withdrew to the Philadelphia suburb of Byberry, and the activities of the Vigilance Committee gradually declined. By 1844, the Association and its committee had ceased to function. From that time until December 1852, the work of the Vigilance Committee was carried on by individuals. In December 1852, a group of abolitionists reported that the old Vigilance Committee "had become disorganized and scattered" and that its affairs were being conducted in a very irregular manner, causing "much dissatisfaction and complaint." The group decided to organize the General Vigilance Committee with an acting committee of four, which would have the authority to attend "to every case that might require their aid," "to raise necessary funds and to keep a record of all their doings," especially their receipts and expenditures. They appointed William Still chairman of the acting committee.

The General Vigilance Committee was the offspring of the former Vigilance Association of Philadelphia and the Pennsylvania State Anti-Slavery Society. The society appears to have pursued a somewhat inconsistent role on the question of fugitive aid. On the one hand, of the fifteen persons present at a meeting of the Vigilance Committee on May 31, 1840, seven are known to have been members of the Anti-Slavery Society, and it is likely that most of the others belonged as well. The minutes of the Philadelphia Female Anti-Slavery Society (auxiliary to the State Anti-Slavery Society) show that at most of its meetings during the years 1840–1842, contributions were made to the Vigilance Committee. Meetings of the state society in 1841, 1843, and 1844 singled out the Vigilance Committee for special praise and pledged to support that organization. Finally, the center of the Vigilance Committee's activities was the antislavery office of the Pennsylvania Society, under the supervision of J. Miller McKim and William Still.

On the other hand, a distinct group within the State Anti-Slavery Society felt that fugitive aid work "does not come particularly within our province as a society" and opposed all institutional support to the Underground Railroad. However, the enactment of the Fugitive Slave Act of 1850 ended this inconsistency in Pennsylvania antislavery thought. By 1852, the society was united in support of the Underground Railroad.

In selecting William Still to be the acting chairman of the body of four members to carry out its work, the General Vigilance Committee chose the most energetic of the many Philadelphians who operated the Underground Railroad.

Still had been born free, but his parents had undergone the hardships of escape, his father being forced to work for many years to purchase his freedom from the master who had recaptured him. William Still spent his life helping other escapees, so effectively, it was said, that nineteen of every twenty fugitives passing through Philadelphia stopped at his home.

After his father had purchased his freedom, his mother ran away with two of her four children. The family set up farming near Medford, New Jersey, where William was born on October 7, 1821, the youngest of eighteen children. With a bare minimum of formal schooling, he continued his own education by extensive reading, including copies of the *Colored American*, to which he subscribed. He worked as a farm hand and became an excellent wood cutter. When he was twenty, Still left home and three years later moved to Philadelphia. After his first venture in an oyster cellar failed, he obtained work as a waiter and butler for a socially prominent aged widow, Mrs. E. Langdon Elwyn, who made him overseer of her properties. In this position, he was able to further his education by reading books from the Elwyn private library. Still's employment terminated when Mrs. Elwyn left the city to reside with her daughter in New York. In the fall of 1847, he learned of a vacancy in the office of the Pennsylvania State Anti-Slavery Society. He was interviewed by J. Miller McKim and hired as clerk.

Still quickly became involved in the affairs of the Underground Railroad, and he and McKim were unquestionably the masterminds behind most of the organized efforts to aid fugitives in the Philadelphia area from 1847 to 1861. They were associated with the fantastic escapes from Georgia of William and Ellen Craft and of Henry "Box" Brown from Virginia (sealed up in a box barely large enough to hold him). One arrival from the South, who had purchased his freedom, proved to be Still's own brother, Peter Still, left behind years earlier when his mother fled to the North.

Still was in charge of boarding fugitives with families of free blacks. Sometimes they stayed for as long as thirteen days, but usually it was for only a few days. As the black secretary of the Vigilance Committee, Still was able to gain the confidence of the fugitives and to know where to find them board and lodging in Philadelphia's black community. This was of great importance for the committee's work, for a white host might well have been an object of suspicion for the fugitive. When William and Ellen Craft were placed with Barkley Ivens, a white abolitionist, Ellen complained to Still: "I have no confidence whatever in white people. They are only trying to get us back into slavery." When Philadelphia papers charged that white abolitionists housed and fed fugitives free of charge while blacks insisted on payments, Still replied:

. . . it is not common in this city for colored people from the South, who are in distress, to "stop with white people." Fearless of successful contradiction, I will affirm that, during the twelve years that I have been in the Anti-Slavery office, not one such person in a hundred has stopped with white people. Not that white people would not take care of them—not because they do not generously furnish means to all the oppressed—do I thus affirm, but simply because it is an undeniable fact, pertinent to make clear a point that otherwise might be left in obscurity.

Still also cared for blacks stranded in the city by their former owners. In one instance, Samuel H. Barrott, a black barber, called his attention to the plight of a mother and daughter who had been brought to Philadelphia by a white family from Georgia and who had purchased their freedom, having left their husband and father behind in bondage. The white family had gone on to New York, leaving the mother and daughter at the hotel with $15, in a city where they did not know anyone. Still offered them a home in his boardinghouse, free of charge, until some other arrangements could be made for them.

Part of Still's duties for the Vigilance Committee was to obtain from the newly arrived fugitives their names, the names of their masters, where they had come from, the severity of their servitude, and the escape route they had taken from the South. These measures were taken partly to protect the Vigilance Committee from imposters who might try to pass themselves off as fugitives in need of money for passage to Canada. More than once, William Lloyd Garrison had to warn Negroes to "be on your guard. There are many deceivers going abroad as fugitive slaves, to impose on your generosity."

In one case, Still was sued for libel. Ellen Wells, a former slave from St. Louis, was traveling throughout the country raising funds to purchase her mother, her children, and several other relatives from slavery. She stayed in Still's rooming house in Philadelphia, and her conversation convinced him that she was an imposter. After leaving, she went on to Boston, where she raised money from members of the legislature, from religious conventions, and from other sources. A Philadelphian who was in Boston wrote to Still, inquiring as to the validity of her claim. Answering in a private letter, Still replied that she was an imposter and a prostitute. The letter was shown to Wells by a party into whose hands it had accidentally fallen, and she was allowed to make a copy of it. Wells sued Still for scandalous and malicious libel. Because the letter was legally and technically libelous, Still was advised by his counsel to plead guilty and offer proof of character and absence of malicious intention, in mitigation of sentence, which he did. The court ordered him to pay a fine of one hundred dollars and spend ten days in prison.

Philadelphia blacks announced a "Public Meeting of Sympathy With Wm. Still!" inviting the public to hear "a proper and public expression of sympathy to Mr. Still, for the recent persecution to which he has been subjected for conscientiously discharging his duty, and to give him satisfactory assurance of the unshaken confidence reposed in him by the friends of humanity, and particularly the unabated respect of his colored brethren." (Among the signers were Williams Wells Brown, Charles H. Bustill, Jonathan C. Gibbs, Stephen Smith, N. W. Dupee, and Peter Gardiner.) In publishing the call for the meeting, the

National Anti-Slavery Standard observed that "one of the most difficult and at the same time most delicate duties that certain Abolitionists have to perform is that of exposing the false pretenses of a class of mendicants who live by ground-less appeals to anti-slavery sympathies. We perceive that our highly-esteemed and valued coadjutor, William Still, of Philadelphia, has been getting into diffi-culty by his efforts rightly to discharge this thankless function." How highly esteemed Still was is indicated in the concluding section of the editorial: "Of all the estimable colored men we know, and their number is not small, there is not one who, in concientiousness, kindness of heart, devotedness to the interests of his race, and to the cause of Freedom, stands higher than William Still of Philadelphia."

Robert Purvis destroyed many of the records of the Vigilance Association of Philadelphia because he feared that its members might be prosecuted or those that it helped recaptured. But Still, at great personal risk, kept the records of the General Vigilance Committee. He later wrote that he did this for possible use in helping to reunite relatives and friends, which was one of the most humanitarian aspects of fugitive aid. Often members of the same family who escaped from slavery and changed their names upon reaching freedom had no way of knowing how to contact each other. The heartbreak involved in this situation was spelled out in a letter Frederick Douglass wrote to Mrs. S. J. Leslie of Philadelphia:

It will give me pleasure to serve you and your friend in bringing Mother and Son together as far as I am able. At present I am totally ignorant of the young man's whereabouts—but I have Several acquaintances on different parts of the Country from North Carolina of whom I will gladly make enquiries—and should any trace of him reach me, I will gladly inform you of the facts. It is however, exceeding difficult to find colored people from the South. They change their names—and conceal their origin for obvious reasons. I have been looking for a friend of mine from Slavery this 10 years—and in a measure, know how to Sympathize with your poor friend in Search of her Son.

William Still's "Autograph Manuscript Journal of Fugitive Slaves Who Passed Through Station No. 2 of the Underground Railroad, Philadelphia, De-cember 25, 1852–February 22, 1857" (the original of which is in the Historical Society of Pennsylvania) is an incredible document. In it, Still set down sketches of all the escaped slaves who came under the care of the Vigilance Committee, designated as "Station No. 2, U.G.R.R." The journal, supplemented by oral narratives, letters, and pamphlets, formed the basis of Still's classic work, *The Underground Railroad*. His extensive records reveal that the Philadelphia Vig-ilance Committee assisted about one hundred escapees a year during the 1850s. The majority of the fugitives came from Virginia and Maryland and were young men, although there are also records of escaping women and children. Most usually got as far as Pennsylvania on their own by pretending to be either white or free, by traveling on foot at night, or by hiding on ships that had sailed from the South. A number were brought to Pennsylvania by the Underground Railroad conductors. For the most part, the slaves took the initiative themselves and, with courage and daring, fled to freedom in new and unfamiliar surroundings. Still's records also show that the fugitive slaves who were shipped from Philadelphia by the Vigilance Committee were not all sent by the same route. Frequently they were passed on to the New York Vigilance Committee; at other times, they were sent northwestward, with the aim of entering Canada between Lake Erie and Ontario. The fugitive usually traveled on foot or in a wagon, driven by a conductor, although he also traveled by rail as a regular passenger or a baggage car stowaway. The Philadelphia & Reading Railroad carried fugitives to Phoenixville and Reading. From Harrisburg, they usually rode the North Central Railroad toward Elmira, New York, and between Philadelphia and New York City, they would use the Pennsylvania Railroad. Still's records indicate how much the Vigilance Committee spent for clothing, medicine, and the fugitive's railroad fare to Canada. In most cases, the committee spent money in small amounts; very few items in the financial reports involved payments of more than five dollars.

Still's *The Underground Railroad* pays great tribute to black and white stationmasters, conductors, and stockholders. But there are also villains—the informers who guided fugitives into the hands of slaveowners and their agents for a price. Throughout, however, it is the fugitives themselves who are the heroes and heroines. Here is a typical entry, which records the escape of Harry Predo:

Broke Jail, jumped out of the window and made his escape.

Henry fled from Buckstown, Dorchester Co., Md., March, 1857. Physically he is a giant. About 27 years of age, stout and well-made, quite black, and no fool, as will appear presently. Only a short time before he escaped, his master threatened to sell him south. To avoid that fate, therefore, he concluded to try his luck on the Underground Rail Road, and, in company with seven others—two of them females—he started for Canada. For two or three days and nights they managed to outgeneral all their adversaries, and succeeded bravely in making the best of their way to a Free State.

In the meantime, however, a reward of $3,000 was offered for their arrest. This temptation was too great to be resisted, even by the man who had been intrusted with the care of them, and who had faithfully promised to pilot them to a safe place. One night, through the treachery of their pretended conductor, they were all taken into Dover Jail, where the Sheriff and several others, who had been notified beforehand by the betrayer, were in readiness to receive them. Up stairs they were taken, the betrayer remarking as they were going up, that they were "cold, but would soon have a good warming." On a light being lit they discovered the iron bars and the fact that they had been betrayed. Their liberty-loving spirits and purposes, however, did not quail. Though resisted brutally by the sheriff with revolver in hand, they made their way down one flight of stairs, and in the moment of excitement, as good luck would have it, plunged into the sheriff's private apartment, where his wife and children were sleeping. The wife cried murder lustily. A shovel full of fire, to the great danger of burning the premises, was scattered over the room; out of the window jumped two of the female fugitives. Our hero Henry, seizing a heavy andiron, smashed out the window entire, through which the others leaped a distance of twelve feet. The railing or wall around the jail, though at first it looked forbidding, was soon surmounted by a desperate effort.

At this stage of the proceedings, Henry found himself without the walls, and also lost sight of his comrades at the same time. The last enemy he spied was the sheriff in his stockings without his shoes. He snapped his pistol at him, but it did not go off. Six of the others, however, marvellously got off safely together; where the eighth went, or how he got off, was not known.

Published in 1872, Still's *The Underground Railroad* was honored by being exhibited at the Philadelphia Centennial Exposition of 1876.

VIGILANCE COMMITTEES: BOSTON

Although the Boston Vigilance Committee was late in being organized, its activities were not the first in that city to protect fugitives. When in the summer of 1836, Eliza Small and Polly Ann Bates, fugitives from Baltimore, were captured by slave hunters and brought before a judge to be returned to their master, blacks acted to save them. At a given signal, a group of black women rushed into the state supreme judicial court, took the fugitives from their captors, whisked them into a waiting carriage, and carried them to Canada. A key role in the daring rescue (which came to be known as the "abolition riot") was played by a black cleaning woman "of great size," who subdued a court officer long enough for the rescue to be effected. The fugitives were never captured and the rescuers never arrested.

It was a failure, however, that led to the formation of the Boston Vigilance Committee. The organization was founded late in 1842 as a reaction to the reenslavement of John Torrence, who had stowed away on the schooner, *Wellington,* in New Bern, North Carolina, was carried to Boston, and was then returned to slavery when the captain sailed out of Boston harbor with Torrence aboard.

The main objectives of the Boston Vigilance Committee were "to rescue from bondage persons of color who are entitled to be free" and "to secure to persons of color the enjoyment of their constitutional and legal rights . . . [by employing] every legal, peaceful and Christian method and none other." Within a short time, the committee had 168 members, including most of Boston's leading white and black abolitionists—William Lloyd Garrison, Theodore Parker, Wendell Phillips, Francis Jackson, John A. White, Richard Dana, Charles Torrey, John Hilton, Peter Howard, Thomas Cole, William C. Nell, Robert Morris, Joshua B. Smith, and Lewis Hayden. Hayden and Smith ("Prince of the Caterers") were members of the executive committee, and Morris was a member of the finance committee. Five percent of the organization's 168 members were black, a percentage more than double that of blacks in the city's population. Included were such black women as the daughters of the Reverend Samuel

Snowden, Mrs. Charles D. Williams, whose husband was the proprietor of a popular clothing shop, and Jane Putnam, wife of one of Boston's wealthiest black hairdressers.

The records of the Boston Vigilance Committee (in the Massachusetts Historical Society) reveal that many black women provided aid to fugitives through the committee even though they were not members. So, too, did black workers. Thus, George Johnson, a seaman, provided board for fugitive Fielding Banks and was reimbursed $5.50 by the Vigilance Committee for two flannel shirts and other expenses incurred in the process.

Lewis Hayden was almost a vigilance committee by himself, in the mold of William Still, although not his equal. His home was the main Boston depot of the Underground Railroad. When Harriet Beecher Stowe once visited Hayden, she was amazed to find a group of thirteen fugitives being fed, clothed, and sheltered. Hayden's custom and ready-made clothing business provided garments for fugitives, and the profits were used to feed runaway slaves during their stay in Boston.

Because supporters of both the old and new antislavery organizations were members of the Boston Vigilance Committee, it was decided that "the association shall have no connection with any anti-slavery or other society to promote the welfare of the people of color." The committee's plan was to raise money and organize auxiliary vigilance committees all over the state to make sure that no Negro coming into Massachusetts, fugitive or not, was denied his rights.

The Massachusetts Anti-Slavery Society quickly gave its sanction to the organization, passing a resolution at its quarterly meeting in Worcester affirming

that the people of Massachusetts are bound by their own professed principles of liberty, justice, humanity, and religion, to succour and protect all fugitives from slavery, who may come within their borders; and we hereby solemnly pledge ourselves never to obey any mandate that requires us to aid in returning such fugitives back to the Southern prison-house of bondage.

Early in 1842 at a rally at Faneuil Hall, a resolution was passed urging the people of Massachusetts to flood both houses of the legislature, calling on them "to pass a declaratory law, that no slave can breathe on the soil of Massachusetts, and that every bondsman shall become free on arriving within her jurisdiction." By then, the movement for passage of a personal liberty law of some kind was picking up support from increasing numbers of people who did not want to see a repetition of the events in the Torrence case. Just at this point, news reached Boston of the Supreme Court decision (in the case of *Prigg* v. *Pennsylvania*) that the free states could pass no legislation depriving a slaveholder of his right to take back his slave property—thus invalidating personal liberty laws. Enraged, William Lloyd Garrison wrote in the *Liberator:*

The Rubicon is passed, if the slaveholding power is permitted to roam without molestation through the Northern States . . . dragging into its den the victims of its lust. . . . The enormity of this decision of the Supreme Court cannot be exhibited in words. . . . *It is not law*—for the entire system of slavery is at war with the rights of man. . . . It is to be spit upon, hooted at, trampled in the dust. . . . The people of Massachusetts will scorn to regard it. The soil of Massachusetts shall be consecrated ground, and the victim of oppression who flies to it for shelter . . . no matter what complexion . . . SHALL BE FREE!

Meeting to protest the Prigg decision, Boston blacks vowed to petition the Massachusetts legislature "to prohibit their officers and citizens from interfering to aid slaveholders in seizing and returning fugitive slaves" and to petition Congress "to secure the right of trial by jury for fugitive slaves." But blacks were aware that with the decision, the slaveowners would intensify their efforts to recapture runaways, and they were increasingly skeptical of the Boston Vigilance Committee's Garrisonian pledge to use only "legal, peaceful and Christian methods, and none other" to resist the reenslavement of fugitives. In July 1842, Boston blacks joined with other Negroes in the region to form the New England Freedom Association, "the object of which is, to protect themselves, and to aid such runaways from Southern bliss as may happen to pass through this region on their way to Canada." The aim was to provide fugitives with food, clothing, shelter, and all other aid, legal or illegal, that might be necessary to ensure their freedom. The membership included two women and at least two staunch black Garrisonians—Henry Weeden and William C. Nell. The illegal aspect of the association's pledge, with the implication of violence if needed, did not deter the black Garrisonians.

The Freedom Association was a distinctly black fugitive aid operation. Funds for its activities came from black contributions, many raised at black social and cultural functions, and substantial sums were collected through the black churches. The association appears to have influenced the formation in the same year of the Colored Vigilance Committee of Detroit, which maintained an independent existence until the Civil War.

THE LATIMER CASE

Three months after the New England Freedom Association was organized, the storm that had been gathering since the *Prigg* decision broke. In October 1842, George Latimer, a slave from Norfolk, Virginia, fled to Boston with his family after his owner, Norfolk merchant James B. Gray, accused him of burglary. Gray, following Latimer to Boston, seized him on October 19 and had him jailed, first on the charge of larceny and later on the charge of being a fugitive. Abolitionists, black and white, rallied to Latimer's side and demanded that he be freed on a writ of habeas corpus. On the day of the hearing before Chief Justice Lemuel Shaw, some three hundred people, mostly blacks, milled about the courthouse, while inside Judge Shaw ruled that, based on the recent *Prigg* decision, Latimer should be given over to Gray's custody. A group of blacks tried to rescue Latimer as he was brought out of the courthouse by the police. Several officers were hurt, but the rescue attempt failed, and eight blacks were arrested. Meetings by Boston blacks, held to raise funds for Latimer's defense, angrily resolved that

the recent seizure and imprisonment of George Latimer, by the authorities of this city, within sight of Bunker Hill, and on the soil that drank the *first* blood that was shed in the revolution that secured the independence of these United States,—WHICH BLOOD FLOWED IN THE VEINS OF A COLORED MAN,—affords convincing proof of the hollow professions of the Americans for democracy, and of the appalling state of that public sentiment which can see unmoved a fugitive from slavery . . . dragged back to his prison-house, to be scourged and tortured, and probably . . . put to death.

The reference to "the *first* blood" was to the death of Crispus Attucks, a fugitive slave in the "Boston Massacre."

The Boston Vigilance Committee and the New England Freedom Association quickly established a Latimer Committee to coordinate statewide protest meetings and published a specially printed newspaper, which appeared every day— the *Latimer Journal and North Star*—protesting the impending return of the fugitive.

Boston was wild with excitement. Placards were distributed, and handbills were posted throughout the city denouncing the police as "Human Kidnappers." "For the Rescue of Liberty! Agitate! Agitate!" cried the *Liberator* of November 11, 1842. "*Latimer shall go free!* . . . Be vigilant, firm, uncompromising, friends of freedom! friends of God!" John Greenleaf Whittier sent a clarion call from Massachusetts to Virginia:

> No slave hunt in our borders,
> no pirate on our strand!
> No fetters in the Bay State,
> no slave upon our land!

In the first public letter he ever wrote, dated Lynn, November 8, 1842, Frederick Douglass informed Garrison that he and Remond had spoken in New Bedford day and night during the first week of November in behalf of "our outraged brother" who had been "hunted down like a wild beast and ferociously dragged through the streets of Boston." But it was not only Massachusetts that was aroused. All New England was aflame. The *People's Advocate* of Concord, New Hampshire, devoted almost the entire issue of November 18, 1842, to "The Case of George Latimer" and introduced it with the note: "The Case seems destined to be like that of Somerset in England, a turning point in the world's progress toward liberty. No apology or explanation therefore will be necessary for occupying a large part of this paper with the various documents necessary to a complete history of the case."

But it was Boston that remained the center of protests, and particularly the black community where so many meetings were being held that the pro-Southern *Boston Daily Bee* blamed the abolitionists for stirring up the Negroes: ''Nothing has ever equalled in our city the state of excitement into which the black population are thrown, by . . . a clique of party zealots, anxious to . . . further their own selfish ends by pretense to . . . love of liberty, in relation to . . . Latimer.''

In mid-November, Latimer was purchased from Gray for four hundred dollars, part of the sum having been raised in the black community. A few weeks after his release, Latimer went on a lecture tour with Douglass, speaking at a series of celebrations hailing his freedom. Following each meeting, they distributed petitions, sponsored by the Latimer Committees, to be presented to the state legislature. The petition asked that fugitive slaves never again be arrested by town or city officials, or held as prisoners in the jails of Massachusetts, and that the state constitution should be ''so amended as shall forever separate the people of Massachusetts from all connection with slavery.''

The petition, bearing 64,526 signatures, headed by that of George Latimer himself, and weighing 150 pounds, was presented to the Massachusetts legislature and resulted in the passage of the 1843 Personal Liberty Act. The law forbade any magistrate or executive officer of the state to assist in the arrest or delivery of any person claimed as a fugitive slave and prohibited those having charge of the jails and other places of confinement to use them for such a person's detention. This was the first personal liberty law passed after the United States Supreme Court invalidated such laws in *Prigg,* and it represented a major victory for the Boston Vigilance Committee and New England Freedom Association. As we shall see in our discussion of resistance to the Fugitive Slave Act of 1850 in the next volume, it was not to be the last.

In the midst of the panic of 1857, J. Miller McKim wrote to Maria Weston Chapman: ''Other railroads are in a declining condition and have stopped their semi-annual dividends, but the Underground has never before done such flourishing business.'' This ''flourishing business'' continued until the Civil War, when the United States government finally took steps to prevent the return of fugitive slaves to their owners. In the period of its existence, the Underground Railroad played a major role in helping slaves escape to freedom and preventing their reenslavement once they achieved it. It was also the one antislavery organization in which blacks and whites functioned in complete harmony—the one in which, more than any other, blacks played the dominant role in both leadership and membership and the one in which old and new antislavery men and women, black and white, could unite, despite their differences on other issues.

Since its activities and membership were often secret, it is difficult to demonstrate the full extent of individual black participation in the Underground Railroad. But there is enough evidence to conclude that more blacks participated in Underground Railroad activity than has been hitherto believed and that such work attracted the broadest spectrum of the black population in the North. Men and women, working-class and middle-class blacks, participated in Underground

Railroad activity, although the precise nature of their work may have differed. Generally, working-class blacks might be more likely to take part directly in fugitive slave rescues and protecting the runaways, while middle-class blacks more often participated in fund-raising and organizational work.

Black churches in the Northern cities and towns supported fugitive aid work, and Underground Railroad meetings commonly used Negro church buildings. In Philadelphia and Boston many Negro clergymen sanctioned Underground Railroad activities, and several belonged to the Vigilance Committees in these cities. Meetings were held at black churches to solicit contributions for the Vigilance Committees, and the churches themselves made financial contributions. Membership in black benevolent and self-improvement societies frequently overlapped with that of the Vigilance Committees, and members and officers of self-improvement societies often served as members or officers.

While many fugitives could not remain in stations on the Underground Railroad for long, in the time they were there, not a few met free blacks and a fellowship emerged that was to strengthen the struggle to free the chains of the millions still in bondage. And since blacks of all classes, religious denominations, fraternal and self-help societies, and of both sexes, united in the protection of fugitives, work in the Underground Railroad strengthened the bonds of the black community.

24

Black-White Relations in the
Antislavery Movement

In his book, *The Antislavery Appeal: American Abolition after 1830*, published in 1976, Ronald G. Walters defined an abolitionist as one whose principal beliefs included a "commitment to the creation of a society in which blacks would have civil equality with whites." The acceptance of such a definition would sharply reduce the number of those who thought of themselves as active abolitionists. Yet this type of commitment was a basic feature of the new abolitionism.

WHITE ABOLITIONISTS AND FREE BLACKS

The constitutions of antislavery societies usually included a resolve to work toward "uplifting the Free People of Color," while their gatherings frequently adopted resolutions attacking "Negrophobia." These actions were inspired in part by humanitarianism, but they were also motivated by a desire to demonstrate that the Negro was capable of becoming a valuable citizen of any community. In the beginning, when many of the new abolitionists confidently expected immediate emancipation to be accomplished in about ten years, they felt that it was necessary to prepare free blacks to assume leadership in the new era that would emerge after that great day when all the slaves were emancipated. At the same time, they believed that the elevation of free blacks would deal the final blow to the "colonization delusion" predicated on the assumption that Negroes, whether slave or free, were inferior beings and would remain a burden on American society unless they were returned to their native Africa.

Many of the new abolitionists believed that by fighting for racial integration on moral grounds, they could pierce the consciences of a complacent white majority and move in the direction of immediate emancipation. They felt that even a limited success in achieving desegregation would soon demonstrate the equality of blacks and would help destroy the racial myths supporting slavery. When

white consciousness about blacks was educated to a new sensitivity and awareness, the belief went, slavery would collapse under the weight of moral criticism.
"Northern prejudice," Angelina Grimké argued, "is grinding the colored man
to the dust in our free states, and this is strengthening the hands of oppressors
continually." "We must eat, walk, travel, and worship with people of color,"
Lewis Tappan insisted, "and show to the slaveholders and their abettors at the
North that we will recognize them as brethren." And William Goodell believed
that as long as Northern laws, institutions, and customs rendered "the freedom
of the colored people but an empty name—but the debased mockery of true
freedom," it would be difficult for abolitionists to condemn Southern practices.

The solution, they believed, was at hand. Treat blacks as equals, Angelina
Grimké advised: "Multitudes of instances will continually occur in which you
will have the opportunity of *identifying yourself with this injured class* of our
fellow beings; embrace these opportunities at all times and in all places." Elizur
Wright, Jr., expressed the belief that if "every man [would] take his stand, turn
out this prejudice, live it down, talk it down, everywhere consider the colored
man as a man, in the church, the stage, the steamboat, the public house, in all
places . . . the death blow to slavery will be struck." The delegates to the 1834
New England Anti-Slavery Society convention passed a resolution stating that it
was

the duty of all the friends . . . of the anti-slavery cause to . . . encourage with their
custom and their influence, those taverns, stages, and steamboats which receive and
accommodate our fellow colored citizens, without making an illiberal and disgraceful
distinction either of charges or of treatment on account of color.

At Sarah Grimké's suggestion, the 1838 Anti-Slavery Convention of American Women adopted a comprehensive direct action resolution, asserting that it
was "the duty of abolitionists to identify themselves with these oppressed Americans, by sitting with them in places of worship, by appearing with them in the
streets, by giving them our countenance in steamboats and stages, by visiting
with them at their homes and encouraging them to visit us, receiving them as we
do our white fellow citizens." At the 1841 Massachusetts Anti-Slavery Society's
annual meeting, Stephen S. Foster proposed a similar resolution:

We recommend to abolitionists as the most consistent and effectual method of abolishing
the "Negro-pew" to take their seats in it, wherever it may be found, whether in
a . . . church, a railroad car, a steamboat, or a stagecoach.

The society did not approve Foster's resolution, but it did require members to
protest against segregation and work "in some way" to abolish it.

The American Anti-Slavery Society was constantly on the lookout for examples of Negroes who were equal in ability to whites. This was one of the reasons
for its interest in Haiti, which it hoped would prove the Negroes' capacity for

self-government. The society's antislavery tracts argued that even though millions of enslaved blacks in the United States had not yet had a real opportunity to prove they were the equals of whites, there were thousands

who are living proofs that slaves of African descent can shake off degradation with their chains, and win respect even from stubborn prejudice. Toussaint and Petion, Dumas the general and Dumas the author, Placid the Cuban poet, Wheatly, Banneker, Horton, Osborn, Jordan and Hill, are a few among the many witnesses, that neither learning, taste, nor talent, nor skill to rule, nor warlike prowess, nor eloquence, nor wisdom, nor sagacity, nor any element of human greatness, is incompatible with negro blood.

In their effort to combat discrimination by personal example, leading abolitionists frequently mingled with blacks in social gatherings. Some lived with Negro families. Augustus Wattles chose to do so in Cincinnati while teaching Negro children there. So, too, did Theodore Weld, whom Gerda Lerner correctly describes as "outstanding among abolitionist leaders in his intellectual understanding of the damaging role of race prejudice and in his alertness and constant vigilance against all evidences of it." While in New York working at the American Anti-Slavery Society office, Weld lived in the attic of editor Samuel Cornish's home, attended Negro church services, and asked a Negro minister to help officiate at his wedding to Angelina Grimké, itself an interracial social affair.

Boston's white abolitionists' favorite meeting places were Lewis Hayden's home and store. "So much time did they spend in these two places," notes Hayden's biographers, "that friends always knew where to find them." When white abolitionists traveled, they sometimes stayed with black families during their stopovers. Garrison often stayed at Charles Remond's house in Salem, and Samuel J. May was put up at the Forten's in Philadelphia. Blacks were also the house guests of the Garrisons. Charlotte Forten reported that not only was the evening enjoyable but that Mrs. Garrison was "one of the loveliest persons I have ever seen, worthy of such a husband."

Garrison and his associates boycotted segregated public transportation in their trips between Philadelphia and New York. They believed, Garrison wrote to the *Liberator,* that if their action was "extensively imitated by anti-slavery men . . . every barrier of caste will soon be overthrown."

Black abolitionists traveled widely in discharging their organizing activities, and when they returned to the black communities, they often brought news of the support they had received from their white friends in the movement. Typical was this report by John Bowers of a stopover in a Lancaster, Pennsylvania, hotel, en route from an antislavery meeting in Harrisburg:

I finished my breakfast. . . . rose and the white Abolitionist friends in company (which they certainly were) gave the landlord to understand . . . that if I could not sit there, they would not . . . thus proving to the colored men, and to the world, that they were not Abolitionists in word, but in deed, and determined to carry out these principles which they profess.

Together, white and black abolitionists used the technique of "ride-ins" to desegregate railroad transportation in Massachusetts. Many times, white abolitionists attempted to ride in the black sections of trains, and blacks tried to ride in the white sections of the railroad cars. Both were assaulted by railroad employees, although blacks were always treated more severely. Their efforts, however, were not without results. Not only did they succeed in abolishing segregation on Massachusetts' railroads, but James N. Buffum, one of the whites engaged in the "ride-ins," believed that the actions had a stimulating effect on the abolitionist movement generally: "In Lynn, it has been the means of bringing new converts to the cause. . . . People are roused into active discussion."

Another primary target of white abolitionists was the abolition of the Negro pew in churches. After the Grimké sisters became Quakers, they insisted on sitting with black women in a Philadelphia Friends' meeting house. When they were scolded by white Quakers for this, they replied, "While you put this badge of degradation on our sisters, we feel it is our duty to share it with them." Lucretia Mott was another abolitionist Quaker who insisted on the abolition of the Negro pew in her meeting house, and she personally invited blacks to attend meetings she addressed. A reporter for the *Nantucket Inquirer* who attended a meeting at the Friends' meeting house on the island at which Lucretia Mott spoke found the presence of "more than a hundred neatly-clad people of color . . . cheering, eminently so. . . . There, for the first time, I saw a practical recognition, on anything like a large scale of that which the Christian Church professes to regard as a truth, viz: that 'God is no respecter of persons.'"

Most blacks preferred to seek religious consolation in their own churches rather than fight to end segregated seating in white churches. Yet there was progress in reducing segregation by the "pray-ins." Thus, even though by the end of the 1840s most churches in the North still had segregated seating, hundreds had abolished the Negro pew system.

White abolitionists, like Weld, Garrison, or Phillips, would never allow black colleagues to suffer discrimination alone. Once, on hearing that Frederick Douglass was compelled to ride in a filthy Jim Crow box car, Phillips stepped to his friend's side in the presence of a group of cultivated spectators and walked with him straight into the miserable car, saying, "Douglass, if you cannot ride with me, I can ride with you." Men like Phillips would give up their staterooms on steamers and share the sleeping accommodations provided for black abolitionists on the decks. They would go hungry rather than eat in a dining room from which blacks were excluded.

And yet there are few aspects of abolitionism that have become more shrouded in controversy than the racial attitudes of white abolitionists. In *Plantation to Ghetto,* August Meier and Elliott M. Rudwick charge that most of the white abolitionists, and particularly Garrison, were "paternalistic and prejudiced," despite their "egalitarian rhetoric." William H. Pease and Jane H. Pease, using the term "the Boston Clique" to describe Garrison and his white followers, assert that "despite the Clique's public and ardent campaign against overt discrimination, they displayed both a social distaste for and an underlying distrust of the individual Negroes they encountered.'' The Garrisonians, they maintain, seldom saw the Negro as ''a complex person or as an equal. He was an ex-slave, or black man, essentially a public exhibit in the antislavery crusade.''

THE CASE OF GARRISON

Certainly Garrison had weaknesses as a human being, and he did not easily brook challenges to his antislavery doctrines by black abolitionists. But the ironic truth is that his reputation has suffered at the hands of the bulk of historians precisely because he had, as Wendell Phillips put it, forgotten ''that he was white.'' In fact, it might be said that as far as the history of the race to which he belonged in its relation to black people was concerned, he was ashamed of being white. As he told a meeting of free blacks in 1832:

I never rise to address a colored audience, without feeling ashamed of my color; ashamed of being identified with a race of men, who have done you so much injustice, and who yet retain so large portion of your brethren in servile chains. To make atonement, in part, for this conduct, I have solemnly dedicated my health, and strength, and life, to your service. I love to plan and to work for your social, intellectual, and spiritual advancement. My happiness is augmented with yours; in your sufferings I participate.

Henceforth I am ready, on all days, on all convenient occasions, in all suitable places, before any sect or party, at whatever peril to my person, character or interest, to plead the cause of my colored countrymen in particular, or of human right in general. For this purpose, there is no day too holy, no place improper, no body of men too inconsiderable to address.

In saying that he loved ''to plan and to work'' for the elevation of the free blacks, Garrison was not suggesting that the Negroes were to be passive and submissive. On the contrary, he felt that they had to stand up for their rights; they had to work together to elevate themselves, and they had to take an active role in the fight to end slavery in the South and segregation in the North. ''Our colored population . . . ought to cooperate like a band of brothers, and depend upon themselves to raise their own character.''

Garrison was thoroughly convinced that the struggles for immediate emancipation and for an end to prejudice were intertwined; both slavery and discrimination were sins. The essential point, Garrison insisted, was that it was a sin to be prejudiced against the Negro: ''Who made him what he is? God. Who gave him his complexion? God. Do these presecutors believe in the power and justice of the Almighty Ruler of the Universe? Then they must know that they have a heavy sin to answer for.'' Therefore, men and women who had not conquered their own prejudices were sinners in need of conversion.

Garrison was under no illusion that the purification of the land from prejudice would come swiftly. In January 1842, he observed: ''The overthrow of American prejudice . . . must necessarily be the work of many years, even under the most favorable circumstances.'' But in speeches to blacks in different parts of the North, Garrison urged them ''never, never despair of the complete attainment of your rights.'' There was only one solution: to fight day in and day out ''to get a full and immediate recognition of your rights.'' His paper, he assured them, would be their staunch ally in this struggle. And after publishing the *Liberator* for little over a month, Garrison wrote in a letter to Samuel J. May: ''This then is my consolation. If I cannot do much in this quarter toward abolishing slavery, I may be able to elevate our free colored population in the scale of society.''

Garrison practiced what he preached. Not only did he mingle socially with blacks, but soon after he began publication of the *Liberator,* he hired a young black, Thomas Paul, Jr., the minister's son, to serve as a general apprentice and learn the printing trade. This may at first glance appear very trifling indeed, but many whites were shocked at the action. As a colleague of Garrison wrote later, ''In that day no colored boy could be apprenticed to any trade in any shop where white men worked; still less could he find a place, except as a menial, in any store or office.'' But Garrison hoped his example and the publicity it received would help break down existing barriers to black apprenticeship in the trades. He must have been pleased to receive the following letter of congratulation:

It must be very gratifying to all the friends of the blacks to know that you, Mr. Editor, are so true to your principles as to have a colored apprentice. . . . I should rejoice . . . if I could believe that before this generation has passed away, reason and religion will have gained so complete a victory over prejudice . . . that half our officers of government may be of African race.

Garrison not only tried, unsuccessfully, to insert into the constitution of the American Anti-Slavery Society a clause advocating social equality of blacks and white, but he also championed the fight to repeal the Massachusetts law forbidding interracial marriage, refusing to yield to the racists on this issue. This was at a time when New York abolitionists were distributing literature to disassociate themselves from the charge that they favored ''amalgamation.'' In a handbill headed ''American Anti-Slavery Society—Disclaimer,'' circulated after the New York riot of 1834, they announced that the society did not favor either the social mixing of the two races or the admittance of blacks to civil rights in the white society beyond what their ''intellectual and moral worth'' made advisable. The society especially pleaded not guilty to possessing ''any desire to promote or encourage intermarriage between white and colored persons.'' A few days later, its members sent a letter to the mayor of New York, which began: ''We disclaim any desire to promote or encourage intermarriage.''

Edward Abdy, a British visitor in New York, was furious that the abolitionists ''should have stooped to recognize the 'amalgamation' complaint as valid enough to disavow,'' and he expressed his gratification over the fact that Garrison shared his views.

In his study of Boston's black community in the antebellum era, Donald M.

Jacobs concludes that "Garrison can in no way be faulted in focusing throughout his lifetime upon the twin goals of humanity and equality for men everywhere." But it was perhaps the *Anti-Slavery Bugle,* published in Ohio, that proposed the real test when it said that it was the Negroes themselves who were in the best position to judge prejudice in the antislavery movement. Measured by this standard, Garrison receives very high marks indeed. In *Black Bostonians,* still another study of Boston's black community before the Civil War, James Oliver Horton and Lois E. Horton note:

While most white abolitionists were received with appreciation and honor by the black community, Garrison held a special place in the hearts of blacks. His vehement denunciation of the institution of slavery and those who supported it, and his willingness to work for racial justice and equality in Boston were significant factors in explaining his special importance to the black community. It was, however, his willingness to associate with blacks as human beings on the basis of social equality which made Garrison most unique. He listened to and seriously considered arguments put forth by the black community at a time when many whites believed blacks incapable of rational and intelligent argument.

"Mr. Garrison," recalled William C. Nell, "has at times, been supposed to be a colored man because of his long, patient and persevering devotion to our cause."

AMBIVALENCE AMONG WHITE ABOLITIONISTS

Yet it cannot be denied that even in the case of Garrison, there was a definite ambivalence in his and his followers' relations with blacks in the antislavery movement. While no antislavery societies excluded blacks—several members of the New England Anti-Slavery Society were voted down when they indicated that they did not want any blacks to serve in the organization with them, even though Negroes were in the minority—there was an unwillingness to view blacks as capable of filling important leadership roles or of participating in the formulation of antislavery strategy. Blacks were officers of the American Anti-Slavery Society, but they never held any top position. The appointment of Frederick Douglass as temporary president in 1847 was only an act of tokenism. Commenting on the experience, Douglass later wrote: "We are too few and too feeble to bear up under the neglect of our friends, though we can perchance stand the insults of our enemies."

Even though Boston's black community had too much affection and respect for Garrison to voice its criticism publicly over the issue, there was a good deal of private resentment over the fact that a black, William C. Nell, who had held a responsible position for a number of years and seemed to be next in line for the position of general agent or "chief man" of the *Liberator,* was passed over in 1853 in favor of Robert P. Wallcut, a white man and comparative newcomer to the firm. To blacks, Garrison appeared to be displaying a lack of confidence in

Nell's ability for a leadership position and to be duplicating the practice of many other white abolitionists, who allowed their enemies to set the terms of their relations with blacks.

The unwillingness of white abolitionists to challenge racist practices was usually justified on the ground that they were simply showing consideration for the feeling of the community. Some who owned houses with apartments for rent refused to lease to blacks, giving as their reason the attitude of their neighbors or the excuse that the value of their property would decline, a rationalization for racism that was to find echoes far into the succeeding century. Arthur Tappan conceded that the attitude of his neighbors had influenced his own conduct:

Though I advocated the sentiment that as Christians we were bound to treat the colored people, without respect to color, yet I feel that great prudence was required to bring about the desired change in public feeling on the subject; and therefore, though I would willingly, so far as my own feelings were concerned, have publicly associated with a well educated and refined colored person, male or female, I felt that their best good would be prompted by refraining from doing so till the public mind and conscience were more enlightened on the subject.

Like his brother and many other white abolitionists, Lewis Tappan was also prone to calculate carefully the expediency of demanding social equality in a Northern society obsessed with fears of amalgamation. "When the subject of acting out our professed principles in treating men irrespective of color is discussed, heat is always produced," he noted in commenting on the shortcomings of his fellow evangelists. But he insisted on practicing his principles, and, unlike his brother, was ready to be seen in public with blacks and to associate with them on all occasions. Although severely handicapped by elitist notions of society and by a rigid and obsessive piety, Lewis Tappan did manage (albeit painfully at times) to react to blacks with something approaching understanding.

However, many white abolitionists were closer to Arthur than to Lewis Tappan in their approach to the question of prejudice. Some even believed that it was a mistake to mix the struggle against prejudice based on race and color with the battle against slavery, which, they felt, was "the great object," and that it would be wisest to leave secondary questions like prejudice "to time to resolve." Others excused their inaction on a different ground by arguing that it was a waste of time to combat prejudice while slavery existed, since the two were inextricably connected. "There is but one remedy [for prejudice]," Edmund Quincy, a New England Garrisonian, argued. "That is emancipation. The prejudice will not cease while slavery lasts; men always hate those they injured."

WHITE PATERNALISM

On November 4, 1837, the *Colored American* carried a brief but significant editorial:

Our white friends, unfortunately, expect less of negro students in the classroom, and speak exultantly of the academic work of negroes which would be barely passable if performed by whites and willingly tolerate negro teachers who fall short of the qualifications of whites for the same position.

Our white friends are deceived when they imagine they are free from prejudice from color, and yet are content with a lower standard of attainment on the part of colored men. That is, in our view, the worst feature of abolitionism—the one which grieves us most. It is the highest rock of danger; the only one in which we fear a shipwreck of our high and holy cause.

This tendency among white abolitionists to praise black accomplishment, regardless of its quality, "as if in surprise that he [the Negro] revealed any ability at all," was part of a pattern of white paternalism that permeated interracial relationships in the antislavery movement. Frederick Douglass observed in 1860 that "consciously or unconsciously, almost every white man approaches a colored man with an air of superiority or condescension"—and he exempted very few abolitionists, even the most well meaning, from this charge.

White abolitionists revealed their paternalistic attitudes in their reminiscences. Levi Coffin, for example, viewed black-led Underground Railroad activities with a good deal of condescension. "Most of the colored people were not shrewd managers," he wrote, complaining that until he came to the rescue, they often lost fugitives to slave catchers. After admitting that "there were a few wise and careful managers among the colored people," Coffin went on to assert that "it was not safe to trust all of them with the affairs of our work," since most blacks were "too careless" and some "could be bribed . . . to betray" the fugitives. Coffin pictured himself as the paternal organizer who often hired "teams from a certain German livery" and sent "some irresponsible though honest colored man to procure them." When it was necessary to transport fugitives from Cincinnati to some other station, Coffin used one of "several trusty colored men . . . as drivers," because they "owned no property" and "could lose nothing in a prosecution." "There seems to be no doubt," writes Richard A. Falk in *Black Man's Burden in Ohio, 1849–1863*, "that Levi Coffin placed most black people in a category little different from the stereotyped image held by most white Ohioans."

Samuel Ringgold Ward and Martin R. Delany, both active black abolitionists, blamed just this brand of paternalism for the tendency among white antislavery men to expect blacks to follow the path that they marked out for them—a path which, Delany contended, excluded Negroes from leadership in the cause. Delany, particularly, resented the paternalistic attitudes of antislavery society members. He charged that white friends "presumed to think for, dictate to, and *know* better what suits colored people" than blacks did themselves. After years of hearing extravagant promises that were seldom kept, Delany came to the conclusion that blacks occupied the "same position in relation to our anti-slavery friends, as we do in relation to the pro-slavery part of the community—a mere secondary, underling position."

Delany's conclusion was especially influenced by the fact that only a few blacks were employed in abolitionist-owned businesses. In an early assertion of the principle of "affirmative action," he wrote:

It was to be expected that Anti-Slavery, according to its professions, would extend to colored persons, as far as the power of its adherents, those advantages nowhere else to be obtained among white men. That colored boys would get situations in the shops and stores, and every other advantage tending to elevate them as far as possible, would be extended to them. At least, it was expected, that in Anti-Slavery establishments, colored men would have the preference. . . . It was urged, and it was true, that the colored people were susceptible of all that the whites were, and all that was required was to give them a fair opportunity, and they would prove their capacity. That it was unjust, wicked and cruel, the result of an unnatural prejudice, that debarred them from places of respectability, and that public opinion could and should be corrected upon this subject. . . .

Thus was the cause espoused, and thus did we expect much. But in all this, we were doomed to disappointment, sad, sad, disappointment.

In truth, little more than a pitiful beginning was even made by the antislavery movement in improving the economic plight of northern blacks. At its 1832 convention, the New England Anti-Slavery Society resolved to request "the parents or guardians of colored lads, who may wish to learn trades in this city [Boston] and its vicinity to make application to this Society for that purpose, and that a committee shall be appointed to provide places for such persons." A five-member Committee on Trades was appointed, headed by Garrison, and the parents and "young lads themselves" were requested to enter their names and places of residence with the chairman of the Apprentices Committee, "whose duty shall be to register the applicants made." Blacks did register, but no businesses were found ready to accept them. Even abolitionists shopowners pleaded that the presence of a black in the shop would lead to the loss of both white mechanics and customers.

Four years later, at its third anniversary meeting, the American Anti-Slavery Society recommended that the auxiliaries determine the number of "our colored brethren" in their districts desirous of learning the "useful arts" and of "mechanics . . . willing to teach them trades, and treat them as they do other apprentices." However, the local societies took no action on the suggestion. There was an American Anti-Slavery Society scheme to settle the unemployed free blacks of the North on new lands in the Old Northwest. Augustus Wattles, a Lane student who had worked among the free blacks of Cincinnati, assumed direction of this project and managed to solicit enough funds to buy a large tract of land, where he set up a land office for prospective Negro farmers. But lack of funds for transportation, implements, and sustenance for the first few years until enough food could be grown to feed the participants and pay expenses, combined with the hostility to the scheme expressed by the inhabitants of the local communities, effectively doomed the venture. A handful of blacks did settle on land offered free by Gerrit Smith in upstate New York.

Thus in the important areas of economic equality, the efforts of white antislavery adherents were fitful and ineffective. Garrison's *Liberator* office included a Negro Employment Office, managed by William C. Nell, to direct blacks to available jobs. In Ohio, the *Philanthropist* also operated a referral agency to which employers willing to hire black apprentices might apply and at which black parents with sons available for apprenticing might leave their names. But while blacks did leave their names at the offices of both papers, few employers, including those with antislavery sentiments, were willing to hire them.

Blacks were painfully aware of the failure of abolitionism to make even a dent in their job problem. When the *Colored American* reviewed the economic plight of the Negro in the wake of the national economic crisis of 1837, it noted that not one abolitionist had placed a black man in any position in his business establishment.

In an extensive survey of the strained relations that had emerged between white abolitionists and blacks over the years, James McCune Smith attacked the former for failing to deal adequately with the economic needs of the free Negro. He was critical of Garrison for having played a major role in ending the career of the American Union for the Relief and Improvement of the Colored Race, founded in Boston in 1835 for the purpose of teaching trades to blacks. Because the American Union refused to declare itself for immediate emancipation and favored colonization, Garrison charged that the real purpose of the organization was to hasten the expatriation of free Negroes rather than to improve their economic prospects in this country. He thereafter called upon the black community to have nothing to do with the project. Smith pointed out that the American Union was forced to dissolve within two years because of lack of cooperation from the Negro people, but that during the brief period of its existence, it had begun to train several blacks for skilled positions and to find employment for them. However, because it was viewed as "an Anti-Garrison Society," it could not be allowed to continue. Unfortunately, he noted, it had not been replaced by any "Garrison Society" doing the type of work it had set out to accomplish. He pointed out that the "New England Anti-Slavery Society and its agent in this matter, Wm. Lloyd Garrison, solemnly pledged themselves as men, Christians and abolitionists, to establish a Manual Labor School for colored youth," and that the American Anti-Slavery Society had also endorsed the project; but he went on to complain:

Twenty odd years have elapsed since these pledges were made and published: how have they been fulfilled? Twenty years have elapsed, during which the American Anti-Slavery Society has expended at least half a million of dollars, in agencies, editors' salaries, newspaper publishing, &c., &c., and has controlled two millions of dollars more, in the business relations of its supporters; how many colored youth has this organization or any portion of it, or its supporters, helped to "trades" or to the higher departments of business as clerks, or editors, or merchants? . . .

To be sure, with some of the rich business men who belonged and still belong to the

American Anti-Slavery Society, a colored man did now and then get a place as porter, but never, never was he raised above it, no matter what his talents or acquirements. And if colored men did seek at the hands of abolitionists situations for their well accomplished sons, they were told, as Mr. Robert Purvis, Esq., of Byberry, was told by Mr. Davis, the merchant abolitionist, "No sir; it would injure my business."

Frederick Douglass, who had been rejected for a job as a caulker in New Bedford by an abolitionist shipbuilder on his arrival from slavery on the same grounds raised by "Mr. Davis," wrote bitterly of such antislavery men: "They might employ a colored boy as a porter or packer. But would as soon as put a hod-carrier to the clerk's desk as a colored boy, regardless of the black's qualifications."

GROWING TENSIONS

To the general feeling that too many of their "white friends" were far from free of the racial prejudice that permeated American society, blacks grew increasingly alarmed by the addition to the abolitionist ranks of white men and women who joined the cause as a result of the civil rights controversy. While they welcomed any growth in the ranks of the antislavery movement, they were concerned that those who joined because slavery was destroying the civil rights of white Americans would be either indifferent or hostile to implementing one of the announced purposes of the movement: the elevation of the free Negro. In their concern over the impact of slavery in the South on white Americans, "they half overlooked slavery in the North," one black editor wrote in 1839. These were the kind of abolitionists, said Nathaniel Paul, who hated slavery, "especially that which is 1,000 or 1,500 miles off," but who hated even more "a man who wears a colored skin." Or, as Samuel Ringgold Ward put it, they were the kind of abolitionists who "love the colored man at a distance."

The issue came to a head at the 1837 convention of the New York Anti-Slavery Society. Theodore Weld welcomed the fact that the ranks of antislavery were being increased as a result of the bitter struggle over civil rights but expressed alarm that, as a result of the influx of the new recruits, there were now "constitutions of abolition societies, where nothing was said about the improvement of the man of color! They have overlooked the giant sin of prejudice. They have passed by this foul monster, which is at once the parent and offspring of slavery."

But it was the Reverend Theodore S. Wright, pastor of the First Presbyterian Church in New York City and a leading black abolitionist, who hit out most sharply on this issue in two dramatic speeches. In the first, he attacked racist thinking present within the antislavery movement and questioned whether new recruits who had recently entered the ranks, could really be called abolitionists:

Three years ago, when a man professed to be an Abolitionists we knew where he was. He was an individual who recognized the identity of the human family. Now a man may call himself an Abolitionist and we know not where to find him. Your tests are taken away. . . . Why, sir, unless men come out and take their stand on the principle of recognizing man as man, I tremble for the ark, and I fear our society will become like the expatriation society—everybody an Abolitionist. These points which have lain in the dark must be brought out to view. The identity of the human family, the principle of recognizing all men as brethren—that is the doctrine, that is the point which touches the quick of the community. It is an easy thing to ask about the vileness of slavery at the South, but to call the dark man a brother, heartily to embrace the doctrine advanced in the second article of the Constitution, to treat all men according to their moral worth, to treat the man of color in all circumstances as a man and brother—that is the test.

Wright's second speech followed the introduction of a resolution declaring that prejudice against colored people was "nefarious and wicked and should be practically reprobated and discountenanced." "Prejudice must be killed," Wright asserted, speaking in favor of the resolution (which was passed), "or slavery will never be abolished." Abolitionists had to "annihilate in their own bosom the cord of caste." This would be the best answer to the slaveholder who said: "Where is your love for the colored man who is crushed at your feet? Talking to us about emancipating our slaves when you are enslaving them by your feelings, and doing more violence to them by your prejudice, than we are to our slaves by our treatment." Only "by treating man as man, the colored man as a man, according to his worth," could the antislavery movement effectively respond.

THE SPLIT BETWEEN DOUGLASS AND THE GARRISONIANS: I

Given the complexities of the relationship between whites and blacks in the antislavery movement, it was inevitable that abolitionists of different colors should have at times had sharply differing opinions. Although black abolitionists agreed with the general principles of white antislavery societies, they disagreed with their white contemporaries on the question of the needs of the Negro people. For example, they were far less fond of moral abstractions than white abolitionists. Or, as Benjamin Quarles writes: "Their interest was more personal. A Negro could scarcely muster enough detachment to live in the realms of pure principle, the world being too much with him."

The Garrisonians were on the lookout for deviations by blacks who spoke or wrote for the cause. Although William Wells Brown stated his sympathy for Garrisonian abolitionism in his lectures, the Garrisonians had doubts about him. When Brown left for England in 1849, Samuel J. May, Jr., wrote to a British friend: "He is a good fellow, of very fair abilities, and has been quite true to the cause. But he likes to make popular and taking speeches, and keeps a careful eye upon his own benefit. The Anti-Slavery cause has been everything to him, in point of elevating and educating him; and giving him a respectable position, etc. He owes much to it and he ought to be true to it.''

It seems incredible that an abolitionist leader would write in such condescending terms about a man who had made his own way from slavery, had singlehandedly assisted many fugitives in achieving freedom as a conductor on the Underground Railroad, and was already proving himself to be an outstanding orator and writer. But this attitude was not uncommon, and it helps to explain much about the famous split between Frederick Douglass and the Garrisonians.

At first, Douglass' differences with the Garrisonians were not ideological. In the 1840s, Douglass was a faithful Garrisonian and revealed this most clearly in his conflict with the Reverend Henry Highland Garnet. A former slave in New Market, Kent County, Maryland, Garnet escaped in 1824, and after living in New York, entered Oneida Institute and became a Presbyterian minister and lecturer. Garnet was an agent of the American Anti-Slavery Society until 1843, when he delivered a militant speech at the convention of Colored Americans at Buffalo, New York. This speech, entitled ''An Address to the Slaves of the United States,'' was a call to the slaves to rebel:

Brethren, arise, arise! Strike for your lives and liberties. Now is the day and the hour. Let every slave throughout the land do this, and the days of slavery are numbered. You can not be more oppressed than you have been—you cannot suffer greater cruelties than you have already. Rather die freeman than live to be slaves. Remember that you are four millions.

Still under the influence of the Garrisonian principles of nonresistance, nonviolence, and moral suasion, Douglass took issue with Garnet. He observed that there was ''too much physical force both in the address and remarks of Garnet; that the address, could it reach the slaves, and the advice . . . be followed, while it might not lead the slaves to rise in insurrection, for liberty, would nevertheless, and necessarily be the occasion for insurrection.'' And that, Douglass concluded, was what he wished ''in no way to have any agency in hurrying about and what we were called to avoid.''

For several days, the convention debated Garnet's proposal, and finally, by the narrow majority of one vote, eighteen in favor and nineteen against, Douglass' position was sustained.

Later in the convention, Douglass proposed a plan of moral suasion to induce the slaveowners to release their slaves from bondage. Garnet objected bitterly to reliance on such tactics and asked that the plan be rejected. Douglass resumed the floor in defense of his report and won a majority vote in the final count. But the convention broke with Garrisonianism when it resolved to support the Liberty party. Douglass, Charles Lenox Remond, and William Wells Brown were among the seven dissenters.

After the 1843 convention, Garnet no longer served as an agent of the American Anti-Slavery Society, but Douglass continued speaking in that capacity in behalf of Garrisonian doctrines. Still, beneath the surface, a conflict was beginning to simmer. In his second autobiography, *My Bondage and My Freedom,* published in 1855, Douglass claimed that he had received patronizing advice from the Garrisonians, including "my then reverend friend, William Lloyd Garrison," never to forget that he was an escaped slave and that if he were to be an effective and believable black antislavery spokesman, he should appear less learned, "have a little of the plantation manner of speech than not," expose his whip-scarred back, and confine his speeches to personal experiences. "Give us the facts," Douglass quotes John A. Collins as telling him, "we will take care of the philosophy!" Whether Douglass was exaggerating (as John W. Blassingame believes), he did move beyond just telling the story of his slave experiences and was soon discussing the "progress of the cause." In 1845, during his English tour, it became clear that his independent attitude was worrying a number of Garrisonians. Maria Weston Chapman, leader of the Boston Female Anti-Slavery Society and editor of its gift book, *The Liberty Bell,* wrote to Richard D. Webb warning the Irish abolitionist to keep an eye on Douglass and his companion, the white abolitionist Robert Buffum, lest they be won over by the anti-Garrisonian wing of the British antislavery movement. Chapman, it seemed, was not too concerned about Buffum, who was wealthy, but was worried that Douglass "might be bought up by the London committee." When he was shown the letter, Douglass was furious at the lack of faith in his integrity and sent a sharp rebuke to Mrs. Chapman, assuring her that he was still a Garrisonian but pointing out in clear and decisive language that he would not tolerate any efforts to supervise and control his activities. "If you wish to drive me from the Anti-Slavery Society," he wrote, "put me under overseership and the work is done. Set some one to watch over me for evil and let them be so simple minded as to inform me of their office, and the last blow is struck."

While in Edinburgh, Douglass was invited to speak at a mammoth public meeting to be arranged in London under the auspices of the British and Foreign Anti-Slavery Society, which had broken away from the Garrisonians. Even though he was well aware that his friends in America would look with disfavor upon his presence at the meeting, Douglass believed that it was his duty to "speak in any meeting where freedom of speech is allowed and where I may do anything toward exposing the bloody system of slavery." He therefore accepted the invitation, making it clear that his presence did not signify an endorsement of the doctrines of the organization. Nevertheless, soon afterward, the pro-Garrison *National Anti-Slavery Standard,* the journalistic organ of the American Anti-Slavery Society, attacked Douglass for sitting in on the meeting.

The split between Douglass and the Garrisonians intensified as a result of the purchase of Douglass' freedom by his English friends late in 1846. While Garrison supported the move and even "gladly contributed" his "mite" to the purchase fund, many of his followers accused Douglass of having violated a cardinal principle of the antislavery creed. They charged that the purchase was a recognition of the "right to traffic in human beings." They also regarded it as "impolitic and inexpedient" because by the ransom, Douglass had "lost much of that moral power which he possessed, as the representative of the three millions of his countrymen in chains, taking, as he did, his life in hands, appearing, wherever he appeared, with all the liabilities which the law laid upon him to be returned to stripes, torture and death."

The controversy raged for more than three months in the columns of the *Liberator* and other antislavery journals. In a reply to Henry C. Wright, who had urged him to repudiate the transaction and had added that if he refused, Wright would never write to him again, Douglass stressed the practical importance of the purchase, called Wright's attention to the fact that as a fugitive slave, he could be seized by his master and returned to slavery the moment he set foot in the United States, and assured him that his changed status would not weaken the bonds that connected him with the slaves. "I shall be Frederick Douglass still," he concluded, "once a slave still. I shall neither be made to forget nor cease to feel the wrongs of my enslaved fellow-countrymen. My knowledge of slavery will be the same and my hatred of it will be the same." But his masterly reply convinced few of the white critics of the transaction, who evidently preferred Douglass as a slave to a man—an attitude that Douglass believed smacked at best of paternalism and at worst of racism.

THE SPLIT BETWEEN DOUGLASS AND THE GARRISONIANS: II

When Douglass returned from abroad in April 1847, he was not only a free man but one with a firmly established international reputation as the outstanding spokesman for black people and as an important advocate of the antislavery movement. The independence he had already displayed in his relationship with the white Garrisonians, and the annoyance this had produced in them, were bound to continue and increase.

When he returned to America, Douglass brought with him £500 ($2,175) from his British friends with which to purchase a printing press to start his own newspaper. Garrison and other Garrisonians advised against such a publication on the ground that there were already many antislavery papers (even several edited by Negroes), that it was doubtful that enough subscribers could be found to sustain it, and that Douglass' greatest talent lay in lecturing, not editing. Garrison pleaded with Douglass to reject the editorial chair and continue his work on the platform:

With such powers of oratory, and so few lecturers in the field where so many are needed, it seems to us as clear as the noon-day sun, that it would be no gain but rather a loss, to the anti-slavery cause, to have him withdrawn to any considerable extent from the work of popular agitation, by assuming the cares, drudgery and perplexities of a publishing life. It is quite impracticable to combine the editor with the lecturer, without either causing the paper to be more or less neglected, or the sphere of lecturing to be severely circumscribed.

Douglass could have replied (as did some abolitionists critical of Garrison's reasoning) that the editor of the *Liberator* seemed to be capable of combining lecturing and editorial duties, but he was unwilling to offend Garrison, his mentor, and abandoned his plan. In the *Liberator* on July 9, 1847, it was announced that Douglass had decided against publishing his own paper. Garrison was relieved. The truth is that he had good reason to be concerned over the fact that the foremost Negro in the North was preparing to publish his own paper, since the bulk of the *Liberator*'s readers were black and Garrison could ill afford to lose many of them. While he admitted that blacks were "poor and trodden down" and could not rise up "without having a press to lift up its voice in their behalf," he maintained that they already had that voice in the *Liberator*. Either Garrison had never read or was little impressed by the opening statement of *Freedom's Journal,* in which the editors explained the reason for the launching of the first black newspaper in these words: "We wish to plead our own cause. Too long have others spoken for us."

But Douglass, agonizing over his decision, reached the conclusion that blacks did need another journalistic voice. ("The man who suffers the wrong is the one who must speak out," was a sentence bound to appear in nearly all of Douglass' speeches.) While lecturing with Garrison in Cleveland in September 1847, he made his final decision and decided to "combine the editor with the lecturer." Douglass moved to Rochester, New York, and the first issue of the *North Star* appeared on December 3, 1847, its masthead proclaiming the slogan: "Right is of no Sex—Truth is of no Color—God is the Father of us all, and we are all Brethren." The role of the paper was to be that of a "terror to evil doers," and while it would be "mainly Anti-Slavery," it would also devote itself to advancing the welfare of the "nominally free" men and women of color, and its columns would be "freely opened to the candid and decorous discussion of all measures and topics of a moral and humane character, which may serve to enlighten, improve and elevate mankind." With Martin R. Delany as coeditor for the first two years, the publication continued for seventeen years—although under different names (*Frederick Douglass' Paper* and *Douglass' Monthly*)—making it the longest-lasting black paper published in the United States before the Civil War.

Douglass' decision to reject Garrison's advice reflected the growing rift between the two men. Garrison was considerably angered, and the fact that the black editor succeeded in putting out a paper of high quality and in keeping it alive further irritated him. However, in the *Liberator* of January 28, 1848, Garrison praised the first issues of the *North Star* and wished it success, indicating that he had lost some of his resentment. Other Garrisonians, however, neither welcomed the new arrival on the antislavery journalistic front nor wished it success. Once again, they complained, Douglass had acted independently. "Confidentially," wrote Abby Kelly Foster, a confirmed Garrisonian, to Maria Weston Chapman, "*I have always feared him.*" It was a sentiment Chapman understood very well and with which she agreed.

Douglass and Garrison continued to share the same platform at the annual meetings of the American Anti-Slavery Society, but their courteous references to each other lacked the old warmth. Within a few years, this strained relationship turned into bitter antagonism, and the antislavery press, much to the dismay of its subscribers and to the delight of its enemies, was treated to a unique spectacle as the participants in the controversy hurled charges and countercharges against each other. Personal antagonisms, often of the pettiest character, became so deeply intertwined with ideological issues that it became virtually impossible to separate them. Yet at this point, the conflict flowed from a sharp difference of opinion over questions of vital importance to the antislavery movement.

During the first years of his work as an abolitionist, Douglass had accepted all of the doctrines of the Garrison school. In his speeches, letters, and early editorials in the *North Star,* he reiterated his belief that the Constitution was wholly a proslavery document; he called for the destruction of the American Union, reaffirmed his opposition to the formation of antislavery political parties, and asserted his conviction that moral suasion was the major instrumentality for ending slavery. "I am willing at all times to be known as a Garrisonian Abolitionist," he wrote on September 4, 1849.

But as he moved outside the orbit of the Massachusetts abolitionists and came into contact with antislavery men who differed with the Garrisonian school, Douglass began, for the first time, to examine his beliefs critically. After considerable study and extensive reading in law, political philosophy, and American government, he concluded that there were serious flaws in the Garrisonian doctrines. Gradually he formulated a new antislavery creed.

First came a weakening of Douglass faith in the Garrisonian principle of nonresistance. To be sure, Douglass had never been a thoroughgoing believer in this doctrine. In a letter written late in his life and dated January 17, 1893, he explained his views as follows: "I was a Non-Resistant til I got to fighting with a mob at Pendleton, Ind. in 1843 . . . I fell never to rise again, and yet I cannot feel I did wrong." Still, Douglass did endorse the nonviolence principle in the constitution of the American Anti-Slavery Society, which pledged that its members would never "countenance the oppressed in vindicating their rights by resorting to physical force." Moreover, he opposed Garnet's call for mass violent uprisings among the slaves, and after 1843 he continued his efforts to persuade fellow black abolitionists to refrain from such encouragement. As late as October 1847, he was still maintaining that any action by a slave to "take vengeance on his guilty master" would be "*folly* and *suicidal* in the extreme."

It was John Brown who led Douglass to doubt the value of relying mainly on moral suasion and caused him to question seriously the Garrisonian concept that slavery could be ended by peaceful persuasion. In the *North Star* of February 11,

1848, Douglass wrote of having a "private interview" with Brown in Springfield, Massachusetts. He said that Brown, "though a white gentleman, is in sympathy a black man, and as deeply interested in our cause, as though his own soul had been pierced with the iron of slavery." Douglass did not reveal the nature of the interview, merely reporting Brown's joy at the appearance of men "possessing the energy of head and heart to demand freedom for their whole people," the result of which "must be the downfall of slavery." Years later, he filled in the details. After dinner at Brown's simple home, his host expounded his views on slavery. He not only condemned the institution but added that the slaveholders "had forfeited their right to live, that the slaves had the right to gain liberty in any way they could." Moral suasion, he insisted, could never liberate the slaves, nor could political action alone abolish the system. Brown outlined a plan to set up five bands of armed men in the Allegheny Mountains who could effect the escape of large numbers of slaves.

Douglass thought that Brown's plan had "much to commend it," but he was still convinced that moral suasion would succeed in converting the entire nation, including the slaveholders, to the antislavery position. Nevertheless, Brown's belief that slavery was actually a state of war profoundly impressed him. "My utterances," Douglass wrote later, "became more tinged by the color of this man's strong impressions." A year after his visit, he was echoing Brown's language, writing editorially that slaveholders had "no rights more than any other thief or pirate. They have forfeited even the right to live, and if the slave should put every one of them to the sword tomorrow, who dare pronounce the penalty disproportionate to the crime, or say that the criminals deserved less than death at the hands of their long-abused chattels?" In June 1849, he astonished a Boston antislavery audience in Fanueil Hall with the announcement: "I should welcome the intelligence tomorrow, should it come, that the slaves had risen in the South, and that the sable arms which had been engaged in beautifying and adorning the South, were engaged in spreading death and devastation."

This still did not mean that Douglass had entirely abandoned his faith in moral suasion; indeed, two months later, he issued the following disclaimer: "It is one thing to assert the right of a slave to gain his freedom by force, and another thing to advocate force as the only means of abolishing slavery. We . . . assert the former . . . but . . . deny the latter. . . . We contend that the only well-grounded hope of the slave for emancipation is in the operation of moral hope."

But step by step, Douglass was abandoning his belief in the effectiveness of moral persuasion and was coming to accept violence as a useful tool in the effort to abolish slavery. In 1856, he wrote that while it was still necessary to use "persuasion and argument" and every other means that promised to destroy slavery "peacefully," he was convinced that "its peaceful annihilation is almost hopeless." Four years later, he no longer had any doubts. "I have little hope of the freedom of the slave by peaceful means," he wrote on June 29, 1860.

As Douglass abandoned his sole reliance on moral power for the overthrow of slavery, he was forced to reexamine his attitude toward political action. Like all other abolitionists under the influence of the Garrisonian wing of antislavery thought, he would have nothing to do with a government and a Constitution framed and administered by men who "were and have been until now, little better than a band of pirates." Like them, too, he believed that until the government and the Constitution were replaced by institutions that would "better answer the ends of justice," no true friend of liberty in the United States could either vote or hold office.

The key to Douglass' antipolitical views lay in his interpretation of the Constitution "as a most foul and bloody conspiracy against the rights of three millions of enslaved and imbruted men." As a former slave and a black abolitionist lecturer who had suffered years of being pelted, harassed, and spit upon by mobs, he was only too ready to accept the Garrisonian doctrine that the Constitution was "a Covenant with death and an agreement with hell." By swearing to uphold the American Constitution and the American Union, the people of the North had sworn before God that the slave would be kept a slave. As long as they accepted the Constitution and its compromises in favor of the slaveholders, they were responsible for the existence of slavery in the United States and must share the guilt for that great crime.

Operating in central New York State, where he published his paper, Douglass came among men who adhered to an antislavery constitutional interpretation, and he was constantly being called upon to justify his view that the Constitution was a proslavery document. This led him to study the writings of Gerrit Smith and William Goodell, both of whom held to an antislavery interpretation. Goodell based his constitutional argument on numerous provisions of the Constitution. In addition to the due-process clause of the Fifth Amendment, he cited the guarantee clause of the Constitution, which provided for a republican form of government for all states and which he considered inconsistent with slavery. Since the Constitution did not qualify its provisions with the word *white,* it obviously applied to all persons regardless of color. In addition, Goodell argued, the commerce clause of the Constitution gave Congress the right to determine what was property and to prohibit the slave trade among the states. Finally, Goodell argued that the Declaration of Independence was a part of the nation's constitutional law and that slavery was therefore prohibited by its equality clause.

Through these readings and discussions with Goodell and Gerrit Smith, Douglass became convinced that the Constitution was, by its avowed purpose, antislavery and that slavery neither was nor could become legalized; it was therefore the duty of the federal government to eradicate it. Political action to secure that end was both warranted and necessary.

Step by step, Douglass also arrived at the conclusion that there was no need to dissolve the Union. He saw clearly that disunion would only isolate the slaves and leave them at the mercy of their masters. For the North to secede, as the Garrisonians advocated, would relieve it of its share of responsibility for slavery and deny the slaves their most important allies. For the Garrisonian slogan, "No union with slaveholders,'' Douglass substituted the motto, "No union with slaveholding.''

While Douglass did not relinquish his belief in the value of moral suasion as an antislavery tactic, he had arrived at the conclusion that it was the duty of everyone in the movement to pursue any course that would bring terror to the slaveholders. This change in Douglass' antislavery creed had been developing over a number of years, but it did not become public until the 1851 meeting of the American Anti-Slavery Society. There Douglass shocked the Garrisonians by announcing publicly that he no longer adhered to the view that the Constitution was proslavery or that political action was incompatible with pure antislavery principles. Garrison immediately reacted by exclaiming that "there is roguery somewhere," and he moved to have the *North Star* stricken from the list of newspapers that merited the support of antislavery men and women. This was promptly carried into effect by the convention.

Douglass was now a heretic. In vain, he denied that he had become a renegade. "We have got to regard Douglass as an enemy, for he is an enemy," a loyal Garrisonian wrote in 1852. Garrison agreed and refused to attend any gathering if he knew Douglass would be present.

Although the formal break between Douglass and the Garrisonians occurred in 1851, the warfare continued, with verbal hostilities replacing issues as the heart of the controversy. They centered largely around the charge that Douglass had sold out his principles for financial and other support from the political abolitionists, headed by Gerrit Smith, and around Douglass' relationship with Julia Griffiths, the white woman who had come from England to help him publish his paper and had become his able assistant and secretary while living in the same house with his wife, Anna Murray Douglass, and their children. Garrison and his followers charged that Griffiths had caused and was continuing to cause discord in the Douglass household. Douglass denied this, but once the personal attacks began, the die was cast. The split between Douglass and Garrison was now complete and irrevocable.

The breach in the relationship between Douglass and the Garrisonians illustrates the complexity of the relations between blacks and whites in the antislavery movement. The basic reasons for the split are not difficult to understand. Garrisonian white paternalism during Douglass' emergence as an antislavery spokesman, Garrisonian hostility to his assertion of independence, and Garrisonian unwillingness to countenance differences in ideas and strategy—all had combined to make the conflict inevitable. Once the side issues and personal recriminations are disposed of, the basic fact remains that however much the Garrisonians protested that their hostility did not stem from Douglass' conversion to new antislavery principles, their words revealed how bitterly they resented his independent thinking as to what constituted the best policies for the movement. The effort to prove that Douglass had sold out to the political abolitionists was merely a manifestation of this resentment. Fundamentally, Douglass' differences with the Garrisonians came about after a careful study on his part of every facet of the antislavery movement. But to men under the influence of white paternalism, the only explanation that made sense was that Douglass had become the puppet of the anti-Garrisonians. If all Douglass had been influenced by was to advance his own interests, he could, as he pointed out, have taken advantage of many opportunities to do so. It would have been much easier for him to have remained with the Garrisonians as an antislavery lecturer than to move to a new community, start a new career, and become involved in the struggle to publish a new newspaper. But Douglass believed that the most important contribution he could make was to demonstrate that the Negro people were active participants in the battle, had their own spokesmen, and were not simply passive bystanders watching the white humanitarians relieve them of their burdens. For all their sincerity and goodwill, what Garrison and his closest associates resented most was this emphasis on the important contribution that the Negro himself should make through his own independent efforts—that and the fact that they were convinced that Douglass was ungrateful. Years later, Garrison's son, recalling the controversy between his father and the black leader, spoke of "Mr. Douglass's animus toward those to whom he owed everything but his native talent for oratory." It was this attitude on the part of Garrison and many of his associates that had much to do with provoking the controversy.

Beriah Green, the Presbyterian minister and abolitionist, advised all Northern people, including those abolitionists who reflected American society's prejudices, to "act as if you felt that you were bound with those who are in bonds; as if their cause was all your own; as if every blow that cuts their flesh lacerated yours." But Frederick Douglass knew that "Facts are Facts. White is not Black, and Black is not White. There is neither good sense nor common honesty in trying to forget this distinction." Hence, even after his bitter feud with the Garrisonians, he was not surprised by the ambivalence among white abolitionists and adopted an understanding attitude toward it. "It is not easy," he wrote in *Frederick Douglass' Paper* of February 17, 1854, "for any white abolitionist to stand with, and to share the bitter cup commended to the lips of our outcast race. The wonder is that any are found to be able to stand this trial of their anti-slavery faith. To do this, the heart must be strong, the eye single, and the whole body full of light."

Yet the truth is that there were not only "any," but many. White abolitionists as a whole were far ahead of the rest of their generation in their willingness to combat discrimination. In an era when virulent antipathy to blacks was endemic in American society and at a time when their own actions often provoked violent opposition, these men and women steadfastly kept up their attacks on prejudice and sought to educate the people on the connections between the sin of slaveholding and "Negrophobia." Many even learned to conquer their own hesitations on the issue. In 1834, the American Anti-Slavery Society publicly disassociated itself from the advocacy of social relationship between whites and blacks. By 1840, however, it was arranging for delegates, black and white, to dine together during the annual meeting in New York, defying a mob that threatened to make trouble over this first integrated meal. And by the end of the decade, such interracial meals were a feature of the annual meetings of both the American Anti-Slavery Society and the American and Foreign Anti-Slavery Society.

Yet the composite picture is deeply complex, tinged with hesitancy and confusion about the relationship with blacks in the antislavery movement, and even with elements of "colorphobia," with the result that even as blacks were fighting their enemies in the South, they ran into the problem of racism among their white friends in the North. Blacks came to see that one of their chief tasks in the antislavery movement was to make sure that white abolitionists never forgot the immediate practical needs of the persecuted "free people of color." If the goal of abolitionism was to teach the white community that a society based on racial justice and brotherly love was possible, white abolitionists would have to be pressured to eliminate the poison of racism from their own bosoms and to act consistently with their stated beliefs. Nor was this a matter that involved only the well-being of the free blacks, for, as Samuel Cornish reminded the white abolitionists, until they judged blacks "as they do other men," they could never succeed in breaking the chains of the slaves. Nor could they expect to enjoy the unqualified support of the black community. The editor of the *Northern Star and Freeman's Advocate,* a black weekly, put it concisely: "Until abolitionists eradicate prejudice from their own hearts, they can never receive the unwavering confidence of the people of color."

Some blacks, influenced by Martin R. Delany, despaired of ever seeing the day when white abolitionists would succeed in eradicating prejudice in their ranks and therefore argued against any further cooperation with whites. They called upon blacks to "act for themselves" in all-black antislavery societies. But the majority agreed with Frederick Douglass that such a policy was suicidal. They were convinced that while all-black action was both fruitful and necessary in such areas as religion, fraternal organizations, and self-improvement societies, by itself it possessed neither the numbers nor the influence to exert the power needed to end slavery. Therefore, to reject cooperation with whites in the antislavery movement would remove from that movement a vital element.

Although the relationship between blacks and their white allies in the antislavery movement had both sweet and bitter elements, it was their joint action that contributed to the emergence of a force in the North powerful enough to bring an end to the "peculiar institution" in the South. Blacks understood that even though the whites in the movement had failed in many ways to conduct a consistent and persistent battle against racism as well as slavery, it was unrealistic to expect more from a great number of them. They were, after all, the products of more than two centuries of racist tradition. Still, they stood far ahead of the others produced by that racist society. In March 1860, the militant black abolitionist and fighter for black equality, Dr. John S. Rock, declared:

The only class who avow themselves openly as the friends of the black man are the Abolitionists; and it would be well for the colored people to remember the fact. . . . I place no one before the leading Abolitionists in this country—they who have spoken for the dumb, and who have braved the storms in their fury. . . . It is the Anti-Slavery men and women, who have made our cause a holy thing. I always feel proud of my community, after an interview with anyone of them.

On June 22, 1894, six months before his death, speaking at the commencement of the Baltimore Colored High School, Douglass recounted the difficulties he and other black abolitionists had undergone in seeking to be recognized as equals with whites in the antislavery movement and how blacks had had to combat prejudice against color in the ranks of white abolitionists. But he concluded:

We should never forget that the ablest and most eloquent voices ever raised in behalf of the black man's cause were the voices of white men. Not for race, not for color, but for man and manhood, they labored, fought, and died. Away, then, with the nonsense that a man must be black to be true to the rights of black men.

25

Blacks and Antislavery Political Parties, 1840–1848

FORMATION OF THE LIBERTY PARTY

By 1840, many abolitionists had come to believe that moral suasion alone was ineffective. They turned, some optimistically, many reluctantly, to antislavery politics. Some of the abolitionists who later became leaders in political action were initially hesitant. Thus, James G. Birney wrote in the *Philanthropist* in 1838: "We are utterly opposed to every measure that looks toward a separate political organization. . . . We should as much regret to see abolitionists drawing off from the parties to which they belong as we should to see them leaving the churches of which they are members to build up a separate anti-slavery church." Two years later, Birney was the presidential candidate of the Liberty party. Gerrit Smith, the Liberty party candidate for governor of New York in 1848, also had written in 1838 that the sole job of the abolitionists was to "publish the truth about slavery." Later that year, however, Smith associated himself with Myron Holley, who already had a long career in public affairs, and Alvin Stewart, a leading New York lawyer, in initiating what they saw as a strategy to achieve a political balance of power.

In order to determine which candidates abolitionists should support at the polls, Smith agreed to ask a series of questions of New York political leaders. The questions, published in the *Emancipator* of October 30, 1838, were:

Are you in favor of granting trial by jury to persons in New York claimed as fugitive slaves?

Do you favor the removal of all distinctions which are "founded solely on complexion" in the constitutional rights of citizens of New York?

Do you favor repeal of the law which now makes it possible for persons to bring slaves into New York and hold them for not more than nine months?

Outside of New York, abolitionists were asking similar questions. In 1839, Arthur Livermore Porter, a leading Michigan abolitionist, was delegated to ask the following questions of office seekers in his state:

Are you in favor of removing from our State Constitution the article which makes color a condition of the right of the suffrage . . . ?

Are you in favor of securing to *all* persons, irrespective of color, the right of trial by jury in all questions?

Not surprisingly, abolitionists were dissatisfied with the evasive answers they usually received from politicians. In addition to desiring to keep the slavery issue out of politics in order to reduce any sectional conflict, all of the major party candidates refused to identify themselves openly with a pro-Negro, abolitionist position. Any gains an office seeker might achieve by satisfying the abolitionists were likely to be more than offset by the losses resulting from antagonizing the many foes of both abolitionism and equality for blacks.

By late 1839, a number of abolitionists were forced to admit that the questioning technique was a failure and called for the nomination of abolitionist candidates independent of the major parties. In October 1839, Myron Holley introduced a resolution that was passed at the Monroe County (New York) Anti-Slavery Convention calling for the creation of an abolitionist party. He was joined by others, and the group of New York antislavery men who recognized that the tactics of moral suasion and of questioning the candidates of the major parties had failed to produce significant results, founded the Liberty party late in 1839. In its first address, written by Alvin Stewart, the new party announced itself as an abolitionist party, denounced slavery, and demanded its immediate eradication as a crime against both man and God. In April 1840, at an organizational meeting in Albany, New York, the Liberty party nominated James G. Birney and Thomas Earle for president and vice-president. The party pledged itself not only to the "overthrow of slavery" within the limits of national jurisdiction but also to the "restoration of equality of rights among men, in every state where the party exists or may exist." It also announced the purpose of its members: "whether as private citizens or as public functionaries sworn to support the Constitution of the United States, to regard and to treat the third clause of the fourth article of that instrument [relating to the return of fugitive slaves] whenever applied to the case of a fugitive slave as utterly null and void, and consequently as forming no part of the Constitution of the United States, whenever we are called upon or sworn to support it."

In accepting the nomination, Birney declared that one of his objectives would be to remove the national government from the hands of the slave power. He also announced that "the grant of the Elective Franchise to the colored people" was a primary goal of the Liberty party.

ELECTION OF 1840

"I was the first colored man that ever attached his name to that party," Henry Highland Garnet declared in 1843, in defending his position as a Liberty party man. Actually he was not the first, for as late as May 6, 1840, Garnet was a committee member of the Pittsburgh and Allegheny Anti-Slavery societies, which "heartily disapproved" of a third political party. These societies voted to ignore the Liberty party and to encourage their members to refrain from active participation in it.

The earliest blacks to rally to the new party were those in Albany, New York, where the Liberty party convention had been held. Meeting at the Baptist church in that city that same month, they called upon all black voters to support Birney and Earle in the coming election. The Albany blacks urged Negroes throughout the North to be politically active in order to "hasten the consummation of our disenthralment from partial and actual bondage."

But even though the Liberty party had come out unequivocally for the overthrow of slavery and for "equal rights for all," blacks were divided over whether to support its candidates. Very few of Boston's Negroes joined the new party, the majority choosing to remain with the Garrisonians. As Thomas Cole, a leader of the Boston black community, explained: "Political parties of the present day give no encouragement to the cause of emancipation, morality, and religion. . . . Political parties, as they now exist, are undoubtedly hostile to the interest of the slaves and the nominally free." Even though the Liberty men had adopted a far-reaching platform, Cole was not impressed: "I firmly believe the majority of politicians would sacrifice their principles rather than their popularity."

Even in New York, where Garrisonian influence was much weaker among blacks, some blacks were ambivalent toward the Liberty party. Charles B. Ray, editor of the *Colored American,* which was soon to support the new party enthusiastically, was at first indecisive: "We go for thorough-going political action; but whether an independent general ticket will best meet the circumstances of the case now, we have many reasons for and many against." Thomas Van Rensselaer was more decisive; he vehemently opposed the Liberty party. Van Rensselaer resented the fact that the party had refused to place a Negro on its ticket where he could plead the cause of his people. He conceded that it would be regarded by many as "contrary to the usages of civilized society to place a colored man on a ticket with a white man." But he reminded the Liberty party there were about 40,000 blacks in New York State while there were only about "5,000 professed [white] abolitionists," and yet "not a single colored man's voice is to be heard in this new anti-slavery legislature." Van Rensselaer, therefore, urged his brethren in New York not to lend their support to the Liberty party.

But as the campaign proceeded, more and more blacks came out in support of the party. For one thing, Ray abandoned his misgivings and strongly supported the new party. To blacks who asked, "For Whom Shall We Vote," Ray urged them to vote for the Liberty ticket. He based his stand, first, on the conviction that the party's candidates were "men of unimpeachable integrity, of sound mind and morals, devoted to *all the interests* of their country, and especially to the paramount interest of Liberty and equal rights to all." His second reason was that neither of the candidates of the major parties—Martin Van Buren, the Democratic nominee, or William Henry Harrison, the Whig candidate—was acceptable to blacks. How could any black vote for Van Buren, who, in the interest of counteracting sectional antagonisms, had yielded to the slaveowners on every issue, had helped rally Northern support for such proslavery measures as the ban on abolitionist literature in Southern mails and the gag rule, and had publicly pledged to veto any bill to abolish slavery in the District of Columbia? Ray, moreover, could not forgive Van Buren because, as a delegate to the New York Constitutional Convention of 1821, he had hedged on the question of equal suffrage for blacks.

The Whig party was not much better, even though it did include a number of influential leaders like William H. Seward and Horace Greeley in New York, who opposed slavery and favored some extension of the elective franchise to the Negro. But how could any black vote for William Henry Harrison, whose only response to contemporary issues was to boast about his record in the War of 1812?

Ray's opinions were influential because the *Colored American* carried considerable weight in the black communities of the North outside of Boston. (Benjamin Quarles believes that the paper's support for the new party "generally furnished an accurate barometer of Negro thought.") But this influence did little to rally white support, and most blacks were disfranchised anyway. Only about 7,100 votes were cast for the Liberty party candidates. The Garrisonians were overjoyed by the poor electoral returns for the antislavery party and predicted that it would not be long before "all who are sincerely attached to the cause of human freedom will return to the primitive faith."

But the size of the Liberty party vote was no barometer of its significance. Like the gag rule, the emergence of an abolitionist party had injected slavery into the political life of the North. Not a few Americans who had voted for the major party candidates were disgusted by the election because these parties had neglected the slavery issue, and they decided to identify themselves with the party of abolition.

POSTELECTION DEVELOPMENTS

After the 1840 election, the Liberty party continued to stimulate considerable discussion within the black communities of the North, and three points of view emerged. One insisted that blacks should remain aloof from all parties; the second maintained that blacks should continue to support the Liberty party; and the third considered it dangerous for blacks to identify themselves too closely with any single party. But the fact that the majority viewpoint was moving toward support for the Liberty party was clearly illustrated at the National Convention of Colored Citizens, held in Buffalo, New York, in mid-August 1843 where the subject of the Liberty party came up for debate. One resolution declared that the convention delegates "hail with pleasure news of the organization of the Freeman's Party, based upon the great principles contained in the Declaration of Independence, that all men are created equal, and that we cheerfully enroll ourselves under its broad banner." The opposition, led by Frederick Douglass, still at that time a Garrisonian, maintained that the Freeman's party was merely the Liberty party by another name, that all political parties were corrupt, and that real enemies of slavery neither believed in nor would enroll themselves in such organizations. Henry Highland Garnet admitted that the Freeman's party was really the Liberty party and insisted that the majority of blacks in the North support its principles. After considerable discussion on both sides, the resolution was overwhelmingly adopted.

Adopted, too, was a resolution stating: "That it is the duty of every lover of liberty to vote the Liberty ticket so long as they are consistent to their principles." The Garrisonians among the delegates again objected, but the convention voted them down and went on to recommend that blacks organize Liberty Associations in their respective communities and support "tried friends of liberty" for office. Thus, while Douglass, Remond, William Wells Brown, and a few others remained true to their Garrisonian principles, the tendency among the majority of blacks outside of Boston was to support the Liberty party.

This trend was strengthened by events at the Liberty party convention in September 1843. Reverend Samuel Ringgold Ward led the convention in prayer, Charles B. Ray served as one of its secretaries, and Henry Highland Garnet was on the committee to nominate officers. This, Charles H. Wesley has noted, "was the first time in American history that Negro citizens were actively in the leadership of a political convention." Garnet also introduced the following resolution: "Resolved, That the Liberty Party has not been organized for any temporary purpose by interested politicians, but has risen from among the people, in consequence of a conviction hourly gaining ground, that no other party in the country represents the true principles of American Liberty or the true spirit of the Constitution of the United States." The resolution was unanimously adopted.

Several papers noted that blacks were present in sizable numbers at the convention and that men like Garnet and Ray had played significant roles in its proceedings. "A large number of colored persons were present," the *Emancipator* noted, and it predicted that their contributions would increase the determination of the Liberty men "to resist more resolutely . . . this national curse."

In the election of 1843, the Liberty party increased its vote in New York to over 16,000, and it appeared that it might well hold the balance of power in that state in the presidential election of 1844. The Liberty party men were making it clear to the Whigs and Democrats that unless the two parties made concessions to antislavery sentiments, they would face defeat at the polls. The leaders of the major parties were quick to get the message, which grew louder and clearer during the ensuing few years—years marked by the annexation of Texas and the Mexican War.

THE ANNEXATION OF TEXAS ISSUE

In Mexico City's Chapultapec Park, a diorama portrays the history of Mexico. A map dated 1819 is followed by one thirty years later, showing Mexico with more than half its national territory of 1819 missing. This land had once comprised an area larger than France and Germany combined and included the present states of Texas, California, New Mexico, Arizona, Nevada, Utah, and parts of Wyoming and Colorado. These had been Mexico's richest farming, cattle-grazing, and fruit-raising lands—lands that bore immense oil and natural gas deposits, as well as incalculable amounts of other natural resources. Fifty five million dollars' worth of gold was extracted from California alone in the ten years after gold was discovered there in 1849. The 1849 map bears the inscription: "The result of robbery by the United States!"

The tragic chain of events underlying this inscription began on January 17, 1821, when Moses Austin, a United States merchant and mine owner, received permission from the Spanish commandant-general of the Eastern Interior Provinces of Mexico to settle three hundred families in Texas. After Austin's death, his son, Stephen Fuller Austin, took over the grant, and in January 1822, he established the first legal settlement of North Americans in Texas. In 1829, Vicente Guerrero, president of the newly independent Mexico, proclaimed the abolition of slavery throughout that country. Local officials immediately petitioned to have Texas exempted from the emancipation decree. Failing that and faced with the necessity of freeing their slaves, the Americans declared their independence from Mexico on March 2, 1836. At the Battle of San Jacinto on April 21, 1836, Texas forces routed the Mexican army and conquered its commanding general, Mexican President Antonio López de Santa Anna.

On March 1, 1837, the United States Senate recognized the "independent political existence" of the Republic of Texas. Its position on slavery was set forth by Stephen F. Austin: "Texas must be a slave country. It is no longer a matter of doubt."

Mexico never recognized this independence but made no serious effort to reconquer Texas. But it did warn the United States that it would not accept its former territory's annexation by the North American republic. Since many Americans did not want to risk war with Mexico and others opposed extending the boundaries of slavery, the question of annexation was put off in 1836—but not abandoned.

Seven years later, in 1843, the question of the annexation of Texas reemerged, but before it became a burning political issue, Stephen Pearl Andrews, a native of Massachusetts who had emigrated to Texas, journeyed to England together with Lewis Tappan to present a plan to the British government which agreed to the proposal that it finance the purchase through the London Anti-Slavery Society. But by the time Andrews returned to Texas, the news of his negotiations in England had become public knowledge, and a proslavery mob drove him out of the Republic of Texas, warning him never to return on the threat of death.

In April 1844, the pro-Southern Tyler administration presented the Senate with a treaty for the annexation of Texas as a slave state. At the same time, Secretary of State Calhoun's letter to the British ambassador, Richard Pakenham, was released, in which Calhoun bluntly based the case for annexation on the need to protect and preserve the institution of slavery.

ELECTION OF 1844

The Liberty party was the first to raise a concerted outcry against the annexation of Texas "as a slaveholders' conspiracy to extend slavery." The new party's platform in the presidential election of 1844 demanded an end to slavery in the District of Columbia and no further expansion of slavery. It declared itself opposed to slavery everywhere as "against natural rights." The party again called for defiance of the Fugitive Slave Law of 1793 and again declared the fugitive slave clause of the Constitution to be null and void. It spoke of free labor, free speech, and the right to petition. In answer to those who feared that a vote for the Liberty party would be thrown away, the party's platform resolved:

That we can never lose our vote, although in ever so small a minority, when cast for the slave's redemption; as each vote for the slave, whether in minority or majority, is a part of that great mass of means which will work out his final deliverance.

That the Whig and Democratic parties always throw away their votes, whether in a majority or minority, and do worse than throw them away, as long as they cast them for binding the slave with fetters, and loading him with chains . . . which these parties have always done, in bowing down to the slaveholding portions of said parties.

Martin Van Buren was generally expected to be the Democratic candidate for president. However, on April 20, 1844, he came out against the annexation of Texas, warning that annexation without Mexican consent inevitably meant war, and opposing the entrance of another slave state into the Union. At one stroke, the years of appeasing the Southern Democrats came to naught, and on the first ballot at the Democratic party convention, Van Buren received only a handful of votes from below the Mason-Dixon line. The Democrats then proceeded to nominate James K. Polk, a Tennessee slaveholder, on a platform calling for immediate annexation of Texas. A few days later, a combination of enraged Van Burenite Democrats and Whigs defeated the Texas treaty in the Senate.

Although Henry Clay, the Whig candidate for president, opposed the annexation of Texas, the Liberty party refused to endorse him because he was a slaveholder, and it continued its campaign to gain votes for James G. Birney, once again its presidential candidate. In this work, Henry Highland Garnet was especially active. Garnet spoke at the Massachusetts State Liberty Party convention in January 1844 and warned black Garrisonians that they were running a great risk in refusing to support the third party, for "if the hope which the Liberty Party held out for speedy and peaceful emancipation of the slaves was taken away, bloody revolution would inevitably follow." But this did not seem to sway the Bostonians. Nor did the fact that the convention officially condemned the decision of the Supreme Court in *Prigg* v. *Pennsylvania* as proslavery and a denial of the fugitive slaves' civil liberties. Special concern was voiced concerning their right of habeas corpus.

At the fifth Annual Convention of the Colored Citizens of the State of New York, held in Schenectady, September 18–20, 1844, the question of endorsing the Liberty party's presidential candidates provoked a debate, with the New York City delegation, led by James McCune Smith and Ulysses S. Vidal, arguing that it would be a mistake for blacks, in their efforts to secure equal suffrage, to antagonize the major parties. Garnet took issue with this position, and Charles B. Ray, in a letter to the convention, emphatically urged support for the Liberty party. But Theodore S. Wright disagreed. While he believed that "the principles upon which the Liberty Party is based" were "just," he did not feel blacks should be identified with one political party. In the end, no specific resolution was adopted endorsing the Liberty party. But since neither of the two major parties was endorsed either, the champions of the abolition party took it as a victory for their cause.

They received no consolation, however, from the State Convention of Colored Citizens of Ohio, held in Columbus in late September 1844. Not only was no resolution adopted endorsing the Liberty party candidate, but in the convention's address, there was an appeal to all citizens, "Whigs, Democats, and Liberty men," to take the lead in eliminating the state's black laws, indicating that there was no special enthusiasm for the third party.

While the Liberty party's vote for James G. Birney of 62,000 in 1844 was less than 3 percent of the total of the votes cast, the party drew enough votes from Clay in crucial states to ensure Polk's victory. In the view of Abraham Lincoln, the Illinois Whig, the Liberty men had made a great mistake in not voting for Clay, even if he was a slaveowner: "If the fruit of electing Mr. Clay would have been to prevent the extension of slavery, could the act of electing have been evil?" Evidently many blacks who voted in the election agreed with Lincoln's position, for Henry Highland Garnet charged later that "for every Birney vote cast by a Negro, five went to the pro-slavery Henry Clay."

WAR WITH MEXICO

Two months before Polk's inauguration as the eleventh president on March 4, 1845, the Senate passed a bill that excluded slavery from any states created from the area of Texas above the Missouri Compromise line of 36° 30′. Even though this area was so small as to be inconsequential, the slaveowners would have none of it. Immediately after Polk took office, the new Congress passed a joint resolution under which the territory "rightfully belonging to the Republic of Texas" was to be set up into a new state called the state of Texas (with slavery), subject to the adjustment by the United States government of "all questions of boundary that may arise with other governments." This amounted to a tacit acknowledgment of the fact that the Republic of Texas might have claimed boundaries that did not rightfully belong to it.

Blacks had opposed the annexation of Texas as soon as the issue arose in 1836. That year, at its first annual meeting, the American Moral Reform Society went on record opposing Texas annexation. A year later, the New York Vigilance Society opened a book at the Broadway Tabernacle at which passersby could sign a petition against the admission of Texas. Blacks were present in large numbers at the Convention of the People of Massachusetts held in Faneuil Hall, January 29–30, 1845, to take action against the proposed annexation and were among the signers of the "Address to the People of the United States," which opposed annexation not only because it was unconstitutional but because it would further spread slavery. In the summer of 1845, booths were set up in Boston's black community to obtain signatures for the "Anti-Slavery Peace Pledge." Signers of the pledge were obliged "not to countenance or aid the United States Government in any war which may be occasioned by the annexation of Texas, or in any other war, foreign or domestic, designed to strengthen or perpetuate slavery."

Texas was formally annexed in December 1845 by an act of Congress. But as early as March of that year, Polk already regarded it as part of the United States and, as such, entitled to protection, including the territory Texas claimed as far south as the Rio Grande. The fact that Mexico claimed that the southern boundary of Texas was the River Nueces and that every map in existence at the time showed the territory between the Rio Grande and the Nueces as belonging to Mexico meant nothing to Polk. Therefore, in mid-June 1845, a month before Texas ratified its annexation and six months before it became a state, Polk and his secretary of war, William Marcy, ordered an army under General Zachary Taylor to take a position south of the river. At the same time, Polk called on Texas, Mississippi, Alabama, Georgia, Arkansas, Kentucky, Missouri, Illinois, Indiana, and Ohio to provide 17,000 volunteers. His objective was to get 50,000 men under arms, half from the South and half from the North.

Clearly the purpose of the Polk administration was to settle the boundary dispute, by armed force if necessary, before the annexation of Texas was ratified, and if Mexico resisted, so much the worse for it. On August 23, Taylor received the following instructions: "Should Mexico assemble a large body of troops on the Rio Grande, and cross it with a considerable force, such a movement must be regarded as an invasion of the United States and the commencement of hostilities."

On April 25, 1846, a detachment of Mexican troops crossed the Rio Grande and ambushed two companies of American soldiers on the left bank of the river. In the ensuing skirmish, eleven Americans were killed, five wounded, and the remainder taken captive. Word of the attack reached the White House at about six o'clock in the evening of Sunday, May 9, 1846. The cabinet met the same night, and agreed that a war message should be presented to Congress the following day.

On Monday morning, May 10, 1846, President Polk sent Congress a special message announcing war with Mexico. Regretting that he had had to use the Sabbath to write a war message, Polk gave as the main reason for declaring war the commencement of hostilities "by Mexico . . . which had invaded American territory and by whose acts had shed American blood upon the American soil."

The war message evoked considerable opposition in Congress. Instead of being, as Polk called it, a defensive war, the conflict was assailed as one of aggression, forced upon Mexico by the president when he ordered an American army into the area between the Nueces and the Rio Grande, which was clearly Mexican soil, and then took possession of it. But the imposition of a virtual prohibition on debate rendered the opposition fruitless. Debate on the war bill in the House was limited to two hours, and in the Senate, only one day was allowed for discussion. Operating under this stampede and with the cry of patriotism in the air, both houses of Congress approved the bill within two days by lopsided majorities: 114 to 14 in the House and 40 to 2 in the Senate. On May 15, 1846, Polk signed the bill authorizing him to enlist 50,000 more troops and appropriating $10 million for national defense. The war was now official.

Throughout the South and West, the war was popular; of 69,540 volunteers who enlisted, at least 40,000 were from these areas, whereas the more populous and wealthy North furnished only 7,930. Northern opposition to the war was immediately expressed and continued to be voiced throughout the conflict in newspapers, churches, antislavery societies, workingmen's conventions, and literary works. Frederick Douglass denounced the "disgraceful, cruel and iniquitous war" that doomed Mexico to be "victim of Anglo-Saxon cupidity and love of dominion." He deplored the innocent blood being shed in the cause of slavery and declared that the nation's only hope of national redemption lay in a united demand of press, pulpit, and public for the "instant recall of our forces from Mexico." James Russell Lowell, Ralph Waldo Emerson, William Ellery Channing, Wendell Phillips, Horace Greeley, Henry Thoreau, and Charles Sumner were among the others who expressed their opposition to the war with voice and pen. In his satirical *Bigelow Papers,* Lowell directed caustic gibes at the war hawks:

> They may talk o Freedom's airy
> Till they're purple in the face,—
> It's a grand gret cemetary
> For the barthrights of our race,
> They just want this Californy

So's to lug new slave states in
To abuse ye, an' to scorn ye,
An' to plunder ye like sin.

Lowell's view that the war was fundamentally one for the expansion of slavery was enunciated at meetings of blacks in Philadelphia, New York, Boston, Cincinnati, and other Northern cities. It was also voiced by New York workingmen at a meeting called in May 1846 to oppose the war. The meeting branded the war a scheme of slaveowners and their allies who lived "in such luxurious idleness on the products of the workingmen" and demanded of President Polk that further hostilities be avoided by withdrawing American troops "to some undisputed land belonging to the United States." Speaking through their delegates at the 1846 convention of the New England Workingmen's Association, the organized workers of New England took a similar stand. They denounced "the foul disgrace of extending the area of slavery through war," and pledged that they would "not take up arms to sustain the Southern slaveholder in robbing one-fifth of our countrymen of their labor."

In Congress, Abraham Lincoln, a freshman congressman from Illinois, pressed for an inquiry as to whether the spot on which American and Mexican forces first clashed was not in fact Mexican territory. As for himself, he was convinced that Polk had ordered American soldiers into a peaceful Mexican community in a deliberate effort to provoke war. Consequently his efforts to blame the conflict on Mexico amounted to "the half insane mumbling of a fever-dream" and the product of "a bewildered, confounded, and miserably perplexed man," whose mind had been "tasked beyond its power."

William Wells Brown, the black abolitionist, urged all Negroes who were called into the armed services in the Mexican War "to fight against the United States." But no blacks served in the American armed forces in the war. Federal law barred Negroes from state militias, and while the U.S. Navy accepted a limited quota of blacks, the army excluded them after the War of 1812 until well into the Civil War.

In January 1847, after three days of fighting at Monterey, the Mexican army capitulated to Zachary Taylor, commander of the army of the Rio Grande, and an eight weeks' armistice was drawn up. But the relatively lenient terms of the treaty were unacceptable to President Polk, who ordered hostilities with the Mexicans resumed. And so the fighting continued until September 1847 when, in the final battle for Mexico City, American troops took the heights of Chapultepec and entered the city. Mexico then surrendered.

The demand was voiced that the United States seize all of Mexico. On March 10, 1848, the Treaty of Guadalupe-Hidalgo was ratified by the United States Senate, officially ending the war with Mexico. Under it, the United States took only half of Mexico. "Peace! Peace! Peace!" the American newspapers rejoiced. But Frederick Douglass wrote in the *North Star* that the celebrations were not for peace but *plunder*. They have succeeded in robbing Mexico of her territory, and we are rejoicing over their success under the hypocritical presence of a regard for peace. . . . Our soul is sick of such hypocrisy. . . . That an end is put to wholesale murder in Mexico, is truly just cause for rejoicing; but we are not the people to rejoice, we ought rather blush and hang our heads for shame, and in the spirit of profound humility, crave pardon for our crimes at the hands of a God whose mercy endureth forever.

President Polk saw no need either to blush or hang his head in shame. In his final message to Congress, he told the American people that due to "the benignant Providence of Almighty God . . . our beloved country presents a sublime moral spectacle to the world."

THE WILMOT PROVISO

The view popularly held by historians of the late nineteenth and early twentieth centuries that the war with Mexico was primarily caused by a concerted drive by the slave power to acquire new territory for slavery is now rejected by a number of scholars. There is substantial evidence, however, that the administration's real intention in the war was not its announced aim of repelling a Mexican intrusion onto American soil but rather the swallowing up of part or all of Mexico, thereby further extending slavery and Southern power. In July 1846, Polk sent his request to Congress for an appropriation of $2 million, and it was universally understood that the money was to be used to purchase land from Mexico. Indeed, Polk's diary reveals that he recognized that a peace treaty ceding land to the United States would be unpopular in Mexico. He intended to use the money as a payment to the Mexican government, enabling it to retain the support of the Mexican army and stay in power.

In Congress, it was charged that the president's request for funds proved that the Mexican War was being waged for conquest—for "buying territory at the South." It was at this point that Congressman David Wilmot, a Democrat from Pennsylvania, along with a few of his associates, decided to act out of their fear that the war would result in the acquistion of territory for slavery and an increase in the number of slaveholding states. When President Polk requested $2 million with which to make peace, Wilmot, with the support of Jacob Brinkeroff of Ohio, introduced the Wilmot Proviso, which would have the effect of excluding Negro slavery from all territory acquired from Mexico—and, as Wilmot phrased it, save that virgin soil for free white labor, for "the sons of toil of my own race and color." The proviso, Wilmot explained in Congress, was not motivated by any "squeamish sensitiveness upon the subject of slavery, [or] morbid sympathy for the slave"; in fact, he objected strenuously when, as he put it, an attempt was made "to bring odium upon this movement, as one designed especially for the benefit of the black race." Instead, he insisted, "I plead the cause and rights of the free white man." The question was simple: should the territories be reserved for the white laborer, "or shall [they] be given up to the African and his descendants." Wilmot's answer was empahtic—white labor must not be degraded by association with "the servile labor of the black."

But the slaveowners were not so sensitive about having blacks associate with whites, provided that the Negroes were slaves, and they called the proviso unconstitutional and even treason. The Wilmot Proviso passed the House twice, but each time it failed in the Southern-controlled Senate, thereby leaving unresolved the status of slavery in Mexican-conquered territory.

The idea embodied in the Wilmot Proviso of no slavery in the territories (and, unfortunately, no blacks either) did not die. Out of the furor over the proviso rose the Free Soil party. But before we turn to this new third-party movement, let us return to the Liberty party.

SPLITS IN THE LIBERTY PARTY

The vote cast for James G. Birney in the 1844 presidential election represented the Liberty party's high point. After 1844, it rapidly lost strength, in large part because many of its adherents, especially in the West, left the party and labored to build a mass political movement directed against slavery. Western Liberty men, especially Salmon Portland Chase of Ohio, felt that the abolition party would get nowhere as long as it was organized and conducted mostly as a religious crusade rather than a political party, as long as the movement was led by ministers instead of more practical men, and as long as its appeal to the electorate was based on an "abstract commitment to abolition" rather than on specific political and economic issues related to slavery and the slave power. Chase's efforts to broaden the Liberty party's political base aroused little positive response from the organization's leaders in the East, and soon after the election of 1844, the western Liberty men, led by Chase, decided that the Liberty party could never achieve mass support. They began to work to build a coalition between the third party and the steadily increasing antislavery wings of the two major parties.

Meanwhile a somewhat similar split was developing among Liberty party men in the East, further weakening the organization; in this case, however, it did not lead to a coalition with antislavery men of the two major parties. The conflict was between the advocates of the "one idea" policy and those who, under the leadership of William Goodell and Gerrit Smith, wished to broaden the party's platform to include other reforms. The advocates of the "one idea" policy insisted that the only program to be presented to the voters was a call for the overthrow of slavery "within the limits of national jurisdiction." Their opponents, aware that the voters wanted to know the party's stand on the tariff, the bank, and the distribution of public lands, called for a broad platform.

The division over issues in the Liberty party inevitably led to a split in the East. Early in June 1847, about forty prominent Liberty party men, all calling for a more comprehensive program, met at Macedon Locke in Wayne County, New York, and, under the leadership of Goodell and Smith, formed the Liberty League. Separating itself from the Liberty party, the convention nominated Gerritt Smith and Elihu Burritt, "the learned blacksmith," for president and vice-president, respectively, of the United States.

In October 1847, the Liberty party held its national convention in Buffalo. Ignoring the platform and candidates of the seceders, the delegates reaffirmed the "one idea" policy and chose John P. Hale of New Hampshire and Leicester King of Ohio as their candidates. Not so easily downed, Gerrit Smith issued a call for another convention to be held in Buffalo on June 14, 1848.

Both Frederick Douglass and Henry Highland Garnet spoke at the Buffalo Convention of the Liberty League, or National Liberty party, the political name assumed by the group to distinguish it from the "one idea" Liberty party. (Indeed, the convention was the first official political gathering Douglass ever attended.) But each presented opposite interpretations of the federal Constitution. Douglass, still faithful to his Garrisonian views, argued that the document showed no regard for the slaves, while conferring political power upon the slaveholders in proportion to the number of humans they could plunder and rob. Under its provisions, he maintained, slaveholders were enabled to recapture their slaves anywhere in the United States, and the national government was empowered to suppress slave insurrections. In rebuttal, Garnet, among others, stressed that the objects for which the Constitution was written were stated in the preamble; they pointed to the absence of the word *slave* in the document and the use in its stead of the word *person*.

While Douglass was mainly an onlooker, Garnet was a member of the Business Committee, and he prepared the *Address of the Liberty Party to the Colored People of the Northern States,* in which he charged the latter with not doing enough for the emancipation of the slaves. "It remains true," the *Address* declared, "that, as a people, you are doing far less than you should, to shame the slaveholders out of their wicked and absurd doctrine, that the negro is fit for slavery only." Garnet urged his fellow blacks in the North "to prove their superiority to the whites in industry, economy, temperance and education, in order to disprove the frequently repeated charge that Negroes were only fit for slavery," and he advised them to withdraw "from pro-slavery political parties and churches." Garnet was disturbed by the fact that many blacks had voted for Henry Clay, the slaveowner, rather than Birney in the previous presidential election, and he ended the *Address* by stating that slavery would cease to exist only after the Negro had established himself as a vigorous opponent of the institution.

Douglass informed his readers that he had been impressed by the *Address* and by the fact that the convention went on record for free public lands to actual settlers, for women's political rights, for the ten-hour system of labor, and for the right of workers to organize into trade unions—in addition to opposition to slavery wherever it existed and equal rights for free blacks. But this initial contact with a political convention made no dent in his confidence in the Garrisonian creed, and he refused to endorse the candidates of the National Liberty party.

Garrison, however, was concerned when he heard that Douglass had taken an active part in the proceedings, believing that it indicated a willingness "to give his influence" to further the objects of the National Liberty party. Douglass reminded his critics that he was still a Garrisonian and could well do without a "diplomatic reproof."

Garrison had more to concern himself with in Boston. A group of the city's blacks had begun holding a series of meetings to discuss plans for forming a subsidiary organization to the Liberty party. Boston's Negro leadership, including Robert Morris and John Hilton, refused to abandon Garrison and go along with the plan. But when the two groups met together, a resolution was adopted asserting that "the people are under the highest obligation to remove slavery by moral and political action." Garrison published a letter from "A Colored Citizen" voicing his doubt that "this movement will meet with much favor among the intelligent portion of the colored people." The editor of the *Liberator* added an attack of his own aimed at "the falsely styled Liberty Party, the successful candidates of which swear to support a Constitution, by which . . . the whole physical force of the nation is pledged to suppress every attempt of the slaves, to obtain their freedom. Away with such a party! Down with such a Constitution."

It turned out that there was only one presidential candidate with a Liberty party label in 1848. In 1847, John P. Hale had been nominated for the presidency by the original Liberty party, but when the Free Soil party absorbed this party in 1848, he withdrew in favor of Martin Van Buren, the Free Soil candidate. The surviving Liberty party, headed by Gerrit Smith as its presidential candidate, remained in existence through the 1850s. But before we say farewell to the original Liberty party, we should note that it was the first among all political parties in the United States to adopt political and social equality for Negroes as one of its major goals, the first specifically to invite the participation of the Negro people, and the first to bring them into its leadership.

The Liberty party was not entirely free of racism. At a Michigan convention of the party, two Negro delegates were denied the right to participate in the nomination of candidates on the ground that they were not legal voters. Senator Thomas Morris, the Liberty party's vice-presidential candidate in 1844, was a staunch foe of Negro suffrage. More typical, however, was the fact that the Liberty party led the fight for equal suffrage. When Connecticut voters defeated a Negro suffrage proposal in 1847, the *Hartford Charter Oak*, a Liberty party newspaper, declared: "There is not, we affirm, a Liberty man in Connecticut who did not desire that the amendment should prevail." In general, the Liberty party consistently avowed its commitment to "the principles of Equal Rights" and urged its supporters to combat "any inequality of rights and privileges . . . on account of color." Almost without exception, the state and national Liberty platforms included such resolutions, and throughout the North the party was a fervent opponent of political and social discrimination against the free Negro.

THE FREE SOIL PARTY

On May 22, 1848, the Democratic National Convention nominated Lewis Cass of Michigan for president on a platform framed to suit the South. On June 10, the Whig National Convention nominated Zachary Taylor, a Louisiana slaveholder, for president and howled down the Wilmot Proviso. Immediately, Garrison called the Whig party the "Bloodhound Party" and Taylor the "Bloodhound candidate." This was a reference to the fact that in 1839, as an officer in the stuggle between the United States and the Seminole Indians, many of them fugitive slaves adopted by the Seminoles, Taylor found it necessary to recruit a pack of bloodhounds from Cuba to track down the Indians.

Democrats and Whigs who opposed the extension of slavery met along with Liberty party men in Buffalo in the summer of 1848 and organized the Free Soil party. They chose Martin Van Buren, who had become convinced that the Northern Democrats had yielded to the slave power long enough, as their presidential candidate. Charles Francis Adams was nominated for the second highest office. The platform proposed no interference with slavery in the states but demanded that Congress halt its advance into the territories. It also called for abolition of slavery in the District of Columbia. The slogan of the new party was: "Free Soil, Free Speech, Free Labor and Free Men."

Blacks had mixed feelings about supporting the Free Soil party. Some felt that merely opposing slavery in the territories and the District of Columbia was hardly enough to warrant their endorsement. Others believed, however, that restricting slavery to the South and halting its further advance would bring about its natural death through exhaustion of the soil. But a major reason for black interest in the new party was the composition of its leadership. In Massachusetts, the major role in the Free Soil party was played by such antislavery figures as Charles Sumner, Charles Francis Adams, and John Gorham Palfrey. While not all were believers in equality for blacks, they (and especially Sumner) were far in advance of the white community on this issue.

With such men associated with the Free Soil party, it is not surprising that even staunch Garrisonian Boston blacks should show interest in the new party. Taking issue with Wendell Phillips' attacks on the Free Soil movement, Robert Morris announced that he believed "in the use and necessity even of political efforts and political machinery to accomplish objects needed for public welfare. . . . He looked with interest to the Buffalo Free Soil Convention." Morris, however, qualified his support, vowing that if Martin Van Buren were the Free Soil candidate for president, he would not support him.

It soon became apparent, however, that the presidential candidate was the least of the problems that concerned blacks about the Free Soil party. In Pennsylvania, David Wilmot was the leader of the group within the Democratic party that moved into the Free Soil party. The author of the Wimot Proviso was a fervent white supremacist and notorious in Pennsylvania as a foe of equal rights for blacks, and especially for his opposition to extending the franchise to blacks. He took the same position in Congress. When a Southern congressman charged that he favored political and social equality between the races, Wilmot cried out indignantly, "My vote shows no such thing." And when Joshua Giddings proposed that all the residents of the District of Columbia vote in a referendum to determine the fate of slavery in the nation's capital, Wilmot was incensed. He found it "highly objectionable," he wrote, "to admit the blacks, bond and free, to vote upon the question." The abolitionist *Pennsylvania Freeman* described the Keystone State's congressman as a man who believed that it was "the negro and not slavery which degraded labor." Wilmot's attitude "seemed the result of an old and unconscious prejudice in his mind."

While Pennsylvania's blacks were disfranchised and could not express their views at the ballot box on the presence of a man like Wilmot in the leadership of the Free Soil party, it became clear that other blacks who could vote might find it difficult to support the new party. What created an even greater difficulty for blacks was the fact that the New York Barnburners, the leading organizers of the Free Soil party, had a long history of Negrophobia. This faction of the Democratic party in New York opposed the further extension of slavery, and when in September 1847 the state Democratic convention tabled a resolution demanding that slavery be excluded from the territory acquired from Mexico, the Barnburners walked out. Like Wilmot, the Barnburners made it clear that they opposed slavery in the territories because they did not want white labor to be degraded by association with blacks. Moreover, the Barnburners were in full agreement with the Hunkers, the dominant faction in the New York Democratic party, on opposition to equal rights for blacks in general and extension of the franchise to Negroes in particular. Indeed, because of the opposition of the Barnburners, an effort by former Liberty party men to include a call for equal rights for free blacks in the North in the Free Soil platform was defeated.

But the press devoted more attention to the presence at the convention of such Negro leaders as Samuel Ringgold Ward, Henry Highland Garnet, Charles Lenox Remond, Henry Bibb, and Frederick Douglass, with Garnet and Ward as official delegates. The fact that Douglass was warmly applauded when called upon to address the convention, even though he was not a delegate, overshadowed the anti-Negro feelings among white delegates in the press reports. One abolitionist wrote enthusiastically that "men of all political and religious complexions and of all *colors* were called to the platform to address the Convention."

Douglass was seated in the convention hall, when a Mr. Husband of Rochester, in the course of addressing the delegates, announced that he saw "Frederick Douglass here." The delegates responded with three cheers. The next day there were loud calls for Douglass to speak. He took the stand and stated that he was grateful for the opportunity to address the delegates but deeply regretted his inability to speak since he had only recently had an operation on his throat. "One thing, however, I want to say, God speed your noble undertaking." The official reporter added: "The audience appeared to feel a great disappointment when they learned that Mr. Douglass could not address them." But what the reporter did not disclose was that it was only after a bitter argument among the Barnburners, and at the insistence of Martin Van Buren (increasingly sensitive to criticism of his record on Negro rights), that blacks had been invited at all. Years later, Francis W. Bird, presiding officer at the session at which Douglass spoke, recalled how, when the black abolitionist came forward to the platform, Barnburners surrounded him and urged him not to give Douglass the floor. "They didn't want a 'nigger' to talk to them," he recalled. "I told them," Bird continued, "we came there for free soil, free speech and free men; and I gave a hint to Mr. Douglass that if he would claim the floor when the gentleman who was then speaking gave it up, he should certainly have it." When Samuel Ringgold Ward spoke, one Ohio delegate complained that he resented "taking his cue from a 'nigger.' "

While blacks did not know of these behind-the-scenes maneuverings, they did know that missing from the Free Soil platform was any statement like that of the Liberty party's stand in behalf of the "principles of Equal Rights" or that party's pledge to combat "any inequality of rights and privileges . . . on account of color."

ELECTION OF 1848

Yet many blacks felt that the expeditious approach was to support a party that went further than any other in the campaign on the slavery issue, even though it did not maintain the Liberty party's forthright stand on the question of equal rights. Such black political pragmatism, however, did not sit well with the leaders of the National Liberty party. When Thomas Van Rensselaer, editor of the *Ram's Horn,* a New York black weekly, endorsed Van Buren, his action brought a sharp rebuke from Gerrit Smith. The National Liberty party's presidential candidate pointed out that the Free Soil standard-bearer shared the prevailing prejudices of the "vast majority of Americans in his views and treatment of the colored race." Blacks, Smith contended, could not expect any better treatment from a Free Soil government than from a Democratic or a Whig administration. In conclusion, he urged blacks not to vote for Free Soilers who "acquiesce and even take part in the proscription and crushing of your race." Instead, they should cast their votes for Smith, who was running on a ticket that both opposed slavery wherever it existed and declared itself for equal rights for all men.

Samuel Ringgold Ward, fresh from the Free Soil convention, endorsed Smith's advice. Some might believe, he wrote, that the absence of a plank advocating equal rights in the Free Soil platform was an oversight, but actually "it has the appearance of a studied and deliberate design." The Free Soilers of New York, he went on, were men who had always opposed Negro suffrage; they were the leading exponents of anti-Negro prejudice and were "as ready to rob black men of their rights now as they ever were." Ward urged blacks to vote for "Smith and Equal Rights."

So, too, did Henry Highland Garnet. Garnet, morever, took on the task of meeting the charge that Smith was "a pseudo-abolitionist" because he had advanced the position that throughout the world, land monopoly was a greater source of suffering and debasement than slavery. Even without slavery in Ireland, Garnet reminded blacks, land monopoly had subjected the Irish to famine and driven thousands upon thousands into exile. Unless the question of land monopoly was settled first, he continued, freedom would be but an illusion to the emancipated slaves: "The chains of the last slave on earth may be broken in twain, and still, while the unholy system of landlordism prevails, nations and people will mourn. But the moment that this widespread and monstrous evil is destroyed, the dawn of the gospel day will break forth, and the world will have rest." The fact that Smith had freely given land to free Negroes was evidence, Garnet insisted, that he was more of a friend to blacks than many abolitionists who denounced him.

Garnet's defense of the presidential candidate of the National Liberty party appeared in Frederick Douglass' *North Star*. But the editor of that journal, though still a nonvoting Garrisonian, was urging all friends of the slave who did vote to cast their ballot for Van Buren, contending that since the Free Soilers were the only openly antislavery party, it was the duty of political abolitionists to support their presidential candidate. The Constitution might be proslavery, Douglass conceded, but the tactical exigencies of the struggle made it necessary that every possible weapon be utilized. The adherents of slavery were gathering around Taylor and Cass, while the forces of freedom were hesitant and disunited. What should the friends of the slave do in this crisis? What should be the response of those blacks who believed in voting to the failure of the Free Soil party to come out in favor of equal rights for all regardless of color?

. . . We may stand off and act the part of fault finders—pick flaws in the Free Soil platform, expose the weakness of some persons connected with it—suspect and criticize their leaders, and in this way play into the hands of our enemies, affording the sticks to break our own heads. Or we may consign ourselves to oblivion . . . remain silent as if we were speechless, and let things take their own course, and thus morally to commit suicide. In neither of these ways can we go. We feel it our duty to pursue the course which will make us in some degree a terror to evil doers, and a praise to all that do well . . . to be a worker on the anvil now before us—that whatever influence we may possess, it shall be given in the right direction.

In September 1848, between sixty and seventy delegates met in Cleveland and chose Douglass as president of the National Negro Convention. The Free Soil movement was the main topic of discussion. John Hilton headed the Boston delegation and fought against any resolutions expressing support for the party. Douglass tried to convince the delegates to put the convention on record as backing the principles of the Free Soil party. The delegates decided to steer a middle course; on the one hand, they recommended that "our brethren throughout the several States . . . support such persons and parties alone as have a tendency to enhance the liberty of the colored people of the United States." But they also passed a resolution stating that "while we heartily engage in recommending to our people the Free Soil Movement . . . nevertheless we . . . are determined to maintain the higher standard and more liberal views which have heretofore characterized us as abolitionists."

Douglass had been wrestling with the problem of whether to endorse the Free Soil candidates in his paper, a position that would have definitely conflicted with his Garrisonian beliefs. Less than a week after the Cleveland convention, he made his decision. On September 10, 1848, the *North Star* editorially recommended the Free Soil candidates, Martin Van Buren and Charles Francis Adams.

Although Van Buren did not carry a single state, the Free Soil party received 291,678 votes out of the 2,882,120 that were cast and elected five men to Congress. Apparently the enfranchised blacks cast their votes in accordance with the image of the Free Soil party in their particular states. In New York, many followed the advice of Ward and Garnet and voted "for Smith and Equal Rights." Outside of New York, where Free Soil leaders were mostly former Liberty men or antislavery (Conscience) Whigs, more favorable to Negro rights than were the New York Free Soilers, blacks overwhelmingly supported the new party. In Boston, Martin Van Buren ran third to Taylor and Cass but polled his highest percentage of votes in Ward Six, the ward with the largest concentration of Negroes.

Considering that this was its first campaign, the Free Soil party did well. The *Liberator,* in fact, sought to interpret its large vote as an evidence of the influence of Garrisonian principles: "The Slave Power is beginning to falter—fresh adherents are daily rallying around the standard of Liberty, and the cry of 'No Union with Slaveholders' is causing the knees of the oppressor to tremble." To Garrison, the votes cast for the election of antislavery candidates in traditionally conservative constituencies was "unmistakable proof of the progress we have made, under God, in changing public sentiment." The Garrisonians distinguished between Liberty men, whom they saw as deserters from the cause of moral suasion abolitionists, and newly awakened Free Soilers, whose more moderate stand on antislavery, Garrisonians optimistically believed, marked not a retreat from but an advance toward abolitionism. The Garrisonians were cheered by the fact that the rise of the Free Soil party signaled the demise of the Liberty party, "this preposterous faction," as Edmund Quincy, a leading Garrisonian, described that political movement.

The Garrisonians still believed that the struggle against slavery would only be corrupted by the everyday world of political compromise; they still opposed an antislavery political party and would not themselves vote. However, they did not oppose a properly cast ballot. Wendell Phillips wrote to John G. Palfrey, one of the Conscience Whigs who moved into the Free Soil party: "Could I conscientiously throw a ballot, I would . . . have the pleasure of voting for a man who nails his color to the mast."

The fact that the Free Soil party had won the support of many thousands of northerners had made it clear that a battle to incorporate the Liberty party position on equal rights for all in the new party's platform might be a difficult undertaking. But it had to be done. On December 7, 1848, the *Pennsylvania Freeman* addressed an eloquent appeal to the entire Free Soil party:

The colored people . . . are calling for their rights, and contending with long-seated prejudices. We have a right to expect Free Soil men to encourage and assist them; if they will not do this, we ask them in the name of humanity, that they will not feed the popular prejudices against this outcast class.

Reprinting this appeal in the *North Star*, Frederick Douglass called upon all antislavery men to promulgate their principles—abolition of slavery everywhere and equal rights for all—among the Free Soilers, so that gradually "a true Free Soil Party" could be established. "We must go on and lead the Free Soilers," he told the audience at the Thirteenth Annual Meeting of the Rhode Island Anti-Slavery Society a month after the election.

First things first, however, Douglass emphasized. A new struggle was shaping up in Congress, a struggle to prevent slavery in the territories taken from Mexico. Although for the abolitionists, he emphasized, the true radical principle was not opposition to the extension of slavery but complete extermination of every vestige of human bondage throughout the entire nation, nevertheless the impending struggle in Congress was of major importance: "Should the North gain in this contest, it will be the first victory gained since the formation of the Government."

Bibliography and Sources

1. AMERICAN HISTORIANS AND ANTEBELLUM SLAVERY

Ulrich B. Phillips and the Phillips School

For James Ford Rhodes' racist views, see *History of the United States from the Compromise of 1850 to the Final Restoration of Home Rule to the South in 1877* (New York, 1892–1906), 1:26, 303, 379, 380; 7:485, and Robert Cruden, "James Ford Rhodes and the Negro: A Study in the Problem of Objectivity," *Ohio History* 7 (Spring 1962): 129–37. A complete list of Ulrich Bonnell Phillips' writings may be found in David M. Potter, Jr., comp., "A Bibliography of the Printed Writings of Ulrich Bonnell Phillips," *Georgia Historical Quarterly* 18 (September 1934): 270–82; Fred Landon and Everett E. Edwards, comps., "A Bibliography of the Writings of Professor Ulrich Bonnell Phillips," *Agricultural History* 7 (October 1934): 196–218. Accounts of Phillips' life are in Wood Gray, "Ulrich Bonnell Phillips," in W. T. Hutchinson, ed., *The Marcus W. Jernegan Essays in American Historiography* (Chicago, 1937), pp. 357–73; E. Merton Coulter, "Ulrich Bonnell Phillips," *Dictionary of American Biography* 21 (Supplement 1): 597–98; Wendell Holmes Stephenson, *The South Lives in History: Southern Historians and Their Legacy* (Baton Rouge, La., 1955), chap. 3, "Ulrich B. Phillips: Historian of Aristocracy," pp. 58–94. Phillips' views are summarized in E. Merton Coulter, ed., *The Cause of the South to Secession: An Interpretation by Ulrich Bonnell Phillips* (New York and London, 1939); Sam E. Salem, "U. B. Phillips and the Scientific Tradition," *Georgia Historical Quarterly* 44 (June 1960): 172–85; Daniel Joseph Singal, "Ulrich B. Phillips: The Old South as the New," *Journal of American History* 43 (March 1977): 871–95: Allan M. Winkler, "Ulrich Bonnell Phillips: A Reappraisal," *South Atlantic Quarterly* 71 (Spring 1972): 234–48; Ruth Hutchinson Crocker, "Ulrich B. Phillips: A Southern Historian Reconsidered," *Louisiana Studies* 15 (Summer 1976): 113–30; Ruben F. Kugler, "U. B. Phillips' Use of Sources," *Journal of Negro History* 47 (Spring 1962): 153–68; and Burton M. Smith, "A Study of American Historians and Their Interpretation of Negro Slavery in the United States" (Ph.D. diss., Washington State University, 1970), pp. 61–75. In presenting Phillips' views on slavery, I have relied mainly on *American Negro Slavery: A Survey of the Supply, Employment and Control of Negro Labor as*

Determined by the Plantation Regime (New York and London, 1918) since the chapter in his *Life and Labor in the Old South* (Boston, 1929) is largely drawn from the earlier volume.

Criticism of Phillips

W.E.B. Du Bois' review of *American Negro Slavery* appears in *American Political Science Review* 12 (November 1918): 722–23; the review by Carter G. Woodson is in *Mississippi Valley Historical Review* 5 (March 1919): 480–82. See also John David Smith, "Du Bois and Phillips—Symbolic Antagonists of the Progressive Era," *Centennial Review* 24 (Winter 1980): 88–102. State histories of slavery written by Phillips' disciples include Ralph Flanders, *Plantation Slavery in Georgia* (Chapel Hill, N.C., 1933); Charles S. Sydnor, *Slavery in Mississippi* (New York, 1933); J. Winston Coleman, *Slavery Times in Kentucky* (Chapel Hill, N.C., 1935); V. Alton Moody, *Slavery on Louisiana Sugar Plantations* (Baton Rouge, La., 1924); Caleb E. Patterson, *The Negro in Tennessee, 1790–1865* (Austin, Tex., 1927). For Ramsdell, see Charles W. Ramsdell, "The Natural Limits of Slavery Expansion," *Mississippi Valley Historical Review* 16 (September 1929): 151–71. Frederick Bancroft's criticism of Phillips may be found in his *Slave Trading in the Old South* (Baltimore, 1931), pp. 68, 271, 208, 235, 298. For the works on slave resistance, see Joseph S. Carroll, *Slave Insurrections in the United States, 1800–1865* (Boston, 1938); Raymond A. Bauer and Alice H. Bauer, "Day to Day Resistance to Slavery," *Journal of Negro History* 27 (October 1942): 388–419, and Herbert Aptheker, *American Negro Slave Revolts* (New York, 1943). Aptheker's criticism of Phillips is on pp. 13, 16. Hofstadter's criticism is in Richard Hofstadter, "U. B. Phillips and the Plantation Legend," *Journal of Negro History* 29 (April 1944): 109–44, and John Hope Franklin's is in his *From Slavery to Freedom: A History of Negro Americans* (New York, 1947), pp. 167–68, 178–79, 181–82, 184, 210. For Morison and Commager, see Samuel Eliot Morison and Henry Steele Commager, *The Growth of the American Republic*, 4th ed. (New York, 1950), 1:537. Lewis C. Gray's differences with Phillips on the unprofitability of slavery may be found in his *History of Agriculture in the Southern States to 1860* (Washington, D.C., 1933), 1:470–71, 473, 474–75, 476–78; 2:33–34, 940–42. For the work of the Owsley school, see especially Frank L. Owsley, *Plain Folk of the Old South* (Baton Rouge, La., 1949); Frank L. Owsley and Harriet C. Owsley, "The Economic Basis of Society in the Late Ante-Bellum South," *Journal of Economic History* 6 (February 1940): 24–45; and "The Economic Structure of Rural Tennessee, 1850–1860," *Journal of Southern History* 8 (May 1942): 161–82. For Govan's views, see Thomas P. Govan, "Was Plantation Slavery Profitable?" *Journal of Southern History* 8 (November 1942): 513–35.

Kenneth M. Stampp's The Peculiar Institution

For Stampp's early criticism of Phillips, see Kenneth M. Stampp, "The Historian and Southern Negro Slavery," *American Historical Review* 57 (April 1952): 13–24. The discussion of Stampp's views on slavery is based on his *The Peculiar Institution: Slavery in the Ante-Bellum South* (New York, 1956). A brief summary of some of his views may be found in Smith, op. cit., pp. 97–100. For criticism of Stampp's views, see Bennett H. Wall, "African Slavery," in Arthur S. Link and Robert W. Patrick, eds., *Writing Southern History: Essays in Historiography in Honor of Fletcher M. Green* (Baton Rouge, La., 1962), pp. 182–83.

Stanley M. Elkins' Slavery

For Elkins' fundamental thesis, see Stanley M. Elkins, *Slavery: A Problem in American Institutional and Intellectual Life* (Chicago, 1959), pp. 102, 104, 118, 119–22, 123–31, 137–39. For a review praising Elkins, see Sidney Mintz in *American Anthropologist* 63 (Spring 1961): 579–85. For critical responses, see "The Question of 'Sambo,'" *Newberry Library Bulletin* 5 (December 1958): 14–41; Harvey Wish in *Mississippi Valley Historical Review* 47 (September 1960): 319–20, and especially Ann J. Lane, ed., *The Debate over Slavery: Stanley Elkins and His Critics* (Urbana, Ill., 1971). Stampp's conclusion on the validity of the Sambo hypothesis is in Kenneth M. Stampp, "Rebels and Sambos: The Search for the Negro's Personality in Slavery," *Journal of Southern History* (August 1971): 368.

Eugene D. Genovese and Slavery

For Stephenson's judgment on Phillips' lack of objectivity, see Stephenson, op. cit., p. 62, and for the view that Phillips was no worse or even better than others in the Progressive era, see Singal, op. cit., p. 895. Eugene D. Genovese's defense of Phillips may be found in Eugene D. Genovese, Foreword to *American Negro Slavery* (Baton Rouge, La., 1967); Introduction to *The Slave Economy of the Old South: Selected Essays in Economic and Social History* (Baton Rouge, La., 1968); "Race and Class in Southern History: An Appraisal of the Work of Ulrich Bonnell Phillips," *Agricultural History* 41 (October 1967): 345–58, and Elinor Miller and Eugene D. Genovese, eds., *Plantation Town, and Country: Essays in the Local History of American Slave Society* (Urbana, Ill., 1974).

Most of the material is drawn from Eugene D. Genovese, *The Political Economy of Slavery: Studies in the Economy and Society of the Slave South* (New York, 1961), esp. pp. 3, 4, 7, 26–28, 34–36, 43–61, 180–208, but some of it also appears in his *The World the Slaveholders Made* (New York, 1969), pp. 21, 195–202, and in his *In Red and Black: Marxian Explorations in Southern and Afro-American History* (New York, 1971), pp. 21, 23, 276–95. For Gramsci, see John Cammett, *Antonio Gramsci and the Origins of Italian Communism* (Palo Alto, Calif., 1967). The article by Alfred H. Conrad and John A. Meyer is "The Economics of Slavery in the Ante-Bellum South," *Journal of Political Economy* 66 (Fall 1958): 95–130. Thomas P. Gowan's review of *The Political Economy of Slavery* appeared in *Journal of Southern History* 31 (May 1969): 230–34; Stampp's review of *The World the Slaveholders Made* is in *Agricultural History* 44 (October 1970): 409–10, and Arthur Zilversmith's is in *Labor History* 22 (Spring 1970): 367–70.

For Genovese's earlier views on black resistance and slave militancy, see his "The Legacy of Slavery and the Roots of Black Nationalism," *Studies on the Left* 6 (Fall 1967): 3–26, 55–65. For his changed views, see *Roll, Jordan, Roll: The World the Slaves Made* (New York, 1974), pp. xv, xvi, 161, 284, 659. For critiques of Genovese's Marxism, see Herbert Aptheker, "Comment," *Studies on the Left* 6 (Fall 1967): 27–34; Donald M. Bluestone, "Marxism without Marx," *Science and Society* 33 (Spring 1970): 231–43; Robert M. Krim, "Eugene D. Genovese, An Historian and His Historiography" (honors paper, University of California, Berkeley, 1971); and Herbert Shapiro, "Eugene Genovese and the Study of Slavery" (Paper presented at the 1979 meeting of the Organization of American Historians) and published as "Genovese, Marxism and the Study of Slavery," *Journal of Ethnic Studies* 9 (Winter 1982): 87–100. For criticism of Genovese's paternalism theory, see Paul D. Escott, *Slavery Remembered: A Record of Twentieth Century Slave Narratives* (Chapel Hill, N.C., 1979), and James Oakes, *The Ruling Race:*

A History of American Slaveholders (New York, 1982). See also Martin A. Kilian and E. Lynn Tatom, "Marx, Hegel, and the Marxian of the Master Class: Eugene D. Genovese on Slavery," *Journal of Negro History* 66 (Fall 1981): 189–203. Other critics of Genovese, apart from those already mentioned, include James D. Anderson, "Aunt Jemima in Dialectics: Genovese on Slave Culture," *Journal of Negro History* 61 (1976): 94–114, and Earl Smith, "Roll, Apology, Roll!" a review of *Roll, Jordan, Roll,* in *A Freedomways Reader: Afro-America in the Seventies,* ed. Ernest Kaiser (New York, 1977), pp. 175–79.

Time on the Cross

The exposition of the themes in *Time on the Cross* is based on Robert William Fogel and Stanley L. Engerman, *Time on the Cross,* Vol. 1: *The Economics of American Negro Slavery,* pp. 49, 115, 130, 133, 239, 259; Vol. 2: *Evidence and Methods* (Boston, 1974). For a detailed survey of the reception to *Time on the Cross* and a summary of reviews, see Charles Crowe, "*Time on the Cross:* The Historical Monograph as Pop Event," *History Teacher* 9 (August 1976): 588–630. Reviews mentioned in the discussion include Peter Russell's in *New York Times Book Review,* April 28, 1974; C. Vann Woodward, *New York Review of Books,* May 2, 1974; Herbert Aptheker, "Heavenly Days in Dixie," *Political Affairs* 53 (June–July 1974): 40–54, 44–57; Eric Foner, *Labor History* 16 (Winter 1976): 127–38; Paul A. David, Herbert Gutman, Richard Sutch, Peter Temin, and Gavin Wright, *Reckoning with Slavery* (New York, 1976); Herbert G. Gutman, *Slavery and the Numbers Game: A Critique of* Time on the Cross (Urbana, Ill., 1975). Gutman's monograph is an expanded version of his article, "The World Two Cliometricians Made," *Journal of Negro History* 60 (January 1975): 53–227. For critical reviews by blacks, see Lloyd Hogan in *Review of Black Political Economy* 5 (1975): 103–4; *Black Books Bulletin* 7 (1975): 68–72; Brenda C. Jones in *Freedomways* 15 (1975): 26–33; Mildred C. Fierce in *Phylon* 36 (March 1975): 89–91; Julius Lester in *New Politics* 11 (1975): 93; Ted Bassett in *Daily World* (New York), September 12, 1974, and John W. Blassingame, "The Mathematics of Slavery," *Atlantic Monthly* 118 (August 1974): 78–82. For support of the dissenting reviews, see Thomas C. Maskell, "The True and Tragic History of *Time on the Cross,*" *New York Review of Books,* October 2, 1975, 33–39.

RECENT DEVELOPMENTS

For a discussion of post-World War I scholarship on slavery, see David Brion Davis, "Slavery and the Post-World War II Historians," *Daedalus* 103 (1947): 1–16. In addition to the books cited above, the list of significant studies published in the 1970s includes David Brion Davis, *The Problem of Slavery in the Age of Revolution, 1770–1823* (Ithaca and London, 1975); Peter H. Wood, *Black Majority: Negroes in Colonial South Carolina from 1670 through the Stono Rebellions* (New York, 1974); Ira Berlin, *Slaves without Masters: The Free Negro in the Antebellum South* (New York, 1974); John W. Blassingame, *The Slave Community; Plantation Life in the Antebellum South* (New York, 1972); Leslie Howard Owen, *This Species of Property: Slave Life and Culture in the Old South* (New York, 1976); Herbert G. Gutman, *The Black Family in Slavery and Freedom, 1750–1925* (New York, 1976). Among the leading historians of slavery in this period, in addition to those mentioned above, were Robert S. Starobin, Willie Lee Rose, Lawrence Levine, Earl Thorpe, Sterling Stuckey, Mina Davis Caufield, Roy S. Bryce-Laporte, Franklin W. Knight, Carl Degler, and Gilbert Osofsky.

For the history of the slave testimony collection, see Lawrence D. Reddick, "A New Interpretation for Negro History," *Journal of Negro History* 22 (January 1937): 1–20; Benjamin A. Botkin, "The Slave as His Own Interpreter," *Library of Congress Quarterly Journal of Current Acquisitions* 2 (November 1944): 30–48; Norman R. Yetman, "The Background of the Slave Narrative Collection," *American Quarterly* 19 (Fall 1963): 530–54; Randall M. Miller, "When Lions Write History: Slave Testimony and the History of American Slavery," *Research Studies* 44 (March 1976): 13–23. The volumes edited by Rawick are George P. Rawick, ed., *The American Slave: A Composite Autobiography*, series 1–2 (Westport, Conn., 1972). Blassingame's discussion is in John Blassingame, "Using the Testimony of Ex-Slaves: Approaches and Problems," *Journal of Southern History* 41 (November 1975): 473–92, which is also part of the introduction to the work he edited: *Slave Testimony: Two Centuries of Letters, Speeches, Interviews, and Autobiographies* (Baton Rouge, La., 1977). Another collection worth consulting is Robert S. Starobin, ed., *Blacks in Bondage: Letters of American Slaves* (New York, 1974). Useful discussions appear in Frances Smith Foster, *Witnessing Slavery: The Development of Antebellum Slave Narratives* (Westport, Conn., 1979); Paul D. Escott, *Slavery Remembered: A Record of Twentieth-Century Slave Narratives* (Chapel Hill, N.C., 1979), and David Thomas Bailey, "A Divided Prism: Two Sources of Black Testimony on Slavery," *Journal of Southern History* 46 (November 1980): 381–404.

For discussion of the slave drivers, see William L. Van Deburg, *The Slave Drivers: Black Agricultural Labor Supervisors in the Antebellum South* (Westport, Conn., 1979), and the review by Melvin Drimmer in *Journal of Negro History* 65 (Winter 1980): 80–83.

For criticism of studies of slave culture on the issue of time and space, see Herbert G. Gutman, "Slave Culture and Slave Family and Kin Network: The Importance of Time," *South Atlantic Urban Studies* 2 (1978): 73–88, and Ira Berlin, "Time, Space, and the Evolution of Afro-American Society on British Mainland North America," *American Historical Review* 85 (February 1980): 44–78.

An interesting discussion of the recent literature on slavery is Bruce Collins, "American Slavery and Its Consequences," *Historical Journal* (Cambridge, England) 22 (December 1979): 997–1015.

2. RISE OF THE COTTON KINGDOM

The Industrial Revolution

For the development of the factory system in cotton textiles in the United States, see W. R. Bagnall, *Samuel Slater and the Early Development of Cotton Manufacture in the United States* (Middletown, Conn., 1890); Caroline F. Ware, *The Early New England Cotton Manufacture* (Boston, 1931); and Victor S. Clark, *History of Manufactures in the United States* (New York, 1939), 1:379–80.

Attempts to develop a cotton gin before Whitney are discussed in Daniel H. Thomas, "Pre-Whitney Cotton Gins in French Louisiana," *Journal of Southern History* 31 (May 1965): 135–48; Jeanette Mirsky and Allan Nevins, in *The World of Eli Whitney* (New York, 1968), present a detailed treatment of Whitney's two great enterprises, the cotton gin and the manufacture of small arms for the U.S. government. See also Brother O. Edward, "Eli Whitney: Embattled Inventor," *American History Illustrated* (February 1974): 4–9, 44–47. For the story of Catherine Greene's being the inventor of the cotton gin, see *Boston Globe* June 29, 1980.

Westward Expansion

The expansion of cotton production to the Southwest is discussed in Ulrich Bonnell Phillips, *American Negro Slavery* (New York, 1918), pp. 39, 171–78; Lewis Cecil Gray, *History of Agriculture in the Southern United States to 1860* (Gloucester, Mass., 1958), 2:691, 698–99, 895; and Clement Eaton, *The Growth of Southern Civilization, 1790–1860* (New York, 1961), pp. 44–46. For the removal of the Indians, see Michael Paul Rogin, *Fathers and Children: Andrew Jackson and the Subjugation of the American Indians* (New York, 1974); Mary E. Young, "Indian Removal and Allotment: The Civilized Tribes and Jacksonian Justice," *American Historical Review* 74 (February 1971): 99–118.

The Illegal African Slave Trade

The illegal African slave trade is discussed in W.E.B. Du Bois, *The Suppression of the African Slave Trade to the United States of America, 1638–1870* (Millwood, N.Y., 1973), pp. 109–12, 162–66, and Warren S. Howard, *American Slavers and the Federal Law, 1837–1862* (Berkeley, Calif., 1963), pp. 26–28. For differing views on the extent of the illegal trade, see Du Bois, op. cit., pp. 119–23; 178; W. H. Collins, *The Domestic Slave Trade of the Southern States* (New York, 1904), pp. 12–20; Peter Dugnan and Clarence Clendenen, *The United States and the African Slave Trade, 1619–1862* (Stanford, Calif., 1963), pp. 9–10; Daniel P. Mannix and Malcolm Cowley, *Black Cargoes: A History of the Atlantic Slave Trade, 1518–1865* (New York, 1962), pp. 266–68; Howard, op. cit., pp. 256–57; Kenneth Stampp, *The Peculiar Institution* (New York, 1956), p. 271; Phillips, *American Negro Slavery*, pp. 147–48; Eugene D. Genovese, "American Slaves and Their History," *New York Review of Books*, December 3, 1970, 35. The African Squadron is discussed in Robert S. Wetherall, "The African Squadron, 1843–1861" (master's thesis, University of Delaware, 1968).

For the effect of the panic of 1819 on the South, see Francis Butler Simkins, *A History of the South* (New York, 1967), p. 97.

The Domestic Slave Trade

The decline of tobacco production is discussed in Joseph Clarke Robert, *The Tobacco Kingdom* (Gloucester, Mass., 1965), pp. 136–41, who, however, contends that the extent of the decline has been exaggerated because of an error in calculating hogsheads in view of the fact that the hogshead had become larger since the American Revolution. Gray, op. cit., 2:767, makes the decline clear, however, as do Edward S. Abdy, *Journal of a Residence and Tour in the United States of America, From April, 1833 to October, 1834* (New York, 1969), 2:183, and H. C. Carey, *The Slave Trade, Domestic and Foreign: Why It Exists and How It May Be Extinguished* (Philadelphia, 1862), p. 103. For the description of the slave coffle, see James Silk Buckingham, *Slave States of America* (New York, 1968), 2:553.

Evaluations of the extent of the internal slave trade are to be found in W. H. Collins, *The Domestic Slave Trade of the Southern States* (Port Washington, N.Y., 1904), pp.

61–77; Frederick Bancroft, *Slave Trading in the Old South* (Baltimore, 1931), pp. 383–85; Stampp, op. cit., p. 238.

The challenge to the traditional view of the extent of the domestic slave trade appears in William Calderhead, "How Extensive was the Border State Slave Trade? A New Look," *Civil War History* 18 (March 1972): 42–55; Robert William Fogel and Stanley L. Engerman, *Time on the Cross* (Boston, 1974), 1:46–48. For the figures on slave trading in Alexandria, see Michael A. Ridgeway, "A Peculiar Business: Slave Trading in Alexandria, Virginia, 1825–1861" (master's thesis, Georgetown University, 1976), pp. 156–57.

Organization of the Domestic Slave Trade

The most extensive discussion of the organization and mechanics of the slave trade is contained in Frederic Bancroft's *Slave Trading in the Old South*. Shorter accounts can be found in Phillips, *American Negro Slavery*, pp. 187–204, Stampp, op. cit., pp. 237–45, and Collins, op. cit., pp. 120–24. For a contemporary account, see Ethan A. Andrews, *Slavery and the Domestic Slave Trade in the United States* (Boston, 1836). A recent study is Robert Evans, Jr., "Some Economic Aspects of the Domestic Slave Trade, 1830–1860," *Southern Economic Journal* 27 (April 1961): 329–37. The discussion of the organization of the slave trade in Alexandria, Virginia is based on Ridgeway, op. cit., Wendell Holmes Stephenson, *Isaac Franklin, Slave Trader and Planter of the Old South* (Gloucester, Mass., 1968), Moncure D. Conway, *Testimonies Concerning Slavery* (London, 1865), and William T. Laprade, "The Domestic Slave Trade in the District of Columbia," *Journal of Negro History* 11 (January 1926). For the protest of the Benevolent Society of Alexandria for Ameliorating and Improving the Condition of the People of Color, see *Alexandria Gazette*, June 22, 1827.

The shipment of slaves to the Deep South by ships is discussed in Ridgeway, op. cit., pp. 58–62, and Charles H. Wesley, "Manifests of Slave Shipments along the Waterways 1808–1864," *Journal of Negro History* 28 (April 1942). The description of the slave coffle by a British visitor is in G. W. Feathersonhaugh, *Excursion through the Slave States* (London, 1844), 1:119–22. Charles Ball's account of a slave coffle is in *Narrative of the Life and Adventures of Charles Ball, a Black Man* (Pittsburgh, Pa., 1854), pp. 30–85. Reverend W. B. Allen's reminiscences are in J. Ralph Jones, "Portraits of Georgia Slaves," edited by Tom Landess, *Georgia Review* 16 (May 1972): 268. For William Wells Brown's description, see *Narrative of William Wells Brown, a Fugitive Slave, Written by Himself* (New York, 1855), pp. 50–51. For the use of railroads in the domestic slave trade, see Frederick Law Olmsted, *A Journey in the Seaboard Slave States with Remarks on Their Economy* (New York, 1859), pp. 55–56; Bancroft, op. cit., pp. 289–91; Charles W. Turner, "Railroad Service to Virginia Farmers, 1828–1836," *Agricultural History* 22 (October 1948): 240–42.

For New Orleans as a major slave trading city, see Bancroft, op. cit., pp. 113, 312; "Slave Market of New Orleans," *Chambers's Edinburgh Review*, n.s. 16, July 19, 1851, pp. 47–48; Richard C. Wade, *Slavery in the Cities: The South 1820–1860* (New York, 1967), pp. 198–200, and Judith Kelleher Schafer, "New Orleans Slavery in 1850 as Seen in Advertisements," *Journal of Southern History* 47 (February 1981): 33–56. The discussion of the slave pens and the slave auctions is based on a wide variety of material including the following slave narratives: Ball, op. cit., pp. 72–73; William Anderson, *Life and Narrative of William Anderson, or Dark Deeds of American Slavery Revealed,*

Written by Himself (Chicago, 1857), pp. 14–16; John Brown, *Slave Life in Georgia: A Narrative of Life, Suffering and Escape of John Brown, A Fugitive Slave, New in England*, edited by L. A. Chamerovzow (London, 1855), pp. 123–24; Josiah Henson, *The Life of Josiah Henson, Formerly a Slave Now an Inhabitant of Canada, as Narrated by Himself to Samuel Eliot* (Boston, 1849), pp. 11–13; Solomon Northup, *Twelve Years a Slave*, with a new introduction by Philip S. Foner (New York, 1970), pp. 78–82; Henry Watson, *Narrative of Henry Watson, a Fugitive Slave* (Boston, 1850), pp. 8–9. For a case involving warranties of soundness, see 15 Missouri 453 (1853).

The determination of slave prices is discussed in Phillips, op. cit., pp. 368–75, and Eugene D. Genovese, *Roll, Jordan, Roll* (New York, 1970), pp. 390–92. The prices of slaves in the 1830s and 1840s are set forth in Ridgeway, op. cit., pp. 42, 70, 102. Specific sales cited are in the University of Virginia Slave Trade Papers, Gilliam Family Papers, Harris-Brady Collection, Morton-Halsey Papers. The list of prices in 1853 is in Gray, op. cit., 2:790. For the prices from 1849 through 1860 in the lower South and New Orleans, see Robert Evans, Jr., "The Economics of American Negro Slavery, 1830–1860," in *Aspects of Labor Economies, A Conference of the Universities—National Bureau Committee for Economic Research* (Princeton, N.J., 1962), pp. 199, 202, and Randolph Campbell, "Local Archives as a Source of Slave Prices, Harrison County, Texas as a Test Case," *Historian* 36 (August 1974): 660–69. The prices for the Pierce Butler sale are in *Manuscript Catalogue of Pierce Butler's Share of the Slaves to be Sold at Auction, with Appraised Prices*, Savannah, February 21, 1859.

For the effect of high prices on stealing of blacks, see Earl W. Fanell, "The Abduction of Free Negroes and Slaves in Texas," *Southwest Historical Quarterly* (January 1957): 385–86, and Norman R. Yetman, ed., *Voices from Slavery* (New York, 1970), p. 206. Fanell is also the scholar who argues that the rise in prices was "a blessing" to the slave.

Slave Breeding

Thomas Jefferson's letter is published in Edwin M. Betts, ed., *Thomas Jefferson's Farm Book with Commentary and Relative Extracts from Other Writings* (Princeton, N.J., 1953), p. 43. The statements of Thomas Drew, Thomas Jefferson Randolph, and Edmund Ruffin are in Henry Wilson, *Rise and Fall of the Slave Power* (New York, 1962), 1:100–101, and John Elliott Cairnes, *The Slave Power: Its Character, Career and Probable Designs*, 2d ed. (London, 1863), pp. 127–28. Edward S. Abdy's comment is in his *Journal of a Residence and Tour in the United States of America from April, 1833 to October, 1834* (London, 1835), 2:90, and Olmsted's appears in Olmsted, op. cit., pp. 57–58, 60–61. Fanny Kemble's comment is quoted in Herbert G. Gutman, *Slavery and the Numbers Game: A Critique of* Time on the Cross (Urbana, Ill., 1975), pp. 97–98. For the accounts in the autobiographies of ex-slaves, see Fisk University, *Unwritten History of Slavery: Autobiographical Account of Negro Ex-Slaves* (Nashville, Tenn., 1962), pp. 1–2; Frederick Douglass, *Narrative of the Life of Frederick Douglass, an American Slave, Written by Himself* (Boston, 1854), p. 45; and J. Ralph Jones, "Portraits of Georgia Slaves," *Georgia Review* 22 (October 1970): 407.

For twentieth-century historians, see Bancroft, op. cit., pp. 67–68; Stampp, op. cit., pp. 241–51; Alfred H. Conrad and John R. Meyer, "The Economics of Slavery in the Ante Bellum South," *Journal of Political Economy* 66 (April 1958): 82, 112–14; Richard C. Sutch, "The Breeding of Slaves for Sale and the Westward Expansion of Slavery, 1850–1860," in Stanley L. Engerman and Eugene D. Genovese, eds., *Race and Slavery in the Western Hemisphere: Quantitative Studies* (Princeton, N.J., 1975), 175–240;

Gutman, op. cit., p. 97. For critics of the slave breeding thesis, see Gray, op. cit., pp. 662–63; J. G. Randall and David Donald, *The Civil War and Reconstruction*, 2d ed. (Lexington, Mass., 1969), p. 65; Fogel and Engerman, op. cit., p. 78; Richard G. Lowe and Randolph B. Campbell, "The Slave-Breeding Hypothesis: A Demographic Comment on the 'Buying' and 'Selling' States," *Journal of Southern History* 42 (August 1976): 401–12.

Separation of Families

Blassingame's conclusion is in John Blassingame, *The Slave Community* (New York, 1972), p. 89. See also Justin Labingjohn, "The Sexual Life of the Oppressed: An Examination of the Family Life of Ante-Bellum Slaves," *Phylon* 35 (1974): 394–95. Stampp's analysis is in Stampp, op. cit., pp. 204, 257–58. For Fogel and Engerman, see *Time on the Cross*, 1:49. For criticism of their conclusions, see Sutch, op. cit., p. 174, and Gutman, op. cit., pp. 10–13. See also Genovese, op. cit., p. 332. For ex-slaves' accounts of separation of families, see John Thompson, *The Life of John Thompson, A Fugitive Slave, Containing His History of Twenty-Five Years in Bondage and His Providential Escape* (Worcester, Mass., 1856), p. 112; Brown, op. cit., pp. 89–90; *An Autobiography of the Rev. Josiah Henson* (London, 1877), p. 18–19; Northup, op cit., pp. 85–87; Lydia Maria Child, *Authentic Anecdotes of American Slavery* (Newburyport, Mass., 1838), p. 18. For Still's account, see William Still, *Underground Rail Records, Revised, with a Life of the Author . . .* (Philadelphia, 1872), p. 111. For the callous remark on the temporary nature of the "disconsolate" state of the Negroes whose families had been separated, see Willie Rose, ed., *A Documentary History of Slavery in North America* (New York, 1976), p. 377.

The Missouri case involving the gift of the watch is *Fodden v. Hendrick*, 25 Mo. 411 (1854). For the Charleston Presbytery, see Haven P. Perkins, "Religion For Slaves: Difficulties and Methods," *Church History* 11 (September 1941): 238–39.

Two recent studies depicting the tragic aspects of the domestic slave trade are Donald M. Sweig, "Reassessing the Human Dimension of the Interstate Slave Trade," *Prologue* 12 (Spring 1980): 5–21, and Schafer, op. cit., pp. 33–56.

3. URBAN AND INDUSTRIAL SLAVERY

Urban Slavery

The two major books on slavery in the cities are Richard C. Wade, *Slavery in the Cities* (New York, 1964), and Claudia Dale Golden, *Urban Slavery in the American South, 1820–1860: A Quantitative Study* (Chicago and London, 1976). The two scholars disagree as to the reasons for the decline of urban slavery between 1850 and 1860. Specialized articles dealing with urban slavery are: Terry L. Seip, "Slaves and Free Negroes in Alexandria, 1850–1860," *Louisiana History* 32 (Spring 1969): 148–65; Robert C. Reinders, "Slavery in New Orleans before the Civil War," *Mid-America* 44 (1962): 215–24; William L. Richter, "Slavery in Baton Rouge, 1820–1860," *Louisiana History* 32 (Spring 1969): 131–42; Clement Eaton, "Slave-Hiring in the Upper South: A Step toward Freedom," *Mississippi Valley Historical Review* 46 (March 1960): 663–78; Jane Riblett Wilkie, "The Black Urban Population of the Pre-Civil War South," *Phylon* 37 (September 1976): 250–62. See also Edna Bonacich, "A Theory of Ethnic Antagonism:

The Split Labor Market," *American Sociological Review* 37 (October 1972): 547–49. Herman C. Woessner, "New Orleans, 1840–1860: A Study in Urban Slavery" (Ph.D. diss., Louisiana State University, 1967), directly challenges the assumption that the viability of slavery was dependent on the plantation. See also Claudia Goldin, "A Model to Explain the Relative Decline of Urban Slavery," in Eugene D. Genovese and Stanley L. Engerman, eds., *Race and Slavery in the Western Hemisphere* (Princeton, N.J., 1975).

Slave Hiring

The hiring system is discussed in Wade, op. cit.; Robert Evans, Jr., "The Economics of American Negro Slavery, 1830–1860" (Ph.D. diss., University of Chicago, 1959); Clement Eaton, "Slave-Hiring in the Upper South," *Mississippi Valley Historical Review* 46 (March 1960); Richard B. Morris, "The Measure of Bondage in Slave States," *Mississippi Valley Historical Review* 41 (March 1954); Robert S. Starobin, *Industrial Slavery in the Old South* (New York, 1970); Frederic Bancroft, *Slave Trading in the Old South* (Baltimore, 1931); and Maximilian Reichard, "Black and White on the Urban Frontier: The St. Louis Community in Transition, 1800–1830," *Missouri Historical Society*, bulletin 33 (October 1976). For the origins of slave hiring in the eighteenth century, see Sarah S. Hughes, "Slaves for Hire: The Allocation of Black Labor in Elizabeth City County, Virginia, 1782 to 1810," *William and Mary Quarterly*, 3d ser., 35 (April 1978): 260–86; Edna Chappel, "Self-Hire among Slaves, 1820–1860" (Ph.D. diss., University of Pittsburgh, 1973).

Industrial Slavery

The view that slaves were not suited for industrial work is discussed in Clement Eaton, *A History of the Old South* (New York, 1949), pp. 424–29. The work of Robert S. Starobin is summed up in his *Industrial Slavery*. However, see also his "The Economics of Industrial Slavery in the Old South," *Business History Review* 44 (Summer 1970): 131–74, "Disciplining Industrial Slaves in the Old South," *Journal of Negro History* 53 (April 1968): 111–28, and "Race Relations in Old South Industries," in Allan Weinstein and Frank Otto Gatell, eds., *American Negro Slavery: A Modern Reader* (New York, 1968), pp. 299–309. For the view of Eugene D. Genovese, see his *The Political Economy of Slavery: Studies in the Economy and Society in the Slave South* (New York, 1965), pp. 221–39, and for Hammond's comment, see *DeBow's Review* 8 (June 1850): 518. The beginnings of the textile industry in South Carolina and the importance of slave labor are discussed in Ernest M. Lander, Jr., "Manufacturing in Ante-Bellum South Carolina" (Ph.D. diss., University of North Carolina, 1956), and in his "Slave Labor in South Carolina Cotton Mills," *Journal of Negro History* 38 (April 1953): 160–63. For the comment on integrated cotton mills in Georgia, see James S. Buckingham, *The Slave States of America* (London, 1842), 2:111–12. For the use of slave labor in Southern textiles during the 1830s and the declining use after that decade, see Norris W. Preyer, "The Historian, the Slave and the Ante-Bellum Textile Industry," *Journal of Negro History* 46 (April 1961): 67–82.

For the iron industry in Lexington, see Richard C. Wade, *The Urban Frontier: Pioneer Life in Early Pittsburgh, Cincinnati, Lexington, Louisville, and St. Louis* (Chicago, 1959), p. 126. The story of the Tredegar Iron Works may be found in Kathleen Bruce, *Virginia Iron Manufacture in the Slave Era* (New York, 1931), pp. 220–38; Ronald L. Lewis, "The Use and Extent of Slave Labor in the Virginia Iron Industry: The Ante-Bellum Era," *West Virginia History* 38 (January 1977): 149–51; Philip S. Foner and

Ronald L. Lewis, eds., *The Black Worker: A Documentary History*, Vol. 1 (Philadelphia, 1978), pp. 34–37, and Barbara Green, "Slave Labor at the Maranec Iron Works, 1828–1850," *Missouri Historical Review* 79 (1979): 150–64. For the use of slaves in mines, see Starobin, *Industrial Slavery*, pp. 23–26, and Ronald L. Lewis, " 'The Darkest Abode of Man': Black Miners in the First Southern Coal Field, 1760–1860" (unpublished paper in my possession).

The use of slave labor in the salt industry is fully discussed in John Edmund Stealey III, "Slavery and the Western Virginia Salt Industry," *Journal of Negro History* 59 (April 1974): 105–31. For the use of slave labor in the hemp industry, see James F. Hopkins, *A History of the Hemp Industry in Kentucky* (Lexington, Ky., 1951), pp. 24–30, 132–46. Negro slaves as cowboys is discussed in Philip Durham and Everett Jones, *The Negro Cowboys* (New York, 1968), pp. 13–19. The story of Simon Gray may be found in John Hebron Moore, "Simon Gray, Riverman: A Slave Who Was Almost Free," *Mississippi Valley Historical Review* 49 (December 1962): 472–84. For the use of slave labor in the tobacco industry, see Joseph Clarke Robert, *The Tobacco Kingdom: Plantation, Market and Factory in Virginia and North Carolina, 1800–1860* (Gloucester, Mass., 1938, reprint ed., 1965), pp. 197–208, and J. Alexander Patten, "Scenes in the Old Dominion. Number Two—A Tobacco Market," in Eugene L. Schwabb, ed., *Travels in the South Selected From Periodicals of the Times* (Lexington, Ky., 1973), 2:535–42. The use of slave labor in construction, railroad, and canal works is discussed in "Slave Labor Upon Public Works at the South," *DeBow's Review* 12 (July 1854): 76–82; Starobin, *Industrial Slavery*, pp. 160–67.

Control and Treatment of Industrial Slaves

For the view of Kenneth Stampp on treatment of hired slaves, see *The Peculiar Institution*, p. 84. For the view that slave hiring was a step toward freedom, see Eaton, op. cit., pp. 668–69, Morris, "Measure of Bondage," pp. 231–39, and Edman McKenzie, "Self-Hire in the Upper South" (master's thesis, University of Pittsburgh, 1974), pp. 52–76.

Robert Starobin's analysis of control and discipline of slaves in Southern industry is in his article, "Disciplining Industrial Slaves in the Old South," *Journal of Negro History* 53 (April 1968): 111–28. The control and discipline of slaves in the iron industry are discussed in Charles B. Dew, "Disciplining Slave Ironworkers in the Antebellum South: Coercion, Conciliation and Accommodation," *American Historical Review* 79 (April 1974): 393–418, and Samuel Sydney Bradford, "The Negro Ironworkers in Ante-Bellum Virginia," *Journal of Southern History* 25 (1959): 194–206. See also Randall M. Miller, "The Fabric of Control: Slavery in Antebellum Southern Textile Mills," *Business History Review* 55 (Winter 1981): 471–90, and Barbara L. Green, "Slave Labor at the Marzmee Iron Works, 1828–1850," *Missouri Historical Review* 73 (1979): 150–64. For the experience of Moses Grandy, see Moses Grandy, *Narrative of the Life of Moses Grandy, Late a Slave in the United States of America* (Boston, 1964). The most famous account of an attack on a slave mechanic by white workers is in Frederick Douglass, *Life and Times of Frederick Douglass* (London, 1892), pp. 178–93. William Wells Brown's account is in *Narrative of William W. Brown: A Fugitive Slave* (Boston, 1848).

On the dangers of work in industrial slavery, see Starobin, *Industrial Slavery*, pp. 37–48. For the factors retarding industrialization in the antebellum South, see Eugene D. Genovese and Elizabeth Fox-Genovese, "The Slave Economies in Political Perspective," *Journal of American History* 66 (June 1979): 11–17; Jay Mandle, *The Plantation Econo-*

my (Philadelphia, 1973), pp. 120–25; Starobin, "Economics of Industrial Slavery," pp. 172–74.

A number of the themes discussed in this chapter are developed in James E. Newton and Ronald L. Lewis, eds., *The Other Slaves: Mechanics, Artisans and Craftsmen* (Boston, 1978).

4. PLANTATION SLAVERY

The Pyramid of Authority

A good discussion of the structure of the plantation may be found in John W. Blassingame, "Status and Social Structure in the Slave Community: Evidence from New Sources," in Harry Powers, ed., *Perspectives and Irony in American Slavery* (Jackson, Miss., 1976), pp. 137–51. For black drivers, see Shirley M. Jackson, "Black Slave Drivers in the Southern United States" (Ph.D. diss., Bowling Green State University, 1977); William L. Van Deburg, *The Slave Drivers: Black Agricultural Labor Supervisors in the Antebellum South* (Westport, Conn., 1979); William L. Van Deburg, "Who Were the Slave Drivers?" *Negro History Bulletin* 41 (March–April 1978): 808–11; Frederick Law Olmsted, *A Journey in the Seaboard Slave States with Remarks on their Economy* (New York, 1859), p. 439.

The Work Systems

For the gang and task systems, see Francis P. Gaines, *The Southern Plantation: A Study in the Development of a Tradition* (New York, 1924), pp. 124–56. Work on a sugar plantation is described in J. Carlyle Sitterson, *Sugar Country* (Lexington, Ky., 1953), and V. Alton Moody, "Slavery on Louisiana Sugar Plantations," *Louisiana Historical Quarterly* 7 (April 1924): 200–211. The use of Irish laborers is described in William Howard Russell, *My Diary North and South* (Boston, 1863), pp. 372–73. For the work program on tobacco and rice plantations, see Lewis Cecil Gray, *History of Agriculture in the Southern States to 1860* (Washington, D.C., 1933), 2:723–35, and for cotton see ibid., pp. 703–4, 720–26; James Lawrence Watkins, *King Cotton: A Statistical Review* (New York, 1908), pp. 13, 72, 100, 139, 147, 194; and Charles Shepard Davis, *The Cotton Kingdom in Alabama* (Montgomery, Ala., 1939), pp. 68–79.

Women and Children

The discussion of slave women is based on the following sources: Eugene D. Genovese, *Roll, Jordan, Roll: The World the Slaves Made* (New York, 1947), pp. 495, 497; Gerda Lerner, ed., *Black Women in White America: A Documentary History* (New York, 1972), pp. 7, 65; Benjamin A. Boskin, ed., *Lay My Burden Down: A Folk History of Slavery* (Chicago, 1945), 189; Dorothy Burnham, "The Life of the Afro-American Woman in Slavery," *International Journal of Women's Studies* 1 (July–August 1978): 363–77; Philip S. Foner, *Women and the American Labor Movement: From Colonial Times to the Eve of World War I* (New York, 1979), pp. 98–103; *Age*, April 10, 1889. The quotation from Jacqueline Jones' article is from "'My Mother Was Much of a Woman': Black Women, Work and the Family Under Slavery," *Feminist Studies* 8 (Summer 1980): 243.

For the use of children on the plantations to do odd jobs, see Norman R. Yetman, ed.,

Life under the "Peculiar Institution": Selections from the Slave Narrative Collection (New York, 1970), pp. 58, 182, 232. Olmsted's division of field hands appears in Frederick Law Olmsted, *A Journey in the Seaboard Slave States, with Remarks on Their Economy* (New York, 1856), p. 433. For Mary Chesnut's comment, see Mary Boykin Chesnut, *A Diary from Dixie; as Written by Mary Boykin Chesnut,* edited by Isabella Martin and Myrtle Lockett Avery (New York, 1905), p. 187. See also Catherine Clinton, *The Plantation Mistress: Another Side of Southern Slavery* (Princeton, N.J., 1980), pp. 120–30. For Pennington's comment on overseers, see James W. C. Pennington, *The Fugitive Blacksmith; or, Events in the Life of James W. C. Pennington, Pastor of a Presbyterian Church, New York, Formerly a Slave in the State of Maryland, United States* (New York, 1850; reprint ed., Westport, Conn., 1971), pp. 2–3. Henson's experience is in Josiah Henson, *The Life of Josiah Henson, Formerly a Slave, Now an Inhabitant of Canada* (Boston, 1849), p. 1, and Brown's is in William Wells Brown, *Narrative of William Wells Brown, A Fugitive Slave, Written by Himself* (Boston, 1847), p. 16. For Webber's comment, see Thomas L. Webber, *Deep Like the Rivers: Education in the Slave Quarter Community, 1831–1865* (New York, 1978), p. 21.

Slave Productivity

For Henry Bibb, see *Narrative of the Life and Adventures of Henry Bibb, an American Slave, Written by Himself* (New York, 1849). The best discussion of the overseer is William Kaufman Scarborough, *The Overseer: Plantation Management in the Old South* (Baton Rouge, La., 1966).

Food and Clothing

Information on the usual diet of slaves may be found in George P. Rawick, ed., *The American Slave: A Composite Autobiography* (Westport, Conn., 1972), Vols. 6, 7, 12, 13; Genovese, op. cit.; John W. Blassingame, *The Slave Community: Plantation Life in the Ante-Bellum South (New York, 1972); Leslie Howard Owens, This Species of Property: Slave Life and Culture in the Old South* (New York, 1976), and Kenneth M. Stampp, *The Peculiar Institution: Slavery in the Ante-Bellum South* (New York, 1956). For the comment on slave stealing, see Reverend Peter Randolph, *From Plantation Cabin to Pulpit: The Autobiography of Peter Randolph* (Boston, 1893), pp. 27–28. The account of the sour milk is by Mrs. Sutton in *Unwritten History of Slavery. Autobiographical Account of Negro Ex-Slaves,* Social Science Institute. Fisk University, Nashville, Tenn., 1945, Social Science Documents No. 1. The one about cornmeal is in Benjamin Drew, *The Refugee: A North-Side View of Slavery* (reprint ed., 1969), pp. 194–95. Robert Fogel and Stanley Engerman's picture of the slave diet is in *Time on the Cross* (Boston, 1974), 1:129–30. For the view that the slaves' caloric intake was insufficient, see Owens, op. cit. For the feeding of infants, see Genovese, op. cit., pp. 498–99. Charles Ball, *Fifty Years in Chains* (New York, 1837; reprint ed., New York, 1970), p. 151; Thomas L. Webber, *Deep Like the Rivers: Education in the Slave Quarter Community, 1831–1865* (New York, 1978), pp. 10–12. Frederick Douglass' recollection is in *Narrative of the Life of Frederick Douglass* (Boston, 1845); Louisa Adams' is in Rawick, op. cit., 14:310, and that of Lizzie Williams is in *Southern Exposure* 1 (Winter 1974): 86. For the clothing of slaves, see Gray, op. cit., 1:565; Federal Writer's Project, "Slave Narratives: A Folk History of Slavery in the United States from Interviews with Former Slaves," typewritten records, microfilm records, Reel 51.

Housing and Health

For slave housing, see Blassingame, *Slave Community,* p. 159; John Brown, *Slave Life in Georgia* (London, 1855), p. 191; Austen Steward, *Twenty-Two Years a Slave* (Rochester, N.Y., 1859), p. 19; James C. Smith, *Autobiography of James C. Smith* (Norwich, Conn., 1881), pp. 1–9; Pennington, op. cit., p. 66; Charles Ball, *Slavery in the United States. A Narrative of the Life and Adventures of Charles Ball, A Black Man* (Pittsburgh, Pa., 1853), pp. 36–37; Henson, op. cit., p. 120; Robert Anderson, *From Slavery to Affluence: Memoirs of Robert Anderson, Ex-Slave* (Steamboat Springs, Colo., 1927), p. 56; Benjamin Drew, ed., *A North-Side View of Slavery, The Refuge: or the Narratives of Fugitive Slaves in Canada* (Boston, 1856), p. 105; Webber, op. cit., pp. 13–14.

The discussion of health care is based on the following: Phillips, op. cit., p. 264; Genovese, op. cit., pp. 498–99; Webber, op. cit., pp. 10–11; Leslie Howard Owen, *This Species of Property: Slave Life and Culture in the Old South* (New York, 1976), pp. 64–69; Felice Swados, "Negro Health on the Ante-Bellum Plantations," *Bulletin of the History of Medicine* 10 (1941): 450–72; William Postell, *The Health of Slaves on Southern Plantations* (Baton Rouge, La., 1951). Glowing reports on medical attention may be found in Lewright Sikes, "Medical Care for Slaves: A Preview of the Welfare State,"*Georgia Historical Quarterly* 22 (December 1968): 405–13. For a picture in one state, see Todd L. Savitt, *Medicine and Slavery: The Disease and Health Care of Blacks in Antebellum Virginia* (Urbana, Ill., 1978). For expenditures on health care for slaves, see Arthur Everett Tiedemann, "Slavery in Rural Louisiana 1840–1860" (master's thesis, Columbia University, 1949). On the annual expenditures for the upkeep of slaves, see Olmsted, *Seaboard Slave States,* p. 431; Stampp, op. cit., pp. 232–33; "On the General Mangement of a Plantation," *Southern Agriculturist* 4 (July 1831): 352; John S. Wilson, "The Negro-His Diet, Clothing, Etc.," *American Cotton Planter and Soil of the South,* n.s., 3 (July 1859): 197.

The Lash

For Mary Boykin Chesnut's comment, see Sudie Duncan Sides, "Southern Women and Slavery, Part I," *History Today* 20 (January 1970): 57; for the grand juries, see Richard D. Younger, "Southern Grand Juries and Slavery," *Journal of Negro History* 25 (Fall 1952): 167–74. The terrible story of the murder of George is presented in Boynton Merrill, Jr., *Jefferson's Nephews: A Frontier Tragedy* (Princeton, N.J., 1976). For the incident reported by Olmsted, see *Seaboard Slave States,* pp. 275–76. The information on reports of whippings in the diary of Bennett H. Barrow is in Tiedemann, op. cit., pp. 125–26. The reports based on advertisements for fugitive slaves are in *Vicksburg Register,* December 5, 1838; *New Orleans Commercial Bulletin,* July 21, 1837; *Little Rock (Ark.) State Democrat,* December 24, 1847. The reports on the black recruits during the Civil War are in Bell Irwin Wiley, "Billy Yank and the Black Folk," *Journal of Negro History* 56 (1951): 234. The report of the British consul in Charleston is in Laura W. White, "The South in the 1850's as Seen by British Consuls," *Journal of Southern History* 1 (1935): 33 (emphasis in original). Olmsted's report appears in Frederick Law Olmsted, *A Journey in the Back Country in the Winter of 1853–4* (New York, 1860), p. 82. For advertisements for whips, see Genovese, op. cit., 649. Frances Foster's report of being beaten by her mistress appears in "Do Lord Remember Me" by James de Jongh, a dramatic presentation based on the firsthand memories of former slaves, recorded in the late 1930s under the Federal Writers Project.

For Escott's conclusions on the basis of his statistical survey of slave narratives, see Paul D. Escott, *Slavery Remembered: A Record of Twentieth-Century Slave Narratives* (Chapel Hill, N.C., 1979). David Brion Davis' estimate of the consensus of the twenty years' historiographical debate is in his review in the *New York Review of Books*, June 26, 1980, p. 14.

5. THE TECHNIQUES OF CONTROL

For Stampp's comment, see Kenneth M. Stampp, *The Peculiar Institution* (New York, 1956), p. 143. For the origins and significance of the curse of Ham, see Philip S. Foner, *History of Black Americans: From Africa to the Emergence of the Cotton Kingdom* (Westport, Conn., 1975), pp. 90, 107, 135, 245, 268, and William McKee Evans, "From the Land of Canaan to the Land of Guinea: The Strange Odyssey of the Sons of Ham," *American Historical Review* 85 (February 1980): 15–43.

Respect for Whites

John Brown's comment appears in John Brown, *Life in Georgia: A Narrative of the Life, Sufferings and Escape of John Brown* (London, 1955), and Frederick Douglass' is in *Narrative of the Life of Frederick Douglass* (Boston, 1845), p. 79.

Role of Religion

The discussion of religion is based on the following sources: J. H. Thornwell, *Sermon Preached at the Dedication of a Church Erected in Charleston, South Carolina for the Benefit and Instruction of the Population* (Charleston, S.C., 1850), p. 9; South Carolinian, *Practicable Considerations Founded in the Scriptures Relative to the Slave Population of South Carolina* (Charleston, S.C., 1823), p. 33; "The Colored Man's Catechism," *Douglass' Monthly* (October 1860); *The Negro in Virginia*, comp. Works of the Writers' Project of the Works Projects Administration in the State of Virginia (New York, 1940), p. 108; Philip Slaughter, *Memoir of the Life of the Rt. Rev. William Meade, F.F.* (Cambridge Mass., 1885), pp. 112–28; Samuel Brooke, *Slavery and the Slaveholder's Religion as Opposed to Christianity* (Cincinnati, 1848), p. 30. The comment of the South Carolina planter appears in Janet Daitman Cornelius, "God's Schoolmasters: Southern Evangelists to the Slaves, 1830–1860" (Ph.D. diss., University of Illinois, 1977), pp. 201–10. For the manipulation of slaves' superstitions, see Gladys-Marie Fry, *Night Riders in Black Folk History* (Nashville, Tenn., 1975), p. 56. For the letters of the slaves, see Robert S. Starobin, ed., *Blacks in Bondage: Letters of American Slaves* (New York, 1974), pp. 57–58, 67. For a general discussion, see L. B. Washington, "The Use of Religion for Social Control in American Slavery" (master's thesis, Howard University, 1939). The material on education is derived from Carter G. Woodson, *The Education of the Negro Prior to 1861* (New York, 1915).

Rewards and Incentives

Solomon Northup's comment is in Solomon Northup, *Twelve Years a Slave*, with a new introduction by Philip S. Foner (New York, 1970). For the comment of the Georgia slaveholder, see Stampp, op. cit., p. 163. For the use of incentives, see Eugene Genovese, *Roll, Jordan, Roll* (New York, 1956), p. 539; Guion S. Johnson, *Ante-Bellum North Carolina* (Chapel Hill, N.C., 1937), p. 530; Arthur Everett Tiedemann, "Slavery in Rural Louisiana, 1840–1860" (master's thesis, Columbia University, 1949), pp. 130–32, and Roderick A. McDonald, "To Have and To Hold: The Economic Activities of Black Slaves on Louisiana Sugar Plantations" (Paper presented at meeting of Association for the Study of Afro-American Life and History, New Orleans, October 1980).

Divide and Rule: Privileged Bondsmen

For the role of the driver and house servant as part of the apparatus of control, see Shirley H. Jackson, "Black Slave Drivers in the Southern United States" (Ph.D. diss., Bowling Green State University, 1977); William L. Van Deburg, *The Slave Drivers* (Westport, Conn., 1979); Howell Henry, *Police Control of the Slave in South Carolina* (Emery, Va., 1914); *DeBow's Review* 22 (1857): 376–79; James H. Hammond Papers, Hammond Plantation Manual, Microfilm in Library of Congress, Manuscripts Division; Robert S. Starobin, "Privileged Bondsmen and the Process of Accommodation: The Role of Houseservants and Drivers as Seen in Their Own Letters," *Journal of Social History* 50; E. Ophelia Settle, "Social Attitudes During the Slave Regime: Household Servants versus Field Hands," *Publication of the American Sociological Society* 28 (May 1934): 95–99; C. W. Harper, "House Servants and Field Hands: Fragmentation in the Antebellum Slave Community," *North Carolina Historical Review* 53 (Spring 1978): 42–59; *Narrative of the Life and Adventures of Henry Bibb* (New York, 1894), p. 136; Frederick Law Olmsted, *The Cotton Kingdom* (New York, 1860), 2:202, and William L. Van Deburg, "Slave Drivers and Slave Narratives: A New Look at the 'Dehumanized Elite,'" *Historian* 39 (August 1977): 717–31.

Slave Patrols

For the slave patrols, see E. Russ Williams, Jr., ed., "Slave Patrol Ordinances of St. Tammany Parish Louisiana, 1835–1838," *Louisiana History* (Fall 1972): 399–411; Ray Grande, "Slave Unrest in Florida," *Florida Historical Quarterly* 55 (July 1976): 21–22. Olmsted's comment is in *Journey in the Back Country in the Winter of 1853–4* (New York, 1860), p. 444, and the remark of Governor Haynes is quoted in Harvey Wish, "American Slave Insurrections before 1861," *Journal of Negro History* 22 (1937): 306. The efforts to win over full support among poor whites is discussed in Bertram W. Doyle, *The Etiquette of Race Relations in the South* (Chicago, 1937); W. B. Benn, "Anti-Jeffersonianism in the Ante-Bellum South," *North Carolina Historical Review* 12 (1937): 103–24; James B. Ranck, *Albert Gallatin Brown* (New York, 1937). For DeBow, see J. D. B. DeBow, *The Interest in Slavery of the Southern Non-Slaveholder* (Charleston, S.C., 1860). For Douglass' comment, see *The Life and Times of Frederick Douglass* (Hartford, Conn., 1883), p. 284.

Slave Codes and the Courts

For Douglass' description of slavery, see Philip S. Foner, *Selections from the Writings of Frederick Douglass* (New York, 1945), p. 45. The discussion of the slave codes and the legal status of slaves is based on the following: Helen T. Catterall, ed., *Judicial Cases Concerning American Slavery and the Negro* (Washington, D.C., 1926–1937), esp. 1:150, 223–24; 2:168; 3:571–73; John Codman Hurd, *The Law of Freedom and Bondage in the United States* (Boston, 1858–1863); Barnett Hollander, *Slavery in America: Its Legal History* (New York, 1963); Wilbert E. Moore, "Slave Law and the Social Structure," *Journal of Negro History* 25 (April 1941): 191; Florence R. Beatty-Brown, "Legal Status of Arkansas Negroes before Emancipation," *Arkansas Historical Quarterly* 23 (Spring 1969): 6–13; *Mundeville* v. *Cookenderbert* (CC D.C. 1827), 16 Fed. Cas. 582; Clement Eaton, *A History of the Old South* (New York, 1966), pp. 254–55; Joseph Brevard, *The Statute Law of South Carolina* (Charleston, S.C., 1814), 2:105, 253–55; Joseph C. Robert, *The Tobacco Kingdom* (Durham, N.C., 1938), p. 56; George M. Stroud, *A Sketch of the Laws Relating to Slavery* (Philadelphia, 1856); Stampp, op. cit., pp. 224, 226; Ulrich B. Phillips, *American Negro Slavery* (New York, 1918), p. 502; Maurice S. Hindus, "Black Justice under White Law: Criminal Prosecutions of Blacks in Antebellum South Carolina," *Journal of Southern History* 63 (December 1976): 594–95. For the case of Celia, see Hugh P. Williamson, "The State against Celia: A Slave," *Midwest Journal* 8 (Spring–Fall 1956): 408–20. A. E. Keir Nash has written four articles on this issue: "A More Equitable Past? Southern Supreme Courts and the Protection of the Antebellum Negro," *North Carolina Law Review* 48 (1969–1970): 197–242; "Fairness and Formalism in the Trials of Blacks in the State Supreme Courts of the Old South," *Virginia Law Review* 56 (1970): 64–100; "Negro Rights, Unionism, and Greatness on the South Carolina Court of Appeals: The Extraordinary Chief Justice John Belton O'Neall," *South Carolina Law Review* 21 (1968): 141–90; "The Texas Supreme Court and the Trial Rights of Blacks, 1845–1860," *Journal of American History* 58 (December 1971): 622–42. See also Daniel J. Flanigan, "Criminal Procedure in Slave Trials in the Antebellum South," *Journal of Southern History* 40 (August 1974): 537–64. Higginbotham's criticism of these contentions appears in A. Leon Higginbotham, Jr., "Racism and the Early American Legal Process, 1619–1896," *Annals of the American Academy of Political and Social Science* 407 (May 1973): 9–10. For Cobb's comment, see Thomas Read Roots Cobb, *An Inquiry into the Law of Negro Slavery in the United States of America: To Which Is Prefixed an Historical Sketch of Slavery* (Philadelphia, 1858). For the case of *Peter* v. *Hargrave*, see 46 Va. (5 Grattan) 12 (1848), and Wayne Edward Barry, "Slaves Against Their Master's Will: A Judicial History of Virginia's Manumission Law, 1800–1860," (unpublished M.A. thesis, University of Minnesota, 1979), pp. 56–60.

6. THE SLAVE COMMUNITY

The Quarters

The basic work on the slave community is John Blassingame, *The Slave Community: Plantation Life in the Antebellum South* (New York, 1972, rev. ed., 1979). For a range of critical responses, see Al-Tony Gilmore, ed., *Revisiting Blassingame's "The Slave Community": The Scholars Respond* (Westport, Conn., 1978). For a study of origins of earlier slave communities, see Allan Kulikoff, "The Origins of Afro-American Society in Tidewater Maryland and Virginia 1700 to 1790," *William and Mary Quarterly*, 3d ser. 35 (April 1978): 226–59. For interesting and valuable insights into the operation of the slave community, see Thomas L. Webber, *Deep Like the Rivers: Education in the Slave Quarter Community, 1831–1865* (New York, 1978).

For Harriet M. Farlin's recollection, see B. A. Botkin, ed., *Lay My Burden Down: A Folk History of Slavery* (Chicago, 1945), pp. xi–xii. Henry Bibb's view on stealing is in Henry Bibb, *Narrative of the Life and Adventures of Henry Bibb, An American Slave*

(New York, 1849), p. 166; Charles Ball's view is in Charles Ball, *Fifty Years in Chains*, with a new introduction by Philip S. Foner (New York, 1970), pp. 298–99. John Brown's comment is in John Brown, *Slave Life in Georgia: A Narrative of the Life, Sufferings and Escape of John Brown* (London, 1855), pp. 82–83. See also George P. Rawick, *From Sunup to Sundown: The Making of the Black Community* (Westport, Conn., 1972), p. 69. For the education of slaves, see Carter G. Woodson, *The Education of the Negro Prior to 1861* (New York, 1918), pp. 208–15.

Drivers and Field Hands

The discussion of the slave drivers is based on Shirley M. Jackson, "Black Slave Drivers in the Southern United States" (Ph.D. diss., Bowling Green State University, 1977); William L. Van Deburg, *The Slave Drivers: Black Agricultural Labor Supervisors in the Antebellum South* (Westport, Conn., 1979); William L. Van Deburg, "The Slave Drivers of Arkansas: A View from the Narratives," *Arkansas Historical Quarterly* 35 (Spring 1976): 238–45; Robert S. Starobin, *Blacks in Bondage: Letters of American Slaves* (New York, 1974); Robert S. Starobin, "Privileged Bondsmen and the Process of Accommodation: The Role of House Servants and Drivers as Seen in Their Own Letters," *Journal of Social History* 5 (Fall 1971): 41–70; George Rawick, *The American Slave: A Composite Autobiography* (Westport, Conn., 1971–1972), *South Carolina Narratives*, Pt. I:197–98; Pt. II:166; *Georgia Narratives*, Pt. IV:356–57; Solomon Northup, *Twelve Years a Slave*, with a new introduction by Philip S. Foner (New York, 1970), pp. 367–68; James Williams, *An American Slave Who Was for Several Years a Driver on a Cotton Plantation in Alabama* (New York, 1838), pp. 64–68; Josiah Henson, *The Life of Josiah Henson, Formerly a Slave* (Boston, 1849), p. 21; Peter Randolph, *From Slave Cabin to the Pulpit, The Autobiography of Rev. Peter Randolph* (Boston, 1893), p. 213; Works Project Adminstration, *The Negro in Virginia* (New York, 1969), p. 156.

House Servants and Field Hands

The discussion of the house servants is based on the following sources: Kenneth M. Stampp, *The Peculiar Institution* (New York, 1956), pp. 41–42, 337–39; Joel Gray Taylor, *Negro Slavery in Louisiana* (Baton Rouge, La., 1963), p. 85; James Benson Sellers, *Slavery in Alabama* (University, Ala., 1950), p. 74; Ulrich Bonnell Phillips, *Life and Labor in the Old South* (Boston, 1929), pp. 206–7; Eugene D. Genovese, *Roll, Jordan, Roll* (New York, 1947), pp. 327–65; C. W. Harper, "House Servants and Field Hands: Fragmentation in the Antebellum Slave Community," *North Carolina Historical Review* 55 (January 1978): 42–59; Starobin, *Blacks in Bondage*, p. 11; *The Negro in Virginia*, pp. 41, 43, 148; Rawick, ed., *Mississippi Narratives*, Pt. II:7: 26–130.

The best study of education in the slave community is Webber, op. cit. For Lane's account, see *Narrative of the Life of Lunsford Lane* in William Loren Katz, ed., *Five Slave Narratives* (New York, 1969). See also *Unwritten History of Slavery: Autobiographical Account of Negro Ex-Slaves* (Nashville, Tenn., 1945), and *God Struck Me Dead: Religious Conversion Experiences and Autobiographies of Negro Ex-Slaves* (Nashville, Tenn., 1945), p. 198. For a moving picture of women field hands under slavery, see Angela Y. Davis, *Women, Race and Class* (New York, 1981).

Religion in the Quarters

The discussion of religion in the slave quarter is based on the following sources: Genovese, op. cit., pp. 159–284 and passim; Vincent Harding, "Religion and Resistance

Among Antebellum Negroes, 1800–1860," in August Meier and Elliott Rudwick, eds., *The Making of Black America* (New York, 1969), 1:179–97; Kenneth Baily, "Protestantism and Afro-Americans in the Old South: Another Look," *Journal of Negro History* 56 (November 1971): 451–72; Luther P. Jackson, "Religious Development of the Negro in Virginia from 1760–1869," *Journal of Negro History* 16 (April 1931): 203–4, 209–12; W. Harrison Daniel, "Virginia Baptists and the Negro in the Antebellum Era," *Journal of Negro History* 56 (January 1971): 71–76; Randall M. Miller, "Black Catholics in the Slave South: Some Needs and Opportunities for Study," *Records of the American Catholic Historical Society of Philadelphia* 86 (March–December 1975): 100–101; Rawick, ed., *Texas Narratives*, 4:132. An excellent study also used in this discussion is Albert J. Raboteau, *Slave Religion: The "Invisible Institution" in the Antebellum South* (New York, 1978), esp. pp. 212–51. For slave burials, see David R. Roediger, "And Die in Dixie: Funerals, Death, & Heaven in the Slave Community, 1700–1865," *Massachusetts Review* 12 (Spring 1980): 163–83.

The Spirituals

For Negro spirituals and slave songs, see Thomas W. Higginson, "Negro Spirituals," *Atlantic Monthly* 29 (June 1867): 670–85; Thomas W. Higginson, *Army Life in a Black Regiment* (Boston, 1870), p. 260; William Francis Allen, comp., *Slave Songs of the United States* (New York, 1867), p. 45; Lawrence W. Levine, *Black Culture and Black Consciousness: Afro-American Folk Thought from Slavery to Freedom* (New York, 1977); Lawrence W. Levine, "Slave Songs and Slave Consciousness: An Exploration in Neglected Sources," in Tamara K. Hareven, ed., *Anonymous Americans: Explorations in Nineteenth Century Social History* (Englewood Cliffs, N.J., 1971), pp. 99–130; Miles Mark Fisher, *Slave Songs in the United States* (New York, 1963): Lydia Parrish, *Slave Songs of the Georgia Sea Islands* (Hatboro, Pa., 1965); *Life and Times of Frederick Douglass* (Hartford, Conn., 1882), p. 181. For Douglass' observation on the real meaning of slave songs, see *Narrative of the Life of Frederick Douglass* (Boston, 1845), p. 27. John Little's statement is quoted in Howard Zinn, *A People's History of the United States* (New York, 1980), p. 168.

The Slave Family

For the traditional view of the Negro slave family, see E. Franklin Frazier, "The Negro Slave Family," *Journal of Negro History* 15 (Spring 1930): 198–259; E. Franklin Frazier, *The Negro Family in the United States* (New York, 1932); Stampp, op. cit., pp. 130–32; Stanley M. Elkins, *Slavery: A Problem in American Intellectual and Institutional Life* (Chicago, 1959), pp. 53–54; Richard C. Wade, *Slavery in the Cities: The South, 1820–1860* (New York, 1964), pp. 117–21; Daniel P. Moynihan, *The Negro Family: The Case for National Action* (Washington, D.C., 1965). See also William P. Rainwater and W. L. Yancey, *The Moynihan Report and the Politics of Controversy* (Cambridge, Mass., 1967). The discussion of the new interpretations of the slave family is based on the following sources: Eugene D. Genovese, *Roll, Jordan, Roll*, pp. 442–523; Eugene D. Genovese, "American Slaves and Their History," *New York Review of Books*, December 3, 1970, pp. 34–43; Blassingame, op. cit., pp. 41, 59, 76, 78–79; Rawick, *From Sunup to Sundown*, pp. 112–28; and, of course, Herbert G. Gutman, *The Black Family in Slavery and Freedom, 1750–1925* (New York, 1976), and Herbert G. Gutman, "Slave Family and Its Legacies," *Historical Reflections* 6 (Summer 1979): 183–211. For an incisive criticism of Gutman's *Black Family*, see review by Dan T. Carter in *Reviews in*

American History (June 1977): 166–73. The advertisements in the *Lynchburg Virginian* are in the issues of August 8, 1836, and October 31, 1850. For the frequency of marriage among first cousins among Southern upper-class whites, see Bertran Wyatt-Brown, *Southern Honor: Ethics and Behavior in the Old South* (New York, 1982).

For an interesting discussion of slave folk tales, see Richard Chase, comp., *Joel Chandler Harris, The Complete Tales of Uncle Remus* (Boston, 1955), pp. 6–8, 12–14; David A. Walton, "Joel Chandler Harris as Folklorist: A Reassessment," *Keystone Folklore Quarterly* 11 (Spring 1966): 23–42.

7. SLAVE RESISTANCE IN THE ANTEBELLUM SOUTH

The full text of Paul Laurence Dunbar's poem, "We Wear the Mask," is in Paul Laurence Dunbar, *Lyrics of a Lordly Life*, with an introduction by W. D. Howells (New York, 1926), p. 167.

Day-to-Day Resistance

For a discussion of such slave tactics as malingering, destruction of tools and implements, inefficient working habits, and the like, see Raymond A. Bauer and Alice H. Bauer, "Day to Day Resistance to Slavery," *Journal of Negro History* 27 (October 1942): 388–49; Marion J. Russell, "American Slave Discontent in Records of High Courts," *Journal of Negro History* 31 (October 1946): 411–34; and Herbert Aptheker, *American Negro Slave Revolts* (New York, 1943), pp. 140–49. For criticism of the view that these tactics constituted, in the main, conscious resistance to slavery, see George M. Fredrickson and Christopher C. Lash, "Resistance to Slavery," *Civil War History* 13 (December 1967): 317–19.

Annie Coley's reminiscences are in WPA Collection, Mississippi Department of Archives and History, Box 2262. For the complaint of the whites of Onslaw County, see Donnie D. Bellamy, "Slavery in Microcosm: Onslaw County, North Carolina," *Journal of Negro History* 62 (October 1977): 346. The letter describing the incident involving Summer is in the Weeks Hall Memorial Collection, William Jacobs to Mrs. Mary C. Weeks, November 29, 1837, Department of Archives and Manuscripts, Louisiana State University, Baton Rouge. Discussion of Frederick Douglass' battle with Edward Covey will be found in Philip S. Foner, *Frederick Douglass* (New York, 1964), pp. 19–20, and the full account is in *Narrative of Frederick Douglass*, 70–73. Solomon Northup's battle with his master is in *Solomon Northup, Twelve Years a Slave*, with a new introduction by Philip S. Foner (New York, 1970), pp. 89–90. The testimony of Albert Forester in the murder of Samuel is in Concordia Parish Inquest Case file, Louisiana State University, Department of Archives and Manuscripts, Baton Rouge, July 5, 1857. W.E.B. Du Bois' comment is in W.E.B. Du Bois, *John Brown*, with an introduction by Herbert Aptheker (Millwood, N.Y., 1973), p. 81. The account of the poisoning in Virginia appears in the *Lynchburg Virginian*, November 24, 1834. For Mays' comment, see Robert E. May, "John A. Quitman and His Slaves: Reconciling Slave Resistance with the Proslavery Defense," *Journal of Southern History* 46 (November 1980): 554, 560, 561.

Fugitive Slaves

Daniel Goodard's comment appears in WPA Files, "Slave Narratives," South Carolina, Library of Congress. The view of the significance of escape as a form of resistance to slavery is that of James M. McPherson, Lawrence B. Holland, James M. Banner, Nancy J. Weiss, and Michael D. Bell, *Blacks in America: Bibliographical Essays* (Garden City, N.Y., 1971), p. 94. The Charleston paper of 1827 is the *Charleston* (S.C.) *Observer*, July 21, 1827, reprinted in John R. Commons et al., eds., *A Documentary History of American Industrial Society* (Cleveland, 1910), 2:90–91. The maroons are treated in two articles by Herbert Aptheker—"Maroons within the Present Limits of the United States," *Journal of Negro History* 24 (April 1939): 167–84; "Slave Guerilla Warfare," in *To Be Free: Studies in American Negro History* (New York, 1948), pp. 11–30; and in Michael P. Johnson, "Runaway Slaves and the Slave Communities in South Carolina, 1799–1830," *William and Mary Quarterly*, 3d ser. 38 (July 1981): 418–41. For fugitive slaves in Canada, see Robin Wink, *The Negro in Canada* (New Haven, Conn., 1972), pp. 144–56. For the full text of "I'm on My Way to Canada" (written to the tune of "Oh, Susannah") see Philip S. Foner, *American Labor Songs of the Nineteenth Century* (Urbana, Ill., 1975), p. 90. The account of the fugitive escape to Mexico is in Frederick Law Olmsted, *A Journey Through Texas: or, a Saddle-Trip in the Southwestern Frontier* (New York, 1857), pp. 256–57. William Still, *The Underground Railroad* (Philadelphia, 1872), and Larry Gara, *The Liberty Line: The Legend of the Underground Railroad* (Lexington, Ky., 1961) are the two books discussed on the issue of the role of the Underground Railroad.

For the reports of fugitive slaves in the federal census, see J.D.B. DeBow, *The Seventh Census of the United States, 1850* (Washington, D.C., 1853), pp. 220, 222, and *Preliminary Report of the Eighth Census* (Washington, D.C., 1862), pp. 137, 263, and in Michael P. Johnson, "Runaway Slaves and the Slave Communities in South Carolina, 1799–1830," *William and Mary Quarterly*, 3d ser., 38 (July 1981): 418–41. Harriet Tubman's planning for her escape is discussed in Earl Conrad, *Harriet Tubman* (Washington, D.C., 1943), pp. 37–38. For the assistance given to fugitive slaves by black seamen, see Benjamin Quarles, *Black Abolitionists* (New York, 1969), p. 147. For the accounts of fugitives who escaped from the lower South, see Gilbert Barnes and Dwight L. Dumond, eds., *Letters of Theodore Dwight Weld, Angelina Grimké Weld, and Sarah Grimké, 1822–1844* (New York, 1934), 2:512–13, and Larry Gara, "Some Self-Help Plans of Fugitive Slaves," *Negro History Bulletin* (January 1952): 75–76. The handbill listing a reward for "Esther" is in the Maryland Historical Society, Baltimore, and is reprinted in Elwood L. Bridner, Jr., "The Fugitive Slaves of Maryland," *Maryland Historical Magazine* 66 (Spring 1971): 33. For the sex and ages of Maryland's three hundred fugitives, see ibid, pp. 36–38.

Frederick Douglass' escape from slavery is discussed in Foner, *Frederick Douglass*, pp. 22–23. For the escape of Ellen and William Craft, see William Craft, *Running a Thousand Miles for Freedom, or, The Escape of William and Ellen Craft from Slavery* (London, 1860), and Still, op. cit., pp. 608–10. Henry "Box" Brown's escape is described in Charles Stearns, *Narrative of Henry Box Brown, Who Escaped from Slavery Enclosed in a Box 3 Feet Long and Wide* (Boston, 1849), pp. 59–62; Still, op. cit., pp. 81–84. For the full text of the song, "Escape from Slavery of Henry Box Brown," see Foner, *American Labor Songs*, pp. 91–92. The group escapes are described in Sidney Gallway, *The Underground Railroad in Tompkins County* (Ithaca, N.Y., 1963), pp. 6–7; Tendai Mutunhu, "John W. Jones: Underground Railroad Station-Master," *Negro History Bulletin* 41 (March–April 1978): 815–16; Levi Coffin, *Reminiscences of Levi Coffin* (Cincinnati, 1880), p. 179; and R. C. Smedley, *History of the Underground Railroad in Chester and the Neighboring Counties of Pennsylvania* (Lancaster, Pa., 1883), p. 228.

The accounts of family escapes are in Bridner, op. cit., pp. 40–41, and Still, op. cit., p. 143. On the difficulties of successful escape from slavery, see W. W. Siebert, *The Underground Railroad from Slavery to Freedom* (New York, 1899), pp. 28–29, 152. Harriet Tubman's jubilant comment appears in Conrad, op. cit., p. 38.

Slave Conspiracies and Revolts

For the banning of slaves from practicing medicine in Tennessee, see Helen T. Caterall, *Judicial Cases Concerning American Slavery and the Negro* (New York, 1926–1937), pp. 520–21. The pioneering articles on slave revolts are Harvey Wish, "American Slave Insurrections before 1861," *Journal of Negro History* 22 (July 1937): 299–320, and Herbert Aptheker, "American Negro Slave Revolts," *Science and Society* 1 (1936–1937): 512–38, and "More on American Negro Slave Revolts," *Science and Society* 2 (January 1938): 386–91. Carroll's study is Joseph C. Carroll, *Slave Insurrections in the United States, 1800–1865* (Boston, 1938). Aptheker's full-length study, *American Negro Slave Revolts* (New York, 1943), originally was his doctoral dissertation at Columbia University. His criterion for determining a slave revolt is on pages 162–63. The criticism of Aptheker is in Chase C. Mooney, "The Literature of Slavery: A Reevaluation," *Indiana Magazine of History* 47 (September 1951): 255, and Kenneth M. Stampp, "Rebels and Samboes: The Search for the Negro's Personality in History," *Journal of Southern History* 37 (August, 1971): 370. For Gabriel Prosser's conspiracy, see Philip S. Foner, *History of Black Americans: From Africa to the Emergence of the Cotton Kingdom* (Westport, Conn., 1975), pp. 453–56.

Denmark Vesey's Conspiracy

The discussion of Denmark Vesey's conspiracy is based on the following sources: Lionel H. Kennedy and Thomas Parker, *An Official Report of the Trials of Sundry Negroes Charged with an Attempt to Raise an Insurrection in the State of South Carolina* (Charleston, S.C., 1822); William W. Freehling, *Prelude to Civil War; the Nullification Controversy in South Carolina, 1816–1836* (New York, 1966); John Oliver Killens, ed., *The Trial Record of Denmark Vesey* (Boston, 1970); Herbert Aptheker, *American Negro Slave Revolts* (New York, 1943), pp. 15, 65, 81, 98, 106, 115, 219, 268–75; John Lofton, *Insurrection in South Carolina: The Turbulent World of Denmark Vesey* (Yellow Springs, Ohio, 1964); Joesph G. Carroll, *Slave Insurrections in the United States* (New York, 1938), pp. 83–117; Robert S. Starobin, ed., *Denmark Vesey: The Slave Conspiracy of 1822* (Englewood Cliffs, N.J., 1970); and Max L. Kleinman, "The Denmark Vesey Conspiracy: An Historiographical Study," *Negro History Bulletin* 37 (February–March 1974): 225–29. Higginson's comment appears in Thomas W. Higginson, "Denmark Vesey," *Atlantic Monthly* 7 (June 1861): 730, and Aptheker's is in *American Negro Slave Revolts*, p. 268. Richard C. Wade's revisionist article on the Vesey conspiracy appears in "The Vesey Plot: A Reconsideration," *Journal of Southern History* 30 (May 1964): 143–61.

Interlude

For the discussion in this section, see the following: Herbert Aptheker, "Negro Slave Revolts in the United States, 1526–1860," in *Essays in the History of the American Negro* (New York, 1948), pp. 40–44, 47; Herbert Aptheker, "Slave Guerrilla Warfare," in *To Be Free: Studies in American Negro Slavery* (New York, 1952), pp. 24–25; James

Taylor, "Slave Conspiracies in North Carolina," *North Carolina Historical Review* 5 (January 1928): 24; *African Repository* 6 (February 1831): 383–84.

Nat Turner's Rebellion

In reconstructing the Nat Turner insurrection, I have relied on the following sources: Thomas R. Gray, ed., *The Confessions of Nat Turner, the leader of the late insurrection in Southampton (County) Va.* (Baltimore, 1831); "The Nat Turner Insurrection," *Anglo-African Magazine* 1 (1959): 387–97; Thomas Wentworth Higginson, "Nat Turner's Insurrection," *Atlantic Monthly* 8 (August 1861): 173–87, reprinted in Higginson, *Travellers and Outlaws* (Boston, 1889); William S. Drewry, *The Southampton Insurrection* (Washington, D.C., 1900); Herbert Aptheker, *Nat Turner's Slave Rebellion* (New York, 1967); Henry I. Tragle, "Southampton Slave Revolt," *American History Illustrated* 6 (November 1971): 4–11, 44–46; Stephen B. Oates, "Children of Darkness," *American Heritage* 24 (October 1973): 42–47, 89–91; Stephen B. Oates, *The Fires of Jubilee: Nat Turner's Fierce Rebellion* (New York, 1975). Two volumes of collections of documents have been published: Eric Foner, ed., *Nat Turner* (Englewood Cliffs, N.J., 1971), and the book by Henry Irving Tragle, *The Southampton Slave Revolt of 1831: A Compilation of Source Material* (Amherst, Mass., 1971). Although the latter is the most comprehensive collection of documents, covering virtually all aspects of the rebellion, it does not include any black perspectives on Turner, which are available in the letters of black abolitionists, speeches of black abolitionists, and in fugitive slave narratives.

Reaction to the Rebellion

For the reaction to Turner's revolt, see in addition to the works cited above, John Cromwell, "The Aftermath of Nat Turner's Insurrection," *Journal of Negro History* 6 (May 1920): 218–32; Elizabeth Lawson, "After Nat Turner's Revolt," *Daily Worker*, August 21, 1936, p. 7; Robert N. Elliott, "The Nat Turner Insurrection as Reported in the North Carolina Press," *North Carolina Historical Review* 38 (January 1961): 1–17; James Newton, "Delaware's Reaction to the Nat Turner Rebellion," *Negro History Bulletin* (December 1974–January 1975): 328–31; Ira Berlin, ed., "After Nat Turner: A Letter from the North," *Journal of Negro History* 55 (April 1970): 145–51.

For the slave song on Nat Turner, see Philip S. Foner, *American Labor Songs*, pp. 93–94. The continuing interest in Nat Turner among black Americans is set forth in Philip S. Foner, ed., *The Voice of Black Americans: Major Speeches by Negroes in the United States, 1797–1971* (New York, 1972), pp. 3, 88, 203, 264, 538–40, 822, 843, 1031. See also William Wells Brown, *The Black Man, His Antecedents, His Genius* (reprint ed., New York, 1968), p. 7; George Williams, *History of the Negro Race in America* (reprint ed., New York, 1968), 2:91; "Nat Turner," a poem by T. Thomas Fortune, *New York Globe*, October 18, 1884; Sterling Brown, "Remembering Nat Turner," *Crisis*, February, 1939, p. 48; Eric Foner, op. cit., pp. 158–77.

William Styron's Confessions of Nat Turner

The literature of the controversy over William Styron's novel *The Confessions of Nat Turner* is extensive. The following are especially useful: C. Vann Woodward, *New Republic*, October 7, 1967; Herbert Aptheker, *Nation*, October 16, 1967, and "Styron-Turner and Nat Turner: Myth and Truth," *Political Affairs* 46 (October 1967): 40–50; Henry Irving Tragle, "Styron and His Sources," *Massachusetts Review* (Winter 1970):

135–53; William Styron, reply to Aptheker, *Nation*, April 22, 1968; William Styron in *New York Times*, August 5, 1967, February 11, 1968; *New York Review of Books*, November 19, 1970; Gertrude Wilson, "Styron's Folly," *New York Amsterdam News*, December 30, 1967; Charles V. Hamilton in *Saturday Review*, June 22, 1968; James D. Bilotta, in *Negro History Bulletin* (December 1974–January 1975); John Henrik Clarke, ed., *William Styron's Nat Turner, Ten Black Writers Respond* (Boston, 1968); Eugene D. Genovese's critical review in *New York Review of Books*, September 12, 1968, and response by Vincent Harding, one of the ten black writers, November 7, 1968; Martin Duberman's critical review of *Ten Black Writers* in *New York Times Sunday Book Review*, August 11, 1968, and response in ibid., September 1, 1968. Articles in scholarly journals on the controversy include: Seymour L. Gross and Eileen Bender, "History, Politics and Literature: The Myth of Nat Turner," *American Quarterly* 23 (October 1971): 487–518; John White, "The Novelist as Historian: William Styron and American Negro Slavery," *Journal of American Studies* 4 (February 1971): 233–45, and Arthur D. Casciato and James C. W. West III, "William Styron and the Southampton Insurrection," *American Literature* 52 (January 1981): 563–77. A summary of the controversy may be found in J. Duff and P. Mitchell, ed., *The Nat Turner Rebellion: The Historical Event and the Modern Controversy* (New York, 1975), and Herbert Shapiro, "*The Confessions of Nat Turner:* William Styron and His Critics," *Negro American Literature Forum* 9 (Winter 1975): 99–104. Shapiro himself criticizes Styron's historical accuracy.

More Conspiracies and Revolts

A listing of most of the rumors and reports of conspiracies from 1835 to the outbreak of the Civil War may be found in Aptheker, *American Negro Slave Revolts*, pp. 325–59. The account of the conspiracy led by Uncle Isaac is in James Redpath, *The Roving Editor* (Boston, 1858), pp. 269–83. The Maryland event of 1845 is discussed in Jeffrey Brackett, *The Negro in Maryland: A Study of the Institution of Slavery* (Baltimore, 1889), p. 96 and in Aptheker, *American Negro Slave Revolts*, p. 337. For the Kentucky event of 1848, see ibid., p. 338 and J. Winston Coleman, Jr., *Slavery Times in Kentucky* (Chapel Hill, N.C., 1940), p. 88. The slave insurrection panic of 1856 is discussed in Aptheker, *American Negro Slave Revolts*, pp. 347–54; Harvey Wish, "The Slave Insurrection Panic of 1856," *Journal of Southern History* 5 (May 1939): 207–22; Robert S. Starobin, *Industrial Slavery in the Old South* (New York, 1970), pp. 89–90; Caleb P. Patterson, *The Negro in Tennessee, 1790–1865* (Austin, Tex., 1922), pp. 49–50; Chase C. Mooney, *Slavery Times in Tennessee* (Bloomington, Ind., 1957), pp. 62–63; Coleman, op. cit., pp. 107–10; Clement Eaton, *The Freedom-of-Thought Struggle in the Old South* (New York, 1964), pp. 99–102; Charles B. Dew, "Black Ironworkers and the Slave Insurrection Panic of 1856," *Journal of Southern History* 41 (August 1975): 321–38. Aptheker, Wish, Starobin, and Patterson are convinced that a real insurrection was planned; Mooney and Coleman are noncommittal; and Eaton and Dew reject the genuineness of the 1856 insurrection.

The slave revolt on the *Amistad* is discussed in Philip S. Foner, *History of Black Americans*, 1:126–27. There are three scholarly studies of the slave revolt on the *Creole:* Wilburn Williams, Jr., "The *Creole* Revolt: New Directions for the History of Slave Rebellions" (honors thesis, Amherst College, 1971); Howard Jones, "The Peculiar Institution and National Honor: The Case of the Creole Slave Revolt," *Civil War History* 20 (March 1975): 28–50; and Edward D. Jervey and C. Harold Huber, "The *Creole* Affair," *Journal of Negro History* 65 (Summer 1980): 196–211. See, in addition, Annie

Heloise Abel and Frank J. Klingberg, eds., *A Side-Light on Anglo-American Relations, 1839–1858: Furnished by the Correspondence of Lewis Tappan and Others with the British and Foreign Anti-Slavery Society* (New York, 1970). Frederick Douglass, who admired Madison Washington, wrote a short story about him and the *Creole* revolt which was entitled, "The Heroic Slave." Julia Griffiths, ed., *Autographs for Freedom* 1 (1853–1854): 174–239, and reprinted in Philip S. Foner, *The Life and Writings of Frederick Douglass*, Vol. 5: *1844–1860* (New York, 1975), pp. 473–506. Sections of the short story also appeared in *Frederick Douglass' Paper*, March 11, 1853. For a fairly complete documentary collection on the *Creole* affair, see Senate Documents, 27th Cong., 2d sess., II, no. 51, pp. 1–46.

The escape of slaves from Key West to the Bahamas is discussed in Julia Floyd Smith, *Slavery and Plantation Growth in Antebellum Florida, 1821–1860* (Gainesville, Fla., 1973), p. 106. For Raboteau's point on religion as a form of resistance, see Albert J. Raboteau, *Slave Religion: "The Invisible Institution" in the Antebellum South* (New York, 1978), p. 318.

For Genovese's discussion of slave rebellions in the New World, see Eugene D. Genovese, *From Rebellion to Revolution: Afro-American Slave in the Making of the Modern World* (Baton Rouge, La., 1979).

The relationship of resistance to slave survival and independence is discussed in Keith Andrew Winsell, "Black Identity: The Southern Negro, 1830–1845" (Ph.D. diss., University of California, Los Angeles, 1971).

For Cartwright's treatise on the Negro diseases he had discovered, see Samuel Cartwright, "Diseases and Peculiarities in the Negro Race," *DeBow's Review* 11 (September 1851): 331–34.

8. FREE BLACKS IN THE ANTEBELLUM SOUTH

Earlier studies of the free Negro include the following works: John H. Russell, *The Free Negro in Virginia, 1619–1865* (Baltimore, 1913); James M. Wright, *The Free Negro in Maryland, 1634–1860* (Baltimore, 1921); Charles S. Sydnor, "The Free Negro in Mississippi before the Civil War," *American Historical Review* 32 (July 1927): 769–88; Luther P. Jackson, *Free Negro Labor and Property Holding in Virginia, 1830–1860* (Chapel Hill, N.C., 1943); E. Horace Fitchett, "The Traditions of the Free Negro in Charleston, South Carolina," *Journal of Negro History* 25 (April 1940): 139–51, "The Origins and Growth of the Free Negro Population of Charleston, South Carolina," *Journal of Negro History* 26 (1941): 421–37, and "The Status of the Free Negro in Charleston, South Carolina and His Descendants in Modern Society," *Journal of Negro History* 32 (1947): 430–51.

The best recent study of the free Negro in the South is Ira Berlin, *Slaves without Masters: The Free Negro in the Antebellum South* (New York, 1974). Recent state studies include Letitia Woods Brown, *Free Negroes in the District of Columbia, 1790–1846* (New York, 1972); Herbert E. Sterkx, *The Free Negro in Antebellum Louisiana* (Rutherford, N.J., 1972), and Marina Wilkramangrake, *A World in Shadow—The Free Black in Antebellum South Carolina* (Columbia, S.C., 1973).

Several articles dealing with the free Negro in a number of Southern states and cities have been reprinted in John H. Bracey, Jr., August Meier, and Elliott Rudwick, eds.,

Free Blacks in America, 1800–1860 (Belmont, Calif., 1971). Recent comparative studies of the free Negro include David W. Cohen and Jack Greene, eds., *Neither Slave Nor Free: The Freedman of African Descent in the Slave Societies of the New World* (Baltimore, 1972), and Laura Foner, "The Free People of Color in Louisiana and St. Domingue, A Comparative Portrait of Two Three-Caste Slave Societies," *Journal of Social History* 3 (1970):406–30.

Statistics for the free black population in the upper and lower South in 1820 and 1860 are derived from *Population of the United States in 1860* (Washington, D.C., 1864), pp. 598–604. On the greater number of free black women, see Berlin, op. cit., p. 177.

Restrictions on Freedom Routes and Self-Purchase

For the changes in manumission and freedom suits in the Southern states after the post-Revolutionary decades, see Berlin, op. cit., p. 138, and ibid., p. 153, for the manumission of decrepit slaves. For the manumission of Jenny and her son, see Joel Gray Taylor, *Negro Slavery in Louisiana* (Baton Rouge, La., 1963), p. 159. For the law in Raleigh, see John Spencer Bassett, *Anti-Slavery Leaders of North Carolina* (Baltimore, 1898), pp. 60–74.

The only biography of George Moses Horton is Richard Walser, *The Black Poet* (Chapel Hill, N.C., 1968). There is also an article on Horton: Blyden Jackson, "George Moses Horton, North Carolinian," *North Carolina Historical Review* 41 (Spring 1976): 140–47. Horton is discussed in Sumner Eliot Matison, "Manumission by Purchase," *Journal of Negro History* 33 (January 1948): 157–58; and his poem is published in Sterling A. Brown, Arthur P. Davis, and Ulysses Lee, eds., *The Negro Caravan* (New York, 1941), pp. 288–89. Theodore Weld's account of the situation in Cincinnati is in his letter of March 18, 1834, in Gilbert H. Barnes and Dwight L. Dumond, eds., *Weld-Grimké Letters* (New York, 1934), 1:134. For the other report on Cincinnati, see Herbert Aptheker, "Buying Freedom," in *To Be Free: Studies in American Negro History* (New York, 1948), p. 197. For the cases of Samuel Martin and John B. Meachum, see *Journal of Negro History* 3 (1918): 91; 13 (1928): 534. For the self-purchase of Peter Still, see Kate E. R. Pickard, *The Kidnapped and the Ransomed. Being the Personal Recollections of Peter Still and His Wife "Una" After Forty Years of Slavery* (Syracuse, N.Y., 1856); John Fowler, "Peter Still versus the Peculiar Institution," *Civil War History* 13 (December 1967): 342–43. For the free Negro's role in such arrangements, see Mattison, op. cit., pp. 165–66. The discussion of appeals for help in purchasing one's family is based on Aptheker, op. cit., pp. 36–39; *Narrative of the Life of Rev. Noah Davis* (Baltimore, 1859), preface; Pickard, op. cit.; Martin W. Hawkins, *Lunsford Lane* (Boston, 1863), pp. 132–33; Martin Luther King, Jr., *Why We Can't Wait* (New York, 1964), pp. 120–21. The case of Edward Brown is discussed in *Boston Commonwealth* reprinted in *Liberator*, September 8, 1854.

Fear of and Restrictions on Free Blacks

The memorial of Charleston citizens is in John R. Commons, ed., *A Documentary History of the American Industrial Society* (Cleveland, 1910), 2:108–9. The *Charleston Mercury* is reprinted in *National Anti-Slavery Standard*, March 1, 1852. For the *Jackson Semi-Weekly* Mississippian, see Berlin, op. cit., p. 341. The comment of the New Orleans editor is in Richard Wade, *Slavery in the Cities* (New York, 1967), pp. 250–51. The discussion of the 1840 census is based on Alexander Thomas and Samuel Sillen, *Racism and Psychiatry* (New York, 1972), pp. 16–19.

For restrictions on free blacks, see Berlin, op. cit.; Russell, op. cit., pp. 122–25; Sydnor, op. cit., pp. 769–72; Brown, op. cit., pp. 118–25; Wilkramangrake, op. cit., pp. 73–82; Andrew Forest Muir, "The Free Negro in Galveston County, Texas," *Negro History Bulletin* 22 (December 1958): 68.

Economic Status of Free Blacks

The discussion in this section is based on the following sources: Berlin, op. cit., pp. 235–38, 320–24; John A. Munroe, "The Negro in Delaware," *South Atlantic Quarterly* 56 (Autumn 1958): 428–34; John Hope Franklin, *Free Negro in North Carolina, 1790–1860* (Chapel Hill, N.C., 1943), p. 47; Robert E. Reinder, "The Free Negro in the New Orleans Economy, 1850–1860," *Louisiana History* 61 (Summer 1965): 274–76; Philip S. Foner and Ronald L. Lewis, eds., *The Black Worker: A Documentary History from Colonial Times to the Present* (Philadelphia, 1978), 1:196–235; M. Ray Della, Jr., "The Problems of Negro Labor in the 1850's," *Maryland Historical Magazine* 66 (Spring 1971): 13–20, 28; Donald E. Everett, "Free Persons of Color in New Orleans, 1803–1865" (Ph.D. diss., Tulane University, 1952), pp. 44–55.

Education for Free Blacks and Persecution of Margaret Douglass

The discussion in this section is based on the following sources: E. Franklin Frazier, *The Free Negro Family: A Study of Family Origins before the Civil War* (Nashville, Tenn., 1932), pp. 12–16; Nathan Willey, "Education of the Free Colored Population of Louisiana," *Harper's New Monthly Magazine* 33 (July 1, 1866): 245–48; Russell, op. cit., pp. 142–45; *Richmond Enquirer*, March 4, 1853; Daniel D. Bellamy, "The Education of Blacks in Missouri Prior to 1861," *Journal of Negro History* 59 (April 1974): 143–57; Margaret Douglass, *The Personal Narrative of Mrs. Margaret Douglass, a Southern Woman Who Was Imprisoned for One Month in the Common Jail of Norfolk, under the Laws of Virginia, for the Crime of Teaching Colored Children to Read* (Boston, 1854); *American Beacon* (Norfolk), November 26, 1853; *Norfolk Argus*, February 9, 1854; *Liberator*, March 7, December 8, 1854; *New York Times*, November 29, December 6, 1853; *National Anti-Slavery Standard*, February 8, 1854.

On education in Washington, D.C., see Lillian G. Davney, *The History of Schools for Negroes in the District of Columbia, 1807–1947* (Washington, D.C., 1949), pp. 12–21; Carter G. Woodson, *Education of the Negro Prior to 1861* (New York, 1915), pp. 133–44, 266–67. For Myrtilla Miner, see Ellen O'Connor, *Myrtilla Miner* (New York, 1889); Henry Barnard, "Education in the District of Columbia," *American Journal of Education* 19 (1870): 201, 206–9. For Frederick Douglass' tribute to Myrtilla Miner, see Philip S. Foner, ed., *Frederick Douglass on Women's Rights* (Westport, Conn., 1976), pp. 160–62.

Black Churches and Black Social Fraternal, and Benevolent Organizations

This section is based on the following sources: Berlin, op. cit., pp. 241–42, 296–99, 302–05; *Acts Passed at a General Assembly of the Commonwealth of Virginia . . . in the Year of our Lord, One Thousand Eight Hundred and Thirty-One* (Richmond, Va., 1832), pp. 20–22; E. Franklin Frazier, *The Negro in the United States* (New York, 1957), pp. 98–125; Janet Duitman Cornelius, "God's Schoolmasters: Southern Evangelists to the Slaves, 1830–1860" (Ph.D. diss., University of Illinois, 1977), pp. 130–54.

For black organizations, see E. Horace Fitchett, "The Free Negro in Charleston, South

Carolina'' (Ph.D. diss., University of Chicago, 1950), pp. 29–56; Berlin, op. cit., pp. 309–16; Henry S. Robinson, ''Some Aspects of the Free Negro Population of Washington, D.C., 1800–1862,'' *Maryland Historical Magazine* 64 (Spring 1969): 60; Foner and Lewis, op. cit., 1:109–13: Norfolk *American Beacon,* April 21, 22, 25, 1854.

Deterioriation of the Status of Free Blacks

This section is based on the following sources: Berlin, op. cit., pp. 131–37, 312–16; Helen T. Caterall, *Judicial Cases Concerning American Slavery and the Negro* (Washington, D.C., 1932), 3:601; Annie Lee Stahl, ''The Free Negro in Ante-Bellum Louisiana'' (master's thesis, Louisiana State University, 1934), pp. 23–32; Robert C. Reinders, ''The Decline of the New Orleans Free Negro in the Decade before the Civil War,'' *Journal of Mississippi History* 24 (April 1962): 89–94; Laura Foner, op. cit., pp. 427–28; Julia Floyd Smith, *Slavery and Plantation Growth in Antebellum Florida 1821–1860* (Gainesville, Fla., 1973), pp. 119, 121; Wade, op. cit., p. 269; Virginia C. Moore, ''The Free Negro in Texas, 1845–1860'' (master's thesis, Lamar State College of Technology, 1969), pp. 54, 57; *Texas Almanac for 1858* (Galveston, Tex., 1857), pp. 132; *National Anti-Slavery Standard,* February 18, 1860.

9. FREE BLACKS IN THE ANTEBELLUM NORTH I

William Hamilton, *An Oration Delivered in the African Church, on the Fourth of July, 1827, in Commemoration of the Abolition of Slavery in the State* (New York. 1827), pp. 5–6; William Chambers, *Things as They Are in America* (New York, 1968), p. 357.

Segregation and Exclusion: East and West

For the populations of Philadelphia, Boston, and New York City, see U.S. Bureau of the Census, *Negro Population, 1790–1915* (Washington, D.C., 1918), pp. 60–62; J. D. B. DeBow, *Statistical View of the United States* (Washington, D.C., 1854), p. 63; U.S. Census Office, *Population of the United States in 1860* (Washington, D.C., 1864), p. 337. For Douglass' comment on Philadelphia, see Philip S. Foner, *Essays in Afro-American History* (Philadelphia, 1978), pp. 22–23. Tocqueville's comment is in George Wilson Pierson, *Tocqueville in America* (New York, 1959), p. 33. The ''Last Supper'' incident is reported in *Pennsylvania Freeman,* September 25, 1845; the incident involving Purvis' son is in *The Non-Slaveholder,* new ser., 1 and 2 (1853–1854): 101. For Sarah Forten's letter, see Gilbert Barnes, ed., *Letters of Theodore Dwight Weld, Angelina Grimké Weld, and Sarah Grimké* (New York, 1934), pp. 273, 379–81.

The discussion of legislation affecting free blacks in Ohio is based on the following sources: Frank U. Quillen, *The Color Line in Ohio: History of Race Prejudice in a Typical Northern State* (Ann Arbor, Mich., 1913), pp. 38–45; Alan Peskin, ed., *North into Freedom: The Autobiography of John Malvin* (Cleveland, 1966), pp. 6–8, 30–40; Stephen Bennett Hanin, ''The Free Negro in Ohio, 1829–1839'' (master's thesis, University of Pittsburgh, 1961), pp. 24–37; Richard A. Folk, ''Black Man's Burden in Ohio, 1849–1863'' (Ph.D. diss., University of Toledo, 1972), pp. 22–138. For the auction in Chicago, see the article by Marion Neville in *Butcher Workman,* reprinted in *Daily Worker,* July 25, 1965.

Eugene H. Berwanger's comment is in his *The Frontier against Slavery: Western Anti-Negro Prejudice and the Slavery Extension Controversy* (Urbana, Ill., 1968), p. 62. For Illinois, see Franklin Johnson, *The Development of State Legislation Concerning the Free Negro* (New York, 1918), pp. 96, 99; James Freeman Clarke, *Present Condition of the Free People of Color of the United States* (New York, 1859), pp. 3–4. For Oregon, see Archie Mares Henderson, "Introduction of the Negroes into the Pacific Northwest, 1788–1842" (master's thesis, University of Washington, 1949), p. 36; Franz M. Schneider, "The 'Black Laws' of Oregon" (master's thesis, University of Santa Clara, 1970), pp. 16–18; *Frederick Douglass' Paper,* November 13, 1851, August 31, 1855; Daniel G. Hill, "The Negro as a Political and Social Issue in the Oregon Country," *Journal of Negro History* 33 (1948): 130–45. The discussion of California is based on: Mifflin Wistar Gibbs, *Shadow and Light: An Autobiography* (Washington, D.C., 1901; reprint ed., New York, 1968), pp. 42–68; Delilah C. Beaseley, *Negro Trail Blazers in California* (Westport, Conn., 1969), pp. 72–85; Roger Daniels and Spencer C. Olin, Jr., *Racism in California: A Reader in the History of Oppression* (New York, 1972), pp. 20–54. Rudolph M. Lapp, "Negro Rights Activities in Gold Rush California," *California Historical Society Quarterly* 45 (March 1966): 9.

Negro Ghettoes

The discussion in this section is based on the following sources: Seth M. Scheiner, *Negro Mecca, A History of the Negro in New York City 1865–1920* (New York, 1965), p. 16; W.E.B. Du Bois, *Some Notes on the Negroes in New York City* (Atlanta, Ga., 1903), pp. 1–2; Charles Dickens, *American Notes for General Circulation* (London, 1846), 1:191–92, 211–18; New York City, *City Inspector Annual Report* (1842), p. 165, *Annual Report* (1857); George E. Walker, "The Negro in New York City, 1827–1860" (Ph.D. diss., Columbia University, 1972), pp. 14–15; Sam Bass Warner, Jr., *The Private City: Philadelphia in Three Periods of Its Growth* (Philadelphia, 1968), pp. 126–27; Kenneth L. Kusmer, *A Ghetto Takes Shape: Black Cleveland, 1870–1930* (Urbana, Ill., 1976), p. 31; James Oliver Horton and Lois E. Horton, *Black Bostonians: Family Life and Community Struggle in the Antebellum North* (New York and London, 1979), pp. 5–6.

Jim Crow Transportation

For the origins of Jim Crow, see Hans Nathan, *Dan Emmett and the Rise of Early Negro Minstrelsy* (Norman, Okla., 1962), pp. 72–85; James H. Dormon, "The Strange Career of Jim Crow Rice (with apologies to Professor Woodward)," *Journal of Social History* 3 (Winter 1969–1970): 109–22. The story of Mrs. Wright is in *Colored American,* October 24, 1840; that of Thomas Downing is in ibid., January 16, February 20, 1841; that of Frederick Douglass is in *Life and Times of Frederick Douglass,* rev. ed. (New York, 1962), pp. 223–25; that of Reverend Pennington is in *New York Evangelist,* reprinted in *African Repository* 29 (March 1853): 82; that of Richard Warner is in *New York Tribune,* reprinted in *Frederick Douglass' Paper,* May 27, 1853, and that of Elizabeth Jenkins, is in *Frederick Douglass' Paper,* June 29, 1854; *National Anti-Slavery,* March 3, 1855. For the experience of William Wells Brown, see his *The American Fugitive in Europe: Sketches of Places and People Abroad* (New York, 1855), pp. 312–13. The discussion of the Philadelphia streetcar ban against Negroes is based on Philip S. Foner, "The Battle to End Discrimination against Negroes on Philadelphia's Streetcars: Part I: Background and Beginning of the Battle," *Pennsylvania History* 40

(July 1973): 261–90, reprinted in Philip S. Foner, *Essays in Afro-American History* (Philadelphia, 1979), pp. 19–50. See also *Goin* v. *McCandless*, 4 Philadelphia Reports 255–58 (1861).

Antiblack Riots

For the attacks on black women in Philadelphia, see *Philadelphia Gazette*, June 30, 1819, November 21, 1825; *National Enquirer*, April 8, 1837; Edward Raymond Turner, *The Negro in Pennsylvania: Slavery-Servitude-Freedom, 1639–1861* (Washington, D.C., 1911), p. 145; The discussion of the Hardscrabble riot in Providence is based on: Julian Rammelkamp, "The Providence Negro Community, 1820–1842," *Rhode Island History* 7 (January 1948): 26–28; reprinted in John H. Bracey, Jr., August Meier, and Elliott Rudwick, eds., *Free Blacks in America, 1800–1860* (Belmont, Calif., 1971), pp. 90–91; *Liberator*, October 1, 1831; J. A. Randall to Mowry Randall, September 25, 1831, MS., Brown University Library, Providence; Philip S. Foner and Ronald L. Lewis, eds., *The Black Worker: A Documentary History from Colonial Times to the Present* (Philadelphia, 1979), 1:167–69; Robert J. Cottrol, *The Afro-Yankees: Providence's Black Community in the Antebellum Era* (Westport, Conn., 1982), pp. 53–55. The discussion of the riots in Philadelphia is based on the following sources: *Philadelphia Public Ledger*, August 2–4, 1842, October 10, 12, 13, 1849; Emma Jones Lapsansky, " 'Since They Got Those Separate Churches': Afro-Americans and Racism in Jacksonian Philadelphia," *American Quarterly* 32 (Spring 1970): 54–78; Warner, op. cit., pp. 126–27; Nicholas B. Wainwright, *A Philadelphia Perspective: The Diary of George Sidney Fisher Covering the Years 1834–1871* (Philadelphia, 1967), p. 135; W.E.B. Du Bois, *The Philadelphia Negro: A Social Study* (Philadelphia, 1899), pp. 27–28; George Fisk, "Hunting the 'Nigs': The 1842 Riot in Philadelphia," *Pennsylvania History* 40 (July 1973): 188–205; Robert Purvis to Henry C. Wright, August 22, 1842, Anti-Slavery Letters to William Lloyd Garrison and Others, Boston Public Library, Rare Book Room.

Disfranchising the Black Voter

This section is based on the following sources: James T. Adams, "Disfranchisement of Negroes in New England," *American Historical Review* 30 (April 1924): 545–56; *Journal of the Proceedings of the Convention of Delegates, Convened at Hartford, August 26, 1818, for the Purpose of Forming a Constitution of Civil Government for the People of Connecticut* (Hartford, Conn., 1901), pp. 46, 90; *Proceedings of the New Jersey Constitutional Convention of 1844* (n.p., 1942), pp. 39–40, 76–111; Charles Z. Lincoln, *The Constitutional History of New York from the Beginning of the Colonial Period to 1905* (Rochester, N.Y., 1906), 1:198–99; *Constitution of the State of New York, Adopted in Convention, November 10th, 1821* (Hudson, N.Y., 1822), p. 8; Edward Price, "The Black Voting Rights Issue in Pennsylvania, 1780–1900," *Pennsylvania Magazine of History and Biography* 100 (July 1976): 357–63; *Hobbs* v. *Fogg*, 46 Pennsylvania Supreme Court Reports, 553–60 (1838); *Proceedings and Debates of the Convention of the Commonwealth of Pennsylvania to Propose Amendments to the Constitution, Commenced and Held at Harrisburg on the Second Day of May, 1837* (Harrisburg, Pa., 1837–1839), 1:233–36, 472–84; 3:82–83; 7:3, 295, 357, 384; 8:40, 91; 11:66; Robert Purvis, *Appeal of Forty Thousand Citizens, Threatened with Disfranchisement, to the People of Pennsylvania* (Philadelphia, 1838); Charles H. Wesley, "Negro Suffrage in the Period of Constitution Making, 1787–1861," *Journal of Negro History* 32 (April 1947): 130–38; Emil

Olbrich, *The Development of Sentiment on Negro Suffrage to 1860* (Madison, Wis., 1912), pp. 53–64; *Report of the Debates and Proceedings of the Convention for the Revision of the Constitution of the State of Indiana, 1850* (Indianapolis, 1950), pp. 232, 233–34; Arthur C. Cole, ed., "The Constitutional Debates of 1847," *Collections of the Illinois State Historical Library* 14 (Constitutional Series), 2 (Springfield, Ill., 1919), pp. 217, 226–27; John G. Gregory, "Negro Suffrage in Wisconsin," *Transactions of the Wisconsin Academy of Science, Arts, and Letters* 11 (1896–1897): 94–98; David McBride, "Black Protest against Racial Politics: Gardner, Hinton and Their Memorial," *Pennsylvania History* 46 (April 1979): 149–62; Phyllis F. Field, *The Politics of Race in New York: The Struggle for Black Suffrage in the Civil War Era* (Ithaca, N.Y., 1982), pp. 19–42.

10. FREE BLACKS IN THE ANTEBELLUM NORTH II

Earning a Living

The discussion in this section is based on the following sources: Carter G. Woodson, "The Negroes of Cincinnati Prior to the Civil War," *Journal of Negro History* 1 (January, 1916): 122–27; Allan Peskin, ed., *North into Freedom* (Cleveland, 1966), pp. 91–92; Richard A. Folk. "Black Man's Burden in Ohio" (Ph.D. diss., University of Toledo, 1972), pp. 34–42; Ohio Anti-Slavery Society, *Report on the Conditions of the People of Color in the State of Ohio* (Boston, 1836), pp. 3–4; Philip S. Foner and Ronald L. Lewis, eds., *The Black Worker* (Philadelphia, 1979), 1:154–57; Robert Ernst, "The Economic Status of New York City Negroes, 1850–1863," *Negro History Bulletin* 12 (1949): 139–43; John Campbell, *Negromania* (Philadelphia, 1851), p. 32; John Daniels, *In Freedom's Birthplace: A Study of the Boston Negro* (Boston and New York, 1914), pp. 21, 26; James Oliver Horton and Lois E. Horton, *Black Bostonians* (New York, 1979), pp. 7–15; Frederick Douglass, "My Escape to Freedom," *Century Magazine* 23 (November 1881): 125–31; Michael Fielding, *The Philadelphia Riots of 1844: A Study of Ethnic Conflicts* (Westport, Conn., 1975), pp. 7–8; Philadelphia *Public Ledger*, September 16, 1834; Theodore Hershberg, "Slavery and the Northern City: Ante Bellum Black Philadelphia: An Urban Perspective" (Paper presented at Association for the Study of Negro Life and History, 1970), pp. 11–13; Theodore Hershberg, "Free Blacks in Antebellum Philadelphia," in Allen F. Davis and Mark H. Haller, eds., *The People of Philadelphia: A History of Ethnic Groups and Lower-Class Life, 1790–1940* (Philadelphia, 1973), pp. 132–37; *Pennsylvania Society for Promoting the Abolition of Slavery, The Present State and Condition of the Free People of Color of the City of Philadelphia* (Philadelphia, 1837), pp. 9–10; *Statistical Inquiry into the Condition of the People of Color of the City and Districts of Philadelphia* (Philadelphia, 1849), pp. 17–18; *Statistics of the Colored People of Philadelphia, Taken by Benjamin C. Bacon* (Philadelphia, 1859), pp. 25–26; *Frederick Douglass' Paper*, March 4, 1853; Philip S. Foner, ed., *The Life and Writings of Frederick Douglass* (New York, 1950), 2:224; *New York Tribune*, September 30, 1857; Carter G. Woodson and Lorenzo J. Greene, *The Negro Wage Earner* (Washington, D.C., 1930), p. 213; Philip Taft, *Organizer Labor in American History* (New York, 1964), p. 664; Philip S. Foner, *Organized Labor and the Black Worker, 1619–1973* (New York, 1974), pp. 4–5, 10.

Blacks and Public Schools

The discussion in this section is based on the following sources: M. H. Freeman, "The Educational Wants of the Free Colored People," *Anglo-African Magazine* 1 (April 1859): 115; Horton and Horton, op. cit., pp. 70–71; *Tenth Annual Report of the Controller of the Public Schools* (Philadelphia, 1828), p. 6; *Twentieth Annual Report of the Controllers of the Public Schools* (Philadelphia, 1838), pp. 4–20; *African Observer* (Philadelphia), July 18, 1827, pp. 122–23; *Laws of the General Assembly of the State of Pennsylvania* (Harrisburg, Pa., 1854), pp. 622–25; *A Memorial to the Honorable Senate and House of Representatives of the Commonwealth by the Colored Citizens of Philadelphia* (Philadelphia, 1854); *Freedom's Journal*, June 1, 1827, emphasis in original; Carter G. Woodson, *The Education of the Negro Prior to 1861* (New York, 1915), pp. 313–15; *New York Tribune*, April 21, 1855, March 8, 1859; Superintendent of Schools (V. M. Rice), *Seventh Annual Report* (Buffalo, N.Y., 1854), p. 28; Arthur O. White, "The Black Movement against Jim Crow Education in Lockport, New York, 1835–1876," *New York History* 50 (July 1969): 268–69; *Rochester Daily Advertiser*, May 7, 8, 1830, October 7, 1834; *North Star*, January 31, 1848; George E. Walker, "The Afro-American in New York City, 1827–1860" (Ph.D. diss., Columbia University, 1972), pp. 79–86; Thomas Boese, *Public Education in the City of New York* (New York, 1969), pp. 146–47; Eve Thurston, "Ethiopia Unshackled: A Brief History of the Education of Negro Children in New York City," *Bulletin of the New York Public Library* 59 (April 1965): 219–21; *Douglass' Monthly*, March 1859; Folk, op. cit., pp. 233–58; Frederick A. McGinnis, *The Education of Negroes in Ohio* (Blanchester, Ohio, 1962), pp. 21–32, 49–55; L. D. Easton, "The Colored Schools of Cincinnati," in Isaac M. Martin, ed., *History of the Schools of Cincinnati and Other Educational Institutions, Public and Private* (Cincinnati, Ohio, 1900), pp. 185–89; *Biennial Report of the Superintendent of Public Instruction of the State of Illinois, 1859–60* (Springfield, Ill., 1861), pp. 15–17; *Minutes and Proceedings of the Second Annual Convention for Improvement of the Free People of the Color in These United States* (Philadelphia, 1832), p. 39.

Blacks and Colleges

The discussion in this section is based on the following sources: "The First Black American College Graduate," *Middleburg College News Letter* (Spring 1974); Hugh Hawkins, "Edward Jones, First Negro American College Graduate?" *School and Society*, November 4, 1961, pp. 34–39; William M. Brewer, "John B. Russwurm," *Journal of Negro History* 21 (1928): 122–34; Philip S. Foner, ed., "John Browne Russwurm: A Document," *Journal of Negro History* 62 (October 1969): 108–15; Jno. B. Russwurm to Col. Jno. S. Russwurm, Bowdoin College, January 9, 1826, original in Ms. section, Tennessee State Library and Archives, copy in Bowdoin College Library; Philip S. Foner, ed., *The Voice of Black America: Major Speeches by Negroes in the United States, 1797–1971* (New York, 1972), pp. 33–36; Robert Samuel Fletcher, *A History of Oberlin College* (Oberlin, Ohio, 1943), 1:169–78; Benjamin P. Thomas, *Theodore Weld, Crusader for Freedom* (New Brunswick, N.J., 1950), pp. 167–71; Folk, op. cit., pp. 39, 157; William Francis Cheek III, "Forgotten Prophet: The Life of John Mercer Langston" (Ph.D. diss., University of Virginia, 1961), pp. 14–15, 38–39, 45–47; Philip S. Foner, "The First Publicly-Elected Black Official in the United States Reports His Election," *Negro History Bulletin* 37 (April–May 1974): 337; Leonard W. Johnson, Jr., "History of the Education of Negro Physicians," *Journal of Medical Education* 42 (1967): 440; Benjamin Quarles, ed., "Letters from Negro Leaders to Gerrit Smith," *Journal of Negro*

History 27 (October 1942): 338–39. For the situation in Plainfield, New Jersey, see George Fishman in *Negro History Bulletin* 31 (January 1968): 18–19. For the exclusion of Thomas Paul, Jr., from Dartmouth's literary society, see *Liberator,* October 26, 1838.

Black Colleges

For the founding of Ashmun Institution, see Horace Mann Bond, *Education for Freedom: A History of Lincoln University, Pennsylvania* (Princeton, N.J., 1976), pp. 208–56; Andrew E. Murray, "The Founding of Lincoln University," *Journal of Presbyterian History* 5 (Winter 1973): 392–410; George B. Car, *John Miller Dickey, D.D.; His Life and Times* (Philadelphia, 1929), pp. 220–48; Ralph Randolph Curley, *Life of Jehudi Ashmun* (Washington, D.C., 1835), Ashmun Institute Records, Langston Hughes Memorial Library, Lincoln University, Pennsylvania; Lincoln University, *Alumni Magazine* 1 (November 1884): 1–15; John Miller Dickey, *Ethiopia Shall Stretch Out Her Hands Unto God* (Philadelphia, 1853). For the founding of Wilberforce University, see Frederick A. McGinnis, *A History and Interpretation of Wilberforce University, Wilberforce, Ohio* (Blanchester, Ohio, 1941), pp. 24–92; Folk, op. cit., pp. 21–22.

11. THE FREE BLACK COMMUNITY IN THE ANTEBELLUM NORTH

For the contemporary analysis of the status of free blacks in the North, see Charles H. Wesley, *Negro Labor in the United States, 1850–1925* (New York, 1927), p. 30.

The Black Church in the North

For Delany's comment on the church, see *North Star,* February 6, 1849; Benjamin Quarles, *Black Abolitionists* (New York, 1969), p. 69. The development of the AME church is set forth in Daniel A. Payne, *History of the African Methodist Episcopal Church* (Nashville, Tenn., 1891); Carol G. George, *Segregated Sabbaths: Richard Allen and the Emergence of the Independent Black Churches, 1760–1840* (New York, 1973); Christopher Rush, *A Short Account of the Rise and Progress of the African Methodist Episcopal Church in America* (New York, 1843). For the African Methodist Episcopal Zion church, see Bishop J. W. Wood, D.D., L.L.D., *One Hundred Years of the African Methodist Episcopal Zion Church* (New York, 1955); John Greenleaf, *A History of the Churches of All Denominations in the City of New York, From the First Settlement to the Year 1846* (New York, 1846), pp. 320–25; *National Anti-Slavery Standard,* April 19, 1849; *North Star,* July 14, 1848; George E. Walker, "The Afro-American in New York City, 1827–1860" (Ph.D. diss., Columbia University, 1972), pp. 125–28. For black Presbyterian churches, see Lewis Evans Jackson, *Walks About New York. Facts and Figures Gathered from Various Places* (New York, 1865), p. 23; Walker, op. cit., pp. 134–35. Cornish's complaint against the Presbyterian church is in *Emancipator,* November 2, 1837. For the Episcopalians, see Robert A. Bennett, "Black Episcopalians," *Historical Magazine of the Protestant Episcopal Church* 43 (September 1974): 236–39. The role of the black church in fostering cooperation is in W.E.B. Du Bois, *Economic Cooperation among American Negroes* (Atlanta, Ga., 1907), p. 10.

The account of the black female minister is in *National Anti-Slavery Standard,* May 1, 1843. For the varied activities of black ministers, see *Freedom's Journal,* April 6, 1827,

January 25, 1828, January 11, 1829; *Rights of All,* June 12, 1829; *Colored American,* October 17, 1840; *National Anti-Slavery Standard,* April 7, 1842; Walker, op. cit., pp. 141–42; James Oliver Horton and Lois E. Horton, *Black Bostonians* (New York, 1979), pp. 32–33, 40–43; Carter G. Woodson, *History of the Negro Church,* 2d ed. (Washington, D.C., 1924), p. 110; E. Franklin Frazier, *Black Bourgeoisie* (New York, 1969), p. 101; E. Eric Lincoln, *The Black Experience in Religion* (New York, 1974); Charles V. Hamilton, *The Black Preacher in America* (New York, 1972). For the Institute of Colored Youth in Philadelphia, see Charline F. A. Conyers, "A History of Cheyney State Teachers College, 1837–1851" (Ph.D. diss., New York University, 1960); *Objects and Regulations of the Institute for Colored Youth with a List of Officers and the Students, and the Annual Report of the Board of Managers for the Year 1860* (Philadelphia, 1860); *Pennsylvania Freeman,* April 7, 1853; *Liberator,* September 29, 1853; *National Anti-Slavery Standard,* May 16, 1857.

Black Mutual Aid and Benevolent Societies

Information on black mutual aid and benevolent societies in Philadelphia may be found in Edward Needles, *Statistical Inquiry into the Condition of People of Colour, of the City and Districts of Philadelphia* (Philadelphia, 1849); Benjamin C. Bacon, *Statistics of the Colored People of Philadelphia* (Philadelphia, 1856); *Philadelphia Press,* September 12, 1860; *North Star,* February 2, 1849. For the African Humane Society of Boston, see *Liberator,* August 4, 1832, November 22, 1861. For mutual aid and benevolent societies in New York City, see Daniel Perlman, "Organizations of the Free Negro in New York City, 1800–1860," *Journal of Negro History* 54 (July 1971): 182–92; Karl Bernhard, Duke of Saxe Neiman-Eisenach, *Travels through North America* (London, 1826), 1:126; Walker, op. cit., pp. 91–92, 283–85; *Freedom's Journal,* January 9, 1829. The Colored Orphan Asylum is discussed in (Rev.) J. F. Richmond, *New York and Its Institutions, 1609–1872* (New York, 1872), pp. 302–3; Association for the Benefit of Colored Orphans, *First Annual Report* (New York, 1837), p. 13; *National Anti-Slavery Standard,* June 24, 1852. For the Society for the Relief of Aged, Indigent Colored Persons, see Mary W. Thompson, *Sketches of the History, Character, and Dying Testimony of the Beneficiaries of the Colored Home in the City of New York* (New York, 1851), pp. 75–76; Walker, op. cit., pp. 188–90. The discussion of black seamen and the Colored Seamen's Home is based on Samuel Eliot Morison, *Maritime History of Massachusetts* (Boston, 1921), pp. 110–11, 257; Philip S. Foner, "William P. Powell, Militant Champion of Black Seamen," in Philip S. Foner, *Essays in Afro-American History* (Philadelphia, 1978), pp. 89–98; *North Star,* February 11, 1848, April 7, 1849. For black mutual aid societies of black workers, the American League of Colored Laborers, and the action of the black waiters of New York, see Philip S. Foner, *Organized Labor and the Black Worker, 1619–1973* (New York, 1974), pp. 10–11; *New York Daily Tribune,* July 3, 1850; Philip S. Foner and Ronald L. Lewis, eds., *The Black Worker: A Documentary History,* Vol. 1 (Philadelphia, 1978), pp. 220–23.

Black Fraternal Societies

The discussion of black Masons is based on Harold Van Buren Voorhis, *Negro Masonry in the United States* (New York, 1940), pp. 203–35; Martin R. Delany, *The Origin and Objects of Ancient Free Masonry; Its Introduction into the United States and Legitimacy Among Colored Men* (Pittsburgh, Pa., 1853), pp. 8–26. For the black Odd Fellows, see *Ram's Horn,* November 5, 1847; Perlman, op. cit., pp. 195–96; Horton and Horton, op.

cit., pp. 33–34; Richard Bardolph, *The Negro Vanguard* (New York, 1959), pp. 28, 31; *New York Tribune*, September 5, 1856.

Black Self-Improvement Societies

The discussion in this section is based on the following sources: Dorothy B. Porter, "The Organized Educational Activities of Negro Literary Societies, 1822–1846," *Journal of Negro Education* 51 (October 1936): 558–76; *Colored American*, April 15, 29, 1837, May 2, 1840; Perlman, op. cit., p. 193; Walker, op. cit., pp. 100–106; *Liberator*, May 3, December 18, 1840, January 21, 1842; Horton and Horton, op. cit., pp. 31, 91; Quarles, op. cit., pp. 104–5; Banneker Institute Lecture and Debates, 1859–1861, February 2, 16, 23, 1859, pp. 8–9, Gardiner Papers, Historical Society of Pennsylvania; Banneker Institute Minutes for May 20, 1858, pp. 142–43, Historical Society of Pennsylvania; Harry C. Silcox, "Philadelphia Negro Educator: Jacob C. White, 1837–1902," *Pennsylvania Magazine of History and Biography* 97 (January 1973): 82–83; *Anglo-African*, January 26, February 16, 1861.

Black Temperance Societies

Black temperance societies are discussed in Quarles, op. cit., pp. 92–100, and Richard A. Folk, "Black Man's Burden in Ohio, 1849–1863" (Ph.D. diss., University of Toledo, 1972), pp. 225–28. See also *Anti-Slavery Bugle* (Salem, Ohio), August 10, 1850, January 14, 1854; *Cincinnati Daily Enquirer*, January 9, 1950. For the number of black societies in New York and Philadelphia, see Perlman, op. cit., p. 182; E. Franklin Frazier, *The Negro in the United States* (New York, 1849), p. 270.

The Black Press: Freedom's Journal *and* Rights for All

A study of the first Negro paper in the United States, though poorly organized, is Bella Gross, "Freedom's Journal and the Rights for All," *Journal of Negro History* 17 (July 1932): 110–36. Most of the discussion in the section is based on the files of *Freedom's Journal*, which is available on microfilm in many libraries. Extracts from *Freedom's Journal* and *Rights for All* appear in Martin E. Dann, ed., *The Black Press, 1827–1890* (New York, 1971). The report by Cornish on Phillis Wheatley is in the issue of January 23, 1827; "The Black Beauty" is in that of June 8, 1827; the attack on the New York press is in the issue of May 11, 1827; and the attack on *Freedom's Journal* by Reverend Miller of Princeton is in the issue of October 12, 1827. For the articles on Haiti, see issues of April 20, 27, May 4, June 15, 26, 29, 1827; those on Touissaint L'Ouverture, see issues of May 4, 11, 18, 1827. Russwurm's conversion to colonization is discussed in J. Staudenraus, *The American Colonization Movement, 1816–1865* (New York, 1961), pp. 191–92. For other discussions of the first two black papers, see Frederick Cooper, "Elevating the Race: The Social Thought of Black Leaders, 1827–1850," *American Quarterly* 24 (1972): 607; Lawrence Fortenberry, "Freedom's Journal: The First Black Medium," *Black Scholar* 6 (November 1974): 33–37; and David E. Swift, "Black Presbyterian Attacks on Racism: Samuel Cornish,Theodore Wright and Their Contemporaries," *Journal of Presbyterian History* 57 (Winter 1973): 437–51.

The Black Press: Other Black Papers

For the *Colored American*, see *Weekly Advocate*, February 25, 1837; *Colored American*, September 1, December 23, 1837, January 13, 1838; Swift, op. cit., pp. 436–43, 446–48. Black papers published in the 1840s and 1850s are listed in I. G. Penn, *The Afro-*

American Press and Its Editors (Springfield, Mass., 1897), pp. 25–57; Martin E. Dann, *The Black Press, 1827–1890* (New York, 1972), pp. 18–20, 46–54. References to Benjamin Roberts' *Anti-Slavery Herald* appear in the *Liberator,* May 4, October 12, 1838.

Frederick Douglass and His Paper

For the career of Frederick Douglass up to his founding of the *North Star,* see Philip S. Foner, *Frederick Douglass* (New York, 1962), pp. 5–100; Frederick Douglass, *Life and Times of Frederick Douglass* (Hartford, Conn., 1881), pp. 3–225; Philip S. Foner, ed., *Frederick Douglass on Women's Rights* (Westport, Conn., 1976), pp. 8–11. For the *Afro-American Magazine,* see issue of January 1859, and C. S. Johnson, "Rise of the Negro Magazine," *Journal of Negro History* 13 (October 1929): 11–15, and Penelope L. Bullock, *Afro-American Political Press, 1838–1909* (Baton Rouge, 1981), pp. 54–63. The statement of the Pennsylvania State Convention is in Philip S. Foner and George E. Walker, eds., *Proceedings of the Black State Conventions, 1840–1865* (Philadelphia, 1979), p. 114. John Hope Franklin regards Samuel E. Cornish as the outstanding Negro journalist of the pre-Civil War period—*From Slavery to Freedom,* 3d ed. (New York, 1967), p. 252—but I believe this honor should be accorded Frederick Douglass.

In concluding the study of the free Negro before the Civil War, it is worth noting that in 1961 Leon F. Litwack's *North of Slavery,* the pioneer study of the free Negro in the North appeared, followed in 1974 by Ira Berlin's *Slaves without Masters: The Free Negro in the Antebellum South.* In 1981 there appeared Leonard P. Curry, *The Free Black in Urban America, 1800–1850: The Shadow of the Dream* (Chicago, 1981). Curry adds some useful information to both of the previous works, especially on housing and residential patterns and on a number of race riots heretofore neglected. But in the main, the book adds little to what is already available, and on such subjects as black employment, it is decidedly inferior. The final chapter on black participation and protest is so summarized as to be almost useless. What is missing, moreover, is a picture of everyday life in the black community—how blacks lived and worked, organized for mutual aid, survival, and social action, as well as the network of family and community that surrounded and strengthened the free blacks. Finally, no attempt is made to note any divisions among the free blacks, the split over fundamental issues, social differences, and the degree to which these tended to disappear in time of crisis.

12. THE FREE BLACK ELITE

Black Trailblazers

Frederick Douglass' observation appears in *Frederick Douglass' Paper,* April 12, 1853. The only biography of James P. Beckwourth is Elinor Wilson, *Jim Beckwourth: Black Mountain Man and War Chief of the Crows* (Norman, Okla., 1972). A critical edition of Beckwourth's "autobiography" is *The Life and Adventures of James P. Beckwourth,* introduction, notes, and epilogue by Delmont P. Oswald (Lincoln, Neb., 1972). For the other trailblazers, see Dale T. Schoenberger, "The Black Man in the American West," *Negro History Bulletin* 32 (March 1969): 7–11.

Black Men of Wealth

The discussion in this section is based on the following sources: Martin R. Delany, *The Condition, Elevation, Emigration, and Destiny of the Colored People of the United States*

(Philadelphia, 1852), pp. 90–108; Eugene Monroe Boykin, "Enterprise and Accumulation of Negroes prior to 1860" (master's thesis, Columbia University, 1934), pp. 30–42; Richard A. Folk, "Black Man's Burden in Ohio, 1849–1853" (Ph.D. diss., University of Toledo, 1972), pp. 34–38; James F. Clarke, "Condition of the Free Colored People of the United States," *Liberator*, March 18, 1859; George Washington Williams, *A History of the Negro Race in America from 1619 to 1880* (New York, 1883), 2:138–45; *Colored American*, May 22, 1837, January 13, July 7, 1838, May 11, July 13, September 28, 1839, June 27, 1840; *Emancipator*, October 19, 1837; *National Anti-Slavery Standard*, March 20, 1862; *Anglo-African Magazine* 1 (July 1859): 222–23; Robert Ernst, "The Economic Status of New York City Negroes," in August Meier and Elliott Rudwick, eds., *The Making of Black America* (New York, 1970), pp. 258–59; James Oliver Horton and Lois E. Horton, *Black Bostonians* (New York and London, 1979), pp. 9, 10, 11–13; Daniel Alexander Payne, *Recollections of Seventy Years* (New York, 1888), p. 46; W. H. Boyd, *New York City Tax Book* (New York, 1857), p. 184; George E. Walker, "The Afro-American in New York City, 1827–1860" (Ph.D. diss., Columbia University, 1972), pp. 42–54; *New York Tribune*, March 20, 1851; Arnett G. Lindsay, "The Negro in Banking," *Journal of Negro History* 14 (April 1929): 158; Richard P. McCormick, "William Whipper: Moral Reformer," *Pennsylvania History* 43 (January 1976): 39; Stanley J. and Anita W. Robboy, "Lewis Hayden: From Fugitive Slave to Statesman," *New England Quarterly* 46 (December 1973): 593–98.

Black Teachers, Doctors, and Lawyers

The discussion in this section is based on the following sources: Arthur O. White, "Salem's Antebellum Black Community: Seedbed of the School Integration Movement," *Essex Institute Historical Collections* 108 (April 1972): 101; John B. Shotwell, *A History of the Schools of Cincinnati* (Cincinnati, 1902), pp. 447–61; Folk, op. cit., pp. 40–41; Philip S. Foner, "Peter H. Clark: Pioneer Black Socialist," *Journal of Ethnic Studies* 5 (1977): 17–35; Philip S. Foner, *The Voice of Black America: Major Speeches by Negroes in the United States, 1797–1971* (New York, 1972), pp. 215–27; *New York Tribune*, June 12, 1853; James Still, *Early Recollections of and Life of Dr. James Still* (New Brunswick, N.J., 1973), fascimile reprint of 1877 edition; Louis Placide Canonge, "Louis Charles Rondanez," *L'Abeille* (New Orleans), March 13, 1890; Horton and Horton, op. cit., pp. 55–57; "Robert Morris, Sr., In Memoriam" (1882), Massachusetts Historical Society, Boston; *Chelsea Telegraph and Pioneer* reprinted in *Liberator*, September 24, 1858; *New Bedford Standard* reprinted in *National Anti-Slavery Standard*, October 2, 1858; George W. Forbes, "Typescript Biographical Sketch of John S. Rock" (n.d.), Boston Public Library, Rare Book Room; Eugene P. Link, "The Civil Rights Activities of Three Great Negro Physicians (1840–1940)," *Journal of Negro History* 52 (July 1967): 172–75; George A. Levesque, "Boston's Black Brahmin: Dr. John Rock," *Civil War History* 26 (1980): 326–46.

Black Artists

The discussion in this section is based on Alain Locke, *The Negro in Art* (Washington, D.C., 1940); Romare Bearden and Harry Henderson, *Black Masters of American Art* (New York, 1972); Isaiah A. Woodward, "Joshua Johnston: Baltimore's First Slave Artist of Distinction," *Negro History Bulletin* 21 (April 1958): 166; James A. Porter, "Robert Duncanson, Midwestern Romantic Realist," *Art in America* 39 (October 1951): 97–154; Folk, op. cit., pp. 37–38; James A. Porter, "Edmonia Lewis," *Negro History Bulletin* 1 (November 1937): 6–7; Philip S. Foner, "Black Participation in the Centennial of 1876," in Foner, *Essays in Afro-American History* (Philadelphia, 1978), pp. 137, 138, 140, 141; Edward Strickland, "Our Forgotten Negro Artists," *Masses and Mainstream* (September 1954): 34–40.

Black Composers, Musicians, and Singers

The discussion in this section is based on the following sources: Eileen Southern, *The Music of Black Americans: A History* (New York, 1971), pp. 105–71; "The Black Swan," *Crisis* (March 1941): 212–13; Harold C. Schonberg, "The Black Swan That Sang for the Nobility," *New York Times*, April 12, 1970; *Cincinnati Daily Times* reprinted in *Liberator*, July 31, 1857; *National Anti-Slavery Standard*, January 20, February 20, June 30, 1855; Richard Bardolph, *The Negro Vanguard* (New York, 1959), pp. 58–60.

Black Actors

On the beginning and development of the African Grove Theater, see Philip S. Foner, *History of Black Americans: From Africa to the Emergence of the Cotton Kingdom* (Westport, Conn., 1975), pp. 539–40, 548–49; and for Ira Aldridge, see Herbert Marshall and Mildred Stock, *Ira Aldridge, The Negro Tragedian* (Carbondale, Ill., 1958); Owen Mortimer, "Ira Aldridge, Shakesperean Actor," *Crisis* (April 1855): 203–15; *New York Sunday Atlas* reprinted in *Liberator*, June 26, 1857.

Black Authors

For the slave narratives, see Charles H. Nichols, *Many Thousands Gone: The Ex-Slaves' Account of Their Bondage and Freedom* (Leiden, 1963); John W. Blassingame, "Black Autobiographies of History and Literature," *Black Scholar* (December 1973–January 1974): 2–4. A study of the evolution of the slave narrative is Ramond Hedin, "The American Slave Narrative: The Justification of the Picaro," *American Literature* 53 (January 1982): 630–45.

Frederick Douglass' "The Heroic Slave" was originally published in *Autographs for Freedom*, ed. Julia W. Griffiths (Rochester, N.Y., 1853), pp. 174–238. Sections of the short story also appeared in *Frederick Douglass' Paper*, March 11, 1853. The story is reprinted in Philip S. Foner, ed., *The Life and Writings of Frederick Douglass* (New York, 1975), 5:473–505. The poem "America" by James M. Whitfield and the poem "The Slave Auction" by Frances E. W. Harper appear in Sterling A. Brown, Arthus P. Davis, and Ulysses L. Lee, eds., *The Negro Caravan* (New York, 1941), pp. 290–92, 295. For the career of William Wells Brown, see William Edward Farrison, *William Wells Brown, Author and Reformer* (Chicago and London, 1969). Farrison is also the author of "The Origin of Brown's *Clotel*," *Phylon* (fourth quarter 1954): 347–54, and "Brown's First Drama," *CLA Journal* 2 (December 1958): 104–10. *Clotel or the President's Daughter* was reprinted in 1969 by the Citadel Press with an introduction by William Edward Farrison. An old biography of Martin R. Delany is Frank A. Rollin (pseud.) (Francis E. Rollin Whipper), *Life and Public Services of Martin R. Delany* (Boston, 1868). This has been supplanted by Victory Ullman, *Martin R. Delany* (Pittsburgh, Pa., 1970). The first publication of *Blake, or the Huts of America* in book form was by Beacon Press in 1970 and contains a useful introduction by Floyd J. Miller, who discovered the unknown texts in the *Weekly Afro-American*. An earlier study of the novel, written before Miller's discovery, is John Zeugner, "A Note on Martin Delany's *Blake*, and Black Militancy," *Phylon* 32 (1971): 98–105. For the story of Placido, see Philip S. Foner, *A*

History of Cuba and Its Relations with the United States (New York, 1962), 1:212–16. For an interesting discussion of these writers, see James Fulcher, "Black Abolitionist Fiction: The Formulaic Art of Douglass, Brown, Delany and Webb," *Journal of American Culture* 2 (Winter 1980): 583–97. For the discovery of the novel *Our Nig,* whose title page states that it was by an author named "Our Nig," for the identification of Harriet E. Wilson as the author, and for the claim that it is the first black novel published in the United States, all by Henry Louis Gates, Jr., see *New York Times,* November 8, 1982.

For the criticism of Elizabeth Greenfield and the events surrounding the charges against her, see *North Star,* February 26, 1852; *Aliened American* (Cleveland), April 9, 1853; *National Anti-Slavery Standard,* July 31, 1857; *Anglo-African,* January 22, 1861.

13. THE COLONIZATION CONTROVERSY

Growth and Ideology of the American Colonization Society

An important source for this section is the *African Repository and Colonial Journal,* published by the American Colonization Society from 1825 to 1892. There are sixty-eight volumes in all, but only the first thirty-six were consulted. The *Repository* is a primary source containing a large variety of materials, including letters, reports, and records. Its greatest single defect as a source is that it was a propaganda device of the Colonization Society. As a result, the materials published are usually favorable to the progress of the society's activities; everything unfavorable was suppressed. Also important as a source for this section is the *Annual Report* of the American Colonization Society, 1818–1910. The first forty of the ninety-two volumes were consulted. The reports suffer from the same fault as the *Repository.* The American Colonization Society Papers, Manuscript Division, Library of Congress, Washington, D.C., is a vast collection. The collection has been microfilmed, and there are 323 reels.

The best study of the early growth of the Colonization society is P. J. Staudenraus, *The African Colonization Movement, 1816–1865* (New York, 1961), pp. 42–128. The most perceptive discussions of the Colonization Society and the colonization movement in the South are: Ira Berlin, "Slaves Who were Free: The Free Negro in the Upper South, 1776–1861" (Ph.D. diss., University of Wisconsin, 1970), and Gordon Esley Finney, "The Anti-Slavery Movement in the South, 1787–1836: Its Rise and Decline and Contribution to Abolitionism in the West" (Ph.D. diss., Duke University, 1962). For Southern emancipationist support of colonization as a way of ending slavery, see especially John H. B. Latrobe to R. R. Gurley, January 27, 1827, and Latrobe to A. C. S. Board of Managers, December 29, 1834, American Colonization Society Papers, Library of Congress. For colonization propaganda to assure slaveowners that they had no intention to interfere with slavery, see *Proceedings of the Colonization Society of Kentucky, with an Address of Hon. Daniel Mayes* (Frankfort, Ky., 1831), and Philip Slaughter, *The Virginia History of African Colonization* (Richmond, Va., 1855). For the instruction of the Maryland Society to its agents not to deal with slavery, see William McKinney to Moses Shephard, October 30, 1832, Agent's Letterbook; J. H. Latrobe to William Handy, October 20, 1827, Latrobe Letterbook, Maryland State Colonization Papers, Maryland Historical Society. Robert Y. Haynes' attack on the ACS is in *Annals of Congress,* 19th Cong., 2d sess., p. 328. For the colonizationist view that Negroes could never be equal to whites and that blacks were a dangerous and inherently inferior element in American society, see *Thirteenth Annual Report, Fourteenth Annual Report,* and *Fifteenth Annual Report* of the American Colonization Society, and the files of the *African Repository*; Charles I. Foster, "The Colonization of Free Negroes in Liberia, 1816–35," *Journal of Negro History* 38 (October 1953): 62–65.

Attitude of Free Blacks toward the American Colonization Society

For a general discussion of this subject, see Louis R. Mehlinger, "The Attitude of the Free Negro toward Colonization," *Journal of Negro History* 1 (July 1916): 284–98. The opposition to the Colonization Society in Philadelphia is discussed in Philip S. Foner, *History of Black Americans: From Africa to the Emergence of the Cotton Kingdom* (Westport, Conn., 1975), pp. 589–94. For economic competition from white immigrants and the inability of black artisans and mechanics to obtain work as a motive for emigration to Liberia, see John Hanson to Rev. Gurley, Baltimore, September 19, 1828, American Colonization Society Papers, and U.S. House of Representatives, Committee on Commerce, *Report of Mr. Kennedy of Maryland on the Memorial of the Friends of African Colonization assembled in Convention in the City of Washington,* May 1842 (Washington, D.C., 1843), pp. 415–18. The 1824 Hardscrabble anti-Negro riot in Provience is discussed in I. H. Bartlett, *From Slave to Citizen, The Story of the Negro in Rhode Island* (Providence, R.I., 1954), pp. 25–27; in Julian Rammelkamp, "The Providence Negro Community, 1820–1842," *Rhode Island History* 7 (January 1948): 21–22, and in Robert J. Cottrol, *The Afro-Yankees: Providence's Black Community in the Antebellum Era* (Westport, Conn., 1982), pp. 53–55. For the emigration of Newport blacks, led by Newport Gardiner, to Liberia, see J. Parker, "Slavery in Rhode Island" (master's thesis, University of Rhode Island, 1959), pp. 30–35. The story of Abd al-Rahman is discussed in Staudenraus, op. cit., pp. 128–46, and in Louis Harlan, "The Prince: The Biography of a Slave," in *Job Ben Solomon and Abd al-Rahman: The Stories of Two Men in Slavery* (American Historical Association, Washington, D.C., 1970), pp. 13–19. For the poem and action at the meeting in Boston's African Masonic Hall, see *Boston Columbian Centinel,* October 20, 1828, and *Freedom's Journal,* October 24, 1828.

John Browne Russwurm's explanation for his conversion to colonization is in the *African Repository,* 12:86, 88. For criticism of Russwurm for his procolonization stand, see Carter G. Woodson, *The Mind of the Negro as Reflected in Letters Written during the Crisis, 1800–1860* (Washington, D.C., 1926), pp. 160–65. In her study *Maryland in Africa: The Maryland State Colonization Society, 1831–1857* (Urbana, Ill., 1971), Penelope Campbell gives Russwurm high marks for his work in Liberia. The arguments advanced by free blacks in opposition to the American Colonization Society and emigration to Liberia are in William Lloyd Garrison, *Thoughts on African Colonization* (Boston, 1832), Pt. I: 5–15; Pt. II: 21–44. For the Maryland plan, see Berlin, op. cit., pp. 212–14, and Ira Berlin, *Slaves Without Masters: The Free Negro in the Antebellum South* (New York, 1976), pp. 204–7. For the opposition of Baltimore free blacks to the ACS, *see* C. R. Harper to R. R. Gurley, August 1, 1832, State Manager's Letterbook, and John Kennard to J.H.B. Latrobe, April 30, 1838, Maryland State Colonization Papers, Maryland Historical Society; Garrison, op. cit., pp. 21–22. The complaints of the Virginia colonizations are in D. Meade to R. R. Gurley, April 8, 1830, and Benjamin Brand to R. R. Gurley, January 8, 1827, American Colonization Society Papers, Library of Congress. Reverend Peter Williams, Jr.'s address attacking the Colonization Society is in Philip S. Foner, ed., *The Voice of Black America* (New York, 1972), pp. 43–46.

For the 1824 correspondence between the ACS and the government of Haiti to further black emigration to Haiti, see *Correspondence Relative to the Emigration to Haiti of the Free People of Colour, in the United States* (New York, 1824). Granville's speech to the New York blacks and Reverend Paul's endorsement of Haitian emigration are published in *Boston Columbian Centinel*, July 3, 31, 1824. For black emigration to Canada, see *Rights of All*, August 14, 1829; Henry N. Sherwood, "The Movement in Ohio to Deport the Negro," *Quarterly Publication of the Historical and Philosophical Society of Ohio* 7 (June, 1912): 102–26; Garrison, op. cit., pt. II: 26, 33; James Oliver Horton and Lois E. Horton, *Black Bostonians* (New York, 1979), pp. 91–92.

The meeting of Providence blacks in opposition to emigration to Liberia is in Rammelkamp, op. cit., p. 91. The poem of a "Poor Colored Man" is in the *Man* (New York), August 9, 1934.

Liberia as Utopia

The address from the "citizens of Monrovia" is in *House Reports* No. 283, 27th Cong., 3d sess., 2:965–66. This 1,088-page Report is a documented account of African colonization from about 1812 to 1842. For Reverend John T. Matthias' report, see *Colored American*, October 20, 1838. Descriptions of the conditions in Liberia in 1838 appear in the *African Repository*, 36:120–22, 145–48, 164–69. Reverend Sawyer's report on tension between native Africans and black Americans in Liberia is in Arthur E. Murray, "Experiment in Equality—Liberia, 1843–44" (unpublished paper), p. 7. Reports of meetings of blacks in the North opposing emigration are in Samuel E. Cornish and Theodore S. Wright, *The Colonization Scheme Considered in Its Rejection by the Colored People* (Newark, N.J., 1840), pp. 4–6, 12–16, 20–21, 26; *Colored American*, May 9, 1840; Richard A. Folk, "Black Man's Burden in Ohio, 1829–1853" (Ph.D. diss., University of Toledo, 1972), p. 182; R.J.M. Blackett, "Anglo-American Opposition to Liberian Colonization, 1831–1833," *Historian* 41 (1978–1979): 276–94.

Emigration to Trinidad

For the emigration to Trinidad, see *Emancipator*, July 25, September 5, 12, 26, 1839; *Colored American*, October 5, 1839; *New York Sun*, January 11, 1840; *African Repository* 15:28; 16:22, 115–17; 17:194; Emanuel Saunders, "Efforts to Recruit Black Americans as Laborers for Trinidad, 1839–1842," *Hampton Institute Journal of Ethnic Studies* 7 (December 1978): 60–81.

Rejuvenation of Colonization Activities and Colonization Rejected

For the formation of the Republic of Liberia, see David Lindsay, " 'The Land of Their Fathers,' Liberia," *American History Illustrated* (May 1972): 32–34. Court decisions facilitating manumission in the South if the liberated slaves left the state and the effect of this on the Colonization Society are discussed in Memory F. Mitchell, "Off to Africa— with Judicial Blessing," *North Carolina Historical Review* 53 (Summer 1976): 265–87. The semiliterate letters of Southern free blacks to the Colonization Society are in Woodson, op. cit., pp. 93, 107, 125, 130–32, and in Tom L. McLaughlin, "Sectional Responses of Free Negroes to the Idea of Colonization," *Research Studies* 34 (September 1966): 126–28. For "Ohio in Africa," see Philip S. Foner, *Essays in Afro-American History* (Philadelphia, 1978), p. 159; *African Repository*, 27:20–21; Folk, op. cit., pp. 174–83. Frederick Douglass' stand against colonization is in *Frederick Douglass' Paper*, January 26, 1849.

14. THE CONVENTION MOVEMENT

The First National Negro Convention

The major work on the National Negro Convention movement is Howard H. Bell, *A Survey of the Negro Convention Movement, 1830–1861* (New York, 1969). Bell has also edited the *Minutes of the Proceedings of the National Negro Conventions, 1830–1863* (New York, 1969), although the almost complete lack of editorial annotations and introductory information reduces the value of the publication. Also useful, though marred by poor organization, is Bella Gross, *Clarion Call: The History and Development of the Negro People's Convention Movement in the United States from 1817 to 1840* (New York, 1847). A useful examination of ideas in the convention movement is William H. Pease and Jane H. Pease, "The Negro Convention Movement," in Nathan I. Huggins, Martin Kilson, and Daniel M. Fox, eds., *Key Issues in the Afro-American Experience* (New York, 1971), 1:191–209.

The National Negro Convention of 1830 is discussed in John W. Cromwell, "The Early Negro Convention Movement," *Occasional Papers of the Negro Academy No. 9* (Washington, D.C., 1904); Bell, *Survey*, pp. 20–32; Bella Gross, "The First National Negro Convention," *Journal of Negro History* 21 (October 1946): 120–38. The proceedings of the convention are in Bell, *Minutes*, which also reprints the article in the 1859 issue of the *Anglo-African Magazine* that discusses the origin of the 1830 convention and the role played by Hezekiah Grice as the founder of the convention movement. This article is also reprinted in Herbert Aptheker, ed., *A Documentary History of the Negro People in the United States* (New York, 1951), 1:98–102, which also publishes the address of the 1830 convention, pp. 106–7.

Other Conventions of the 1830s

For the national conventions of 1831–1835, see Bell, *Proceedings*. For the unsuccessful effort to establish a manual labor college in New Haven, see *Liberator*, August 20, November 26, December 3, 1831. The views of William Whipper are discussed in Richard P. McCormick, "William Whipper: Moral Reformer," *Pennsylvania History* 43 (January 1976): 30–33.

American Moral Reform Society

The best study of the society is Howard H. Bell, "The American Moral Reform Society, 1836–1841," *Journal of Negro Education* 27 (Winter 1978): 34–40, and McCormick, op. cit., pp. 34–40. See also *Colored American*, September 2, 9, 16, 23, 30, November 11, 1837, February 10, March 29, 1838, and *National Reformer*, March, September, December 1839. Also worth consulting are Jane H. Pease and William H. Pease, *Bound with Them in Chains* (Westport, Conn., 1972), pp. 140–61; Sterling Stuckey, *The Ideological Origins of Black Nationalism* (Boston, 1972), pp. 118–46; and *National Anti-Slavery Standard*, October 1, 1840.

Revival of the Negro National Conventions

The discussion in this section is based on *Minutes of the National Convention of Colored Citizens* (Buffalo, N.Y., August 1843), pp. 8, 10, 13–15, 24, 37–39; *Proceedings of the National Convention of Colored People and Their Friends held in Troy, N.Y., . . . October, 1847*, pp. 7–8, 31–32; *North Star*, January 14, September 19, 1848;

Report of Proceedings of Colored National Convention, Held at Cleveland, Ohio, on Wednesday, September 6, 1848 (Rochester, N.Y., 1848), pp. 8, 12.

The 1853 Rochester Convention and Its Aftermath

The discussion in this section is based on the following sources: *Proceedings of the Colored National Convention Held in Rochester, July 6th, 7th, and 8th, 1853* (Rochester, N.Y., 1853), pp. 6–9, 33–38; *Proceedings of the Colored Convention Held in Franklin Hall, Sixth Street, Below Arch, Philadelphia, October 16th, 17th and 18th, 1855* (Salem, N.J.); Philip S. Foner, *The Life and Writings of Frederick Douglass* (New York, 1950), 2:28–37; *Frederick Douglass' Paper*, August 29, October 2, 9, 16, 1853; Jane H. Pease and William H. Pease, *They Who Would Be Free* (New York, 1974), pp. 170–73.

Black State Conventions

The discussion in this section is based on Philip S. Foner and George E. Walker, eds., *Proceedings of the Black State Conventions, 1840–1865.* Volume 1 (Philadelphia, 1979) includes New York, Pennsylvania, Indiana, Michigan, Ohio; volume 2 (Philadelphia, 1980) includes New Jersey, Connecticut, Maryland, Illinois, Massachusetts, California, and New England. Volume 2 also includes black state conventions in Kansas, Louisiana, Virginia, Missouri, and South Carolina during and immediately after the Civil War.

15. THE BATTLE FOR EQUALITY

The Twin Battle in Massachusetts

The discussion in this section is based on the following sources: *Liberator*, June 19, 1840; June 19, July 9, November 4, 1841; April 8, December 1, 1843; Philip S. Foner, *The Voice of Black America* (New York, 1972), pp. 72–76; Louis Ruchames, "Jim Crow Railroads in Massachusetts," *American Quarterly* 8 (July 1956): 61–75; Louis Ruchames, "Race, Marriage and Abolition in Massachusetts," *Journal of Negro History* 40 (January 1955): 250–73. For the Massachusetts General Colored Association, see John Daniels, *In Freedom's Birth Place: A Study of the Boston Negroes*, 2d ed. (New York, 1968), p. 455.

The Battle for Equal Education: Massachusetts

The 1851 meeting in Boston is reported in *Liberator*, April 4, 1851. For William C. Nell's account of his experience in 1829, see *Triumph of Equal School Rights in Boston: Proceedings of the Presentation Meeting Held in Boston, December 17, 1855* (Boston, 1856). The discussion of the desegregation of public schools in Salem and Nantucket is based on the following sources: Arthur O. White, "Salem's Antebellum Black Community: Seedbed of the School Integration Movement," *Essex Institute Historical Collections* 118 (April 1972): 99–118; *Salem Register*, March 7, 14, 21, 1844; *Salem Register*, reprinted in *Liberator*, March 26, 1858; *Nantucket Islander* in *Liberator*, March 18, 1842.

For the struggle for equal education in Boston in its early stages, see Louis Ruchames, "Race and Education in Massachusetts," *Negro History Bulletin* 24 (December 1949): 13–18; Arthur O. White, "Blacks and Education in Antebellum Massachusetts: Strategies for Social Mobility" (Ph.D. diss., State University of New York at Buffalo, 1975), pp. 208–35; *Report of the Minority of the Committee of the Primary School Board on the Caste Schools of the City of Boston* (Boston, 1846); Charles H. Wesley, "The Negro's Struggle for Freedom in Its Birthplace," *Journal of Negro History* 30 (January 1945): 73–78. For the Roberts case, see *Roberts* v. *City of Boston*, 5 Cush. 198; *The Works of Charles Sumner* (Boston, 1874), 2:327–29, 357, 364; *Liberator*, December 28, 1849, January 11, 1850; *Boston Post*, November 10, December 27, 1849; Leonard W. Levy and Harlan B. Phillips, "The Roberts Case: Source of the 'Separate but Equal' Doctrine," *American Historical Review* 56 (April 1951): 511–14; *Argument of Charles Sumner against the Constitutionality of Separate Schools* (Boston, 1849), pp. 3–4, 10–12, 20. For the controversy over the appointment of Thomas Paul as master of the Smith School, the role of Thomas Paul Smith, and Dr. James McCune Smith, see *Liberator*, September 7, October 5, November 23, 1849, January 4, February 15, 1850; Arthur O. White, "Antebellum School Reform in Boston: Integrationists and Separatists," *Phylon* 34 (1973): 203–14. For the passage of the law desegregating public schools in Massachusetts and the events that followed, see *Liberator*, March 30, 1855; *Boston Evening Telegraph*, August 28, 1855; *New York Herald* in Leon F. Litwack, "The Abolitionist Dilemma: The Anti-Slavery Movement and the Northern Negro," *New England Quarterly* 34 (March 1961): 72; Arthur O. White, "Integrated Schools in Antebellum Boston: The Implications of the Black Victory," *Urban Education* 6 (July–October 1971): 140–41; *Triumph of Equal School Rights*, pp. 5–11; Foner, op. cit., pp. 164–68.

The Battle for Equal Education: Rochester, New York

The discussion in this section is based on Philip S. Foner, *Life and Writings of Frederick Douglass* (New York, 1950), 2:39–41; *North Star*, August 10, 17, 1849; *Douglass' Monthly*, March 1859; Judith Polgar Ruchkin, "The Abolition of 'Colored Schools' in Rochester, New York: 1832–1856," *New York History* 47 (June 1973): 377–93. For the observation of the New York teacher on the outlook for a black school graduate, see Charles C. Andrew, *The History of the New York-African Free Schools* (New York, 1830; reprint ed., New York, 1969), pp. 117–18.

The Battle for Equal Education: Rhode Island

The discussion in this section is based on the following sources: *Liberator*, January 29, June 10, 1859; *Providence Journal*, March 28, 29, 1859; *Minority Report of the Committee on Education of the General Assembly of the State of Rhode Island on the Abolition of Caste Schools* (Providence, 1858); *Minority Report of the Committee on Education upon the Petition of Isaac Rice and Others* (Providence, 1859); George Downing et al., *Will the General Assembly Put Down Caste Schools* (n.p., n.d., but signed December 1857); George Downing et al., *To the Friends of Equal Rights* (n.p., n.d., but signed Providence, 1859); Lorenzo Greene, "Protest against Separate Schools in Rhode Island, 1859," *Midwest Journal* 1 (Summer 1949): 102–6; Robert J. Cottrol, *The Afro-Yankees: Providence's Black Community in the Antebellum Era* (Westport, Conn., 1982), pp. 95–101.

The Battle for Equal Suffrage: New York

For the petitions to the state legislature, the address of the 1840 state convention, the appeal of the *Colored American*, the testimony of Henry Highland Garnet, and the refusal of the state legislature to act, see the *Colored American*, March 1, December 9, 16, 1837; December 12, 1840; February 13, March 13, 1841; Philip S. Foner and George E.

Walker, eds., *Proceedings of the Black State Conventions, 1840–1865* (Philadelphia, 1979), 1:1–20; George E. Walker, "The Afro-American in New York City, 1827–1860" (Ph.D. diss., Columbia University, 1972), pp. 157–76; Joel Schor, *Henry Highland Garnet* (Westport, Conn., 1977), p. 43. For the 1846 Constitutional Convention and the events following, see *Herkimer Journal* reprinted in *National Anti-Slavery Standard*, May 4, 1843, and the battle for equal suffrage from that point to the Civil War, see *Debates and Proceedings in the New York State Convention for the Revision of the Constitution* (Albany, N.Y., 1846), pp. 775, 785–87, 842, 852; I. G. Penn, *The Afro-American Press and Its Editors* (Springfield, Mass., 1890), pp. 61–63; Benjamin Quarles, *Black Abolitionists* (New York, 1969), p. 173; *Weekly Anglo-African*, March 31, 1860; *New York Tribune*, September 6, 1855; Walker, op. cit., pp. 170–85; Emil Olbrich, *The Development of Negro Suffrage to 1860* (Madison, Wis., 1901), pp. 30–38, 126–28; *Brooklyn Daily Times* reprinted in *Principia*, October 20, 1860; Philip S. Foner, *Frederick Douglass* (New York, 1964), pp. 186–87; Phyllis F. Field, *The Politics of Race in New York: The Struggle for Black Suffrage in the Civil War Era* (Ithaca, N.Y., 1982), pp. 114–46.

The Battle for Equal Suffrage: Pennsylvania

The discussion in this section is based on the following sources: Foner and Walker, op. cit., 1:xvii, 104, 130; *Memorial of Thirty Thousand Disfranchised Citizens of Philadelphia to the Honorable Senate and House of Representatives* (Philadelphia, 1855); *Pennsylvania Freeman*, December 21, 1848; Edward Price, Jr., "Let the Law Be Just: The Quest for Racial Equality in Pennsylvania, 1780–1915" (Ph.D. diss., Pennsylvania State University, 1973), pp. 123–27; Edward Price, Jr., "The Black Voting Rights Issue in Philadelphia, 1780–1900," *Pennsylvania Magazine of History and Biography* 100 (July 1976): 362–70; Ann Greenwood Wilmoth, "Negro Suffrage in Nineteenth Century Pennsylvania: A Study in Politics and Prejudice" (master's thesis, Pennsylvania State University, 1970), pp. 40–42.

The Battle for Equal Suffrage: Rhode Island

The discussion of the reenfranchisement of blacks in Rhode Island is based on the following sources: Marvin C. Gettleman, *The Dorr Rebellion: A Study in American Radicalism, 1833–1849* (New York, 1973); Julian Rammelkamp, "The Providence Negro Community, 1840–1842," *Rhode Island History* 7 (January 1948): 20–33; U.S. Congress, *Interference of the Executive in Affairs of Rhode Island, Rpt. 546*, 28th Cong., 1st sess., 1844, pp. 111–13; Rhode Island, House of Representatives, *Journal of the Convention, Assembled to Frame a Constitution for the State of Rhode Island at Newport, Sept. 12, 1842* (Providence, 1859), pp. 22, 36–37, 45, 48, 51, 57; Foner, *Life and Writings of Douglass*, 1:48–49; *The Life and Times of Frederick Douglass* (Hartford, 1882), pp. 250–52; Quarles, op. cit., pp. 170–75; Peter J. Coleman, *The Transformation of Rhode Island, 1790–1860* (Providence, R.I., 1963); Arthur May Mowry, *The Dorr War: or, The Constitutional Struggle in Rhode Island* (Providence, R.I., 1901), pp. 34–44; J. Stanley Lemons and Michael A. McKenna, "The Re-Enfranchisement of Rhode Island Negroes" (unpublished paper).

The Militia Issue

For William J. Watkins' speech, see Foner, *Voice of Black America*, pp. 130–43. The parade of the independent Negro militiamen in Boston is reported in *Boston Herald*, reprinted in *Liberator*, November 27, 1857, and Watkin's query is in ibid., July 15, 1853.

For judicial decisions in San Francisco accepting Negro testimony against whites despite the state law banning such testimony, see Rudolph M. Lapp, "Negro Rights Activities in Gold Rush California," *California Historical Society Quarterly* 45 (March 1966): 10–11. For "An Address to the Colored People of the United States," written by Frederick Douglass in 1848, see Foner, *Life and Writings of Douglass*, 1:331–35.

16. "A FIREBELL IN THE NIGHT"

Antislavery after the War of 1812

For the contributions of George Bourne to abolition and the complete text of the rare 1816 edition of Bourne's antislavery treatise, see John W. Christie and Dwight L. Dumond, *George Bourne and "The Book and Slavery Irreconcilable"* (Wilmington, Del., 1969). For the action of the 1818 general assembly of the Presbyterian church against Bourne, see *Extracts from the Minutes of the General Assembly of the Presbyterian Church of the United States of America* (Philadelphia, 1818), pp. 20–21; Andrew E. Murray, *Presbyterians and the Negro—A History* (Philadelphia, 1966), pp. 98–101. For the failure of antislavery in the South between 1800 and 1820 to make any real impact, see Gordon Esley Finnie, "The Anti-Slavery Movement in the South, 1787–1836" (Ph.D. diss., Duke University, 1962); John Michael Shay, "The Anti-Slavery Movement in North Carolina" (Ph.D. diss., Princeton University, 1971); Kenneth M. Stampp, "The Fate of the Southern Anti-Slavery Movement," *Journal of Negro History* 28 (January 1943): 10–22. For the view that a flourishing and effective antislavery movement existed in the South during this period, see William M. Boyd, "Charles Osborn: Pioneer American Abolitionist," and "Southerners in the Anti-Slavery Movement, 1800–1831," *Phylon* 8 (second quarter 1947): 101–22, 154–66. For James Jones' proposal to Congress to abolish the internal slave trade, see Larry Gara, "A Southern Quaker's Plan to Abolish Slavery," *Quaker History* 58 (Autumn 1969): 104–7, and for the Union Humane Society, see Randall M. Miller, "The Union Humane Society," *Quaker History* 61 (Autumn 1972): 91–106. The resurgence of slavery is discussed in David Brion Davis, *The Problem of Slavery in the Age of Revolution, 1770–1823* (New York, 1978).

The Missouri Controversy and the Missouri Compromise

The events leading up to the Missouri Compromise are discussed in Glover Moore, *The Missouri Controversy, 1819–1821* (Lexington, Ky., 1953), and in Donald C. Robinson, *Slavery in the Structure of American Politics, 1765–1820* (New York, 1971), pp. 408–23. See also William R. Johnson, "Prelude to the Missouri Controversy," *Arkansas Historical Quarterly* 24 (Spring 1965): 47–56. The article deals with the effort, which failed, to exclude slavery from Arkansas Territory. For contemporary sources, see L. Shaw, "Slavery and the Missouri Question," *North American Review* 10 (1820); Thomas Hart Benton, *Thirty Years View* (New York, 1854), Vol. 1; Charles Francis Adams, ed., *Memoirs of John Quincy Adams* (Philadelphia, 1875), Vol. 4; *Niles' Weekly Register* 17. The debates in Congress cited in the discussion are in *Annals of Congress*, 15th Cong., 1st sess., pp. 974–75; 2d sess., pp. 122, 238, 251, 272–73, 279, 280–83; 418, 1166, 1170, 1434–38; 16th Cong., 1st sess., pp. 70–72, 119, 123, 124, 153, 179, 184, 210, 217, 229, 247, 266, 331–83, 987–95, 1089, 1134, 1231–34, 1263, 1299–1300, 1311–15, 1497, 1537, 1820; 16th Cong., 2d sess., pp. 79, 1022–24, 1107–11, 1102–7, 1144, 1784–86. Cushman's and Taylor's speeches are in ibid., 15th Cong., 2d sess., pp.

1191–93, and 16th Cong., 1st sess., pp. 952, 964–65. For Rufus King's speeches and the reaction to them, see Charles R. King, ed., *Life and Correspondence of Rufus King* (New York, 1894–1900), 6:700; *Niles' Weekly Register* 17, pp. 218–19; Adams, op. cit., 4:517; Gaillard Hunt, ed., *The Writings of Madison* (New York, 1900–1910), 9:517; Frederick J. Turner, *Rise of the New West, 1819–1829* (New York, 1906), pp. 155–58. The pamphlet containing King's speeches is Rufus King, *Substance of Two Speeches Delivered in the Senate of the United States on the Subject of the Missouri Bill* (New York, 1819).

The influence of the Declaration of Independence on the debates is discussed in Philip F. Detweiler, "Congressional Debate on Slavery and the Declaration of Independence, 1819–1821," *American Historical Review* 63 (April 1958). For meetings in the North, and the memorials adopted, see *Niles' Weekly Register* 17, pp. 200, 241–42, 296, 297, and Moore, op. cit., pp. 190–232. For efforts of antislavery forces in Missouri to restrict slavery in the 1820 constitution, see John Merkel, "The Anti-Slavery Movement in Missouri, 1819–1865" (Ph.D. diss., Washington University, 1939), pp. 21–22, and for the Missouri constitution, see *State Papers, Senate Doc. 1, House Doc. 2.*, 16th Cong., 2d sess.; for the Missouri question, see *Annals of Congress*, 16th Cong., 2d sess., pp. 1019, 1219–40, 1784–86; *Niles' Weekly Register* 20, p. 388. John Quincy Adams' observation of the threat to the Union in the Missouri debates is in Adams, op. cit., 4:260, 502, 528, and Thomas Jefferson's is in Paul L. Ford, ed., *Writings of Thomas Jefferson* (New York, 1892–1899), 10:156–58, and Philip S. Foner, ed., *Basic Writings of Thomas Jefferson* (New York, 1950), pp. 767–68. Accounts of the petitions to Congress and meetings in opposition to slavery in Missouri and the entrance of Missouri into the Union as a slave state are in the *Philanthropist*, January 1, 1820.

For the anger of the South over the Missouri settlement, see Richard H. Brown, "The Missouri Crisis, Slavery and the Politics of Jacksonianism," *South Atlantic Quarterly* 65 (Winter 1966): 80–98. The reaction of the abolitionists may be found in Samuel Eddy to Moses Brown, April 4, 1820, Moses Brown to Nathaniel Hazard, April 12, 1820, Moses Brown Papers, XIV, #3940–3941, Rhode Island Historical Society, and Miller, op. cit., pp. 98–99.

The Closed Southern Mind

For the influence of the Vesey conspiracy, see William W. Freehling, *Prelude to Civil War: the Nullification Controversy in South Carolina, 1816–1836* (New York, 1966), pp. 53–61. George Logan's observation is in George Logan, *Autograph Letter Signed to Caesar A. Rodney* (Charleston, S.C., 1822). The minutes of the 1828 American Convention of delegates from abolition societies are published in *Freedom's Journal*, February 15, 22, 1828. For the proposal of the Ohio General Assembly of 1824, see Richard F. O'Dell, "The Early Antislavery Movement in Ohio"(Ph.D. diss., University of Michigan, 1948), pp. 290–94, 298–305. For Benjamin Lundy's antislavery role, see Merton L. Dillon, *Benjamin Lundy and the Struggle for Negro Freedom* (Urbana, Ill., 1966), pp. 32–85.

Nullification and the Slavery Issue and Decline of Abolition Societies

For the discussion of the relationship between the nullification controversy and the slavery issue, see Freehling, op. cit., and Major L. Wilson, "A Preview of Irrepressible Conflict: The Issue of Slavery during the Nullification Controversy," *Mississippi* 9 (Fall 1966): 12–29. For criticism of the Freehling thesis, see Eugene D. Genovese, *The World the Slaveholders Made* (New York, 1969), p. 134; Paul H. Bergeron, "The Nullification

Controversy Revisited,'' *Tennessee Historical Quarterly* 35 (Fall 1976): 263–75. For support of the Freehling thesis, see James M. Benner, Jr., ''The problem of South Carolina,'' in Stanley M. Elkins and Eric McKitrick, eds., *The Hofstadter Aegis: A Memorial* (New York, 1974), p. 67. In his article, ''Paranoia and American History,'' *New York Review of Books*, September 23, 1971, p. 36n., Freehling indicated he may have gone too far in his discussion of paranoid feelings in South Carolina over slavery. For John Randolph's statement, see his letter to Andrew Jackson, March 18, 1832, in John Spencer Bassett, ed., *Correspondence of Andrew Jackson* (Washington, D.C., 1931), 4:421–22. Other Southern statements of a similar nature may be found in William Sumner Jenkins, *Pro-Slavery Thought in the Old South* (Chapel Hill, N.C., 1935), pp. 76–77.

David Walker's Revolutionary Appeal

For Garrison's Fourth of July 1829 speech, see W. P. and F. J. Garrison, *William Lloyd Garrison: The Story of His Life as Told by His Children* (New York, 1885–1889), 1:134–35. The best study of David Walker is Donald M. Jacobs, ''David Walker, Boston Race Leader, 1825–1830,'' *Essex Institute Historical Collections* 107 (January 1971). An earlier study is George Forbes, ''David Walker,'' unpublished ms., Boston Public Library. The various editions of *Walker's Appeal* may be conveniently found in Herbert Aptheker, ed., *''One Continuous Cry,'' David Walker's Appeal to the Colored Citizens of the World, 1829–1830), Its Setting and Its Meaning* (New York, 1965); Charles M. Wiltse, ed., *David Walker's Appeal in Four Articles: Together with a Preamble to the Coloured Citizens of the World, But in Particular, and Very Expressly, to Those of the United States of America* (New York, 1965), and the reprint of the 1848 edition published by Henry Highland Garnet (New York, 1969), which also includes Garnet's 1843 *Address to the Slaves of the United States of America*. Extracts of Walker's *Appeal* appear in Aptheker's *Documentary History*, 1:93–97, and in Benjamin Brawley's *Early American Negro Writers* (Chapel Hill, 1935), pp. 125–46. Walker's speech before the Massachusetts General Colored Association is in Philip S. Foner, ed., *The Voice of Black America: Major Speeches by Blacks in the United States, 1797–1973* (New York, 1975), 1:51–56. For the reaction in the South to the *Appeal*, see Clement Eaton, ''A Dangerous Pamphlet in the Old South,'' *Journal of Southern History* 2 (Winter 1936): 180–96, and William H. Pease and Jane H. Pease, ''Walker's Appeal Comes to Charleston: A Note and Documents,'' *Journal of Negro History* 59 (July 1974): 287–92. Pease and Pease tell the story of the arrest and imprisonment of Edward Smith. The *Boston Daily Courier's* note to its readers doubting the ability of Walker to be the author of the pamphlet is in the issue of March 22, 1830. For relations between Lundy and Garrison, see Dillon, op. cit., pp. 126–80, and Walter M. Merrill, *Against Wind and Tide: A Biography of Wm. Lloyd Garrison* (Cambridge, Mass., 1963), pp. 50–61. Garrison's reaction to Walker's pamphlet in the *Genius of Universal Emancipation* is in Forbes, op. cit., p. 6. For Walker's death, see Forbes, op. cit., p. 8. For the theory that Walker's *Appeal* was written for Northern abolitionists rather than for Southern slaves, see Peter Buckingham, ''David Walker: An Appeal to Whom?'' *Negro History Bulletin* 42 (January, February, March 1979): 24–26.

Walker and Garrison

The best study of Garrison's stay of less than one year in Baltimore is David K. Sullivan, ''William Lloyd Garrison in Baltimore, 1829–1830,'' *Maryland Historical*

Magazine 56 (Spring 1973): 64–79. See also Dillon, op. cit., pp. 131–46; John L. Thomas, *The Liberator: William Lloyd Garrison* (Boston, 1963), pp. 74–81, 89–101; Walter M. Merrill, ed., *The Letters of William Lloyd Garrison: I Will Be Heard, 1822–1835* (Cambridge, Mass., 1971), pp. 1–93.

17. THE PROSLAVERY ARGUMENT

George M. Fredrickson's point is made in his *The Black Image in the White Mind: The Debate on Afro-American Character and Destiny, 1817–1914* (New York, 1971), pp. 43–45. For the proslavery argument in the 1790s, see Philip S. Foner, *History of Black Americans: From Africa to the Emergence of the Cotton Kingdom* (Westport, Conn., 1975), pp. 406–20. Stampp's argument is in Kenneth M. Stampp, "An Analysis of T. R. Drew's *Review of the Debates in the Virginia Legislature*," *Journal of Negro History* 27 (October 1942): 380–86. For Governor McDuffie's defense of slavery in his message to the South Carolina legislature of 1835, see William W. Freehling, *Prelude to Civil War: The Nullification Controversy in South Carolina, 1816–1836* (New York, 1965), pp. 144–48, 192–96, 340–46; Edwin L. Green, *George McDuffie* (Columbia, S.C., 1936), pp. 146–55; William S. Jenkins, *Pro-Slavery Thought in the Old South* (Chapel Hill, N.C., 1935), pp. 285–95.

An interesting view of the controversy over the proslavery argument is presented in John David Smith, "A Different View of Slavery: Black Historians Attack the Proslavery Argument, 1890–1920," *Journal of Negro History* 65 (Fall 1980): 298–311. A valuable discussion of the proslavery argument may be found in Drew Gilpin Faust, ed., *The Ideology of Slavery: Proslavery Thought in the Antebellum South, 1830–1860* (Baton Rouge, La., 1980).

A School for "Barbarians"

The discussion in this section is based on the following sources: Jenkins, op. cit., pp. 62–84, 285–308; Thomas R. Drew, *Review of the Debate in the Virginia Legislature of 1831 and 1832* (Richmond, Va., 1932), pp. 12–15, 43–46, 64–68. William J. Grayson, *The Hireling and the Slave, Cherocra and Other Poems* (Charleston, S.C., 1856). Grayson's poem runs to 1,576 lines, of which about a quarter are reprinted in Eric L. McKitrick, ed., *Slavery Defended: The Views of the Old South* (Englewood Cliffs, N.J., 1963), pp. 57–68. See also Thomas D. Jarrett, "The Literary Significance of William J. Grayson's *The Hireling and the Slave*," *Georgia Review* 5 (Winter 1951): 487–94; Edmund Wilson, *Patriotic Gore: Studies in the Literature of the Civil War* (New York, 1962), pp. 336–64; Arthur Y. Lloyd, *The Slavery Controversy, 1831–1860* (Chapel Hill, N.C., 1939), pp. 139–45.

The Pseudoscientific Argument

The discussion in this section is based on the following sources: Chancellor Harper, Governor Hammond, Dr. Simms, and Professor Drew, *The Pro-Slavery Argument* (Charleston, S.C., 1852), pp. 40–71; Alexander H. Stephens, *African Slavery: The Cornerstone of the Southern Confederacy* (Savannah, Ga., 1861), pp. 14–32; Jenkins, op. cit., pp. 112–41; F. A. Ross, *Slavery Ordained of God* (Philadelphia, 1857), pp. 6–22; J. Priest, *Bible Defense of Slavery* (Glasgow, Ky., 1852), pp. 34–45.

Chattel Slavery and Wage Slavery

The most recent analysis of this issue is Marcus Cunliffe, *Chattel Slavery and Wage Slavery: The Anglo-American Contest, 1830–1860* (Athens, Ga., 1970). For an older discussion, see Wilfred Carsel, "The Slaveholders' Indictment of Northern Wage Slavery," *Journal of Southern History* 6 (November 1940): 504–20. For the views of George Fitzhugh, see *Cannibals All! or Slaves Without Masters*, ed. with an introduction by C. Vann Woodward (Cambridge, Mass., 1960); George Fitzhugh, *Sociology for the South* (Richmond, Va., 1854). Selections from Fitzhugh may be found in Harvey Wish, ed., *Ante-Bellum* (New York, 1960). Wish is also the author of *George Fitzhugh, Propagandist of the Old South* (Baton Rouge, La., 1943). An appreciative analysis of Fitzhugh is in Eugene D. Genovese, *The World the Slaveholders Made* (New York, 1969), which takes issue with Wish. See also Fredrickson, op. cit., pp. 59–70. Finally, see George Fitzhugh, "The Conservative Principle; or, Social Evils and Their Remedies," *DeBow's Review* 22 (April 1857): 249–65. John C. Calhoun's speech is published in John C. Calhoun, *Speech on the Slavery Question* (Washington, D.C., 1850).

Northern Echoes

The discussion in this section is based on the following sources: William Gouge, *A Short History of Paper Money and Banking in the United States* (Philadelphia, 1833), pt. 1: 98–99; *Boston Quarterly Review* 1 (April 1838): 260, Cunliffe, op. cit., pp. 32–48; Robert Spiller, "Fenimore Cooper's Defense of Slave-Owning America," *American Historical Review* 35 (April 1930): 580; James K. Paulding, *Slavery in the United States* (New York, 1836), pp. 177–78; Seth Luther, *An Address to the Working-Men of New England on the State of Education, and on the Condition of the Producing Classes in Europe and America* (Boston, 1832), p. 37; *Working Man's Advocate*, June 22, 1844; Philip S. Foner, *History of the Labor Movement in the United States* (New York, 1947), 1:272–75; Eugene H. Beridinger, "Negrophobia in Northern Proslavery and Antislavery Thought," *Phylon* 13 (Fall 1972): 266–85; Gerald S. Henig, "The Jacksonian Attitude toward Abolitionism in the 1830's," *Tennessee Historical Quarterly* 24 (Spring 1969): 51–53; William Stanton, *The Leopard's Spots, Scientific Attitude toward Race in America, 1815–1859* (Chicago, 1960), pp. 33–41; Calvin Colton, *Abolition a Sedition, by a Northern Man* (Philadelphia, 1839), pp. 127, 189; Alfred A. Cave, "The Case of Calvin Colton," *New-York Historical Society Quarterly* (July 1969): 215–28; Ronald T. Takaki, *Iron Cages: Race and Culture in Nineteenth Century America* (New York, 1979).

18. AMERICAN HISTORIANS AND THE ABOLITIONISTS

Traditional Interpretation of Abolitionists

The discussion in this section is based on the following sources: T. Harry Williams, *Lincoln and the Radicals* (Baton Rouge, La., 1961), passim; Samuel Eliot Morison and Henry Steele Commager, *The Growth of the American Republic*, 4th ed. (New York, 1950), pp. 216–18; Arnold Whitridge, *No Compromise! The Story of the Fanatics Who Paved the Way to the Civil War* (New York, 1960), passim; Avery Craven, *The Coming of the Civil War* (Chicago, 1942), pp. 134–50; David Donald, "Toward a Reconsideration of Abolitionists," in his *Lincoln Reconsidered: Essays in the Civil War* (New York, 1956), pp. 33–38; Hazel C. Wolf, *On Freedom's Altar, The Martyr Complex in the*

Abolitionist Movement (Madison, Wis., 1952), pp. 8–16. William H. Pease and Jane H. Pease, "Antislavery Ambivalence: Immediatism, Expediency, Race," *American Quarterly* 17 (Winter 1965): 693; Stanley M. Elkins, *Slavery: A Problem in American Institutional and Intellectual Life* (Chicago, 1959), pp. 193–206.

For a useful synthesis of the scholarship on abolitionists, see James Brewer Stewart, *Holy Warriors: The Abolitionists and American Slavery* (New York, 1976).

The Traditional View of William Lloyd Garrison

The discussion in this section is based on the following sources: Allan Nevins, *Ordeal of the Union* (New York, 1964), pp. 132–34; Dwight L. Dumond, *Antislavery: The Crusade for Freedom in America* (New York, 1961), p. 174; Gilbert Hobbs Barnes, *The Antislavery Impulse, 1830–1844* (New York, 1933), pp. 51, 192–94; Wendell Phillips, *Speeches, Lectures, and Letters*, 1st ser. (Boston, 1863), p. 152; Merton L. Dillon, "The Abolitionist: A Decade of Historiography, 1959–1969," *Journal of Southern History* 35 (1969): 504–5; Walter M. Merrill, *Against Wind and Tide: A Biography of William Lloyd Garrison* (Cambridge, Mass., 1963), pp. 14–23, 117–50; John L. Thomas, *The Liberator: William Lloyd Garrison* (Boston, 1963), pp. 12–15, 162–78. David Donald, *Charles Sumner and the Coming of the Civil War* (New York, 1960); Dwight L. Dumond, *Antislavery Origins of the Civil War* (Ann Arbor, Mich., 1959), p. 87; Leon F. Litwack, *North of Slavery: The North in the Free States, 1790–1860* (Chicago, 1961), pp. 243–44.

A New Look at the Abolitionists

The discussion in this section is based on the following sources: Benjamin P. Thomas, *Theodore D. Weld: Crusader for Freedom* (New Brunswick, N.J., 1950), pp. 4–5; Louis Filler, *The Crusade against Slavery: 1830–1860* (New York, 1960), pp. 32–48; Louis Ruchames, "The Historian as Special Pleader," *Nation*, November 24, 1962, pp. 352–56; Louis Ruchames, *The Abolitionists: A Collection of Their Writings* (New York, 1963), pp. 15–18; Martin Duberman, ed., *The Antislavery Vanguard: New Essays on the Abolitionists* (Princeton, N.J., 1965), passim.

An effort, not entirely successful, to update the Duberman volume of essays by various scholars is Lewis Perry and Michael Fellman, eds., *Antislavery Reconsidered: New Perspectives on the Abolitionists* (Baton Rouge, La., 1979). A more important recent work, unfortunately mainly unpublished, is Ronald Gordon Walters, "The Antislavery Appeal: American Abolitionism after 1831" (Ph.D. diss., University of California, Berkeley, 1971). The part published is Ronald G. Walters, *The Antislavery Appeal: American Abolitionism After 1830* (Baltimore, 1976). See also for the discussion in this section, Bertram Wyatt-Brown, "Abolitionism: Its Meaning for Contemporary Reform," *Midwest Quarterly* 8 (October 1966): 41–55; Betty Fladeland, "Who Were the Abolitionists?" *Journal of Negro History* 49 (April 1964): 99–115; Martin Duberman, "The Abolitionists and Psychology," *Journal of Negro History* 47 (July 1962): 183–91, and in Hugh Hawkins, ed., *The Abolitionists, Means, Ends, and Motivation* (Lexington, Mass., 1942), pp. 142–50; Dillon, op. cit., p. 502; Bertram Wyatt-Brown, "New Leftists and Abolitionists: A Comparison of American Radical Types," *Wisconsin Magazine of History* 53 (1970): 256–58.

The New View of Garrison

The discussion in this section is based on the following sources: *William Lloyd Garrison: I Will Be Heard, Letters*, Vol. 1:*1822–1835*, edited by Walter M. Merrill; *William*

Lloyd Garrison: A House Divided Against Itself, 1836–1840 Letters, Vol. 2, *1836–1840*, edited by Louis Ruchames; *William Lloyd Garrison: No Union with Slave-Holders, Letters*, Vol. 3: *1841–1849*, edited by Walter M. Merrill (Cambridge, Mass., 1971, 1974); Truman Nelson, ed., *Documents of Upheaval* (New York, 1964), pp. 12–13; Bertram Wyatt-Brown, *Lewis Tappan and the Evangelist War against Slavery* (Cleveland, 1969), pp. 19–23; Bertram Wyatt-Brown, "William Lloyd Garrison and Antislavery Unity: A Reappraisal," *Civil War History* 13 (March 1967): 5–24; James B. Stewart, "The Aims and Impact of Garrisonian Abolitionism, 1840–1860," *Civil War History* 15 (September 1969): 203; David A. Williams, "William Lloyd Garrison, the Historians, and the Abolitionist Movement," Essex Institute, *Historical Collections* 98 (April 1962): 84–99; Aileen S. Kraditor, *Means and Ends in American Abolitionism: Garrison and His Critics on Strategy and Tactics, 1834–1850* (New York, 1969), pp. 76–108; Aileen S. Kraditor, "The Abolitionists Rehabilitated," Review of James M. McPherson, *The Struggle for Equality: Abolitionists and the Negro in the Civil War and Reconstruction*, in *Studies on the Left* 5 (1965): 99–102; Aileen S. Kraditor, "A Note on Elkins and the Abolitionists," *Civil War History* 13 (December 1967): 102–12; Barrington Moore Jr., *Social Origins of Dictatorship and Democracy: Lord and Peasant in the Making of the Modern World* (Boston, 1966), chap. 3.

A Revolutionary Movement

See Herbert Aptheker, "The Abolitionist Movement," *Political Affairs* (February 1976): 29–33. See also Margaret Shortreed, "The Antislavery Radicals: From Crusade to Revolution, 1840–1868," *Past and Present* 16 (November 1959): 65–87.

Blacks and the Antislavery Movement

For criticism of the abolitionists for their racism and refusal to battle discrimination, see Merton L. Dillon, "The Failure of the American Abolitionists," *Journal of Southern History* 35 (May 1959): 159–77; Leon F. Litwack, *North of Slavery: The Negro in the Free States, 1790–1860* (Chicago 1961), pp. 214–30; Jane H. Pease and William H. Pease, *Bound with Them in Chains: A Biographical History of the Antislavery Movement* (Westport, Conn., 1972), pp. 162–90; Pease and Pease, "Ends, Means and Attitudes: Black-White Conflict in the Antislavery Movement," *Civil War History* 18 (1972): 117–28; Pease and Pease, "Antislavery Ambivalence," pp. 682–95. For Quarles' view, see Benjamin Quarles, *Black Abolitionists* (New York, 1969), p. 132. McPherson's analysis is in James M. McPherson, "A Brief for Equality: The Abolitionist Reply to the Racist Myth, 1860–1865," in Duberman, *Antislavery Vanguard*, pp. 156–77; the quotation from Aptheker is from his review in *Masses and Mainstream* (May 1951): 87; W.E.B. Du Bois, *John Brown* (New York, 1962), pp. 5, 7, 42; W.E.B. Du Bois, "The Liberator," *Crisis* 39 (February 1931): 69.

19. THE *LIBERATOR* AND THE AMERICAN ANTI-SLAVERY SOCIETY

Launching the Liberator

For Garrison's plans to start a paper in Washington and the decision to launch the *Liberator* in Boston, see Garrison to George Sheperd, September 13, 1830; Garrison to Ebenezer Dale, July 14, 1830; Garrison to Ephraim Allen, September 30, 1830, in Walter

M. Merrill, ed., *The Letters of William Lloyd Garrison: I Will Be Heard, 1822–1835* (Cambridge, Mass., 1971), pp. 104, 109–11. For the contributions and comments of James Forten, see Forten to William Lloyd Garrison, December 31, 1830, February 2, 1831, Anti-Slavery Letters Addressed to William Lloyd Garrison, Boston Public Library, Rare Book Room; *William Lloyd Garrison, 1805–1879, The Story of His Life Told by His Children* (New York, 1885–1889), 1:433. On the Support of Boston blacks, see *Liberator*, August 20, September 3, 1831, and Donald M. Jacobs, "William Lloyd Garrison's Liberator and Boston Blacks, 1830–1865," *New England Quarterly* 26 (Spring 1971): 259–61. For the importance of black subscribers and the view that the *Liberator* was the organ of blacks, see *Liberator*, December 10, 1831, December 29, 1865; John L. Thomas, *The Liberator, William Lloyd Garrison* (Boston, 1963), p. 31.

Revivalism

The discussion in this section is based on the following sources: Gilbert Hobbs Barnes, *The Anti-Slavery Impulse, 1830–1844* (New York, 1933), pp. 15–38; John C. Hammond, "Revival Religion and Antislavery Politics," *American Sociological Review* 39 (April 1974): 175–86; Donald G. Mathews, *Slavery and Methodism: A Chapter in American Morality, 1780–1845* (Princeton, N.J., 1965), pp. 86–105; William G. McLaughlin Jr., *Modern Revivalism: Charles Grandison Finney to Billy Graham* (New York, 1959), p. 115; Andrew G. Murray, *Presbyterians and the Negro—A History* (Philadelphia, 1966), pp. 94–110; William H. Pease and Jane H. Pease, eds., *The Anti-Slavery Movement* (New York, 1967), pp. 72–80; Robert H. Abuzy, "The Influence of Garrisonian Abolitionists' Fears of Slave Violence on the Antislavery Argument, 1829–40," *Journal of Negro History* 55 (January 1970): 16–17. For Finney's backwardness on the issue of equal rights for blacks, see Garth Mervin Russell, "Charles G. Finney and the Rise of the Benevolence Empire" (Ph.D. diss., University of Minnesota, 1971), pp. 175–78.

The "Lane Rebels"

The discussion in this section is based on the following sources: Bertram Wyatt-Brown, *Lewis Tappan and the Evangelical War against Slavery* (Cleveland, 1969), pp. 32–54, 74–81; Robert Samuel Fletcher, *A History of Oberlin College* (Oberlin, Ohio, 1943), pp. 34–35, 153, 162, 168, 170–71; Benjamin P. Thomas, *Theodore D. Weld: Crusader for Freedom* (New Brunswick, N.J., 1950), pp. 18–26, 48, 73–93; Barnes, op. cit., pp. 38–40, 55–58; Gilbert H. Barnes and Dwight L. Dumond, eds., *Letters of Theodore Dwight Weld, Angelina Grimké Weld, and Sarah Grimké 1822–1844* (New York, 1934), 1:32–36, 48–51, 63–67 (hereafter cited as *Weld-Grimké Letters*). The most recent study of the Lane rebels, which, however, does not add much new to what is already known, is Lawrence Thomas Lesick, *The Lane Rebels: Evangelicalism and Antislavery in Antebellum America* (Metuchen, N.J., 1980).

New England Anti-Slavery Society

For the British antislavery movement and its influence in the United States, see Barnes, op. cit., 29–37; Annie H. Abel and Frank J. Klineberg, *A Side-Light on Anglo-American Relations, 1839–1858* (Lancaster, Pa., 1927), pp. 11–15. On the formation of the New England Anti-Slavery Society, see *Liberator*, February 2, 1833; John Daniels, *In Freedom's Birthplace: A Study of the Boston Negroes* (Boston, 1914), p. 47; George W. Williams, *History of the Negro Race from 1619 to 1880* (New York, 1883), 2:78–79; Donald M. Jacobs, "A History of the Boston Negro from Revolution to Civil War" (Ph.D. diss., Boston University, 1968), p. 107.

Formation of the American Anti-Slavery Society

For Garrison's trip to England, see *Liberator*, March 23, April 3, May 11, 1833. There are several versions of the speech by the unknown Negro in New York City. The one reproduced here is from Lewis Tappan, *Life of Arthur Tappan* (New York, 1885), p. 7, and reprinted in Herbert Aptheker, "The Negro in the Abolitionist Movement," *Science and Society* 12 (Spring 1952): 168–69. For other versions, see Henry Wilson, *History of the Rise and Fall of the Slave Power in America* (New York, 1872), 1:231–32; Clarence Winthrop Brown, *Arthur and Lewis Tappan* (New York, 1883), pp. 5–7; *New York Evangelist*, October 5, 1833. For the conflict over immediate emancipation between Garrison and the New York abolitionists, see Abel and Klineberg, op. cit., pp. 11–12, 420–43, and David Brion Davis, "The Emergence of Immediatism in British American Antislavery Thought," *Mississippi Valley Historical Review* 49 (September 1962): 209. The Declaration of Sentiment of the American Anti-Slavery Society and the proceedings of the founding convention are in *Liberator*, December 14, 1833; American Anti-Slavery Society, *Declaration of the Anti-Slavery Convention. Assembled in Philadelphia, December 4, 1833* (Philadelphia, 1833); American Anti-Slavery Society, *First Annual Report* (New York, 1834), pp. 30–36. The formation of the Massachusetts Anti-Slavery Society is discussed in Elaine Brooks, "Massachusetts Anti-Slavery Society," *Journal of Negro History* 30 (July 1945): 312.

Female Antislavery Societies

The discussion in this section is based on the following sources: *Liberator*, March 30, 1833, September 13, 1834, July 14, 1835, March 4, June 2, October 6, 1837; Philip S. Foner, ed., *Frederick Douglass and Women's Rights* (Westport, Conn., 1976), pp. 3–4; Filler, op. cit., pp. 34–38, 129–36; Dwight L. Dumond, *Anti-Slavery: The Crusade for Freedom in America* (Ann Arbor, Mich., 1961), pp. 275–86; Charles H. Wesley, *Richard Allen, Apostle of Freedom* (Washington, D.C., 1935), pp. 239–40; Constitution and Minutes of the Society for the Encouragement of Free-Labour, Delaware Historical Society, Wilmington; *North Star*, December 8, 1848, March 20, 1851; *National Anti-Slavery Standard*, March 3, 1860; Norman B. Wilkinson, "The Philadelphia Free Produce Attack upon Slavery," *Pennsylvania Magazine of History and Biography* 56 (July 1947): 294–313; *New York Commercial Advertiser*, May 17, 1837.

Antislavery Agents

Elizur Wright's letter to Weld is in *Weld-Grimké Letters*, 1:121; for the work of the various agents, see Benjamin P. Thomas, *Theodore Weld, Crusader for Freedom* (New Brunswick, N.J., 1950), pp. 100–21; Dumond, *Anti-Slavery*, pp. 183–89; John L. Myers, "The Beginning of Anti-Slavery Agencies in New York State, 1833–1836," *New York History* 42 (April 1962): 149–81, "Anti-Slavery Activities of Five Lane Seminary Boys in 1835–1836," *Historical and Philosophical Society of Ohio Bulletin* 21 (September 1963): 128–49, and "The Beginning of Antislavery Agencies in New Hampshire, 1832–1835," *Historical New Hampshire* 25 (Fall 1970): 120–45; *Liberty Bell*, 1842, pp. 64–66; *Fourteenth Annual Report of the Massachusetts Anti-Slavery Society*, 1846, p. 48; Elizur Wright to James G. Birney, July 16, 1836, in Dwight L. Dumond, ed., *Letters of James Gillespie Birney* (New York, 1938), 1:334; Ira V. Brown, "An Antislavery Agent: C. C. Burleigh in Pennsylvania, 1836–1837," *Pennsylvania Magazine of History and Biography* 105 (January 1981): 66–84.

"The Seventy"

The discussion in this section is based on the following sources: Maria W. Stewart, *Productions of Mary W. Stewart* (Boston, 1835); *Liberator*, March 17, 1832; Philip S. Foner, ed., *The Voice of Black America: Major Speeches by Blacks in the United States, 1797–1973* (New York, 1975), 1:63–70; Barnes and Dumond, eds., *Weld-Grimké Letters*, 2:564; Gerda Lerner, *The Grimké Sisters of South Carolina: Pioneers for Women's Rights and Abolition* (New York, 1968), pp. 120–35; John L. Myers, "The Organization of 'the Seventy,': To Arouse the North against Slavery," *Mid-America* 48 (January 1966): 29–46; Janet Wilson, "The Travelling Agents Convert the Countryside," *More Books* 12 (January, 1968): 123–40; John L. Myers, "American Antislavery Society Agents and the Free Negro, 1833–1838," *Journal of Negro History* 52 (July 1967): 200–219; Herbert Aptheker, *The Negro in the Abolitionist Movement* (New York, 1944), p. 169.

Antislavery Pamphlets and Tracts

For Weld's work as an editor, see Janet Wilson, "The Early Antislavery Propaganda," *More Books* 12 (March 1968): 357–59; *Weld-Grimké Letters*, 1:479–80, 505; 2:526, 621, 717. For Dickens' use of *American Slavery As It Is*, see Louise H. Johnson, "The Source of the Chapter on Slavery in Dickens' *American Notes*," *American Literature* 14 (January 1943): 427–30. For a brief sketch of Lydia Maria Child, see *Dictionary of American Biography*, 4:67–69. The discussion of her *Appeal* is based on: Lydia M. Child, *An Appeal in Favor of That Class of Americans Called Africans* (New York, 1836), pp. 7–37, 81, 101, 105–22, 148; Lydia M. Child, *Letters*, with an introduction by John G. Whittier and an appendix by Wendell Phillips (Boston, 1883), pp. 41, 194–95; J. W. Chadwick, *A Life for Liberty, Anti-Slavery and Other Letters of Sally Holley* (New York, 1899), p. 175; Hilda Marie Sampey, "Lydia Maria Child and the Female Anti-Slavery Movement" (master's thesis, New York University, 1946), pp. 24–27. For the quotation from *Slavery and the North*, see Charles C. Burleigh, "Slavery and the North," *Anti-Slavery Tracts*, No. 10:9–10.

Antislavery Fairs

The discussion in this section is based on the following sources: *Liberator*, October 6, December 15, 1837, December 14, 1838, November 29, 1839, January 1, 1841, January 12, 1855, January 30, 1857; *National Anti-Slavery Standard*, September 21, 1843, November 11, 1851, September 2, 1854; *Weld-Grimké Letters*, 2:541. For a detailed study of Abolitionist finances, see Benjamin Quarles, "Sources of Abolitionist Income," *Mississippi Valley Historical Review* 32 (June 1945): 63–76. The development of the American Anti-Slavery Society may be followed in Dumond, *Anti-Slavery*, chap. 20; Filler, op. cit., pp. 66–67; and Janet Wilson, "The Network of Anti-Slavery Societies," *More Books* (February 1945): 51–53.

20. CIVIL RIGHTS AND ANTISLAVERY

For Mary Parker's letter, see Liberator, April 30, 1836. A discussion of the civil liberties issue and the antislavery movement is in Russell B. Nye, *Fettered Freedom:*

Civil Liberties and the Slavery Controversy, 1830–1860 (East Lansing, Mich., 1949). For bitter denunciations of the abolitionists quoted, see James K. Paulding, *Slavery in the United States* (New York, 1836), pp. 302–3; speech of Ely Moore, *Congressional Globe*, 25th Cong., 3d sess., Appendix, p. 240. For a discussion of Moore, see Philip S. Foner, *History of the Labor Movement in the United States* (New York, 1947), 1:151–53, 268, 564. The comment of the *New York Courier and Enquirer* is in the issue of July 22, 1834; that of James Buchanan is in *Lancaster Intelligencer*, August 18, 1838, reprinted in *Niles' Weekly Register*, October 6, 1838. For Leland's comment, see Charles Godfrey Leland, *Memoirs* (London, 1893), 1:301. For the restrictions on civil liberties in the South, see Clement Eaton, *The Freedom-of-Thought Struggle in the Old South* (New York, 1964), pp. 162–95; Clement Eaton, "The Freedom of the Press in the Upper South," *Mississippi Valley Historical Review* 18 (March 1932): 479–99; William W. Freehling, *Prelude to Civil War: The Nullification Controversy in South Carolina 1816 to 1836* (New York, 1965), pp. 255, 257, 259. The Georgia law against the *Liberator* is discussed in Walter M. Merrill, *Against Wind and Tide: A Biography of William Lloyd Garrison* (Cambridge, Mass., 1963), pp. 53–55. For the efforts to keep news of slave revolts and conspiracies quiet before the 1830s, see James Monroe to Thomas Jefferson, September 15, 1800, Stanislaus M. Hamilton, ed., *The Writings of James Monroe* (New York, 1898–1903), 3:201; Thomas W. Higginson, "Gabriel's Defeat," *Atlantic Monthly* 10 (September 1862): 337–45, which refers to Vesey. Garrison's poem is in the *Liberator*, January 1, 1831. Thomas Sydenham Witherspoon's letter to the *Emancipator* is reprinted in James G. Birney, *The American Churches, the Bulwarks of American Slavery* (London, 1840), pp. 42–43.

Causes of Antiabolitionist Violence

The observation of the Mississippi slaveowner is in Matthew Estes, *A Defense of Negro Slavery As It Exists in the United States* (Montgomery, Ala., 1946), pp. 230–31. For the connection between New York City and the South, see Philip S. Foner, *Business and Slavery: New York Merchants and the Irrepressible Conflict* (Chapel Hill, N.C., 1940), pp. 1–6; Barnes and Dumond, eds., *Weld-Grimké Letters*, 1:363; on Boston and Lowell, see Samuel Eliot Morison, *The Maritime History of Massachusetts* (Boston and New York, 1930), pp. 298–99. For the card of the New York merchants, see Foner, *Business and Slavery*, p. 14, and for the comment to May, see Samuel J. May, *Some Recollections of Our Anti-Slavery Conflict* (Boston, 1869), pp. 127–28. Hubbard's, Moore's, and Leggett's remarks on the threat of emancipation to white workers in the North are in *Congressional Globe*, 24th Cong., 1st sess., Appendix, p. 5; 25th Cong., 3d sess., Appendix, p. 240; *New York Evening Post*, February 10, 1835. For Fisk, see Theophilus Fisk, *The Banking Bubble Burst: Being a History of the Enormous Legalized Frauds Practiced upon the Community by the Present American Banking System* (Charleston, S.C., 1837), pp. 184–85; *Boston Courier*, March 12, 1837; Lydia Maria Child, *Letters* (Boston, 1883), p. 18; William Goodell, *Slavery and Anti-Slavery* (New York, 1853), p. 407. For Ratner's conclusion, see Norman Ratner, *Powder-Keg: Northern Opposition to the Anti-Slavery Movement, 1831–1840* (New York, 1968), pp. 215–17; and for Henig's, see Gerald S. Henig, "The Jacksonian Attitude toward Abolitionism, in the 1830's," *Tennessee Historical Quarterly* 16 (Spring 1969): 56. For the view of John B. Jentz, see his article "The Antislavery Constituency in Jacksonian New York City," *Civil War History* 27 (June 1981): 104.

The "Mob Years"

Two accounts of antiabolitionist riots are Ratner, op. cit., which concentrates on fundamental factors behind hostility to abolitionists, and Leonard L. Richards, *"Gentlemen of Property and Standing": Anti-Abolition Mobs in Jacksonian America* (New York, 1970), which presents an in-depth analysis of three particular riots in Utica, New York City, and Cincinnati. For the 1834 riot in New York City, see also *New York Courier and Enquirer*, July 4, 8, 9, 10, 11, 22, 1834; *New York Mercantile Advertiser*, July 12, 14, 15, 18, 22, 24, 1834; Linda K. Kerber, "Abolitionists and Amalgamators: The New York City Riots of 1834," *New York History* 48 (January 1967): 28–39. For the Utica riot, see also Benjamin Savitch, "The Well-Planned Riot of October 21, 1835: Utica's Answer to Abolitionism," *New York History* 50 (July 1969): 251–63; May, op. cit., p. 164; Octavius Brooks Frothingham, *Gerrit Smith* (New York, 1979), pp. 164–66. The events surrounding the visit of George Thompson to the United States are discussed, although with an antiabolitionist bias, in C. Duncan Rice, "The Anti-Slavery Mission of George Thompson to the United States, 1834–1835," *Journal of American Studies* 2 (April 1968): 13–31; but see also *Liberator*, August 23, September 27, 1834, May 30, July 18, 25, August 8, October 10, 24, December 5, 1835; George Thompson to William Lloyd Garrison, September 24, December 6, 1834, Anti-Slavery Letters Addressed to Garrison, Boston Public Library, Rare Book Room; Wendell P. and Francis J. Garrison, *William Lloyd Garrison, 1805–1879* (New York, 1885–1889), 1:434–67. The Boston riot and the near-lynching of Garrison is discussed in Louis Filler, *The Crusade against Slavery, 1830–1860* (New York, 1960), pp. 76–80; Russell B. Nye, *William Lloyd Garrison and the Humanitarian Reformers* (Boston, 1955), pp. 96–98; Garrison and Garrison, op. cit., 1:434–51, 486–92. See also *Liberator*, April 18, May 23, October 24, November 23, December 19, 1835; *Boston Commercial Gazette*, October 1, 1835. For the attacks on Negroes in Boston, see Donald M. Jacobs, "A History of the Boston Negro from Revolution to Civil War" (Ph.D. diss., Boston University, 1968), pp. 132–33. Seward's recollection is in Frederick W. Seward, ed., *An Autobiography of William H. Seward from 1810 to 1834 with a Memoir of His Life and Selections from His Letters, 1831–1846* (New York, 1891), p. 291. The attack on abolitionist mailings is discussed in Nye, *Fettered Freedom*, pp. 54–69; Freehling, op. cit., pp. 279–92; Clement Eaton, *Freedom of Thought in the Old South* (New York, 1964), pp. 200–205; William Thomas ("Defensor"), *Enemies of the Constitution Discovered, or, an Inquiry into the Origin and Tendency of Popular Violence* (New York, 1835), pp. 125–30; Clement Eaton, "Censorship of the Southern Mails," *American Historical Review* 48 (January 1943): 260–78. For the incident involving Amos Dresser, see *The Narrative of Amos Dresser* (New York, 1836), pp. 3–15.

Freedom of the Press

The attack on the *Philanthropist* is discussed in Betty Fladeland, *James Gillespie Birney: The Slaveholder to Abolitionist* (New York, 1969), pp. 82–83, 125–60. The discussion of Elijah P. Lovejoy is based on the following sources: Melvin Johnson, *Elijah Parish Lovejoy* (Rochester, N.Y., 1910 [?]), pp. 38–68; John Gill, *Tide without Turning: Elijah P. Lovejoy and Freedom of the Press* (Boston, n.d.), pp. 51–56, 62; Edward Beecher, *Narrative of Riots at Alton*, introduction by Robert Meredith (Alton, Ill., 1838; reprint ed., New York, 1965); Merton L. Dillon, *Elijah P. Lovejoy, Abolitionist Editor* (Urbana, Ill., 1961), pp. 40–86; *Liberator*, November 24, December 1, 1837, January 5,

February 16, 1838. For the editorial of the *Colored American* and the reports of Negro meetings, see Herbert Aptheker, ed., *A Documentary History of the Negro People in the United States* (New York, 1951), 1:174–75. Aptheker publishes the resolutions adopted at the New York Negro meeting in honor of Lovejoy. For the debate over Lovejoy's resort to the use of guns to defend himself, see Carleton Mabee, *Black Freedom: The Nonviolent Abolitionists from 1830 through the Civil War* (New York, 1970), pp. 38–50.

Freedom of Assembly

For Wendell Phillips' comment on the threat to blacks for permitting abolitionists to use their churches and halls, see Carol Martyn, *Wendell Phillips* (New York, 1890), p. 303. The discussion of Pennsylvania Hall is based on the following sources: *Pennsylvania Hall Association, History of Pennsylvania Hall Which Was Destroyed by A Mob on the 17th of May 1838* (Philadelphia, 1838); Minutes, Board of Managers, Philadelphia Female Anti-Slavery Society and Minute Book of the Pennsylvania Hall Association, both in Historical Society of Pennsylvania. Ms. Diary of General August J. Pleasanton, 1838–1844 (May 17, 1838), ibid.; William N. Needles to Wendell P. Garrison, Germantown, June 23, 1885, Abolition Society Papers, ibid.; Samuel G. Packard, *The Life and Letters of John Greenleaf Whittier* (Boston and New York, 1894), 1:233–34; *Weld-Grimké Letters*, 1:275–76; 2:511–12, 651; *Niles' Weekly Register*, February 3, May 26, 1838; *Pennsylvania Freeman*, May 12, 17, 24, October 25, November 25, 1838; *Philadelphia Public Ledger*, May 14, 20, 22, 24, 30, July 18, 1838; Merton L. Dillon, *Benjamin Lundy and the Struggle for Negro Freedom* (Urbana, Ill., 1969); Anna Davis Howell, ed., *James and Lucretia Mott, Life and Letters* (Boston, 1884), pp. 131–35. Two important studies of the burning of Pennsylvania Hall are William P. Lloyd, "Roots of Fear: A History of Pennsylvania Hall" (master's thesis, Pennsylvania State University, 1963), and Ira V. Brown, "Racism and Sexism: The Case of Pennsylvania Hall," *Phylon* 37 (June 1976): 126–35.

Freedom of Petition

The discussion in this section is based on the following sources: Nye, *Fettered Freedom*, pp. 32–54; Barnes, *Anti-Slavery Impulse*, pp. 100–145; Merton L. Dillon, *The Abolitionists: The Growth of a Dissenting Minority* (DeKalb, Ill., 1974), pp. 100–106; Samuel Flagg Bemis, *John Quincy Adams and the Union* (New York, 1956), pp. 326–83; *Congressional Globe*, 24th Cong., 1st sess., Appendix, pp. 225–26; Samuel J. Kline, "The Old Man Eloquent," *American Historical Magazine* 21 (1927): 479–97; Oscar Sherwin, "Old Man Eloquent," *Phylon* 5 (1944); Frederick Douglass, *My Bondage and My Freedom* (New York, 1855), pp. 164–65; *Pennsylvania Freeman*, October 20, 1841; B. C. Clark, *John Quincy Adams* (Boston, 1932), p. 368.

Civil Liberties and Antislavery Growth

Frederick Douglass' speech appeared in *Renfrewshire Advertiser*, April 11, 1846. For the comment of the *Boston Commercial Gazette*, see New York *Courier and Enquirer* of July 18, 1834 which reprints it, and also Kerber, op. cit., pp. 37–38. For the number of antislavery riots, see Theodore D. Weld, *In Memory: Angelina Grimké Weld* (Boston, 1880), p. 2. William Ellery Channing's comments are in W. E. Channing to Jonathan Phillips, July 24, 1834, see Weld to James G. Birney, August 7, 1834, in Dwight L. Dumond, ed., *Letters of James G. Birney, 1831–1857* (New York, 1938), 1:128. The comment of the head of the Pennsylvania militia is in diary of Colonel Pleasanton, May

20, June 23, 1838, Historical Society of Pennsylvania, Philadelphia. On William Jay, see Bayard Tuckerman, *William Jay and the Constitutional Movement for the Abolition of Slavery* (New York, 1894), p. 56. For Lewis Tappan and Schuyler Colfax, see *Weld-Grimké Letters*, 1:153; Lewis Tappan, *The Life of Arthur Tappan* (New York, 1870), p. 420. On the *Philanthropist* and Lovejoy's comment and the effect of Lovejoy's death on Bryant, see Fladeland, op. cit., p. 146; Dillon, op. cit., pp 178, 192. Southern comments on the burning of Pennsylvania Hall are reprinted in *Pennsylvania Freeman*, May 31, June 21, 1838. See also Lloyd, op. cit., pp. 66–67 and Brown, op. cit., p. 15. The reaction of labor to the civil liberties issue is discussed in Foner, *History of the Labor Movement in the United States*, 1:267. See also *National Laborer*, March 26, 1836. For Williams' resignation from the Anti-Slavery Society, see George Walker, "The Afro-American in New York City Before the Civil War, 1827–1860" (Ph.D. diss., Columbia University, 1972), pp. 220–21. For Ward, see Samuel R. Ward, *Autobiography of a Fugitive Negro* (New York, 1872), p. 46. The conservative reaction of the Society of Friends to the burning of Pennsylvania Hall is discussed in Thomas E. Drake, *Quakers and Slavery in America* (New Haven, Conn., 1950), pp. 156–57. See also *An Address to the Quarterly, Monthly and Preparative Meetings, and the Members thereof, Composing the Yearly Meeting of Friends, Held in Philadelphia, by the Committee Appointed at the late Yearly Meeting to Have Charge of the Subject of Slavery* (Philadelphia, 1839), p. 8. For Furness' different reaction, see William Henry Furness, *A Sermon Occasioned by the Destruction of Pennsylvania Hall* (Philadelphia, 1838), p. 3; Lloyd, op. cit., pp. 68–69. For Gerrit Smith, see *Liberator*, February 6, 1836. For John Quincy Adams' opposition to slavery, see John Quincy Adams, Autograph Letter Signed to E. P. Atlee, Washington, June 25, 1836, Historical Society of Pennsylvania; Allan Nevins, ed., *Diary of John Quincy Adams* (New York, 1929), pp. 126–28, 138–48; Sherwin, op. cit., pp. 133–34. For the Amistad case, see *U.S.* v. *Amistad* in Richard Peters, *Reports of Cases Argued and Adjudged in the Supreme Court of the United States, January Term, 1841* (Philadelphia, 1840), 15:519–98; *Argument of John Quincy Adams, before the Supreme Court of the United States, in the case of the United States, Appellants, vs. Cinque, and others, Africans* (New York, 1841); Edwin P. Hoyt, *The Amistad Affair* (London, 1970). For Wendell Phillips, see Louis Ruchames, "Wendell Phillips' Lovejoy Address," *New England Quarterly* 47 (March 1974): 108–17, and for Phillips' earlier antislavery activity, see also *Liberator*, January 21, March 31, April 14, July 7, 14, August 4, 27, 1837. The "Prospectus" for 1836 appeared in the *Liberator* of December 19, 1835. Calvin Colton, *A Voice from America to England* (London, 1839), pp. 273–74.

21. THE SPLIT IN THE ANTISLAVERY MOVEMENT

Moral Suasion, Nonresistance, and Come-Outerism

For the charge against Garrison, see Massachusetts Abolition Society, *The True History of the Late Division in the Anti-Slavery Societies* (Boston, 1841), p. 6. The discussion of moral suasion and nonresistance is based on the following sources: Henry Wilson, *History of the Rise and Fall of the Slave Power in America* (Boston and New York, 1872), 1:405–12; Garrison to Henry E. Benson, August 29, 1831, Walter M. Merrill, ed., *The Letters of William Lloyd Garrison: I Will Be Heard, 1822–1835* (Cambridge, Mass., 1971), p. 128. Oliver Johnson, *William Lloyd Garrison* (Boston, 1881), p. 314. *Fourth*

Annual Report of the American Anti-Slavery Society (Boston, 1839), p. 23; Wendell Phillips to the *Liberator*, December 2, 1841, in *Liberator*, December 31, 1841; E. N. Elliot, ed., *Cotton Is King* (Augusta, Ga., 1860), pp. 140–41; John Demos, "The Anti-Slavery Movement and the Problem of Violent Means," *New England Quarterly* 27 (December 1964): 503.

Women's Rights

The discussion in this section is based on the following sources: Barnes and Dumond, eds., *Weld-Grimké Letters*, 2:415, 424, 428, 441; *Liberator*, July 14, 1832, March 1, May 23, July 19, 1839; Gerda Lerner, *The Grimké Sisters from South Carolina, Pioneers for Women's Rights and Abolition* (New York, 1971), pp. 116–82; Philip S. Foner, ed., *Frederick Douglass and Women's Rights* (Westport, Conn., 1976), pp. 5–7; *New York Commercial Advertiser*, May 25, 1838; *Liberator*, October 24, 1835, September 15, 1837.

Political Action

Garrison's views are set forth in William Lloyd Garrison, *An Address to the Abolitionists of Massachusetts on the Subject of Political Action* (n.p., n.d.), pp. 7, 15; Aileen Kraditor, *Means and Ends in American Abolitionism: Garrison and His Critics on Strategy and Tactics, 1834–1850* (New York, 1969), pp. 16–19, 162–68. For the advice by Garrison to Boston blacks in the election of 1839, see *Liberator*, November 8, 1839; Donald M. Jacobs, "William Lloyd Garrison's *Liberator* and Boston's Blacks, 1830–1865," *New England Quarterly* 45 (June 1971): 265. For the controversy over an antislavery political party, see James B. Stewart, "The Aims and Impact of Garrisonian Abolitionism, 1840–1860," *Civil War History* 15 (September 1969): 197–209; Bertram Wyatt-Brown, "The Abolitionists' Postal Campaign of 1835," *Journal of Negro History* 50 (October 1965): 227–38; James M. McPherson, "The Fight against the Gag Rule: Joshua Leavitt and Antislavery Insurgency in the Whig Party, 1835–1842," *Journal of Negro History* 48 (July 1963): 77–75.

The Pastoral and Clerical Appeals

The discussion in this section is based on the following sources: Russell B. Nye, *William Lloyd Garrison and the Humanitarian Reformers*, pp. 109–16; Oliver Johnson, *William Lloyd Garrison and His Times* (Boston, 1880), pp. 258–70; Lerner, op. cit., pp. 163–294; *Liberator*, October 6, 20, 1837; Gilbert Hobbs Barnes, *The Antislavery Impulse, 1830–1844* (New York, 1933), pp. 156–57; Jacobs, op. cit., pp. 158–59.

The First Split

For the discussion in this section, see *Massachusetts Abolitionist* reprinted in *Liberator*, March 8, 1839, and *Liberator*, May 23, June 21, July 19, 1839; Elaine Brooks, "The Massachusetts Anti-Slavery Society," *Journal of Negro History* 30 (July 1945): 320–31; *The True History of the Late Division*, pp. 10–45.

The Split in the American Anti-Slavery Society

The discussion in this section is based on the following sources: *Liberator*, August 23, 30, September 19, 1839, April 24, 1840; Wilson, op. cit., 1:415–20; W. P. and F. J. Garrison, *Life of William Lloyd Garrison*, 2:347; Staughton Lynd, "The Abolitionist

Critique of the United States Constitution," in Martin Duberman, ed., *The Antislavery Vanguard: New Essays on the Abolitionists* (Princeton, N.J., 1965), pp. 209–37; Barnes, op. cit., pp. 153–60; Barnes and Dumond, eds., *Weld-Grimké Letters*, 2:849.

World Anti-Slavery Convention

For the events at the convention, see Louis Filler, *The Crusade against Slavery, 1830–1860* (New York, 1960), pp. 137–38; Walter M. Merrill, *Against Wind and Tide: A Biography of William Lloyd Garrison* (Cambridge, Mass., 1963), pp. 161–69; Miriam C. Usrey, "Charles Lenox Remond, Garrison's Ebony Echo, World Anti-Slavery Convention, 1840," *Essex Institute Historical Collections* 106 (April 1970): 112; Herbert Aptheker, ed., *A Documentary History of the Negro People in the United States* (New York, 1951), 1:196–98; Truman Nelson, ed., *Documents of Upheaval* (New York, 1966), p. 17. For Garrison's comment on the results of the election of 1840, see *Liberator*, December 4, 1840.

Blacks and the Antislavery Split

The discussion in this section is based on the following sources: Aptheker, ed., *A Documentary History of the Negro People in the United States* (New York, 1951), 1:192–96; *Liberator*, April 3, 1840; Dwight L. Dumond, ed., *Letters of James G. Birney* (New York, 1938), 1:575–79; Joel Schor, *Henry Highland Garnet: A Voice of Black Radicalism in the Nineteenth Century* (Westport, Conn., 1977), pp. 38, 44.

22. BLACK ABOLITIONISTS

For Wesley's statement, see Charles H. Wesley, "The Negroes of New York in the Emancipation Movement," *Journal of Negro History* 24 (April 1939): 66. Elizur Wright's appears in *First Annual Report of the American Anti-Slavery Society* (New York, 1834), p. 45.

Black-White Joint Activity

James Forten's role is discussed in Ray Allen Billington, "James Forten: Forgotten Abolitionist," *Negro History Bulletin* 13 (1949): 36–45. The *Harvardiana* statement and the *Liberator*'s on *The Liberty Bell* are in *Liberator*, February 21, 1835. For a detailed account of antislavery gift books, see Ralph Thompson, *American Literary Annuals and Gift Books* (New York, 1936). Frederick Douglass' "The Heroic Slave" is reprinted in Philip S. Foner, *The Life and Writings of Frederick Douglass* (New York, 1975), Vol. 5 (Supplementary Volume, 1844–1860), pp. 473–506. See *Pennsylvania Freeman*, November 9, 1836, November 30, 1837, January 17, 1839, and *Liberator*, June 20, 1835, for the joint activities of black and white women in female antislavery societies.

Independent Black Activity

The discussion in this section is based on the following sources: Herbert Aptheker, "The Negro in the Abolitionist Movement," *Science and Society* 13 (Spring 1941): 153–58; Florence Ray, *Life of Charles B. Ray* (New York, 1872), pp. 128–29; Gerald Sorin, *The New York Abolitionists* (Westport, Conn., 1971), pp. 81–93; Dorothy B. Porter, "The Organized Educational Activities of Negro Literary Societies, 1826–1836,"

Bibliography and Sources

Journal of Negro Education 5 (1936): 557–58; *Pennsylvania Freeman*, November 30, 1837, August 4, 1841.

Contributions of Ex-Slaves: The Narratives

For a general discussion, see Larry Gara, "The Professional Fugitive in the Abolition Movement," *Wisconsin Magazine of History* 26 (Spring 1965): 196–204; Aptheker, op. cit., pp. 163–64. For Angelina Grimké's comment, see Gilbert Barnes and Dwight L. Dumond, eds., *Letters of Theodore Dwight Weld, Angelina Grimké Weld, and Sarah Grimké 1822–1844* (New York, 1934), 2:523. On Harriet Beecher Stowe and Josiah Henson, see Eileen Ward, "In Memory of 'Uncle Tom,'" *Dalhousie Review* 20 (1940): 335–38. On sales of Douglass' autobiographies, see Philip S. Foner, *Frederick Douglass* (New York, 1964), pp. 59–60; on the impact of Douglass' autobiographies, see Ephraim Peabody, "Narratives of Fugitive Slaves," *Christian Examiner* 47 (July 1849): 64.

Contributions of Ex-Slaves: The Speakers

For Collins' comment, see John A. Collins to William Lloyd Garrison, January 18, 1842 in *Liberator*, January 21, 1842 and reprinted in Foner, *Douglass*, p. 46. For the fugitives who found lecturing very difficult, see John W. Blassingame, ed., *Slave Testimony* (Baton Rouge, La., 1977), p. 151; *Liberator*, June 4, 1841; Patrick C. Kennicott, "Negro Antislavery Speakers in America" (Ph.D. diss., Florida State University, 1967), pp. 171–201. For the effect of the fugitive slave speakers in overcoming proslavery arguments, see Gara, op. cit., pp. 200–202. On Douglass' view on the importance of speaking, see *North Star*, November 23, 1849. For Lunsford Lane, see Lunsford Lane, *The Narrative of Lunsford Lane* (Boston, 1842), and William G. Hawkins, *Lunsford Lane: Another Helper from North Carolina* (Miami, Fla., 1969). For the importance of self-improvement societies in the development of ex-slave speakers, see *Liberator*, July 9, 1841; *National Anti-Slavery Standard*, December 23, 1841. For Garrison's comment, see W. P. and T. J. Garrison, *Life of William Lloyd Garrison* (Boston, 1885–1889), 3:311. For the comments on Brown, Bibb, and Douglass as speakers, see Gara, op. cit., pp. 201–2. For comments on Anthony Burns, see *National Anti-Slavery Standard*, January 24, 1857; *Liberator*, August 13, 1858.

Frederick Douglass: Antislavery Agent

The discussion in this section is based on the following sources: Foner, *Frederick Douglass*, pp. 24–27, 45–52; *Life and Times of Frederick Douglass* (Hartford, Conn., 1881), pp. 183–95; Frederick Douglass, "Reminiscences," *Cosmopolitan* 7 (August 1889): 378–79; *Liberator*, July 9, August 20, September 3, 17, 24, October 15, 29, November 12, 19, December 3, 14, 1841, January 14, August 26, September 2, November 18, 1842; *National Anti-Slavery Standard*, August 26, December 23, 1841, October 25, 1847; *Herald of Freedom* (Concord, N.H.), November 12, 1841, June 3, 1842; *Providence Journal*, January 1, 1842; Frederic May Holland, *Frederick Douglass* (New York, 1891), pp. 68–69; *Tenth Annual Report of the Board of Managers of the Massachusetts Anti-Slavery Society* (Boston, 1841), pp. 105–6; *Eleventh Annual Report* (Boston, 1843), pp. 45–46; John W. Blassingame, ed., *The Frederick Douglass Papers: Series One* (New Haven, Conn., 1979), 1:xxi–lii.

A new detailed study of Douglass' early life as a slave is Dickson J. Preston, *Young Frederick Douglass: The Maryland Years* (Baltimore, 1980). While correcting some errors in Douglass' own narratives of his life in slavery, the author finally concedes that most of the former slave's perceptions were accurate. Frequently, moreover, the author contradicts himself, and his picture of the slaveholders of Maryland's Eastern Shore under whom the young Douglass worked as a slave is overly romanticized.

Trials of Black Antislavery Agents

For Robert Purvis, see Joseph A. Borome, "Robert Purvis and His Early Challenge to American Racism," *Negro History Bulletin* 30 (May 1967): 8–10; Pauline C. Johnson, "Robert Purvis," *Negro History Bulletin* 5 (December 1941): 65–66; Benjamin Quarles, *Black Abolitionists* (New York, 1969), pp. 24–25, 35–56; for Charles Lenox Remond, see James Oliver Horton and Lois E. Horton, *Black Bostonians: Family Life and Community Struggle in the Antebellum North* (New York and London, 1979), pp. 61–62; Quarles, op. cit., pp. 50, 56–58; for Nell, see Robert P. Smith, "William Cooper Nell: Crusading Black Abolitionist," *Journal of Negro History* 55 (July 1970): 182–99. For the comment of the *Buffalo Courier* on Remond and Douglass, see Blassingame, op. cit., p. xxxviii. William Wells Brown's experience is described in William E. Farrison, "William Wells Brown in Buffalo," *Journal of Negro History* 39 (October 1854): 312–13. Remond's letter to Phillips is in *Liberator*, April 18, 1845. For experiences of Douglass on the antislavery circuit, see Foner, *Frederick Douglass*, pp. 56–57; *National Anti-Slavery Standard*, August 19, 1847; Aaron M. Powell, *Personal Reminiscences of the Anti-Slavery and Other Reforms and Reformers* (New York, 1899), p. 71; William A. White to Garrison, September 22, 1843 in *Liberator*, October 13, 1843; Douglass to William A. White, July 30, 1846, Douglass Ms., Library of Congress, Manuscript Division.

Sojourner Truth

For Frances Ellen Watkins, see Quarles, op. cit., p. 178. For Sarah P. Remond, see Dorothy B. Parker, "Sarah Parker Remond, Abolitionist and Physician," *Journal of Negro History* 20 (1935): 287–93; Ruth Bogen, "Sarah Parker Remond: Black Abolitionist from Salem," *Essex Institute Historical Collections* (April 1974): 12–30. For Sojourner Truth, see Sojourner Truth, *Narrative of Sojourner Truth, A Northern Slave, Emancipated from Bodily Servitude by the State of New York, in 1828* (New York, 1853); Arthur H. Fauset, *Sojourner Truth* (Chapel Hill, N.C.), pp. 2–37.

Black Abolitionists and Women's Rights

For Sojourner's Truth's speech at the 1851 convention, see Philip S. Foner, ed., *The Voice of Black America: Major Speeches by Blacks in the United States 1798–1973* (New York, 1975), 1:122–24. The speech is published here without the dialect. For the Hortons' comment, see *Black Bostonians*, 66. For McCrummell and the Philadelphia Female Anti-Slavery Society, see Lloyd C. Hare, *Lucretia Mott* (New York, 1937), p. 92, and Aptheker, op. cit., p. 166. Brown's statement is in William Wells Brown, *A Lecture Delivered Before the Female Anti-Slavery Society at Salem, at Lyceum Hall, Nov. 14, 1847* (Boston, 1847), p. 4. For the role of Frederick Douglass in the movement see Philip S. Foner, ed., *Frederick Douglass on Women's Rights* (Westport, Conn., 1976), pp. 12–19; Benjamin Quarles, "Frederick Douglass and the Women's Rights Movement," *Journal of Negro History* 25 (1940): 35–39; Adelaide Elizabeth Dorn, "A History of the Anti-Slavery Movement in Rochester and Vicinity" (master's thesis, University of Buffalo, 1949), p. 51; Elizabeth Cady Stanton, Susan B. Anthony, and Matilda Joslyn Gage, eds., *History of Woman Suffrage* (New York, 1881), 1:70–71; Helen T. Shea, "The

Woman's Rights Movement in New York State, 1848–1854'' (master's thesis, Columbia University, 1940), p. 15; *New York Herald*, September 12, 1852.

Black Abolitionists Abroad

The discussion in this section is based on the following sources: Quarles, *Black Abolitionists*, pp. 129–39; Benjamin Quarles, "Ministers without Portfolio," *Journal of Negro History* (January 1954): 27–42; Claire Taylor, ed., *British and American Abolitionists* (Edinburgh, 1974), pp. 230–341; Claire Taylor, "Notes on American Negro Reformers in Victorian Britain," *Bulletin of the British Association for American Studies* n.s. 2 (March 1961): 40–51; Foner, *Frederick Douglass*, pp. 62–75; Blassingame, op. cit., pp. liii–lxi; Gerald Falkerson, "Exile as Emergence: Frederick Douglass in Great Britain, 1845–1847," *Quarterly Journal of Speech* 60 (February 1974): 69–82; Philip S. Foner, "William P. Powell: Militant Champion of Black Seamen," *Essays in Afro-American History* (Philadelphia, 1978), pp. 98–99; Ruth Bogin, "Sarah Parker Remond, Black Abolitionist from Salem," *Essex Institute Historical Collections* 110 (April 1974): 131–38; "Miss Remond in London," *London Morning Star*, July 22, 1859; *National Anti-Slavery Standard*, August 27, 1859; Blassingame, op. cit., pp. 398–400; William Wells Brown, *Sketches of People and Places Abroad* (Boston, 1855), p. 140.

For Davis on conservative trends in British antislavery, see especially David Brion Davis, *The Problem of Slavery in the Age of Revolution* (Ithaca, N.Y., 1954), pp. 346–47, 350, 361–85, 450–54. For a different picture, see Patricia Hollis, "Anti-Slavery and British Working-Class Radicalism in the Years of Reform," in Christine Bolt and Seymour Drescher, eds., *Anti-Slavery, Religion and Reform* (Hamden, Conn., 1980), pp. 294–315, and Seymour Drescher, "Cart Whip and Billy Roller: Antislavery and Reform Symbolism in Industrializing Britain," *Journal of Social History* 15 (1981): 3–24.

23. BLACK ABOLITIONISTS AND THE UNDERGROUND RAILROAD

For a discussion of the Fugitive Slave Act of 1793, see Philip S. Foner, *History of Black Americans: From Africa to the Emergence of the Cotton Kingdom* (Westport, Conn., 1975), pp. 473–75.

The Underground Railroad: Fact or Myth

The major books on the Underground Railroad are: William Still, *The Underground Railroad* (Philadelphia, 1872); William Still, *Still's Underground Railroad Records* (Hartford, Conn., 1886); Wilbur H. Siebert, *The Underground Railroad from Slavery to Freedom* (New York, 1898); R. C. Smedley, *History of the Underground Railroad in Chester and in the Neighboring Counties of Pennsylvania* (reprint ed., New York, 1968); Henrietta Buckmaster, *Let My People Go* (New York, 1941); William A. Breyfogle, *Make Free: The Story of the Underground Railroad* (Philadelphia and New York, 1958); Sidney Gallwey, *Underground Railroad in Tompkins County* (Ithaca, N.Y., 1936); Larry Gara, *The Liberty Line: The Legend of the Underground Railroad* (Lexington, Ky., 1961); Marion Gleason McDougall, *Fugitive Slaves: 1619–1865* (New York, 1967). For examples of omission of all but a small number of black activists in their accounts, see Siebert, Breyfogle, and Smedley.

For the comment of Levi Coffin, see *Reminiscences of Levi Coffin* (Cincinnati, 1876),

p. 106; and for Birney's see James G. Birney to Lewis Tappan, February 27, 1837, in Dwight L. Dumond, ed., *Letters of James Gillespie Birney* (New York, 1938), 2:376. For information on some of the individuals mentioned as involved in the Underground Railroad, see Benjamin Quarles, *Black Abolitionists* (New York, 1969), pp. 143–53; Still, *Underground Railroad*, pp. 735–40; Clarice A. Richardson, "The Anti-Slavery Activities of Negroes in Pennsylvania" (master's thesis, Howard University, 1931), pp. 13–23.

The Underground Railroad: Routes, Stations, and Stationmasters

For the origin of the term *Underground Railroad*, see Linda McCabe McCurdy, "The Underground Railroad," *Historic Pennsylvania Leaflets*, no. 29 (1969): 1. For the routes and stations, see Siebert, op. cit., pp. 120–21; Smedly, op. cit., pp. 31–35; Marianna Gibbons Brubaker, "The Underground Railroad," *Lancaster County Historical Society Papers* 15 (1911): 95–98; Thomas Whitson, "The Early Abolitionists of Lancaster County," *Lancaster County Historical Society Papers* 15 (1911): 69–85. Richard P. McCormick, "William Whipper: Moral Reformer," *Pennsylvania History* 43 (January 1976): 39–40; John W. Heisy, "William Whipper," August 31, 1968—The Underground Railroad file at the York Historical Society, York, Pennsylvania; Siebert, op. cit., pp. 738–39; Colonel Thomas W. Lloyd, *History of Lycoming County, Pennsylvania* (Indianapolis, 1929), pp. 128–32; John Gibson, *History of York County* (York, Pa., 1886), pp. 440–50; Tendal Mutunhu, "John W. Jones: Underground Railroad Station-Master," *Negro History Bulletin* 22 (March 1972): 814–18; Ebner C. Wright, "Underground Railroad Activities in Elmira," *Chemung Historical Journal* 20 (September 1974): 2422–26; Philip S. Foner, *Frederick Douglass* (New York, 1964), pp. 129–35, 398–99; Amy Post, "The Underground Railroad," in William Peck, ed., *Semicentennial History of Rochester* (Rochester, N.Y., 1924), pp. 458–60; Douglass to Anna H. Richardson, July 2, 1860, in Still, *Underground Railroad*, p. 598; *Life and Times of Frederick Douglass*, pp. 329–30.

Underground Railroad Conductors: North

For William Wells Brown's activities in the Underground Railroad, see *Narrative of William W. Brown* (Boston, 1847), pp. 109–10; William E. Farison, "William Wells Brown in Buffalo," *Journal of Negro History* 39 (October 1954): 300–303; Josephine Brown, *Biography of an American Bondsman* (Boston, 1856), pp. 52–53. Farison doubts the authenticity of the story of the painting of the fugitive with white paint.

Underground Railroad Conductors: South–Whites

For the experiences of Calvin Fairbank, see Calvin Fairbank, *How the Way Was Prepared* (Chicago, 1890), pp. 46–93; Siebert, op. cit., pp. 117–19; Stanley J. and Anita W. Robboy, "Lewis Hayden: From Fugitive Slave to Statesman," *New England Quarterly* 46 (December 1933): 595–96; J. W. Coleman, Jr., *Slavery Times in Kentucky* (Chapel Hill, N.C., 1940); 80–88; *Voice of Fugitive*, January 15, 1852. For Jonathan Walker's experiences, see Jonathan Walker, *Trial and Imprisonment of Jonathan Walker* (Boston, 1845); *Renfewshire Advertiser*, April 25, 1846, reprinted in John W. Blassingame, *The Frederick Douglass Papers (1841–1846)* (New Haven, Conn., 1979), 1:226. For the story of John L. Brown, see Betty Fladeland, *Men and Brothers: Anglo-American Anti-Slavery Cooperation* (Urbana, Ill., 1972), pp. 295–98; *Charleston Mercury*, April 7, August 30, 1844; John B. O'Neall, *The Negro Law of South Carolina* (Columbia, S.C., 1848), pp. 30–35; *Liberator*, April 2, 9, 16, 1844. For John Brown's raid into Missouri to liberate slaves, see F. B. Sanborn, *The Life and Letters of John Brown* (Boston, 1885), p. 482. For the story of Charles T. Torrey, see J. C. Lovejoy, *Memoir of Rev. Charles T. Torrey, Who Died in the Penitentiary of Maryland, Where He Was Confined for Showing Mercy to the Poor* (Boston, 1847); Filler, *Crusade against Slavery*, pp. 163–64; Benjamin Quarles, *Black Abolitionists* (New York, 1969), pp. 164–65; *Liberator*, July 10, August 7, 1846; William Lloyd Garrison to Samuel E. Sewall, May 18, 1846; Walter M. Merrill, ed., *The Letters of William Lloyd Garrison* (Cambridge, Mass., 1979), 4:133. For the story of Robert Morris and Captain Drayton, see Donald M. Jacobs, "A History of the Boston Negro from Revolution to Civil War" (Ph.D. diss., Boston University, 1968), pp. 267–68; *Liberator*, December 1, 1848, July 3, 1857; Quarles, op. cit., pp. 163–64; *Pennsylvania Freeman*, January 6, 1853; *Frederick Douglass' Paper*, September 14, 1855.

Underground Railroad Conductors: South—Black (Harriet Tubman)

For Josiah Henson's role as a conductor, see Breyfogle, op. cit., pp. 189–91; for Henry Bibb, see Quarles, op. cit., pp. 61, 62, 65–66; for Leonard A. Grimes, see William Wells Brown, *The Rising Sun; or the Antecedents and Advancement of the Colored Race* (Boston, 1874), pp. 534–35; James Oliver Horton and Lois E. Horton, *Black Bostonians* (New York, 1979), p. 54. The discussion of Harriet Tubman is based on the following sources: Sarah H. Bradford, *Scenes in the Life of Harriet Tubman* (Auburn, N.Y., 1869); Earl Conrad, *Harriet Tubman* (New York, 1943); Frederick Douglass, *Life and Times of Frederick Douglass*, p. 266; Breyfogle, op. cit., pp. 176–86; Still, *Underground Railroad*, pp. 296–306; John Bell Robinson, *Pictures of Slavery and Anti-Slavery* (Philadelphia, 1863), pp. 323–24; Mary Thacher Higginson, *Letters and Journals of Thomas Wentworth Higginson* (Boston, 1921), p. 81; Buckmaster, op. cit., pp. 150–51; Philip S. Foner, *Frederick Douglass and Women's Rights* (Westport, Conn., 1976), p. 159.

Vigilance Committees: New York City

For the description of the work of a Vigilance Committee, see Quarles, op. cit., p. 150; for the action of the 1848 National Negro Convention, see *Liberator*, June 8, 1849. The discussion on the New York Committee of Vigilance is based on the following sources: *The First Annual Report of the New York Committee for the Year 1837, Together with Important Facts Relative to Their Proceedings* (New York, 1837), pp. 11–12; Quarles, op. cit., p. 151; Helen Boardman, "David Ruggles," *Negro History Bulletin* 5 (November 1941): 39–40; Dorothy B. Parker, "David B. Ruggles, An Apostle for Human Freedom," *Journal of Negro History* (January 1943): 23–50; Foner, *Frederick Douglass*, pp. 23, 26; *Emancipator*, July 28, August 4, September 1, October 6, 1836, March 2, 1837, June 17, 1841, and *New York Express* reprinted in *Emancipator*, August 30, 1838; *National Anti-Slavery Standard*, August 20, 1840; *Fifth Annual Report of the New York Committee of Vigilance, for the Year 1842, with Interesting Facts Relative to their Proceedings* (New York, 1842), p. 38.

Vigilance Committees: Philadelphia

The discussion in this section is based on the following sources: Joseph A. Borome, "The Vigilance Committee of Philadelphia," *Pennsylvania Magazine of History and Biography* 92 (July 1968): 320–52; William D. Fergusson, "A Black Underground: The Underground Railroad in Philadelphia, 1836–1954," *Pennsylvania History* 44 (January 1977): 128–49; Quarles, op. cit.; *Pennsylvania Freeman*, April 19, July 4, 1838, December 29, 1841, May 12, 1842, August 22, 1844; McDougall, op. cit., p. 64; Gara, op. cit.,

p. 124; *Annual Reports* (Scrapbooks), December 1841, August 1843, August 1844; "Minutes of the Vigilance Committee of Philadelphia, 1839–1844," Pennsylvania Historical Society; "Minutes of the Philadelphia Female Anti-Slavery Society, September 9, 1841, January 20, 1842, June 9, 1842," Pennsylvania Historical Society; *National Anti-Slavery Standard*, April 28, May 15, 1860; *Liberator*, August 30, 1844; Larry Gara, "William Still and the Underground Railroad," *Pennsylvania History* 28 (January 1961): 33–45; "Vigilant Committee of Philadelphia, Original Manuscript Book and Record of Cases, kept by Jacob C. White, Jr., Philadelphia, 1839–1844"; William Still, "Autograph Manuscript Journal of Fugitive Slaves Who Passed Through Station No. 2 of the Underground Railroad, Philadelphia, December 25, 1852–February 22, 1857," both in Historical Society of Pennsylvania.

Vigilance Committees: Boston

The discussion of the Boston Vigilance Committee is based on the following sources: Francis Jackson, "Vigilance Committee Account Book" and "Members of Committee of Vigilance," Massachusetts Historical Society, Boston; Horton and Horton, op. cit., pp. 37, 42, 47, 50, 53, 55, 65–66, 80, 95, 101; Wilbur H. Siebert, *The Vigilance Committee of Boston* (Boston, 1953), pp. 1–23; Wilbur H. Siebert, "The Underground Railroad in Massachusetts," *Proceedings of the American Antiquarian Society* 45 (1936): 25–100; Donald M. Jacobs, "A History of the Boston Negro from Revolution to Civil War" (Ph.D. diss., Boston University, 1968), pp. 209–12; Austin Bearse, *Reminiscences of Fugitive Slave Law Days in Boston* (Boston, 1880), pp. 3–6; Robboy, op. cit., p. 598; "Old Passages of Boston's Underground Railroad," *Magazine of History* 3 (1926): 221; Leonard W. Levy, "The Abolition Riot: Boston's First Slave Rescue," *New England Quarterly* 25 (1952): 85–92; Joseph Nogee, "The Prigg Case and Fugitive Slavery," *Journal of Negro History* 39 (July 1954): 197–99; *Liberator*, June 4, 11, July 2, August 27, 1841, March 11, 18, 1842. For the New England Freedom Association, see *Liberator*, July 15, 1842; Horton and Horton, op. cit., pp. 58, 99.

The Latimer Case

The discussion in this section is based on the following sources: *Liberator*, October 21, 28, November 4, 25, December 2, 16, 23, 1842; *Boston Daily Bee*, reprinted in *Liberator*, November 11, 1842; Jacobs, op. cit., pp. 2, 212–18; Horton and Horton, op. cit., pp. 99, 105; Foner, *Frederick Douglass*, pp. 54–55, 385; *Latimer Journal and North Star*, November 18, 23, 1842; *Twelfth Annual Report of the Massachusetts Anti-Slavery Society* (Boston, 1844), p. 45. The Somersett case is discussed in Foner, *History of Black Americans*, 1:194, 296. See also Reginald Coupland, *The British Anti-Slavery Movement* (London, 1933), pp. 45–65. For J. Miller McKim's letter see J. Miller McKim to Mrs. M. W. Chapman, November 19, 1857, Maria W. Weston Papers, Boston Public Library.

24. BLACK-WHITE RELATIONS IN THE ANTISLAVERY MOVEMENT

White Abolitionists and Free Blacks

For Walters' comment, see *The Antislavery Appeal: American Abolitionism after 1830* (Baltimore, 1976), p. 12. For the ideology behind antislavery devoting special attention to elevating free blacks, see *Liberator*, December 12, 1835; Barnes and Dumond, eds.,

Weld-Grimké Letters, 1:232–34; Lewis Tappan in *Emancipator*, November 14, 1834; William Goodell in *Anti-Slavery Bugle*, August 14, 1848; Elizur Wright, Jr., in *Liberator*, October 15, 1846. For the New England Anti-Slavery Society position, that of the Anti-Slavery Convention of American Women, and the 1841 Massachusetts Anti-Slavery Society's annual meeting, see *Liberator*, June 14, 1834, October 17, 1838, March 12, 1841. For the quotation from the Anti-Slavery Tract, see Charles C. Burleigh, "Slavery and the North," *Anti-Slavery Tracts, No. 10*, p. 4. For Gerda Lerner's comment on Theodore Weld, see Gerda Lerner, *The Grimké Sisters of South Carolina* (New York, 1968), p. 132. For the use of Hayden's store and home, see Stanley J. and Anita W. Robby, "Lewis Hayden: From Fugitive Slave to Statesman," *New England Quarterly* 46 (December 1973): 598. See also Wendell Phillips Garrison and Francis Jackson Garrison, *William Lloyd Garrison, The Store of His Life as Told by His Children* (Boston, 1894), 3:324. For Charlotte Forten's comment, see Ray Allen Billington, ed., *Journal of Charlotte Forten* (New York, 1967), p. 45. For the "ride-ins" and the efforts to abolish the Negro pew, see Carlton Mabee, *Black Freedom: The Non-violent Abolitionists from 1830 Through the Civil War* (New York, 1970), pp. 127–58. For the opposition of white abolitionists to segregation and racism, see ibid., pp. 91–111. For Wendell Phillips' action, see Philip S. Foner, *Frederick Douglass* (New York, 1964), p. 53. The report on Lucretia Mott is reprinted in *National Anti-Slavery Standard*, September 8, 1842. For John Bowers' report see *Colored American*, February 25, 1837. For Meier and Rudwick, see August Meier and Elliott M. Rudwick, *From Plantation to Ghetto* (New York, 1967), p. 58, and for the Peases' statement, see William H. Pease and Jane H. Pease, "Bostonian Garrisonians and the Problem of Frederick Douglass," *Canadian Journal of History* 2 (September 1967): 47–48.

The Case of Garrison

For Garrison's statements to free blacks, see *Liberator*, February 12, 1831, January 21, February 25, March 12, May 19, June 2, 1832; Donald M. Jacobs, "A History of the Boston Negro from Revolution to Civil War" (Ph.D. diss., Boston University, 1968), pp. 88–90, 112–13. For Garrison's letter to May, see William Lloyd Garrison to Reverend Samuel J. May, February 14, 1831, Anti-Slavery Papers, Boston Public Library, Rare Book Room. For Garrison's view of prejudice as a sin, see *Liberator*, December 10, 1841, and his view that it would take a long time to eradicate prejudice, ibid., January 28, 1842. For the comment on the hiring of Thomas Paul, Jr., see Oliver Johnson, *William Lloyd Garrison and His Times* (Boston, 1880), p. 101; and for the congratulatory letter to Garrison, see *Liberator*, March 12, 1831. The handbill of the American Anti-Slavery Society following the New York 1834 riot is discussed in Linda B. Kerber, "Abolitionists and Amalgamators: The New York City Race Riot of 1834," *New York History* 48 (1966): 35; the text of the handbill and letter to the mayor of New York are reprinted in Lewis Tappan, *The Life of Arthur Tappan* (New York, 1870), pp. 201–2, 215–16. For the *Anti-Slavery Bugle's* comment, see issue of February 17, 1855. Donald M. Jacobs' assessment of Garrison is in *New England Quarterly* 45 (December 1971): 277. The Hortons' estimate is in James Oliver Horton and Lois E. Horton, *Black Bostonians* (New York, 1979), p. 84. For Nell's comment, see William C. Nell, *The Colored Patriots of the American Revolution* (Boston, 1855), p. 369.

Ambivalence among White Abolitionists

For the New England Anti-Slavery Society action on black members, see George W. Williams, *History of the Negro Race from 1619 to 1880* (New York, 1883), 2:80;

Liberator, June 2, 1837. For Douglass' incident, see *North Star*, January 8, 1848; *Frederick Douglass' Paper*, February 17, 1854. For the William C. Nell incident, see Horton and Horton, op. cit., p. 83; George W. Forbes, "Typescript Biographical Sketch of William Cooper Nell," n.d., Boston Public Library, Rare Book Room. For Arthur Tappan's statement, see Tappan, op. cit., p. 132, and for Lewis Tappan's position, see Bertram Wyatt-Brown, *Lewis Tappan and the Evangelist War against Slavery* (Cleveland, 1969), pp. 46–52. For the position that the fight against prejudice should be abandoned see Mabee, op. cit., p. 92. For Edmund Quincy's statement, see *Liberator*, December 10, 1841, and John S. Patterson, "A Garrisonian Discussion of Prejudice: 'No One Dare to Rise,' " *New England Quarterly* 48 (December 1975): 566.

White Paternalism

For Frederick Douglass' comment, see *Douglass' Monthly* (October 1860). For Coffin's comments, see Levi Coffin, *Reminiscences of Levi Coffin (Cincinnati, 1876)*, pp. 297–399. For Richard A. Falk's comment, see his "Black Man's Burden in Ohio, 1849–1863" (Ph.D. diss., University of Toledo, 1972). For the comments of Ward and Delany, see *Liberator*, May 28, 1852, and Pease and Pease, op. cit., p. 43n. Delany's comment on the economic treatment of blacks by white abolitionists is in Martin R. Delany, *The Condition, Elevation, Emigration and Destiny of the Colored People of the United States* (Philadelphia, 1852), pp. 10, 27; *Frederick Douglass' Paper*, May 18, 1855. The action of the New England Anti-Slavery Society is reported in *Liberator*, March 10, 1832, and ibid., June 12, 1836, for the action of the American Anti-Slavery Society. See also Benjamin Quarles, *Black Abolitionists* (New York, 1969), pp. 48–55 for discussion of economic relations between white and black abolitionists. For the *Colored American*, see issue of November 15, 1837. J. McCune Smith's analysis is in *Frederick Douglass' Paper*, February 16, 1855. For the American Union, see *Exposition of the Objects and Plans of the American Union for the Relief and Improvement of Race* (Boston, 1835). Douglass' comment is in *Frederick Douglass' Paper*, May 18, 1855.

Growing Tensions

For Paul and Ward's statements, see Quarles, op. cit., pp. 47–48. Weld's and Wright's statements are reported in *Liberator*, October 2, 1837, and *Colored American*, October 4, 1837. Wright's speeches are reprinted in Philip S. Foner, ed., *The Voice of Black Americans: Major Speeches by Blacks in the United States, 1798–1973* (New York, 1975), pp. 83–88.

The Split between Douglass and the Garrisonians: I

For Quarles' statement, see op. cit., p. 53. For May's letter on Brown, see Samuel J. May, Jr., to Joseph Estlin, May 21, 1849, cited in Larry Gara, "The Professional Fugitive in the Abolition Movement," *Wisconsin Magazine of History* 48 (Spring, 1965): 201.

The story of the Douglass-Garrison split can be found in Benjamin Quarles, "The Breach between Douglass and Garrison," *Journal of Negro History* 23 (April 1938): 144–54; Foner, *Frederick Douglass*, pp. 136–54; Pease and Pease, op. cit., pp. 29–48, and Tyrone Tillery, "The Inevitability of the Douglass-Garrison Conflict," *Phylon* 37 (June 1976): 137–49. For discussions of the National Convention of Colored Citizens of 1843, see *Liberator*, September 22, 1843; Charles Wesley, "The Participation of Negroes in Anti-Slavery Political Parties," *Journal of Negro History* 29 (January 1944): 43–45, Joel Schor, *Henry Highland Garnet* (Westport, Conn., 1977), pp. 56–57. For the full text of Garnet's "An Address to the Slaves of the United States of America," see Philip S. Foner, *Voice of Black Americans*, 1:103–12. For Douglass' observations on restrictions placed on his early antislavery speeches, see Frederick Douglass, *My Bondage and My Freedom* (New York, 1855), pp. 361–62. Blassingame's interpretation is in *The Frederick Douglass Papers (1841–46)* (New Haven, Conn., 1979), 1:xlviii–xlix. For Maria Weston Chapman's letter to Richard D. Webb and Douglass' reaction, see Douglass to Richard D. Webb, March 29, 1846; Douglass to Maria W. Chapman, March 29, 1849, Anti-Slavery Letters to Garrison, Boston Public Library, Rare Book Room. On the reaction of the *National Anti-Slavery Standard*, see issue of July 24, 1846. For the controversy over Douglass' freedom by purchase, see Liberator, January 15, March 19, 1847; Garrison to Elizabeth Pease, April 1, 1847, Garrison Ms., Boston Public Library, Rare Book Room; Douglass to Henry C. Wright, December 22, 1846, *Liberator*, January 29, 1847. For a discussion of paternalism in the white woman antislavery groups, see Angela Y. Davis, *Women, Race and Class* (New York, 1982).

The Split between Douglass and the Garrisonians: II

For the events leading up to the publication of the *North Star*, see Foner, *Frederick Douglass*, pp. 75–84; Pease and Pease, op. cit., pp. 34–37; Abby Kelly Foster to Maria Weston Chapman, October 5, 1847, Weston Papers, Boston Public Library, Rare Book Room. For Garrison's view that blacks needed a paper but that the *Liberator* served that purpose, see his letter to Robert Purvis, December 10, 1832, Anti-Slavery Papers, Boston Public Library, Rare Book Room. For Douglass' changing views on reliance on moral suasion and opposition to violence, see Foner, *Frederick Douglass*, pp. 137–39, and Leslie F. Goldstein, "Violence as an Instrument for Social Change: The Views of Frederick Douglass, 1819–1895," *Journal of Negro History* 41 (January 1976): 61–69. Douglass' changing views on the Constitution are discussed in Foner, *Frederick Douglass*, pp. 139–41. For a discussion of Goodell's interpretation of the Constitution, see M. Leon Perkal, "William Goodell: A Life of Reform" (Ph.D. diss., City University of New York, 1972), and William Goodell, *Slavery and Anti-Slavery* (New York, 1897). The controversy over Julia M. Griffiths is discussed in Philip S. Foner, ed., *Frederick Douglass and Women's Rights* (Westport, Conn., 1976), pp. 19–24. Garrison's son's statement appeared in *Nation* 52 (1891): 388.

For Beriah Green's statement, see Mabee, op. cit., pp. 36–37; Douglass' statement about facts is in *North Star*, January 8, 1848. For Cornish and the *Northern Star and Freeman's Advocate*, see Quarles, op. cit., pp. 47–48. Dr. John S. Rock's statement on the abolitionists is in *Liberator*, March 16, 1860, and Douglass' statement before the Baltimore Colored High School is published in *Baltimore American*, June 23, 1894.

25. BLACKS AND ANTISLAVERY POLITICAL PARTIES, 1840–1848

Formation of the Liberty Party

For the factors leading up to the formation of the Liberty party, see Theodore T. Smith, *The Liberty and Free-Soil Parties in the Northwest* (New York, 1897), pp. 27–39; John R. Hendricks, "The Liberty Party in New York State, 1838–1848" (Ph.D. diss., Fordham University, 1959), pp. 10–35; The platform of the Liberty party is in Kirk M. Porter and Donald Bruce Johnson, eds., *National Party Platforms, 1840–1956* (Urbana, Ill., 1956), pp. 4–5. For early black support of the Liberty party, see Benjamin Quarles, *Black Abolitionists* (New York, 1969), pp. 183–84.

Election of 1840

For Garnet's statement, see *Liberator*, December 8, 1843, and Joel Schor, *Henry Highland Garnet* (Westport, Conn., 1977), p. 33. For Thomas Cole's position, see *Liberator*, December 4, 18, 1840. For Charles B. Ray's stand, see *Colored American*, April 18, October 3, 10, 1840. For the position of Thomas Van Rensselaer, see ibid., October 10, 31, 1840. See also for role of blacks in the campaign, Charles H. Wesley, "The Participation of Negroes in Anti-Slavery Political Parties," *Journal of Negro History* 29 (June 1844): 44–46; Eric Foner, "Racial Attitudes of the New York Free Soilers," *New York History* 46 (October 1965): 313.

Postelection Developments

For the Buffalo National Negro Convention, see *Liberator*, September 1, 18, 1843; Wesley, op. cit., pp. 43–45; *Minutes of the National Convention of Colored Citizens Held at Buffalo, on the 15th, 16th, 17th, 18th & 19th of August, 1843, for the Purposes of Considering Their Moral and Actual Conditions as American Citizens* (New York, 1843), pp. 15–22.

The Annexation of Texas Issue

For events in Texas, see Eugene C. Barker, *The Life of Stephen F. Austin, Founder of Texas, 1793–1836* (Dallas, 1923), pp. 147, 237–42, 254–56, 324; Eugene C. Barker, ed., *The Austin Papers* (Washington, D.C. and Austin, Tex., 1919–1926), 3:101–2; James K. Greer, "The Texas Declaration of Independence," in Eugene C. Barker, ed., *Readings in Texas History* (Dallas, 1929), pp. 234–45, and Annie Middleton, "The Last Stage in the Annexation of Texas," in ibid., pp. 86–102. For the effort of Andrews and Tappan to have Britain purchase the slaves in Texas and grant them freedom, see Charles Shively, "An Option for Freedom in Texas, 1840–1844," *Journal of Negro History* 50 (April 1965): 77–96. For the antislavery peace pledge, see *Liberator*, June 27, 1845, and for black opposition to annexation of Texas, see Quarles, op. cit., pp. 192–93.

Election of 1844

For Liberty party opposition to the annexation of Texas, see Joseph G. Raybec, *Free Soil: The Election of 1848* (Lexington, Ky., 1970), p. 57. For the stand of James McCune Smith and the New York City delegation against endorsing the Liberty party, see *National Anti-Slavery Standard*, October 17, 24, 1844, and Wesley, op. cit., p. 46. For Gay's statement, see *National Anti-Slavery Standard*, October 24, 1844. For Lincoln's criticism of Liberty party refusal to support Henry Clay, see Roy P. Basler, Marion Dolores Pragtt, and Lloyd A. Dunlap, eds., *The Collected Works of Abraham Lincoln* (New Brunswick, N.J., 1953–1955), 1:347–48, and Stephen B. Oates, *With Malice toward None: The Life of Abraham Lincoln* (New York, 1977), p. 69. For Garnet's statement, see *Proceedings of the National Liberty Party Convention, Held at Buffalo, New York, June 14th and 15th, 1848; Including the Resolutions and Addresses Adopted by That Body, and Speeches of Beriah Green and Gerrit Smith on That Occasion* (Utica, N.Y., 1848), pp. 12–13; Schor, op. cit., p. 95.

War with Mexico

The discussion in this section is based on the following sources: Frederick Merk, *Slavery and the Annexation of Texas* (New York, 1972), pp. 13–46. Alfred Hoyt Bill, *Rehearsal for Conflict: The Story of Our War with Mexico, 1846–1848* (Indianapolis, 1950), pp. 12–35; Philip S. Foner, ed., *Life and Writings of Frederick Douglass* (New York, 1950), 1:182–83, 187–88, 291–96; J. D. P. Fuller, *The Movement for the Acquisition of All Mexico, 1846–48* (Baltimore, 1936), pp. 128–34; Albert K. Weinberg, *Manifest Destiny: A Study in Nationalist Expansionism* (New York, 1935), pp. 45–52; Eugene Irving McCormack, *James K. Polk: A Political Biography* (Berkeley, 1922), pp. 77–82; John H. Schroeder, *Mr. Polk's War: American Opposition and Dissent, 1846–1848* (Madison, Wis., 1973), pp. 104–12; Frank Friedel, *Dissent in Three American Wars* (Cambridge, Mass., 1976), pp. 13–23. Two recent studies of the Mexican war are Norman A. Graebner, "The Mexican War: A Study in Causation," *Pacific Historical Review* 22 (1980): 405–26, and Ernest McPherson Lander, Jr., *Reluctant Imperialists: Calhoun, the South Carolinians, and the Mexican War* (Baton Rouge, La., 1980).

The Wilmot Proviso

The discussion in this section is based on the following sources: Eric Foner, "The Wilmot Provision Revisited," *Journal of American History* 56 (September 1969): 269–79; Eric Foner, "Racial Attitudes of the New York Free Soilers," *New York History* 46 (October 1965): 317–18; Charles B. Going, *David Wilmot: Free Soiler* (New York, 1924), pp. 174–75; Margaret Koshinski, "David Wilmot and Free Soil" (master's thesis, Columbia University, 1949), p. 25; *Congressional Globe*, 29th Cong., 2nd sess., Appendix, p. 317; 30th Cong., 1st sess., Appendix, pp. 1076–89.

Splits in the Liberty Party

For the views of the Ohio Liberty party men, see Joseph G. Rayback, "The Liberty Party Leaders of Ohio: Exponents of Anti-Slavery Coalition," *Ohio Archeological and Historical Quarterly* 57 (April 1947): 165–78; Eric Foner, *Free Soil, Free Labor, Free Men: The Ideology of the Republican Party before the Civil War* (New York, 1970), pp. 73–80. For the opponents of the "one idea" in the Liberty party, see William Goodell, *Slavery and Anti-Slavery* (New York, 1853), p. 425; *North Star*, June 23, July 12, August 4, 1848; Henry Wilson, *History of the Rise and Fall of the Slave Power in America* (Boston, 1872–1877), 2:109–14; Schor, op. cit., pp. 93–95; Foner, *Frederick Douglass*, pp. 156–57; *Proceedings of the National Liberty Party Convention* (Utica, N.Y., 1848), pp. 1–13; Garnet on land monopoly in *North Star*, September 15, 1848.

The Free Soil Party

For the views of Robert Morris, see *Liberator*, August 25, 1848, and for the role played in Massachusetts by the Free Soil party, see Donald M. Jacobs, "A History of the Boston Negro from Revolution to Civil War" (Ph.D. diss., Boston University, 1968), p. 305. For the formation of the Free Soil party, see Gerald Sorin, *Abolitionism: A New Perspective* (New York, 1972), pp. 114–20. For David Wilmot's position on Negro suffrage, see *Congressional Globe*, 31st Cong., 1st sess., Appendix, p. 943; 32d Cong., 2d sess., p. 405; Eric Foner, "Racial Attitude of New York Free Soilers," p. 318, and *Pennsylvania Freeman*, December 7, 1848. For the role of the Barnburners, see Eric Foner, "Racial Attitude of New York Free Soilers," op. cit., pp. 314–18; Herbert D. A. Donovan, *The*

Barnburners (New York, 1905), pp. 92–94. For the blacks at the Buffalo convention, see Oliver Dyer, *Phonographic Report of the Proceedings of the National Free Soil Convention* (New York, 1848), pp. 4, 21; W. E. Smith, *The Francis Blair Family in Politics* (New York, 1933), 1:236; *Reunion of the Free Soilers, at Dover Landing, Higham, Massachusetts* (Boston, 1877), p. 43; Foner, *Frederick Douglass*, pp. 158–59; *Frederick Douglass' Paper*, August 20, 1852. A recent examination of the issues discussed in this section is John Mayfield, *Rehearsal for Republicanism: Free Soil and the Politics of Antislavery* (Port Washington, N.Y., 1980).

Election of 1848

For Edmund Quincy's view, see *Liberator*, September 15, 1848, and for Garrison on the Whig party and Taylor, see *Liberator*, July 7, 1848. For Smith's reply to Van Rensselaer, see Foner, "Racial Attitudes," p. 320. For Garrison on the results of the election, see *Liberator*, January 19, 1848, and for Phillips on voting, see Wendell Phillips to John Gorham Palfrey, December 9, 1847, John Gorham Palfrey Papers, Houghton Library, Harvard University. For Douglass' position during the election of 1848, see Foner, *Frederick Douglass*, pp. 158–61, and *North Star*, August 18, September 1, 29, November 10, 1848; see Schor, op. cit., pp. 95–97.

Index

About the Author

PHILIP S. FONER is Professor Emeritus of History at Lincoln University in Pennsylvania. Before undertaking the massive *History of Black Americans* Foner wrote numerous books including *American Socialism and Black Americans* (Greenwood Press, 1977) and *The Democratic-Republican Societies, 1790–1800* (Greenwood Press, 1976).